Transformation of cities in central and Eastern Europe

# Transformation of cities in central and Eastern Europe: Towards globalization

Edited by F.E. Ian Hamilton, Kaliopa Dimitrovska Andrews, and Nataša Pichler-Milanović

**United Nations University Press**

TOKYO · NEW YORK · PARIS

The views expressed in this publication are those of the authors and do not necessarily reflect the views of the United Nations University.

United Nations University Press
United Nations University, 53–70, Jingumae 5-chome,
Shibuya-ku, Tokyo, 150–8925, Japan
Tel: +81-3-3499-2811 Fax: +81-3-3406-7345
E-mail: sales@hq.unu.edu general enquiries: press@hq.unu.edu
http://www.unu.edu

United Nations University Office at the United Nations, New York
2 United Nations Plaza, Room DC2–2062, New York, NY 10017, USA
Tel: +1-212-963-6387 Fax: +1-212-371-9454
E-mail: unuona@ony.unu.edu

United Nations University Press is the publishing division of the United Nations University.

Cover design by Andrew Corbett

Printed in India

ISBN 92-808-1105-3

Library of Congress Cataloging-in-Publication Data

Transformation of cities in Central and Eastern Europe : towards globalization / edited by
    F.E. Ian Hamilton, Kaliopa Dimitrovska Andrews, and Nataša Pichler-Milanović.
      p. cm.
    Includes index.
    ISBN 9280811053 (pbk.)
        1. Cities and towns—Europe, Central. 2. Cities and towns—Europe, Eastern.
        3. Globalization. 4. Post-communism—Europe, Central. 5. Post-communism—
        Europe, Eastern. I. Hamilton, F.E. Ian. II. Andrews, Kaliopa Dimitrovska.
        III. Pichler-Milanović, Nataša.

HT145.E8T7 2004
307.76'0943—dc22
                                                                        2004017311

# Contents

# List of tables and figures

## Tables

## Figures

# Preface

Shortly after I became the Rector of the UNU, I was introduced to this research project, then entitled "Globalization and Urban Transformations in Central and Eastern Europe". It was one of the projects initiated and organized by Fu-chen Lo, the successful manager of the Mega-cities and Urban Development programme at the UNU-IAS. I was delighted to see such an effort, as I had been involved in the study of the socialist countries of Central and Eastern Europe since I became a professor in the Geographical Institute of Utrecht University, the Netherlands.

At that time, I concentrated on questions such as what made socialist agriculture different, how could this difference be seen in the landscape, and how successful was it? In the same vein, the Institute began studies of socialist cities, comparing them to the cities of Western Europe, developing countries, and North America. We assumed that differences in economic and political systems, socio-cultural backgrounds, and histories made a major impact on the layout and functioning of cities. In that context, studying Central and Eastern Europe, I also met Ian Hamilton and we discussed in particular the development of socialist cities. At Utrecht, we focused our research on the bigger, long-established cities and their changes during socialist times, as well as on new towns founded or established during socialism. It was clear that the new towns and cities reflected the basic tenets of socialist thinking much more than the former group. The pre-socialist heritage has continued to weigh down heavily on both the appearance and development of the cities that already existed. Nevertheless, looking at (East) Berlin, or Warsaw, the influence of socialist thinking and planning after more than four decades, though now rapidly disappearing, is undeniable.

In the present project, the discussion is pushed forward one stage further, as many of these cities have entered a new stage in their development. Specifically, since the fall of the Wall in Berlin they entered almost immediately the new era of globalization. The variety of contributions in this publication provides an excellent overview of what really happened to cities, and in particular to the main cities of the region, as they gained their new growth momentum. Indeed, the cities in Central and Eastern Europe changed much more slowly and less profoundly during socialism, but at the same time this trajectory provided certain advantages. As those of us that still visit the region have noticed, having an "old", even deteriorated, housing and building stock is an asset when it comes to using tourism as a way to develop economically. As the recent histories of Prague and Budapest demonstrate, this has contributed in an important way to make them major magnets for international tourism. With the building stock intact, some of these cities have been able to capitalize on their advantages: their attractive situation and city-scape, their traditional urban streets, squares, and parks, and their historical buildings. Prague and Budapest are competing with Paris and Rome in terms of attracting tourists from all around the world, illustrating in a most vivid way the increasing impact of globalization in cities that some 15 years ago were still difficult to visit.

These cities have maintained a human scale of development lost to many Western European cities. Their more advantageous starting point, in this regard, affords them opportunities to grow, while preserving a physical environment more inclusive for citizens and better for urban conviviality. It is interesting to note how Western European cities are now spending money on reshaping their centres and attempting to bring people back to the city. It would be wise for Central and Eastern European city governments to fully appreciate and use the advantages that history has brought them – as, I know, many do.

Gradually the pressure to transform to modern types of cities with greater diversity of infrastructure, housing, and buildings is being felt by all Central and Eastern European cities. This most interesting volume, based on rich contributions from true experts on the cities studied and portrayed, provides many good examples of the transformation in which all these cities are engaged. It seems as if they are leap-frogging, now, in their extreme efforts to catch up and make up for the precious time lost. The national economies and the activity levels in the individual cities are rapidly improving, creating many new opportunities and enhancing the drive for further urban development. This new pace of development will invigorate and energize living and working conditions and appeal to the imagination and ambitions of the people. However, dependent on their respective situations and histories, cities will grow at different paces and in different directions, adding to an ever-growing, diverse European and worldwide system of cities. The different orientations of these cities under these conditions are still open to question. It will, in particular, be interesting to see to what extent the different cities of Central and Eastern Europe in their specific locations will continue to orient themselves towards the West, and to occupy a peripheral position in a heavily Western-centred European Union, or in the process will rather shift to their more traditional bridging position, linking "Europe" to the East.

Many of the issues just touched upon in this preface, and many more, are elaborated in rich detail in the chapters of this book. The depth and breadth of the descriptions, observations, and analyses are both inspiring and impressive. We are grateful to Fu-chen Lo for his efforts in bringing the volume's contributors together. We would also like to thank Peter Marcotullio, who shortly after the project began, took over the programme from Dr Lo. Peter demonstrated a strong commitment to the project, which helped to see that it continued and was completed despite the great losses of Ian Hamilton and Frank Carter and the change in direction of the UNU-IAS urban programme itself. As we know at the UNU, this type of initiative, support, and encouragement, from the true experts, is crucial for seeing projects through to completion.

I highly regard Ian Hamilton's personal contribution in initiating and developing this project. In particular, I would like to thank Kaliopa and Nataša for their patience and perseverance, as without them this book would not have come to fruition. I think that their efforts, time, and energy paid off with the publication of this important text, essential for our understanding of the development of the cities studied in a crucial time of change. Together these studies published here are an apt tribute to Ian's long and productive career.

*Hans van Ginkel*
*Rector, United Nations*
*University*

# Acknowledgements

The preparation of this volume has been a collective effort of the contributors and institutions involved – Institute of Advanced Studies, United Nations University (IAS/UNU), Department of Geography and Environment at the London School of Economics and Political Sciences (LSE), the Urban Planning Institute of the Republic of Slovenia (UPIRS), and a number of others – all of whom we must thank for their help and advice. As editors, we would like to thank the other contributors to this book for responding to our frequent requests for new data, amendments, and additional information. Funding provided by the United Nations University made this book possible from the start, but thanks are due in particular to Professor Tarcisio Della Senta, Professor Fu-chen Lo, and Dr Peter J. Marcotullio from the IAS.

The two instigating project meetings, in London, 21–23 March 1999, organized by LSE, and a mid-project meeting in Bled, 15–18 December 1999, organized by UPIRS, helped us to shape the book based on the authors' cross-cultural perspectives. Unfortunately, the whole project and production of the final manuscript was marred and delayed by the tragic deaths of Frank Carter in May 2001 and of Ian Hamilton in March 2002. We have been honoured by the opportunity to work closely with Ian and the involvement that he gave to us as mentor and co-editor of this book, and trust that our joint publication, in addition to adding to knowledge of Central and Eastern Europe, will keep Ian's memory alive and will, as he would have wished, stimulate further studies in the fields to which he made great contributions during his lifetime.

At the LSE, thanks are due to Mrs Ann Seal for her efforts in transcribing and typing Ian's editorial notes on different draft chapters with accuracy and consistency, and to Professor Emeritus Michael Wise for helping us to write the tributes for Frank and Ian.

Crucial technical assistance with the preparation of the manuscript, and production of maps and diagrams, has been provided by the technical and administrative staff at the Urban Planning Institute of the Republic of Slovenia under the supervision of Ivan Stanič and Igor Bizjak, to whom we are enormously grateful. In addition, it should be acknowledged that without support in the concluding phase of this project from the Urban Planning Institute of the Republic of Slovenia and research funds from the Ministry of Education, Science and Sport, this book could not have finally been completed.

We also wish to extend our appreciation to two anonymous referees for their invaluable comments on the draft manuscript and to the editors at the United Nations University Press for the final production of this book. We are responsible for any remaining errors and shortcomings.

*The editors*
*Ljubljana*

# Part 1

## Towards globalization

# 1

# Introduction

*F.E. Ian Hamilton, Nataša Pichler-Milanović, and Kaliopa Dimitrovska Andrews*

At the turn of the millennium, "globalization" has become a very fashionable topic of research and debate, and the subject of a burgeoning international literature. This book, one of a series initiated by UNU/IAS on the interrelationships between globalization and metropolitan or urban change, contributes to that debate and focuses on a hitherto neglected part of the world: the transition economies of Central and Eastern Europe (CEE). The idea of globalization embodies an increasingly widespread perception or conviction that "the world is getting smaller" or, as Held et al. (1999: 1) express it, that "the world is rapidly being moulded into a shared social space by economic and technological forces". Metropolitan regions located around the world, including those in Europe, are becoming increasingly interdependent as rising international flows of capital, information, people, and trade make the global economy more tightly integrated. Developments in one city or metropolitan region can have cumulative and far-reaching impacts on the lives and work of populations in cities and their regions elsewhere across the globe. Indeed, globalization can be defined as a process which is diffusing, deepening, and accelerating the functional integration, competition, cooperation, dependency, and interdependency of cities and their regions, across international borders, continents, and oceans.

"Thinking globally", however, is not new: the forces leading to globalization that have been at work and gathering momentum during the past few decades have attracted a growing body of analytical research and discussion. By the 1970s, studies by Vernon (1966, 1971) were recognizing and identifying multinational enterprises (MNEs) as a key force in the development of what he

3

termed "globalism" through foreign direct investment (FDI) in host countries. At the same time, Wallerstein (1974) was propagating a "world systems approach" to the operation of the capitalist system in which the "dependency theory" was evolved to argue that the "third world" or "world periphery" was being maintained perpetually in a state of underdevelopment by the advanced "core" capitalist countries by substituting economic mechanisms for former "imperial-colonial" politico-economic power relations. The structuralist–Marxist ideology underpinning such an approach, however, meant that its advocates excluded the communist arena from their "world". Some steps were taken towards correcting this in the sphere of economic geography by the International Geographical Union (IGU) Commission on Industrial Systems, which, in the late 1970s, initiated research on international industrial systems. It identified

a myriad of interrelationships entangling "North" and "South," "East" and "West," or states grouped into such international organisations as the CMEA or the EEC . . . [while] the erosion or loss of the "national" identities of a multitude of manufacturers have been demonstrating to ordinary folk . . . that "their street" is but one lane of circulation in a global village. (Hamilton and Linge, 1981: 15)

The conclusion drawn from this work, however, was that while "dependency" remained significant, the global economy was becoming more "interdependent" as a result of commercial trade and competition, the armaments trade, multinational enterprise and FDI, the operation of financial markets, and the strategies of national or city state governments – especially in the "semi-periphery" – to replace import-substitution industrial development policies by export-orientated industrialization targeted at the global market (Hamilton and Linge, 1981). Although much of this work referred implicitly only to cities, the IGU Commission's predecessor, the IGU Working Group on Industry, had initiated research earlier to show that the growth of non-manufacturing functions related to industry and the associated growth in the importance of information and innovation diffusion, especially in large cities, were significantly modifying the inherited understanding of "Christallerian" urban hierarchies (Christaller, 1933, 1966) by creating new, more global, inter-metropolitan interdependencies (see Hamilton, 1974).

Yet, although these lines of enquiry were addressing "global issues", they did not address or use the term "globalization" as such; this had to wait until the 1990s, when broader, more comprehensive approaches stimulated by the ending of the Cold War began to encompass a multiplicity of interrelated cultural, economic, environmental, political, social, and technological dimensions. While these aspects have come together to generate a growing literature investigating "globalization", researchers have simultaneously created a good deal of controversy over the topic and even in some cases question its relevance or existence.

Recently, therefore, controversy over globalization has been expressed through the identification of three broad schools of thought on the subject (Held et al., 1999).

First, there are those so-called "hyperglobalizers" who, like Ohmae (1990, 1995), are dedicated to the idea of an all-powerful, all-pervasive globalization process. They discern a "borderless world" in which global market and technological forces are subjugating nation states, deconstructing their national sovereignty, and – by extension – affecting trends in their constituent cities and regions.

A second stance is adopted by the so-called "sceptics", such as Hirst and Thompson (1996). They argue that globalization was already well established by the end of the nineteenth century, when it reached a peak, and that in recent decades the world is rather being reorganized into a few major regional–international blocs (such as the EU or NAFTA) which exhibit intensifying internal cohesion and interdependence and lesser external interdependence. For the sceptics, therefore, the world economy is more fragmented today and national or local cultural and political forces can wield substantially more power than in earlier epochs. The classic case is Japan, where the government, supported by powerful business interests, pursues rigorous and changing policies to severely restrict import penetration and inward FDI while aggressively supporting exports (Longworth, 1998).

Third, there are the "transformationalists", like Giddens (1990, 1996) or Rosenau (1997), for whom globalization is a very contemporary phenomenon without historical precedent, because most nations and cities are undergoing profound changes as they attempt to adapt and adjust not only to a more interdependent but also a less predictable world.

In one sense, the virtually parallel or simultaneous development and coexistence of these diverse viewpoints on the globalization debate itself underlines that globalization is a reality – it expresses an environment which favours the instantaneous, interactive transmission and diffusion of ideas and knowledge, and their empirical testing. This is very healthy – ideas, concepts, or policies which become "fashionable bandwagons" can be very dangerous, especially if they are cast in narrow frameworks of bounded ideologies, since these can and do exclude "uncomfortable" information or findings and can thus distort or over-generalize the complexities of the real world. Thus, the rapid evolution of a plurality of approaches yielding diverse findings, both within and between these three broad schools of thought, provides a useful starting point for evaluating that complex reality in the case of the current transformation of cities in Central and Eastern Europe.

This book, therefore, attempts to provide some insights into whether cities in this region are experiencing the globalization process and being integrated into the world economy, or whether they are, rather, more strongly subject to regional–international forces such as European enlargement and integration

("EU-ization"). In either case, they are undoubtedly undergoing various transformations which embody outcomes of the interaction of both "internal" city or national processes and "external" international processes. In other words, the book attempts to evaluate the interplay of the global and regional–international forces with the internal local and national forces of political and economic transition, in shaping the transformation of cities in the former socialist countries in Central and Eastern Europe.

## The Region Defined

Through long periods of history, the Central and Eastern European region has been plagued by contested definitions, claims, and counter-claims to territorial identity and affiliation, and nationalist conflict, as well as frequent use of these to propagate geopolitical and geo-strategic power interests. Frequent wars and changing political boundaries, and the "relocating" of territory from one empire or state to another, have stunted or distorted urban development, creating real functioning environments of poverty and economic, military, and political instability for cities, whose people have had to adjust and readjust to new circumstances. Few cities in the region have enjoyed a stable interaction with the same territory; most have had to adapt to new political, social, and economic relationships in space, like Posen as part of Germany before 1919, or Poznan in Poland since 1919; or like Uzhgorod, part of Austro-Hungarian Monarchy before 1919; Ruthenia in Czechoslovakia, from 1919 to 1939; German-occupied Europe from 1940 to 1944; the Soviet Union from 1944 to 1991; and today, a border town of Ukraine (Fig. 1.1).

The ending of the Second World War and the emplacement of the "Iron Curtain" effectively destroyed the historic concepts and functional reality of Central Europe, dividing it between East and West.

Thus, during the socialist period, it became common in the Western world to refer to the region as "Eastern Europe", an area encompassing Albania, Bulgaria, Czechoslovakia, East Germany (the German Democratic Republic or GDR), Hungary, Poland, Romania, and Yugoslavia, as distinct from the Soviet Union – that is, the area lying between the (then) USSR to the east and the civil societies or market economies of Western Europe, or the member countries of NATO to the west (Fig. 1.2). The dramatic changes which have occurred since 1989 – the collapse of communist power, the break-up of the Soviet Union, Czechoslovakia, and Yugoslavia, and the end of the Cold War – have "reconfigured" this region.

"Central Europe" (or more precisely Central-East Europe) has re-emerged as a distinctive subregion embracing the Czech Republic, Hungary, Poland, Slovakia, and Slovenia (Fig. 1.3). Although the former East Germany is now within the European Union, it is also in some respect part of this zone because of Berlin's potential wider regional influence. Very distinctive, too, is the Balkan

Fig. 1.1 "Eastern Europe" before and after the First World War.

region, or "South-east Europe", comprising the former Yugoslav republics of Bosnia-Herzegovina, Serbia and Montenegro, and the Former Yugoslav Republic of Macedonia (FYRoM), as well as Albania, Bulgaria, and Romania, although Croatia may consider itself marginal and more part of Central Europe despite its

Fig. 1.2 "Eastern Europe" before 1989.

division between areas focusing respectively on the southern Pannonian plain and those focusing on the Adriatic (Mediterranean) Sea coast.

With the break-up of the USSR, however, two other distinct subregions have emerged: first, the Baltic states of Estonia, Latvia, and Lithuania; and second, "East Europe", which is used nowadays to describe the western areas of the former Soviet Union, namely Belarus, Moldova, and Ukraine, and in some respect also the European part of Russia (as far east as the Urals). These regional

Fig. 1.3 "Eastern Europe" after 1989: "subregionalization".

subdivisions suggest initially that cities in Central and Eastern Europe, which were subjected to a relatively high level of uniformity in their development under communism (see French and Hamilton, 1979), may be experiencing much more divergent forces and trends in the 1990s and will do so in the foreseeable future. The situation, however, is dynamic and fluid, not static, because the preparations for accession to the European Union in 2004 have already shaped

Fig. 1.4  EU enlargement towards Central and Eastern Europe.

trends in cities in much of Central Europe (Poland, Czech Republic, Hungary, Slovenia) and in Estonia (i.e. those countries known as "first-wave" EU candidates since *Agenda 2000* in 1997), and also in Slovakia and two other Baltic states of Latvia and Lithuania that became EU members in 2004 (Fig. 1.4). There could also be spillover effects on cities in adjacent EU candidates such as Croatia, Bulgaria, and Romania (which are known as "second-wave" EU candidates), and "long-term excluded" territories from the EU enlargement such as other former republics of Yugoslavia (Bosnia-Herzegovina, Serbia and Montenegro, and FYRoM), Albania, or the East European states of Belarus, Moldova, and Ukraine.

## Transformation

In the early 1990s, it was assumed, perhaps in both the East and West, that "transition" from a centrally managed state-owned socialist economy, within the context of a single (communist) party system, towards a market economy and a civil, democratic society, would project cities in Central and Eastern Europe rather uniformly along a linear trajectory, which would result in their "convergence" through time towards the spatial–structural and functional characteristics of cities in advanced market economies, or at least of those in Western Europe. Such thinking, however, was not only naive in the light of subsequent reality, but was often based on a lack of understanding of the "power of the past" to differentiate city trends: to varying degrees, contemporary developments in, and the characteristics of, cities in Central and Eastern Europe are "path dependent" on their pre-socialist as well as their socialist-period legacies. Thus, as a starting point, one can argue that current spatial patterns of integration among cities in the region reflect the impacts of at least three "layers" of influences.

The first is the highly differentiated pattern of historical legacies before 1945–1949, including imperial division (see Fig. 1.1) of the region through much of the nineteenth century (in some cases until 1914–1918), the effects of the processes of nationalism and the creation of "nation" states between 1918 and 1939–1941, and the variable effects of the Second World War on individual countries and their cities.

The second is the socialist period from the late 1940s to 1989–1991. While being characterized by both a high degree of isolation or closure from the rest of the world (as well as from other socialist states) and the integrating influences of the Soviet Union, this period did, nevertheless, also yield some important variations between cities in different states, as governments either initiated modified "paths to socialism" such as the Yugoslav "self-management model", or more strictly adhered to the Soviet model.

The third set of influences embody the effects of the opening up of cities to wider European and global forces – during the post-socialist period since the end of 1980s – through the adoption of more market-orientated principles and practice, leading to their greater or lesser integration or reintegration into a broader European and world urban system.

During the past decade, the paths of city development and change between those in Central, South-east, and East Europe appear to be diverging significantly. This is occurring in different ways, to different degrees, and on different levels. Globalization and leadership in restructuring national economies is usually creating significant divergence between (a) capital cities and their capital city regions on the one hand, where the effects of reforms and restructuring are most marked, and (b) second- or third-order, smaller cities where change is or may be less marked and more narrowly confined. And yet significant international differentiation is also occurring between urban systems in different states as a result of major variations in the speed and depth of, and commitment or resistance to, reform by national, city, or local governments. As a result, one may initially differentiate the following groups of territories according to their distinctive features and trends in city transformation:

Cities in former East Germany which became integrated overnight into the German "social market" economy and the EU "single market". Instantaneous "shock therapy" has radically altered East German cities as a result, although the regeneration and reintegration of Berlin is a special case since it has also been acquiring the capital functions of a reunified Germany within the European Union, while also lying close to the frontier with Poland;

Cities in the "fast-track" reforming states in Central Europe, which were aspiring to EU membership, such as the Czech Republic, Hungary, Poland, and Slovenia, together with Estonia among the Baltic states. These cities have been experiencing varying degrees of "commodification" of production factors and productive capacities, and have been amongst cities in the region which are most exposed to globalization and "EU-ization" influences through flows of capital, information, people, technology, and trade. Such cities are more firmly on a path of "convergence" towards cities in market economies as a result of de-industrialization or industrial restructuring, the growth of producer and consumer services, the implementation of diversified foreign investment, and the emergence of small firms and entrepreneurship within the context of reorganization of production systems. Indeed, cities in these states have been playing the leading role in achieving a major shift in economic trends from recession and decline in the early to mid-1990s to significant economic growth in the mid- to late 1990s, some more recently than others;

Cities in states of South-east Europe where attempts to introduce "transition" have largely "stalled" in the breadth and depth of real implementation by government and people alike and where, therefore, foreign investors have been more reluctant to establish any major facilities. These cities in Romania, Bulgaria, or Baltic states like Lithuania or Latvia may exhibit at best intermediate levels of transformation because economic decline continues with the result that informal sector activities may be developed significantly, while any evidence of globalization or "EU-ization" is very limited;

Cities in the Russian Federation in which apparent attempts at "fast-track" reform have not been matched by reality. There, the following features seem to be significant. First, a "virtual economy" has been created which is controlled by oligopolists and mafia-style elements and is effectively moving away from market reform. Second, with the collapse of a strong central government, Russia is characterized by a "mosaic" of city and regional economies, ranging at one extreme from cities like Moscow or St Petersburg, which are experiencing very significant transformation and integration/reintegration into the European or global economy, through to cities where barter and the informal economy predominate, alongside state or unrestructured "privatized" enterprises;

Cities in states of East Europe where, in effect, the state socialist economy has continued to be nurtured (Belarus), or has not really been dismantled or subject to real market reforms (Moldova, Ukraine). These cities are still largely isolated from global influences;

Cities in states which have experienced war destruction or war-related chaos and which effectively are either cities in ruins (such as Sarajevo in Bosnia and Herzegovina) where life is attempting to return to normal, or are still shaped by the legacies of a military economy (such as Belgrade in Serbia) or refugee problems. In these cases there is a high level of isolation from developments in neighbouring regions, let alone from those in the wider world. And yet these cities are also, in part, subject to the operations of international processes, not least those carried out by UN forces;

Cities in territories which are adjacent to those which have been the object of military action and hence are, or may be, experiencing spillover effects of the Balkan conflict. In particular, one must single out the Former Yugoslav Republic of Macedonia, where cities have been influenced by the break-up of Yugoslavia, embargoes on trade with Serbia, and refugee and ethnic problems, not to mention political isolation from Greece. This environment of instability or potential instability combines with geographic isolation (except from Greece) to foster specific conditions of city transformation (especially, but not only, in Skopje, the capital of FYRoM);

Cities in Albania, where rapid transformation into an unregulated "third world" development model has taken place, following the end of the isolation of the former socialist countries.

However, one must also take into account the effects of politico-territorial reorganization in Central and Eastern Europe in the 1990s, as this is reshaping the roles of many cities in the region in various ways, and not only those of the capital cities. Nevertheless, since these capital cities are the focus of the case studies in this book, it is necessary to attempt an initial classification of them.

**Berlin**, it must be reiterated, is unique because it is the only city which has resumed its role as a capital within a larger, reintegrated socio-economic and political space – that of a reunited Germany. In principle, this should result in major changes in the city since it is now the capital of the largest European economy (in GDP) and is the second largest in Central and Eastern Europe after Moscow (Table 1.1).

Five capital cities perform their functions within the context of unchanged state boundaries – these are **Bucharest**, **Budapest**, **Sofia**, **Tirana**, and **Warsaw**. Even so, their experiences are quite diverse. Budapest, the capital of Hungary, and Warsaw, the capital of Poland, are playing leading roles in economies which have been growing and restructuring strongly or quite strongly. They are also capitals of states adjacent to the European Union and soon to be incorporated into it. On the other hand, the other three capital cities of Albania, Bulgaria, and Romania are located in states which have been, or still are, suffering from economic decline (for various reasons), and which are more isolated or distant from the European Union and may be excluded from it in the foreseeable future.

Another group of cities have had their functional status significantly upgraded since 1991, as the territories over which they have jurisdiction were transformed from "semi-autonomous" regions of republics within larger "federated" states into independent sovereign states in their own right. These are **Bratislava** (Slovakia), **Kiev** (Ukraine), **Ljubljana** (Slovenia), **Minsk** (Belarus), **Riga** (Latvia), **Sarajevo** (Bosnia and Herzegovina), **Skopje** (Macedonia), **Tallinn** (Estonia), **Vilnius** (Lithuania), and **Zagreb** (Croatia). In these cases, the changing patterns of spatial and functional integration must be addressed to see how, why, and to what extent the acquisition of capital city status has affected their developmental paths in comparison with their former integration into larger states. Again, however, the contexts of proximity to or distance from the European Union, impending accession to or exclusion from the European Union, and specific circumstances such as location within or near the recent Balkan war zones also play significant roles.

Much the same can be said about the next group of cities which were capital cities of larger states, and continue to perform capital city functions but have found themselves, since 1991 or so, presiding over "shrunken" former sovereign states: **Belgrade** (Yugoslav Federation), **Moscow** (Soviet Union), and **Prague** (Czechoslovakia). It would be interesting to see how their experiences compare with those of, say, Budapest after the loss of the Hungarian empire following the First World War. One would expect a decline in economic activity and functions, but the questions then are, to what extent has "transition" facilitated restructuring, even growth, certainly in the cases of Moscow and Prague, and how has Belgrade been affected by the military situation and international sanctions, during the 1990s, in the former Yugoslavia?

Table 1.1  Changes in population in key Central and Eastern European cities (in 000s).

| City | Year Population | Year Population | Year Population | Year Population |
|---|---|---|---|---|
| Baltic States | | | | |
| ESTONIA | 1956 | 1970 | 1990 | 2000 |
| *Tallinn* | 257 | 363 | 484 | 408 |
| LATVIA | 1956 | 1970 | 1990 | 1999 |
| *Riga* | 565 | 732 | 917 | 793 |
| LITHUANIA | 1956 | 1970 | 1990 | 1999 |
| *Vilnius* | 200 | 372 | 593 | 578 |
| Central Europe | | | | |
| CZECH REPUBLIC | 1956 | 1970 | 1990 | 1999 |
| *Prague* | 979 | 1,080 | 1,215 | 1,193 |
| Brno | 306 | 334 | 392 | 385 |
| Plzeň | 134 | 148 | 175 | 168 |
| EAST GERMANY (FORMER GERMAN DEMOCRATIC REPUBLIC) | 1956 | 1970 | 1989 (East & West) | 1999 (East & West) |
| Berlin (East) | 1,120 | 1,084 | 3,409 | 3,387 |
| Dresden | 492 | 501 | 501 | 477 |
| Karl-Marx-Stadt (Chemnitz) | 288 | 298 | 302 | 263 |
| Erfurt | 186 | 195 | 217 | 201 |
| Halle | 285 | 258 | 231 | 254 |
| Leipzig | 608 | 585 | 530 | 490 |
| Magdeburg | 259 | 270 | 288 | 235 |
| Rostock | 150 | 197 | 253 | 203 |
| HUNGARY | 1956 | 1970 | 1989 | 1999 |
| *Budapest* | 1,850 | 1,940 | 2,117 | 1,825 |
| Debrecen | 130 | 155 | 220 | 204 |
| Győr | 59 | 100 | 132 | 127 |
| Miskolc | 150 | 173 | 207 | 173 |
| Pecs | 110 | 145 | 184 | 158 |
| Szeged | 100 | 119 | 191 | 159 |
| POLAND | 1957 | 1970 | 1990 | 1999 |
| *Warsaw* | 1,031 | 1,308 | 1,656 | 1,615 |
| Bialystok | 69 | 167 | 269 | 284 |
| Bydgoszcz | 213 | 280 | 382 | 387 |
| Bytom | 179 | 187 | 230 | 205 |
| Częstochowa | 155 | 188 | 258 | 257 |
| Gdańsk | 262 | 364 | 465 | 458 |
| Gdynia | 135 | 190 | 251 | 254 |
| Katowice | 204 | 303 | 367 | 345 |

Table 1.1 (*continued*)

| City | Year Population | Year Population | Year Population | Year Population |
|---|---|---|---|---|
| Kielce | 61 | 126 | 214 | 212 |
| Kraków | 456 | 583 | 750 | 740 |
| Łódz | 686 | 762 | 850 | 803 |
| Lublin | 143 | 236 | 351 | 356 |
| Poznań | 379 | 469 | 590 | 578 |
| Radom | 80 | 159 | 227 | 232 |
| Sosnowiec | 96 | 145 | 260 | 243 |
| Szczecin | 239 | 337 | 413 | 417 |
| Wrocław | 390 | 523 | 643 | 637 |
| Zabrze | 185 | 197 | 204 | 200 |
| SLOVAKIA | 1956 | 1970 | 1990 | 2000 |
| *Bratislava* | 246 | 306 | 443 | 447 |
| Košice | 63 | 144 | 237 | 242 |
| SLOVENIA | 1956 | 1971 | 1991 | 2002 |
| Ljubljana | 115 | 174 | 267 | 257 |
| Maribor | 73 | 97 | 104 | 92 |
| South-east Europe | | | | |
| ALBANIA | 1955 | 1970 | 1990 | 2002 |
| *Tirana* | 108 | 169 | 244 | 700 |
| BULGARIA | 1956 | 1971 | 1990 | 2000 |
| *Sofia* | 592 | 898 | 1,141 | 1,142 |
| Plovdiv | 163 | 255 | 379 | 346 |
| Varna | 120 | 235 | 315 | 293 |
| ROMANIA | 1956 | 1970 | 1990 | 2001 |
| *Bucharest* | 1,237 | 1,475 | 2,127 | 1,917 |
| Arad | 106 | 137 | 203 | 183 |
| Bacău | 34 | 108 | 197 | 207 |
| Brăila | 102 | 152 | 248 | 231 |
| Braşov | 83 | 182 | 264 | 307 |
| Cluj – Napoca | 155 | 203 | 329 | 332 |
| Constanţa | 79 | 172 | 355 | 336 |
| Craiova | 85 | 175 | 317 | 311 |
| Galaţi | 80 | 179 | 326 | 325 |
| Iaşi | 113 | 184 | 347 | 349 |
| Oradea | 82 | 138 | 171 | 221 |
| Ploieşti | 115 | 163 | 259 | 248 |
| Sibiu | 61 | 120 | 188 | 167 |
| Timişoara | 142 | 193 | 351 | 328 |
| FORMER YUGOSLAVIA: BOSNIA AND HERZEGOVINA | 1956 | 1971 | 1991 | 2001 |
| *Sarajevo* | 99 | 244 | 529 | 401 |

Table 1.1 (*continued*)

| City | Year Population | Year Population | Year Population | Year Population |
|---|---|---|---|---|
| CROATIA | 1956 | 1971 | 1991 | 2001 |
| *Zagreb* | 351 | 566 | 704 | 779 |
| Rijeka | 69 | 132 | 168 | 144 |
| Split | 64 | 153 | 190 | 175 |
| FORMER YUGOSLAV REPUBLIC OF MACEDONIA | 1956 | 1971 | 1991 | 2002 |
| *Skopje* | 122 | 313 | 393 | 471 |
| SERBIA AND MONTENEGRO | 1956 | 1971 | 1991 | 2002 |
| *Belgrade* | 470 | 746 | 1,137 | 1,574 |
| Niš | 49 | 128 | 176 | 235 |
| Novi Sad | 69 | 141 | 179 | 298 |
| Podgorica | 60 | 98 | 118 | 162 |
| Priština | 61 | 105 | 108 | 242 |
| East Europe | | | | |
| BELARUS | 1956 | 1970 | 1990 | 1999 |
| *Minsk*** | 412 | 907 | 1,613 | 1,729 |
| MOLDOVA | 1956 | 1970 | 1990 | 1997 |
| *Kishniev* | 190 | 356 | 676 | 658 |
| UKRAINE | 1956 | 1970 | 1990 | 1999 |
| *Kiev* | 991 | 1620 | 2616 | 2590 |
| RUSSIA | 1956 | 1970 | 1990 | 1999 |
| *Moscow* | 4,847 | 6,942 | 8,801 | 8,297 |
| St Petersburg | 2,819 | 3,513 | 4,468 | 4,678 |

Notes:
*Capital cities in italics.
**Urban agglomeration.
*Sources:* Hamilton (1979a: 179–181); Encyclopaedia Britannica, *Britannica Book of the Year World Data 1990*, Chicago: Encyclopaedia Britannica; Department of Economic and Social Affairs, *Demographic Yearbook, 1955, 1957, 1971, 1972, 1973, 1975, 1990, 1991, 1992, 1998, 1999, 2000*, New York: United Nations; Census 2001 for Croatia; Census 2002 (first results) for Macedonia, Serbia and Slovenia; local demographic sources for Albania, Bosnia and Herzegovina, Romania, Bulgaria, Estonia and Slovak Republic.

The great diversity of conditions and trends which has emerged in Central and Eastern Europe in just one decade at the end of the twentieth century thus provides rich opportunities for the comparative study of cities in the region. It is hoped that the following chapters examining broad processes of transformation and detailed case studies of individual capital cities will provide such comparative insights.

## Structure of this Book

The main objectives of this book are, therefore, to identify and describe the relationships among and between:
- the forces that are impacting the development of cities, including those associated with the prevailing historic legacies before the late 1940s, the socialist period of specific development in relative isolation between the late 1940s and 1990s, and the contemporary transition towards market-orientated and democratic systems emphasizing the processes and impacts of integration/ reintegration of Central and Eastern European cities into the European and global economy, and international urban networks;
- the accompanying spatial transformation of the urban-built environment attributed to these changes, including the impact of socio-economic structural changes (i.e. industrial restructuring, privatization, restitution), FDI inflows, changes in spatial organization, land-use patterns, and physical structure; and
- the emerging issues and policy responses to these urban transformations, the success, or otherwise, of national and local governance in organizing appropriate urban planning and management, and the role of the European Union and other international organizations and agencies.

In order to achieve these objectives, a balance between comparative cross-national thematic analyses, in Part One (Chapters 1–6), and case studies of selected representative cities, in Part Two (Chapters 7–14) of this book, was considered desirable, especially in view of the unavailability of comparative and comprehensive studies on inter-urban and intra-urban development in Central and Eastern Europe.

Most of the recent books published on transformation processes in Central and Eastern Europe have been on macro-economic or political issues (with the exception of Andrusz et al., 1996; Enyedi, 1998), but not on their comprehensive effects on urban development, city-competitiveness, and transformation of Central and Eastern European cities (Pichler-Milanović, 1998: 2).

In Part One, the similarities and differences between Central and Eastern European cities' development have been addressed in view of comparisons of the differentiated pattern of historical context and socialist legacies before 1990 (Chapter 2), and the impacts of internal and external forces on (re)shaping these cities and their paths of transformation since 1990. The discussion of the impact of "internal" forces focuses on transformation processes aimed at democratization of society and the liberal – fully market-based – economy, especially changes to the institutional system, the elimination of state control over the land and housing sector, privatization and restitution, and decentralization of decision-making from the central to the municipal level (Chapter 3). The "external" forces – globalization and internationalization – and their effects on city dynamics, structure, functions, spatial organization, spatial forms, and the evolution of city (inter)dependencies have been analysed for the periods before and after 1990 (Chapter 4). The impacts of FDI as the most explicit phenomenon among the "external" forces shaping urban restructuring and development in Central and Eastern Europe have been discussed in terms of international patterns of location and determinants and, in particular, their impacts on the capital and other cities in the region (Chapter 5). Chapter 6 gives a review of the impact of the pressures of globalization, European integration, and general market competition, on the restructuring of the city-built environment, and the transformation of land-use patterns and physical structure. It specifically examines the role of contemporary planning within the overall development of each city.

In Part Two of the book, case studies of many of the capital cities in Central Europe are presented, including examples of the most significant capital cities in the Baltics, South-east, and East Europe, although there are some notable omissions (e.g. Bratislava, Zagreb, Belgrade, Bucharest, Tirana, Minsk) due to limitations of time, space, and programming. Berlin was included as a case study because of its unique transformation, with the reintegration of West and East Berlin into the capital city of a reunified Germany (Chapter 7). Warsaw, Prague, Budapest, and Ljubljana represent capital cities of the "fast-track" reforming post-socialist states in Central Europe (Chapters 8–11). To gain a clearer picture of the diversity of conditions and trends which have emerged in the processes of transformation in the Baltics, and in South-east and East Europe, the capital cities of the Baltic states (Tallinn, Riga, Vilnius), together with Sofia and Moscow, were selected as representative case studies (Chapters 12–14).

In each of these case studies, the authors have reviewed the heritage of past, recent, and likely future trends of the transformation processes, with particular reference to the position of each capital city in relation to its urban region, and national and international context. They have considered the impact of globalization and "Europeanization" or "EU-ization" on urban restructuring and the inter- and intra-urban transformation of each capital city in relation to its functional region and its reintegration into the European city system. They also examine political and geo-strategic changes, local government reforms, the forms that political, economic, and social organizations have taken in recent years, and the implications of these factors on urban governance. They explore economic and demographic trends, the structure and patterns of change of urban economics, sources of capital and labour, privatization reforms, capital investments, and FDI. The processes of land (re)development, land-use changes, and the production of the built environment are also described, as are the resulting issues of social cohesion and changing spatial structure of the city. Planning processes and urban management are also reviewed, city cooperation with global and/or European networks and associations is examined, and finally, prospects – vision and strategy – for the future are identified. The chapters do not cover all the above issues in equal detail, as the authors have been allowed freedom to concentrate on the features of a particular city that they feel are most crucial for understanding the specific impacts of globalization and post-socialist transformation processes, but together they offer a rich source of information and a solid basis for comparison and/or future comparative research.

Some conclusions are presented in the final chapter of this book, as an attempt to draw a summary from the comparative studies presented in Part One and the individual city case studies shown in Part Two. The conclusion shows the main similarities and differences between Central and Eastern European capitals during the process of their intensive inter- and intra-urban transformation in the 1990s from "socialist" to "post-socialist" cities. The impact of globalization, European integration, and the internationalization of their economies and societies, together with national policies and specific regulations, have all had profound effects on inherited local urban structures. The conclusion also states that major policy changes and commitments are needed in Central and Eastern European cities, which should take the necessary initiatives towards improving their competitiveness in "global" city networks, while preserving sustainability and quality of life for their local citizens.

## REFERENCES

Gregory Andrusz, Michael Harloe, and Ivan Szelenyi, eds, *Cities after Socialism: Urban and Regional Change and Conflict in Post-Socialist Societies*, Oxford: Blackwell Publishers, 1996.

Walter Christaller, *Die Zentralen Orte in Süddeutschland*, Lena: Fischer, 1933.

―――, *Central Places in Southern Germany* (translated by C.W. Baskin), Englewood Cliffs: Prentice Hall, 1966.

Györgyi Enyedi, ed., *Social Change and Urban Restructuring in Central Europe*, Budapest: Akadémiai Kiadó, 1998.

R. Anthony French and F.E. Ian Hamilton, eds, *The Socialist City: Spatial Structure and Urban Policy*, Chichester and New York: Wiley, 1979.

Anthony Giddens, *The Consequences of Modernity*, Cambridge: Polity Press, 1990.

―――, "Globalisation: A Keynote Address", *UNRISD News* 15, 1996, p. 15.

F.E. Ian Hamilton, *Spatial Perspectives and Industrial Organisation and Decision-Making*, New York: Wiley, 1974.

F.E. Ian Hamilton and Godfrey J.R. Linge, *Spatial Analysis, Industry and the Industrial Environment Vol. 2: International Industrial Systems*, Chichester and New York: Wiley, 1981.

David Held, Anthony McGrew, David Goldblatt, and Jonathan Perraton, *Global Transformations: Politics, Economics of Culture*, Cambridge: Polity Press, 1999.

Paul Hirst and Graham Thompson, *Globalisation in Question: The International Economy and the Possibilities of Governance*, Cambridge: Polity Press, 1996.

Ron Longworth, "Nowhere are the Winds of Globalization Sensed with more Apprehension than on the Continent of Europe", *Global Squeeze*, 1998, p. 151.

Kenichi Ohmae, *The Borderless World*, London: Collins, 1990.

―――, *The End of the Nation State*, New York: Free Press, 1995.

Nataša Pichler-Milanović, "Globalisation and Transformation of Central and Eastern European Cities", Proposed IAS/UNU Research Project, First Draft (unpublished), 1998.

James N. Rosenau, *Along the Domestic–Foreign Frontier*, Cambridge: Cambridge University Press, 1997.

Raymond Vernon, "International Investment and International Trade in the Product Cycle", *Quarterly Journal of Economics* 80, 1966, pp. 190–207.

———, *Sovereignty at Bay: The Multinational Spread of U.S. Enterprises*, Harmondsworth: Penguin, 1971.

Immanuel Wallerstein, "Dependence in an Interdependent World: The Limited Possibilities of Transformation within the Capitalist World Economy", *African Studies Review* 17, 1974, pp. 1–26.

# 2

# City development in Central and Eastern Europe before 1990: Historical context and socialist legacies

*Jiří Musil*

## Introduction

The aim of this chapter is to describe and interpret urban processes and policies in Central and Eastern Europe during the decades of socialism before 1990. However, as cities and urban systems are typical representatives of that dimension of history, which Braudel (1980) termed the *"long durée"*, it will be necessary to refer also to the more distant urban past of the region. Thus, the resulting picture comprises the basic data about the region's pre-socialist past as well as the socialist transformations of the cities. These data should reveal the past major urban layers and structures with which Central and Eastern Europe enters the contemporary period of deep economic and political changes linked to intensive globalization and European integration. Without combining analytical methods with historical explorations of this kind, it would be impossible to understand the challenges of the urban future in this part of Europe.

### The Main Questions

The central question that the chapter intends to answer can thus be expressed in the following terms: what were the main features of inter- and intra-urban structures in Central and Eastern Europe when this part of the continent entered the complex processes of the political, economic, and social transformations after 1989? Such a general query must be broken down into the following more

specific questions:
- Did urbanization processes under socialism differ from those which previously had taken place and currently are taking place under capitalism? And, if so, in what respect and in what dimensions? And, furthermore, were these differences substantial or small?
- If socialist urbanization did differ from capitalist urbanization, what were the main causes of this difference?
- To what extent did urbanization processes in the socialist countries under study follow basically similar or, conversely, substantially different trajectories?
- How and why did official strategies and policies of urbanization, as well as the norms of town planning, change during the 40 years of socialism? Did continuity of goals and norms exist at all?

## Historical Heritage

It would be a mistake to try to explain present urban patterns in Central and Eastern Europe only in terms of the region's past. On the other hand, the origins of many contemporary urban phenomena specific to this region would remain incomprehensible to us without an elementary summary of the region's urban history. This part of Europe is culturally, socially, and economically a rather heterogeneous area, and therefore it is not easy to regionalize it. Despite the obstacles involved with developing a consistent model for its regionalization, it is nevertheless useful to distinguish at least two macro-zones within this area: Central-East (or Central) Europe, and South-east Europe.

The South-east part of Europe had inherited a network of many trading, administrative, and cultural centres from the Eastern Roman Empire, but these lost their functions and even disappeared during subsequent centuries. There are very few regions in Europe with so many urban relics. But at the same time, until the twentieth century, along with Russia, this region belonged to those zones of Europe where the network of functioning and living urban centres was the least developed. This was especially true of the inland regions. The cities on the Black, Aegean, and Adriatic Seas, some of which were founded in classic antiquity or were relics of the Roman Empire (e.g. Split in Croatia), flourished later on in mediaeval and renaissance times thanks to their links with Venice. By contrast, the wave of German urban colonization (i.e. the foundation of cities endowed with rights and privileges) was restricted only to a few inland areas, such as Transylvania, Transdanubia, Croatia, and Slovenia. Pounds (1971) gives a careful analysis on the urban history of South-east Europe in his summary observations of the region in the following succinct statement:

Urbanisation made very little progress in South-east Europe; indeed it further decayed during the latter middle ages over most of the area. A few of the urban sites of the late classical period continued to be occupied. The cities of the interior had never recovered from their devastation during the period of invasions . . . . Only the mining settlements of Bosnia, Serbia and Montenegro continued as an exception. (Pounds, 1971: 64)

The network of cities, which had become stabilized in this area by the fourteenth century, later changed under Turkish rule, but these changes were definitely not substantial. In any case, the region lacked a network of large cities. Wars and resettlement of the population caused by the expansion of the Ottoman Empire changed the urban network in central and eastern Hungary. Some cities in the regions dominated by the Turks did undergo some growth, however, mainly as a result of the expansion of their administrative functions within the Ottoman Empire. Overall, though, South-east (urban) Europe did not experience any extensive changes between the fourteenth and nineteenth centuries, unlike other parts of Europe, and the weakness of its cities remained its salient feature into the late twentieth century.

This prolonged stagnation was caused by a series of historical processes. Among them were: the general decline of the role of the eastern Mediterranean area in the European economy; the decline of the political and economic power of Venice; the expansion of Turkish rule into the principal parts of the area; the declining impact of economic and political development in Western Europe on the South-east; and, in the nineteenth century, the inability of the region to react effectively to the modernization challenges of West European forms of industrial capitalism.

Thanks to progress made during the last few decades in the urban archaeology of the region north of the Danube, we know that Central Europe had developed its own specific urban network of settlements, which was quite independent of the settlement system of the Roman Empire.

After the collapse of Rome, many Slavonic, "proto-urban" cores emerged in the region, especially on the territories of present-day Poland, Bohemia, Moravia, and north-western Hungary. Paradoxically, these cores proved to be, as Pounds (1971) points out, more stable than the old classical urban settlements of South-east Europe. These proto-urban cores created the framework for the development of Slavic and Hungarian cities in the eleventh and twelfth centuries. Shortly afterwards, this endogenous urban growth was strengthened, especially between the twelfth and the fourteenth centuries, by a new wave of city foundations, known as the German colonization. As many authors, including Pounds (1971, 1973) and Rugg (1985), have stressed, mediaeval German colonization was essentially a complex economic, legal, and political process which can be described as the greatest single transformation of the East European landscape. In the main areas of contemporary Poland and the Czech Republic, as well as in some parts of Slovakia and Hungary, there emerged a specific combination of two urban settlement "layers" – namely, Slavic and Hungarian settlements that started to form a dense network of small and medium-sized cities. This new pattern had already stabilized during the fourteenth century. What the region lacked, however, was large cities, such as those that existed in Western or Southern Europe, like Paris, Bruges, Gent, Milan or Venice, and emerging clusters of large and medium-sized cities similar to those in northern Italy and Flanders. Prague was, however, one exception to this. According to Chandler and Fox (1974), it was ranked in the fourteenth century as Europe's seventh largest city. Nevertheless, the weakness of the region's large cities remained a typical feature of Central and Eastern Europe for centuries.

The historical "watershed" period which again began to separate and distinguish Eastern and Western Europe, and the urban systems of those regions, from each other, included the decades at the turn of the fifteenth and sixteenth centuries. At that time, when commercial capitalism gained strength in the West, states became centralized and better organized, while the nobility began to lose its economic and, to a certain extent, political power. By contrast, Eastern Europe experienced the rise of serfdom, "the rebirth of rigid feudal structures" (see Berend, 1986), the growth of the power of the nobility, the decline of the middle classes, and the stagnation of cities. So, during the relatively short period from the beginning of the sixteenth to the middle of the eighteenth century, Europe became divided into a dynamic Western core area and a semi-peripheral zone in the East. Simultaneously, the Hanseatic League of cities on the Baltic Sea disintegrated and the prolonged wars heavily decimated the population and cities of Central Europe. Nevertheless, the old network of mediaeval cities in the region survived without much change until the second half of the nineteenth century.

New industrial technology and organization then diffused into Central and Eastern Europe, mainly via Saxony and Silesia, and by the intermediary functions of large or growing cities in the region – Vienna, Prague, and Budapest. Yet, this diffusion of industry even benefited the mediaeval network of small towns, especially in northern Bohemia, Silesia, and Galicia. The building of new industrial cities was rather exceptional – in contrast to Western Europe. One of the rare exceptions was the Polish textile city of Lodz. In most cases, new industry developed on the peripheries of old towns or even in rural localities along rivers, which became industrial villages (especially in Silesia, Bohemia, and Moravia). To get a realistic picture of nineteenth-century industrialization in Central and Eastern Europe, one should keep in mind that the decisive part of the region's industry was concentrated before the First World War in a relatively small area, within the triangle formed by Halle, Lodz, and Budapest (Rugg, 1985: 182).[1] Other parts of the macro-region remained predominantly rural and agricultural. This spatial pattern was not significantly changed until the onset of the socialist wave of industrialization.

*Historical Heritage – Main Conclusions*

Despite the fact that both areas, namely Central and South-east Europe, do not form one homogenous cultural and socio-economic region, the main features of their urban developments – which are relevant for the discussion on socialist urbanization in this chapter – can be summarized in the following conclusions:

Firstly, cities of Central Europe were, for long periods of time, part of a socio-economic region which can be described as a semi-peripheral zone to the main European urban core area. The position of South-east European cities during most periods can be described as peripheral. The difference lies in the fact that, from early mediaeval times, Central European cities interacted with the cities of Western Europe through a variety of cultural, technological, economic, and political processes. This applied mainly to large cities, however.

Second, the intensity of contacts between the cities of this semi-periphery and cities within the core areas of Europe fluctuated quite considerably during history and therefore cannot be considered as constant. Epochs of strong interaction (especially from the thirteenth to the fifteenth centuries, in the second half of the nineteenth century and in the initial decades of the twentieth century) were separated by long periods of declining and weak contact. The consequences of these cleavages, which developed mainly in the sixteenth and eighteenth centuries, are still felt in Europe today.

Third, the urban system that evolved in this region remained relatively weak despite its deep historical roots, while in South-east Europe, which went through extreme discontinuities in its political and economic frameworks, the urban system was very weak.

Fourth, Central Europe was, however, not at all homogenous in its economy, intensity of urbanization, and technical and social infrastructure. The western areas such as Bohemia, Moravia, and Slovenia, as well as western parts of Poland and Hungary, did not, up to the Second World War, differ substantially from Western Europe, and in some respects these were more developed than some regions of southern Europe.

Fifth, when evaluating the development of urban systems in different parts of Europe, it is necessary to analyse a relatively long period. From this perspective, even the 40 years of socialism – even though it was indeed a system which aimed at radical political and economic changes – were not a sufficiently long period to change substantially the basic macro-regional structures and hierarchies of cities in Central and Eastern Europe, though 70 years of socialism had more impact on Soviet cities. The intra-urban structure changes proved to be more significant throughout the region.

## Socialist Urban Futures in Soviet Politics

In those countries with centrally planned economies, which also declared that they intended to establish harmonious and cooperative societies with minimum social inequalities, and create "a new person", it proved necessary to supplement economic planning with more subtle instruments of management. These supplementary instruments often consisted of strategies and policies for the planned development of settlement systems and individual cities. Thus, one must examine the main lines of the evolution of ideas that gave direction to the strategies of urban development in the Central European socialist countries. And as they were rooted in the Soviet planning ideology, at least at the beginning, it is necessary to start with a short review of the Soviet (communist) concepts.

All rational forms of planning presuppose that the politicians will supply the planners with relatively specific statements on intended goals. The concepts of the aims of the patterns of settlement systems to be developed remained, however, quite ambiguous many years after the establishment of socialist regimes. The situation in Central European socialist countries after 1945 was comparable to that of the Soviet Union after 1917. One of the main causes of this ambiguity was the fact that the founders of the socialist doctrine never expressed quite unequivocally their views on the spatial organization of the new society. And in a political system that Raymond Aron called "ideocratic", this caused many troubles.

From the works of Marxist classics, indeed, only a few general principles for the spatial organization of a socialist society could have been deduced. The basic ideas were rejection of the market, elimination of social differences between town and country, a more even spatial distribution of industry and population and, last but not least, stress on intentional spatial integration of agriculture and industry. V.I. Lenin, in his "Draft Plan for Scientific and Technical Work", written in April 1918, laid down slightly more specific guidelines. In setting out the main principles for reorganizing industry, Lenin wrote that the plan should include:

the rational location of industry in Russia from the standpoint of proximity to raw materials and the lowest consumption of labour-power in the transition from the proceedings of semi-manufactured goods, up to and including the output of the finished product; the rational merging and concentration of industry in a few big enterprises from the standpoint of the most up-to-date large-scale industry, especially trusts . . . . (Lenin, 1918: 684)

Most of the above-mentioned ideas remained, however, mere exercises in theoretical and utopian thinking. But even the decisions of the Communist Party Congresses in the 1920s still recommended de-concentration policies (i.e. more even distribution of industry in 1925, and in 1927 industrial development in less advanced regions).

The Soviet communists, under the leadership of J.V. Stalin, decided to start rapid industrialization and ruthless collectivization of agriculture. Utopian, social-orientated, and to some extent even political principles (such as the removal of the remnants of national inequalities by a quick industrialization of the non-Russian parts of the Soviet Union) lost their priority. Pragmatic economy (i.e. economic considerations coupled with military concerns) started to be the dominant idea. The 1931 Central Party Committee resolution rejected the decentralization theory and recommended that the town–country gap should be eliminated not by abolishing cities but by transforming them, while simultaneously carrying out a socialist transformation of the countryside, bringing it under the influence of progressive urban culture. The resolution also said that industrial construction must be directed at establishing new industrial centres in agricultural areas in the future, which would ultimately bring about the day when the gap between town and country would be closed. In parallel, it was decided to stop building new industrial plants in the largest cities of Moscow and Leningrad (St Petersburg). As a result of these policies of "accelerated industrialization" and the guidelines applied concerning the location of industry, the Soviet Union, during the first three five-year plans, achieved the highest urbanization rates ever recorded in any major country. Before the Second World War, between 1929 and 1939, urban population increased from 28.5 million to 60.5 million. In that decade, the growth of urban population was caused mainly by demand for labour for the new industries and was made possible by an unprecedented migration of rural population into the cities. However, corresponding infrastructure and house building did not accompany this. Due to the poor quality of the transport infrastructure and the impossibility of improving it quickly, at least around the largest cities, for lack of resources, the Soviet planners could not rely on extensive commuting to rapidly industrializing cities from surrounding rural areas. It is therefore evident that they quite consciously accepted the typical Soviet solution of moving several rural households into one urban flat. This form of common housing, in flats designed for only one family, produced specific anthropological patterns of urban life and human behaviour, with long-term consequences.

Efforts were made to stop the growth of the largest cities by not allowing the building of new industrial plants in Moscow and Leningrad. This followed a decision by the Central Committee of the Communist Party in 1931, and the ban was later extended to five other large cities (Kiev, Kharkov, Sverdlovsk, etc.). But these administrative measures proved to be only partially effective, and all these cities continued to grow (Harris, 1970; French and Hamilton, 1979). The internal mechanisms of industrial–urban growth were already too strong by then.

In spite of enormous human and material losses during the Second World War, the Soviet Union continued the trend of rapid urbanization in the decades that followed. So between 1950 and 1995 the urban population of the Russian Federation rose from 45.7 million to 112.7 million. A similar development was observed in Ukraine, and the result of these processes was that by the 1960s the Soviet Union had achieved world primacy in the number of cities with more than 100,000 inhabitants, while a whole series of large industrial agglomerations had been constructed. The uncontrollable growth of large cities on the one hand, and the decay of small and medium-sized cities, especially in many rural regions, on the other, increasingly became the main problem for Soviet planners. Hundreds of thousands of small settlements disappeared.

In the middle of the 1970s – when two-thirds of the Soviet population were urban – Belousov (1974) described the problems of the Soviet settlement system in the following critical words:

The historically developed system of settlement is still marked by unequal distribution of population over the country, by the existence of two settlement systems that are not yet sufficiently linked with each other – the urban and the rural – by unequal development of towns and settlements of different sizes, by fragmentation or scattering of rural settlements. ... The development of urban agglomerations, based on the largest and large towns, is still under only weak town-planning control and has been accompanied by a number of undesirable economic effects. An autonomous approach to urban development still prevails, without regard for the relationships actually existing in economic life and in employment and public amenities among whole groups of settlements. Insufficient attention is paid to the progressive process of opening branches of enterprises, workshops, and auxiliary industries attached to large firms in the small and medium-sized towns that lie in the hinterland zones of large cities. (Belousov, 1974: 5)

During this whole period, when one of the most dramatic processes of European urbanization was taking place, Soviet urbanologists were divided into several groups. Quite conspicuous were the group of "liberals", and the group of "conservatives" who represented the orthodox Marxist stream. The liberals accepted rapid urbanization, and for them, the growth of large cities seemed to provide an opportunity for the deeper transformation of Soviet society. By contrast, the conservatives perceived the growth of large cities as a dangerous phenomenon that threatened the achievement of socialist goals, so they energetically supported the strengthening of the network of small and medium-sized cities as a means of transforming an essentially "peasant" society.

In most theoretical conceptions and in normative projects worked out in the 1970s and later, one can observe several important shifts:
– first, a retreat from purely normative concepts to strategies which take into account the analysis of actual trends in the settlement system; this implicitly meant a retreat from the post-revolutionary and utopian socialist ideas on the future of cities;
– second, the application of the theory of regional urban systems to planning implementation, especially through the territorial division of labour, and through the specialization of individual centres; particularly through the concept of the "group settlement system" as developed by the Central Research and Design Institute of Town Planning in Moscow; and
– third, a retreat from a one-sided emphasis on the determining role of industry in forming new regional types of urban systems. These studies were modern,

based on analytical procedures, and stressed the role of information, science, and interactions between individual elements of urban regions. As to the contents, they did not differ much from Western regional science approaches, or from the neo-classical version of human ecology. The utopianism of the first Soviet urban strategies had practically disappeared. Territorial planning was understood as a harmonization of different types of regional processes (economy, social needs, environmental aspects, demographic growth, etc.). A more radical endeavour to control these processes reappeared only when the environmental hazards of large urban regions became obvious (Musil, 1980: 65–74).

Even our short and selective account of urban strategies in the history of the Soviet Union highlights some generally valid conclusions. First, the strategies changed in accordance with the transformations of the urban system itself; second, the strategies evolved in discernable separate phases; and third, with rising urbanization and industrialization, Soviet urban strategies began to converge with those which had evolved in capitalist countries. However, it should be stressed that they never became mere copies or modifications of the theories developed in the West.

## Urbanization Strategies in Central and Eastern European Socialist Countries: From Utopia to Realism

The countries of Central Europe started their socialist transformation at different stages in their economic and settlement development. Some entered the socialist period with relatively advanced industrial bases, which had originated under capitalism – as in western Czechoslovakia or in the former East Germany. Some entered socialism as agrarian or semi-agrarian societies – as did the former Yugoslavia, Bulgaria, and Romania. And yet, other states, while having inherited strong industrial centres or agglomerations, also included quite backward areas where industry was almost entirely lacking and urban settlement was sparse – as in Poland and Hungary. In those countries that started socialist transformation as predominantly agricultural societies, urbanization coincided almost completely with the processes of socialist industrialization. These countries therefore represent relatively "pure" examples.

The Eastern European socialist countries also inherited differing settlement and demographic structures, and they varied considerably in size. But the main dissimilarities were found in their distinctive institutional patterns, political culture, and traditions inherited from the past. Some of the countries, like Czechoslovakia or Poland, developed and preserved democratic political institutions and regimes during the inter-war period, but it was more common in other countries of the region to become dominated by authoritarian or semi-fascist regimes.

## The First Years of Socialism (1945–1960)

After 1948, all of these countries, except Yugoslavia, went through a kind of political and economic homogenization through a process of "Sovietization". The crucial part of this process was the establishment of a centrally planned "command" economy, which modified many features of the urbanization processes observed under capitalism. In this context, it is necessary to mention those elements of the command economy which were the most relevant for the socialist modifications of urbanization processes:
- all significant means of production – except in agriculture in some countries – were nationalized or collectivized;
- economic decision-making was hierarchical, and was determined through the respective administrative hierarchies and not through the market;
- prices were set by administrative procedures, and did not reflect costs and demand or supply pressures;
- planning was pervasive and was expressed mainly in physical units rather than in value terms (see also Rugg, 1985: 284).

This imposed Soviet system of command economy, however, did not sufficiently include guidelines for urban strategies applicable in Central Europe. Soviet authorities were probably aware of this fact. Therefore, they allowed politicians, geographers, and planners of the "satellite" countries to conceptualize their own specific urban strategies. This naturally engendered a wide variety of conceptions, and only 10 to 15 years after the communist takeover were opinions on urban futures seen as official policies.

In this first period of socialist development, emphasis was laid primarily on rapid industrialization. According to Enyedi (1987), long-term production goals were stressed as a priority, because it was assumed that industrial growth would lead automatically to the improvement of living conditions. At the same time, the thinking of the planners was still strongly influenced by ideological motives that stressed the social role of industrial development. Attention was focused mainly on the problems of allocating new investments, especially in industry. Decentralization tended to be the dominant theme, and further accumulation of industrial investment in areas where resources had been under capitalism was opposed. Some writers recommended that workplaces should be evenly spread, and that small industrial enterprises should be used for this purpose. Such approaches were soon criticized by economists, who emphasized that the planned industrialization of economically weak regions had its limits, and that certain decisions on the location of new industrial plants should always be guided by economic considerations and national interests. Thus, new industries were to be planned not only to benefit the regions where they were to be located, but also to favour the general advance of the national economy.

The ad hoc decisions made in the first phases of this "socially orientated" industrialization became the first targets of criticism. The second wave of criticism was aimed, by contrast, at the shortcomings of narrowly conceived economic planning. These critiques were obviously promoted by growing difficulties in the daily life of ordinary citizens. However, this dissatisfaction reflected a deeper layer of intellectual troubles and uncertainties. It highlighted the fact that without deeper knowledge of the nature of the relationship between the economy and the spatial system of society, no effective planning is possible. To what extent is it possible to reduce the "urban question" to mere economy or to the relations between classes? To what extent does an independent urban (i.e. socio-spatial) dimension form an analytically separable part of the social systems? The answers to such questions became a precondition for effective intervention in urban processes.

In the first phase of the centrally planned economy – which was later on labelled by the planners themselves as the "phase of extensive development" – the relation between physical and economic planning was one-sided in the sense that the economic plan formed the basis from which specific regional solutions were derived. Physical planning only located investments that had already been included in economic plans. In this context, physical planning was described as "projection" of economic planning. The feedback links that existed between territorial conditions, social potential, and the consequences of placing investment in a particular location and the economic plan was then not sufficiently understood. But the need to supplement the mechanisms of a planned command economy with more subtle instruments was felt quite strongly in Hungary, Poland, and Czechoslovakia. And, as happened several decades earlier in the Soviet Union, the analysts and planners of the new socialist countries were confronted with the question of the degree to which settlement should be concentrated or dispersed. Essentially, the answers reflected the search for the best balance between economic efficiency and the social goals of the emerging "new society". Unfortunately, in the discussions of that time, not enough attention was given to the distinction between the regional impacts of the economic processes of production and distribution, and the planners lacked a deeper knowledge of urban sociology as well as of the interaction between economy, society, and space. They were in the difficult situation of somebody who has the power to decide and to order, but does not have a deep knowledge of the object that is to be regulated.[2]

## The First Generation of Urbanization Strategies (1960s)

The first urbanization strategies started to function as official regulative instruments at the beginning of the 1960s in Hungary, somewhat later in Czechoslovakia, and at the beginning of the 1970s in the former East Germany, Poland, and Yugoslavia.

A kind of normative version of modified Christaller theory of central places served as a theoretical basis of the settlement strategies in Czechoslovakia,

Hungary, and Slovenia. The underlying idea was the desire to implement one of the traditional normative principles of socialist planning, namely to eliminate or at least reduce the social differences dividing various territorial units. Therefore, the concept emphasized that the "centres" containing the basic components of the facilities with which their inhabitants and those of the hinterland zones could satisfy their rights and claims to education and health care, should be spread as evenly as possible throughout the country. At the same time, the three-tier system would help on the economic side and strengthen the concentration of output and investment in the non-production sector. One of the authors of the Hungarian strategy, Perczel (1972), stressed even more explicitly the social dimension of this aim, stating: "It was necessary to propose a system of urban centres and their hinterland zones in which every citizen, wherever he lived or worked, would share equally in modern public facilities at all levels, these being at readily accessible distances."

Hungarian regional policy at that time was decisively decentralist, with five regional centres designated as "counter poles" to Budapest. The establishment of new industrial plants in Budapest was prohibited, and modern industry was located in a number of provincial cities as well as in agricultural regions.[3] Politically, this strategy was implemented by governmental decrees deciding which settlements were to have the status of the first, second, or the third level. This hierarchy was to be a guideline not only for the allocation of direct state investments, but also for the location of industry, commercial services, and so on.

Strategies developed in Poland and the former East Germany also stressed the need to balance economic efficiency and social goals. But the settlement structures inherited from the past, with the great Upper Silesian industrial agglomeration on the one hand and underdeveloped agricultural regions in north-east Poland on the other, necessitated a different approach, as applied, for example, in the Czech Lands. In Poland, the solution to the conflict between concentration and dispersal was being sought in the idea of a "belt" or "corridor" settlement development and planned urban regions and agglomerations. A similar situation also existed in East Germany, but on a different level than in Poland.

## The Second Generation of Urbanization Strategies (1970s)

Some years later, when the effects of the strategies approved by the government were analysed, it turned out that in many instances in Czechoslovakia the administratively selected central places grew at a slower pace than other towns. A similar discrepancy was found in Poland, where the settlements within the main traffic corridors did not grow as quickly as had been expected. Clearly, spontaneous and unpredicted changes were stronger than planners had assumed.

Thus, both theoretical criticism and empirical analyses of the real settlement processes began to call for new ideas and approaches, which were soon translated into new strategies. It was typical for the period that when work started on the second generation of strategies, greater weight was given to the concentration of population and to social activities in cities than had been the case in the previous period – there was a growing acceptance of a positive role of "planned industrial agglomerations". This shift was most spectacular in the intellectual atmosphere among planners in Czechoslovakia, where the normative central place theory had functioned for many years as part of official planning policy. The new generation of strategies worked out in the Czech and Slovak Republics in the 1970s stressed the processes of planned urbanization. Existing regional agglomerations, which formed the main poles of development, plus lower-level agglomerations, technically labelled as "important centres of the settlement system", could be considered as a framework of these processes.

Less conspicuous were the shifts in this respect in Poland, East Germany, and Hungary, because from the very beginning of socialist planning the planners there had faced the difficult task of organizing and regulating the large industrial agglomerations inherited from capitalism, or regulating the development of a large capital city. In this context, one fact was important: many Polish planners *via facti* accepted the universal model of urbanization processes. They ceased to distinguish between socialist and capitalist urbanization. For them it was a universal process modified more or less by socio-economic systems of capitalism and socialism. They considered metropolitan areas, urban regions, and urban agglomerations to be a ubiquitous spatial form of higher stages of urbanization. Other groups of planners tried to save parts of older concepts, which had stressed a third way between economic efficiency and social equity. In the settlement plan for the year 2000 they proposed to combine the spontaneous growth of certain metropolitan areas with a pro-growth policy supporting middle-sized agglomerations in less developed parts of the country. The basic common idea was to maximize interaction among large proportions of the population. To describe this third way, the term "moderate polycentric concentration" was used.

Planners in East Germany were more cautious in their statements than their Polish colleagues, but the substance of their pronouncements was almost identical. Let us add that the thinking of planners and geographers of the Soviet Union during that period moved in the same direction – towards the concept of a "group settlement system" developed in the 1970s, which became a semi-official theory but was in fact only another term for planned urban agglomeration.

In all these shifts in thinking, certain factors were especially important: a declining emphasis on normative and utopian concepts, more attention to actual forms of urbanization processes, the de facto acceptance of the universal nature of urbanization processes, greater emphasis on the active economic role of the settlement structures (which can contribute to a higher efficiency of the economy in the whole country), and more stress on rational concentration of economic and social activities as a means of achieving economic efficiency.

*The Years of Pragmatic Planning (1980s)*

Neither the end of the 1970s nor the 1980s brought any new and innovative models for the future of urban settlement in Central Europe and South-east Europe. The radical processes of "systemization" that occurred in Romania may be considered as the only exception. Most of the measures implemented at that time were only modifications of existing guidelines and the very few new elements were responses to new challenges.

In spite of the explicit policy of the Soviet Union aimed at the reduction of socio-economic disparities among the members of the Council for Mutual Economic Assistance (CMEA or Comecon), the differences between Central Europe and South-east Europe continued to be quite considerable. This was also reflected in the diversity of problems with which individual countries were faced. In Central Europe, however, there existed some new common challenges to which regional and urban planners were obliged to react:

– economic reforms leading to the decline of central planning and to the growth of economic decentralization;
– the growth of "parallel" economics (i.e. the informal economy);
– an unusually rapid growth of urban population, especially in the Czech Lands (Bohemia, Moravia), Slovakia, and Hungary, together with a quick depopulation of rural areas;
– the growth of the service (tertiary) sector of the economy;
– symptoms of stagnation or even decline of old industrial regions based on coal mining and metallurgy;
– the formation of inner peripheries, in the Czech Lands along the western border and in some rural regions; and, last but not least,
– a slow but systematic retreat of the state from some economic spheres such as housing.

These challenges were reflected in new accents in urban and regional policies. They were, however, of a standard and pragmatic nature, similar to those used in non-socialist countries. The first group of policies concerned itself with various forms of state subsidies to the stagnating and depopulating peripheral regions (e.g. higher state subsidies to private house builders in Western Bohemia) and various forms of state support of industrial firms in those regions. Second, programmes for the conversion and revitalization of old industrial regions began to be drafted in Hungary and Czechoslovakia. The development potentials of non-industrial regions for the expansion of new industries were assessed. The use of the concept of "regional potential", which originated in German and Swiss planning systems, remained, however, only an analytical device used, for example, by Czech planning institutes. In Hungary, new stimuli for regional development were sought for the same reasons. Most often, the planners concentrated on the potential of new technologies.

At present, when looking back at this period, it is obvious that most of the measures mentioned were only reactive policies and not robust strategic concepts. The time of great projects and strategies was over.

## Urban Systems: The Reality

After summarizing the evolution of planning ideologies that served or were to serve as guidelines for developing the "socialist" settlement system, it is useful to compare these ideologies with what actually happened. This enables us to answer the four questions put at the beginning of the chapter. When studying the urban phenomena from the sociological perspective, there are four main aspects – the morphological, the institutional, the cultural, and the behavioural aspects – which should be discussed. With the morphology of urbanization processes, it is useful to distinguish three levels of analyses: the inter-urban (i.e. the macro-study of urban and settlement systems), the regional (i.e. "mezzo"), and the intra-urban (i.e. the "mezzo-micro") dimensions.

It seems that there exists a correlation between the *pace* of possible changes and the amount of possible *structural modifications* on the one hand, and dimensions (orders) of urban phenomena on the other. It can be assumed that large factors such as urban hierarchies will be transformed with more difficulty and at a slower pace than smaller (micro- or mezzo) elements of cities or urban regions. Past history, namely the "maturity" of individual urban systems, also plays an important role here. To change an existing settlement system requires more effort and time than to structure a completely new one.

### Socialism and Changes in the Inter-urban Structures of Cities

After the Second World War, when countries of Central and Eastern Europe began the socialist transformation of their political and economic systems, the urban structures that they had inherited were rather diverse. In the Central European countries of Czechoslovakia, Hungary, and Poland, about 40 per cent of the population in the year 1950[4] were already concentrated in urban areas. In South-east Europe, in Albania, Bulgaria, Romania, and Yugoslavia, only 20 per cent of the population lived in urban areas (see Tables 4.1 and 4.2 in Chapter 4). Despite the inherited difference in urbanization levels, all Central and Eastern European countries underwent an impressive wave of urbanization during socialism. The main cause of these urban concentrations was the intensive industrial growth that occurred after the Second World War. Enyedi (1972) described this process in the following terms:

industry and the traditional industrial local elements (i.e., raw materials, manpower, transport facilities) were the driving forces for regional structuring and for urban development. Only a few large metropolitan areas . . . have shown tertiary and quaternary development. (Enyedi, 1992: 871)

For all these countries, especially Poland, Bulgaria, and Yugoslavia, this was the period of the most rapid urbanization in their history. Czechoslovakia and East

Germany, however, were already experiencing their second or even third wave of urbanization, and the process in these countries, despite its importance, was relatively slower.

From data published by the United Nations (1997), it is evident that within Europe the processes of urban growth between 1950 and 1990 were the most rapid in that region which the United Nations defines as "Eastern Europe". The growth index for this period and for "Eastern Europe" equalled 245, for "Southern Europe" 187, for "Western Europe" 148, and for "Northern Europe" 35.[5] It should also be mentioned that the increase in urban population in Eastern Europe was partly caused by high post–Second World War birth rates in the region.

In most of these countries, the growth of urban population was the most dynamic in the first 10 to 15 years of socialism (between 1950 and 1965). But there were also interesting deviations from this pattern. In Czechoslovakia and Hungary, the highest urban growth rates were observed in the 1970s. It is not easy to explain these different patterns of urban growth. One can, for example, hypothesize that the delayed wave of socialist urbanization was caused in Czechoslovakia and Hungary by a combination of multiple factors, such as changing investment policies, changing migration patterns, declining need for labour in agriculture, etc. Thus, "non-systemic" factors probably played an important role. In the first few years after the Second World War, the settlement system of the Czech Lands was strongly influenced by the transfer of German inhabitants from the border regions and the subsequent resettlement processes that this caused. Another "non-systemic" factor was the industrialization of Slovakia, which redirected some investments from Czech to Slovak cities. This example has an instructive methodological role. It points to the fact that the model of urbanization – which should be conceived as a Weberian ideal type – is always modified by empirical realities.

In all countries, it is possible to discern factors that, like in Czechoslovakia, modified the model trajectory of urbanization. In Poland, it was modified by extensive changes in the country's borders, by transfer of German population, and by extensive migration. In Hungary, the "model" process was modified by the unusual size of the capital city, Budapest, and in East Germany by the division of Germany and the specific status of Berlin. Nevertheless, the system logic of the urbanization processes asserted itself in this subregion as well.[6] This is illustrated by the fact that in the period from 1950 to 1990, it was possible to distinguish two groups of countries: those which in the year 1950 were still in the first phases of urbanization, and where during the following decades a rapid concentration of population into cities was taking place; and those which by 1950 had already reached a medium or high level of urbanization, and where consequently the rate of concentration was much lower.

Different dynamics of these processes in individual Central and Eastern European countries homogenized the whole region known as "Eastern Europe" during the 40 years of socialism. Eastern Europe, as a macro-region, never included areas with a great number of large cities and metropoles. In Central Europe, these categories were only weakly represented. For a long time, the only "metropoles" in the region were Vienna and Budapest. During the socialist period, however, some capital and other large cities began to grow quite rapidly. This happened mainly in countries with generally high rates of urbanization processes. In 1950, there were only five urban agglomerations with more than 500,000 inhabitants in the whole region; by 1990, their number grew to nine rapidly growing cities: Belgrade, Warsaw, Sofia, Bucharest, Riga, Zagreb, Katowice, Lodz, and Crakow. With the exception of Riga, all these cities are located in countries with originally low urban concentration. By contrast, the "old" metropoles like Prague and Budapest did not grow substantially during the socialist period.

*Socialism and Urban Regions*

Even more complex and more diversified were the urban processes that took place on the "mezzo" level, namely the formation of urban regions. Strictly comparable information describing the situation in individual former socialist countries in this respect is not available, but some general conclusions can nevertheless be derived from the existing data. Let us examine, first of all, the suburbanization processes.

In some countries, the suburbanization of large cities was practically stopped in the early years of socialist development. This was caused by a host of factors, the most effective being the administrative regulation of in-migration to large cities, and the restrictive policies governing the construction of private family houses in the hinterlands of large cities. Ideological motives played their role here. Another factor was that housing and living costs in suburban communities under socialism did not differ notably from those in inner cities. The suburbs ceased to be attractive in economic terms to most households. Between 1950 and 1970, for example, the population growth rates in suburban communities around Prague were not only lower than in the 1920s, but even lower than in the last few decades of the nineteenth century (Musil and Ryšavý, 1983).[7] A similar phenomenon was observed in the former East Germany. According to Mackensen (1991), "there was no decentralization of agglomerations, neither any expanding agglomerations, but only rather concentric agglomerations". An analogous control of suburban growth most probably also blocked the suburbanization process in large cities in Poland and the Baltics (Tallinn, Riga).

On the other hand, there are countries (such as the former Yugoslavia) in which the politicians and planners encouraged commuting to large cities and employment centres. As a result of these policies, former agricultural communities around Budapest, Belgrade, Sofia, etc., turned into "dormitories" for the new industrial labour force. According to Fuchs and Demko (1977), who studied commuting in the socialist countries, the number of commuters in

Hungary doubled from 613,000 to 1,300,000 between 1960 and 1973, while 35 per cent of all commuters needed more than one hour to reach their workplaces. Commuting in Czechoslovakia and Slovenia (see also Chapter 11 on Ljubljana) was also quite extensive, but most commuters there travelled daily to nearby small or medium-sized cities. In Poland, the number of commuters was somehow lower than in Czechoslovakia and Hungary.

## Changes in the Intra-urban Structure of Cities

Forty years is rather a short period in the history of cities. Nevertheless, the policies of the socialist regimes had had some undeniable effects on the intra-urban structure of Central and Eastern European cities. Among the most important factors of the "socialization" of cities are the following:
- abolition of the land and property market and the introduction of fixed land prices;
- location within a specific part of the city became an almost irrelevant economic variable from the point of view of a user (i.e. firm, enterprise, office) or a potential investor or developer;
- redistribution of existing housing space by dividing large upper- and middle-class houses (i.e. family houses and apartments) into two or three dwellings;
- the introduction of legal norms, which allowed the local authorities to regulate the housing system; and
- the nationalization of retail shops, businesses, trades, services, and restaurants, coupled with the policy of merging small premises into larger shops or trade units.

All these changes occurred during the period of intensive industrialization that took place in the 1950s. Resources were thus channelled away from investments in housing and building infrastructure and into industry, at a time of rapid population growth and creation of new households. Housing construction rates were low and did not even cover replacement needs, let alone rising demographic needs. Thus, massive housing shortages were created in most socialist countries during the first few decades after the Second World War.

These policies also began to change urban spatial patterns. City centres, mainly in those cities which had not been destroyed during the Second World War, ceased to evolve. Due to the irrelevancy of location within these cities (brought about as a result of the state monopoly), there were almost no incentives to invest in the city centre, to build new firm headquarters, hotels, banks, department stores, etc. This contributed to the stability of the physical patterns of urban cores and to the preservation of many historical buildings, but also to the decay of the city centres. From the 1960s onwards, a new factor emerged in most Central and Eastern European former socialist countries: the construction of large housing estates. Those were built most often in the outer zones of cities and changed their structure quite considerably.

The main socio-spatial effects of socialist planning and building on the intra-urban level can be summed up in the following way:
– in city centres, far less physical and functional change occurred than in cities of a similar size in countries with market economies;
– "socialist" cities changed radically through the construction of new housing estates, which were substantially larger than similar housing projects in capitalist cities;
– the role of socio-economic status in the socio-spatial differentiation of socialist cities was less pronounced than in capitalist cities, and was often less important than the role of the family cycle.

Due to changes in socialist housing policies in the 1960s, growing differences in income, and the emergence of a "socialist mixed" housing system with strong "marketization" elements (although often those of a "black" market), new trends in socio-spatial differentiation emerged. On the one hand, old people, low-income households, and Roma people were concentrated (even trapped) in the deteriorating city centres, and in many older residential areas in central urban zones; on the other hand, new housing developments in Czechoslovakia, East Germany, and Slovenia (but not in Poland and Hungary) showed a relatively high degree of social heterogeneity. A new differentiation also started to evolve in the older pre–Second World War villa districts, and in new housing developments built on the outskirts of cities. Some new elements of differentiation were linked to a slow revival of suburbanization processes from the end of the 1970s onwards.

## Conclusion

The main questions formulated at the beginning of this chapter can be summarized in the following basic query: did urbanization processes under socialism differ from those under capitalism? There is a temporal and a dimensional aspect to this question. Urbanization trajectories in socialist countries differed from those in capitalist countries, most notably in the first phase after the socialist takeover. After 10 to 15 years of socialist rule, however, urbanization trends in Central and Eastern European countries began to converge with those in Western Europe.

As regards the dimensional aspects, empirical analyses have shown that the differences in urban patterns between countries with planned economies and those with market economies were increasing from the "macro" to the "micro" level. Inter-urban processes in Central and Eastern European cities did not differ in principle from similar processes in Western European cities. The differences between European capitalist and former socialist countries, ascertained in the current levels of urbanization, express to a large extent the different developmental phases of the countries compared. The "logic" of industrialization and urban growth probably led to analogous effects concerning the "macro" spatial patterns. In both types of society, industrialization caused a concentration of human activities and population, prompted by a desire to minimize the costs and efforts necessary for the functioning of the society in question.

In spite of this basic similarity, the socialist period has left, even on the macro-dimensional level, some noticeable modifications of the ideal-type model of urbanization. Proportionally fewer people lived in the capital cities of the former socialist countries, and in the larger cities of those countries in general, than under similar developmental conditions in countries with market economies. There was less "metropolization" in the socialist countries than in the capitalist ones. On the other hand, the concentration of population in medium-sized cities was higher in the socialist countries. Moreover, a specific feature of socialist settlement processes was rapid depopulation of the small rural communities. This was caused by collectivization of agriculture and by resulting shifts in people's attitudes to land and locality. Peasants lost their deep bonds with the land.

More evident than the factors just listed were differences in urban processes at the regional (i.e. "mezzo") level. In the former socialist countries, suburbanization and metropolization processes did not play an important role in shaping the growth patterns of cities, as they did in the capitalist countries. Socialist cities in general were more compact than capitalist cities, and densities in urban areas were generally higher. It is also obvious that in former socialist countries the "polarization" effects of the growth poles (i.e. larger cities) upon smaller settlements and towns around them were much weaker than in the countries with market economies.

The most pronounced effects, however, were differences on the intra-urban (i.e. "micro") level. The socialist economy and its redistributive nature, the non-existence of a land market, and the specific features of socialist housing policies (i.e. the decommodification of housing in the first few decades of socialism) had discernible socio-spatial effects. The smaller the size of the rapidly growing cities, the more evident were the spatial, physical, and cultural effects of socialist planning and building. Some of these cities were completely rebuilt by means of new construction technologies that had been developed for larger socialist cities.

Therefore, the urban settlement systems that emerged in the former socialist countries of Central and Eastern Europe represented only a modification of a universal model of urbanization (see also Friedrichs, 1985; Kennedy and Smith, 1989; Enyedi, 1992). Modification on the macro level was not significant and will probably be rectified in a relatively short period. This also applies to the mezzo level. Socialism has left its most lasting imprint on individual cities, mainly on their peripheral zones. By contrast, these cities' inner areas have stagnated and many of them have decayed into historical slums.

Three main groups of factors engendered the differences between socialist and capitalist urbanization. The first was the substitution of market allocation mechanisms with central planning. As Claval (1998: 250) stressed, "central planning extended the circuits of information, harmed their quality and considerably encumbered the process of arriving at decisions". Socialism also underestimated the role of the transport and communication sectors. The second was excessive political centralization and the suppression of local and regional autonomy. The third factor was excessive redistribution of resources, also in the regional dimension.

Urbanization processes in individual socialist countries were caused, on the one hand, by inherited urban patterns and different levels of development, and on the other, by different types of economies and cultures. In spite of all these differences, it is evident, however, that in all these countries the "systemic logic" of the general urbanization model asserted itself. This reduced the differences among urban structures in Central and Eastern European countries. The official strategies and policies concerning urbanization changed quite considerably during the 40 years of socialism. The structure of the goals of planned urbanization changed also. All these shifts can be described as a change from the predominance of social services and redistribution-orientated goals to the predominance of economic, technological, and production goals. In fact, this was a form of adapting concepts, strategies, and policies to what was actually happening with the urban system itself.

## Notes

1 See map in Dean S. Rugg (1985: 182), which was adapted from a map by Mellor (1975).
2 In the well-known discussion on "new urban sociology" which took place in the 1960s and 1970s, very few Western sociologists were aware of the fact that an analysis of the difficulties of planning socialist cities would offer many theoretical insights. And those who lived under socialist rule were, for understandable reasons, generally not able to take part in the discussion and to reflect explicitly the dilemmas they faced.
3 For more details see Enyedi (1987: 256–259).
4 It should be mentioned that at the same time in many Western European countries – i.e. Portugal (19.2), Greece (37.3), Finland (32.0), Ireland (41.1) and Switzerland (44.3) – the percentage of population residing in urban areas was lower or similar.
5 The slower pace of urban growth in these parts of Europe was also due to the already achieved high levels of urbanization.
6 Under the term "system logic" of urbanization processes, we understand lawful changes in spatial distribution of population in individual countries (i.e. from a dispersed settlement form to a less dispersed and more concentrated form, and to a hierarchically organized distribution of population). This process is a typical example of a transition from a relative equilibrium to a different state, and its course corresponds to the "S-shaped" (logistic) curve.
7 Thanks to a detailed analysis in this study on the impact of location of communities on their growth rates under capitalism and socialism, it was discovered that those communities located near large cities grew in the Czech Lands (Bohemia, Moravia) much more quickly in the period of market economy than during a centrally planned economy after the Second World War.

# REFERENCES

Tertius Chandler and Gerald Fox, *3000 Years of Urban Growth*, New York: Academic Press, 1974.

Boris Belousov, "Osnovnye problemy sovershenstvovanija sistemy rasselenija" [The Main Problems of the Settlement System in the Soviet Union], *Architektura SSSR 3*, 1974, pp. 3–12.

Ivan T. Berend, *The Crisis Zone of Europe*, Cambridge: Cambridge University Press, 1986.

Fermand Braudel, *On History*, Chicago: University of Chicago Press, 1980.

Paul Claval, *An Introduction to Regional Geography*, Oxford: Blackwell, 1998.

György Enyedi, "Urbanization in East Central Europe: Social Processes and Societal Responses in the State Socialist Systems", *Urban Studies* 29(6), 1992, pp. 869–880.

———, "Regional Development Policy in Hungary", *International Social Science Journal* 112, 1987, pp. 256–259.

R. Anthony French and F.E. Ian Hamilton, eds, *The Socialist City: Spatial Structure and Urban Policy*, New York: John Wiley, 1979.

Jürgen Friedrichs, ed., *Stadtentwicklungen in West- und Osteuropa* [Urban Change in West and East Europe], Berlin, New York: Walter de Gruyter, 1985.

Roland J. Fuchs and George J. Demko, "Commuting and Urbanization in the Socialist Countries of Europe", *Bulletin of the Association for Comparative Economic Studies* 19, 1977.

Chauncy D. Harris, *Cities of the Soviet Union*, Chicago: Chicago University Press, 1970.

Michael Kennedy and David A. Smith, "East-Central European Urbanization: A Political Economy of the World-System Perspective", *International Journal of Urban and Regional Research* 13(4), 1989, pp. 597–624.

Vladimir Ilich Lenin, *Selected Works, Vol. 2*, Moscow: Progress Publishers, 1967.

Roy Mellor, *Eastern Europe: A Geography of the Comecon Countries*, New York: Columbia University Press, 1975.

Rainer Mackensen, *Urbanization under Federalist and Centralist Government: The Case of Two German States 1980–1988*, Budapest: IGU Commission on Urban Systems and Urban Development, 1991.

Jiří Musil, *Urbanization in Socialist Countries*, White Plains, New York: M.E. Sharpe Inc., 1980.

Jiří Musil and Zdeněk Ryšavý, "Urban and Regional Processes under Capitalism and Socialism", *International Journal of Urban and Regional Research* 7(4), 1983, pp. 515–516.

Károly Perczel, "A városközpontok országos rendszere és munkamegosztása" [The National System of City Centres and their Division of Labour], *Területrendezés 3*, 1972, pp. 16–28.

Norman J.G. Pounds, *A Historical Geography of Europe, 450 B.C.–1330 A.D.*, Cambridge: Cambridge University Press, 1973.

———, "The Urbanization of East-Central and South-east Europe: A Historical Perspective," in George Hoffman, ed., *Eastern Europe: Essays in Geographical Problems*, London: Methuen, 1971, pp. 45–78.

Dean S. Rugg, *Eastern Europe*, London and New York: Longman, 1985.

United Nations, *World Urbanization Prospects: 1996 Revision*, New York: United Nations, 1997.

# 3

# City development in Central and Eastern Europe since 1990: The impacts of internal forces

*Iván Tosics*

## Introduction

By the end of the 1980s, Central and Eastern European cities had for four decades been part of the socialist political and economic system. Although there were visible differences in their outlook and level of development, the common elements of the socialist system still dominated the institutional structure and the major decision-making processes within these cities. The collapse of socialism in 1989–1990 brought about a totally new situation in which strong external and internal forces started to exert their influence.

This chapter analyses the transition from centrally planned to other, more or less market-orientated urban systems, concentrating on the internal forces of this process. By "internal forces", we mean all the efforts made by different actors within these countries or from elsewhere to dissolve the "old" socialist system and create new elements. In contrast, "external forces" refer to broader processes, not specifically connected to the transition of the Central and Eastern European countries, such as globalization of the economy or extension of the European Union; these are discussed in the next two chapters.

To understand the logic of transition, an interpretation of the "socialist city-development model" dominated by state control and non-market institutional forms must be given first. This provides the basis for analysing the transformation of one system into another, in which both market and private, non-market elements are present. Subsequently, this chapter discusses different aspects of the dissolution of the socialist city-development model in more detail.

The focus is on the internal factors of change, such as the elimination of state control over the land and housing sector, privatization and restitution, and decentralization of decision-making from the central towards the municipal (in larger cities, even sub-municipal) level. Changes in the institutional system engendered the disappearance of the key actors of the socialist system (central planning agencies, monopolistic planning developer management organizations) and the emergence of new actors, such as the market-orientated private developers and commercial banks.

Therefore, this chapter combines theoretical and empirical approaches to the transition period in the large cities of Central and Eastern Europe. The analysis concentrates on changes in the residential sector and also on developments in the commercial and real estate sectors, such as the emergence of shopping centres and large-scale office developments. The final section discusses the future of city development in the Central and Eastern European countries: what kind of model or alternative models will replace the once common socialist city-development model, and how much will these model(s) differ from those which were dominant in the Western (American and European) cities one, two, or three decades ago? In other words, will post-socialist cities follow one given route towards a capitalist, free-market city, dominated by massive suburbanization of the middle classes, growing segregation within the city, and the takeover of non-residential functions in the central business district (CBD), or are other routes also possible or likely? Our initial hypothesis is that different development paths are observable among the post-socialist cities, as they move away from the common socialist city-development model; there are not only differences in the speed of change from the socialist model to another, but also differences in the direction of change – towards different variants of the capitalist city, towards another model in which market elements are mixed with non-market elements, or towards the "third world" model of cities. Thus, the starting point, the socialist city-development model, was common, but the end point is as yet uncertain and will most probably be different in large cities of the different subregions of Central and Eastern Europe.

## Theoretical Background: Was there a Distinctive Socialist Model of City Development at All?

There are debates among urban researchers as to whether or not a "general model" of city development in advanced societies exists (Szelényi, 1996: 286). Those defending the idea of the existence of a general model base it on changes in developed Western (American and West European) cities, describing such changes as sequential periods of urbanization, suburbanization, desuburbanization, and reurbanization. In this model, the process of industrialization is considered to be the decisive factor, while other variables, such as the type of political-economic system involved, are treated as subordinate (see van den Berg et al., 1982).

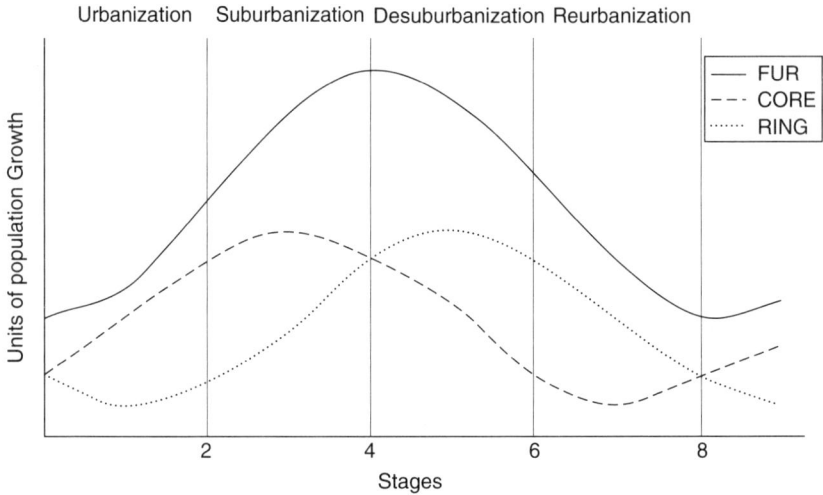

Fig. 3.1 Model of city development.
*Source:* Berg et al., 1982: 38.

This is "a globally applicable model", in which new "stages were first developed in centres of economic and industrial innovation" and later "were transmitted from these core areas to other parts of the world, with different countries embarking on different stages at different times". The case of the development of Central and Eastern European cities is regarded by this approach as part of the general model, being only "deferred" compared to the case of the Western European and especially the American cities, because industrialization is deferred in Hungary compared to the more developed Western countries. Consequently, in this view, "socialist urbanization was not a new model of modern urbanization. Rather, Central European socialist countries replicated stages of a more generally applicable global process of urban development" (see Enyedi, 1996: 102). This model can be called the "ecological" model of city development as it is described in Berg et al. (1982) and in Enyedi (1996).

The other theoretical stance, the "historical" approach, emphasizes the importance of the mode of production (the neo-Marxists) or of the political-economic order (the neo-Weberians) and considers the process of industrialization as of secondary importance. According to this approach, no general, linear model of city development is considered to exist. The starting statement of the historical approach is that "societies with different socio-economic orders will produce qualitatively different urban conditions" (Szelényi, 1996: 290). Thus, one major difference is that the same development phases can occur in different sequences in different cities, depending on the development of the given socio-economic systems.

Consequently, according to the historical approach, it is possible that the Central and Eastern European cities follow a different development path from their Western counterparts. Szelényi raises the hypothesis that in the case of socialist cities, not even the sequencing of urbanization and suburbanization phases resembles those of Western cities. Following the change from a centrally planned into a market society, post-socialist cities (in which some forms of suburbanization have already started) might be dominated again by urbanization, as the lifting of political and planning controls might result in a massive influx of poorer population from less developed regions. Häussermann (1996) also emphasizes the importance of the influence of socio-economic order on city development. The socialist city "could be designed according to theory and . . . realised according to the plan, and the state was in charge of all the means necessary to implement it. In former times, not even sovereign rulers disposed of such great power over urban development" (Häussermann, 1996: 215).

It is not the task of this chapter – or this book – to settle the dispute about the existence and universality of a general city-development model, or to give a final answer to the question of whether socialist cities were only in a deferred stage of their development or developed according to a totally different, distinctive model. The approach of the chapter, however, is not neutral – in fact it is closer to the historical approach and its "neo-Weberian" view, as it starts from an analysis of the most important political, institutional, and economic elements of city development, endowing these elements with the major role in the explanation of the dilemmas of the transition and of the new model(s) to be introduced.

## Key Structural Aspects of the Socialist Development Phase

The historical context and political legacies of the pre-1990 development of socialist cities are discussed in the previous chapter of this book. Here, therefore, it is only necessary to summarize those elements of the socialist city-development model that can be regarded as crucial from the point of view of transition from the original socialist model to other forms of city development.

### Control of the State over Supply and Demand Factors

The socialist model did not ensure free choice between different supply options for consumers. On the one hand, the state strongly determined the income of citizens, defining it on a low level, eliminating from it all those cost components (education, housing, health care) which were to be given free to citizens through state services. At the same time, the state acquired virtually all important means of production and centralized all important investment decisions (Hegedüs and Tosics, 1996: 16; UNECE, 1997: 1). Price control over the whole economy was an additional tool in the enforcement of political goals. The outcome was a planned economy with a primacy of industrial sectors at the expense of service activities. Many social services were provided by state enterprises. The main political goal – general accessibility to social services – was achieved in some of these services (like education and health care), although they were generally of a low standard and required considerable investment from the state budget. As a logical extension of the basic system, the "merit-based" allocation of higher-level services was developed based on the social status and contacts of people.

The control of the state over the demand and supply sides of the economy could not be fully established and could be fully maintained even less during subsequent decades of socialism. The history of the socialist housing model (Hegedüs and Tosics, 1996) illustrates this statement, showing the contrasting development tracks in the different countries and highlighting the case of Hungary, where quite soon, both on the demand and on the supply side, alternative mechanisms ("cracks") have developed, decreasing the efficiency of state control. In any given period, the real strength of state control was the outcome of compromises between conflicting political and economic interests, leading to the almost total elimination of state control before the end of the 1980s.

## The Special Characteristics of Socialist Urban Development

Derived from the socialist political model and the system of planned economy, the following political-institutional factors are considered as important specific determinants of the Eastern European socialist urban and housing policies:
- significant state ownership of the land and housing stock in cities as a consequence of confiscation and nationalization;
- residential incomes under (in the beginning, total) state control;
- strong and direct state control over land use, leading to very specific land-use patterns expressing the preferences of the socialist state (Bertaud and Buckley, 1997: 3);
- administrative limitation of housing consumption (one dwelling per family);
- state control over certain housing policy factors (state-financed housing construction, social housing policy, subsidized private house-building, loan origination, construction industry, and materials);
- control over the private housing market (private rents) and indirect regulation of the self-financed form of housing construction;
- administrative limitation of the size and development (inflow of population, industrial growth) of major cities; and
- direct control over the financial resources of cities, and over the political decision-making process.

Subsequent chapters of this book, describing the development of individual Central and Eastern European cities, will show how these elements were introduced and what effect they had on the development of these cities. There were significant differences in the timing and extent of the measures introduced (e.g. control over urban land was total in Moscow from the 1920s, while in most Central and Eastern European cities it was only partial – concentrating on the most dense core of the city – and in some cases introduced only at the end of the 1950s). Yet the logic of state control was the same, and had very similar consequences.

The institutions and households involved in urban development created specialized reactions and strategies to the listed – and from time to time changing – regulatory elements. For example, the most important state institutions involved in residential construction formed a "housing construction chain" (an institutional trust, a power-group of state planners, investors, developers, financial institutions) to acquire the direct state funds available on the supply side for the construction of new units (Hegedüs, Partos, and Tosics, 1980). Simultaneously, the behaviour of households was dominated by their efforts to obtain major subsidies on the demand side. Clear evidence for this was provided by the "double mobility way" of the better-off households: first, they obtained a state rental or cooperative flat from the state, mostly in less desirable locations but at a containing huge state subsidy. Later they sold these flats and acquired, on the market, the units they preferred. Eventually, strong state control and housing policy built on big subsidies resulted in distorted behaviour of the housing system on both the supply and demand sides, as a result of actions aimed primarily at obtaining the state subsidies provided through the housing sector.

Iván Szelényi, in his study on urban development under state socialism, divides the pre-transition period of the Eastern European (socialist) urban development into two phases (Szelényi, 1996: 304). In his evaluation, the first two-and-a-half decades of the socialist system, namely the period between the late 1940s and the mid-1970s, was dominated by the state, because of its decisive role in financing, constructing and allocating new housing units, and total control over the land market. The second phase, between the mid-1970s and the transition period of 1990s, is evaluated by Szelényi as a period in which market factors gained ground.

Hegedüs and Tosics (1996) analysed the processes from a similar perspective in their study of the "East European housing model". When discussing the peculiarities of the situation in Hungary compared with the general features of the "East European housing model", they state that the private sector economy has always had a role, and that the confiscated (nationalized) stock of units hardly exceeded half of the entire stock even in major cities. Part of the land market was always in private hands, amid quasi-market conditions. Political control was, of course, still the core of the system, within which even in the relatively liberal periods no market sphere could form where economic feedback and the rules of demand and supply could have freely operated: instead, the system was dominated by a kind of political feedback, which is an essential element of planning based on politics.

The distinguishing feature of Hungary, however, was that a limited market was still in operation throughout these housing policy and urban development processes, mainly ruled by politics and planning. The changing power relations of political and planning control and the private sphere necessitate the definition of at least four periods within the socialist system, depending on how much space was allowed to market conditions by politics: the periods of centralization between 1947 and 1956, and 1969 and 1980, were each followed by a relative *détente*, with a better climate for the private sphere. However, Chapter 12 gives a slightly different periodization for the development of Sofia.

Socialist urban development was of course influenced by, besides housing policy, other sectoral development policies, essentially based on the same logic. Here we highlight economic development and infrastructure investments, and their internal relations. In the 1960s and 1970s – when already suburbanization was under way or advanced in some Western countries – in Central and Eastern Europe, centrally planned and spatially concentrated industrial development (in a few new towns, but mainly in some of the already existing cities) brought about rapid growth of urban agglomerations. The "under-urbanization" theory (Szelényi, 1996: 287) based on different patterns of locating economic and infrastructure investments shows, however, how different this development was from Western suburbanization.

The starting point is the concentrated industrial development that took place in urban centres, which was accompanied by relatively slow infrastructural development of these cities. The new industrial workers of new urban enterprises could hardly settle down in the cities themselves, as real estate was more expensive there and permission was needed for purchase. At the same time, workers could commute between their rural residency and the industrial cities by well-developed and cheap public transport, or might settle in the agglomeration where real estate was cheaper and no permission was needed for purchase. As a consequence, increases in population were most significant in the surrounding areas of urban centres. This is a unique development model of the agglomeration, where the source of rapid increase in population in the area surrounding a city was not the residents moving out from the city but those coming in from rural areas, willing but not allowed to move into the city itself. This model may be considered as the "Eastern European type of urbanization" (Ekler, Hegedüs, and Tosics, 1980: 111). The notion of "under-urbanization" did not mean that cities were not increasing at all. From the 1970s on, the development of urban infrastructure was accelerated in socialist cities, mainly in the form of pre-fabricated large housing estates with high density of population. Thus, another important feature of the socialist urban model evolved.

The development features described above are characteristic of most Eastern European socialist countries. There are of course some deviations in details of minor importance between countries, like the amount of subsidies spent and the extent of control exerted on the self-financed forms of housing construction. As a consequence, different patterns have formed in the directions of mobility of the wealthier households (towards condominiums) and the poorer residents (towards single-family housing) within and around the cities.

## The Specific Urban Structure of Socialist Cities

When arguing that the development of cities during the socialist period was significantly different from Western urban development processes, Szelényi considered the following three factors to be the most important distinctive features of socialist city development as a result of different political-economic circumstances (Szelényi, 1996: 287):
– under-urbanization: industrialization following the Second World War was accompanied by a lower degree of urban population growth than in Western countries;
– lower level of urbanization of major cities: as a result of political-economic social development policies, socialist cities were at a lower level of urbanization than Western cities of a similar size (the most obvious illustration being a comparison of the Eastern and Western sectors of the city of Berlin); and
– special urban development features of major cities: socialist cities' internal structures, social segregation, and slums have taken different directions from those in Western cities.

The last distinction mentioned means that a major city in Central and Eastern Europe – which in its structure resembled Western European cities even in the period between the two World Wars – would be marked at the end of the socialist period by different urban development characteristics. The most important urban structural elements of this type of development were:
– inner city areas dominated by a deteriorating stock of old buildings (due to neglect of the confiscated or nationalized stock and rent controls at a low level);
– transitional zones with mixed building dominated by obsolete large industry and other functions;
– concentrated development of high-density housing estates in the *outer zones* (under the given economic and political circumstances, this concentrated form was created to locate the "overheated" public housing investments);
– emergence of elite zones with high housing quality in the *green belt areas* (the opportunity for the political and economic leaders of the period to locate there was created through the nationalization of earlier elite districts, and their promotion was furthered by government and by subsidized private investments); and
– the emergence and relatively rapid growth of settlements in the *suburban region* with low-level infrastructure, largely inhabited by the lower echelons of society (for the new urban workforce, who could not move into the city because of administrative restrictions, this was the only area where they could settle and get housing largely from private resources, accessible to their place of work).

Due to the special features of the individual elements of the urban structure, the housing density gradient of the socialist cities also had specific characteristics.

Western European cities usually have an evenly decreasing density with increasing distance from the city centre. The case of socialist cities is different: the transitional zones have a lower density as compared with the evenly decreasing model (because of under-utilized areas), while the curve jumps upwards in the outer areas of the cities (because of high-density housing estates) (French and Hamilton, 1979). Indeed, Bertaud and Buckley have recently shown in the case of Crakow that land use patterns . . . and the massive housing estates, are not likely to have been situated in their present locations if market forces had governed locational decisions. Indeed, one indication that these locational patterns are unusual is the finding that these investment patterns cause more than half of Crakow's population to live at densities similar to those of New York City, a city ten times its size and one of the densest cities in the world (Bertaud-Buckley, 1997: 3).

The socialist model of housing and urban planning represented a housing and construction policy completely subordinate to a centralized, party-ruled, planned economic system. The socialist state regarded housing and construction policy as a matter of politics. To achieve political objectives it applied every possible form of intervention to regulate both supply and demand. Housing policy and urban planning became attached to power and served as a source of its legitimacy. As a consequence of being embedded in the legitimization of the power structure, the institutional and subsidization elements of the socialist model of housing policy and urban planning (e.g. housing factories, parts of the constructional chain, diversion of prices, subventions) were much more firmly established than their Western equivalents, most of which were abolished after a certain period of time.

The really distinctive marks of the socialist model of urban development are not to be found in specific elements of its structure, but in the system of political, economic, and social relations underlying their emergence: "the essence of socialist housing was its structure of decision-making in which the planning authorities – both party and state – had a decisive role in determining the conditions of informal contracts with the most important institutions and layers of the population" (Hegedüs and Tosics, 1996: 37). Thus, strict state control and centralized, politically motivated planning procedures were the characteristics of the socialist housing system and its urban development as well. These strong institutionalized elements and the procedures of political decision-making in place at the time resulted in the stabilization of many of the above-mentioned elements of urban structure:

– inner districts: the bulk of apartments built around the turn of the century or earlier, and nationalized in the early 1950s, received basically no major maintenance or rehabilitation investment for 40 years. As a result, the inner districts of many of the socialist cities have a huge stock of apartments in bad

condition (these figures run to hundreds of thousands in Budapest, which constitutes the single most serious rehabilitation problem in Europe [Hegedüs et al., 1993: 111]);
– new housing estates: a large share of the housing in socialist cities is located in concentrated, high-density housing estates. The well-known problems of such estates (monotonous environment, huge distance from the inner city, small size of dwellings) are especially true for those constructed with the panel technology of the 1970s. During the socialist period the buildings on these housing estates received no maintenance, so by now hundreds of thousands of apartments are in urgent need of comprehensive rehabilitation; and
– suburban settlements: population growth and intense housing construction from private resources was not matched by proper infrastructure development. In certain poorer sectors, a significant infrastructure backwardness emerged (in the early 1990s, for example, only 49 per cent of the dwellings in the southern Pest sector of the Budapest agglomeration had drinking-water supply pipes and only 12 per cent had proper sewage systems).

As a result of four decades of socialist social, political, and economic relations, the Central and Eastern European cities have developed according to specific political-institutional factors. The cities' populations and institutions have established their strategies in reaction to these circumstances. As a consequence of specific political and economic regulations and reactions to these regulations, the Central and Eastern European cities underwent significant changes and their urban structure became markedly different to the Western European city-model.

## The Transition: Fundamental Changes in the Political and Economic System

The basic political, institutional, and economic conditions of the former Eastern European socialist city-model were abolished when the political regime changed at the end of the 1980s. Overall state control was terminated and long-term politically motivated planning was been replaced by short-term (at most, one-year) planning. Other important factors of city development have changed, such as the main actors in decision-making positions, and ownership of the means of production and urban housing and land. This sudden change in all the fundamental conditions of city development made the period of transition one of the most turbulent and interesting phases of development in Central and Eastern European cities. Some of these countries started the transition, in an economic sense, years before the political changes took place. The most notable cases are Hungary, where central planning was eliminated in 1986 for local government financing and in 1988 for the housing sector, and Slovenia, where economic, monetary, and enterprise reforms emerged in 1987, marking a definite break-up of the previous "market socialism" (see Chapter 11). The fundamental political changes only came, however, in the course of the early 1990s, with the peaceful transition from a one-party system into a democratic multi-party system with free elections. In most Central and Eastern European countries, this was the change that opened up the way for fundamental shifts in the economic system, and for the creation of more independent local governments as well.

## The New Political Systems

Parallel to the establishment of democratic multi-party parliamentary systems with free elections, the key question for the political transition was decentralization. In all socialist countries, subnational levels of government (regional/counties, local authorities) existed, but these had not been at all independent – political and financial decisions were directed from above and were controlled by the party apparatus. "Subnational governments were essentially deconcentrated units (or branch offices) of the central government and had little or no financial autonomy" (Bird et al., 1996: 1). Very soon after the establishment of the new democratic government at the central level, totally new legislation was adopted for local self-governments (in Poland and Hungary in 1990, in Bulgaria and Romania in 1991, in Albania, Russia, and Ukraine in 1992, in Slovenia in 1994). In most countries, the new legislation ensured, in principle, the establishment of independent local self-governments, and much of the public sector decision-making rights (and responsibilities) could be transferred from the central to the local government level. "Decentralization is a key dimension of the national transition from a command to a market economy. The total level of public sector activity must be dramatically reduced, but at the same time the new subnational governments must be allowed to build staff and institutional capacities" (Bird, Ebel, and Wallich, 1996: 2).

It is not the aim of this chapter to evaluate the decentralization processes of the post-socialist countries. It is unquestionably a large measure of success that during the course of the first decade of the new political system, independent local governments have been developed in most of these countries. "There is no direct involvement of any central government officers or politicians in local decision-making and central supervision is restricted to checking the legality of procedures" (Bennett, 1998: 38). In many countries the number of local governments increased dramatically (in the Czech Republic and Hungary the figure doubled, and in Bulgaria and Slovenia it more than doubled), which means that the new local governments became small in number of population, even smaller than before (e.g. average size in Hungary 3,000, and in the Czech Republic and Slovakia below 2,000, with 50 to 80 per cent of settlements below 1,000 population). Consequently, the new communes became too small to be able to administer some services, and this became a serious obstacle to real decentralization within the state as a whole (see Bennett, 1998: 41). Central governments were not keen to allow the local governments to develop into powerful political entities. Therefore, no substantial financial autonomy was given to local governments: where local taxes were established at all, their magnitude was strongly limited and settlements continued to depend mainly on central transfers.

Furthermore, in many countries, the intermediate level (counties) of subnational government was terminated or made insignificant as a reaction to the substantial role these entities played in the socialist system in the allocation of political directives. All these facts prove that decentralization of political power was limited in the post-socialist countries. Although power-sharing between the national and local levels changed substantially compared to the socialist period, the central state managed to preserve a large amount of its power. The establishment of independent local governments "has been accompanied by a higher degree of centralism than was first intended . . . as a consequence of the fragmentation of the local level, the weakness (absence) of an intermediate level and as a result of the desire for efficiency and expedience in the context of economic transition" (Michalski and Saraceno, 2000: 19). In this situation, the role of the large cities, especially the capitals, increased as the only potential alternative power centres.

The decentralization process is applied in a very differentiated way to the individual countries of Central and Eastern Europe. Differences range from Hungary, where central government and legal regulation on local governments were more or less stable in the last decade, to Albania, where various crisis situations periodically led to huge changes. There are also big differences in changes to institutional structure; in some countries, the "old" political forces – the parties, the big state enterprises, the "interest associations" of the power elite – disappeared, and the newly elected local governments were given substantial power, while in others the old structures are still alive and continue to hold sway. An illustration of this "power play" was the deeply discussed question of the restructuring of the monopolistic state enterprises. Arguments were raised for compromising solutions between keeping these enterprises in an unchanged form, and the radical approach of privatization (or even total dissolution) of the companies. In the public utility sector, for example, the idea was raised to create non-profit companies from the state-owned utility companies. However, attempts at such a "third way" produced very controversial results.

For example, at the 1988–1989 Noszvaj (Hungary) conferences on the restructuring of the public rental sector, an idea was discussed that the Hungarian state-owned monopolistic public maintenance companies could be easily restructured into non-profit housing associations. Experience since then has not supported this belief, as companies did not become more efficient with small reorganizations. The reason behind this was simple: new rules cannot be introduced efficiently if the old institutional structure – with the old interest relations and the old leaders – remains. In Hungary, with few exceptions, real changes only occurred if these companies were dissolved and new private ventures were established, or total privatization was carried out. The Polish approach was different and many of the old cooperatives continued in the new market-orientated system (there are, however, controversial evaluations about their efficiency). Probably the most successful example of this special type of restructuring was the German model, where all top managers of state-owned utility companies were replaced by experienced managers of similar, market-based Western companies. This happened in parallel to the change of ownership relations of the company from a state-owned to a local-government-owned limited liability company, functioning according to non-profit principles.

Besides decentralization, which is a phenomenon often discussed in Western European countries as well, Central and Eastern European countries had to solve another, special problem: compensating for political suppression. The new political system, of course, made it possible for suppressed political forces to come back to the political arena. Moreover, in most countries, direct financial compensation was given to those groups that suffered the most during the socialist period. In regard to urban development real-estate transfers, restitution of urban land and existing residential real estate was the most important method used.

*Economic Transformation*

The details of the various economic transformations that occurred, dominated by privatization, have been discussed in many books and journals (e.g. for an analysis of the privatization of the economy see UNECE, 1997: 4–5; for privatization processes in the housing sector see Hegedüs, Mayo, and Tosics, 1996), and also in Chapters 4 and 5 of this book. Central and Eastern European countries differ from each other regarding the method used for the privatization of the economy. Privatization strategies range from employee and management buyout schemes through voucher systems to cash privatization. Chapter 11 of this book describes briefly the different methods used, such as the case of Slovenia, where the law made it possible for economic enterprises to select their own privatization strategy. Most recent economic data tend to show the advantages of those countries that used cash privatization against those where vouchers were allocated among the population (in this latter case the real ownership of economic enterprises was not clarified, and this postponed the necessary market decisions).

It is clear that both the method and the pace of privatization were politically determined. A good illustration of this is the case of housing: Hungary and Budapest, for example, could have kept more public rental housing instead of virtually privatizing the entire sector; the transformed housing sector could have worked well with a substantial public rental sector (Hegedüs et al., 1993). Under the pace of political changes in Hungary, however, these alternatives were soon swept away and replaced by more radical, market-orientated solutions. This was not the case in all of the Central and Eastern European countries, as in some of them the restructuring process happened at a considerably slower pace.

# The Development of Post-Socialist Cities in the 1990s:
## New Public Policies and Emerging Market Processes

In the course of 1989–1991, all the important factors of city development were changed in the Central and Eastern European countries. In general, planning and development commands/instructions and restrictions coming from the central level terminated, a practice similar to that of sending central budget transfers to the local level tied to prescribed interventions. Most cities became much more independent in the political, administrative, and economic sense than before in determining the development of their area and population. As a result, all cities of the Central and Eastern European region moved substantially towards the direction of the "market city": they became more decentralized and privatized, with growing differentiation between different parts of the city. Below this common surface, however, very different circumstances, aims, and real processes can be discovered in the different cities of the region. The following sub-sections aim to conceptualize the most important changes in city development. Discussed first are the changes that occurred in the political, administrative, and financial framework of the cities; this is followed by an analysis of the main market processes at work, and finally we analyse the consequences of these changes in connection with mobility processes.

## The Changing Regulatory and Institutional Environment of City Development

It is not easy to elaborate the real changes that took place in the framework of local urban development in different Central and Eastern European countries. Despite a general tendency towards decentralization, the central (country) level had the opportunity to retain substantial influence over local urban development by introducing central regulation of public control over market processes, retaining some elements of direct central political control over local governments, and inter-governmental financing, regulating the level and proportion of public financial means transferred to the local levels.

When analysing changes in the role of the public sector, we must distinguish between two factors: first, the change in the regulation of general public control over market processes, and second, the allocation of the remaining elements of public control between the central and local government levels.

### The Regulation of General Public Control over Market Processes

As already discussed, the essence of the socialist model was strong state control over urban development processes, both on the demand and on the supply side. The change from the socialist model towards market-orientated model(s) means in general the elimination of this control or the replacement of its elements by less direct methods.

Changes in state control on the demand side:
- no state determination of the income of citizens;
- no state limitation on consumption at the higher end (unlimited consumption of housing, land, and means of production for citizens); and
- less state control over consumption at the lower end (homelessness and unemployment become much more common, and social services for homeless and unemployed are weak).

Changes in state control on the supply side:
- level of control: as a consequence of decentralization, many elements of public control were transferred to the local level (e.g. rent setting) or disappeared entirely (e.g. long-term planning for industry or housing);
- content of control: as a consequence of privatization, state ownership of production factors, housing, and land diminished or disappeared, state monopoly over important investment decisions became limited, and price control over the economy was lifted;
- main institutional elements of control: state-owned institutions have been privatized or their monopolistic positions have been restricted; and
- means of control: direct methods of public control were replaced by much more indirect methods (less central allocation of funds, more local taxes; no centrally determined long-term plans, only some control over yearly local budgets; weaker legal rights to constrain unwanted development, through building codes and zoning plans; weaker position for those wishing to carry out development in the public interest, through limited rights for expropriation).

Looking at this list, which is far from exhaustive, it is clear that the processes of democratization, decentralization, and privatization were responsible for the destruction of the main pillars of the socialist city-development model. The role of state control and long-term planning decreased in all transition countries, and totally new, more market-related actors (landlords, land-owners, enterprises, financial institutions) emerged as important decision-makers. More detailed examination of these changes, however, will reveal important differences between countries, leading perhaps to different new models of city development.

### The Allocation of the Remaining Elements of Public Control between the Different Levels of Government

The main goal of the new political forces, besides democratization, was decentralization. Two important questions that had to be answered were: how many levels of administration should exist, and how should large cities be ruled or administered?

### How many Levels of Administration?

Regions were not given substantial power after 1990 as there had not been regional self-governments in the socialist period but rather "multi-purpose deconcentrated state administrations perfectly corresponding to the organizational principle of 'democratic centralism' under communist rule" (COR, 1999: 17). Therefore, it was the local government level in most of the Central and Eastern European countries that gained substantial strength as a consequence of decentralization. Local governments could, in fact, start to work as real decision-makers within their territory as the meso (or regional) level of administration was abolished or made insignificant. Central government transferred many public rights and responsibilities to the local level (e.g. public rental housing, ownership of "state" enterprises or public utilities). The new division of duties between central and local government made it possible for central government to withdraw from many tasks. The belief was that the local level would make wiser decisions, and more could be done with less money. In most of the countries in question, however, no calculations were made about the amount of public money needed to fulfil given tasks, so that generally the local level did not receive sufficient funds. An example of this is public rental housing in Hungary: after the transfer of the ownership (landlord) role from the central to the local level, the central budget subsidy earmarked for maintenance of public rental housing was terminated. Substantially different models can only be seen in Germany, where public rental housing was turned into a non-profit housing association sector, and a comprehensive subsidy system has been created to rehabilitate housing in inner city areas and on large housing estates.

*The Special Problem of the Government Structure of Large Cities*

There exist various possible models of government structure in large cities:

... one in which there is a single level of government consisting of numerous local authorities, each responsible for the urban area, a second in which there is a single level of government consisting of one authority for the entire urban area, and a third in which there are two levels of government, one being a city-wide authority, and the other consisting of numerous local units. These may be described as the "poly-centric" model, the "unicity" model, and the "two-tier" model. (Barlow, 1994: 125)

In most large cities of Central and Eastern Europe, two levels of administration exist: there are district governments, and also one municipal (metropolitan) government (Bennett, 1998: 44). All the large cities, therefore, belong to the two-tier governmental model. The real functioning of these cities is quite different, however, and in reality, which model the city belongs to depends on power-sharing within layers of the city:
– Prague, a city of 1.2 million people, consisting of 56 districts, represents the case of a relatively strong upper (municipal) level, as the lower-level units are too small.
– Budapest, a city of 1.8 million people, consisting of 23 districts, represents the case of an "equal-power" two-tier system, in which both levels, the upper (municipal) level and the lower district level, are strong and can block each other.

– Warsaw, a city of 1.6 million people, comprises 11 districts and represents the case of a relatively strong lower (district) level, with strong planning power and resources, while the upper municipal level has only a coordinating role and no power for implementation.

Thus, these three cities represent three different models of the two-tier local government system. Further research is needed to show the pros and cons of these different administrative models, in which the upper municipal level plays a respectively dominant, equal, or even subordinate role to the districts.

## Market Processes in the Transition Period

The decade that has passed since the collapse of socialism has brought significant changes in the outlook of post-socialist cities. The most visible changes are the products of market forces: foreign investors, domestic entrepreneurs, and private persons acting as developers. The public sector does not play a major role in development, but its indirect role in making private investment possible and shaping its outcome is crucial. Enyedi (1998: 32) suggests a distinction between the main agents and main coordinators of urban development in the post-socialist cities. The main agents are found in the private sector and are manifest in economic decisions "ranging from the location of the investment of trans-national companies to the personal strategies of self-employed entrepreneurs". Households are also important actors, putting their savings and investments into production, commerce or residential development, or even in their decisions whether to stay in the city or to move out of it. As the main coordinators of urban development, local governments have the task of creating the framework (regulations, incentives, services) for local development, and redirect a portion of the profit created by the local economy to the improvement of conditions in their city.

## Changing Conditions for Real-estate Investments

### Changes in the Urban Land Market

Ownership relations and planning (zoning) regulations of urban land are among the most important factors shaping city development. The first years of transition brought about fundamental changes in this sphere in all post-socialist cities. One of the cornerstones of the socialist city-model was the elimination of an urban land market. Nationalization drastically reduced private ownership of land (limiting it to single-family fringe areas of cities), and in the public sphere, land values were not taken into account at all. "*Cities without land markets* had a spatial organization in which the needs of a supply-driven economy were accommodated. In the absence of economic incentives and land markets, the system produced land-use patterns characterised by a number of inefficiencies"

(UNECE, 1997: 18). Socialist cities, compared to Western cities, had much higher shares of industrial land use, less land used by public services, and much lower shares of residential land use. Due to a total lack of economic incentives, population density gradients – as already mentioned – were also very different to those of Western cities: inefficiencies can be shown in the very low density of the transitional belt areas close to the centre, in the extremely high density of the large housing estates on the urban fringe, and in the sudden decrease of density in agglomerations, immediately beyond the city border. This spatial model of socialist cities required high investments in urban infrastructure to make it possible to build the outer housing estates, and public transport to make it possible for the residents to travel to their far-away working places.

Urban land and property rights reforms were the subject of serious political consideration after 1989. In many post-socialist countries, compensation was given to reverse earlier confiscation. The injustice of socialism was either reversed by payments/vouchers, or in kind. In some countries (e.g. East Germany, Czech Republic, Slovenia, Albania and Bulgaria), in-kind restitution has even been extended to the urban land market; land (urban plots) was restituted to the heirs of the previous owners from whom the land had been confiscated. There is a general view that this restitution procedure created a lot of difficulties and slowed down the privatization process. In exceptional cases, like the inner city of Prague, restitution led to rapid investments, but otherwise its effect was to deter potential investors, as property relations were unclear.

Unfortunately, there are no reliable data on the magnitude of restitution in the land market. It is easier to measure this process in relation to housing stock. According to data from 1994 (Hegedüs, Mayo, and Tosics, 1996), restitution amounted to 3 per cent, and privatization (to sitting tenants) to 30 per cent of the 1990 public rental housing stock in Central and Eastern capital cities. As a result of restitution, privatization, and the introduction of market elements into land regulation, within the course of the first half of the 1990s, the land–price gradient turned from a flat line into a sharply decreasing line; in Cracow, for example, price differentiation between the centre and the periphery grew to 10 : 1 (UNECE, 1997: 19). Such differentiation is now much bigger than in Western cities as a result of exploding land prices in the CBD areas, in contrast with only slowly increasing land prices on the periphery of Central and Eastern European cities; even though suburbanization has started, it takes a long time to develop a stable, high-quality suburban ring.

## The Changing Role of Urban Planning

Parallel to restitution and privatization, the planning system must also be discussed, as the positive elements of the market (i.e. clear valuation, efficient allocation) can easily be countered by its potential negative elements. The less planning control, the more the emerging market tendencies change the city towards the uncontrolled market-type city, with huge contradictions: office and commercial functions crowd out residential functions from the CBD area with the highest land values, upper-income families move out from the city to suburban locations with the highest value compared to other residential areas, and huge areas of previous industrial use within the existing fabric of the city remain derelict as the costs of recycling exceed the costs of establishing new functions in the green-field areas around the city.

Thus, urban planning has a very important role to play: it "has to ensure that urban land markets serve the economic and social needs of urban residents and businesses" (UNECE, 1997: 21). Besides economic considerations – attracting investment, rationalizing the use of infrastructure – issues of traffic optimization and social criteria also have to be taken into account, such as avoiding urban decline in given areas, minimizing negative environmental externalities, avoiding suburban sprawl, and protecting the existing values of the physical and natural environment. The new roles that urban planning has to play require new tools, as the direct regulation of the socialist period (i.e. very detailed zoning ordinances, direct state intervention on plot level to determine new use) is not in accordance with the challenges posed by market-orientated development. Urban planning has to operate more with indirect planning tools, such as framework-type regulations (e.g. maximum density permitted, specific effects excluded) and sophisticated and differentiated taxation methods.

## The Economic Conditions for Investments in Urban Areas

As a logical consequence of the collapse of the socialist economy and the deep restructuring procedure of the public sector, the public sphere lost its previously dominating role in the economy. Within the first four to five years of transition in many post-socialist countries, more than half of GDP was already produced by the private sector. Investments flowing into urban areas are also mainly products of market forces: foreign investors, domestic entrepreneurs, and private persons. There are, of course, huge differences in levels of investment among the various post-socialist countries, as economic conditions for urban development vary greatly.

Chapter 5 of this volume gives a detailed analysis of the magnitude of foreign direct investments and types of investors. In the first years of the transition (apart from the former East Germany, which is a totally different case), Hungary was the main target of FDI, while in the second half of the 1990s, Poland and Russia took over the leading role in this "competition". Foreign investors valued political stability, general economic development, and some other specific conditions (i.e. the size of the internal market, solvent demand of the population and geographical location) when deciding where to put their investments. It is clear that the "economic restructuring that took place was largely left to market forces as the legacy of central planning had discredited top-down policies of economic

Table 3.1  The level of economic performance in the post-socialist countries in the 1990s

| Countries | GNP/capita (US$) | | Real GDP/capita PPP (US$) | | | Consumer price index | | |
|---|---|---|---|---|---|---|---|---|
| | 1992 | 1996 | 1991 | 1996 | 2001 | 1992 | 1997 | 2001 |
| Germany* | 23.030 | 28.741 | 19.770 | 21.200 | 26.500 | 5,3 | 3,2 | 2,4 |
| Slovenia | 6.540 | 9.448 | 9.878 | 11.248 | 16.100 | 201,3 | 8,6 | 8,4 |
| Czech Republic | 2.746 | 5.446 | 7.812 | 11.329 | 15.100 | 11,1 | 8,5 | 4,7 |
| Slovakia | 1.930 | 3.530 | | 8.058 | 11.600 | | 6,0 | 7,3 |
| Hungary | 2.970 | 4.402 | 6.080 | 7.035 | 12.400 | 23,0 | 18,3 | 9,2 |
| Poland | 1.910 | 3.480 | 4.500 | 5.991 | 9.600 | 43,0 | 14,8 | 5,5 |
| Bulgaria | 1.330 | 1.028 | 4.813 | 4.241 | 6.800 | 82,6 | 123,0 | 7,4 |
| Romania | 1.130 | 1.571 | 3.500 | 4.646 | 6.200 | 210,9 | 154,8 | 34,5 |
| Albania | | | 3.500 | | | 226,0 | 33,2 | |

Note: *Data for Germany refer to the whole country, after unification.
*Source:* Trends in Europe and North America. The Statistical Yearbook of the Economic Commission for Europe, UN, 1995 and international statistics. Main Economic Indicators, Paris: OECD, 2002/6.

and regional development. As a result of transition regional and social inequalities have risen substantially within the Central and Eastern European countries" (Michalski and Saraceno, 2000: 21). As a general rule, it has been the largest cities who have been the winners and gained the most FDI, and who have thus managed to carry out economic restructuring in the shortest time (see Table 3.1).

Real-estate investments have the most direct effect on the urban restructuring of cities, while macro-economic conditions determine the supply of investors and the likelihood of financing being allocated to given projects. In the case of Hungary, it is easy to show how the "waves" of economic development relate to foreign investments. After the 1995–1996 fiscal reforms (a kind of shock therapy, to reverse negative budgetary processes), confidence has grown again in the macro-economic situation of the country, so that at the end of the century it is easy to get financing for sound development projects, and there is a tendency – also in connection with NATO membership – for Hungarian projects to be considered lower-risk than those in many other Eastern European countries. The result is seen in decreasing interest rates on large loans and in the activity of foreign financial institutions, which are starting to look for development projects in Hungary.

*The Main Types of New Real-estate Investments*

There are numerous accounts of developments in the non-residential real-estate markets. Sýkora (1997: 109) gives an overview of commercial property development in some Central European capital cities, concentrating mainly on the office market and paying much less attention to retailing, industry, and warehousing (see also Pütz, 1997; Barta, 1998).

*Commercial real-estate investments: Offices*

The commercial property market is flourishing in all post-socialist cities. The unprecedented speed of refurbishment and creation of commercial real estate has highlighted the peculiarities of this process, especially its spatial selectivity; "new commercial property development ... focused on major urban centres; even within those it helped to revitalise only certain parts of their urban space" (Sýkora, 1998: 110). Sýkora considers privatization, price liberalization, rent deregulation, liberalization of foreign trade, and satisfactory property-orientated legislation as the most important preconditions for the functioning of real-estate markets. Most of these factors were quickly introduced in Central and Eastern European countries, with the exception of the last – the establishment of good property legislation, which took a much longer time. This factor, along with differences in national political and economic circumstances, explains the huge variation in the magnitude of real-estate investment across the big cities of the region.

*Commercial Real-estate Investments: Retail Sector*

It was around the middle of the 1990s that the first large shopping centres were erected in Central Europe. International retail chains concentrated their efforts in the first period almost exclusively on the Central European capital cities with the biggest purchasing power; investments in "secondary" cities followed with at least three years' delay. Investment decisions came in a period when both the purchasing power of the population and the turnover of the existing retail sector were declining as part of the early economic transformation. The "brave" decisions of investors in the retail sector came somewhat unexpectedly for the urban planners; by the time Budapest developed and passed its strategy for the regulation of the retail sector, the first 500,000 sq.m of new retail space had already been built or had acquired building permission (Baross, 1999). The retail sector has special importance in the restructuring of post-socialist cities. On the one hand, retailing was very underdeveloped in the socialist cities both in quantitative and qualitative terms: in 1994, retail space per capita was more than three times higher in Berlin than in Moscow (UNECE, 1997: 22). On the other hand, this sector exhibits in market economies the fastest restructuring in accordance with a high level of capital concentration and rapid globalization. As a result of rapid restructuring of the retail sector, the "break-in" of newly built, high-tech, professionally organized shopping centres became one of the most visible signs of the market-orientated development of the post-socialist cities. The new retail sector is more based on car use, needs bigger buildings, and is therefore more orientated towards the transitional zones and outskirts of cities, and to suburban areas. This is a huge change for Central and Eastern European cities, in which the administrative centre of the city was traditionally also the centre of retail activities, a scheme that was only partially modified by the socialist city planning of retail sub-centres on new housing estates (Baross, 1999; French and Hamilton, 1979).

Although shopping centres have in many cases shorter "life expectancy" than residential or office developments, they are a crucial factor regarding where new retail investments are concentrated. If they are concentrated in suburban areas instead of the inner parts of cities, this can have a huge impact on traffic flows and can speed up residential suburbanization. In this regard, there is a big difference between Budapest and Prague, for example, in the proximity of shopping centres to the inner areas of the city.

*Real-estate Investments in the "Productive" Sectors*

The restructuring of the once-dominant socialist industrial system is a long story, starting with the closure of many outdated state-owned enterprises and continuing with different phases of privatization, the recovery of some brown-field areas, and much more substantial new green-field investments. The industrial sector, once the biggest employer, underwent dramatic changes, losing many workers. According to Barta (1998: 196), for instance, the industrial workforce of Budapest decreased from 602,000 in 1970 to 427,000 in 1980, 277,000 in 1990, and 117,000 in 1996. It is not the intention of this chapter to discuss the de-industrialization process in detail. Note, however, that changing employment patterns might seriously influence mobility: if out-of-town green-field investments become dominant, suburbanization might increase; furthermore, the problem of brown-field areas (derelict industrial areas) might become a major question in city (re)development (see Misztal, 1996: 125; and Chapter 5).

*Investment in the Residential Real-estate Market*

The transition towards market-type housing systems was slow in Central and Eastern Europe. The share of owner-occupied housing forms, which were really functioning as market commodities (i.e. in cases where the title was clear, the unit on the open housing market could serve as collateral for a bank loan), was low in most countries. This was one of the main reasons why profit-orientated housing (construction for sale) played only very limited role: low income levels and limited opportunities for bank financing meant that only the highest strata of society could afford to buy new housing units built by developers for cash. Thus, in most Central and Eastern European cities, speculative housing has played only a minor role, concentrating on the best areas of the city and on the highest-income households. Speculative residential real-estate investments were usually small, and not many developers existed who specialized only in residential construction.

By the end of the 1990s, this situation started to change in Central and Eastern Europe because of improved macro-economic conditions and a rise in incomes, as a consequence of which more banks and developers turned to the residential real-estate market. As usual, the former East Germany differs significantly from this general picture. As a consequence of a dynamic rise in incomes and the generous tax-deduction possibilities offered by the federal government to all investments in the new states, market-led residential investments have been booming in and around eastern German cities. Based on the belief that there would be huge demand for suburban housing, substantial numbers of new units were built by investors for sale, mainly in suburban neighbourhoods. According to an analysis of the Leipzig housing market (Pfeiffer, 1995), there was an unprecedented wave of housing construction between 1990 and 1996 in the rental sector as a result of tax exemption: while 4,000 new flats were built between 1992 and 1994, some 11,000 were delivered in 1995, and 25,000 in 1996–1997. Nearly 80 per cent of new apartments are built in the suburbs. Another analysis (Pfeiffer, 1999) shows that the supply of new single-family houses also grew rapidly around the city. This supply already exceeds demand: 45,000 dwellings are empty in Leipzig, of which 9,000 are freshly renovated and 5,000 are newly built. Forecasts expect an excess supply of 85,000 housing units in the city by the year 2010.

Another clear exception from the general picture of a slow housing construction market in the post-socialist countries during the 1990s is Tirana. This city, accommodating 300,000 people before the political changes, exploded to 700,000 by 1998 and is expected to reach a million by 2006 (Aliaj et al., 2003: 83). According to estimates, 8,000 to 9,000 new households move to Tirana each year from other parts of Albania. Regarding housing supply, the legal market is hardly functioning, while the irregular constructions are very developed. About 70 per cent of the housing supply is provided by the informal sector, and 25 per cent of the population is living in the irregular settlements. The main reason for the high share of the informal sector is the poverty of the migrants. According to surveys, "60 per cent of the demand comes from low income groups; 26 per cent of households in Tirana live below the poverty line of 119 US$ per month and this figure increases to 35 per cent in the periphery; a family in this category will need 30–40 years to buy an apartment in the formal market" (Misja, 1998: 57). The unprecedented growth of the city, based almost entirely on house building by the population itself and without real intervention by the authorities, leads to the "densification of the city within the boundaries of 1990 and the process of extension of the city outside these boundaries" at the same time (Slootweg, 1998: 138).

## Consequences of Transition on Social and Spatial Relations

This section summarizes new tendencies in residential mobility as the key variable in the city-development model, and offers some explanations to enable us to elaborate a hypothesis on the link between city development and public policy.

## Tendencies in Residential Mobility: The Spatial Restructuring of the Population

Despite strong urbanization tendencies after the Second World War, at the end of the 1980s, Central and Eastern European countries were still very much behind Western Europe and Northern America regarding share of urban population: this was around 63 per cent in Central Europe, 55 per cent in South-east Europe, almost 80 per cent in Western Europe, and 75 per cent in Northern America (UNECE, 1997: 11). As discussed earlier, an important component of the socialist city-development model was the attempt to limit city growth. Yet, growing employment in socialist cities came into conflict with the deferred development of infrastructure and housing, so some part of urbanization was "indirect" – people employed by urban industry could only get accommodation outside urban centres, in suburban zones from where they commuted to work.

After 1989, all the earlier political–administrative barriers to internal population flows were eliminated. If all other aspects were left unchanged, this would have led to increased migration towards the cities, i.e. to a late wave of urbanization. However, other aspects of the situation changed substantially: the number of industrial workplaces decreased, many big state-owned employers in the cities closed down, and unemployment increased dramatically (although it was still the lowest in the largest cities). Additionally, the price of residential real estate increased faster in metropolitan areas than elsewhere and urban public transport fares started to rise. Thus, the question is: which aspect was becoming stronger – incentives to move into the city, or incentives to leave (see Table 3.2)?

All the cities investigated in more detail in this volume have been losing population in recent years, as a result of demographic decline and migration losses to their hinterlands. The available forecasts for the next decades are not very optimistic, suggesting further losses for Budapest, Prague, and Ljubljana, coupled with strong suburbanization processes (see Table 3.2). Moscow and

Table 3.2 Forecasts of population increase in some Central European metropoles

| Population | 1995 | | 2010 (1995 = 100) | | |
| --- | --- | --- | --- | --- | --- |
| | City | Agglo.* | City % | Agglo.% | Together % |
| Budapest | 1,906 | 599 | 79 | n.a. | n.a. |
| Prague | 1,210 | 170 | 97 | 112 | 99 |
| Warsaw | 1,629 | 782 | 101 | 109 | 104 |

Note: *"Agglo." refers to the suburban belt around the city.
*Sources:* Budapest, 2002 (forecast refers to 2015); for Prague: Turba and Mejstrik (1999), and Warsaw (1999).

Tirana exhibit different trends. In Moscow, the previously positive demographic balance of births and deaths became negative around 1990, leading to almost 1 per cent (almost 100,000 people) yearly loss of population by the middle of the decade. The fact that the population of Moscow decreased by only 235,000 people (2.5 per cent) between 1992 and 1998 is due to the increasing positive migration balance of the city (the yearly migration surplus increased from 13,000 to 51,000 during this period (see Chapter 14, Table 14.5).

The most unique case is without doubt Tirana. In the 1990s, Tirana experienced an extremely quick population growth that can be called an "East European type of suburbanization", which means the growth of the suburbs (and also of the population of the city itself) from outside, as a consequence of positive migration balance from the rest of the country. This tendency will most probably continue, and the growth of population in Tirana and its agglomeration for the period 1995–2015 is expected to be 286 per cent, increasing from 508,000 to 1,452,000 (Aliaj and Aliaj, 1998: 110)! This dramatic increase of population both inside and around the city is a net result of high birth rates and inward migration.

This comparative analysis has illustrated the significant differences that exist between cities in the different subregions: in Central Europe, both demographic and migration data show losses; Tirana in South-east Europe is the opposite case, where both data show increases; and in Moscow, demographic losses are partly counter-weighted by a positive migration balance. Among the factors influencing future changes in population, the most difficult to estimate is the balance of external (foreign) migration. This is the only factor which could offset demographic and internal migration losses: the number of foreign citizens moving to these cities, as they become the new border cities of the European Union, is expected to grow. Yet, the most optimistic future scenarios for population in Budapest and Prague suggest that even intensive foreign in-migration will only help keep the population of the city stable.

The balance of external migration depends on a number of factors that have become the subject of intense debate. One question is the number of citizens of Central and Eastern European countries who will emigrate to other countries of the European Union when free movement of labour takes effect (probably some years after accession). According to most analysts, the fears of present border countries, especially Austria, are exaggerated. In any case, it is more likely that migration into the Central and Eastern European metropoles from outside the European Union will outweigh the number of citizens leaving these cities for other EU countries. In fact, "unwanted immigration flows from far afield is a challenge at least as great to the countries of Central and Eastern Europe as to the Western European countries, with the former having less resources and experience to manage them. It pleads for a balanced view on migration within the enlarged EU and for a common European approach to border management" (Michalski, 1999: 8).

## Explanations and Hypotheses on the Causes of Suburbanization

Analysis of post-socialist city development is most advanced in Germany, where the eastern region is in a stage of accelerated change, while the scholars of the western part have the necessary expertise, interest, and finance to study the turbulent urban development of the region.

### The Transformation of East German Cities

Spatial developmental tendencies in East German cities have been widely discussed by Western scholars following the reunification. Their most important theoretical hypothesis (Fassman, 1997) states that in Eastern European post-socialist countries, while less advanced compared with Western Europe, spatial development is being created in a special way: capital moves to the suburbs first, and the population then follows it. This hypothesis might be paraphrased thusly: the economic and commercial development of Central European cities as a result of large-scale foreign capital investment has occurred mainly in the immediate vicinity of the cities. Foreign investors locate developments less in the deteriorating inner city brown-field areas than in the less inhabited suburban green-field areas, and these office and commercial developments form a comparatively much bigger proportion than suburban housing within overall suburban development.

Herfert (1996) shows that commerce and jobs began moving out of East German cities as early as 1990–1991, while the population followed only in 1992–1993. Losses of population from former East German cities after 1994 reached the levels of West German cities in the early 1970s (the annual amount of emigrants was 3 per cent in smaller cities and 1–2 per cent in larger ones). A factor specific to Germany, namely the special subsidy (tax exemption) for housing and economic investments until the end of 1998, contributed largely to this tendency. It is peculiar to East German suburbanization that, in the final balance, the agglomerations as a whole are losing population. This results from the ongoing migration from East to West Germany and thus cannot be generalized for the whole of Central Europe. Most of the emigrants own two cars, which signifies that the ones who move to the suburbs do not belong to the lower layers of society. On the Berlin housing market (Pfeiffer, 1995), dominated by rental units, the demand for owner-occupied dwellings is high; according to a sample of households, demand for private apartments amounts to 160,000, but only half of these expect to actually have an apartment within two years. According to the demand analysis, most of such richer families are from West Berlin and want to get private property in the inner districts. Since this is not possible in West Berlin, they try to move to East Berlin or to the suburbs.

### Transformation Processes in other Central European Capital Cities

The hypothesis of Fassman – that the movement of capital to the suburbs proceeds that of the population – might not be equally valid across the different

Central and Eastern European countries. Germany might be the only country experiencing this effect, and the other Central European cities seem to differ from this model. In the case of Budapest, commercial development concentrates on the city and less on the suburbs, and there is, as yet, no strong link between the out-migration of economic and housing investments. Suburban settlements with the most dynamic economic development are usually not identical to those that have the highest population increase. The link between the two processes might be the development of basic infrastructure, necessary for both economic and housing investments. There are, however, different ideas in many suburban settlements as to whether economic or population growth is their main development aim (Tosics et al., 1998: 189).

One analysis of the Budapest housing market (Tosics et al., 1998) was based on a sample of families who wished to change their flat in the near future. To move out from Budapest to the suburban belt was a definite wish of 17 per cent of the families surveyed. Another 23–26 per cent of families thought that the suburban belt would become the most likely place where they would find their new housing unit. These families were bigger than average, lived in crowded conditions, and were thus strongly motivated to move to bigger housing units. Starcevic (1996) offers an overview of Prague's development in the last decades and its effects on the dilemmas of today. The development of Prague was artificially restrained for 45 years and new construction was permitted only in the form of apartment housing estates. This led to a distorted development, the result of which is that one-fifth of the population own a weekend house, 60 per cent of which are in the suburbs. Following the change of regime, better-off families had the opportunity to move out from the city. Trends suggest, however, that these families tend to remain in their small rental dwellings in the inner city. The author accounts for this by the influence of the younger generation: children prefer the inner city because of the attractiveness of the urban environment there (proper public transport, cultural and entertainment opportunities, etc.). The Master Plan of Prague remains cautious with regard to the suburbs (it predicts 30,000 new apartments by 2010), but new projections for the metropolitan area suggest much faster migration. Furthermore, projects in the suburban areas themselves reflect enormous potential for development: they expect their population to grow somewhere between 100 and 1,000 per cent! Thus, Prague is threatened by rapid uncontrolled suburbanization, the dangers of which are yet to be recognized by urban planners.

*Differences in the Forces of Suburbanization*

The analysis above has shown important differences in the causes of suburbanization in the former East German cities compared with other Central European capital cities, the most important of which are the level of state subsidy given for and capital invested into suburban development. On the other hand, there are also some similarities: housing market analyses of Berlin and

Budapest revealed the fact that the motives for suburbanization in many cases are not the positive features of the suburb or the negative conditions of the inner city, but certain expectations with regard to the new dwellings which can only be matched in the suburbs. In the case of Berlin this was because owner-occupied housing is more readily available in the suburbs, while in the case of Budapest it is the large size and the good environmental quality of the new dwelling relative to its price that is important. Families looking for housing with such attributes are not able to pay the inner city Budapest price of these dwellings, and hence they search for them in the suburban belt at a much cheaper price. If the cities could change these imbalances, the speed of suburbanization could be reduced substantially.

## Transition of City Development: From the Socialist Model – Towards What?

There was once a socialist city-model, dominated by state control over all actors of development, and by non-market mechanisms that integrated these actors (see the logic of this model in Hegedüs and Tosics, 1998). This city-model has been dissolved since the end of the 1980s in a transitionary process in which control on both the demand and supply sides has changed substantially. The changes leading to the dissolution of the socialist city-model, initiated partly by the state, partly by the market, and partly by spontaneous processes, occurred in different forms across the Central and Eastern European countries. In some countries decentralization has been quick and comprehensive (even leading to extreme situations), while in others the reinforcement of local governments is slower and real power is still kept at the national level. The same applies to changes in property relations: in some countries private ownership is almost totally dominant, while in others public or non-profit forms have retained a significant role. There are also differences in the "aggressiveness" of foreign development capital, which depends very much on political stability, on the speed of economic restructuring in the country, and on the geopolitical position of the city.

The question raised in this chapter is the following: what are the possible ways of transition from the socialist city into different, market-orientated or other city-types, and what are the potential outcomes?

As a result of differences in political, economic, and society-related factors, in some countries and cities quick changes lead towards a pure, free-market version of the capitalist city-model; in other cities, regulatory, equalizing elements remain or become strong and the outcome is closer to a more regulated version of the capitalist city-model or even to a different ("third world") city-model. The outcomes are "path-dependent", determined both by the starting position of the city, and by political and economic development factors. As a result, there are very different sub-types of city development emerging in the transition period, differing in the level of state control, the functioning of the land market, the magnitude of investments, and the activity of citizens. There is one common fact: a radically different type of public control over the city as compared with the central planning of the socialist period. Differences in types of city development relate to the strength and direction of this new public control.

Ten years after the collapse of socialism, significantly different processes of post-socialist city development are observable mostly in the capital cities of Central and Eastern Europe. On the basis of empirical facts and those also presented in Chapters 7–14, we can hypothesize the following sub-types of development in post-socialist cities:[1]

(1) *East German cities:* quick transition from the socialist into the capitalist city-model. Extraordinary influx of capital investments into the office, commercial, and housing market, quickly increasing population incomes. Strong central and local public control: no privatization of housing to sitting tenants, and carefully established, new types of public control over the land market, and over the planning and building process. Huge public investments in infrastructure, public transport, and renewal of large housing estates. The outcome might be somewhere between the unregulated and regulated capitalist city-model, depending on "competition" between investment lobbies and the public sector.

(2) *Hungarian (and in some respect Slovenian) cities:* relatively quick transition from the socialist towards the capitalist city-model. Huge capital investments into the office and commercial market, rapid differentiation of incomes with a thin layer of very rich people and a wide layer of people in poverty. Dissolution of previous types of public control at both the national and local levels, rapid and total privatization of housing to sitting tenants, very slow establishment of new type of local public control over the land market, planning and building process. The outcome might be the unregulated capitalist city-model, unless the newly developing public control becomes strong enough to limit free-market processes.

(3) *Czech, Slovakian, Polish cities:* relatively quick transition from the socialist to a "mixed" model with some remnants of state control. Growing capital investments into the office and commercial market, slow differentiation of population incomes. Partial dissolution of the previous types of public control, slow privatization of housing to sitting tenants, very slow establishment of new type of public control over the land market, planning, and building process. The outcome might be somewhere between the unregulated and regulated capitalist city-model, depending on the strength and direction of public control.

(4) *Bulgarian, Romanian cities:* slow transition from the socialist towards the capitalist city-model. Very limited capital investments in the office and commercial market, stagnating but differentiating population incomes. Dissolution of previous type of public control, quick and total privatization

of housing to sitting tenants, very slow establishment of new type of public control over the land market, planning, and building process. The outcome might be the unregulated capitalist city, with some elements of the "third world" type of city development.

(5) *Albanian cities:* quick transition from the socialist into an unregulated "third world" city-development model. Very limited formal capital investments, but substantial population investments into the illegal or unofficial commercial and housing market, decreasing and quickly differentiating official population incomes. Total dissolution of all previous types of public control, quick and total privatization of housing to sitting tenants, no new type of public control over the land market, planning, and building process. The outcome is the parallel process of densification and sprawl in urban areas in a quick, unregulated development.

(6) *Other ex-Yugoslav cities:* slow transition from the socialist towards the capitalist city-model due to armed conflict in the 1990s, mass refugee movements, and destroyed urban centres. Very limited capital investments at first, but substantial population investments into the illegal or unofficial property market. Relatively quick privatization of public housing to sitting tenants at the beginning of the 1990s, but deferred restitution, privatization of enterprises, and other public assets due to the war and unsettled disputes over property. Huge differentiation in incomes between the "formal" and "informal" sectors, and very slow establishment of new type of public control over the land market, planning, and building processes. The outcome is the parallel process of densification and sprawl through unregulated development, with some elements of the "third world" type of city development.

(7) *Baltic cities:* relatively quick transition from the socialist (and ex-Soviet) into a "mixed" ("Scandinavian") model with some elements of state control. Growing capital investments into the property market, slow differentiation of rather low population incomes. First slow, but from 1996 accelerated privatization of housing to sitting tenants, and establishment of new type of public control over the land market, planning, and building process. The outcome might be somewhere between the unregulated and regulated capitalist city-model, depending on the strength and direction of public control.

(8) *Russian (and to some extent other East European) cities:* transition from the socialist towards a locally controlled, mixed city-model. Limited foreign capital investments into the office and commercial market, stagnating but extremely differentiated population incomes. Rich and very powerful public sector on the local level. Dissolution of the previous type of general public control was replaced by political power concentrated at the local level, functioning along political and personal lines and not adapting itself to the indirect regulation of market processes. Quick privatization of housing to sitting tenants, new type of public control over the land market, planning, and building process based on political decisions taken by the very strong

local government. The outcome is local government and investment-led city development, a curious mixture of political and market elements of (un)regulated development.

This hypothetical classification is based on available information mainly from the capital cities of Central and Eastern European countries. It is also possible that significant differences emerge within the same country between the largest (capital) city and other cities, as only the former can really participate in competition with European cities, which has special consequences on city development.

From the facts summarized in this chapter, the socialist period of city development can be evaluated as a substantially different model compared to the "general development model" of the cities of market-economy countries. The development of the socialist cities was in many aspects unique, which also means that socialist cities arrived with many similarities to each other at the beginning of the transitional period. Thus, the starting position had many common aspects. Our analysis indicates that the end point of the transition from the socialist towards other city-models is as yet uncertain and might vary throughout the different subregions of Central and Eastern Europe. The future of the post-socialist cities can be hypothesized in the following way:

– for Central European cities – the first three sub-types listed above – and to some extent *Baltic cities*, there will be a differentiation typical of the market-orientated capitalist city: the less public intervention occurs, the more these cities will approach the American, "sprawl-type" city-model, while new types of public control will encourage a move towards the European "compact city" model. This means that if a post-socialist city wants to avoid some unwanted phases of development (e.g. the phase dominated by massive suburbanization), strong public intervention must be established, to be able to control market processes;

– cities in South-east Europe (sub-type 4) and *East Europe* (sub-type 8) are somehow limited in their development towards the capitalist city-model. There are elements of other city-development models that could potentially influence the direction taken by these cities;

– the Albanian and some ex-Yugoslav cities are completely different from all the others, leading towards a different outcome than the capitalist city-model.

The further development of the post-socialist cities depends on a number of factors. Probably the most important of these is the need for a new type of public control over market processes, parallel to a transition from the socialist system into democratic, market-based systems. Central and Eastern European cities also face two other types of transformation: changing from the industrial into the post-industrial phase, and becoming emerging participants in the globalization process (Enyedi, 1998: 30). To manage successfully the challenges posed by the last two types of transformation it is essential to complete the first, i.e. to establish a new institutional framework and a new system of public control over market processes, which is the prerequisite for the establishment of a long-term strategy of city development and is key to success in the globalizing, competitive world.

The key question for the future development of post-socialist cities is: how and on what level can an efficient new public leadership be established? As Bennett (1998: 53) argues, "the reform and development of the upper tier . . . represent perhaps the most crucial development required to enhance the capacity of the local governments of cities". As "upper-tier", Bennett understands subnational, regional governments or agencies, and the metropolitan (municipal) government in the case of the large cities. On this level, a new type of public leadership should be developed, which should be based on the partnership of the enabling state, business, third sectors, and local associations. Those cities which joined the European Union in the first wave, in May 2004, will get a special push.

Therefore, the specific model of city development in post-socialist cities will depend very much on the strength and quality of this new public leadership, and its cooperation with the other actors in the partnership. For post-socialist cities, the whole range of present city-development models (American, Western European, or third world type) will be available. The impact of the past will gradually diminish, and new forms of public leadership will gradually gain in strength to determine the future of these cities.

## Note

1 Special thanks to Nataša Pichler-Milanović for her contribution to this typology with the case of ex-Yugoslav and Baltic cities.

## REFERENCES

Besnik Aliaj and Elvira Aliaj, "Organization and Financing of Public Utilities in Albania" [The Case of Roads in Tirana], in *City Made by People: New ideas to manage urban realities*, Tirana: IHS Alumni, IHS, Co-Plan, 1998, pp. 97–117.

Besnik Aliaj, Keida Lulo, and Genc Myftiu, *Tirana, the Challenge of Urban Development*, Tirana: Seda and Co-Plan, 2003.

Max Barlow, "Alternative Structures of Government in Metropolitan Areas", in Max Barlow, Peter Dostál, and Martin Hampl, eds, *Development and Administration of Prague*, Prague, Amsterdam: University of Amsterdam, Charles University, Institute of Sociology, 1994, pp. 38–56.

Pál Baross, "Kiskereskedelem: átalakuló kínálati struktúra?" [Retail Sector: Changing Structure of Supply?], in *Budapest Városfejlesztési Koncepciója*, Kézirat [Budapest Strategic Development Concept, manuscript], 1999.

Györgyi Barta, "Industrial Restructuring or Deindustrialisation?", in Enyedi György, ed., *Social Change and Urban Restructuring in Central Europe*, Budapest: Akadémia Kiado, 1998, pp. 189–208.

Robert J. Bennett, "Local Government in Postsocialist Cities", in György Enyedi, ed., *Social Change and Urban Restructuring in Central Europe*, Budapest: Akadémia Kiado, 1998, pp. 35–54.

Alain Bertaud and Robert Buckley, Cracow in the Twenty First Century: Prince of Merchants? A City's Structure under the Conflicting Influences of Land Markets, Zoning Regulations and a Socialist Past, Budapest: Mimeo, 1997.

Leo van den Berg, Roy Drewett, Leo Klaassen, Angelo Rossi, and Cornelis Vijverberg, *A Study of Growth and Decline* (Urban Europe, Volume 1), Pergamon Press, 1982.

Robert M. Bird, Robert D. Ebel, and Christine I. Wallich, Decentralization of the Socialist State. Intergovernmental Finance in Transition Economies, Washington D.C.: The World Bank, 1995.

*Budapest Városfejlesztési Koncepciója*, [The Strategic Development Concept of Budapest], Budapest: Budapest Municipality, 2002.

"Preparing for EU Enlargement. Devolution in the First Wave Candidate Countries" (COR Studies E-4/99), Brussels: EU Committee of the Regions, September 1999.

Dezsõ Ekler, József Hegedüs, and Iván Tosics, *A városfejlõdés társadalmi-térbeli összefüggései Budapest példáján* [The Socio-spatial Relations of City Development. On the Example of Budapest], Budapest: Mimeo, 1980.

György Enyedi, "Urbanization under Socialism", in Gregory Andrusz, Michael Harloe, and Iván Szelényi, eds, *Cities After Socialism: Urban and Regional Change and Conflict in Post-socialist Societies*, Oxford: Blackwell Publishers, 1996, pp. 100–118.

György Enyedi, ed., Social Change and Urban Restructuring in Central Europe, Budapest: Akadémia Kiado, 1998.

Heinz Fassmann, "Veranderung des Stadtesystems in Ostmitteleuropa" [The Changing Urban System in East Central Europe], in Zoltán Kovács and Reinhard Wiessner, eds, *Prozesse und Perspektiven der Stadtentwicklung in Ostmitteleuropa*, Münchener Geographische Hefte 76, Passau: L.I.S. Verlag, 1997, pp. 49–62.

R. Anthony French and F.E. Ian Hamilton, eds, *The Socialist City*, Chichester: John Wiley, 1979.

Hartmut Häussermann, "From the Socialist to the Capitalist City", in Gregory Andrusz, Michael Harloe, and Iván Szelényi, eds, *Cities After Socialism: Urban and Regional Change and Conflict in Post-socialist Societies*, Oxford: Blackwell Publishers, 1996, pp. 214–231.

Patsy Healey, Abdul Khakee, Alain Motte, and Barrie Needham, eds, *Making Strategic Spatial Plans. Innovation in Europe*, London: UCL Press, 1997.

József Hegedüs and Iván Tosics, "Disintegration of East-European Housing Model", in David Clapham, József Hegedüs, Keith Kintrea, and Iván Tosics, eds, with Helen Kay, *Housing Privatisation in Eastern Europe*, Westport: Greenwood Press, 1996, pp. 15–40.

József Hegedüs and Iván Tosics, "Towards New Models of the Housing System", in György Enyedi, ed., *Social Change and Urban Restructuring in Central Europe*, Budapest: Akadémia Kiado, 1998, pp. 137–168.

József Hegedüs, Gyula Pártos, and Iván Tosics, *A lakáskínálattal kapcsolatos MT program véleményezése* [Opinion about the Government Programme on the Supply of Housing], Budapest: Mimeo, 1980.

József Hegedüs, Katharine Mark, Raymond Struyk, and Iván Tosics, "Local Options for the Transformation of the Public Rental Sector: Empirical Results from Two Cities in Hungary", *Cities* 10(2), 1993, pp. 257–271.

József Hegedüs, Stephen E. Mayo, and Iván Tosics, "Transition of the Housing Sector in the East Central European Countries", *Review of Urban & Regional Development Studies* 8, 1996, pp. 101–136.

Günter Herfert, "Wohnsuburbanisierung in Grossstadtregionen der neuen lander", paper presented at the Internationales Symposium Prozesse und Perspektiven der Stadtentwicklung in Ostmitteleuropa, Budapest, October 1996.

Ulrich Jürgens, "Der Aufholprozess ostdeutscher Innenstadte gegenüber Einkaufszentren auf der Grünen Wiese: Erfolge und Fehlschlage" [The Catching-up Process of Eastern German Inner Cities against the Green-field Shopping Centres: Successes and Failures], paper presented at Internationales Symposium Prozesse und Perspektiven der Stadtentwicklung in Ostmitteleuropa, Budapest, October 1996.

Zoltán Kovács and Reinhard Wiessner, eds, *Prozesse und Perspektiven der Stadtentwicklung in Ostmitteleuropa* [Processes and Perspectives of City Development in Central Eastern Europe], Münchener Geographische Hefte 76, Passau: L.I.S. Verlag, 1997.

Walter Kunz, "Einkaufszentren auf der 'Grünen Wiese' – Lehren aus westeuropaischen Erfahrungen" [Shopping Centres and Retail Outlets in Green-field Areas – The Lesson from West European Experience], paper presented at IFHP Conference, Eastern European Cities in Transition, Warsaw, May 1997.

Anna Michalski, "Long-term Implications of EU Enlargement: The Nature of the New Border," *Carrefours Newsletter*, October 1999.

Anna Michalski and Elena Saraceno, "Regions in the Enlarged European Union", Background Note prepared for the 18th European Carrefour on Science and Culture, Forward Studies Unit, Budapest, 20–21 March 2000.

Alketa Misja, "Organizing Tirana's Land and Housing Markets", in *City Made by People: New Ideas to Manage Urban Realities*, Tirana: IHS Alumni, IHS, Co-Plan, 1998, pp. 51–66.

Stanislaw Misztal, "Deindustrialization of Warsaw and Problems of Redevelopment of the Derelict Industrial Areas", paper presented at International Symposium: Prozesse und Perspektiven der Stadtentwicklung in Ostmitteleuropa, Budapest, October 1996.

Ulrich Pfeiffer, *Akzeptanz und Vermarktbarkeit neu gebauter Wohnanlagen im Berliner Umland* [The Acceptance and Marketability of New Residential Real-estate in the Surrounding Area of Berlin], Bonn: empirica, 1995.

———, *Evaluation und Perspektiven der Stadterneuerungspolitik in Ostdeutschland. Erfahrungen aus der Stadt Leipzig* [Evaluation and Perspectives of Urban Renewal Policy in Eastern Germany. Experiences from the City of Leipzig], Endbericht (manuscript), March 1999.

Robert Pütz, "Transformation des polnischen Einzelhandels zwischen interner Restrukturierung und Internationalisierung. Das Beispiel Wroclaw" [Transformation of Polish Small Commerce Activity between Internal Restructuring and Internationalization], in Zoltán Kovács and Reinhard Wiessner, eds, *Prozesse und Perspektiven der Stadtentwicklung in Ostmitteleurop*, Münchener Geographische Hefte 76, Passau, L.I.S. Verlag, 1997, pp. 141–156.

Helga Schmidt, "Veranderungen auf dem ostdeutschen Wohnungsmarkt – das Beispiel Leipzig", in Zoltán Kovács and Reinhard Wiessner, eds, *Prozesse und Perspektiven der Stadtentwicklung in Ostmitteleuropa*, Münchener Geographische Hefte 76, Passau: L.I.S. Verlag, 1997, pp. 171–188.

Sef Slootweg, "Statements on urban reality in Tirana, Albania", in *City Made by People. New Ideas to Manage Urban Realities*, Tirana: IHS Alumni, IHS, Co-Plan, 1998, pp. 137–152.

Peter Starcevic, "Suburbanisation in Prague Metropolitan Region (Housing Aspects)," paper prepared for the Internationales Symposium Prozesse und Perspektiven der Stadtentwicklung in Ostmitteleuropa, Budapest, October 1996.

Ludék Sýkora, "Commercial Property Development in Budapest, Prague and Warsaw", in György Enyedi, ed., *Social Change and Urban Restructuring in Central Europe*, Budapest: Akadémiai, 1998, pp. 109–136.

Iván Szelényi, "Cities under Socialism – and After", in Gregory Andrusz, Michael Harloe, and Iván Szelényi, eds, *Cities after Socialism: Urban and Regional Change and Conflict in Post-socialist Societies*, Oxford: Blackwell Publishers, 1996, pp. 286–317.

Iván Tosics, with Judit Bányai, Éva Geroházi, Judit Kálmán, Róbert Kovács, Csilla Sárkány, and Zoltán Török, *Szuburbanizációs tendenciák és településfejlesztési stratégiák Budapesten és agglomerációjában* [Tendencies of Suburbanization and Urban Development Strategies in Budapest and its Agglomeration], Metropolitan Research Institute, January 1998.

Milán Turba and J. Mejstrik, *Strategy Report. Metropolitan Region Prague*, Contribution to the European Metropolitan Regions Project, Prague, 1999.

United Nations Economic Commission for Europe (UNECE), *Trends in Europe and North America: The Statistical Yearbook of the Economic Commission for Europe*, New York and Geneva: UNECE, 1995.

———, *Human Settlement Trends in Central and Eastern Europe*, New York and Geneva: UNECE, 1997.

*Warsaw Development Strategy until the Year 2010, A Synthesis*, Warsaw: Warsaw City Hall, Department of Land Development, 1999.

# 4

# The external forces: Towards globalization and European integration

*F.E. Ian Hamilton*

## Introduction

The preceding chapter outlined the internal forces that have been operating within states and localities during the past decade to shape the development characteristics and paths of transformation of Central and Eastern European cities. This chapter focuses on the "external forces"; in reality, the two interact in varying degrees and in complex and diverse ways. "External forces" can be defined in a spatial context as those emanating either from outside the borders of the post-socialist arena as a whole, such as from the market economies of Western Europe, North America, East Asia, or elsewhere, and which may be thus treated as being "global"; or from outside the borders of individual post-socialist states, from neighbouring territories and cities, and which may be considered more as "regional" or "regional-international" forces. In fact, both the definition and the operation of "globalization" and "internationalization" forces are rather blurred and interactive (Painter, 1995; Ó Tuathail, 1996). "Globalization" refers to a range of processes, which operate above the scale of the nation state as capital mobility, foreign direct investment, free trade agreements, information society etc., while "internationalization" refers to the growing porosity of the boundaries and borders of national economies (Jessop, 1995). In functional terms, these forces are, or can be, very diversified and include cultural, economic, ideological, institutional, political, social, strategic-military, and technological factors. One can hypothesize that through time, the geographic scope or territorial or spatial "range" of the forces operating will change, as will the functional characteristics or balance of such forces. This applies anywhere in the world, and Central and Eastern Europe is no exception.

In fact, external forces have long shaped the growth, development, and salient features of cities in Central and Eastern Europe, but the changing origins, nature, intensity, and impact of those forces have resulted in both continuities and discontinuities through time. Undoubtedly, the years 1989 to 1991 represent a watershed in the region's history, with significant breaks or discontinuities from the preceding socialist period being effected: cities have become opened up to market forces, to the intensified and diversified interests of globalization, to NATO enlargement and to European integration. These factors are having increasingly important effects on city dynamics, structure, functions, spatial organization and spatial forms, and on the evolution of city interdependencies and dependencies. Yet, it would be erroneous to believe that external forces had not played a role – even a significant role – in earlier periods, even if the power and characteristics of those forces differed from those operating today in the region.

## External Forces before 1989

The relevance of external forces operating in the region before 1989 lies in the preconditions, continuities, and legacies that they created, and which have been shaping the transformation of cities in the post-socialist period since 1989. A brief survey is necessary in as much as present transformations may embody a dimension of "back to the future", i.e. whether pre-socialist period developments, trends, or influences are, or have been, re-establishing themselves, or whether there are also legacies from the socialist period itself which have long-term consequences affecting city transformation.

### External Forces in the Pre-socialist Period

As far as most of Central and Eastern Europe is concerned, it is useful to distinguish the operation of external forces in three broad periods: before the First World War; the "inter-war" period (1918 to 1939); and the Second World War period.[1]

Before the First World War – in contrast to Western Europe, where urbanization and "metropolitanization" were shaped in the formative years of the nineteenth century either by stable nation states such as Great Britain, France, or the Netherlands which were "mother countries" of far-flung empires, or by enlarging and unifying states such as Germany and Italy – the development of cities in the present-day territories of much of Central and Eastern Europe was subject to foreign imperial influences that were political, military, cultural, and economic in character.

The very establishment of town status in the region's central and northern areas was determined by the conferment of German town law and privileges. Settlements receiving such status could begin to prosper from trade, crafts, and industries. Some key centres of markets or trade fairs such as Crakow (Poland), Dubrovnik (Croatia) and the Baltic Hanseatic ports engaged in international trade with significant parts of the known world in mediaeval times, but after 1492 cities in the region became more isolated from the broader "global" developments associated with the opening up of the New World and the growth of trade with Africa, Asia, and the Pacific. More significantly, from the late eighteenth century, the division of the region between four empires – the Prussian, Russian, Habsburg (Austro-Hungarian from 1867), and Ottoman – largely deepened this isolation and reinforced trends towards the emergence of a highly uneven pattern of urbanization linked to the railway network. This division remained, by and large, strongly reflected in the very differentiated levels of urbanization across the region into the 1940s. The proportion of the population living in urban areas declined from more than 60–70 per cent in the north-west (eastern Germany, Bohemia) along broadly west–east and north-west–south-east axes to 25 per cent in eastern Poland (including those areas which since 1945 are in present-day Lithuania, Belarus, and Ukraine) and in most of South-east Europe, i.e. the Balkan peninsula (Hamilton, 1979a: 168) (see also Table 4.1).

The strong economic development of the Prussian Empire in the nineteenth century, and the parallel emergence of Berlin as a major industrial and prime market centre, influenced the development of the present-day western and northern territories of Poland and Upper Silesia (southern Poland), a trend which was reinforced by the centripetal rail network focusing on Berlin and supported by earlier tributary canal links to that city. A similar situation prevailed in

Table 4.1 Urban population change in Eastern Europe before and after the Second World War

| Country | Pre–Second World War | | | Post–Second World War | | |
|---|---|---|---|---|---|---|
| | Year | 000 | % | Year | 000 | % |
| Poland* | 1939 | 11,944 | 37.3 | 1946 | 7,425 | 31.0 |
| Czechoslovakia | 1938 | 5,798 | 39.7 | 1949 | 5,446 | 44.1 |
| Hungary | 1930 | 2,881 | 33.2 | 1949 | 3,341 | 36.3 |
| Romania | 1930 | 3,051 | 21.4 | 1948 | 3,713 | 23.4 |
| Bulgaria | 1934 | 1,303 | 21.4 | 1946 | 1,735 | 24.7 |
| Yugoslavia | 1931 | 1,839 | 13.2 | 1948 | 3,117 | 19.7 |
| Albania | 1938 | 160 | 15.4 | 1945 | 239 | 21.3 |

Note: *Figures relate to the present-day territory of Poland.
*Source:* Hamilton (1979a: 168).

Bohemia (Czech Republic) which became the "factory backyard" of Vienna, the capital and market centre of the Habsburg Empire. After the creation of the Austro-Hungarian Monarchy in 1867, Budapest experienced rapid industrialization and metropolitanization. There, a strong centralizing and agglomerating force was the centripetal rail network, a distorted rail tariff regime which comprised lower rates to and from Budapest irrespective of distance and higher rates between any other locations in the Empire. The imperial policy for "spatial–ethnic division of labour" encouraged manufacturing diversity in Hungary, especially in Budapest itself, and relegated the roles of towns located in the colonial areas of Slovakia, Slavonia (northern Croatia), Vojvodina (northern Serbia), and Romania largely to mining, agriculture and raw material processing (Hamilton, 1968). Imperial policy also attempted to delay the construction of a rail link between Zagreb and Belgrade, for instance, for fear of stimulating "pan-Slavic" nationalism directed against imperial rule. City development was also generally discouraged in the Russian colonial zones of central and eastern Poland for similar reasons: railways were usually aligned to bypass all towns by several kilometres to prevent or discourage an industrialization process which was perceived as creating a revolutionary urban proletariat that could further fuel Polish nationalism. The outstanding exception to this, however, was the growth of Lodz (Poland) into the "Manchester of Eastern Europe" to supply the Russian market with textiles and clothing. In this case, much German and Jewish capital – in effect, FDI – "leap-frogged" the Prussian–Russian border to establish production inside a Russian Empire that was protected from textile and clothing imports by high tariffs. Finally, in the Balkans, the Ottoman Empire left a legacy of very limited city development centred around handicrafts and Islamic culture, but with long-term consequences for the attitudes and behaviour of the people.

The "external forces" that operated between the First and Second World Wars were mainly political and economic. The re-drawing of the Central and Eastern European map by the Great Powers, following the outcome of the First World War (and before it the Balkan Wars), created a "tier" of independent "buffer" states between Russia (after 1922, the Soviet Union) and the Germanic states. The effects on cities were broadly twofold:

(i) enhancement of the roles of those cities which became capitals of new, "reborn" or enlarged sovereign states: Belgrade (the Kingdom of Serbs, Croats and Slovenes, renamed in 1929 as Kingdom of Yugoslavia), Bucharest (Romania), Kaunas (Lithuania), Prague (Czechoslovakia), Riga (Latvia), Sofia (Bulgaria), Tallinn (Estonia), and Warsaw (Poland). These experienced the creation of administrative functions and services and some market-led or state-stimulated industrialization; and

(ii) the decline of cities whose former food and raw-material or manufacturing supply and market areas were "truncated" by border changes and "shrinkage" of their territorial and administrative range and population size: Budapest and Vienna, and an arc of smaller cities lying on either side of the post-1920 Hungarian border, i.e. in Slavonia (northern Croatia), Vojvodina (northern Serbia), and Transilvania (western Romania).

By the 1930s, however, the region as a whole began to suffer the first major "global" economic effects through the diffusion of the 1929 Wall Street Crash, which seriously depressed agriculture, restricted markets for manufacturers, and deepened poverty in rural and urban communities alike. Indeed, the growth of poverty in the region was such that it stimulated the League of Nations to research the main causes of the problem, the first expression of "global concern" for the region (Moore, 1945). Ensuing "economic nationalist" or "national autarkic" development strategies further curtailed food and manufacturing exports, adding, for instance, to the severe recession in Lodz caused by the loss of the Russian (Soviet) textile market and the loss of the German markets to producer cities in Poland (such as Poznan) and Upper Silesia (Katowice). The "Depression Years" also effectively curtailed any further FDI that had begun to penetrate the region, particularly in natural resource-based industries (Hamilton, 1968), although there was growing German corporate penetration of Central and Eastern European strategic industries as part of Nazi militarization and expansionist plans (Basch, 1944).

The Second World War had highly differential impacts on cities in the region, largely as a result of the varying intensity and character of military operations, which were partly a response to the positions adopted by national governments in either opposing or accepting Axis occupation. On the one hand, cities in the north, especially in the Third Reich east of the Oder River, together with Berlin and Warsaw, were very heavily damaged. By contrast, cities in south Poland, Czechoslovakia, Hungary, Romania, and Bulgaria generally escaped this fate, although their Jewish and other indigenous populations were often decimated or annihilated. In South-east Europe, on the other hand, cities actually grew in population through a combination of rural-to-urban migration and high rates of indigenous growth, though in Yugoslavia population increase in cities was also "fostered" by the concentration of German military action and partisan resistance in more rural areas, especially in Bosnia and Herzegovina. However, the outcomes of the Second World War also had specific impacts on cities in certain countries and regions. The sharp drop in the urban population living on the territory of present-day Poland reflects the post-1944 exodus of Germans from former Third Reich areas lying to the east of the Oder (which became part of Poland in 1945). Similarly, the decline in Czechoslovakia's urban population expresses the German exodus from "Sudetenland" or, more properly, northern Bohemia. On the other hand, it could be argued that the longer time lag between census years (1930–1931 and 1948–1949) in Hungary, Romania, and Yugoslavia provided opportunities for more pre-war urban growth and hence somewhat masks the impacts of the Second World War.

## External Forces during the Socialist Period

In the aftermath of the Second World War, the entire Central and Eastern European arena became subject to "Sovietization". This occurred either directly in the Baltic states and those areas of the former East Prussia, Poland, Czechoslovakia, and Romania that were incorporated into the USSR in 1945, or indirectly in the "independent states" ruled from 1945 by essentially "implanted" communist regimes. The effects on cities were both far-reaching and diverse. Urbanization was intended to be the vanguard process for "socialization" under the Soviet Union. As a result, cities expanded everywhere and, by 1989, all states were far more urbanized than they had been 40 years earlier, although north-west and south-east differentiation still persisted (see Table 4.2). Indeed, by 1989 more than twice as many people lived in cities in Central and Eastern Europe compared to 1950. Rapid urban growth was particularly striking in relatively less urbanized Poland, Romania, Bulgaria, and Yugoslavia.

The elimination of market forces and private enterprise (though not necessarily private ownership) depressed the role of economic factors in shaping city development and, especially in the capital cities, elevated the importance of political, cultural, and social functions significantly. Yet, city growth became primarily driven by industrialization that, until 1958, followed the Stalinist model of autarkic "import-substitution" in each Central and Eastern European country that was bilaterally tied to the USSR. The quest for equality, together with strategic needs, also led to greater spatial dispersion of industrialization, and hence, of city growth. Nevertheless, although most governments adopted some kind of implicit or explicit policy to restrict the rate of growth and scale of development of their capital city, these continued to expand, not least because

Table 4.2  Growth of urban population in Eastern Europe, 1950–1990

| Country | 1950 | | 1970 | | 1990* | |
|---|---|---|---|---|---|---|
| | 000 | % | 000 | % | 000 | % |
| East Germany | 13,040 | 72.0 | 12,592 | 73.8 | 15,759 | 76.8 |
| Poland | 9,605 | 39.0 | 17,088 | 52.3 | 2,310 | 61.3 |
| Czechoslovakia | 6,354 | 51.5 | 8,942 | 62.3 | 11,836 | 75.7 |
| Hungary | 3,553 | 38.6 | 4,992 | 48.2 | 6,295 | 59.5 |
| Romania | 3,713 | 23.4 | 8,335 | 40.9 | 11,723 | 50.6 |
| Bulgaria | 2,001 | 27.5 | 4,510 | 52.9 | 5,967 | 66.4 |
| Yugoslavia | 3,269 | 21.9 | 7,385 | 35.9 | 1,125 | 46.5 |
| Albania | 250 | 20.5 | 800 | 37.4 | 1,135 | 35.5 |
| Total | 41,785 | 39.4 | 64,644 | 51.2 | 83,920 | 60.0 |

Note: *Data refer to years 1988, 1989, or 1990.
*Sources:* Hamilton (1979a: 168); *Encyclopaedia Britannica, Book of the Year: Britannica World Data 1990.*

new industrial development there was supposed to assist in the deconstruction of the bourgeoisie and the construction of an urban proletariat sympathetic to communism. Moreover, a general shortage of skills and transport infrastructure also stimulated the localization (or agglomeration) of the key, and more skill-intensive, machinery, engineering electrical, and pharmaceutical industries in or near capital cities and main second-order cities. Dispersion to less developed regions and smaller cities was often constrained by scarce investment resources and by low investment priorities for agriculture activities. Thus, dispersion tended to occur most strongly where activities based on natural resources could contribute to the overriding "national" planning priorities of capital-intensive or "heavy" industrialization.

The Soviet Union wielded direct control (through its Ministry of Defence) over the location of all new industries or (expanded) capacities in the region which were of direct strategic significance or which could form part of the defence industry "supply chain". That control often resulted in accelerated industrialization in smaller or medium-sized cities, especially in the "safer" eastern or interior regions of Soviet bloc member countries, such south-eastern and eastern Poland (e.g. Lublin) and the "central industrial region", eastern Slovakia (Banská Bystrica, Košice), eastern Hungary (Dunajvaros, Miskolc) (see Bora, 1981), eastern Romania (Iaşi, Galaţi, Braila), and central and eastern Bulgaria (Burgas, Varna, Dimitrovgrad). It also contributed to the construction of more than 40 new towns in the region, usually for basic or defence industries (Shackleton, 1969: 466–468; Szirmai, 1998). Where possible, the border regions in the west were avoided. However, Soviet influence also contributed to relatively faster industrialization and city growth in the less-developed countries of South-east Europe and Poland than in East Germany, Czechoslovakia, and Hungary. This trend was partly assisted by the transfer of equipment for some 300 industrial plants by the USSR to those areas in the late 1940s and early 1950s (Hoffman, 1961).

The legacy of the Stalin years that was most important for city change in the post-socialist period was the duplication between the Central and Eastern European states of many basic, raw-material processing and engineering industries of sub-optimal size and outdated technology built under the "national autarky" regime – a direct transfer of the Soviet experience of "socialism in one country". In other words, this legacy created the core of the problem of "surplus capacities" under the conditions of relative demilitarization and exposure to international competition in the 1990s, and thus has been a contributory factor of de-industrialization in many cities in Central and Eastern Europe, including those which had grown or had been established as new industrial towns after the Second World War.

While Soviet domination imposed isolation on Central and Eastern Europe from many "global" economic urban trends between 1945 and 1990, it did also led to a "partial transition" from the national autarky of the pre–Second World

War period towards a greater degree of international division of labour which began to effect city systems and functions from 1960. This commenced in the "Khrushchev" period (1956–1964) within the framework of the Council for Mutual Economic Assistance. The policy was consolidated during the "Brezhnev" era (1964–1981) within the CMEA and extended to international cooperation between CMEA cities and cities in other regions of the world through "East–West" and "East–West–South" integration (Bora, 1981; Gutman and Arkwright, 1981; Kortus and Kaczorowski, 1981; Linge and Hamilton, 1981).

The "de-Stalinization" process under President Khrushchev was critically important in several ways. Within the USSR, there was a "rebirth of economics", as part of the "de-Stalinization" and "rehabilitation" programmes, which had at least two impacts on the paths and character of city development in the socialist countries of Eastern Europe. Both were related to attempts to make socialist production and economic and social functioning more "efficient". The first concerned the quest for achieving "optimum city size"; the second concerned raising industrial (plant) efficiency.

The question as to whether or not optimum city sizes really exist, or indeed could be achieved, had emerged in town planning debates in the USSR in the 1920s and 1930s. By the 1960s, the debate had been revived within the CMEA; it paralleled similar concerns in Western Europe and shared some common elements at the global level at that time (see Neutze, 1971). Essentially, assessments of optimum city size within the CMEA were tied to industrial needs. Since optimal plant sizes varied between sectors, single-industry or single-enterprise towns ("company towns") should form a hierarchy, somewhat reminiscent of the "rank size rule" or Christaller's "central place hierarchy" (albeit based on market services) that evolved in the West. However, the concept was also applied to underpin the rationale of controlling large cities and especially capital city size, and to disperse industry and other "non-essential" functions away from those cities into the hierarchy of other urban centres. The objective was to forge a "balanced" and "integrated" urban system. This was achieved mostly by central planning decisions to divert new job-creating functions to green-field sites in or near existing regional, provincial, or smaller cities, or to sites where "new towns" were built as "free-standing cities" (often conceived as "model socialist towns") or as "satellites" of major urban areas. Rarely, however, did socialist planning involve either industrial closures in capital cities or relocation to other cities, unlike in Western Europe.

While decentralization was easier in countries with quite dispersed urban systems or networks such as Czechoslovakia, Romania, Bulgaria, and Yugoslavia, it also began to play a role in Hungary, where the major second-order cities (Gyor, Miskolc, Debrecen, Szeged, and Pecs) were designated major "growth poles" to divert development from the capital city of Budapest. The aim of this urban policy was to make more efficient use of scarce resources (capital, materials, labour) in the construction of new housing, education, welfare, and other services, as well as commuter transport and infrastructure, which were funded directly or indirectly by the state to minimize the social costs associated with production. The idea stimulated and in the 1970s was further encouraged by work in Britain on the "costs of urban growth" (CURB). The deepest analysis of the idea, however, emanated from Poland, where it was elaborated into "threshold analysis".[2] Research in Poland demonstrated that the costs of further expansion (mainly of industry, but to a lesser extent, services) were highest in Warsaw and other larger cities, and much less or very low in small and medium-sized cities. This led the government to locate major new manufacturing in such cities in the 1960s. This policy was particularly evident in the location of new petrochemical, chemical, and other industries in small or medium-sized cities along the Vistula river, in south-eastern Poland and, to impose strict controls on growth (employment creation as well as housing), in Warsaw and Upper Silesia in particular. However, the cost data were later found to be erroneous (Hamilton, 1979b).

The issue of plant efficiency had another impact. The "new economics" basically argued that specialized optimal plants allocated the to socialist countries, at least outside the USSR, should counteract the legacy of Stalinist (autarkic) development, which had been inefficient since it had led to the duplication of sub-optimal industries. In the USSR, however, Stalinist socialism had often built excessively large plants in the "gigantomania" period of the 1930s and 1940s, which created transportation inefficiencies with long hauls, and large city expansion with overcrowding. So Khrushchev led a campaign to ensure that industrialization in the socialist countries after 1958 (embedded in the Five Year Plans of 1960–1964 in most Eastern European states, and the Seven Year Plan of 1958–1964 in the USSR) should take the form of larger-scale, efficient, specialized facilities to serve the needs of the whole CMEA[3] (rather than just the national) market. This stimulated the introduction of policies to create "international division of labour" within the CMEA to "share out" development amongst member states and, hence, amongst the region's cities. In practice, this meant that while the USSR could produce the entire range of products planned for the market, the other socialist states needed to specialize on much more restricted ranges of products. Thus, city development in Central and Eastern Europe – except in Yugoslavia and Albania, which were not CMEA members – was shaped by this type of CMEA industrialization policy after 1960. Cities expanded rapidly if they acquired new product lines or could supply enlarged quantities of existing specialized products to the whole CMEA market from existing locations.

Increased engagement of the CMEA in international trade, and the growing need for "fish-factory" ships to meet CMEA food shortages, led to a rapid expansion of shipbuilding and associated marine engineering in and around cities such as Rostock (East Germany), Gdansk, Gdynia and Szczecin (Poland), Constanţa (Romania), and Varna and Burgas (Bulgaria). Port cities tended to experience significant population growth, and suitable ice-free locations were restricted along the Soviet coast to cities like Leningrad (St Petersburg), Arkhangelsk, Murmansk, Vladivostok, and Odessa. Railway equipment manufactured for CMEA markets expanded in Wrocław (Poland), while Prague specialized in the assembly of trams for use in capital and medium-sized city urban transport networks. Steel production to serve the CMEA market led to major plant expansion at Crakow (Poland), Ostrava (Czech Republic), and Kosice (Slovakia). Hungary was allocated the role of CMEA supplier of buses, which led to major development and expansion at Szekerfehervar, Gyor, and Budapest. But Hungary also possessed bauxite resources scarce in the CMEA, so it favoured the growth of aluminium industries, and new chemical complexes were also developed in north-east Hungary as part of CMEA integration (Bora, 1981).

In the Brezhnev period (1964–1981), attempts were made to expand this international division of labour through the development of "new" industries, including those expanded to supply more "consumers" products, drawing partly on Western technology transfer (e.g. synthetic fibres, automotive products, colour televisions). The rapid growth and diversification of the computer and information technology industries, though much slower and more modest than in the West, also enabled most socialist countries to specialize in particular lines of computer hardware and software (Linge and Hamilton, 1981) and so share in their development. This often occurred in or near the capital cities.

But several problems associated with CMEA specialization and cooperation were emerging, too. The development of international organizations within the CMEA, or so-called "socialist internationals" (Linge and Hamilton, 1981), led to the localization of administrative and research facilities mainly in the capital cities, led by Moscow – which, after all, was also the CMEA capital. Of 23 CMEA-wide organizations in existence by the mid-1970s, 11 were located in or near Moscow, the others being dispersed among Warsaw (3), Budapest (3), Prague (2), and Bucharest (1). The other 3 were shared among "second-order" cities: Gdynia and Wroclaw (Poland), and Halle (East Germany). Although hard evidence of the scale of these operations is lacking, there is no doubt that they contributed to the agglomeration of service growth functions in capital cities in this period and hence to a relative shift from manufacturing to services there. This was particularly marked in the case of Moscow (Hamilton, 1976; see also Chapter 14 of this volume).

A contrasting problem can be seen in the CMEA's attempts to develop international specialization in the automotive industry. While Hungary was probably "content" to receive CMEA specialization on large-scale bus production, the same cannot be said for the car industry. Because of its traditional long-established skills, Skoda in Czechoslovakia was deemed by the CMEA administration in Moscow to be the site for the expansion of this industry to serve CMEA markets in private cars. However, the Polish government decided to invite Fiat to invest after 1964 in modernizing the old Soviet-equipped Warsaw plant and later to build green-field facilities in Upper Silesia. The Soviet government responded, attracting Fiat technology to build the Togliatti (new town) plant in the Volga region, while the Romanians, not to be left out, invited Renault to equip the new Dacia plant. Yugoslavia had already been producing Fiat vehicles since the mid-1950s. The point illustrates the way in which "internal" nationalist forces seized on international opportunities, with major impacts on the growth (or creation) of selected cities.

The 1960s and 1970s saw substantial Western technology transfer to the "more liberal" socialist states, especially Poland and Hungary, following the path pioneered by President Tito in Yugoslavia as early as 1953 after the break-up with Stalin. This was not the case in East Germany, Czechoslovakia, or Bulgaria, which were more strongly "pro-Soviet" or "anti-Western" in their stance. Thus began a process of wider global integration of selected cities in more "liberal" socialist states in contrast to the continued greater isolation of cities in the "pro-Soviet" states, which still maintained most of their links within the CMEA, especially with cities in the USSR. And yet industry in East German cities experienced considerable modernization though "industrial espionage" of technologies evolved or located in West Germany.

Much of the technology transfer to Poland, Hungary, and Romania was paid for in "counter-trade", a reverse flow of products to Western Europe, so establishing the first significant East–West trade flows. Since this trade happened to come on stream in the aftermath of the first oil crisis (1974), it either stimulated or accelerated innovation or downsizing in West European industrial cities (e.g. in Torino, Italy, the home of Fiat). The resulting technology transfer and counter-trade flows, therefore, tended towards closer European integration rather than globalization. But "East–West–South" integration, stimulated by the 1970s oil crisis, did bring Central and Eastern European cities into more economic and political interaction with some developing and newly industrializing countries (Gutman and Arkwright, 1981).

Two further points need to be mentioned here. First, policy shifts in the USSR towards more "consumer" goods production did have the effect of bringing more diversified industrialization to cities in regions with few or no natural resources as part of the spatial "division of labour" within the USSR itself. This did have important consequences for the growth of the capital cities of the Baltic republics, especially Riga (Latvia), where significant electrical industry expansion was located, and Minsk (Belarus). The latter, however, also became part of the CMEA engineering "production chain" on the Berlin–Warsaw–Moscow axis. Moreover, the development and expansion of some Soviet cities was also an effect of the energy and raw materials supply chain from the USSR to Central and Eastern Europe.

The second point is that there has been a fairly strong Soviet influence on the spatial form of cities in Eastern Europe during the socialist period. The ideas of the "socialist city" elaborated by Milyutin in the 1930s and incorporated in the Moscow city plan (1935), with subsequent revisions, found expression in Eastern European cities in the "universal" development of residential neighbourhoods with minimal services (i.e. "sleeping quarters") and with green zones separating residential from industrial areas (Milyutin, 1974; French and Hamilton, 1979).

*External Forces since 1989*

There has been both a dramatic rise in, and a change in direction and character of, the operation of international and global forces in the cities of Central and Eastern Europe since the end of the Cold War, the collapse of communism and the break-up of the former Soviet Union in the years 1989–1991. These forces have been "filtered" into cities from outside the region on the waves of a fundamental systemic change from the relatively closed, state-managed socialist economy to much more open systems based on market principles and civil society. "Filtering" has resulted from interactions between global forces and international agencies, and national government policies. However, once the Central and Eastern European countries began to experience a fundamental systemic change, major surpluses, as well as a whole series of wide "gaps" or large "deficits", were exposed in the region compared with advanced and newly industrializing economies. Attempts to narrow, close, or fill these gaps or deficits – in efficiency, technology, production organization, producer services, entrepreneurship, and local empowerment, for instance – have drawn into the region a wide variety of international public and private agencies and corporate actors which have begun to intensify the process of globalization and European integration and enlargement ("EU-ization"). These processes, however, vary between Central and Eastern European countries and subregions, as well as between and within cities in those countries. The next section explores these processes and attempts to throw light on some of their outcomes.

## Systemic Change

Cities have been experiencing far-reaching systemic change since 1989. However, the mood for reform in countries like the former Yugoslavia, East Germany, Czechoslovakia, and Hungary tended to favour a "third way" which would be quite distinctive from the established "socialist" or "capitalist" modes (see Šik, 1992) and closer to the (then) Swedish model of the "social economy" that combined economic efficiency in production with welfare policies in housing and social services, and policies for managed labour markets. In reality, the conjunction of two sets of forces led to an almost outright rejection of state management and even state intervention, and a tendency to "overshoot" to the opposite extreme to favour a more liberal capitalistic market system.

These forces were as follows. First, embryonic democratization enabled popular opinion to feed into national government policies to reject the former authoritarian system. Second, external pressure was applied by Western powers on national governments to adopt a market system, through the medium of experts appointed by international organizations such as the International Monetary Fund (IMF) and the World Bank. The operation of both forces was facilitated by the demise of communism in the USSR and by the break-up of the USSR itself, while the seizure by President Kohl of the unique political opportunity to reunite eastern and western Germany (partly by "buying off" east German voters) led to the rapid integration of the former East Germany into the economic, political, and social space of Germany and the European Union. The replacement in a very short time of the stark old "Iron Curtain" by a perceived glittering "Golden Curtain" between Eastern and Western Europe probably also coloured local opinion in Central and Eastern European countries that following the West European model and closer integration with the European Union could lead to "the promised land" (Smith, 2000) (see Table 4.3).

In any event, systemic change in Central and Eastern Europe geographically reorientated the source of external forces from the "East" to the "West", and it has tended to bear the deep imprint of Anglo-American "neo-classical" or

Table 4.3 Economic performance of Central and Eastern European countries – EU candidates (2000)

| | Population (mil.) | GDP per capita* (US$) | Inflation rate (%) | Agriculture | | Unemployment rate** (%) |
|---|---|---|---|---|---|---|
| | | | | (% of GDP) | (% of employment) | |
| *Baltic states* | | | | | | |
| Estonia | 1.4 | 7,700 | 5.9 | 4.3 | 8.2 | 13.7 |
| Latvia | 2.4 | 5,800 | 2.5 | 3.6 | 18.4 | 13.2 |
| Lithuania | 3.7 | 6,200 | 1.3 | 7.9 | 22.4 | 11.4 |
| *Central-east Europe* | | | | | | |
| Czech Republic | 10.3 | 12,500 | 4.7 | 3.7 | 5.6 | 8.8 |
| Hungary | 10.1 | 10,700 | 9.2 | 5.4 | 10.1 | 7.0 |
| Poland | 38.7 | 7,800 | 5.5 | 5.2 | 25.6 | 16.0 |
| Slovakia | 5.4 | 10,300 | 7.3 | 4.4 | 8.4 | 18.6 |
| Slovenia | 2.0 | 15,600 | 8.4 | 2.9 | 10.7 | 7.0 |
| *South-east Europe* | | | | | | |
| Bulgaria | 8.2 | 4,700 | 7.5 | 15.9 | 21.2 | 17.8 |
| Romania | 22.4 | 5,700 | 34.5 | 13.9 | 35.2 | 7.2 |
| CEEC 10 | 104.6 | 8,005 | 8.7 | 6.7 | 16.6 | 12.2 |
| EU 15 | 375.3 | 21,100 | 2.3 | 2.5 | 5.7 | 8.3 |

Notes:
*GDP per capita at PPP.
**As percentage of the labour force (ILO).
*Sources:* EUROSTAT; ILO, UNCHS.

"neo-liberal" economists (i.e. advisers from IMF, the World Bank, various Western governments, etc.) who persuaded or tried to persuade governments to apply macro-economic stabilization and micro-economic restructuring policies to achieve "transition" to a market economy and more efficient resource allocation to achieve economic growth. Such narrow approaches overlooked the difficulties, time-lags, and importance of institutional restructuring in changing economic systems and in generating growth, and ignored the "frictions" of history and geography. And, in practice, the idea that "transition" across the entire region would follow a linear trajectory has been derailed by (a) democratic changes of government and related policy shifts to "stall" reform, especially when reform did not appear to produce results, and (b) the behaviour of many local actors in the "reform" process. So the pattern of reform has become highly differentiated across Central and Eastern Europe.

Nevertheless, broadly speaking, systemic change is involving increasing "commodification" of the factors of production and of space and spatial relationships, displacing past "socialistic" political, ideological, strategic, social, and economic evaluations by international competitive and comparative advantage or disadvantage (Hamilton, 1995). The inherited assets of location are thus being reappraised according to what they offer or do not offer for profitable production or functioning within the framework of both national and global systems. The growth of market exchange in Central and Eastern Europe embodies increasingly pervasive commodification. This involves a diffusion process which is (i) *structural*, penetrating more sectors and factors of production, and (ii) *geographical*, spreading to more countries, regions, and cities. And yet, it is also a process that is being spearheaded mainly by people and organizations located in the capital and larger cities, which can diffuse commodification through city interdependencies within and across national borders and through their linked regional and national urban hierarchies. Of course, one "indicator" of commodification tendencies is the level of privatization of city economies, but one must note the caveat that private ownership is not necessarily synonymous with the "market economy". Generally, the availability of data on privatization varies between countries and may often apply at the national and regional levels. Variations in methods of privatization also suggest international and sometimes inter-city differentiation in the operation of market-economic forces.

Elsewhere, Hamilton (1995) has elaborated various aspects of commodification. These may be summarized here with regard to their effects on cities and city systems in Central and Eastern Europe. First, by bringing greater exposure to international market competition, commodification is leading to a significant decline or stagnation in cities dominated by natural resources, except in cases such as timber (supporting wood-processing furniture or paper industries) or copper, which are benefiting from expanding local markets and are proving to be more competitive in national, European, or wider global markets,

Table 4.4 Average monthly manufacturing wages in Europe (1992–2000) (US$)

|  | 1992* | 1996 | 2000 |
|---|---|---|---|
| **Selected EU countries** | | | |
| Austria | 2,565 | 3,153 | 2,473 |
| Germany | 1,872** | 2,275 | 2,421 |
| Ireland | 1,487 | 1,552 | 1,632 |
| Spain | 1,535 | 1,507 | 1,535 |
| United Kingdom | 1,786 | 1,852 | 2,107 |
| **Central and Eastern European transition economies** | | | |
| *Baltic states* | | | |
| Estonia | 42 | 256 | 285 |
| Latvia | 34 | 189 | 223 |
| Lithuania | 33 | 164 | 239 |
| *Central Europe* | | | |
| Croatia | 131 | 559 | 495 |
| Czech Republic | 162 | 341 | 341 |
| Hungary | 267 | 309 | 312 |
| Poland | 196 | 309 | 404 |
| Slovakia | 155 | 269 | 254 |
| Slovenia | 533 | 784 | 724 |
| *South-east Europe* | | | |
| Bulgaria | 96 | 87 | 103 |
| Romania | 77 | 138 | 117 |

Notes:
*Introduction of national (new) currencies in newly independent states of Central and Eastern Europe (i.e. Baltic states, Croatia, Slovenia). Data for the EU member states (except Austria) are based on hourly rates. For all other countries data relate to monthly wages.
**West Germany only.
*Sources:* ILO (2002); Holland and Pain (1998); UN Economic Bulletin for Europe (1998) (own calculations).

or where continued state protection has cushioned or delayed the effects of competition. Second, commodification is progressively penetrating labour markets that, while often imperfect, are essentially city-centred within "journey-to-work" areas. For the first time in 50 years, labour markets in Central and Eastern Europe are having to operate in an increasingly competitive international European and global framework. However, low labour costs are a common advantage throughout the region, certainly in sharp contrast to the high labour costs of the more advanced economies of Western Europe, North America, East Asia, and the Pacific.

Table 4.4 uses manufacturing wage data in the 1990s to illustrate:

(a) the huge gap between EU countries and the transitioning economies in general; in other words, the data are a clear expression of the "Golden Curtain" between West and East;

(b) significant variations in wage rates both within the European Union and within the transition economies; and

(c) relative changes in wage rates over time, broadly between the deeper recession year of 1992 (in both East and West Europe) and the period of economic upswing (1996) and stabilization (2000).

It must be recognized, of course, that the data are only indicative of competitiveness and are not a true measure of it – this would require unit labour cost data incorporating productivity etc. Nevertheless, they are a useful guide to international economic differentiation of urban systems and capital cities between the European Union and transition economies as well as within the European Union and within Central and Eastern Europe. Although one should not read too much into the precise figures, it is clear that in 1992, monthly manufacturing wages were 20–120 times greater in Germany and Austria than in the Baltic and South-east European states. In the same year, the lower manufacturing wage rates in the EU periphery (Ireland, Spain, UK) were almost 10 times higher than in several Central European states. The "East–West gap" was narrowest between Slovenia and the EU periphery, although still high between Slovenia and the neighbouring Austria and (West) Germany. With the exception of Hungary, which registered relatively slow growth in manufacturing wages, and Bulgaria, where there was a decline, wages generally rose faster in the transition economies between 1992 and 2000 than in Western Europe, so the gaps have narrowed somewhat. Generally, wages in the expanding services sector are generally lower than in manufacturing, although wages paid in producer services could well be higher. Also, wages tend to be higher in the capital city than in provincial cities.

In assessing competitiveness, however, other factors such as land and property costs need to be taken into consideration. Thus, the attraction of specific labour markets for inward investment within Central and Eastern Europe is determined by cost differentials only in the case of less skilled or unskilled labour-intensive activities. Other factors, such as particular labour skills or human capital resources and the international accessibility of labour markets where labour supplies and the diversity of labour skills are greater, play a much more influential role, especially in cities in western Poland and Hungary, the Czech Republic and Slovenia, compared with more remote labour markets in South-east and East Europe. In other words, globalization and European integration are having a strongly selective impact on city labour markets, given the generally widespread availability of cheap labour. Land and property privatization is an especially diversified phenomenon between Central and Eastern European countries and cities, drawing urban and suburban property into the market exchange process. This is particularly important in reshaping the functional structure, dynamics, and spatial forms of cities, especially in the capital city regions, as their space is transformed from the flat "money valueless" pattern of socialist utility values to market exchange values which show a gradient from high levels in the city centres to lower or low values with increasing distance from or accessibility to those centres.

However, intra-city, intra-regional, and inter-city transport and flows are being significantly reshaped by the fact that, under transition, the cost and time considerations of transport and communications have come to "matter". Business transactions and movements of freight, people, and information have all acquired real costs associated with the decline or removal of artificial state subsidies, and with distance, economies or dis-economies of scale, and infrastructure quality and quantity (density or intensity). The "friction" of time and distance in procuring inputs and in distributing outputs has become significant for the survival, efficiency, competitiveness, and profitability of enterprises. This suggests that, with a general rise in real transport costs (especially road transport, as a result of steep rises in fuel prices in Europe), such forces as external or agglomeration economies are now playing a far more influential role in urban functional change in the Central and Eastern European countries than previously was the case, so favouring larger metropolitan centres and medium-sized cities or clusters of cities occupying nodal locations in the integrating Europe.

Finally, the combination of commodification as a systemic process and the geography of trade integration and city interdependencies has been leading to a fundamental reversal in the "fortunes" of cities located along, in or near the border zones of Central and Eastern European states. For many reasons, under socialism, integration with the former USSR endowed cities in the eastern regions with advantages, stimulating their growth – especially in eastern Poland, Hungary, Slovakia, Romania, and Bulgaria. Although this was less apparent in the Baltic states or in East Europe (Belarus, Ukraine, Moldova), cities in the western regions of Poland, the Czech Republic, and Hungary were considered "less safe" or "more risky" for development. Since 1989, this situation has been reversed, and cities in the western regions of Central and Eastern Europe, and that are close to EU borders, are in most cases experiencing vigorous growth or restructuring of their economies and societies.

## "Surpluses", "Deficits", and City Transformation

The socialist era bequeathed cities in the post-socialist states a whole series of "surpluses" in relation to the needs of national, European, and global markets on the one hand, and "gaps" or "deficits" in Central and Eastern European economic structures on the other. These "surpluses" and "deficits" lay at the very roots of the divergence of the functional and spatial structures of socialist cities from their market-economy counterparts in advanced economies throughout the period from 1950 to the 1980s, and also from many cities in newly industrializing and developing countries. The process of transformation of post-socialist cities since 1989 has essentially involved trends towards the "destruction" of surpluses and the "construction" of capacities to fill the gaps and to correct deficiencies, and hence to begin to bring about greater convergence between East and West European countries. The extent to which these trends have occurred during the 1990s is quite differentiated between cities in various Central and Eastern European states and between cities within individual states. Hence, cities are experiencing differential degrees and types of restructuring, so changing the urban systems of the region. "Surpluses" essentially derive from global market needs, the socialist legacy of "over-industrialization" – creating excess capacities in heavy, capital-goods, and defence industries – and the significant "demilitarization" that has occurred since the end of the Cold War. In general, surpluses are leading to de-industrialization and hence to decline or structural crisis in cities highly dependent on such industries as their economic base (Barta, 1998).

To some extent, de-industrialization has been cushioned by continuity of state ownership, as these industries have been the most difficult to privatize and sell off or to convert from military to civilian purposes. However, liberalization of trade has often also resulted in the downsizing or closure of industries in such consumer sectors as textiles, clothing, and footwear as a result of import penetration from a combination of cheaper goods from newly industrializing and developing economies and higher-quality and more fashionable products from the European Union and other countries. In many cases, also, the engineering and machinery industries have suffered both from declining Central and Eastern European and former Soviet markets, and from import penetration from the European Union and other advanced economies on account of their obsolescence or uncompetitiveness – this links up also with the question of gaps or deficits discussed below. To some extent, however, continued protection of state ownership and low costs of production have enabled cities dependent on such industries as steel to adjust, at least in the shorter or medium term, by exporting to the European Union (despite quotas and controls) or by diverting exports to oil-rich or newly industrializing economies in the Middle East, Latin America, or Asia. Nevertheless, the existence of surpluses has meant that the cities where such capacity is located have had to bear the brunt of the "destructive" de-industrialization forces resulting from systematic change and international trade integration, and this has often affected the capital city regions of Central and Eastern Europe.

On the other hand, "constructive" forces of change have helped the process of filling the large gaps or deficits in the Central and Eastern European economies. The gaps between those economies and the rest of the world have been, and often still are, very wide. They usually represent individual or collective market potentials and express a big structural lag in the Central and Eastern European states behind not only the advanced market economies but also, often, the world's newly industrializing economies in Latin America and Asia as well as the peripheral EU economies.

The first of these "deficits" relates to economic efficiency. At its root is the need for cities in Central and Eastern Europe to adjust to international competitiveness by achieving economies of scale in the operation of enterprises on their territories. As noted earlier, the Stalin period left a very broad industrial base of sub-optimal plants, which was only partially corrected by later CMEA integration policies. The rigidities of bilateral trade, lack of competition, and the absence of economic indicators, as well as sustained planned growth of heavy industrial output, provided a framework within the CMEA for the continued operation of such plants, although new facilities built from the early 1960s through the 1970s may have had more optimal scales. Even so, the liberalization of trade necessitates an increase in scale to achieve cost reductions, but this process has to be selective between facilities in over-developed sectors. Hence, one would expect investments by national or foreign firms to target enterprises with the "best potential", leading to stronger inter-city specialization and to concentration in key nodal city regions with the best transport accessibility to wider European and international markets. Yet, these areas can also attract new activities that operate at large efficient scales, especially in "deficit" warehousing and logistics.

The second "deficit" is technological obsolescence; to be competitive in the globalizing market, cities need to ensure the technological modernization of their enterprises. This might well be aimed at automation to achieve economies of scale but, equally, the modern market also requires the development of more flexible, or minimum-efficient scale, production systems as well as more "knowledge-intensive" functions embodying human capital resources, research and development. It is more likely that such technological modernization will occur in or near key capital or provincial cities with good pools of labour skills, training, and research facilities, including cities with a strong history of relatively skilled engineering. New investment in such activities will, to varying degrees, compensate for de-industrialization in such cities.

The third "deficit" relates to the legacy of the socialist underdevelopment of the service sector; this has caused all cities to experience a "tertiarization" process involving, at least, the growth of a wide range of consumer services, while the capital cities in particular, and some key regional cities, are also experiencing the development, expansion, and diversification of producer services. It is this trend that is beginning to enable cities in Central and Eastern Europe to converge with EU cities with respect to their economic structures.

The fourth "deficit" is both entrepreneurial and organizational. It concerns the need to fill the gaps created by the inherited lack of small and medium-sized enterprises (SMEs) and the "supply" of such enterprises to engage in reorganizing a wide range of production through subcontracting arrangements. Privatization and economic growth in cities has been driven largely by the emergence of small enterprises, especially in services, and to a lesser extent by the development of "embedded", clustered networks of manufacturers and service providers, especially in or around capital cities and key provincial cities which offer the best "seedbed" or "incubator" conditions for such firms through the creation of agglomeration economies.

Although local, indigenous entrepreneurs are playing a key role in this latter development, filling the other "gaps" depends to a very significant extent on foreign sources and hence on the global integration of Central and Eastern European countries through FDI by multinational enterprises, the European Bank for Reconstruction and Development, or other agencies. Hence, the growth of FDI (discussed at length in Chapter 5) is of crucial importance in city transformation. FDI has contributed to the shift in international trade relations of Central and Eastern European cities, though in differing ways and directions, partly according to the integration of new investments into the European or global networks of the firms involved. As research into international trade at the city level is fraught with difficulties, the best that can be done at this juncture is to use national trade patterns as a "proxy". In broad terms, over the period 1988–1997, Central and Eastern European countries have reorientated their trade more strongly to the European Union following the collapse of the Soviet market, even though the latter accounted for only 25–47 per cent of manufactured exports in 1988. What is striking in trade patterns (Smith, 2000) is that while exports to the European Union have risen by about three times, imports from the European Union have increased by five times in this period. In broad terms, therefore, Central and European cities have experienced a greater impact from EU imports of consumer goods relative to capital goods (despite higher aggregate and per capita inward flows of FDI). While cities in South-east Europe (Bulgaria, Romania) and the Baltic States have gained more from exports of labour-intensive consumer goods to the European Union, they have been relatively more deeply affected by imports of capital goods. On the other hand, FDI seems to have contributed to stronger export gains in capital goods, especially intermediate products, from cities in Central Europe (Poland, Czech Republic, Slovakia, Hungary, Slovenia).

This suggests at least two trends in manufacturing restructuring in Central and Eastern European cities. First, cities in Central Europe have gained more from integration into the European production chains of multinational enterprises, although only cities in Hungary, and to a lesser extent the Czech Republic and Slovenia, exhibit restructuring into human capital resources-related manufacturing and are converging with EU cities in this type of production. Cities in Poland, however, are mainly restructuring through FDI into products aimed mostly at the larger national and wider Central European markets. And second, the comparative advantages for the production of less skilled labour-intensive and material-intensive products have shifted relatively from Central European to South-east and East European cities, with a loss of advantages in the latter for more skill-intensive activities (Hamilton, 1995, 1999; Smith, 2000).

*Competition and Changing Spatial Form*

That said, the proximity of the capital cities of Central Europe – Prague, Bratislava, and Budapest – both to each other and to Vienna and Berlin, suggests that these cities are also experiencing more intensified competition between each other, certainly for inward investment. They also are more open to competition from second-order cities which form a relatively dense network in the western regions of Central Europe near the EU border, such as Poznan, Wroclaw, Szczecin (Poland), and an arc of northern Bohemian towns, as well as Brno and Olomouc (Czech Republic), Gyor (Hungary), Leipzig, and Dresden (Germany); this suggests that greater specialization is likely to result in their functions in the longer term. On the other hand, Warsaw is more "shielded" by time and distance and can command high accessibility to a larger national market and perhaps, therefore, may remain more diversified and will experience stronger growth. Warsaw also has the potential advantage of greater proximity to the Baltic cities, Belarus, and western Ukrainian cities. Other capitals in South-east Europe (Bucharest, Sofia) are more remote and less favoured by slow growth or stagnating economies.

Nevertheless, it is in the capital cities and their regions, with their greater diversity of inherited functions and their greater growth potentials, where the sharpest functional changes occur through de-industrialization, some re-industrialization and a marked shift to consumer and producer services. This is contributing to more rapid polarization of growth and change at least at this stage of the transformation. It is, therefore, in the capital cities and to a lesser extent the second-order cities that key contemporary changes, mirroring global trends, are occurring – the transformation of city centres with services and the creation or re-emergence of "central business districts", gentrified "islands", tourist developments and cultural amenities, highlighted by Kunzman (1998) – although the emergence of other phenomena such as modern research and development spaces is as yet very embryonic, as is the development of any "edge cities" and related suburban phenomena. So far the appearance of modern "just-in-time" production complexes is rather restricted to second-order cities in manufacturing, although the development of service complexes occurs in the capital city regions.

## Some Indicators of International Integration and City Transformation

This final section focuses on the evidence of patterns, processes, and changes in the international integration of Central and Eastern European cities. Two indicators have been selected for further discussion and elaboration in this chapter. The first, **trade patterns**, helps us to identify the effects of changing political and economic organization in shaping international integration through freight flows. The second, **air traffic patterns**, provides important insights into the connectivity of these cities in their European and wider global contexts. The following chapter examines FDI, which has become a key force in shaping the evolution of trade flows and expresses "globalization" trends through the decisions and activities of multinational firms with a wide range of functions, including control, finance, and other producer and consumer services, as well as manufacturing. **Real-estate markets**, which provide a strong link between external and internal forces, as an example of the "global–local nexus", linking globalization processes with changing patterns of urban land use and urban landscape features, are also to some extent analysed in Chapters 3, 5, and 6. To a substantial degree, all four indicators are interlinked, and thus potentially can be mutually supportive of this analysis.

## Trade Patterns

Cities and their hinterlands in Central and Eastern Europe have participated in very significant international trade during the transition of the 1990s. Their engagement in trade, of course, is effected through the competitive behaviour and production, purchasing or sales activities of the "populations" of the enterprises that make up their urban and regional productive systems. During the 1990s, cities in the region have been subject to or have implemented geographic, quantitative, and qualitative trade shifts. As already mentioned, the main problem is to obtain data which disaggregate national trade statistics by cities or regions; subsequent chapters of this book provide some insights for capital-city regions, but the lack of accurate collected data at that level precludes any comparative or in-depth analysis. One must therefore begin with a broad picture of national trade shifts. Table 4.5 outlines the geographic shifts of international trade to and from the Central and Eastern European states.

Kornai (1992) demonstrates the "abrupt turnaround" in trade that occurred after the Second World War. The Eastern European socialist countries traded principally with developed capitalist countries in 1938 (75 per cent of exports, 72 per cent of imports), while in 1958 only 20 per cent of their export and import trade was with these countries and over 70 per cent was with the socialist countries (see also Mayhew, 1998). The data for 1988 in Table 4.5 indicate that the former Eastern European socialist countries surveyed already conducted substantial trade (i.e. more than 50 per cent of exports) with the non-socialist world, except for Bulgaria, which sent 61 per cent of its exports to the USSR and Central and Eastern Europe and bought 57 per cent of its imports from socialist countries. To a substantial degree this shift reflected efforts by Eastern European countries in the 1970s and 1980s to import Western technology and consumer goods, to pay for these goods by counter-trade, and to reduce their

Table 4.5 Geographic changes in the directions of trade of Central and Eastern European countries (1988–1997)

| Selection of Central and Eastern European countries | 1988 | | | | | | | | 1997 | | | | | | | | | | | |
|---|---|---|---|---|---|---|---|---|---|---|---|---|---|---|---|---|---|---|---|---|
| | US$ (bn) | | % source destination regions | | | | | | US$ (bn) | | % source destination regions | | | | | | | | | |
| | | | USSR | | CEE | | Rest of the world | | | | CIS | | CEE | | EU-15 | | Rest of the world | | | |
| | E | I | E | I | E | I | E | I | E | I | E | I | E | I | E | I | E | I | | |
| Bulgaria | 6.4 | 6.9 | 47 | 39 | 14 | 11 | 39 | 49 | 3.8 | 3.4 | 18 | 31 | 3 | 5 | 45 | 42 | 31 | 21 | | |
| Czechoslovakia | 10.5 | 10.3 | 29 | 27 | 22 | 22 | 49 | 51 | | | | | | | | | | | | |
| Czech Republic | | | | | | | | | 19.8 | 23.8 | 4 | 7 | 22 | 22 | 60 | 52 | 11 | 26 | | |
| Slovakia | | | | | | | | | 7.8 | 10.5 | 7 | 17 | 36 | 30 | 47 | 46 | 7 | 7 | | |
| Hungary | 8.5 | 8.0 | 26 | 25 | 19 | 19 | 55 | 56 | 16.8 | 18.7 | 7 | 11 | 9 | 8 | 71 | 62 | 8 | 18 | | |
| Poland | 12.3 | 11.0 | 25 | 25 | 18 | 18 | 57 | 57 | 22.7 | 37.3 | 15 | 8 | 8 | 7 | 64 | 64 | 10 | 20 | | |
| Romania | 8.0 | 4.5 | 14 | 23 | 11 | 19 | 75 | 58 | 7.4 | 8.9 | 6 | 15 | 6 | 7 | 57 | 52 | 30 | 25 | | |
| Slovenia** | 3.3 | 2.9 | 12 | 8 | 11 | 11 | 77 | 81 | 9.4 | 10.5 | 4 | 3 | 25 | 15 | 63 | 68 | 8 | 14 | | |

Notes:
*All % rounded; E = exports; I = imports; USSR = Soviet Union; CEE = Central and Eastern Europe; CIS = Commonwealth of Independent States; EU = European Union.
**Half of all Slovenia's trade with CEE in the 1990s was with neighbouring Croatia.
*Source:* UNCTAD (own calculations).

dependency on imports of energy and raw materials from the Soviet Union, or on Soviet export markets. Nevertheless, as Anthony Smith points out:

Even as late as 1989, the structure of trade relations of the socialist states was influenced by the Stalinist concept of "two world" economic systems. This required the socialist states inside and outside the Soviet Union to conduct trade between themselves at the expense of the pursuit of trade flows with non-socialist countries that might have been regarded as more rational from a micro-economic, geographical, or even historical perspective. As a result, the CMEA states were responsible for less than 3 per cent of all international trade flows that were conducted outside the CMEA itself in 1989. (Smith, 2000: 6)

One key feature shown in Table 4.5 is the importance of continued trade flows between states that have become independent of each other since the demise of socialism at the end of 1980s. This demonstrates intertia, the legacies of former trading systems and networks of traders, so that, for instance, Slovak trade with the Czech Republic – which accounted for 26 per cent of all Slovakia's exports and 24 per cent of all Slovakian imports – was 10 times the volume of Slovak trade with neighbouring Hungary. The most important changes during the transition, however, were (i) the marked reduction of trade with the territories of the former Soviet Union, and (ii) the re-emergence of Germany as a trade partner for manufacturing exports and imports. Another feature is that whereas the bilateral trade framework led to a broad, even close, balance between imports and exports under socialism, the opening up of borders to freer trade combined with movement towards a market system, adjustment to market-driven forces, and opportunities for foreign investors to engage in trade and production.

This has led to the appearance of trade deficits in most Central and Eastern European economies, especially with the European Union. The gaps between import costs and export revenues are particularly large in the cases of Poland, Slovakia, the Czech Republic and, to a lesser degree, Hungary. This reflects the substantially faster growth of EU exports to Central and Eastern European countries than vice versa. As Smith (2000) observes, the share of Bulgaria, the former Czechoslovakia, Hungary, Poland, and Romania listed in Table 4.5 in total imports from the EU-15 rose from 3.4 in 1989 to 6.8 per cent in 1995 and has continued to rise, a trend which supports predictions based on "gravity" models which anticipated that a rapid redirection of Central and Eastern European imports and exports would take place when barriers to trade between the two regions were progressively removed. It is significant, however, that trade deficits are especially large in those Central and Eastern European states which are due to join the European Union first, especially Poland and the Czech Republic, while those which will be excluded from EU membership in the first wave either have trade in balance or a surplus. The difference, in part at least, is accounted for in the accelerated inflows of FDI into those states about to join the

European Union as companies prepare to consolidate their productive activities and competitive strategies in readiness for EU membership of the first-tier states. In particular, such FDI results in expanded imports of technologically intensive machinery or equipment and high-quality materials that have high value added.

Smith (2000) also indicates that in general, Central and Eastern European exports to the European Union do not and cannot command high values because most export growth is accounted for by the labour-intensive factor in content (39 per cent from Bulgaria and 75 per cent from Romania) or the resource-intensive factor (15–38 per cent). The sole exception is Hungary where human capital intensity accounts for 48 per cent of export growth since 1988, followed by the Czech Republic (36 per cent), while Bulgaria (23 per cent) and Poland (24 per cent) lag and Romania trails far behind (10 per cent). To a significant degree the low-value, labour-intensive nature of exports is explained by the growth of "outward processing trade" from the European Union of yarns, fabrics, and leather goods. Central and Eastern Europe absorbs around 25 per cent of total EU exports of these goods compared to 10 per cent of manufacturers as a whole, while at the same time accounting for almost 20 per cent of EU imports of clothing, furniture, and footwear, or 10 per cent of all manufacturers. What this means is that cities in Central and Eastern Europe, and especially Romania, have become locations for "putting out" subcontracting from the European Union, especially in textiles, clothing, leather goods, and furniture, to supply the European Union on the basis of local comparative advantages in terms of lower labour costs.[4]

Trade impacts at the city level are difficult to measure, mainly because of data collection deficiencies, so we must rely on enterprise surveys or chambers of commerce information in a supporting role. Conceptually, however, trade shapes the directions of city transformation through the ability of local firms or their component production facilities to exploit export opportunities made available by more open international markets or the effects of barriers to trade, and through import penetration which threatens or undermines the ability of enterprises to supply national markets. On the other hand, while import penetration can lead to the downsizing or closure of indigenous (state-owned or privatized) manufacturing firms, it fosters trading and service establishments, so contributing to structural shifts in the urban economy. In other words, international trade effects contribute towards shaping the changing quantitative and qualitative attributes of the urban and regional (functional urban region) "population" of enterprise and organizations and their performance.

From evidence available from individual city case studies in this book (see, for example, Chapter 11 on Ljubljana), there appears to be a tendency for Central and Eastern European capital cities during the transition to become major foci of import penetration and of FDI, leading to their more radical economic transformation from manufacturing to service centres, conduits for retailing and wholesale distribution and logistics for imported consumer goods destined for the national market. Through economic restructuring, technological modernization, and improved competitiveness, often through FDI, provincial or second-order cities, and small or medium-sized cities in non-metropolitan regions or in the wider functional urban regions of capital cities, have become major sources of manufactured exports. At the same time, however, import penetration or lack of international competitiveness has often had serious or devastating consequences for "one-company, one-industry" cities developed in the socialist period, especially in cases where enterprises were very inefficient or their products and processes were technologically outdated.

*Air Traffic Patterns*

Two sources of information can indicate the emerging patterns in the connectivity and network relationships between cities in Central and Eastern Europe and cities in the wider European and global space. These sources are (i) scheduled passenger flight information contained in airline timetables, and, (ii) data from the International Civil Aviation Organization (ICAO) regarding the numbers of passengers and volumes of cargo handled by city airports, and the numbers of passengers traveling on "flight stages" between cities.

The key point is that these data are "indicative". Several empirical studies in recent years have applied air traffic data to rank cities internationally (using both passenger and freight volumes) or to highlight networks of cities (using airline passenger "flow" or "flight-stage" data) (Kunzmann, 1998; Beaverstock, Smith, and Taylor, 2000). These studies, however, focus on "world cities" or the "top 25" ranked cities. They do not encompass any Central or Eastern European cities. Table 4.6 suggests a reason why: both the passenger and cargo volumes flowing through these cities' airports are but a fraction of traffic flows through airports serving Frankfurt, London, and Paris, cities which are classified as 3 of the 10 "Alpha world cities" (see Beaverstock, Smith, and Taylor, 2000).

Berlin and Vienna are far more significant cities in terms of passenger traffic than other Central and Eastern European cities (most of which are capital cities), except for Moscow, which is a close rival. However, Moscow's airports handle significantly more cargo than Vienna, while Warsaw is placed third in cargo handling – ahead of Berlin. While both Moscow and Warsaw attract greater air cargo movements because of their land transport centrality within their respective national spaces, passenger flows through Moscow are particularly small given the city's size, and this underscores the city's remoteness (as discussed in Chapter 14 on Moscow).

Table 4.6 might suggest that Berlin and Vienna act as important air traffic "hubs" for Central and Eastern European cities. The fact is that, for its size, Berlin has rather limited air traffic, a function of its unattractive "hollow" character (see Chapter 7 on Berlin).

Table 4.6  Ranking Central and Eastern European cities by airport traffic (1997)

| | Passengers (mil.) | | | Cargo (000 tonnes) | |
|---|---|---|---|---|---|
| 1 | Berlin | 10.48 | 1 | Moscow | 122.1 |
| 2 | Vienna | 9.59 | 2 | Vienna | 107.0 |
| 3 | Moscow | 4.82 | 3 | Warsaw | 47.1 |
| 4 | Prague | 4.08 | 4 | Berlin | 33.7 |
| 5 | Budapest | 3.62 | 5 | Budapest | 24.0 |
| 6 | Warsaw | 3.55 | 6 | Prague | 21.4 |
| 7 | St Petersburg | 1.67 | 7 | St Petersburg | 11.6 |
| 8 | Kiev | 1.38 | 8 | Kiev | 11.2 |
| 9 | Bucharest | 1.30 | 9 | Ljubljana | 10.2 |
| 10 | Zagreb | 1.07 | 10 | Kaunas | 5.4 |
| 11 | Ljubljana | 0.71 | 11 | Zagreb | 5.2 |
| 12 | Riga | 0.53 | 12 | Vilnius | 5.1 |
| 13 | Split | 0.47 | 13 | Skopje | 4.5 |
| 14 | Skopje | 0.42 | 14 | Riga | 3.7 |
| 15 | Vilnius | 0.41 | 15 | Brno | 2.8 |
| 16 | Tallinn | 0.38 | 16 | Odessa | 2.5 |
| 17 | Bratislava | 0.28 | 17 | Tallinn | 2.2 |
| 18 | Odessa | 0.26 | 18 | Bratislava | 1.6 |
| 19 | Brno | 0.13 | 19 | Split | 1.4 |
| 20 | Ostrava | 0.13 | 20 | Bucharest | 1.5 |

Leading West European cities by airport traffic (for comparison)

| | | | | | |
|---|---|---|---|---|---|
| 1 | London | 93.9 | 1 | Frankfurt | 1367.9 |
| 2 | Frankfurt | 39.9 | 2 | Amsterdam | 1161.0 |
| 3 | Paris | 35.1 | 3 | London | 1160.0 |

Note: *ICAO sources contain no information for Bulgaria or Serbia.
*Source:* International Civil Aviation Organization (ICAO), *Digest of Statistics* 462 (1997). Data for Ljubljana are provided by Airport Ljubljana.

Moreover, other ICAO data, on international flight stages and domestic flights, show clearly that most of Berlin's inter-city interaction is with other cities in Germany itself, especially in the west and south, or with other EU capital cities. At present Berlin plays a very limited role as a "central place" or "gateway" to cities in the transitional economies, even of Central Europe, let alone South-east or East Europe. In fact, according to the ICAO, Vienna proves to be a far more significant origin and destination, or European "hub", for passengers moving to and from the main Central European capitals of Budapest, Prague, and Warsaw. As Table 4.6 indicates, all these three cities rank among the top six (along with Moscow) within Central and Eastern Europe in terms of both passenger and freight volumes handled.

Many factors, of course, help to determine traffic volumes. Some are "internal forces", such as the size of the national population and economy served by a capital city airport, or national economic performance during the transition period; others are the interactions of "internal" and "external" forces in determining the openness and attractiveness to the wider world of the city and its "catchment area" for foreign trade, investment, and tourism. What is important here is to try to assess the extent to which air transport statistics provide evidence of globalization or European integration, and how the transition has shaped the patterns of such integration.

Globalization or international integration is not synonymous only with "world cities" and "world city formation" processes, even though these cities are the prime initiators, purveyors and recipients. Globalization, albeit in highly varying degrees, is shaping or diffusing into whole national and international space economies and their city systems, creating varying degrees of "globalizing cities" (Marcuse and van Kempen, 2000). So, therefore, tourism has become big international, if not global, business; the rapid growth of international migration, and hence increasing multiculturalism at the city level, generates international, inter-continental, inter-city personal (as well as business-related) travel. Thus, from our perspective, air passenger statistics are a comparatively satisfactory indicator of inter-city relationships.

Table 4.6 also suggests that while the volumes of cargo handled by airports in Warsaw, Budapest, and Prague are relatively more commensurate with the size of their respective national economies, airline passenger flows show a quite different pattern. Despite the fact that Prague is the smallest of the three Central and Eastern European capitals, and capital of the second largest of the three economies, its airport handles significantly more passengers than do either Budapest or Warsaw, which in volume terms are similar to each other. Prague handles far higher volumes of tourist-related passenger movement than either of the other two capitals, and is better connected internationally with direct flights than Budapest or Warsaw. But whereas Budapest has no rival airports in Hungary, Warsaw does have to compete for some international traffic with other expanding airports located in Gdansk, Katowice, Crakow, Poznan, and Wroclaw. Even so, Budapest is clearly relatively more important because of its greater centrality in Central Europe than Warsaw, and the more rapid growth of international trade and FDI in Hungary in the first half of 1990s than in Poland at that time.

Other cities are ranked by air traffic volumes that are broadly commensurate with their relative sizes, or with the economies of which they are an integral part. Nevertheless, there is need to comment on some that are not. For its size, St Petersburg has very low traffic volumes and is clearly very much in the economic "shadow" of Moscow. Bucharest (Romania) and Kiev (Ukraine), capitals of populous states, clearly exhibit very weak international integration, and this reflects their remoteness from Western Europe, the poor performance and limited restructuring of their economies and their limited attractiveness for foreign business. Bratislava, the capital of Slovakia, also has extraordinarily low volumes of passengers and freight passing through its airport, despite the "medium" size of Slovakia in population and economy. The main factor here is that Bratislava is so close to Vienna and so easily accessible from Prague and Budapest that it cannot compete with those nodes.

In Lithuania, Kaunas has a tiny amount of passenger traffic compared to the capital, Vilnius, but complements the capital as a major cargo airport and ranks higher in freight handling than many much larger cities in the region such as Zagreb (Croatia), Riga, Bratislava, and Bucharest. One geopolitical reason for the high volumes of cargo passing through the airports of Vilnius and Kaunas is the sensitive situation that exists between Lithuania and the adjacent East European countries of Belarus and Russia concerning the use of railway transport. On the other hand, Zagreb, the capital city of Croatia, and Ljubljana (Slovenia) rank higher than expected, partly because they act as "gateways" between the former Yugoslav republics of Bosnia and Herzegovina (Sarajevo) and the Former Yugoslav Republic of Macedonia (Skopje) and handle transit tourist traffic en route to and from the Adriatic coast (Split, Dubrovnik). Tourist traffic elevates the status of Split in the Adriatic region, as that city has its own direct flights (e.g. from London); this puts Split on a par with the Baltic state capitals of Riga, Vilnius, and Tallinn.

It is, of course, very instructive to examine the changes that have occurred in air traffic flows through the airports of Central and Eastern European cities since 1990. There are data that permit us to compare trends for seven cities between 1989 and 1997 (see Table 4.7). In general, as one would expect, the opening up of these economies combined with the free potential flow of people has led to a growth in both passenger and cargo traffic through capital city airports. Except in the cases of Prague, however, where passenger and cargo volumes have doubled or more than doubled, and Warsaw, where cargo volume has almost tripled, this growth has been modest and in two cases (Bratislava and St Petersburg) decline has occurred.

A wide range of explanations underlies these trends. As a general rule, modest growth reflects the effects of economic recession during the transition, increased air transport costs associated with the removal of state subsidies and rising world fuel prices, and shifts in the structure of passenger traffic and in city connectivity. In the cases of Budapest and Warsaw, the relatively modest growth of passenger traffic (and cargo through Budapest) reflects earlier relative openness and initiation of transition processes in Hungary and Poland than elsewhere in Central and Eastern Europe. By contrast, the much greater rate of increase in traffic through Prague reflects the higher level of "closure" of the former Czechoslovakia from non-Soviet bloc countries before 1990. Prague's rapid acquisition of greatly enhanced connectivity since 1990 has helped stimulate both tourist and business traffic. Even more dramatic changes have occurred in the Russian cities of Leningrad (St Petersburg) and Moscow. Although the problems of the post-Soviet economy underpin the decline in

Table 4.7 Some comparisons of air traffic at airports of key Central and Eastern European cities, 1989 and 1997

| | Passengers (mil.) | | Cargo (000 tonnes) | |
|---|---|---|---|---|
| City | 1989 | 1997 | 1989 | 1997 |
| Bratislava (Slovakia) | 0.37 | 0.28 | 0.6 | 1.6 |
| Budapest (Hungary) | 2.36 | 3.62 | 19.9 | 24.0 |
| Ljubljana (Slovenia) | 0.73 | 0.71 | 6.8 | 10.2 |
| Moscow (Russia)* | 9.54 | 8.82 | 114.3 | 122.1 |
| Prague (Czech Republic) | 2.01 | 4.08 | 9.8 | 21.4 |
| St Petersburg (Russia)* | 9.55 | 1.67 | 83.2 | 19.6 |
| Warsaw (Poland) | 2.78 | 3.55 | 16.7 | 47.0 |

Note: *Most passenger and flight movements relate to international movements. The exceptions, however, are Moscow and Leningrad (St Petersburg). Significantly, in 1989, only 0.35 million international passengers arrived at, or departed from, Leningrad airport, whereas this number had risen to 1.37 million in 1997, indicating the increased integration of St Petersburg into the international network and, effectively, a collapse of "domestic" passenger movements because of the demise of the USSR and the economic difficulties of the Russian federation. The Moscow figures for 1989 relate only to Sheremetyevo airport, but 4.14 million passenger movements there in that year were international, indicating the global role of Moscow during the communist period. The data for 1997 are for the combined passenger arrivals and departures at Moscow's two main airports, Sheremetyevo and Vnukovo: by 1997 international passenger numbers had grown to 5.72 million, suggesting a strengthened international role for the city.
Sources: ICAO, Digest of Statistics 371 (1989), 403 (1992), 462 (1997). Data for Ljubljana are provided by Airport Ljubljana.

passenger traffic volumes, its impact is actually far more severe than the data indicate. The figures hide a major shift from domestic (intra-Soviet) passenger trips to international trips. There has actually been a rise in the international connectivity of St Petersburg, so that the volume of international traffic through the city's airport is greater now than in 1989 (as connections with the Baltic capitals of Tallinn, Riga and Vilnius became international). The same applies to Moscow. About half of the passenger traffic through the city's two airports in 1989 was domestic (Soviet), while the third airport, Sheremetevo, handled mostly international traffic. The volume of international traffic almost doubled to 8.8 million in 1997. Again, the "conversion" of air links with the capitals of the 14 non-Russian states (former Soviet republics) from "domestic" to "international" only partially explains this growth. There has, therefore, been a very significant rise in international air passenger flows between Moscow and cities outside the former Soviet Union.

Far more significant than the growth in the volume of airline passenger and cargo traffic since 1989 has been the reorientation of flows, leading to new patterns of connectivity between Central and Eastern European cities on the one hand, and networks of cities elsewhere on the other hand. Table 4.6 indicates that there has been a striking increase in the number of foreign destinations served by direct passenger flights (i.e. non-stop flights) from both capital cities and selected second-order cities in the region. While all cities, except possibly Bratislava and Moscow, now have direct flights to and from a much larger network of cities abroad, the most marked growth in international connectivity has occurred in those cities that became capitals of sovereign states in the 1990s, such as Ljubljana, Riga, Tallinn, Vilnius, and Kiev. Second-order cities, too, have become much more "connected" internationally, especially the East German cities of Dresden and Leipzig. Polish cities exhibit the same trend, albeit from a somewhat higher level of international connectivity inherited from the 1980s; this is especially true of Crakow, which is seeking wider business and tourist links.

During the socialist period, nationally owned state airlines flew at subsidized rates primarily to places abroad that conformed to foreign policy interests. Theoretically, subsidization could stimulate greater demand for air travel and certainly did so between cities within the former Soviet Union (where air passenger fare subsidies were aimed at shifting passengers off the congested railroad system) and between the Central and Eastern European capitals. But political and administrative restrictions on people's movements severely constrained international travel. The Iron Curtain was a very powerful factor of control as flights to and from capitalist cities were generally restricted to capital cities only, facilitated by reciprocal agreements with (usually) state-owned Western airlines. Flight paths to socialist (capital) cities were usually strictly confined to designated corridors to minimize the amount of land behind the Iron Curtain over which aircraft could fly (to minimize, for example, potential spying! [5]).

On the other hand, for political reasons, capitals located in the republics of the former Yugoslavia only had connections with Belgrade, not other Central and Eastern European capitals, while cities like Ljubljana, Zagreb, and cities at the Adriatic coast (Rijeka, Split, Dubrovnik) already exhibited a preponderant orientation to Western Europe – in part for tourist purposes. However, Budapest, Moscow, Prague, Sofia, and Warsaw had a wide range of direct flight connections with West European cities and, because of Soviet involvement in Middle East and North African political affairs, also with capital cities in those regions of the world. Warsaw connected Poland to the large Polish diaspora in the USA and Canada through New York, Chicago, and Toronto, but the most "globally connected" city before 1989 was Moscow.

The pattern of connectivity of Central and Eastern European cities is significantly different today. First, as noted above, most cities have a substantially increased number of cities abroad with which they are connected. Established capital cities with a relatively wider range of connections in 1989 have further extended their linkages with European and world city networks. Prague, Warsaw, and, perhaps surprisingly, Sofia have apparently displaced Moscow in terms of the number of city destinations served. And Moscow alone has actually experienced a contraction in the number of cities abroad that its airports serve with direct flights – this is a clear reflection of the "shrinkage" of global power and loss of ideological motivations underpinning Aeroflot services (for instance, to Havana, Cuba) before 1990.

Second, there is today a far wider range of services within Central and Eastern Europe, most notably new routes inter-connecting the capitals of the newly independent successor states of the USSR and Yugoslavia (Ljubljana–Sarajevo, Ljubljana–Skopje, Ljubljana–Podgorica, etc.) and between the Baltic capitals (Riga–Vilnius). And yet, because of the ethnic conflicts in the former Yugoslavia in the 1990s, none of these new capitals appear to have direct connections to other Central and Eastern European capitals. For example, to reach Ljubljana from Budapest it is necessary to fly via the hubs in Vienna or Zurich (see also Chapter 11). Also, while connectivity between Central and Eastern Europe and the Commonwealth of Independent States (CIS) cities is relatively stable, a major shift has been the establishment of new and extended connections with West European cities, including not only capital cities or major airports (e.g. Frankfurt, London, Paris, Amsterdam, Brussels) but also "second-order" cities, especially in Germany (such as Dusseldorf, Hamburg, Munich and Stuttgart), France (Lyon, Mulhouse), and England (Manchester). The growth of passenger traffic on routes to and from these cities has multiple causes, including business, tourism and family connections.

Third, new direct connections with Middle East cities have been introduced, particularly by newly independent states wishing to connect their capitals with the region. This reflects the effects of independence from the Soviet Union – cities in Central and Eastern Europe were only usually linked to this region via Moscow. Fourth, although numbers of destinations in Africa and Asia are mostly similar today to those in 1989, the political changes of the transition have frequently led to the substitution of new destinations for old (e.g. Dubai for Addis Ababa) (see Table 4.8). Fifth, Central and Eastern European cities today have more "global" connections (except with Latin America) than they did before 1990. The most significant growth has been with cities in North America (New York, Chicago, Montreal, Toronto, Edmonton).

Information deduced from the ICAO data provides some insights into whether there are any emerging patterns of stronger "regional" international linkages or "dependency relationships". Capital cities are assessed according to passenger volumes on flight stages (non-stop) to groups or clusters of other major cities. Budapest, Prague, and Warsaw have far stronger interaction with western and north-western European cities (especially London, followed by Amsterdam, Paris, and Brussels) than they have with German cities (despite the prominence of Frankfurt). In turn, passenger flows between German cities and those three Central European capitals exceeded those with the triad of Central European cities in the European Union or European Economic Association (EEA) (i.e. Berlin, Vienna and Zurich), which are nowadays rivaled

Table 4.8 Changes in the number of foreign destinations served by direct scheduled flights from the airports of selected Central and Eastern European cities, 1989 and 1997

| Central and Eastern European cities | Number of destinations (1989) | Cities served (1997) |
|---|---|---|
| *Capital cities* | | |
| Budapest | 41 | 46 |
| Ljubljana | 7 | 21 |
| Kiev | 13 | 46 |
| Minsk | 3 | 7 |
| Moscow | 52 | 50 |
| Prague | 42 | 63 |
| Riga | — | 19 |
| Skopje | 1 | 16 |
| Sofia | 34 | 51 |
| Tallinn | 1 | 11 |
| Vilnius | — | 19 |
| Warsaw | 36 | 53 |
| *Second-order cities* | | |
| Dresden (Germany) | 8 | 20 |
| Katowice (Poland) | 2 | 12 |
| Crakow (Poland) | 13 | 15 |
| St Petersburg (Russia) | 24 | 47 |

*Source:* ICAO, *Digest of Statistics* 371 (1989), 403 (1992), 462 (1997).

in importance by the Nordic cluster of Copenhagen, Stockholm, and Helsinki. By contrast, the Baltic capitals and St Petersburg are strongly tied to the major cities of Scandinavia and Finland, and much less to Germany or north-west European cities, and the Central European cities of Vienna and Zurich interact strongly with the capitals of the republics of the former Yugoslavia, especially Ljubljana, Zagreb, Belgrade, and Skopje. Russian cities are strongly linked to north-west Europe and, secondarily, to Germany. On the other hand, connectivity with, and flows to, southern European capitals is very weak, including the "alpha global city" of Milan in Italy (see Beaverstock, Smith, and Taylor, 2000).

Central and Eastern European connectivity with "alpha global cities" is therefore strongly dominated by passenger flows to and from London and Frankfurt. Milan, as stated above, is playing at best a very marginal role in the international integration of Central and Eastern European cities.[6] Only Warsaw, Moscow, and to a lesser extent Prague generate passenger flows with "alpha global cities" outside Europe, mostly with New York and Chicago, while Moscow maintains air passenger links with Tokyo.[7] Central and Eastern European cities have no direct links with Hong Kong, Singapore, or Los Angeles, and this suggests their limited globalization.

## Conclusion

"External forces" have long shaped the growth and development of Central and Eastern European cities, with continuity and discontinuity through time. The relevance of these forces operating in the region before 1989 lies in the preconditions, continuities, and legacies they have created, which have shaped the transformation of post-socialist cities ever since. Central and Eastern European countries were subject to different foreign imperial influences under the Habsburg, Russian, Prussian, and Ottoman Empires before the First World War, then as a "buffer" zone between Russia and Germany between the First and Second World Wars, and after 1945 to different forces of "Sovietization" and the diverse effects of socialist development until the end of the 1980s. There has been a dramatic rise and change in the direction and character of, and operation of international and global forces in, Central and Eastern Europe since the end of the Cold War, the collapse of the socialist ideology and the break-up of Soviet Union. Since then, Central and Eastern European cities have been affected by diverse forces of globalization, cross-border cooperation, and NATO and EU enlargement and integration. The power and characteristics of these forces differed from those operating in the region in the past, with increasingly important effects on inter-urban and intra-urban dependencies or independencies, dynamics of change, structures, functions, and spatial organization and forms.

The fundamental systemic changes that occurred in the 1990s, moving from a relatively closed, state-managed socialist economy to much more open systems based on market principles and civic society, together with interactions between global forces, international agencies, and national government policies, have begun to intensify the processes of globalization and European integration. These processes of transition and transformation are being differentiated between Central and Eastern European countries and subregions, as well as between and within cities in those countries, favouring large metropolitan centres with proximity to EU markets and capital cities in particular as nodal locations in Europe. Structural adjustment, international integration through trade flows, FDI, joint ventures, transport connections, privatization, de-industrialization and a shift from producer to consumer services are reshaping the functional structure, dynamics, and spatial forms of cities, with selective impact on land, property, and labour markets.

These processes are mirrored in the increased links and connections that exist between Central and Eastern European cities and "global" cities in Europe, such as London, Frankfurt, Paris, and Brussels (as the "EU capital"), and "hubs" in nearby Western European countries such as Munich, Vienna, Zurich and Stockholm. These "regional" or cross-border patterns are also visible in tourism and cultural links and cross-border inter-city cooperation. Uneven spatial development patterns and increased city competition are favouring Central European metropolitan capitals such as Berlin, Prague, Budapest, and Warsaw, and to some extent the Baltic capitals and Ljubljana, the capital city of Slovenia, while urban transformation has been less visible in South-east and East European cities.

Therefore, it can be concluded that the international integration and "globalization" of Central and Eastern European cities in the 1990s has occurred largely through "Europeanization", or most notably through the process of EU integration and enlargement ("EU-ization"), reinforcing cross-border and historic relations with West European cities and regions. The following chapter on the impact of FDIs on city restructuring confirms further these selective impacts of "external" forces on inter- and intra-city transformations in Central and Eastern Europe.

## Notes

1 Of course, cities on the territory of the former Russian Empire and the Soviet Union became subject to socialist processes for most of the latter two periods.
2 In brief, this argued that the growth of city functions in creating jobs could occur efficiently with little additional social investment up to a certain "threshold" or size; but if city growth were to be continued, this would require large-scale state investment in social and technical infrastructure to overcome the "bottlenecks", significantly raising the marginal costs of job creation in the city.
3 Stalin had equated the notion of "international division of labour" with the capitalist–imperialist economic process, relegating low-order functions to "colonies" while "imperial" countries specialized in higher-order functions. He dismissed the idea as irrelevant for the socialist world.
4 The EU supplies materials and yarns of higher quality than those produced locally, and manufacturers in Central and Eastern Europe then process, assemble or work on these materials and send the finished products back to the EU.
5 The Soviet Union did not allow any US airlines to run scheduled flights to or from Moscow for this reason, but from 1970 this was also to ensure that Soviet citizens could not glimpse any Boeing 747s, for which the Soviet Union had (and Russia has) no real equivalent, to avoid any local discontent over what was, patently, a technological aerospace weakness.
6 Paris is underestimated largely because of poor data reporting to the ICAO by Air France and other air carriers using Charles de Gaulle airport.
7 Given that there is so little Japanese FDI in Central and Eastern Europe this is mainly business travel, although it could be for trading.

This paper was edited by Nataša Pichler-Milanović

## REFERENCES

Gyorgy Barta, "Industrial Restructuring or Deindustrialisation?", in Gyorgy Enyedi, ed., *Social Change and Urban Restructuring in Central Europe*, Budapest: Akadémiai Kiadó, 1998, pp. 189–207.

Antonín Basch, *The Danubian Basin and the German Economic Sphere*, London: Kegan Paul, Trench, Trubner & Co. Ltd, 1944.

Jon V. Beaverstock, Richard G. Smith, and Peter J. Taylor, "World City Network: A New Metageography", *Annals of the Association of American Geographers* 90, 2000, pp. 123–134.

Gyula Bora, "International Division of Labour and the National Industrial System: The Case of Hungary", in F.E. Ian Hamilton and Godfrey J.R. Linge, eds, *Spatial Analysis, Industry and the Industrial Environment, Vol. 2: International Industrial Systems*, Chichester and New York: Wiley, 1981, pp. 155–184.

*Encyclopaedia Britannica, Book of the Year: Britannica World Data 1990*, Chicago: Encyclopaedia Britannica, 1990.

R. Anthony French and F.E. Ian Hamilton, eds, *The Socialist City: Spatial Structure and Urban Policy*, Chichester and New York: Wiley, 1979.

Patrick Gutman and Françis Arkwright, "Tripartite Industrial Co-operation between East, West and South", in F.E. Ian Hamilton and Godfrey J.R. Linge, eds, *Spatial Analysis, Industry and the Industrial Environment: Volume 2: International Industrial Systems*, Chichester and New York: Wiley, 1981, pp. 185–214.

F.E. Ian Hamilton, *Yugoslavia: Patterns of Economic Activity*, London: Bell, 1968.

——, *The Moscow City Region*, Oxford: Oxford University Press, 1976.

——, "Transformation and Space in Central and Eastern Europe", *Geographical Journal* 165(2), 1999, pp. 135–144.

——, "Urbanization in Socialist Eastern Europe: The Macro-Environment of Internal-City Structure", in R. Anthony French and F.E. Ian Hamilton, eds, *The Socialist City: Spatial Structure and Urban Policy*, Chichester and New York: Wiley, 1979a, pp. 167–193.

——, "Spatial Structure in Eastern European Cities," in R. Anthony French and F.E. Ian Hamilton, eds, *The Socialist City: Spatial Structure and Urban Policy*, Chichester and New York: Wiley, 1979b, pp. 195–261.

——, "Regional Policy in Poland: A Search for Equity", *Geoforum* 13(2), 1982, pp. 121–132.

——, "Restructuring Space: Locational Change and Adjustment in Central and Eastern Europe", *Geographische Zeitschrift* 83(2), 1995, pp. 67–86.

Eric Hoffman, *Comecon: Das Gemeinsame Market in Osteuropa*, Opladen: Lerke Verlag, 1961.

Dawn Holland and Nigel Pain, "The Diffusion of Innovation in Central and Eastern Europe: A Study of the Determinants and Impact of Foreign Direct Investment", *National Institute for Economic of Social Research Discussion Paper* 137, London: NIESR, 1998.

International Civic Aviation Organization (ICAO), *Digest of Statistics*, London: ICAO (various issues).

International Labour Organization (ILO), *Annual Yearbook of Labour Statistics 2002*, Geneva: ILO, 2002.

Robert Jessop, "Post-Fordism and the State," in Ash Amin, ed., *Post-Fordism: A Reader*, Oxford: Basil Blackwell, 1995, pp. 251–279.

Janos Kornai, *The Socialist System: The Political Economy of Communism*, Oxford: Clarendon Press, 1992.

Bronisław Kortus and Wojciech Kaczorowski, "Polish Industry forges External Links," in F.E. Ian Hamilton and Godfrey J.R. Linge, eds, *Spatial Analysis, Industry and the Industrial Environment: Vol. 2: International Industrial Systems*, Chichester and New York: Wiley, 1981, pp. 119–154.

Klaus R. Kunzman, "World City Regions in Europe: Structural Change and Future Challenges", in Fu-chen Lo and Yuc-Man Yaung, eds, *Globalization and the World of Large Cities*, Tokyo: UNUP, 1998, pp. 37–75.

Godfrey J.R. Linge and F.E. Ian Hamilton, "International Industrial Systems", in F.E. Ian Hamilton and Godfrey J.R. Linge, eds, *Spatial Analysis, Industry and the Industrial Environment, Vol. 2: International Industrial Systems*, Chichester and New York: Wiley, 1981.

Peter Marcuse and Ronald van Kempen, eds, *Globalizing Cities: A New Spatial Order*, Oxford: Blackwell Publishers, 2000.

Alan Mayhew, *Recreating Europe: The European Union's Policy Towards Central and Eastern Europe*, Cambridge: Cambridge University Press, 1998.

Nikolaj AleksandroviT Milyutin, *"Sotsgorod": The Problem of Building Socialist Cities*, Cambridge, MA: M.I.T. Press, 1974.

Wilbert Ellis Moore, *The Economic Demography of Eastern Europe*, Geneva: League of Nations, 1945.

Graeme M. Neutze, *Economic Policy and the Size of Cities*, Canberra: Australian National University Press, 1971.

Gearoid Ó Tuathail, *Critical Geopolitics: The Politics of Writing Global Space*, Minneapolis: University of Minnesota Press, 1996.

Joe Painter, *Politics, Geography and "Political Geography": A Critical Perspective*, New York and London: Arnold, 1995.

Margaret R. Shackleton, *Europe: A Regional Geography*, 7th revised and enlarged edition, New York: Pragger, 1969.

Ota Mik, "Revolutionary Changes in Czechoslovakia", in Huib Ernste and Verena Meier, eds, *Regional Development and Contemporary Industrial Response: Extending Flexible Specialization*, London: Belhaven Press, 1992, pp. 247–259.

Anthony Smith, *The Return to Europe: The Reintegration of Eastern Europe into the European Economy*, Basingstoke: Macmillan, 2000.

Viktoria Szirmai, "Socialist Cities (New Towns) in the Postsocialist Era", in Gyorgy Enyedi, ed., *Social Change and Urban Restructuring in Central Europe*, Budapest: Akadémiai Kiadó, 1998, pp. 169–188.

United Nations Economic Commission for Europe (UNECE), *Economic Bulletin for Europe*, Geneva: UNECE, 1998.

United Nations Centre for Human Settlements (UNCHS – Habitat), *An Urbanising World: Global Report on Human Settlements*, Oxford: Oxford University Press, 1996.

United Nations Conference on Trade and Development (UNCTAD), *World Investment Report*, New York: UNCTAD (various issues).

# 5

# Foreign direct investment and city restructuring

*F.E. Ian Hamilton and Francis W. Carter*

## Introduction

Cites and city systems across the post-socialist states are experiencing a range of restructuring trends. This plurality broadly expresses the varied national, regional, and place-specific outcomes of the interplay between the characteristics, strengths and weaknesses of four sets of forces – three endogenous, one exogenous (Smith and Pickles, 1998; Hamilton, 1999). The first of these forces involves the commitment by, and success of, governments and people to implement real institutional and market reforms since 1989. The second concerns the extent to which, and how, the continuities of the "baggage" of socialist culture, economy, organization, and society are still acting as a drag on reform. The third comprises the spatially diverse legacies of embedded pre-socialist socio-cultural and behavioural environments that have been handed down from generation to generation, survived Sovietization, and now foster, shape, exploit or hinder the reforms and conditions of the transition. The fourth embodies the salient features and influence of exogenous forces through inward flows of capital, ideas, information, innovation, know-how, technology, and trade, i.e. "globalization" forces.

Foreign direct investment is the most important phenomenon among the "external" forces shaping urban development, landscapes, and restructuring in Central and Eastern Europe. It is a major factor helping to propel leading cities and national and regional urban systems along the economic, political, and social paths of transformation from socialism to capitalism. There are two broad sets of reasons for this. FDI transfers much-needed capital into the cities during a period of local scarcity. Yet, it is also a medium for economic integration through bilateral and multilateral trade and information flows, technological innovation, enterprise restructuring, organizational and sectoral modernization, and marketing know-how (Holland and Pain, 1998; Garibaldi et al., 1999). As a result, and given the interaction with the three endogenous forces noted above, FDI symbolizes the complex inter-relationships emerging in the region between globalization and city restructuring.

The effects are visible in the highly differentiated trends in city landscapes, both structurally and spatially. The first, the structural, concerns the position of the cities of transitioning economies on a kind of scale from the "worst-case scenarios" of industrial stagnation, de-industrialization, or rural marginalization to the "best-case scenarios" of (relatively) successful manufacturing adjustment, re-industrialization, and tertiarization (i.e. the growth and diversification of consumer and producer services). The structural position of cities on such a scale has been determined largely by the extent to which market reforms have been introduced, diffused, and adopted to foster FDI, and the extent to which corruption is contained (EBRD, 1997; Bevan and Estrin, 2000; Mickiewicz and Bell, 2000).[1] The second, the spatial dimension, is the "uneven" geographic distribution of the structural scale across the region's cities and city systems. Broadly speaking, real urban change through restructuring towards the "best-case scenarios" is faster and deeper in areas adjacent to, or more accessible from, the European Union; and it declines significantly with increasing distance from the European Union eastwards and south-eastwards into the Balkans and East Europe, where "worst-case scenarios" are more common and corruption is rampant. So, although potential locations for FDI are very numerous throughout the city systems of Central and Eastern Europe, the actual pattern of FDI has been, and remains, very uneven not only between countries, but also between cities within them. In general the larger cities have attracted the most FDI, although more business opportunities are now being sought by foreign investors in smaller cities.

## The International Pattern of FDI Location and its Determinants

A decade ago, Hamilton (1990) predicted that FDI flows into Central and Eastern Europe from firms headquartered in advanced market economies would be essential if the (then) socialist countries were to attempt seriously to bridge the competitive, managerial, organizational, sectoral, and technological "gaps" between them and the dynamic global economy. It is now evident that foreign-owned and "globalizing" or multinational enterprises have indeed become a major force transforming the post-socialist states, especially those within Central Europe and close to the European Union (Hamilton, 1995, 1999, 2000, 2001;

Barta, Kralik, and Perger, 1997; Swain and Hardy, 1998; Hunya, 2000). Nevertheless, FDI flows into the region should be kept in perspective. They have been modest but have grown significantly since 1993. Although FDI is often difficult to measure with precision, the United Nations Economic Commission for Europe (UNECE) estimated the cumulative stock in the region to be US$102 billion in 1999 (UNECE, 2000), while the *Transition Report* Update of the European Bank for Reconstruction and Development puts the figure for 2000 at US$113.3 billion (EBRD, 2001).[2] In fact, data published annually in *The World Investment Report* by the United Nations Conference on Trade and Development (UNCTAD) indicate that Central and Eastern Europe was attracting less than 2.5 per cent of global FDI in the early 1990s but that this share has risen relatively sharply to more than 5 per cent in 2000. Clearly, the significance of FDI for and its impact on the region's cities has grown. Earlier observers such as Sinn and Weichenrieder (1997) argued that FDI levels were low before 1995; more recent data (EBRD, 1999, 2000, 2001) and analysis (Bevan and Estrin, 2000) indicate that FDI is now high relative to GDP and GDP per capita in the region as a whole. These broad statements, however, cloak a very uneven pattern of FDI inflows between host countries. The reasons for this will now be discussed in the contexts of the available literature on FDI and the issue of location within it.

A vast body of literature developed on the determinants of FDI from the late 1950s, especially in economics, much of which was not spatial per se (e.g. Hymer, 1976; Buckley and Casson, 1976; Caves, 1982). The locational aspects were fostered within the realm of economic geography and linked to the decision-making and organizational behaviour of large firms (McNee, 1958; Hamilton, 1974, 1976; Hakanson, 1979; Hamilton and Linge, 1981). Within economics, however, major conceptual contributions of spatial relevance were provided by Vernon's product cycle hypothesis (Vernon, 1966, 1979) and Dunning's eclectic paradigm, which inter-relates the significance of ownership, location, and internalization (OLI) advantages to explain international patterns of FDI (Dunning, 1980, 1988a, 1988b). Although it is necessary to defend the importance of location in economic analysis, there is now a growing body of research which seeks to infuse both the "new economic geography" and the "cultural turn" in geography into conceptual and empirical work on FDI. This seeks to synthesize investment behaviour, economies of scale and scope, international trade and logistics, location, and psychic-distance theory (Krugman, 1991; Meyer, 1998; Morsink, 1998; Deichmann, 1999; Hamilton, 2000).

So why is location important? Three sets of reasons can be given. First, the attributes of place – a city and its region can, for instance, affect an area's business attractiveness through the local mix of competitive advantages or disadvantages in supply conditions. Second, the development of business in a city or its vicinity to exploit these conditions will have various economic and social impacts locally and can generate spillover or multiplier effects. Such effects can, of course, be positive or negative. Third, the selection of a city as a business location will create feedback effects on the local mix of conditions, and alter them, both directly through local impacts and indirectly through trade relations; these processes can propel a city through a series of "life cycles" in a dynamic manner but can also "fossilize" its structure and functioning (Hamilton, 1974).

Since market reforms were introduced after 1989, and governments opened their state borders to FDI, most literature on FDI has attempted to explain why investment has flowed into certain transitioning economies rather than others (Meyer, 1998; Hunya, 2000). The question of why FDI has been located in specific cities and regions within these countries is comparatively neglected. Yet in reality, the two are closely inter-related. The selection of a location for FDI within a state often explains the importance of the host country for inward FDI, and vice versa. Very often, the managements of existing MNEs, and firms entering international production to become MNEs, put first priority on the selection of a host country for investment and tend to treat the issue of the choice of a specific location within it as rather secondary. This may also be because a firm considers the capital city of that country or an area just across the border of a neighbouring state as a "natural" location choice. In the case of Central and Eastern Europe, however, the specific conditions of the transition suggest that, for at least two reasons, firms might select a specific city first, with the host country being considered a secondary concern. A very significant proportion of FDI in the region has been associated with the privatization process. In other words, FDI has flowed into specific "brown-field" sites, i.e. existing enterprises (usually in manufacturing or utilities, but also some service establishments) which, by virtue of their production capacities, profiles, and potentials, MNEs see as "matching" their global or European growth strategies. Thus, FDI location in a city (and a host country) will be defined by the timing of privatization and the "supply" of particular enterprises on the market. The second reason can be seen when a foreign firm seeks to serve the markets of a group of Central and Eastern European states from a new "green-field" facility. In this case the firm is likely to select a location in a very "nodal" city or urbanized region, such as the capital cities of Prague, Budapest, Bratislava, or Upper Silesia (Poland).

Once governments in the region resolved to open their borders to foreign investors, the body of published theoretical, conceptual, and empirical work on the operations of MNEs in the non-socialist world provided insights that, in many respects, have made the character and patterns of FDI in post-socialist states quite predictable. First, and most predictably, it has been large or medium-sized MNEs operating in oligopolistic sectors that first clamoured to acquire privatizing brown-field facilities or to establish new green-field capacities in the region. By extending their oligopolistic behaviour into "virgin market territory", such MNEs aimed to secure significant gains (e.g. increased world market shares) and profits by exploiting lower labour or other input costs or by dominating local markets. Lead firms thus sought to gain a "first-mover advantage" (Lankes and Venables, 1996) in individual, or groups of, national markets through the achievement of monopolistic control over resource inputs, existing production capacities, and markets. Such behaviour, however, induced their European or global competitors to retaliate either to gain a "first-mover advantage" in another national arena or to pursue a "follow-the-leader" strategy and exploit lower costs to be competitive (Knickerbocker, 1973) and so acquire alternative existing, or establish new, production facilities in the same or a neighbouring post-socialist economy. This explains the predominant flows of FDI by manufacturing MNEs into such sectors as processed foods, drinks and tobacco products, vehicles and automotive components, tyres, consumer electronics, heavy electrical engineering, paper, pharmaceuticals, plastics, and some chemical products (see Hamilton, 2001). The trend explains why these industries, and hence the cities in which they are located, have increased their relative importance in the manufacturing profiles of the Central European states during the 1990s.

But the extension of oligopolistic market structures in the region through FDI is not restricted only to manufacturing (see Table 5.1). It also occurs in public utilities and especially underpins the expansion of more advanced producer services such as accountancy and management consultancy, banking, insurance, and real-estate management into selected cities, and of consumer services such as modern retailing (supermarkets, hypermarkets, specialist retailers) and hotel, gas station, and fast-food restaurant chains into many cities. The irony is that MNEs in these sectors have invested in facilities in the post-socialist economic space to exploit their firm-specific ownership and internalization advantages and have done so in markets which were either poorly developed or did not really

Table 5.1 Sectoral composition of inward FDI stock in Central and Eastern Europe (1998)

| Sector | Subsector | Total FDI (%) |
| --- | --- | --- |
| Primary | Farming, fishing, forestry, mining | 4 |
| Utilities | Electricity, water etc. | 4 |
| Secondary | Manufacturing | 41 |
| | Automotive industries | 4 |
| | Chemicals industries | 5 |
| | Food, drink, tobacco industries | 12 |
| | Other manufacturing | 20 |
| Tertiary | Services | 43 |
| | Trade | 13 |
| | Financial services | 12 |
| | Transport and telecommunications | 10 |
| | Business services | 4 |
| | Other services | 4 |
| Unspecified | | 8 |
| Total | | 100 |

Source: UNCTAD, World Investment Report (1999: 73).

exist at all as they remained the province of state-owned monopolies or were underdeveloped "deficit" sectors. In other words, MNEs, which had been perceived by the (neo-classical) economists (such as the IMF, World Bank, or other advisers) and by the new governments of host countries as purveyors of market reforms and competition, in reality often engaged in FDI in Central and Eastern Europe to exploit national or regional market failure!

In a significant number of cases, the Western firms entering these markets to gain "first-mover advantage" included those which had built new or equipped existing factories with new technology in growth sectors during the socialist period and were thus quick to exploit their knowledge of, and contacts with, the region to acquire those facilities as they were privatized.[3] In some instances, firms "returned" to the region by acquiring what had been their own pre-Second World War (and later confiscated or nationalized) facilities; Bata (shoes) in Zlin (Czech Republic) and Josef Meinl (retailing) in Hungary are examples. In other cases, MNEs with no previous significant ties in the region sought "first-mover advantage" through the acquisition of privatized state enterprises with established national or "socialist region" brand names in an attempt to secure "captive markets"; here, Volkswagen (Skoda in the Czech Republic), General Electric (Tungsram in Hungary), Nestlé (several renowned national chocolate manufacturers in the region), and Philip Morris (several state-owned tobacco factories) are cases in point. New green-field investments, however, have been the hallmark of MNEs seeking "first-mover advantage" in the "deficit" service sectors. This has been particularly prevalent in the retail sector, with firms such as Blockbuster, Carrefour, IKEA, Makro, Tesco, and Virgin opening large stores, supermarkets, and hypermarkets.

Once such firms moved in, rival MNEs began to invest in the region in "follow-the-leader" fashion, more commonly in new green-field facilities, to exploit market opportunities or low-cost labour advantages, or both. Some of the most publicized examples are drawn from the automotive sector (Audi, Ford, General Motors/Opel, Suzuki), consumer electronics (Ericsson, Nokia, Philips), foods and drinks (Cadbury-Schweppes, Coca-Cola, Unilever), tobacco (British American Tobacco, Reemstma), and especially retailing (Cora, Metro, Spar, Carrefour, Tesco).

The second predictable feature concerns the broad geographic distribution of FDI across Central and Eastern Europe. Table 5.2 indicates that by the end of 2000, almost 70 per cent of total FDI in the region was concentrated in Central Europe.[4] With the Baltic States, about three-quarters of all FDI is located in countries which lie adjacent to, or highly accessible from, the more advanced economies of the European Union. By contrast, South-east Europe has attracted only 10 per cent, and the European part of the Commonwealth of Independent States, including the entire Russian Federation, just 15 per cent. As a result, the cumulative stock of FDI and annual FDI inflows per capita and as a percentage of GDP tend to be much higher in Central Europe and the Baltic states than in

Table 5.2 International distribution of FDI in Central and Eastern Europe, 1989–2000 (US$)

| Subregion/country | Cumulative stock FDI (1989–1999) | | FDI stock per capita (2000) | FDI stock per head city population (2000) | FDI inflow as % of GDP (2000) |
|---|---|---|---|---|---|
| | (US$ bn) | % | (US$ mil.) | (US$ mil.) | (%) |
| *Baltic states* | 6.7 | 5.8 | 895 | 1.600 | 4.4 |
| Estonia | 1.9 | 1.6 | 1.337 | 1.585 | 4.6 |
| Latvia | 2.4 | 2.1 | 1.027 | 1.920 | 4.8 |
| Lithuania | 2.4 | 2.1 | 642 | 960 | 3.8 |
| *Central Europe* | 80.4 | 70.4 | 1.269 | 2.024 | 5.2 |
| Croatia | 4.1 | 3.6 | 907 | 1.572 | 5.4 |
| Czech Republic | 21.7 | 19.0 | 2.102 | 3.170 | 10.4 |
| Hungary | 19.4 | 17.0 | 1.935 | 2.892 | 3.2 |
| Poland | 29.1 | 25.5 | 751 | 1.145 | 5.0 |
| Slovakia | 3.6 | 3.1 | 669 | 1.095 | 5.5 |
| Slovenia | 2.5 | 2.2 | 1.250 | 2.273 | 1.5 |
| *South-east Europe* | 11.4 | 9.3 | 237 | 380 | 3.5 |
| Albania | 0.5 | 0.4 | 161 | 411 | 1.8 |
| Bulgaria | 3.3 | 2.8 | 407 | 581 | 7.3 |
| Bosnia-Herzegovina | 0.3 | 0.3 | 71 | 164 | 2.5 |
| FR Yugoslavia (Serbia and Montenegro) | 0.1 | 0.09 | 13 | 22 | n/a |
| FYRoM | 0.4 | 0.4 | 219 | 353 | 2.9 |
| Romania | 6.8 | 5.9 | 303 | 521 | 3.0 |
| *East Europe* | 16.8 | 14.5 | 65 | 121 | 2.1 |
| Belarus | 0.8 | 0.7 | 78 | 108 | 1.3 |
| Moldova | 0.4 | 0.4 | 102 | 174 | 4.8 |
| Ukraine | 3.3 | 2.8 | 67 | 92 | 1.8 |
| *Russian Federation* | 12.3 | 10.7 | 9 | 109 | 0.6 |

*Source:* EBRD, *Transition Report* (2000) (own calculations).

countries to the east and south-east. This indicates a marked division of the region in FDI inflows and impacts. Bevan and Estrin (2000) argue that this dichotomous pattern essentially reflects the operation of two quite contrary "circles" which appear to be largely self-reinforcing. First, a virtuous circle of forces fostering FDI in Central Europe and the Baltic states, and second, a vicious circle restraining FDI elsewhere. These "circles" appear to be analogous to Myrdal's "cumulative causation" hypothesis developed to explain the emergence and persistence of "core" as opposed to "peripheral" states or regions (Myrdal, 1956, 1957). There are good reasons why such a dichotomous pattern could be expected.

The first is a greater commitment to, and achievement of, macro- and micro-economic market and institutional reforms, especially in Hungary, Poland, the

Czech Republic, and Estonia. These reforms yielded more sound opportunities for green-field investments by foreign firms and, through more rapid and relatively larger-scale privatization, a greater supply of former state-owned enterprises for brown-field investments. These states offer lower risks to foreign investors, and their operating business environments, protection of property rights, profit repatriation possibilities, lower inflation rates, greater currency stability, and low corruption levels have enabled them to enjoy higher credit ratings in international financial markets. They have thus achieved higher EBRD "transition scores".

Second, these states achieved a significant economic "U-turn" from recession before to real GDP growth after 1993, making their consumer and producer markets far more attractive to diversified foreign investments than those in East and South-east Europe, where recession has been more prolonged. This is particularly evident from Table 5.3 in the cases of Poland, Slovenia, Hungary,

Table 5.3  GDP indicators (US$)

| Subregion/Country | GDP per capita 2000* | Index (1988 = 100) | GDP 2000 (US$ bn) | GDP 2000 (%) |
|---|---|---|---|---|
| *Baltic states* | 3.160 | 70 | 23.29 | 3.3 |
| Estonia | 3.409 | 82 | 4.77 | 0.7 |
| Latvia | 3.019 | 64 | 7.25 | 1.0 |
| Lithuania | 3.045 | 64 | 11.27 | 1.6 |
| *Central Europe* | 5.140 | 105 | 313.22 | 45.0 |
| Croatia | 4.211 | 80 | 18.95 | 2.7 |
| Czech Republic | 4.797 | 98 | 49.41 | 7.1 |
| Hungary | 4.734 | 105 | 47.81 | 6.9 |
| Poland | 4.109 | 127 | 159.00 | 22.8 |
| Slovakia | 3.650 | 103 | 19.41 | 2.8 |
| Slovenia | 9.320 | 114 | 18.64 | 2.7 |
| *South-east Europe* | 1.360 | 65 | 69.53 | 9.9 |
| Albania | 1.195 | 72 | 3.83 | 0.5 |
| Bosnia-Herzegovina | 972 | 45 | 4.18 | 0.6 |
| Bulgaria | 1.484 | 70 | 12.02 | 1.7 |
| FR Yugoslavia (Serbia and Montenegro) | 1.225 | 48 | 10.53 | 1.5 |
| FYRoM | 1.685 | 77 | 3.37 | 0.5 |
| Romania | 1.596 | 77 | 35.60 | 5.1 |
| *East Europe* | 940 | 55 | 258.83 | 41.8 |
| Belarus | 1.104 | 85 | 11.04 | 1.6 |
| Moldova | 326 | 32 | 1.04 | 0.2 |
| Ukraine | 640 | 39 | 31.74 | 4.6 |
| *Russian Federation* | 1.697 | 62 | 246.75 | 35.4 |

Note: *Real prices.
*Source:* EBRD, *Transition Report* (2000) (own calculations).

Slovakia, and the Czech Republic, where GDP per capita exceeds 1989 levels, or is close to it, and is far higher than elsewhere. This underlines the "pull" exerted on FDI by market size and market growth dynamics.

Table 5.3 presents GDP (2000) as a "proxy" for current market size.[5] As one would expect, the Russian Federation, with a population of 145.4 million, ranks first, and is followed in descending rank order of market size by Poland (population of 39 million), the Czech Republic (10 million), Hungary (10 million), and Romania (22 million), which lie ahead of Ukraine (50 million). In fact, as Table 5.3 shows, if Romania is added to Central Europe and the Baltic States, this group has more than half the market of the European transition economies and has attracted more than 81 per cent of the cumulative stock of FDI. This is important because, while literature on the subject, especially in economics, tends to focus on national markets, for many MNEs, FDI in a location in Central Europe is attractive by virtue of the geographic proximity of the combined markets of Poland, the Czech Republic, and Hungary, which form a core market area, and the prospect of high accessibility to smaller but developing markets elsewhere in Central Europe (Croatia, Slovakia, Slovenia), the Baltic States, and South-east Europe (especially Romania and Bulgaria), which provide a further attraction to FDI in or near the core. This also means, however, that MNEs can invest in modernizing brown-field sites with which they have historic (socialist period) links in the smaller Central European economies so as to supply the wider core market. The production of the Clio by Renault in Novo mesto, Slovenia, is an example. These generalizations are supported by more detailed analyses which demonstrate the significance of the business environment, the form and timing of privatization, the size of the market, and market access as the main determinants of FDI across this growth region (Lankes and Venables, 1996; Brenton, Di Mauro, and Lücke, 1998; Holland and Pain, 1998; Meyer, 1998; Garibaldi et al., 1999; Hamilton, 2000).

A third predictable dimension concerns the effects of supra-national trade agreements on FDI, the growing openness of the transitioning realm to trade, the geographic proximity of the European Union, and prospective membership of the European Union. In sum, this underscores the importance of the progressive "reintegration" of the region into Europe (Grabbe and Hughes, 1998; Mayhew, 1998; Smith, 2000) to the attraction of FDI.[6] Indeed, research by Dokopoulou and Hamilton (1988) established that, in the cases of Greece in the 1970s and Spain in the early 1980s, there was a strong tendency for MNEs to invest in a country in advance of its accession to the European Union so as to be in a position to reap the full benefits of access to an enlarged, integrating market from the very beginning rather than to wait until the entry date and possibly lose out to competitors. The prediction that this would be the case in Central and Eastern Europe (Hamilton, 1995) is borne out by recent analysis by Bevan and Estrin (2000).

Within the European Union, the largest domestic markets (like Germany) and the single market itself can encourage MNEs achieving significant economies of scale to concentrate production within Western Europe, and thus to export products eastwards to transition markets. Yet, it is also true that economies of scale and scope in logistics encourage firms to operate multiple facilities and thus locate in Central and Eastern European countries. One would expect this factor to reinforce the decision to locate in the region by two major groups of firms:

(a) MNEs which pursue a horizontal integration pattern of organization to supply similar or identical products, especially bulkier products (drinks), and certainly produced or consumer services from dispersed centres within international, national, or local markets;

(b) one would also expect dispersion of FDI production into Central and Eastern Europe to be stimulated in MNEs with vertically integrated production to "disintegrate" their production chains into the region in the form of smaller "branch", "batch production" or "flexible specialization" facilities. In this latter case, the main attraction of the region lies in its low input costs, especially labour costs; these provide a particularly powerful competitive edge for supplying the EU market, perhaps as the main market, with the Central and Eastern European market as a more peripheral but growing demand component.

In fact, Bevan and Estrin (2000) found that low labour costs, resulting from a combination of both low wages and relatively good productivity, have been a major factor attracting FDI. It is expected that because wage differentials between Central and Eastern Europe and the European Union are substantial, low wage costs will play an enhanced role in attracting FDI both as accession approaches and after accession of these countries as new EU members. If one pursues these various lines of argument, it could be predicted that progress towards accession to the European Union in the case of individual or groups of transition states would have a positive effect on the inflows and location patterns of FDI in the region. That this has indeed been the case is borne out by Bevan and Estrin (2000), who make two pertinent findings:

– there was a large increase in FDI flows into the Visegrad countries (Czech Republic, Hungary, Poland, and Slovakia) between 1995 and 1998 following the Essen European Council (1994), which launched the pre-accession strategy, and the *Amsterdam Treaty* (1997), which re affirmed EU commitment to eastward enlargement;

– the *Agenda 2000* announcement (July 1997) that identified "two waves" of accession led to a significant upswing in the rate of FDI flows into states to be in the "first wave" of EU enlargement (Czech Republic, Estonia, Hungary, Poland, and Slovenia), while states excluded from the first wave but included in the "second wave" (Bulgaria, Latvia, Lithuania, Romania, and Slovakia) at that time experienced a smaller upswing in FDI inflows, and those excluded altogether generally exhibited little or no change. As Table 5.4 indicates, the "first wave" countries, with about 40 per cent of the European transition economy market, had received 65 per cent of the cumulative stock of FDI

Table 5.4 Classifications of Central and Eastern European countries: comparative shares of FDI and GDP (2000)

| Subregion | FDI (%) | GDP (%) |
|---|---|---|
| Baltic states | 5.8 | 3.3 |
| Central Europe | 70.4 | 45.0 |
| South-east Europe | 9.3 | 9.9 |
| East Europe | 14.5 | 41.8 |
| Total | 100.0 | 100.0 |
| Central Europe, Baltic states, and Romania | 82.1 | 53.4 |
| Rest of South-east Europe and East Europe | 17.9 | 46.6 |
| 1st wave EU accession countries* | 65.3 | 40.1 |
| 2nd wave EU accession countries** | 16.0 (19.6) | 12.3 (15.0) |
| Long-term excluded** | 18.7 (15.1) | 47.6 (44.9) |

Notes:
*"First-wave" accession countries as classified in *Agenda 2000* (1997) are Estonia, Czech Republic, Hungary, Poland, and Slovenia.
**Figures in brackets relate to the case where Croatia might be incorporated into the "second-wave" EU accession countries along with Bulgaria, Latvia, Lithuania, Romania, and Slovakia, rather than being "long-term excluded" (other ex-Yugoslav republics, Albania, Belarus, Moldova, Ukraine).
*Sources: Agenda 2000* (1997); EBRD, *Transition Report* (2000); Bevan and Estrin (2000); own calculations.

by 2000. They clearly benefited because of their stronger transition progress, creating a virtuous circle in combination with their closer geographic proximity to the European Union.

The "second-wave" entrants, with about 12 per cent of the market, attracted almost 14 per cent of FDI, and one could say that the upswing in FDI in the late 1990s was connected with their inclusion in the "second wave" of EU enlargements. This has begun to counteract the vicious circle tendencies of former likely exclusion, as arguably has the trend towards greater stability in the Balkans (affecting Bulgaria and Romania) and the fact that, although excluded from the "first wave", these "second-wave" countries lie in close geographic proximity to EU member states (i.e. Bulgaria next to Greece, Latvia and Lithuania close to Sweden and Finland), and certainly lie close to or neighbour "first-wave" accession states (Romania next to Hungary, Slovakia between the Czech Republic, Hungary, and Poland, Lithuania next to Poland). On the other hand, the CIS states continue to suffer the disadvantages for FDI of a vicious circle and longer-term exclusion from the European Union as well as greater distance from it. The former Yugoslav states (except Slovenia, which is in the "first-wave" group) are excluded from both stages of accession and continue to suffer the consequences of the ethnic wars of the 1990s and ongoing political instability. Croatia, however, is an exception; it has attracted rising FDI inflows, peaking in 1999 (UNECE, 2000; EBRD, 2001). The recent stabilization and privatization policies of the new (post-1999) government have contributed to this trend, as has Croatia's proximity to the European Union and adjacency to Hungary and Slovenia. Indeed, the sustenance of inward FDI may also be in anticipation of Croatia's inclusion in the "second-wave" EU accession countries.

The fourth predictable feature concerns the source-country headquarters' location of firms investing in Central and Eastern Europe. One can make several hypotheses about the pattern. The first is that leading investor nations in the region will be the home bases of large numbers of major MNEs and vigorously internationalizing small and medium-sized enterprises. Such nations tend to fall into two distinct groups: (a) those with large and diversified economies and firms, such as the US, Japan, Germany, France, Italy, and the UK; and (b) those with small economies with a high propensity to generate FDI through a few major specialized "lead" MNEs, such as Austria, Denmark, Finland, the Netherlands, Sweden, and Switzerland. The extent to which MNEs from such source countries actually do invest will be determined in large measure by how far their demand for investment in the region can be matched by the host country's supply of brown- and green-field opportunities. The second dimension is that investor (nation) firms are likely to be located in close geographic or psychic proximity to the transition economies in which they invest so as to reduce transaction and transport costs. This applies especially to those EU states adjacent to or very close to transition economies (Austria, Germany, Italy, Sweden, Finland) and those with historical cultural, linguistic, or economic ties with them.[7]

Several publications reveal the actual importance of various FDI source countries, especially UNCTAD (1999) for the entire region, Hunya (2000) and Meyer (1998) for Central Europe, and Hamilton (2000) for Poland. Table 5.5

Table 5.5  Geographical sources of FDI in Central and Eastern Europe (1998)

| Geographical sources | % |
| --- | --- |
| *European Union* | 61 |
| Germany | 19 |
| The Netherlands | 15 |
| Austria | 7 |
| UK | 6 |
| France | 5 |
| Other EU countries | 9 |
| United States | 15 |
| Rest of the world | 22 |
| Central and Eastern Europe | 2 |
| Total FDI in Central and Eastern Europe | 100 |

*Source:* UNCTAD (1999: 72).

provides an overview for the whole region. In keeping with modern global FDI patterns, the region plays host to investors from a plurality of locations. Yet, this also reveals the dominance of the European Union as a source region, and particularly that Germany, the largest economy within the European Union and one located adjacent to Central Europe, is the biggest single source of FDI. The prominence of the US comes as no surprise, although its true importance may be masked by the fact that some US investments have actually been conducted through European subsidiaries, as in the case of Opel (Germany) for General Motors. Even so, it can be argued that US investment has been somewhat restrained by the barriers of transaction costs and geographical and psychic distance from the region. Those barriers certainly explain the relative under-representation of the UK as a source country given that British firms have long rivaled the US and recently actually "outperformed" the US in global FDI. By contrast, the Netherlands, a very small economy which is highly accessible to Central and Eastern Europe (but not so close geographically), has become the second-largest source of FDI in Europe and rivals the US. Hamilton (2000) suggests that this reflects a combination of capitalizing on the information available through trading networks established in the socialist period between the Netherlands and Central and Eastern Europe, and vigorous expansion into the region in the 1990s by leading Dutch firms in a range of manufacturing, consumer and producer service sectors. Significantly, Austrian firms are also major investors, as a result of close geographic and cultural proximity. On the other hand, there is one major absentee – Japan, which still has very limited investments in Central and Eastern Europe, a situation reflecting a combination of business caution towards a rather unpredictable region, and a time of domestic crisis in Japan.

Table 5.6 sheds more light on the geographic sourcing pattern, listing the top five sources of FDI for most of the countries in the region. It reveals that firms from the largest and most diversified economies in the world (Germany and the US) have made significant investments most widely, while Japanese FDI is unimportant throughout the region. The data and information, however, also indicate much geographic clustering of FDI in host countries close to source countries. The high proportions of German and Austrian FDI concentrated in neighbouring Central European countries, Scandinavian and Finnish FDI in the Baltic states, Greek FDI in FYRoM, and Italian FDI in neighbouring Slovenia and relatively nearby FYRoM and Romania are cases in point, signifying the importance of "cross-border regionalization" and Europeanization. Dutch FDI is most prominent in the four major markets outside the Russian Federation that form a continuous geographic area in Central and South-east Europe: the Czech Republic, Hungary, Poland, and Romania. The key exception of note is South Korean FDI in Poland and Romania, where Daewoo has developed the cores of its Central and Eastern European automotive production system.

Table 5.6 The top five source countries of FDI stock in individual Central and Eastern European countries, 1998 (%)

| Host countries | Top five source countries of FDI | | | | |
|---|---|---|---|---|---|
| | 1st | 2nd | 3rd | 4th | 5th |
| *Baltic states* | | | | | |
| Estonia | S (32%) | SF (27%) | DK (5%) | CH (5%) | USA (5%) |
| Latvia | DK (16%) | USA (11%) | RU (9%) | D (8%) | UK (8%) |
| Lithuania | S (22%) | SF (19%) | USA (16%) | D (7%) | UK (5%) |
| *Central Europe* | | | | | |
| Croatia | USA (42%) | A (24%) | CH (6%) | S (4%) | D (3%) |
| Czech Republic | D (31%) | NL (28%) | A (10%) | USA (6%) | UK (5%) |
| Hungary | D (25%) | USA (15%) | NL (14%) | A (11%) | UK (8%) |
| Poland | NL (22%) | D (19%) | USA (15%) | F (10%) | Korea (7%) |
| Slovakia | A (20%) | D (19%) | UK (13%) | USA (11%) | NL (8%) |
| Slovenia | A (31%) | D (14%) | CRO (14%) | I (8%) | F (8%) |
| *South-east Europe* | | | | | |
| Bulgaria | B (18%) | D (16%) | USA (7%) | NL (7%) | Cyprus (7%) |
| Bosnia-Herzegovina | Kuwait (21%) | D (17%) | CRO (17%) | A (4%) | F (3%) |
| FYRoM | GR (39%) | A (21%) | D (17%) | S (5%) | I (3%) |
| Romania | NL (15%) | D (10%) | I (8%) | F (7%) | USA (7%) |
| *East Europe* | | | | | |
| Belarus | D (25%) | NL (25%) | USA (17%) | I (9%) | A (3%) |
| Moldova | RU (29%) | USA (19%) | D (6%) | B (6%) | GR (4%) |
| Ukraine | USA (18%) | NL (9%) | D (8%) | UK (8%) | CH (6%) |
| *Russian Federation* | USA (30%) | Cyprus (26%) | D (8%) | UK (4%) | SF (3%) |

Notes:  A = Austria;  B = Belgium;  CH = Switzerland;  CRO = Croatia;  D = Germany; DK = Denmark;  F = France;  GR = Greece;  I = Italy;  NL = Netherlands;  RU = Russian Federation; S = Sweden; SF = Finland.
*Sources:* UNCTAD, *World Investment Report* (1999); Hamilton (2000: 106); own calculations.

## Cities and FDI Location

Foreign firms locate and operate most of their investments in Central and Eastern Europe in the cities or their immediate hinterlands. Available UNCTAD data indicate that FDI in primary sector activities is insignificant, at only 5 per cent of the region's cumulative inward FDI stock at the end of the 1990s (UNCTAD, 1999; see also Table 5.1). Rural locations (i.e. FDI in farming or forestry) are only important locally in Romania, where such investment accounts for 11 per cent (see Table 5.7). More foreign money has been sunk into natural-resource extraction in mining or oil-drilling towns across the region, but mainly in Belarus (54 per cent) and the Russian Federation (13 per cent). Most FDI stock in Central and Eastern Europe has gone into manufacturing (41 per cent) and services (47 per cent) (UNCTAD, 1999; see also Table 5.1). Thus, it can be inferred that FDI is overwhelmingly city-located. Services are wholly so,

Table 5.7  FDI stock by sectors and countries, 1998 (US$ bn)*

| Central and Eastern European countries | Farming/ Forestry | | Mining | | Manufacturing | | Services | | Unspecified | |
|---|---|---|---|---|---|---|---|---|---|---|
| | Vol. | % | Vol. | % | Vol. | % | Vol. | % | Vol. | % |
| *Baltic states* | | | | | | | | | | |
| Estonia | 0.02 | 1 | 0.02 | 1 | 0.6 | 30 | 1.3 | 66 | 0.04 | 2 |
| Latvia | 0.02 | 1 | — | — | 0.4 | 18 | 1.9 | 79 | 0.05 | 2 |
| Lithuania | — | — | — | — | 0.6 | 25 | 1.6 | 67 | 0.2 | 8 |
| *Central Europe* | | | | | | | | | | |
| Croatia | — | — | — | — | 2.5 | 60 | 0.8 | 18 | 0.9 | 22 |
| Czech Republic | — | — | 0.2 | 1 | 9.8 | 45 | 9.3 | 43 | 2.4 | 11 |
| Hungary | 0.2 | 1 | 0.2 | 1 | 7.6 | 39 | 11.5 | 59 | — | — |
| Poland | — | — | 0.3 | 1 | 13.1 | 45 | 12.8 | 44 | 2.9 | 10 |
| Slovakia | — | — | 0.04 | 1 | 1.7 | 47 | 1.8 | 51 | — | — |
| Slovenia | — | — | — | — | 0.6 | 48 | 0.8 | 51 | — | — |
| *South-east Europe* | | | | | | | | | | |
| Bulgaria | — | — | — | — | 1.8 | 54 | 1.4 | 43 | 0.1 | 3 |
| Bosnia-Herzegovina | — | — | — | — | 0.1 | 33 | 0.2 | 63 | 0.02 | 5 |
| Romania | 0.8 | 11 | — | — | 3.1 | 46 | 2.1 | 31 | 0.08 | 11 |
| *East Europe* | | | | | | | | | | |
| Belarus | — | — | 0.4 | 54 | 0.4 | 46 | — | — | — | — |
| Moldova | — | — | — | — | 0.1 | 33 | 0.2 | 56 | 0.04 | 2 |
| Ukraine | 0.1 | 3 | 0.03 | 1 | 1.4 | 43 | 1.3 | 40 | 0.4 | 12 |
| *Russian Federation* | — | — | 1.6 | 13 | 4.3 | 35 | 4.9 | 40 | 1.4 | 11 |

Notes: *Figures are rounded.
Source: UNCTAD, *World Investment Report* (1999: 435); EBRD, *Transition Report* (2001).

although public utilities serve networks of cities and their regions and some small-scale "workbench"-type industry has also been funded in villages in some regions.

As Table 5.7 reveals, manufacturing and services have absorbed FDI in approximately equal measure in the city systems of the Czech Republic, Poland, and Ukraine. FDI is restructuring mainly manufacturing, more so than services, in Bulgarian, Croatian, and Romanian cities. By contrast, service functions are the main targets of FDI in the remaining nine states. Yet, given the sharp international contrasts in FDI inflows discussed earlier (see Table 5.2), it is clear that foreign firms are most active in restructuring the forms and functions of cities in two states, most notably the Czech Republic and Hungary, followed by Poland. That said, the location and character of FDI are very diversified between several types of cities: (i) leading metropolitan capital-city regions; (ii) other capitals; and (iii) major provincial cities, industrial centres, and small towns.

## FDI in Metropolitan Capital-City Regions

Capital cities throughout Central and Eastern Europe have attracted the biggest shares of FDI flowing into the states they administer. Leadership in transformation emanating from the four capitals in the region that are classified as "world cities" (see Beaverstock, Smith, and Taylor, 2000) – Budapest, Prague, Warsaw, and Moscow – has been instrumental in making their respective states the leading hosts for FDI. The three Central European capitals had already established themselves by 1992 as major competitors in the race to attract FDI. In that year, Budapest received 57.5 per cent of all FDI in Hungary, Prague 45.5 per cent of FDI in Czechoslovakia (60 per cent of that in the Czech Republic), and Warsaw 39 per cent of FDI in Poland. Moscow entered the market for FDI rather later on account of the socio-economic and political upheavals rooted in the simultaneous collapse of communism and break-up of the Soviet Union. Nevertheless, by mid-1999 it was estimated that Moscow received 49 per cent of all FDI in the Russian Federation (http://www.fips.ru).

The magnetism of capital cities for foreign investors, however, resides in their unrivalled advantages within their state territories and in perception and the "eye of the beholder". Rey (1998) proposed a "capital-city hypothesis" to explain that in the initial stages of FDI inflows into a host country, foreign investors tend to cluster their activities in the capital city because it offers the least risky environment, under conditions of limited corporate knowledge of the host country. He argued that as firms gain more knowledge, managements gain in confidence and seek advantages and opportunities elsewhere, so eroding the pre-eminence of the capital city as a location for FDI. The evidence seems to suggest, however, that conditions specific to the transition economies require qualification of this hypothesis in that the initial importance of the capital city might be less than expected, and several factors may combine to maintain or enhance the role of the capital city as a location for FDI, at least during the decade or so since transition began. Some foreign MNE managements already had contacts with enterprise facilities, employees, markets, and supply sources in the region during the socialist period and hence possessed a "ready" stock of information and knowledge pertaining to a range of locations inside and outside the capital region. In most states, the capital city offers major advantages to foreign investors, including:

(i) the largest regional market, the best transport access to the biggest segment of the national market, and the best telecommunications and transport connectivity with facilities or headquarters abroad for transactions and managerial control;

(ii) concentration of state-governmental and private agencies or institutions with which foreign investors need to negotiate or lobby, regarding brown-field joint ventures, acquisitions, or green-field development (Sýkora, 1994);

(iii) the most diversified manufacturing and service opportunities for new investment, and hence scope for exploiting agglomeration economies in supporting and related activities (Porter, 1990; Hamilton, 1991);

(iv) the largest labour market with the widest range of skills, is usually further enhanced by major universities and training establishments which assist recruitment of human capital resources for the more knowledge-intensive and deficit sectors that can attract FDI; and

(v) unrivalled cultural and other "quality-of-life" amenities to attract and hold expatriate and indigenous skilled employees of foreign firms; yet, each capital city is unique and has an ambience of its own.

The timing of privatization of specific sectors and enterprises also shapes the spatial pattern of FDI acquisition or merger opportunities in any year in any transition state. So, in all three Central European states, foreign acquisitions of key industrial enterprises privatized early on resulted in substantial FDI flows into non-metropolitan locations (e.g. Fiat in Bielsko, southern Poland; Volkswagen in Mlada Boleslav, north of Prague) as well as into the capital city. On the other hand, delayed privatization of other state-owned enterprises, public utilities, or producer services (such as banking, electricity, and telecommunications) has led to more recent upsurges of FDI into the capital cities. Thus, for example, the Budapest metropolitan region was estimated recently to localize two-thirds of all FDI in Hungary (Barta, Kralik, and Perger, 1997), while the Warsaw metropolitan region actually increased its concentration of FDI in Poland from 38 per cent in 1994 to 48 per cent in 1998 (Hamilton, 2000). Yet, one must bear in mind that the amounts of FDI quoted as being located in a capital city reflect the location of a foreign firm's host-country or regional-international headquarters and not necessarily the actual location of investments.[8] Nevertheless, the clustering of FDI in a capital-city region does express the locus there of command and control functions and thus expresses the city's ability to match the locational requirements for such functions of foreign investors within the host country and the wider Central and Eastern European region.

FDI has been transforming the functions and space economy of the capital-city regions in several ways. First, the preceding socialist regimes endowed these cities with national leadership roles in industrialization and technological modernization, mainly through the development of key engineering and other producers' goods sectors. Thus, the capital cities have offered foreign investors scope to restructure manufacturing in the 1990s through rationalization of existing enterprises and through "re-industrialization" by building new enterprises to serve deficit markets. The results, however, have been rather patchy; many foreign firms have shunned saving or restructuring whole swathes of metal, machinery, textile, clothing, footwear, and other enterprises, which now present rather desolate zones of de-industrialization in wedges of western Warsaw and the north-east and south-east sectors of Budapest and Csepel Island. Nevertheless, foreign firms have targeted selected enterprises to serve local deficit markets or to export competitive products across Europe.[9] Warsaw has experienced expansion of the automotive sector and related supply industries, with major investments by Daewoo of South Korea in the old Fiat-equipped Zeran plant to make it a hub in the firm's Central European production network (Chae, 1999; Hamilton, 2000). Italian FDI has modernized the Warsaw steelworks to supply the automotive industry with high-quality sheet steel. These investments have helped stimulate a "snowball" effect, with a range of smaller-scale foreign investments in automotive components supply in the suburban zone, together with a growth in food-processing (e.g. Cadbury) and consumer electronics (e.g. Thomson).

The main impact of FDI, however, has been the growth, modernization, and diversification of consumer and producer services. These are transforming the city centres and, to a lesser (yet increasing) extent, the socialist residential neighbourhoods and urban fringes. Given the quantitative and qualitative deficiencies in service provision in the socialist city (Hamilton, 1967; Hamilton, 1976), the scope for foreign development of services is huge, notwithstanding the vigorous growth of indigenous private entrepreneurship in some of these activities. In fact, FDI is making a major contribution to the (re)creation and consolidation of central business districts (CBDs), which now begin to resemble those of Western metropoles. The transformation of the central zones of the four leading capital cities had been fostered by the in-movement of very large numbers of foreign firms to satisfy pent-up services demand, and their simultaneous exploitation of the huge "rent-gap" (Sýkora, 1994) between what Hamilton (1995) described as the previous socialist "use value" and the new potential "commodified" and best "exchange values" of sites in the city. One piece of evidence for this lies in the contrasting yields on investments in prime office or shopping centre sites. In most West European capitals these are currently about 5–7 per cent, whereas in Central and Eastern European capitals they range from 10 to 25 per cent (Jones Lang LaSalle, 2000). Property restitution in the 1990s opened up possibilities for foreign firms to acquire or lease property at attractive rates and for multinational real-estate firms (such as London-based Healey and Baker or Jones Lang LaSalle) and commercial facility developers (like the British firm Regus or Germany's Hochtief) to move in and, given the prevailing local land, labour, and materials prices, to refurbish existing or build new premises at low cost, often speculating on future demand. As a result, substantial growth of new office, retail, and warehouse space has occurred, as Table 5.8 shows, most of it financed by FDI (Enyedi and Szirmai, 1992; Dingsdale, 1997).

Table 5.8 reveals several interesting contrasts. First, the attraction of Budapest, Prague, and Warsaw for new services space is clearly evident, indicating that these three cities are spearheading the "service revolution", while the South east and East European capitals, symbolized by Bucharest and Moscow, lag in new services provision. Yet, second, all capitals of the transition economies lag far behind their West European counterparts, including Berlin, in modern office space. This gap can be explained by the interplay of many factors.

Table 5.8 Modern commercial service space in Central and Eastern European metropolitan capitals: comparisons with selected West European capitals (2000/2001)

| Cities | Offices | | Retail (shopping) centers | | Industrial/ warehouses | |
|---|---|---|---|---|---|---|
| | Volume (000 sq.m) | Sq.m per 1,000 pop. | Volume (000 sq.m) | Sq.m. per 1,000 pop. | Volume (000 sq.m) | Sq.m per 1,000 pop. |
| Bucharest | 390 | 186 | 20 | 10 | 95 | 45 |
| Budapest | 1.570 | 785 | 600 | 300 | 145 | 68 |
| Prague | 1.130 | 920 | 970 | 790 | 360 | 296 |
| Warsaw | 1.815 | 800 | 1.195 | 525 | 780 | 471 |
| Moscow | 2.515 | 270 | 305 | 33 | 600 | 65 |
| Berlin | 16.000 | 4,805 | 900 | 270 | n/a | n/a |
| Brussels | 10.000 | 9,090 | 300 | 273 | n/a | n/a |
| London | 27.100 | 3,545 | 2.100 | 265 | n/a | n/a |
| Madrid | 11.000 | 2,750 | 1.450 | 363 | n/a | n/a |
| Paris | 31.500 | 3,270 | 3.700 | 384 | n/a | n/a |
| Stockholm | 7.500 | 4,747 | 1.300 | 823 | n/a | n/a |
| Vienna | 8.000 | 3,820 | 350 | 167 | n/a | n/a |

*Sources:* Jones Lang LaSalle, *City Profiles* (for commercial floor space data); United Nations world population "urban" data were used for calculating floor space per thousand population.

Delays in property restitution and privatization have meant that new office construction has been concentrated in a very short period, mostly since 1996, in contrast to much longer incremental growth in West European capitals. Even in Budapest, where the process began earlier, 50 per cent of modern office space is less than three years old. Constraints exist on the supply of sites suitable for new construction, especially in the older, densely built-up, pre-1914 areas of central Budapest, Prague, and Moscow, and on opportunities to modernize offices built in the 1950s or 1960s. Scarcities in supply, especially of attractive modern premises, partly explain the high rent levels in Central and Eastern European capitals as compared with many of their EU competitors for regional headquarters functions, like Vienna or Berlin, as Table 5.9 shows. Indeed, new office supply has helped reduce rent levels; for example, in the early 1990s, Prague offices averaged US$83 per sq.m per month (Sýkora and Simonickova, 1994).

On the other hand, buoyant demand by foreign firms maintains high rent levels. According to UNCTAD (1999), Central and Eastern Europe is host to 174,170 affiliates of foreign firms, almost 30 per cent of the world total. How, then, can one reconcile the relatively small modern office space provision in the capitals of the transition economies with such a presence? The answer appears to lie in the small, or very small, size of most foreign affiliate office operations in the region. Most are, in effect, "branches" which gain their infrastructural

Table 5.9 Prime office rent levels in selected European cities, 2000 (US$ per sq.m per month)

| EU cities | Rent level | CEE cities | Rent level |
|-----------|-----------|------------|-----------|
| Amsterdam | 25 | Budapest | 19 |
| Berlin | 27 | Bucharest | 34 |
| Brussels | 18 | Prague | 22 |
| London | 94 | Warsaw | 32 |
| Madrid | 23 | Moscow | 42 |
| Paris | 42 | | |
| Stockholm | 36 | | |
| Vienna | 20 | | |

*Source:* Jones Lang LaSalle, *City Profile* (2000).

support through the corporate networks of facilities located in other European and world cities, including the corporate headquarters, and from local supporting clusters of specialist services provided by clusters of foreign MNEs and local firms; many are little more than "toe-holds" in the doorway, awaiting better future prospects.[10] Thus, most new office buildings constructed in Central and Eastern European cities are for multiple occupancy. Yet, large numbers of foreign firms have also found refurbished office space in the older property stock of the extensive CBDs of Budapest, Prague, and Moscow – space which is not included in the data presented in Table 5.8. In connection with this, it should be noted that the transition towards a market economy and civil society led to substantial "downsizing" of central government, which, while generally still occupying the same pre-socialist or socialist buildings in situ, nevertheless released space for occupancy by private firms as well.

The key force in the transformation of the capital city centres from their socialistic socio-political government, administrative, and cultural character into more fully fledged CBDs is the growth of modern and diverse producer services. Wernerheim and Sharp (1999) have compared 12 sources of classifications and concluded that there is a wide consensus of opinion that "producer services" include accounting, advertising, architectural services and design, banking and financial services, computer services, employment agencies, engineering and research services, insurance, legal services, management consultancy, real-estate management and sales, security and investigation services, and typing and copying services. Many of these are "new" to the former socialist city functional structure or take on new forms of privatized service activity in the post-socialist city. Much of this growth has involved occupancy of space in refurbished nineteenth- and earlier twentieth-century properties in Budapest, Prague, and Moscow, as well as new office premises. In Warsaw, by contrast, it is associated with occupancy of more spectacular high-rise office blocks and towers which in-fill the extensive open spaces and sites on broad avenues created in the 1950s rebuilding of the heavily destroyed central city. Foreign MNEs have been as instrumental in actually constructing new office blocks as in equipping them with furnishings, elevators, computers, and telecommunications facilities.

Demand for office space is being stimulated by the perception of increasing numbers of MNE managements that these leading capital cities can perform crucial roles in wider European and global production and service networks. Budapest functions as a hub between West European and German cities, as well as Vienna, on the one hand, and South-east Europe, on the other (Rey, 1998); Prague as a hub for cities in Germany, west and south-west Poland, and Slovakia (Barlow, Dostal, and Hampl, 1994); and Warsaw between Rhineland cities and Berlin to the west, Scandinavia to the north, and the Baltic states, Russian Federation, and Ukraine to the east (Dangschat, 1993). As Chapter 4 of this volume indicates, however, these three cities, together with Moscow, have strong air transport connections with the global hubs of London, Paris, and Frankfurt, particularly for onward global connections.

Budapest has attracted substantial inward FDI because it is no longer just the capital of a small economy – Hungary, on the eastern margins of the European Union – but because it is a growing competitor in the European metropolitan system by virtue of its proximity to Vienna and Bratislava, and its possession of a well-educated business and professional community with longstanding trading and transactional experience with former socialist countries, including the CIS (Barta, 1992; Enyedi, 1994, 1997). For example, PepsiCo has relocated its regional headquarters from Vienna to Budapest to make its new office a "forward point" for expanding its business into South-east Europe (including former Yugoslav markets) and East Europe (Moldova, Ukraine). Opel, the German subsidiary of General Motors, has established a sales and marketing office in Budapest to serve the same region and to obviate delays in working through its Austrian and German offices (Nicholls, 1998). Royal Dutch Shell and Lucent Technologies have also selected Budapest as their Central European headquarters. These examples emphasize the advantages of the city and its proximity and accessibility to an expanding market area.

When viewing the region as a whole, however, Budapest is in competition with Warsaw for "hub" status, as the Polish capital has attracted major MNEs to supply the large national market. Many of these have subsequently promoted their local Warsaw offices to the international-regional level de facto to exploit the city's nodality (Gaudray-Coudroy, 1998). American corporations like Colgate or Proctor and Gamble thus use their Warsaw bases to coordinate advertising and marketing, at least, more widely across the northern part of Central Europe (the Czech Republic, Hungary, and Slovakia) as well as Russia. Such in-migration of producer services has contributed to the emergence of business centres like the impressive Atrium, which are entirely new elements in Warsaw's urban space. They contain almost 90 per cent of all new high-quality office premises in Poland and create a dispersed pattern of towers to the west and north of the Palace of Culture (Dawson, 1999).

Inward FDI, then, has been a major factor propelling the growth and concentration of advanced producer services in the capital city economies and their CBDs. In-movement early in the 1990s of a range of management consultancy firms – Andersen, Coopers Lybrand, Deloitte Touche, Ernst & Young, KPMG, and Price Waterhouse (some of which subsequently merged operations as part of global consolidation) – is an example of the way in which foreign MNEs sought to exploit new markets created by the learning and information gaps inherent in the implementation of most aspects of transition. Such in-movement was parallelled by international law firms. Later, as new governments expanded the spheres of privatization, the influx of another cluster of foreign firms occurred in financial services, insurance, and banking. Leading firms experienced in stock market transactions, such as BZW, Goldman Sachs, Merrill Lynch, JP Morgan, and Nomura, became active in handling enterprise privatization and helping to raise capital on international markets. Insurance, previously "guaranteed" or deemed unnecessary or undesirable under socialist state ownership and management, suddenly burgeoned as a new and diversified service sphere and attracted FDI by MNEs like Allianz (Germany), Axa (France), Prudential (US), and Winterthur (Switzerland). The more protracted process of privatizing banking has stimulated a rapid insurge of FDI by foreign banks keen to gain market footholds in the region by acquiring local banks or expanding provision of an underdeveloped service sector: ABN Amro, Citibank, Commerzbank, Creditanstalt, Banque Nationale de Paris, and Union Bank of Switzerland are just a few. Although the growth of producer services is localized mainly in the CBDs, the sheer dynamism of their expansion has led to inroads into adjacent areas as a result of the scarcity of suitable CBD sites and escalating land values and rents.[11]

The most publicized and overt expression of the "globalizing" transformation of CBDs, of course, has been the introduction, proliferation, and diffusion along main streets and around squares of the "fast food" revolution, with the capital cities becoming the "forward points" for the "McDonaldization" of Central and Eastern European urban societies, thereby serving and reshaping consumer demand. While the opening of the world's largest McDonald's on Red Square in Moscow opposite the Kremlin is the most blatant expression of the arrival of this new revolution, the cityscapes of all four capitals are now liberally peppered with competing fast-food outlets including, besides McDonald's, Burger King, Dunkin' Donuts, Kentucky Fried Chicken, Pizza Hut, and Subway. But they form merely a part of the broad "cosmopolitanization" of restaurant and catering facilities also being fostered by indigenous entrepreneurs and new immigrant populations (see also Chapter 14 on Moscow).

Prestigious locations for retail space that commanded prime rents of about US$40 per sq.m per month in the mid-1990s now range between US$75 and

US$80 per sq.m per month in Budapest, Prague, and Warsaw, and can reach US$150 per sq.m per month in Moscow in comparison to US$350–380 per sq.m per month in London or Paris (Jones Lang LaSalle, 2000). Such locations as the largely pedestrianized Vaci Utca in Budapest, Arbat in Moscow, and Nowy Swiat in Warsaw have attracted some of the world's leading brand names in clothing, leather goods, footwear, cosmetics, and luxury goods, while all the commercial premises in the city centre of Prague are geared to Western (and Japanese) wallets! In large measure, this reflects the marked growth and concentration in the capital cities of purchasing power from tourism (especially in Prague), the rising volume of business travellers, the expansion of profitable local entrepreneurship (mainly in selected services), and the emergence of some richer echelons of society. These trends are interrelated with the growth of FDI in or near the CBDs in new hotel construction for chains such as Holiday Inn, Ibis, Intercontinental, Marriott, Novotel, Radisson, and Sheraton.

With time, however, FDI has been flowing increasingly into other zones of these capital cities both because property scarcities and high rents in the CBDs are encouraging investors to look elsewhere and because economic growth has been creating demand for more diversified, high-quality offices and services also in "mid-town" areas and suburban locations. In Budapest, for example, the new office space under construction in 2001 outside the CDB (500,000 sq.m) exceeds that being built within the CBD (430,000 sq.m). A more marked shift appears to be occurring in Warsaw, where office floor space in the CBD will rise from 500,000 to 740,000 sq.m while that in the rest of the city will increase to 880,000 sq.m. Much of this more decentralized development is in response to demand for prestigious facilities at lower rents from foreign manufacturers (e.g. PepsiCo, Nokia), telecommunications firms, insurance companies, advertising agencies, management consultants, and IT service providers (Jones Lang LaSalle, 2000).

The trend towards decentralization of FDI and service modernization within these metropolitan areas is being further reinforced by retail developments. FDI is fostering major expansion of shopping and leisure facilities in "mid-town" locations in the extensive socialist residential neighbourhoods which were characterized by very basic consumer services, and in "out of town" suburban sites. New retail facilities essentially comprise two forms. The first involves small or medium-scale "in-fillings" between housing blocks and in open spaces along major thoroughfares. These generally include: supermarkets owned by foreign firms such as Makro, Meinl, or Spar; petrol (gas) stations and mini-markets by AgiP, BP, Exxon, Mobil, Shell, Texaco, and others; car dealerships for all European and Japanese makes, and Daewoo (South Korea); and the conversion of former small state stores at street level under the housing blocks into new specialized retail outlets such as Blockbuster (video).

The second and most striking change consists in the construction of spacious new shopping centres, malls, and leisure complexes along major avenues and near key transport intersections served by buses, trains, metro stations, and, in suburban zones, rail stations and good highways. These facilities are financed by foreign money (direct or indirect investment by individual firms or by consortia) and "populated" by leading foreign enterprises. For example, the Central European Property Fund, sponsored by Jones Lang LaSalle, Lehmann Brothers, and Bouggues, was established in 1999 to fund 8–10 shopping centres in Poland, the Czech Republic, and Hungary, with one to be located in each of the capital city regions. Examples of such centres in Budapest include the Duna Centre (Virgin Megastore, Kookai etc.), built on derelict industrial land to the north-north-east of the CBD, Europark, Albertalva, and the Plus Center (Tesco) in the outer north-east of the city. All have a mix of clothing, footwear, furniture, consumer electronics, and bookstores as well as fast-food restaurants, and some have integrated gas station facilities. Prague has attracted the Swedish furniture firm IKEA, which invested US$101 million in a retail strip mall west of the city, while the Swiss retail chain Intershop has opened Centrum Černý Most to the east, complete with cinemas and a bowling alley, pool hall, and theatre, so contributing to the transformation of the city's suburbs (Kok and van Weesep, 1996). Similar centres exist in Warsaw, notably Galeria Mokotów to the south of the CBD, and others have opened in Praga and Siekierki on the "working class" east bank of the Vistula river. The gradual eastward diffusion of shopping centres is illustrated by the opening of the first IKEA centre in Moscow in March 2000.

Yet, the largest retail developments are occurring in green-field "out of town" locations on the metropolitan fringes, to take advantage of open land and cheaper rents (Wasiuk, 1998) as well as the suburbanisation of wealthier households, improved roads, and rapidly rising car ownership. Thus, the French firm Carrefour and German chain Metro have opened hypermarkets on the outskirts of Warsaw, while the French chains Auchan and Cora have done likewise to the east of Budapest beside the ring road and motorway facilities and close to new executive housing estates which combine apartments, terraced housing, and single villas. It is these large-scale developments in particular which help to explain the high levels of retail floor space per thousand population, especially evident in Prague and Warsaw (Table 5.8) in comparison with West European capitals. The latter, with the exception of Stockholm, concentrate a much bigger stock of older and relatively smaller stores, often arranged along inner city and suburban shopping "high streets". Although Budapest has more of this type of retail facility, especially within pre-1914 Pest, the higher figures for the Central European capitals express a recent "catch-up" in eliminating their historic deficits of modern shopping provision under socialism. Clearly, however, Table 5.8 indicates that Bucharest and Moscow still suffer those deficits.

Table 5.8 also shows a substantial growth of modern warehousing, especially in Warsaw and Moscow, followed by Prague and Budapest. This is new space and does not include conversions of vacated industrial premises, which are more evident in Budapest than elsewhere, following more severe de-industrialization; thus, the data in Table 5.8 partially hide the importance of the growth of this function in and around the city. Two points are important here. First, under socialism, warehousing services were neglected. This was because, under socialist ideology, services were treated as "non-productive" sectors, were thus starved of investment, and so became "deficit" sectors. The command economy was intended to be fully planned and to operate on the basis of direct factory-to-store (or market) delivery. Had this economic model been efficient, it (rather than the Japanese) would have invented "just-in-time" delivery, but in reality, inefficiency, expediency, and deficiency in the system usually meant "delivery if and when ready". This did not matter in the socialist shortage economy, as goods were almost always sold as soon as they were received; this tended to make warehouses redundant (except that consumer "choice" was a matter of whether or not to buy the goods on offer, and rejected goods did fill warehouses or decayed in the open). Transition and privatization had led to the proliferation of firms, fragmentation, and lengthening of the supply chain and, with open borders and rising foreign trade, the multiplication of longer international supply lines. Warehouses have become necessary and, of course, have been developed as an integral part of the market economy culture and organization. Thus, for example, by 1996 foreign-owned stores and manufacturers in Warsaw were already utilizing more than 2,500 retail warehouses in and around the city. Similar conditions prevail in the other capitals. This leads to the second point. The significantly greater expansion of modern warehousing space in Moscow and Warsaw has been a response to two main factors: greater national market size and greater distance from alternative logistics centres. Moscow and Warsaw are the major distribution centres for the two largest Central and East European economies. With its eastward location in Poland, Warsaw also functions as a distribution centre for foreign firms selling in Lithuania, Belarus, and Ukraine. Moreover, both Warsaw and Moscow are much more distant from the European Union, so that air freight is proportionately more important (as already shown in Chapter 4) and hence foreign (and local) firms require greater local warehouse space. This is in contrast to Budapest and Prague, where firms serving the Czech and Hungarian as well as the Slovakian, Slovenian, and Croatian markets can be more quickly and efficiently supplied from logistics centres located in Austria, Germany, and Italy.

## FDI in Other Capital Cities

The remaining Central and Eastern European capital cities perform a key gateway function for channeling FDI into their respective state territories. Bratislava, newly created capital of Slovakia, consistently drew in about 60 per cent of the country's foreign investment throughout the 1990s (Pavlinek and Smith, 1998; Bu3ek, 1999). Sofia localized FDI in Bulgaria: three-fifths of all foreign-owned producer services were located there between 1989 and 1993, while in 1998 the capital still pulled in 58 per cent of the country's FDI (Carter, 1999). Bucharest dominated inflows into Romania, with more than half of all foreign firms in Romania located in the city between March 1990 and February 1997 (Guran-Nicu, 1999). The situation is similar in Slovenia's capital Ljubljana, where almost half of the country's total FDI in the 1990s was located (see Chapter 11 on Ljubljana). In the Baltic states, however, more than 70 per cent of all FDI at the end of the 1990s was absorbed by their respective capital city regions of Tallinn, Riga, and Vilnius (see Chapter 13 on Baltic cities).

Yet, none of the other capitals have been able to attract major FDI. A range of factors explain delayed or limited FDI. Apart from Bucharest and Sofia, all are administrative seats of newly independent (or, in the case of the Baltics, regained independent) states where people have had to try to climb a very steep learning curve to establish national political and economic stability and international credibility. Most capitals are smaller in size, and serve national markets of very limited size and purchasing power, so that any significant scale of foreign investment requires open borders and an environment of international cooperation to facilitate exports. Most often, however, foreign firms have been deterred because post-socialist governments have pursued controversial policies, have vacillated or stalled, or have failed to engender international credibility. Several examples illustrate these points.

For example, Ljubljana, capital of Slovenia, has pulled in FDI despite the sluggishness of the privatization process since 1993. To an extent this disadvantage has been outweighed by the city's excellent location, the inheritance of a more advanced technological base which was embedded from the early post–Second World War socialist period (Hamilton, 1967), and the presence of a community skilled in dealing with other regions of the former Yugoslavia. These factors persuaded Siemens from Germany to establish its local headquarters in Ljubljana as early as 1991 and to supply household appliances and consumer goods, and IBM to open a subsidiary with a Systems Support Center and Personal Computer Institute to bolster IBM Austria's trade with the former Yugoslavia. Indeed, the city has also attracted a software cluster, with Microsoft and Oracle establishing centres to serve the Bulgarian, Hungarian, Romanian, and Slovakian markets.

A more extreme case is Bratislava, the capital of Slovakia. Its city region ought to be among the leading locations of FDI in the region. True, leading firms like Henkel, K-Mart, Volkswagen, and Unilever have invested there in manufacturing (vehicles, chemicals) and retailing. Yet, when the city became the capital of the newly independent Slovakia in 1992, leading foreign management consultancy firms assessed the Bratislava region to have the best location for FDI in the whole of Central Europe, located between Vienna and Budapest, near the borders of four states – Slovakia, the Czech Republic, Hungary, and Austria (which in 1995 became the EU border) – and equidistant from Berlin, central and southern Poland to the north, and Slovenia, Croatia and the Adriatic coast to the south. However, the city has been unable to exploit this potential in large measure because the Vladimir Meciar government of Slovakia (1992–1998) pursued a rather nationalistic policy which engendered domestic ethnic tensions, created friction with Hungary, and discouraged investors. If that were not enough, this government attempted to deflate the capital role and advantages of Bratislava, a multi-ethnic city, by trying to foster key state, university, and financial services functions in Banská Bystrica, a town beneath the low Tatras mountains. Now, though, Bratislava's attraction for FDI is likely to be restored because Slovakia's new government has created political and market confidence through recent reforms, enabling Slovakia to attain Standard & Poor's award of an investment grade rating for the first time since independence (Carter, 1998, 1999).

The lion's share of FDI in the Baltic capitals of Tallinn, Riga, and Vilnius come from either Scandinavia (Sweden, Finland, Norway, Denmark) or other northern European countries such as Germany, the Netherlands, and the UK. Foreign investments also tend to focus on certain sectors of the local economies. The new capital was targeted towards what traditionally were under-developed sectors during the Soviet period, and went hand-in-hand with the break-up of old economic dependencies. Many foreign direct investments were made through takeovers of old manufacturing industries; this enhances productivity and creates important spillover effects from foreign companies to domestic ones. In Tallinn, for example, more than 30 per cent of all FDI between 1992 and 1996 was made in manufacturing, while 25 per cent was made in the wholesale and retail trades. Another 18 per cent went into transportation and telecommunications. The investments by Swedish Telia AB and Finnish Telecom in the Eesti Telefon and EMT AS mobile telephone companies in 1996 were two major undertakings. A similar pattern can be noticed in Riga as well as in Vilnius, although investments in trade play a more prominent role relative to other sectors compared to the case in Tallinn (see also Chapter 13).

By contrast, FDI is being hindered in Bucharest (as in other Romanian cities) because "two facts tarnish Romania's regional reputation. The country is the laggard of the 10 countries of Central and Eastern Europe waiting to join the Eurepean Union. And it is unique among that group in terms of repeatedly failing to fulfil any of the agreements it has entered into with the International Monetary Fund. Unfavourable political environments have had the most detrimental effects in stifling FDI into the other capital cities of South-east and East Europe. Preservation of state control and political centralism in Belarus under President Lukashenko has ensured that Minsk, its capital, is virtually "foreign investment free" (apart from a small Ford assembly operation), while unconvincing reform, slow political democratization and economic pauperization in Ukraine have restricted Kiev's attractiveness. For much of the 1990s, FDI in Zagreb, capital of Croatia, was deterred by late President Tudjman's crony politics, but, of course, the Yugoslav wars made Belgrade, Sarajevo, Podgorica (Montenegro), and to a lesser extent, Skopje, very unattractive for investment. The same is true of Tirana, the Albanian capital. Despite introduction of a privatization programme managed by a National Privatization Agency in 1995, foreign investors have stayed away. While regional political and military instability associated with ethnic conflicts and tensions in Kosovo and FYRoM has been a factor, it is internal conditions which are most detrimental – local corruption; industrial obsolescence; lack of basic urban infrastructure; intense rural to urban migration after 1992, when free population movement was permitted for the first time in half a century; an influx of refugees from the former Yugoslavia; and the explosion of shanty towns on the urban fringe. As already mentioned in Chapter 3, Tirana combines geographical isolation with "third world" conditions (see also Carter, 1999).

So FDI has changed the face of the other Central and Eastern European capital cities much less dramatically than in the leading "world cities" in the region – some hardly at all. FDI is directly evident in new hotels, some restructured industries, public utilities such as telecommunication, refurbished offices, and some consumer services. But generally there has not been the proliferation of foreign consumer goods outlets, hypermarkets, shopping centres, offices, and warehouse construction found in Budapest, Prague, Warsaw, or Ljubljana. In Sofia, for example, small private businesses have flourished as result of ground-floor flats being converted by their owners into small retail outlets, boutiques, and cafés, and some residents renting out property to foreign traders busy introducing Western and Asian goods to the Bulgarian market. Bucharest, like Sofia, escaped the direct effects of the Balkan regional wars of the 1990s, and its wide, tree-lined boulevards endow the city with a deceptively prosperous appearance unmatched elsewhere in Romania – clearly a potential future factor in the city's competitiveness.

## FDI Beyond the Capital Cities

Most foreign investment located outside capital cities has been targeted at rationalizing, modernizing, and expanding manufacturing and boosting the provision of consumer services. That FDI has led to relatively limited producer services growth outside capital cites underlines the continued functional division of labour within the city network. In addition, FDI shows substantial geographical bias between individual cities and levels of the urban hierarchy. Most is localized in larger provincial cities and regional (and some industrial) centres or agglomerations; FDI is much lower in medium-sized and small towns, except near borders with EU member states.

Given the international flow pattern of FDI, foreign firms are having much greater, deeper, more widespread restructuring effects in the city systems of the Czech Republic, Hungary, and Poland than elsewhere. The impacts are far weaker and less diffuse in East and South-east Europe. Thus, for example, towns in north, west, and central Bohemia (including the Prague city region) dominate

FDI in the Czech Republic, with significantly less in east Bohemia or Moravia (except in larger southern cities like Brno and Zlin) (Pavlinek, 1998). Foreign investors in Hungary prefer to be in the triangle of Transdanubia lying between Budapest to the east, Lake Balaton to the south, and the Austrian border to the west. They appear reluctant to locate east of the river Danube in the "agricultural" towns of the Great Plain or older industrial cities of the north-east (Tinee, 1994). Large regional centres in Poland have benefited most from FDI outside Warsaw, especially Poznan, Szczecin, and Wroclaw in the west; the "Three-City" ("*Trojmiasto*") region of Gdansk-Gdynia-Sopot, with Elblag in the north; Bydgoszcz and Lodz in the centre; and Katowice and Crakow in the south (Upper Silesia). By contrast, even larger centres like Bialystok, Lublin, Olsztyn, and Rzeszow lying east of the river Vistula have attracted far less investments (Komorowski, 1998; Domanski, 2000; Hamilton, 2000). In Slovenia, more than 60 per cent of total FDI is concentrated in the six largest cities; more than 50 per cent of total FDI is clustered in four cities in the western part of Slovenia (Ljubljana, Kranj, Novo mesto, Koper) (see Chapter 11 on Slovenia). FDI in Romania tends to cluster in major cities in the west (Arad, Oradea, Timisoara), the south-west (Craiova), and the Prahova valley to the north of Bucharest. FDI is spread more thinly in the centre, north, and east (Guran-Nicu, 1999).

These cities have attracted significant FDI because they offer investors all or most of the following assets:

(a)  good transport accessibility by land, air, or sea to markets, production, and supply chains of MNEs (large or small), and the European management centres of those MNEs;

(b)  proximity to the European Union to minimize transport and transaction costs;

(c)  state enterprises undergoing privatization which offer specific assets, such as market share, product profiles, output capacity, established trade networks, skilled labour, or even technological potential; these factors induce MNEs to make strategic investments with respect to the Central and Eastern European, European Union or global economy;

(d)  availability of cheap and often quite skilled and well-educated labour;

(e)  good local material and technical infrastructure including derelict or unoccupied industrial premises or abandoned military bases to attract major single, or groups of, inward investors;

(f)  a central position in a dynamic regional economy which creates a sufficient market threshold to support substantial growth of consumer services;

(g)  local entrepreneurship in various forms, such as an active indigenous business community keen to upgrade the urban environment or to provide outsourced goods and services for MNEs, or a progressive city authority with innovative policies to attract inward FDI; and

(h)  a core urban heritage of pre-socialist origin, i.e. buildings or zones of Romanesque, Gothic, Renaissance, baroque, classicist, or expressionist architecture etc., which endows a city with a distinctive character, and a potential for tourism, gentrification, and a quality of life not too divergent from cities in EU states.

Cities which have been unable to attract much or any FDI usually lack the above attributes. They may suffer poor accessibility, be run by traditional or unenterprising councils, have less modernized infrastructure from the pre-socialist era, especially in rural regions, or embody predominantly socialist city legacies such as obsolescent state enterprises and a polluted, monotonous, drab, and poorly maintained or serviced urban environment. FDI in manufacturing in the provinces varies enormously in character. At the bottom of the spectrum are relatively short-distance cross-border investments by small foreign firms in "workbench" facilities which employ just a handful of low-cost workers in low value-added assembly or processing operations. For example, many German SMEs have located such outsourcing activities in the small border towns and villages of the Czech Republic (Pavlinek, 1998; Pavlinek and Smith, 1998). At the other end of the spectrum are the major plants of large MNEs that embody rising technological sophistication to serve Europe-wide markets and production chains. As the local spillover effects derive from both the quantitative and the qualitative features of FDI, and are liable to change, the provincial cities form the main stage on which a kaleidoscope of scenarios of MNE strategy and behaviour are played out. These scenarios tend to vary from industry to industry, but there are common ones, too.

Privatization of state-owned enterprises in the transition states provided larger, "global" MNEs with opportunities to achieve "first-mover advantage" and regional monopoly by acquiring entire national networks of plants in several countries. This enabled firms like Asea Brown Boveri, Philip Morris, Nestle, Siemens, and Volkswagen to gain control over multiple locations almost simultaneously and so create a "splashing effect" of FDI among the cities in Central and Eastern Europe. The trend was reinforced by the counter-moves of competitors in acquiring or building alternative plants. In this way, FDI has brought cities into new functional relations and competitive or cooperative national and cross-border interdependencies. Unless the plants acquired can absorb output shifted from the European Union, some will become surplus to requirements and will be downsized or closed. Such a scenario, involving MNEs in decisions to select between plants and cities in making investment or divestment, is most likely in sectors selling long-established branded goods in national markets "protected" by traditional consumer preferences (e.g. chocolate, tobacco) or making engineering goods developed under socialism (e.g. transport equipment). By contrast, the growth of the automotive and electronics industries has occurred to serve real-market expansion in Central and Eastern Europe and to help MNEs lower costs and increase competitiveness in European and global markets. This has not only ensured futures for some former state enterprises, but has required the construction of many new green-field facilities, with direct and indirect spillover effects, in the region's provincial cities.

While FDI converted the auto industry into the biggest in Central Europe, its position is being challenged by the dynamic growth and development of FDI-funded electronics enterprises, most of which are located in provincial cities. This is not surprising, because the region since 1990 has been able to offer MNEs in the sector low, competitive costs within Europe that they previously had to seek out in East and South-east Asia. So MNEs producing consumer electronics, computer hardware and software, and telecommunications equipment, such as Bosch, Ericsson, IBM, Intel, Matsushita, Microsoft, Motorola, Nokia, Philips, Samsung, Siemens, and Sony, have all invested in the region. While such FDI often involves low value-added assembly work using cheap, often female labour, there is also evidence that certain cities with electronics industries, mainly in Hungary, are benefiting from plant restructuring out of labour-intensive into more knowledge-intensive activities. In these cases, initial simple assembly was replaced by more integrated manufacturing, while more recently, on-site functions have been upgraded by the introduction of design, managerial, organizational, and even research and development work. Such "gentrification" of the urban fabric expresses the fierce competition for FDI between cities in Central and Eastern Europe. But because MNEs "play off" one city against another, they often demand concessions or threaten to locate elsewhere. So central or local authorities feel compelled to offer incentives even in very desirable cities which really do not need additional stimuli.

## Conclusion

The impact of "globalization" on city restructuring in Central and Eastern Europe through FDI has been varied, especially between the region's two distinct geographic parts: north and west, and south-east. Economic forces and market opportunities have played the strongest role in the former, geopolitics in the latter.

People in Central Europe have embraced change with great commitment and handled transition very competently, have been rewarded with NATO and OECD membership, and have been offered the opportunity of fully fledged membership of the European Union in 2004. The area is favoured by history and geography and receives the bulk of inward investment. There was a large increase in FDI in the Czech Republic, Hungary, Poland, and Slovakia following the Essen European Council, which launched the pre-accession strategy, and the *Amsterdam Treaty*, which reaffirmed the EU's commitment to eastward enlargement. *Agenda 2000* identified "two waves" of accession and led to a significant upswing in the rate of FDI flows into "first-wave" countries (the Czech Republic, Estonia, Hungary, Poland, and Slovenia), while states included in the "second wave" at that time (Bulgaria, Latvia, Lithuania, Romania, and Slovakia) experienced a smaller upswing in FDI inflows. Those excluded altogether for now from EU enlargement, such as Croatia, Bosnia and Herzegovina, Serbia and Montenegro, Macedonia,

Albania (also known as the "Western Balkans"), and East European countries (Belarus, Ukraine, Moldova), generally exhibit little or no change. Conditions in South-east Europe are more perilous; without radical change in political and economic structures, too much of the past lingers on, the new elites containing many old players keen to protect their privileges and anti-democratic way of life. Large areas of the former Yugoslavia in particular have experienced an even more tragic decline from a functioning multi-ethnic state until 1991 into war, economic collapse, and deprivation in the 1990s.

In keeping with modern global FDI patterns, Central and Eastern Europe play host to investors from a plurality of locations. Most inward investors are likely to be located in close geographic proximity to transition countries in which they invest in order to reduce transaction and transport costs. This applies especially to those EU member states adjacent to or very close to transition economies such as Austria, Germany, Italy, Sweden, and Finland, and those with historical cultural, linguistic, or economic ties with them (e.g. France). This pattern also reveals the dominance of the European Union as a source region of FDI, and particularly that of Germany, the largest economy within the European Union. Germany, as a dominant source of capital and a large market, is vital to many areas in Central and Eastern Europe where FDI has localized. The high proportions of German and Austrian inward investments concentrated in the neighbouring Central European countries, Scandinavian and Finnish FDI in the Baltic states, Greek FDI in FYRoM, and Italian FDI in neighbouring Slovenia and relatively nearby FYRoM and Romania are cases in point, signifying the importance of economic links and cooperation between neighbouring European Union and Central and Eastern European countries, i.e. "cross-border regionalization". By contrast, the Netherlands, a very small economy, highly "accessible" to Central and Eastern Europe (but not so close geographically), has become an important source of FDI in Europe, most prominent in a continuous geographic area in Central and South-east Europe: the Czech Republic, Hungary, Poland, and Romania.

The true importance of the US may be masked by the fact that some US investments have actually been conducted through European subsidiaries. Even so, it can be argued that US investment has been somewhat restrained by the barriers of transaction costs and geographical distance from Central and Eastern Europe. These barriers certainly explain the relative under-representation of the UK as a source country. On the other hand, there is one major absentee – Japan, which still has very limited investments in Central and Eastern Europe. An exceptional case is South Korean FDI in Poland and Romania, where Daewoo developed, in the 1990s, the cores of its Central and Eastern European automotive production system.

All these factors are mirrored in the pace of inter- and intra-urban transformation. It is no coincidence that the "world-cities-in-making" in the region (Berlin, Budapest, Prague, Warsaw) are all located in Central Europe, and that their development owes much to their capacities to attract FDI. Further south, foreign aid, not FDI, and urban "reconstruction" rather than "restructuring" are more common. There, the effects of "globalization" in the 1990s were more readily associated with armed conflict, international peacekeeping forces, mass refugee movements, and destroyed urban centres.

There are also tendencies towards a division of labour between localized producer services in the capital cities and greater emphasis on manufacturing or consumer services elsewhere, with preferred locations being in the west and north, which enjoy better connectivity with markets and corporate headquarters in EU countries. Property investments and different (re)development projects have had the most direct effect on intra-city transformation in Central and Eastern Europe. FDI, as an expression of "globalization" on the transformation of urban land-use patterns and built environment of post-socialist cities, is most visible in residential, commercial, industrial, and leisure property development in city centres, inner city residential neighbourhoods, brown-field industrial sites, and green-field sites on the suburban fringes.

The evidence provided in this chapter supports the uneven spatial patterns of "globalization" in Central and Eastern Europe. First, it reveals the significant concentration of inward investments in Central Europe compared to South-east Europe, the Baltic states, or East Europe. Second, it confirms the importance of FDI flow from EU member states to nearby transition countries, and the process of (selective) economic integration of European markets. Third, it highlights the importance of location of FDI in capital cities and larger regional centres, as opposed to other less favoured locations in more remote areas in transition countries. The challenges of global competitiveness are still to be met by post-socialist cities, especially in terms of attracting international property investments, and directing urban development activities in a more strategic and organized manner to preserve city identity and improve quality of life for local residents.

## Notes

1  Expressed as the average of eight European Bank for Reconstruction and Development (EBRD) performance indicators of transition reforms in Central and Eastern Europe.
2  Yet this volume compares relatively unfavourably with inflows in 1998 of US$193 billion into the US and US$63 billion into the UK (*The Economist*, 2 October 1999).
3  Examples in Poland include Fiat in Upper Silesia, ABB in Wroclaw and elsewhere, Thomson (colour TVs) in Piaseczno (south of Warsaw), and Pilkington (glass) in Sandomierz (south-eastern Poland), or Pepsi-Cola in several states.
4  Croatia is included in Central Europe because of its historic cultural ties to the Austro-Hungarian Monarchy and the fact that it, together with Slovenia, was the most developed part of the former Yugoslavia (Hamilton, 1967; Pichler-Milanović, 1996).
5  This is a rather crude indicator. GDP at PPP (purchasing power parity) would be a better proxy.
6  The experience of Mexican integration into the North American Free Trade Area (NAFTA) and Spain's membership of the European Union provide useful insights.
7  Examples are Austria and Germany through the former Austro-Hungarian and Prussian Empires respectively; Finland's linguistic proximity to Estonia; France's political and cultural ties with Poland; and Italy's mainly socialist-period connections with Poland, Romania, and the former Yugoslavia.

This paper was edited by Nataša Pichler-Milanović

8 For instance, FDI by US corporation General Electric (GE) in Hungary's Tungsram electrical enterprise is registered as located in Budapest, although only one of four Tungsram facilities is actually located in the city.

9 Thus, in Budapest, GE modernized Tungsram and concentrated its European Research and Development Centre on a site in the north-east of the city, while the American firm El Paso and British company PowerGen bought a Csepel Island power plant to share the risks of modernizing and expanding electricity output.

10 Moreover, to meet this kind of demand, a firm like Regus (based in London), for example, manages flexible office buildings in all Central and Eastern European capitals where firms can rent variable amounts of space for as little as a day, or for a week, a month, or longer.

11 Thus in Warsaw, where Centrum concentrates the city's Financial Centre near the Palace of Culture, the zone of Wola to the west of the CBD and main station (Glowny) is now undergoing a transformation from derelict manufacturing to booming banking area (see also Chapter 8).

## REFERENCES

Györgyi Barta, "The Changing Role of Industry in Regional Development and Regional Development Policy in Hungary", *Tijdschrift voor Economische en Sociale Geografie* 58, 1992, pp. 372–379.

Györgyi Barta, Miklós Kralik, and Eva Perger, "Achievements and Conflicts of Modernization in Hungary", *European Spatial Research and Policy* 4(2), 1997, pp. 61–82.

Max Barlow, Peter Dostal, and Martin Hampl, eds, *Development and Administration in Prague*, Amsterdam: Institut voor Sociale Geografie; Prague: Charles University, 1994.

Jon V. Beaverstock, Richard G. Smith, and Peter J. Taylor, "World City Network: A New Metageography", *Annals of the Association of American Geographers* 90, 2000, pp. 123–134.

Alan A. Bevan and Saul Estrin, "The Determinants of Foreign Investment in Transition Economies", *Discussion Paper Series* 9, London: London Business School Centre for New and Emerging Markets, 2000.

Paul Brenton, Francesca Di Mauro, and Matthias Lücke, "Economic Integration and FDI: An Empirical Analysis of Foreign Investment in the EU and Central and Eastern Europe", *Kiel Working Paper* 890, 1998.

Milan Bu3ek, "Regional Disparities in Transition in the Slovak Republic", *European Urban and Regional Studies* 6(4), 1999, pp. 10–21.

Peter Buckley and Mark Casson, *The Economic Theory of the Multinational Enterprise*, London: Macmillan, 1976.

Francis W. Carter, "Geographical Problems in East Slovakia", *Region and Regionalism* 3, 1998, pp. 187–203.

———, "The Geography of Foreign Direct Investment in Central-East Europe During the 1990s", *Wirtschafts Geographische Studien* 24–25, 1999, pp. 40–70.

Richard E. Caves, *Multinational Enterprise and Economic Analysis*, Cambridge: Cambridge University Press, 1982.

Sun Hae Chac, *The Transfer of Korean Passenger Car Production to East-Central Europe: The Case of Direct Investments by Daewoo Motor*, London: University College London, 1999, unpublished Ph.D. dissertation.

Jens S. Dangschat, "Berlin and the German System of Cities", *Urban Studies* 30, 1993, pp. 1025–1057.

Andrew H. Dawson, "From Glittering Icon to . . .", *The Geographical Journal* 165(2), 1999, pp. 154–160.

Joel I. Deichmann, *The Origins, Industrial Composition, and Spatial Distribution of Foreign Direct Investment in Poland: 1989–1998*, Buffalo: State University of New York, 1999, unpublished Ph.D. dissertation.

Alan Dingsdale, "Reconstructing Budapest's Urban Landscape", in Alan Dingsdale, ed., *Urban Regeneration and Development in Post-Socialist Towns and Cities, Trent Geographical Papers* 2, 1997, pp. 73–87.

Evangelia Dokopoulou and F.E. Ian Hamilton, *Development Potentials of the Regions of Spain in the Enlarged EC, Report to the European Commission*, Brussels: Directorate-General for Regional Policy, 1988.

Boleslaw Domański, "Types of Investment and Locational Preferences of European, American and Asian Manufacturing Companies in Poland," in Jerzego J. Parysek and Tadeusz Stryjakiewicz, eds., *Polish Economy in Transition: Spatial Perspectives*, Poznan: Bogucki Wydawnictwo Naukowe, 2000, pp. 29–39.

John H. Dunning, "Toward an Eclectic Theory of International Production: Some Empirical Tests", *Journal of International Business Studies* 11(1), 1980, pp. 9–31.

———, *Explaining International Production*, London: Unwin Hyman, 1988a.

———, "Location and the Multinational Enterprise: A Neglected Factor?", *Journal of International Business Studies* 29(1), 1988b, pp. 45–66.

Györgyi Enyedi, "Budapest and European Metropolitan Integration", *GeoJournal* 32, 1994, pp. 399–402.

———, "Budapest: Return to European Competition", in Chris Jensen-Butler, Arie Schacher, and Jan Van Weesep, eds, *European Cities in Competition*, Aldershot: Avebury, 1997, pp. 274–298.

Györgyi Enyedi and Viktoria Szirmai, *Budapest: A Central European City*, London: Belhaven, 1992.

European Bank for Reconstruction and Development (EBRD), *Transition Report*, London: EBRD, 1997–2001.

Pietro Garibaldi, Nada Mora, Ratna Sahay, and Jeronim Zettelmeyer, "What Moves Capital to Transition Economies", paper presented at the International Monetary Fund Conference "A Decade of Transition", IMF: Washington D.C., 1999.

Lydia Gaudray-Coudroy, "Varsovie: ville capitale," in Violette Rey, ed., *Les territoires centre-Europeens: dilemmes et defis*, Paris: La Decouverte, 1998, pp. 232–245.

Heather Grabbe and Kirsty Hughes, *Enlarging the EU Eastwards*, Chatham House Papers, London: Royal Institute of International Affairs, 1998.

Liliana Guran-Nicu, "Spatial Variations in Foreign Direct Investment", in David Turnock, ed., *Geographical Essays on the Romanian Banat,* Vol. 1, Leicester: Leicester University Department of Geography, 1999, pp. 193–199.

Lars Hakanson, "Towards a Theory of Location and Corporate Growth," in F.E. Ian Hamilton and Godfrey J.R. Linge, eds, *Spatial Analysis, Industry and the Industrial Environment, Vol. 1: Industrial Systems*, Chichester: Wiley, 1979, pp. 115–138.

F.E. Ian Hamilton, "Models of Industrial Location," in Richard J. Chorley and Peter Haggett, eds, *Models in Geography*, London: Methuen, 1967.

———, *Spatial Perspectives on Industrial Organization and Decision-Making*, London, New York: Wiley, 1974.

———, "Multinational Enterprise and the European Community", *Tijdschrift voor Economische en Sociale Geografie* 67(5), 1976, pp. 258–278.

————, "A Global Region in the Melting Pot?", *Geoforum* 21(2), 1990, pp. 145–161.

————, "A New Geography of London's Manufacturing", in Keith Hoggart and David Green, eds, *A New Geography of London*, London: Arnold, 1991.

————, "Re-evaluating Space: Locational Change and Adjustment in Central and Eastern Europe", *Geographische Zeitschrift* 83(2), 1995, pp. 67–86.

————, "Transformation and Space in Central and Eastern Europe", *Geographical Journal* 165(2), 1999, pp. 135–144.

————, "The Locational Impacts of Foreign Direct Investment in Poland", in Marzenna Weresa, ed., *Foreign Direct Investment in a Transition Economy: The Polish Case*, London: School of Slavonic and East European Studies, University College London, 2000, pp. 99–123.

————, "Industrial Restructuring between Magdeburg and Magadan: On the Road from Marx to Market?", in David Turnock, ed., *Environment and Society in Eastern Europe and the Former Soviet Union*, London: Arnold, 2001, pp. 188–129.

F.E. Ian Hamilton and Godfrey J.R. Linge, eds., *Spatial Analysis, Industry and the Industrial Environment, Vol. 2: International Industrial Systems*, Chichester: Wiley, 1981.

Dawn Holland and Nigel Pain, "The Diffusion of Innovations in Central and Eastern Europe: A Study of the Determinants and Impact of Foreign Direct Investment", *NIESR Discussion Paper* 137, London: National Institute of Social and Economic Research, 1998.

Gabor Hunya, "The Role of Foreign Direct Investment in Industrial Restructuring in Central and Eastern Europe", in Marzenna Weresa, ed., *Foreign Direct Investment in a Transition Economy: The Polish Case*, London: School of Slavonic and East European Studies, University College London, 2000, pp. 99–123.

Stephen Hymer, *The International Operations of National Firms: A Study of Foreign Direct Investment*, Cambridge, MA: MIT Press, 1976.

Jones Lang LaSalle, *City Profiles*, 2000 (various issues).

Friderick T. Knickerbocker, *Oligopolistic Reaction and Multinational Enterprise*, Boston: Harvard University Press, 1973.

Herman J. Kok and Jan van Weesep, "After the Velvet Revolution: Neighbourhood Change in Prague", in Proceedings from the Workshop: Transformation Processes in Eastern Europe, The Hague, 1996, pp. 137–154.

Jan Komorowski, "City Marketing and the Need for City Success", *Geographical Journal, Polish Geographical Society* 49, 1998, pp. 275–293.

Paul Krugman, *Geography and Trade*, Cambridge, MA: MIT Press, 1991.

Hans Lankes and Anthony Venables, "Foreign Direct Investment in Economic Transition: The Changing Pattern of Investments", *Economics of Transition* 4, 1996, pp. 331–347.

Alan Mayhew, *Recreating Europe: The European Union's Policy Towards Central and Eastern Europe*, Cambridge: Cambridge University Press, 1998.

Robert B. McNee, "The Functional Geography of the Firm", *Economic Geography* 34, 1958, pp. 321–337.

Klaus Meyer, *Direct Investment in Economies in Transition*, Cheltenham: Edward Elgar, 1998.

Tomasz Mickiewicz and Janice Bell, *Unemployment in Transition: Restructuring and Labour Markets in Central Europe*, Amsterdam: Harwood, 2000.

Robert L.A. Morsink, *Foreign Direct Investment and Corporate Networking. A Spatial Analysis of Investment Conditions*, Cheltenham: Edward Elgar, 1998.

Alexander Murphy, "Western Investment in East-Central Europe: Emerging Patterns and Implications for State Stability", *Professional Geographer* 44(3), 1992, pp. 192–209.

Gunnar Myrdal, *Rich Lands and Poor: The Road to World Prosperity*, New York: Harper, 1956.

———, *Economic Theory and Underdeveloped Regions*, London: Duckworth, 1957.

Alan Nicholls, "Pest Control: Where Best to Locate East European Regional Headquarters", *Business Eastern Europe* 27(31), 1998, p. 7.

Petr Pavlinek, "The Role of Foreign Direct Investment in the Czech Republic's Transition to Capitalism", *Professional Geographer* 50, 1998, pp. 71–85.

Petr Pavlinek and Adrian Smith, "Internationalism and Embeddedness in East-Central European Transition: Contrasting Geographies of Inward Investment in the Czech and Slovak Republics", *Regional Studies* 32, 1998, pp. 619–638.

Natama Pichler-Milanovič, "Slovenia in the New Geopolitical Context", in Francis W. Carter and H.T. Norris, eds, *The Changing Shape of the Balkans,* London: UCL Press Ltd, 1996, pp. 25–51.

Michael Porter, *The Competitiveness of Nations*, London: Methuen, 1990.

Violette Rey, ed., *Les territoires centre-Europeens: dilemmes et defis*, Paris: La Decouverte, 1998.

Hans-Werner Sinn and Alex J. Weichenrieder, "Foreign Direct Investment, Political Resentment and the Privatization Process in Eastern Europe", *Economic Policy* 24, 1997, pp. 177–198.

Adrian Smith, *Restructuring the Regional Economy: Industrial Transformation and Regional Development in Slovakia*, Cheltenham: Edward Elgar, 1998.

Alan Smith, *The Return to Europe*, London: MacMillan, 2000.

Adrian Smith and John Pickles, *Theorizing Transition*, London: Rouledge, 1998.

Adam Swain and Jane Hardy, eds, "Globalization, Institutions, Foreign Investment and the Reintegration of East and Central Europe and the Former Soviet Union within the World Economy", *Regional Studies* 32, 1998, pp. 587–695.

Ludek Sýkora, "Cities in Transition: The Role of Rent Gaps in Prague's Revitalization", *Tijdschrift voor Economische en Sociale Geografie* 84, 1994, pp. 281–293.

Ludek Sýkora and Ivana Simonickova, "From Totalitarian Urban Managerialism to a Liberal Real Estate Market: Prague's Transformations in the Early 1990s", in Michael Barlow, Peter Dostal, and Martin Hampl, eds, *Development and Administration in Prague*, Amsterdam: Institut voor Sociale Geografie, 1994, pp. 47–72.

Tibor Tiner, "Integration Prospects of the Hungarian Transport Network into the More Advanced European Networks", *GeoJournal* 32, 1994, pp. 369–371.

United Nations Conference on Trade and Development (UNCTAD), *World Investment Report*, New York: UNCTAD (annual).

United Nations Economic Commission for Europe (UNECE), *Economic Survey of Europe*, Geneva: UNECE, 2000.

Raymond Vernon, "International Investment and International Trade in the Product Cycle", *Quarterly Journal of Economics*, 1966, pp. 190–207.

Raymond Vernon, "The Product Cycle Hypothesis in a New International Environment", *Oxford Bulletin of Economics and Statistics* 41, 1979, pp. 255–279.

Jósef Wasiuk, "Land Prices", *Warsaw Voice* 10(489), 1998, p. 10.

C. Michael Wernerheim and Christopher A. Sharp, "Producer Services and the 'Mixed Market' Problem: Some Empirical Evidence", *Area* 31(2), 1999, pp. 123–140.

# 6

# Mastering the post-socialist city: Impacts on planning the built environment

*Kaliopa Dimitrovska Andrews*

## Introduction

It has been recognized that the economic strength and vitality of the post-industrial city depends mainly on the quality of its environment, its image, identity, and culture, and its accessibility and safety (Roger and Fisher, 1992; Tibbalds, 1992). Thus, there are many complex factors connected with the increasing demand for innovation in methods to deal efficiently with the evolving problems of (re)development of the built environment and the transformations that inevitably take place in the built fabric of cities. These have been brought on by the rapidly growing processes of globalization, the increasing significance of information technology, a shift in concentration of employment opportunities into the service sector, and the increasing competition for international trade between major cities. The impact of these factors has been particularly significant for many Central and Eastern European (CEE) countries, where rapid political and economic changes since 1990 have raised demands for corresponding changes in established planning systems, especially in development control and urban management processes.

This chapter reviews the impact of the pressures of globalization, the harmonization and expansion pressures of the European Union, and general market competition on the transformation of land-use patterns and physical structure, with a comparative commentary on the similarities and differences between CEE cities. It specifically examines reasons and outcomes relating to those cities which are being most affected, identifying the role of contemporary planning within the overall development of each city.

The first section reviews the impact of the socio-political events of the twentieth century on the evolution of spatial structures of CEE capital cities, and their transformations and changes in the post-socialist era. The main aim of the early part of this chapter is to identify the principle characteristics of the current transformations of urban patterns, and the internal spatial structure of cities, as a product of globalized processes of production and the restructuring of urban activities and social changes.

Contemporary urban development characteristics, including problems relating to privatization and restitution of land, housing, office and commercial property, transport, and infrastructure, are compared, following the political upheavals of 1989–1990, and key problem areas common to all cities are identified. Current changes in physical urban structure, with examples of particular types of new construction and renovation, and design and investment priorities in the field of housing, office and commerce, industry, intra-city transport, and infrastructure, have been reviewed in the second section.

In many CEE countries, as a response to the pressures of globalization and competition, a shift can be seen in the planning process, moving from the more traditional "master plan" model to strategic planning methods with greater flexibility and adaptability. The third section contains a brief assessment of the success or otherwise of particular post-socialist cities in adapting to and developing new approaches and innovatory planning tools to make their plan-orientated systems more effective and responsive to current development needs. The success, or otherwise, of urban governance in organizing appropriate city management (urban development strategies, policies, and programmes) is examined, as is the importance for city competitiveness of factors for attracting international investment.

## City Development

### The evolution of the spatial structure of CEE cities

At the end of the nineteenth century, three main morphological tissues are identified in the majority of CEE cities, similar to other European towns with long urban traditions:
1. the mediaeval town core (tenth to fourteenth century) with its original street pattern and building structure, more or less preserved;
2. baroque and neo-classical inner city (regular grid pattern) developments from the eighteenth and the first half of the nineteenth century; and
3. the expansion of the city beyond its mediaeval perimeter during the second half of the nineteenth century, as a result of the growth of urban populations resulting from industrialization.

To understand the urban morphological patterns that can be seen in the historical development of the various CEE capital cities, and their development over the last 100 years, it is necessary to identify the most significant socio-political events over that period and their impact on urban development generally. When talking about socio-political history, four major periods in the history of the twentieth century in CEE can be identified:

(i)   1900–1918, the period before the First World War up to the collapse of the Austro-Hungarian Empire in 1918; and 1920, the end of the civil war in Russia;

(ii)  1918–1945, the period between the two World Wars, starting with the "jazz" age;

(iii) 1945–1990, the Cold War period from the end of the Second World War to the economic collapse of the eastern socialist world; and

(iv)  post-1990, the decade of historical changes and transition at the end of the century: the post-socialist era.

Within these main periods, which are defined by the major political changes of the twentieth century, shorter episodes can be identified that affected urban and architectural development in general and in different countries in particular.

To expand on this theme requires a brief historical review of the development of urban form and built structures during specific periods. This offers a contextual framework for a more detailed discussion on the urban transformation of CEE cities after 1990, i.e. the post-socialist cities.

*1900–1918*: The period up to the First World War was very much a period of public uncertainty, but also of hopeful expectation in light of the accelerating pace of technological advances during the previous century that appeared to be continuing.

In the late nineteenth century, the Habsburg cities of Central Europe were the sites of modernization, where industry and finance were concentrated, but they were also places of history and accumulated knowledge, with poly-ethnic and multicultural urban societies. Economic modernization in the Austro-Hungarian Monarchy began considerably later than in Germany and France due to factors including, particularly, lack of liquid capital for industrial development (e.g. banks preferring to lend to the state and the aristocracy whose wealth was secured in land holdings), the relatively late construction of railway lines connecting the Empire's coal-producing areas with steel-producing regions and shipping ports, and a shortage of skilled workers caused by regressive educational policies (Blau, 1999: 13). The Monarchy's cities grew in response to imperial policy and inspiration from the centre. The Crown was the principal client for major cultural initiatives and large-scale modernization projects. The network of railway stations, administrative buildings, cultural institutions, universities, and broad new ring-boulevards with distinctive spatial hierarchies (often by way of destroying mediaeval defensive works), patterns of building, and historicist styles, were built in cities across the Empire (from L'vov and Cernivci to Krakow and Zagreb) as an imperial effort to unify the peripheral urban centres of the ethnically diverse state into a homogeneous civilization.

However, as administrative and cultural centers of the multinational Empire, they had also trans-local even trans-national identities and significance.

It is, of course, impossible to generalize in any meaningful way about the range of urban and architectural responses to the lived experience of modernizing urban society in the cities of Central Europe (e.g. Vienna, Budapest, Prague, Krakow, L'vov, Zagreb, Ljubljana) as they had different urban histories (political and economic structures and culture), but it is possible to identify broad cross-cultural currents, especially in terms of city-building and the conceptual models that dominated planning practice at the turn of the century. The first model, "engineer's planning", was a concept that emphasized rationality and functionality in city operation and technical infrastructure: circulation, sanitation, and hygiene. The second model was that of the city as a biological organism (regulatory plan), which considered the city in its entirety, analysing and planning various infrastructure systems, morphological units, and an extendable urban grid. Most often these ideas of urban design are linked with Wagner and Sitte (positivist and future-orientated versus "nostalgic" and traditional). However, as Blau comments, "for both Sitte and Wagner, an underlying objective of urban design was to reconcile the new with the old, to bring the facts of modern urban life into harmony with traditional concepts of place making" (Blau and Platzer, 1999: 17). In direct contrast to these models of compact city development, the garden city model, pioneered by Ebenezer Howard and his followers and based purely on economic modeling, proposed ideas of suburban, anti-city, semi-rural, low-density developments, encouraged by advances in public transport.

The situation was quite different in Russia at the end of the twentieth century. While Russia was, at the time, the biggest European country, it lagged far behind other European countries in an economic sense. However, as a result of the explosive growth of trade and industry at the beginning of the twentieth century, Moscow started to develop into a city of political and cultural importance, a main commercial centre, and an important rail intersection for the Russian Empire. In the city centre, old estates of the nobility made way for enormous apartment buildings, commercial establishments, banks, and the railway station; some of these were designed in Art Nouveau styles of international quality, but the style that prevailed was eclectic (Kopp, 1967: 43–44). Tenement blocks shot up on the edge of the city as a result of the rapid increase in population. The modernization of infrastructure (e.g. water supply, sewers, gas, electricity, traffic) was disrupted, however, by industrial crises between 1900 and 1903, and the recession that followed.

*1918–1945*: Following the Russian revolution of 1917, and the break-up of the Habsburg empire, the post–First World War period was initially one of new nationalistic euphoria in the newly independent countries of Eastern Europe (e.g. Poland, Czechoslovakia, the Kingdom of Yugoslavia), while the reparations demanded of a demoralized and bankrupt Germany ensured the eventual collapse of the reforming Weimar Republic, laying the seeds of right-wing support for the fascist regime that was to follow. The majority of development in these cities was devoted to expressions of their new-found nationhood, and meeting the increasing demand for urban housing as the agrarian economies of the nineteenth century now began to give way to the new industrial and commercial bases for employment centred on expanded urban centres. This was a situation that served to transform the historic cores of the cities by the incorporation of new government and commercial buildings, and reinforced calls for reforms of the city environments as horses gave way to the onslaught of the private car and motor transport generally. Most of the reforms tended to be based on the models, already established in Britain and America, of the rural suburb. This onset of twentieth-century suburbanization began with the "Garden City" models of Letchworth and Welwyn Garden City (1900–1925), followed by the city-peripheral garden suburbs (without supporting facilities and infrastructure) of the 1920s and 1930s (predominant in Britain). At the same time, however, the influence of the Modern Movement was holding sway (the "jazz" age) throughout Europe (e.g. the BABA district in Prague, Czechoslovakia; the Dessau-Torten settlement in Germany; and Batía town, Zlin, Czechoslovakia, built on the *Cité Industrielle* principles of Garnier, reflecting his notion of a "factory in the garden"). In the Soviet Union, a similar model – Milyutin's linear town conception – was considered to be the best form for new Soviet industrial towns (French and Hamilton, 1979: 9; Banik-Schweitzer, 1999: 68).

Other significant urban models and projects originating in Central Europe at that time – from theoretical ones such as Le Corbusier's *Ville Contemporain* (1922) and Hilberseimer's *Hochhausstadt* (1923–1934) – were all host to an ideal of multifunctional urbanity (Banik-Schweitzer, 1999: 58–71). The evolution of a new scale of urban building and architectonic form – the superblock and megastructure – commensurate with the aspirations of newly established governments, strove to reshape the spaces of production, public life, and cultural representation.

In contrast to Western Europe, where modern architectural design blossomed after the First World War, eclectic architecture in Russia survived through the revolutionary period and even fended off modern architecture. What was revolutionary was that, according to Kopp (1967), the date of birth of Soviet urbanism was precisely determined as 19 February 1918, the day when the decree on the nationalization of land was issued. This marked the beginning of planned urbanization, which, by the decree issued at the end of the war, obliged cities and towns to prepare long-term plans for a period of 25 years, as well as partial master plans.

Moscow's urban renewal in the early 1930s, as the new capital of the Soviet Union, was a socialist version of the City Beautiful Movement. The primary objective was to make an impression and to regain Moscow's "Third Rome" image. The irregular street network composed of ring and radials was to be expanded, and a green belt that would accommodate residential garden districts had to be introduced. Housing blocks in neo-classical style were to rise along the broad boulevards, the rings, and the banks of the rivers Moskva and Yauza.

The scenic character of the city's architectural silhouette, and its spatial order, were to be reinforced by several high-rise buildings, erected at the junctions of main traffic arteries.

The best imperial tradition of City Beautiful urban planning was also a basis for the transformation of Berlin, the capital of the Third Reich, into a symbol of National Socialist power. Speer's plan for the Berlin region proposed a green matrix and the improvement of the radial road system, creating a new north–south axis that would accommodate the most important ministries and public institutions.

The political symbols of totalitarian ideology are invariably associated with order, force, power, and strength (Duwel, 1997: 250). Therefore, metaphorically speaking, architecture and urban planning were to become instruments in the political reconstruction of the Soviet Union and Germany, a pattern that was to be repeated many years later in Romania (Bucharest).

During the 1930s, the rise of modern planning concepts based on the thinking of the CIAM group and Le Corbusier (e.g. the Functional Warsaw plan by Syrkus and Chmielewski, 1934) had a major impact on the other CEE cities. These ideas were in contrast to the influences of the Garden City movement, prevalent in Britain and America, although private-sector housing was still developing its "rural idyll"-based dreams. However, the design of social housing was largely influenced by the high-density community blocks that were being developed in Austria (Karl Marx Hof, Viena) and other major Western European cities, except where such development was thwarted by the incessant spread of fascism. City planning had grown to the extent that visions abounded of the "evil" smoke-ridden city, to be destroyed and replaced with new open spaces and broad boulevards for the increasing streams of traffic. Popular culture spilling over from the West through the new international media of film and radio reinforced these visions (e.g. Alexander Korda's "The Shape of Things to Come"). All this was to avail itself of the real opportunities generated by the Second World War.

*1945–1990*: The destruction wrought by Allied and Axis bombing combined with the collapse of the economic structures of many of CEE's major industrial cities was to be met in 1945 with a wholesale "carve-up" of Europe between the two major powers, leading to the imposition of a stern "command economy" within what became known as the "Eastern Bloc". Grand-scale autocratic master planning geared to Marxist-socialist philosophies of state control meant that many modern development ideas proposed for city living by the pre-war internationalist concepts of urban reconstruction were actually to see implementation under state supervision. Especially during the height of the Cold War (1945–1955), the inner parts of major cities in the socialist regions were forcibly reconstructed in the style of "Socialist Realism", using Moscow as a model (e.g. Semenov et al., General Plan for Reconstruction of Moscow, 1935 [see van Es, 1997]). Shops, often with flats over them, and massive office blocks were built to a virtually uniform pattern of continuous street frontages with residential courts behind (e.g. MDM Complex,

Warsaw, 1952; Stalinalle, Berlin, 1952, followed by similar constructions in Dresden, Leipzig, and Magdenburg). Monumental emphasis was provided by "showpiece skyscrapers in a gothic outline and ubiquitous neo-classical detailing" (Alden, 1998: 364) (e.g. Moscow University and Hotel Ukraine Moscow, 1953; the Palace of Culture and Science in Warsaw, 1955; the planned East German government building in Mitte, Berlin, 1951).

In the design of the built fabric of the divided city of Berlin, the influence of politico-cultural propaganda on the two contrasting worlds is clearly evident. In response to the monumental historicism of Stalinalle in East Berlin, the superficially modernist residential area of Hansaviertel was erected in West Berlin as a deliberate contrast. From the 1950s onward, West Berlin had the role of "display window of the West" and playground of the international architectural elite, a status which reached its height in the late 1970s (see Bosma and Hellinga, 1997: 128–136).

The political distortions of urban development brought about by such aberrations as the "siege" of West Berlin and the resultant massive, politically driven subsidies for development in the Western sector, had little or no influence on other Eastern Bloc cities, where the general effects of the command economy were to stifle individual initiatives and investment in small businesses, the lifeblood of any major city. All this led to a general degradation of urban fabric (contrasted by the occasional showcase development to illustrate the "might" of the socialist philosophies) and, more important for the present financial environment, to the complete lack of any financial incentive for new commercial development in these cities, exacerbated by an inability to establish a "gravity model" of land values related to their city centres. Ironically, many of the historic cores (e.g. Warsaw) managed to retain or rebuild their mediaeval built fabric and spatial characteristics, albeit in poor states of maintenance, while new commercial and industrial development was often of a very utilitarian nature, occurring on virgin peripheral sites. The major problems of the largest Eastern Bloc cities were the new processes of re-industrialization and the burgeoning growth of the need for mass housing, the wholesale implementation of which was also heavily influenced by pre-war functionalist principles; this created the soulless, high-density, high-rise suburban housing estates identified with the immediate post–Second World War era, often with less than adequate community facilities.

However, by the late 1950s, the return of modernism was celebrated as liberation from Stalinism. Long-postponed projects for reform of the building industry started and by the early 1960s new housing districts built in five-storey blocks of modern industrialized panel construction had been established all around the socialist countries (e.g. in Moscow, popularly known as "Kruschevki"). Today, these 50-year-old blocks, with flats built to minimum space standards, suffer from all the commonly identified defects associated with this type of construction, making repair or refurbishment economically impossible. Most of these housing estates were located near to old restored or new industrial districts that added even more negative connotations to their image.

In the period from 1960 to 1990, large housing estates with even higher (tower) blocks of flats continued to be erected on peripheral sites, often based on satellite extension within existing settlement cores. These destroyed or damaged the original historic fabric of these settlements and created major dormitory areas, completely ignoring the earlier concepts of "planned communities" that had been established by both the "suburbanite" Garden City advocates and the modern functionalists of "*Ville Radieuse*" high-rise inclination. Meanwhile, the easing of East–West tension, the limited growth of international trade, and the increasing access by all to international information and awareness of attitudes via new media facilities (telecommunications and TV via satellite) led to a growing awareness by the general population in the East of the inappropriateness and inefficiency of many Eastern Bloc economic structures, when compared with the visible signs of Western consumerism. All this, together with student exchange programmes and other interactive means of information awareness, eventually led, by 1989, to the collapse of popular support for the economic and political structures still prevalent in Eastern Europe. The "wall" came down, and the "market" moved in.

## Changes in the Internal Spatial Structure of CEE Cities in the Post-socialist Era

Current changes towards globalization, the concentration of employment opportunities in the service sector, growing awareness of environmental quality, and the new urban/planning paradigms of sustainable development, on the one hand, and the socio-economic transformation of former socialist countries towards pluralistic democracy and market economies on the other, are the major factors connected with changes in the internal spatial and physical structure of cities, most evident in the CEE capital cities. These changes can be observed at the city level (the city as a whole), and at the level of characteristic city areas such as the historic core, inner city areas, and the outer city (suburban zone).

Currently the characteristic changes in the land-use pattern of post-socialist cities are similar to those identified in other European cities (Bourne in Kivell, 1993):

- growth of the urban fringe, or suburbanization;
- reurbanization/revitalization of the central areas;
- growth of need for infrastructure, especially transport; and
- growth and decline of particular nuclei (urban nodes) (e.g. relocation of industry away from city centres, and establishment of shopping centres on the outskirts of towns).

These transformations of urban pattern are mostly a product of the restructuring of urban activities and social changes rather than of demographic growth.

While the density of built-up structures and the preservation of historical heritage in some CEE capital cities (e.g. Prague, Budapest, Ljubljana, Sofia) constrain the possibilities for new development, the largely post-war reconstructed environments of the inner cities of Warsaw and Berlin, with their numerous vacant open spaces, present many opportunities. However, disputes about restitution and unresolved ownership rights have up to now limited more intensive (re)development in the central parts of Warsaw, while Berlin is booming due to the "*Investitionsvorranggesetz*" ("priority of investment law") that "enables the political authorities to grant the land in the city centre to high capital investors, and merely remunerate the former owners" (Keivani, Parsa, and McGreal, 2001; see also Chapter 7).

Current urban changes in CEE capital cities have been associated predominately with changes in land-use patterns and the physical upgrading of the built structure, influenced by the restitution of private property, privatization processes, and the activities of foreign agencies.

Restitution, coupled with land and property market price deregulation, has had significant impacts upon the urban form. However, the effects have mainly been felt in the historic core (central areas) of the capital cities, since the outer urban areas were mainly characterized by their socialist pre-fabricated housing estates and have been subject to privatization (Sòkora, 1999). In Prague, for example, the vast majority of buildings in the city centre (70 per cent) had already been returned to their original owners by 1994. This process, plus high demand for office and retail space in the central areas of the city, has led to a large price differentiation for residential accommodation between the central and peripheral locations (Keivani, Parsa, and McGreal, 2001).

In most of the CEE countries (e.g. Poland, Hungary, Czech Republic), privatization has taken two basic forms: small-scale privatization arrangements and large privatization programmes (Keivani, Parsa, and McGreal, 2001). The former were largely carried out through auction whereby small retail units, restaurants, and service and manufacturing firms were sold to domestic investors (e.g. Prague). The latter, on the other hand, focused on medium-sized and large state-owned enterprises through tenders and direct sale and was open to both domestic and foreign investors (Keivani, Parsa, and McGreal, 2001). The rapid privatization of social housing in the 1990s has substantially increased home ownership in most of the former socialist countries, with levels ranging from 85 to 90 per cent, well above the EU average of 62 per cent (Tsenkova, 2000) (Fig. 6.1).

Internationalization and globalization processes have especially influenced the economy and culture of the capital cities of the post-socialist countries, principally through capital investment as described in Chapter 5.

Foreign activities have been particularly evident in trade and advance services (e.g. financing, real estate, marketing, media), while foreign developers have become very influential actors in the commercial property development process (principally office and retail space).

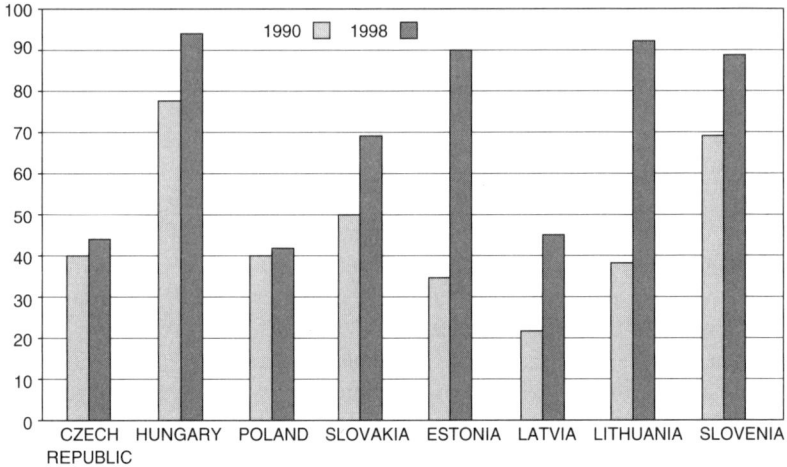

Fig. 6.1  Home ownership, 1990 versus 1998.
*Source:* Tsenkova, 2000; Dimitrovska Andrews, 2002.

Tourism has been one of the most important factors of globalization, usually predominately represented and flourishing in the capital cities of post-socialist countries after the 1990s (e.g. cultural, business, and conference/convention tourism in Prague and Budapest; business tourism in Moscow). It has generated large investments into the accommodation and catering industries. Major international chains have competed to build or acquire hotels in these cities, causing a substantial increase in hotel beds and in the number of restaurants, pubs, and cafés. Contributing to the transformation of the economic base of the cities, these enterprises have also been one of the most important elements of the revitalization of the old parts of the cities.

Internationalization has also had a profound impact on the labour market. The growing number of Western employees working in CEE capital cities (e.g. 50,000 in Prague) is an important force on the residential market, demanding new or reconstructed "up-market" housing and thus contributing to changes in the built environment. Among other factors contributing to internationalization is the growth of cultural tourism and Westernization, in particular Americanization, which has penetrated the daily life of indigenous populations and influenced their consumption preferences and habits. This has invariably been backed up and even driven by "Westernization" of the media (Argenbright, 1999).

Only a minor part of foreign investment has gone into the housing sector. However, such projects can have a considerable influence on social life in particular city areas. The reinforcement of gentrification processes can be expected in inner city areas ("better" status area) and in small projects of "housing for entrepreneurs" that are already being built in the outer city ring or outside the administrative boundaries of capital cities (e.g. Prague, Moscow).

*Commercialization of the Historic Core*

Commercial development constitutes an important force that has substantially contributed to a massive reorganization of land-use patterns in the CEE cities in the post-socialist era. Such development has been recognized as a tool of local economic regeneration and growth, and has often been supported by central government policies as well as by local entrepreneurial-orientated politicians (Sòkora, 1998). Local governments in most of the former socialist countries (especially Hungary and the Czech Republic) have facilitated real-estate and commercial property development using land in their ownership, together with development grants and the easing of planning control and land-use regulation.

A review of the revitalization processes taking place in the historic cores (downtown) of the principle cities in CEE countries reveals comparable similarities, summarized as follows:

- concentration of commercial and government functions;
- development of offices, multipurpose commercial centres, and tourist-orientated facilities, including hotels, restaurants, and retail;
- refurbishment of existing buildings predominates but new development is also present;
- supply of land and buildings for (re)development has resulted from quick privatization of real estate; and the sale or long-term leasing of vacant municipal land has facilitated private commercial development; and
- gentrification promoted by the private sector and city government (luxury municipal dwellings and reconstruction of dilapidated premises and attics into apartments).

Common "negative" consequences of these revitalization processes (showing the inevitable shift to the standard gravity model of values present in cities reacting to market economy pressures) are as follows:

- the decline of residential function (e.g. leasing to commercial uses generates up to 50 times higher revenues than regulated rent from housing);
- non-existence of detailed planning regulation that would constrain these changes: the city government has promoted commercialization by selling or leasing the last empty plots for commercial development, with scant or total lack of recognition of need for public purposes;
- damage to historical heritage: conflicts between the interests of commercial developers and the protection of cultural heritage;
- unsympathetic design of new buildings often does not fit or respect existing morphological context;
- development control procedures have not been well used (e.g. demolition of listed buildings); and
- traffic congestion, parking problems: the decline of public transport caused by an increase in private car ownership and a shift in model split in favour of car use.

*Revitalization of Some Inner City Neighbourhoods*

In the latter half of the 1990s, development interest moved towards certain inner city districts and outer city areas, as a result of structural changes and differentiation in commercial market demand, and the scarcity of available land left in the city centre – for example, rising demand for retail, warehousing, and light industry, and demand for larger-scale office space, now ranging from 1,000 to 15,000 sq.m, previously only up to 500 sq.m.

The urban changes that have occurred in inner city areas can be summarized as follows:

- physical upgrading has been associated more with commercial functions than housing (e.g. secondary business nodes established in strategic locations near public transport and major roads);
- revitalization of older neighbourhoods with higher-quality residential environments, which had retained higher social status during the communist era (e.g. single family houses and villas, and zones of apartment housing dating from the nineteenth century);
- scattered housing (re)development: new apartments for sale in condominiums (virtually no new private rental housing), located in dispersed fashion on vacant zones in the inner city or at the edge of social housing estates. These residential complexes now form well-off residential enclaves within the existing structure of the city;
- residential upgrading and gentrification of small pockets of original village housing in settlements which have been overrun by twentieth-century urban growth of the city;
- differentiation of social housing estates (e.g. revitalization of housing estates in better locations, with improved public transport accessibility and "image"); and
- reduction of industrial uses: large redundant industrial and warehouse zones have been released for other uses, predominantly commercial development, shopping centres, and housing.

Common problems in the restructuring of inner city areas can be identified across most post-socialist capital cities:

- degraded urban areas, areas of former industrial use, barrack sites, and "black" housing (housing built without planning permits);
- undeveloped local centres without clear identities;
- increasing social polarization of housing estates; problems of revitalization, maintenance, and management;
- ad hoc in-fill development jeopardizing continuity of important established city-wide systems (e.g. open space and green areas networks, landscape structure);
- "edge city" development jeopardizing city centre viability, reducing attraction for business and employment (e.g. shopping and business centres on the outskirts of towns); and
- in-fill development with no respect for the characteristic identities of established city areas.

*Residential and Commercial Suburbanization in the Outer City*

The characteristics of urban change in outer city areas are as follows:

- residential suburbanization takes several forms, such as speculatively built housing for sale or sale of plots for housing construction, transformation of existing villages by random developments scattered across the suburban area;
- very limited involvement of foreigners in suburbanization;
- residential suburbanization contributes to a reversal of the traditional socio-spatial pattern of the social city, with the socio-economic status of population declining with distance from the centre;
- commercial development has more significant impact on the transformation of outer city areas than housing construction (e.g. concentration in complexes built along major highways – "ribbon" development – and important transport intersections, and also around subway stations);
- an important proportion of retailing is moving to the suburban zone (e.g. out-of-town shopping centres), and suburban business parks and office complexes are being created (e.g. near to the airport in Prague and Warsaw) – this is largely in response to greater personal mobility with the rise in car ownership;
- no speculative industrial and warehousing development yet, but high potential for development of industrial properties at the major junctions on the motorway network (e.g. Prague, on D1 and D5 highway; Budapest, around M0 and M1 motorways); and
- suburbanization is adding another ring to the existing spatial structure of the city (e.g. Prague, Moscow).

The most significant problems of urban change in inter-city areas can be summarized as follows:

- coalescence of existing traditional village settlements into suburban agglomeration with resultant loss of identity;
- transformation and loss of identity of cultural landscape and cultural heritage;
- pollution of underground water resources due to insufficient technical infrastructure and improper waste management; and
- increase in individual car traffic with resultant congestion and decline in use of public transport, leading to decline in service.

# Restructuring of the Built Environment

## Housing

While the changes introduced in the political and economic systems of former socialist countries have had profound effects on the social and economic situation of their populations, the provision of housing has become one of the spheres to which little or no serious attention has been given in the majority of post-socialist countries. With regard to housing, the most important changes include the withdrawal of direct state financing for new housing construction, the privatization of the previous public housing stock, and the restitution of housing to private owners that had been nationalized during communist rule.

Under the previous socialist systems, housing policy had been aimed at guaranteeing all citizens equal opportunity of access to housing. Although this goal was never entirely achieved in any of the former socialist countries, a varying but continuous supply of housing was nonetheless maintained through the provision of low-cost pre-fabricated high-density housing estates. A substantial amount of the funds required for the construction of these large housing estates was secured through various forms of public financing and state subsidies.

Until 1990, the housing stock of the CEE capital cities, with the exception of Sofia and Ljubljana, was dominated by the public rental sector, although the owner-occupied sector was always substantial, in the form of single private family houses or owner-occupied flats in cooperative or condominium multi-family houses. At this time, because of growing economic problems, public sector housing construction, which in 1980 accounted for between 40 and 60 per cent of new housing production in most of the CEE countries, and even up to 85 per cent in the Baltic countries (Tsenkova, 2000), began to decline, dropping significantly in the early 1990s. Comparative data from 1990 and 1998 (UNECE, 2000) show that the Czech Republic, Slovak Republic, and Bulgaria still managed to maintain a significant public housing supply with more than 20 per cent of total housing stock, followed by Poland, Slovenia, Lithuania, and Estonia with about 10 per cent. However, recent evidence suggests further decline of public supply in this sector; Latvia is the extreme example, with 68 per cent of dwellings completed by the public sector in 1990 dropping to zero per cent in 1998 (Fig. 6.2).

Upon the introduction of housing reforms, post-socialist countries abandoned their previous "provision" role and adopted, instead, the "enabling" principle, which, in theory, requires that households are encouraged to solve their housing problem by themselves (UNCHS, 1992; see also Chapter 3). Under this arrangement, the state has ceased to provide direct financing for housing construction. State intervention, as such, is limited to guaranteeing only the legislative and institutional framework necessary for the efficient operation of the housing market. The state may intervene in exceptional cases only to introduce measures intended to secure market equilibrium in the supply and demand for housing and, in this way, prevent excessive increases in housing prices.

One of the many problems that have arisen after the introduction of these changes has been the failure, in all post-socialist countries, to develop such housing policies as would appropriately replace the dismantled social housing systems. With the exception of the Russian Federation and the former East Germany, a sharp decrease in levels of house construction is characteristic of all CEE countries. The liberalization of the labour market as a consequence of the liberalization of the economy has meant new opportunities for labour mobility

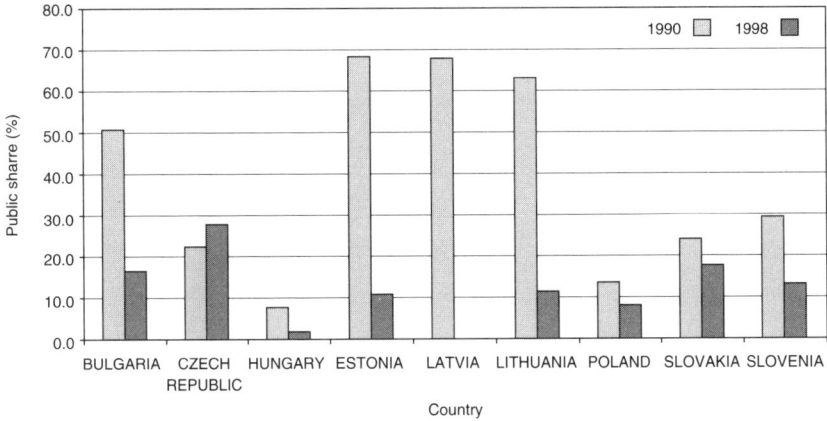

Fig. 6.2 Dwelling completed by type of investor, 1990 and 1998.
*Source:* UNECE, *Annual Bulletin of Housing and Building Statistics for Europe and North America*, Vol. 2000, New York and Geneva: United Nations.

and migration. Due to lack of suitable alternative housing policies to match the new macro-economic situation, however, labour mobility and positive migration have been seriously restricted by growing constraints on the housing market.

Post-privatization housing systems also face a range of new problems. The unsuccessful handling of maintenance and management problems, through inadequate legislative back-up, together with the revival of the general housing market and emerging socio-economic polarization, means that some of the large housing estates are in considerable danger of the effects of ghettoization in the near future. The low share of public housing (usually the worst parts of the housing stock) and the lack of new public housing construction in most of the former socialist countries have left municipalities with no capacity to provide shelter for socially marginalized households. For the first time since 1945, homelessness can be seen as a serious, growing problem in these countries. According to Szemzò (1999), homelessness had reached relatively formidable proportions, by the early 1990s, in Hungary, the Czech Republic, Poland, the Slovak Republic, Russia, and Bulgaria (Fig. 6.3).

*Large Housing Estates*

Large housing estates are the primary innovation of the twentieth century in the search for democracy and humanism in architecture. The bona fide intention was to offer every city dweller pleasant, healthy shelter that could be built quickly and cheaply. Following the extensive damage caused by the Second World War across Europe, and given the high level of population growth and intensive urbanization activity that was occurring, the construction of high-density mass housing offered a very efficient means of satisfying the housing needs of the

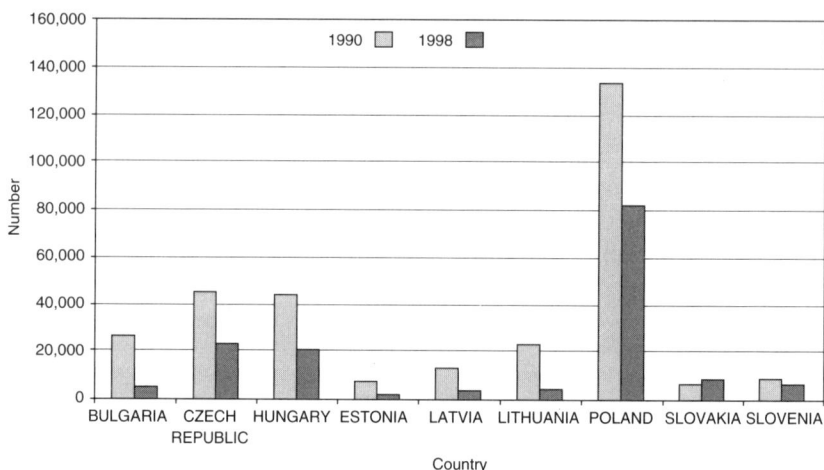

Fig. 6.3 Dwelling stock increase, 1990 versus 1998.

*Source:* UNECE, *Annual Bulletin of Housing and Building Statistics for Europe and North America*, Vol. 2000, New York and Geneva: United Nations.

time, notwithstanding the deficiencies of some low-cost construction. This form of housing provided adequate living standards (sanitation, central heating, and suitably sized flats) to the greater part of the lower- and middle-income populations. Performing the role of dormitory areas, these new residential neighbourhoods were, in most cases, located at the fringes of urban centres, near industrial plants.

While large housing estates (e.g. housing estates with more than 2,500 dwellings) are estimated to account for only 3–7 per cent of the total housing stock in Western Europe, this type of housing construction represents 20–40 per cent of the total housing stock in CEE countries (with the exception of the former USSR) (Knorr-Siedow and Kosiol, 1998). Most of these large housing estates continued to be built in the CEE countries through the late 1970s and 1980s, while in Western Europe the processes of their revitalization and reconstruction were already in full operation.

Nowadays, housing conditions in the majority of these large housing estates are either already very poor or gradually deteriorating. It is estimated, for example, that more than 30 per cent of the dwellings in multi-family housing in Slovakia urgently need extensive repair (Tsenkova, 2000). According to the same source, nearly three-quarters of the dwellings in Lithuania (built between 1961 and 1996) are located in high-rise peripheral housing estates characterized by low energy efficiency, neglected maintenance and repair work, and relatively poor technical quality of buildings and technical infrastructure. In Sofia, where more than 50 per cent of the residents live in large housing estates (see

Chapter 12), professionals have warned of the potential social and functional isolation of these residential neighbourhoods from the rest of the city, should they be allowed to deteriorate further.

As has been explained elsewhere by various authors (Sendi, 1995; Hegedüs and Tosics, 1997; Tsenkova, 2000), the privatization of previous rented social housing at very low cost through capital subsidies has enabled low-income households to become homeowners, oblivious of their inability to meet the current operating costs, let alone the costs for major maintenance and repair work.

By the late 1990s, however, the processes of revitalization and reconstruction of these areas have been present in most of the CEE capital cities.

## Office and Commercial Activities

The most important common feature that has influenced property development in all post-socialist capital cities in the first period of transition is the general lack of premises for commercial use, contrasting with a rapidly growing demand for modern offices and retail space.

In the 1990s, demand for quality office space in city centre locations by foreign and international firms was especially high in Budapest and Moscow, followed by Prague and Warsaw. At that time, there was "virtually no office space of international quality in any of these cities" (Sòkora, 1998), so this demand had a strong impact on the character of property development and redevelopment in their most valuable central locations (e.g. the central business district in Budapest, the business core/historical districts of Prague 1 and Prague 2). Initially, there was a need for smaller units, and this could be accommodated predominantly by refurbishment or/and change of use (from residential to office use) of existing building stock. However, the changing requirements generated by expanding companies demanded larger office space, often in cheaper locations outside the prime property zones, but with good public transportation links (e.g. office park "Graphisoft" and technopark "Infopark" – office and higher education development in Budapest). Probably the most striking example of this kind of development is "The City", the new business centre in Moscow (100 ha), which has been built emulating the design principles of "La Defence" in Paris (see Chapter 14).

By the mid-1990s, a well-established competitive office market was operating in most of the capital cities. In 1995, the total supply of office stock in Budapest and Prague was estimated to be about 2 million sq.m (Incoma, 1996) and in Warsaw about 2.6 million sq.m, with an estimated annual growth in Budapest of 50,000 sq.m; by the second half of the 1990s, the total stock had doubled in Prague and Warsaw (Sòkora, 1998).

At present, as a result of this rapid enlargement, the office market in some capital cities seems now to have developed an oversupply and problems of vacancy (e.g. in Budapest, about 18 per cent of the total stock). In most of the

CEE capital cities, due to a relative lack of financial and technical know-how at the local level, foreign developers/investors have increasingly dominated the development of first-class office space (e.g. in Budapest, 95 per cent of this stock has been financed from abroad; see Chapter 9).

In the mid-1990s, the emerging retail market followed the already developed office market. Notwithstanding the substantial differences in the development of this sector within the post-socialist countries themselves, there are strong similarities in the patterns of distribution of foreign investment in this sector and the consequent effects on the urban restructuring of the capital cities.

In Budapest and Ljubljana, a substantial growth in privately operated retail units had already occurred during the 1980s, while it was not until after 1991 that the development of the retail sector in Prague was strongly influenced by the processes of restitution and small-scale privatization (e.g. 2,500 small retail units were auctioned in the period 1991–1993). In Budapest, however, the "city and district local governments still retain ownership of the majority of small retail units in major shopping streets" (Sòkora, 1998).

Currently, foreign retailers have become a very significant force in all CEE capital cities, either by acquiring existing operations or by establishing joint ventures with local partners. Familiar international retail brands (e.g. Benetton, Max Mara, Marks & Spencers, Tesco, Ikea) and fast-food chains (e.g. McDonald's, Kentucky Fried Chicken, Pizza Hut) can be found not only in the city centres, but also in secondary centres in newer neighbourhoods, changing their image towards a global consumption landscape. Shopping malls in the city centres (e.g. Myslbek Centre, Darex and Koruna Palaces in Prague; Bogusz Centre and Panorama in Warsaw), together with large out-of-town shopping centres located at highway junctions (e.g. Buda Park in Budapest; Janki Retail Centre in Warsaw), can now be found in almost all major CEE cities.

The out-of-town sector has been the most active one, predominantly financed by foreign firms. The domestic retail sector has also been expanding quickly, but most often in downtown locations or residential neighbourhoods and on a smaller scale. Most noticeably, underground passages and basements (e.g. Warsaw, Moscow), even cellars and ground floors of former residential units (e.g. Sofia), have been intensively redeveloped by small private investors.

The biggest retail complexes have been developed with great rapidity on sites of obsolescence; in the case of Hungary, on a reconstructed barracks site vacated by the Soviet Army (the Polus Centre in Budapest) and in the case of Slovenia, in reconstructed warehouses originally used by the former Yugoslav customs service (BTC in Ljubljana).

## Industrial Activities

The reduction of industrial activity after the 1990s, with respect to numbers of employees and industrial land occupancy, is significant for most of the CEE capital cities. In capital cities such as Prague, Budapest, and Ljubljana there is "virtually no demand for speculative industrial and warehousing development yet" (Sòkora, 1998; Dimitrovska Andrews, 2001). In Warsaw, by contrast, demand for new industrial space is very high. There is a strong belief that rapid modernization and increasing direct foreign investment in industrial development will help the Warsaw Metropolitan Area to remain one of the largest industrial concentrations in Poland (see Chapter 8).

The restructuring of the industrial sector has had little impact on the property market (Sòkora, 1998). Privatization of outdated industrial premises and complexes, often in poor condition, has resulted in their lease and sale to multiple private owners, making the subsequent management and maintenance of infrastructure sometimes very difficult (e.g. Warsaw, Ljubljana).

Large, underused (existing or planned) industrial and warehouse zones have been released for other uses, most often for commercial investments and housing.

Currently, these former industrial areas are often seen to represent a problem for the image of major parts of the city, but they also represent a potential land resource for the future (e.g. derelict land along the city centre ring road in Ljubljana; huge areas of derelict land in the "transitional belt" of Budapest, only 4–8 km from the CBD area). Brown-field restructuring for industrial uses is very rare.

Industrial investment is moving out of the capital cities, to green-field locations around motorway junctions just outside the administrative city boundary (i.e. Rudna on D5 and on D1, exit to Ricany, Prague) or even beyond, to agglomerations of smaller settlements ("Western gate", Budapest), or to other regions altogether (e.g. South and West Bohemia in the Czech Republic, the north-western part of Hungary). Other favoured locations for new industrial and warehousing development can be found near to major airport sites (e.g. Warsaw, Prague).

New industrial premises used for production, distribution, and storage operations have usually been built for owner occupation. There has also been a tendency towards the development of combined light industrial, retail, and warehousing zones (e.g. Warsaw Industrial Centre, 36,000 sq.m).

*Transport and Infrastructure*

Increasing efforts to develop international transportation and telecommunication networks have been a common characteristic of most of the post-socialist countries. Priority has been given to the construction of multi-modal transport corridors, to improve connections between national transport networks and those of neighbouring Western countries and to facilitate compliance with higher environmental standards in transport development.

In the last decade, according to results from the *VISION PLANET* project (2000: 33), three main shifts could be observed, determining the role and structure of transport: the shift from railway to road transportation, the shift from public to private and individual transportation, and the shift from domestic to international transportation.

Until the early 1990s, railway transportation played a dominant role in former socialist countries, its share being much higher than in EU countries. Since that time, however, the volume of rail transportation has decreased dramatically in the Eastern countries; in 1994 it was less than 50 per cent of the 1990 level, while road transportation was on the increase. While Western governments are undertaking serious efforts to divert transportation from road to rail, in the Eastern countries a dramatic, market-led shift is still taking place in the opposite direction (*VISION PLANET*, 1999). These shifts are comparable to the shifts that occurred some 40 years previously in Western Europe, now belatedly being countermanded by EU governments.

The same contradiction is reflected in the pattern of projects for transportation network development. While the projects of the Trans-European Transport Network (TEN) in EU member countries are principally focused on modernization and development of high-speed railway networks (80 per cent of financing is devoted to this objective), in the CEE accession countries, 52 per cent of the financing requirement is devoted to motorway construction, while the share for railways is only 36 per cent (e.g. the semi-high-speed railway network in the Czech Republic).

The shift from public to private and individual transport is closely connected with the shift from rail to road. The reasons are also similar: subsidies to public transportation are decreasing, while the number of private cars is increasing dramatically in all post-socialist countries. Apart from environmental and energy efficiency consequences, the public–private shift has additional social consequences – with the decline in public transport, some groups, especially children and elderly people, are left increasingly deprived of the means of mobility. The decline of public transportation is beginning to have serious consequences in the surrounding rural areas of cities and within large urban agglomerations.

The shift from domestic to international transportation is closely connected to structural change of the economy. Within international transportation, another important shift has taken place. In both freight and passenger transportation, the share of transport to and from Western European market economies has increased significantly, while the intensity of transport connections between CEE countries has decreased. In more recent years, however, trade and transport between neighbouring CEE countries has begun to rise again, resulting in a more balanced structure of economic and transport relations.

The concentration of investments in transport in most of the capital cities has focused on the construction of ring roads and expressways for better connection of the city road systems with newly built motorways (e.g. Ljubljana ring road, Moscow third ring). The building and refurbishment of petrol station and parking facilities (e.g. underground and multi-storey garages) can also be observed. Traffic congestion has rapidly become a common problem in all post-socialist capital cities. Thus, in Moscow and Ljubljana, consideration is being given to the possibility of converting the existing traditional rail system into a light rail/ surface metro, while additional metro lines have been built in both Prague and Warsaw (Šašek Divjak, 2002: 1–14).

At present, with regard to infrastructure development, one of the main issues to be addressed is the interconnection of the electricity, oil, and gas pipeline systems of the two halves of Central Europe, which were separated from each other in the past, in order to ensure the diversification of energy sources and security (*VISION PLANET*, 2000: 37).

## Planning and Practices

### Physical Planning and the Development Process

The liberalized thinking of the early years of transition has been characterized by the low political priority given by central government to physical planning, and regional and housing policy (Sòkora, 1994; Dumitrovska Andrews and Ploštajner, 2000). The absence of comprehensive national spatial development strategies and coherent regional policies, together with reforms in local and regional government systems and disputes regarding the basis of new planning legislation, has been significantly evident in many of the former socialist countries (e.g. Czech Republic, Slovenia).

Consequently, land-use planning and the public regulation of the development process and redevelopment at the municipal level since the break-up of the Eastern Bloc has been characterized by the prevalence of ad hoc political decisions and approaches rather than long-term strategic visions, with local governments applying their own strategies, often incorporating elements established under the former systems before 1989. More recently, physical planning at the urban level is now being supplemented by the emerging strategic planning and attempts to implement economic tools for the stimulation and facilitation of local development.

### Physical Planning

Physical planning was introduced or reconstituted in the former socialist countries as a tool for urban development in the early 1960s. The physical plans from that time laid down the macro-spatial structure and general land-use patterns of urban areas, especially focusing on the allocation of land for housing, industrial construction, and transport network arrangements (for more details see Sòkora, 1995). In the former Soviet Union, and most of the CEE countries, town plans had to "nest" within overall national economic plans, translating the requirements of economic planning into land-use proposals, along with centrally prescribed planning and construction standards or "norms".

The amount of services at the city-wide and neighbourhood levels was also planned according to nationally set standards. The protection of agricultural land and the preference for high-density high-rise housing estates on the edges of the inner city led to the creation of compact urban structures and limited urban sprawl. Another characteristic of the urban fabric that can be identified as a result of socialist urban planning is a very low economic utilization of space in city centres due to the insignificance of differential land rents and the absence of a "gravity model" of land values (e.g. lack of definable CBD; see Chapter 3). However, the inadvertent benefits resulting from these processes are the well-preserved historic cores of most of the CEE cities, due to a lack of the type of redevelopment driven by increased land values seen in many West European towns in the post–Second World War period, and also a significant un-redeveloped land-bank of derelict nineteenth-century industry (factories, warehouses, gasworks etc.) that can be released for other uses.

In many former socialist countries, current physical planning and legitimacy of planning development control is characterized by the absence of national and regional spatial development concepts, often with uncoordinated planning efforts by individual municipalities, and inexperienced or weak local governments under strong pressure from developers trying to "cherry-pick" attractive and valuable areas.

The basic regulations governing physical planning and control of the development process in CEE countries are usually provided through parliamentary legislation for physical planning or spatial planning, and building acts or building codes. New laws, which reflect changing conditions, are still under preparation (e.g. in Slovenia) or under discussion by parliamentary committees (e.g. Czech Republic). Physical planning is in the competence of the Ministry of Local Development or Ministry of Environment (see Table 6.1).

Specific examples of recently proposed spatial planning legislation have established the organization of a planning institutional framework on two or three basic levels (local and national for Slovenia and Poland; local, regional, and national for the Czech Republic and Hungary).

In the Czech Republic, the central government has prepared a programme of national development. Regional governments (in operation from 2000) will prepare regional development programmes and regional physical plans, which in particular will specify the organization of regional transport and technical infrastructure and delineate the protected environmental zones. Regional governments will also coordinate the harmonization of municipal physical plans. Municipalities are to be the core institutions for physical planning. The principal planning documents are the Municipal Development Programme, the Land-use Plan for the whole municipal territory, and a detailed Regulation Plan for urban zones. In the case of small municipalities, land use and building regulation principles are applied through a single plan.

In Prague, the old Master Plan from 1986 has been replaced by a provisional plan from 1994. The City Master Plan of 1994 was based on the 1986 plan, from which it takes the idea that areas with relatively fixed urban structures where

Table 6.1 Physical planning and development control

| Country level | Czech Republic | Hungary | Poland | Slovenia | Germany |
|---|---|---|---|---|---|
| Planning legislation | Act on Physical Planning and Building Regulations (Building Act) (1976, last amendment 2000) | Act on Regional Development and Physical Planning (1996, 1999); Building Act (1996) | Building Code (1993); Spatial Planning Act (1994) | Building Act (2002); Spatial Planning Act (2002) | Federal Building Code; Federal Land Utilization Ordinance; sectoral planning low; building low |
| National level | | National physical plan (2002 under consultation with Brussels) | | Spatial development strategy; spatial regulation ordinance | Guidelines for regional planning |
| Regional level | Regional physical plan; strategic plan | Regional development plans; regional physical plans (not legally binding documents) | | Regional development programme; regional concept of spatial development plan | Regional development programme; regional spatial plan |
| Local/municipality level | Master plan (land-use plan for all territory); municipal development programme (strategic plan) | Development Concepts and programmes; master plan | Master plan | Spatial development strategy including concept of urban development and concept of landscape development and protection; spatial regulation ordinance | Land-use plan for cities (FNP); sectoral development plans (STEP); local development plan (Städtebauliche Rahuenplanung, Bebauungsplanung); development programmes (BEP) |
| Communes level (districts, boroughs) | Regulatory plan – detailed regulation plan for urban zone | Detailed local plans (land-use plan) | Detailed local plans (land-use plan/local taxation function) | Local plans (detailed regulation plans for urban zone) | Detailed plans |

Table 6.1 (continued)

| City level | Prague | Budapest | Warsaw | Ljubljana | Berlin |
|---|---|---|---|---|---|
| Formal planning documents | Master Plan (1986) (provisional plan, 1994; new zoning plan, 1999); Prague Strategic Plan (2000); Prague Regional Operational Programme (1999) | Master plan* (1988, 1993, 1998; new zoning regulation); Urban Development Concept | Master plan (1980, 1994, more suited to market conditions); Warsaw Development Strategy 2010 (2001); Spatial Development Plan (under preparation) | Master plan (1986, 1998, minor changes adopted, mainly traffic); new master plan, 1st phase: spatial development concept (2002) | Land Use Plan (FNP); general zoning framework; main transportation network; spatial distribution of public services |
| Informal/ supplementary documents | Urban Study (area-specialised analytical study) | Sustainable development concept, programmes and action plan; rehabilitation programme | Condition and Directions of Spatial Development of the Capital City of Warsaw Study (2001); development condition studies of the individual municipality | Strategy for Sustainable Development of the City (2002) | Development programme (BEP); urban development plans |
| Development control | Planning permits; building permits | Planning permits; building permits | Planning permits; building permits (can be combined in construction permit) | Planning permits; building permits (can be combined) | Building permits |
|  | Plans certificate** |  |  | Plans certificate |  |

Notes:
* Dual nature of municipal system: Municipality of Budapest and 23 district municipalities. Budapest districts have a large autonomy in decision-making process, including the field of planning and development (e.g. development priorities and detailed zoning regulation).
** Certificate of approval for building use and occupation, after the completion of building.

176

major functional changes are not expected should be declared as "Stabilized Zones" (Sòkora, 1995). These Stabilized Zones cover about two-thirds of Prague's territory and have served to create a binding document for the preparation of local regulation plans and for the planning application procedure. Developments proposed in non-stabilized zones will require the preparation of detailed planning documentation (urban studies), financed by the developer. The new Master Plan of 1999 and the plans of Stabilized Zones use a principle of mixed zoning that has replaced the mono-functional zoning used by physical planners in previous decades.

In 1999, Prague adopted another important planning document, the Prague Strategic Plan (PSP) (http://www.praha-mesto.cz/strateg.plan/obsah.asp). This points "a realistic way forward to prosperity and a healthy living environment whilst upholding and developing the values for which Prague is regarded as one of the most beautiful cities in Europe". Its further development in land-use planning and sectoral concepts should redirect mono-centric Prague into becoming poly-centric and into solving "various pressing problems like the provision of housing and transport, or how to balance historical conservation of sites with city expansion and development" (Prague Strategic Plan: 9).

The Strategic Plan for the City of Prague is therefore a specific consensual agreement on what has to be achieved over the next two decades. Together with the Prague Regional Operational Program (ROP), prepared subsequently, it is not merely a political proclamation but is becoming an important tool in city management. It addresses the reintegration of Prague into the wider European structures, as well as giving guidance for support of the housing market, ensuring its availability, and economic and sustainable management of energy, water, and other resources, all working to enable transition from a mono-centric to a poly-centric city structure. Based on these programmes, the city will seek financial support from EU funds for its most important projects.

Now, most of the CEE capital cities have also begun preparation of similar strategic planning policy documentation (e.g. Riga, Budapest, Ljubljana, Moscow).

The City of Riga is at present preparing a comprehensive Economic Development Strategy to supplement the City Master Plan from 1996 (Francis, 2000). Thus, the starting point to planning a better urban environment is to identify the key economic trends that influence the community and to work within these to establish achievable goals.

Strategic planning for Moscow is dominated by concerns over the future size of the city and the pressing need for urban regeneration. The 1992 Moscow structure plan marked the end of restrictive growth policies for the city, but also identified the need to maintain the existing size of the city. The 1996 review of this document has confirmed and reinforced planning policies focused on regeneration and refurbishment, and the need for the city economy to move from an industrial base towards a service-orientated system (Alden, 1998).

In Warsaw, the old plan from the 1980s was considered too rigid, detailed, and outdated. A new Master Plan for Warsaw, more suited to evolving market conditions, was approved under the old legislation in 1992. It divides the city into broad zones that define dominant land-use types. The plan for each land-use zone indicates a series of preferences, allowances, and exclusions. The main function of the Master Plan was to coordinate the local plans of communities within the Warsaw area, including environmental protection. It also established public investment programmes for transport, public infrastructure, and public facilities such as schools and hospitals. In 1999, new principles of spatial development have been presented based on two documents: "A Study of the Conditions and Directions of the Spatial Development of the Capital City of Warsaw" and "Warsaw Development Strategy up to the year 2010". Together with the development condition studies of the individual municipalities, these documents form "the uniform vision of the spatial development of the city as a whole, without neglecting instruments necessary for implementation" (Matusik, 2001). The new policy is intended to reconcile two almost contradictory priorities: the maintenance of the present character of the city's historic tissue and its traditional spatial layout, and growth in the city's development potential (e.g. new urban plans for the Western Centre, Praga Port, and the Siekierkowski Arc) (Matusik, 2001). Planning guidelines divided the city into six types of zone with dominant functions derived from their present or planned development, and with proposed planning instruments that include height zoning and a detailed definition of building density.

The 1980 Budapest Master Plan had concentrated on continued development of housing estates. It also reinforced the decentralization of the central city to district centres. The 1998 revised Master Plan laid emphasis on rehabilitation and growth of the inner city. In 1996, the Master Plan had been supplemented by a plan for the metropolitan region. A new Concept of Urban Development and a new Concept Master Plan were approved in 1998.

The new planning regulations for Budapest are administered by the current dual-municipal system of 23 district municipalities and the Municipality of Budapest. Recent changes in planning legislation also called for a new division of urban planning, which is characterized by a duality of planning by-laws: framework planning regulations by the Municipality of Budapest and detailed physical planning by the district municipalities. The Master Plan defines the framework-zoning aspects: principal function, excluded functions, maximum density, maximum floor area (plot) ratio, and minimum green area ratio. It also defines certain regions of the city as "areas of primary importance" from a city-wide point of view, for which the district planning processes should involve the Municipality of Budapest as well. Because of the dual nature of the municipal system, during the planning phase of the Master Plan, a long harmonizing process was carried out with each of the district municipalities, in consideration of all their development initiatives. Based on this so-called framework-zoning plan, the districts will create their own, detailed zoning plans, adjusted specifically to the specialities of their neighbourhoods (Hegedüs, 1999).

The new Master Plan of Budapest has allocated most of the new development areas, intended for residential development, to the outskirts of the city, in many cases as an extension of existing residential neighbourhoods. Besides their peripheral location, it is significant that almost all these development sites are on non-built-up areas, former allotment gardens, or other uncultivated agricultural land. Although these new residential areas can offer an alternative to the exodus into the suburban region around Budapest, they should not be the only solution the city offers. The map of residential-use areas shows a wide gap in between the inner zone and the outskirts. It is clear by now that greater attention should focus on this transitional zone, and more areas for residential land use should be allocated in this part of the city. The restructuring of this zone is of primary importance, yet it seems that residential developments will only happen with difficulty in this part of the city. In such areas there is often a heavy burden in terms of the additional costs associated with clearing these "brown-land" sites – cleaning contaminated soil, removing derelict industrial structures and machinery, and dealing with run-down industrial buildings – and it is unrealistic to attempt to service these costs from returns generated by residential developments (Hegedüs, 1999).

The new General Plan for Sofia (2000) attempts to address both "the strong chances of the city as a transportation, communication and information centre of integrated Europe" (its role as an international administrative centre of the Balkan region) and problematic aspects of city development such as the revitalization of large housing estates, legislative regularization of "black" neighbourhoods, and new zones for housing within the city limits (see Chapter 12).

Currently, the city of Ljubljana is preparing two important planning documents: A Strategy for Sustainable Development, and the New Master Plan. The first phase of the Master Plan, "The Concept for Spatial Development of the City of Ljubljana", has been prepared, and together with the draft version of the Strategy for Sustainable Development of Ljubljana was issued for public consultation in June 2001. The Concept is innovative in giving more detailed consideration to design issues, issues relating to the city's image, and implementation mechanisms. A City Design strategy for the urban area as a whole is proposed (e.g. enhancement of the local context, identity, and legibility of the public urban space) together with Urban Design Frameworks for characteristic urban areas (e.g. rebuilding of degraded urban sites with respect to the contextual identity of each area). For implementation of the plan, the Concept has proposed three layers of instruments for spatial development: Urban Regulation Plans, Urban Design Projects, and Urban Regulatory Measures (urban land policy) (Cerar et al., 2002).

*The Development Control Process*

Development is regulated through two aspects: planning control (planning permits) and the building application procedure (building permits). Such planning and building permits must be obtained for virtually all developments. In Slovenia and also in Poland, for certain types of development, these two permits may be combined in one to reduce procedural time. Usually, permits are issued by specialized (building) departments of the municipal authorities (except in Slovenia, where central government offices are responsible for issuing such permits). The authorities check that applications are in accord with approved planning documentation, and the procedure requires acquisition of individual permits from organizations such as the water, electricity, and gas supply authorities. Environmental impact assessment is required for larger development projects (e.g. in the Czech Republic, for industrial, trade, and storage complexes with areas of development exceeding 3,000 sq.m) or those that have been specifically defined in the planning acts. In addition, the protection and conservation of historic buildings is regulated by preservation or heritage authorities, which are independent of the local government authorities.

The procedure of issuing planning permits in most of the CEE countries is intended to take two months from the submission of a complete and appropriately prepared application. However, the granting of planning permission can become a bureaucratic and time-consuming procedure, which takes as much as 15–18 months (e.g. Poland, Slovenia) in cases where proposals conflict with current planning policy (Dimitrovska Andrews, 2000).

During the building application procedure, detailed drawings of the proposed building are checked by building officers. The building permit can only be granted to those who have already obtained a planning permit and have provided proof of ownership rights. The processing period should not exceed two months. Building permits entitle the recipient to commence construction work.

Planning and building permits are usually valid for a two-year period. After the completion of a building, certificated plans or a certificate of approval must be issued by the building department in order for the building to be occupied and used.

## City Development Practice and Management

A review of recent planning documents in the post-socialist capital cities shows that in the last decade urban policies have revolved around the search for comparative advantages in order to establish a revitalized role within the European city network, re-establish transportation networks, encourage a shift from antiquated industry to service-based economies, and resolve the problems of efficient guidance and regulation of private initiative in the dynamic process of restructuring. The common characteristics of development practices in post-socialist cities in the first half of the 1990s can be summarized as follows:

- generally, a liberal approach by central government and local politicians when assessing urban development proposals, especially in the field of regulation of development, urban planning, and housing policy;
- reduced state involvement in as many matters as possible;
- short-term, highly individualized, ad hoc decisions by local politicians and administrators taking precedence over the preparation of long-term plans, strategy, or visions of city development;
- the ideological rejection of forward planning as being counter to free market activities, along with unwillingness of urban planners to identify or adapt to

new circumstances – this has fostered unregulated, politicized urban development practice;

- weak development control, of especial concern regarding regulation of redevelopment in the historic cores; and
- suburban projects uncoordinated with development in the city; very little or no coordination between city government and the local governments of surrounding municipalities in the (functional) region of the capital cities.

From the beginning of the 1990s, the "post-socialist era", even the new generation of master plans have been prepared in an old-fashioned spirit of physical planning (e.g. Prague), lacking up-to-date implementation mechanisms. There is very limited use of economic tools to encourage urban development, and consequently, a lack of economic incentives (e.g. the establishment of urban development corporations).

The forces behind the majority of transformation processes at the national level in the areas of economic, political, and technological development have not been matched by equal rates of change at the local city level. There is a need for changes in the field of education and the introduction of new knowledge, new urban management techniques, the development of institutions and use of modern methods in managing local community development, and most significantly, a need to embrace partnerships with the private sector, urban planning by consensus, negotiations with investors, project-orientated work, and market activities.

Invariably, cities did not have at their disposal the full spectrum of necessary land policy instruments (differential taxes, pre-emptive rights, expropriation, compulsory purchase etc.) for use in the area of spatial planning and urban regulation. Therefore, their power to influence local development was impaired. Only Germany is an exception in this respect, where the "priority of investment law" enables the political authorities to grant land to high-capital investors that want to buy to invest in favourable projects in the city centres (see Chapter 7).

However, recent developments in the planning and management of post-socialist capital cities show positive change towards comprehensive strategic approaches to redevelopment, and enhancement of the image of the cities as a whole and of the identities of their characteristic areas. Standardized formats for local plans have been introduced for achieving better quality documentation and consequently better quality physical development (Masrkowski, 2000). Other changes include:

- transparency of planning and management of the city, for better involvement of the general public in the decision-making process;
- greater integration of physical planning and real-estate regulation in order to shape the built environment more efficiently;
- simplification of procedures for planning permission and better responsiveness to developer needs; and
- urban renewal orientated towards reintroduction of vital and liveable public open spaces.

*Impact of the European Union in Physical Planning*

The predominant influence of the European Union on spatial planning in the post-socialist countries (EC, 1997) has occurred directly through:

*1. Legislation, especially harmonization of environmental laws.* Environmental issues are becoming a powerful force in shaping development patterns in Europe, both through their influence on systems and policies for spatial planning, and through the interaction of new mechanisms and policies specifically designed for environmental protection. The concept of "sustainability" is becoming a major factor not only for the formulation and implementation of planning policy, but also for the instruments and procedures of planning.

*2. Policy, on matters with a spatial dimension.* Trans-national policies defined by the European Union have had important implications for planning systems and policies, both in Member States and CEE countries, especially concerning the TEN. National infrastructure plans have been prepared which have important spatial implications for development opportunities along the TEN corridors and their junctions with local motorway systems within each capital city's region.

*3. Policy formulation and implementation, notably cohesion policy supported by Structural and Cohesion Funds.* Funding programmes will have a direct spatial impact on post-socialist countries in the context of regionalization, preparation of regional development plans, and the establishment of regional development agencies for the organization and review of structural fund spending. In most of the CEE accession countries, these processes have intensified over the last few years.

As well as the relatively direct impact of the European Union through law, policy, and funding, the European dimension is reflected in other ways; in changes to planning systems in CEE countries, and indirectly to the physical planning of cities in those countries. Recent changes to planning systems to some extent show an increasing concern with strategic planning, not only at the regional level, which in part reflects the perceived growing importance of European integration, but also at the city level (e.g. Prague, Warsaw, Ljubljana). The problems created by limitations within the spatial planning system have been recognized both by Member States and by CEE countries. These can be identified as:

- the lack of effective plans, mechanisms, or policies to deal with Europe-wide issues;
- the difficulties of tackling cross-border issues within two or more different planning systems;
- the absence of mechanisms to coordinate spatial planning policy and land-use regulation with EU funding programmes. Delays in the production of policies and plans are said to have hindered the implementation of regional policy and the most effective use of funding in some EU regions, and these issues could mean real problems for CEE accession countries (EC, 1997: 40).

On a more positive note, there is evidence of the impact of the European Union and other international policies through:

- the adoption of objectives, guiding principles, and criteria for sustainable development in most of the planning documents and policies of CEE cities (e.g. European Spatial Development Prospective [ESDP], Green Paper on the Urban Environment, Habitat Agenda, Agenda 21);
- the promotion of new planning methods, and exchanges of know-how on city planning and management, through networking of research institutes, city planning departments, city authorities, and other important actors in the planning process; and
- the operation of international real-estate investment (foreign firms; the loan activities of the European Investment Bank, World Bank, and other international banks, particularly German and Austrian); this is dominant in city transformation and restructuring processes, and is influencing morphology and organizational structure within urban areas, especially in Prague, Budapest, and Warsaw – the most important CEE "gateway" cities.

## Conclusion

A historical review of the impact of the socio-political events of the twentieth century on the evolution of Central and Eastern European cities shows great similarities in their internal spatial organization and urban development structures through four distinctive periods: before the First World War (the Austro-Hungarian Empire), between the two World Wars (the newly independent countries), after the Second World War (the socialist period), and after 1990 (the transitional period).

Ten years after the fall of the Iron Curtain, the countries in Central and South-Eastern Europe are still facing huge challenges in economic and social development, most evident in the rapid transformation of urban structure especially in the capital cities. The function and image of downtown districts (historic cores), inner city areas, and the outer city (urban-rural fringe) are changing rapidly. The dangers of damage to historical cultural heritage, uncontrolled urban sprawl, congestion, and social segregation are imminent. Therefore, new types and instruments of urban management and planning are needed to meet these challenges.

Observations of current town planning practices in both EU Member States and CEE countries (EC, 1997; Dimitrovska Andrews, 2000) have revealed that the ideas of the "urban plan" as a fixed blueprint for the future, and the urban designer as a "master" of the city, have been superseded by reality (Bosma and Helinga, 1999). "Master plans" are losing their role, and are being forced to change from "compulsory" guidelines to "strategic" management plans.

Managing change and adapting urban fabric in a responsive manner to rapidly shifting economic goals will be essential for the successful non-destructive revitalization of post-socialist cities in the new millennium.

Within the fast-growing processes of globalization and instability, "mastering" the city has become a more varied and complex process, involving a wide range of actors who must learn to assimilate change into the very processes of managing that change. In this respect, there is a need for the following:

- additional non-statutory planning documentation such as visions of strategic alternatives, scenarios, design briefs, and guides to help architects, developers, and local planning control officers to reach better and more appropriate design standards in development proposals, preserving local identity and context;
- negotiations with local planning officers regarding any planning proposal, to take account of economic viability both of the scheme, and in relation to satisfying relevant local needs (planning gain); and
- involvement of the public in the early stages of preparing statutory development plans through the use of "community planning" approaches such as "Action Planning", "Planning for Real", and "Gaming" techniques (Wates, 1996).

The need for institutional reforms and the lack of strategic planning are regarded as the major obstacles to urban development. In addition, the lack of coordination between local (regional) and central authorities and, in turn, a city's urban services, has major implications for economic competitiveness and the international image of the city. However, there is evidence of increasing concern that these problems can only be resolved by an integrated approach between different actors, at both the local (regional) and central (national/ state) level. It is also increasingly recognized that a fully integrated economy can only be achieved with the support of high-quality, coordinated infrastructure; this requires improvement of the intra- and inter-urban transport systems and environmental quality of the built environment. City governance is becoming more proactive in encouraging economic investment and public–private partnerships, with cooperation between local (and regional/state) politicians and the business community, essential for promoting the city internationally.

## Acknowledgements

This chapter is based on a research programme (Spatial Planning, 1999–2003) funded by the Ministry of Education, Science, and Sport of the Republic of Slovenia. I am indebted to both Dr Breda Mihelic and Dr Richard Sandi, from the Urban Planning Institute of the Republic of Slovenia, for their invaluable contributions and assistance. Thanks also to Professor Georgia Butina Watson, from Oxford Brookes University, and Dr Ludòk Sòkora, from Charles University Prague, for their valuable comments on earlier drafts of this chapter.

# REFERENCES

Jeremy Alden, Stephen Crow, and Yana Beigulenko, "Moscow: Planning for a World Capital City Towards 2000", *Cities* 15(5), 1998, pp. 361–374.

Robert Argenbright, "Remaking Moscow: New Places, New Selves", *Geographical Review* 89(1), 1999, pp. 1–22.

Renate Banik-Schweitzer, "Urban Visions, Plans, and Projects: 1890–1937", in Eve Blau and Monika Platzer, eds, *Shaping the Great City: Modern Architecture in Central Europe 1890–1937*, Munich, Prestel, 1999.

Berlin, *The Land Use Plan for Berlin (FNP 94)*, 1999.

Eve Blau, "The City as Protagonist: Architecture and Cultures of Central Europe", in Eve Blau and Monika Platzer, eds, *Shaping the Great City: Modern Architecture in Central Europe 1890–1937*, Munich: Prestel, 1999.

Koss Bosma and Helma Hellinga, eds, *Mastering the City I: North-European City Planning 1900–2000*, The Hague: NAI Publishers/EFL Publications, 1997.

Budapest, *Városfejlesztléi koncepció* [Strategic Development Concept], 1999.

Marjan Cerar, Kaliopa Dimitrovska Andrews, Mateja Doléal, Ferdo Jordan, Igor Jurańi, Aleš Mlakar, Alenka Pavlin, Andrej Prelovšek, Tomá Souvan, and Ivan Stanic, eds, *Prostorski Plan Mestne obcine Ljubljana, Prostorska zasnova* [Spatial Development Concept for Ljubljana], Ljubljana: Mestna obcina Ljubljana, 2002.

Evelin van Es, "Moscow 1935", in Koss Bosma and Helma Hellinga, eds, *Mastering the City I: North-European City Planning 1900–2000*, The Hague, NAI Publishers/EFL Publications, 1997.

Kaliopa Dimitrovska Andrews, "Mastering the City: Globalisation versus Local Identity", in Ooi Giok Ling, ed., *Model Cities, Urban Best Practices*, Vol. 1, 2000, pp. 52–59.

Kaliopa Dimitrovska Andrews and Zlatka Ploštajner, "Local Effects of Transformation Processes in Slovenia", *Informationen zur Raumentwicklung* 7/8, 2000, pp. 435–449.

Jorn Duwel, "Berlin 1938", in Koss Bosma and Helma Hellinga, eds, *Mastering the City I: North-European City Planning 1900–2000*, The Hague: NAI Publishers/EFL Publications, 1997.

European Commission (EC), *The EU Compendium of Spatial Planning Systems and Policies. Regional Policy and Cohesion*, Luxembourg: Office for Official Publications of the EC, 1997.

R. Anthony French and F. E. Ian Hamilton, eds, *The Socialist City: Spatial Structure and Urban Policy*, Chichester: John Wiley & Sons, 1979.

Victoria Hegedüs, "Restructuring the Former Industrial Belt of Budapest – Attractive Locations for Residential Developments?", paper presented at ENHR-MRI Conference, Balatonfüred, 1999, 25–29 August, unpublished.

József Hegedüs and Iván Tosics, "Transition from the East-European Housing Model – Heading to Where?", in *Housing in Europe*, Hòrsholm: Danish Building Research Institute, 1997.

Ramin Keivani, Ali Parsa, and Stanley McGreal, "Globalisation, Institution Structures and Real Estate Markets in Central European Cities", *Urban Studies* 38(13), 2001, pp. 2457–2476.

Philip Kivell, *Land and the City: Patterns and Processes of Urban Change*, London: Routledge, 1993.

Thomas Knor-Siedow and Barbara Kosiol, eds, *A Future for Large Housing Estates: European Strategies for Pre-fabricated Housing Estates in Central and Eastern Europe*, Berlin: European Academy of the Urban Environment, 1998.

Anatole Kopp, *Ville et Revolution*, Paris: Editions Anthropos, 1967.

Tadesz Markowski, "Recent Developments in Housing and Planning in Poland", *Latest Developments in the Field of Housing and Planning*, The Hague: IFHP, 2000.

Wojciech Matusik, *The Evolution of Spatial Planning in Warsaw and its Metropolitan Area*, Warsaw: Department of Spatial Planning and Architecture, City Hall of the Capital City of Warsaw, 2001.

Anne Power, *Estates on the Edge: The Social Consequences of Mass Housing in Northern Europe*, London: Macmillan Press Ltd, 1999.

*Prague Strategic Plan* [http://www.praha-mesto.cz/strateg.plan/obsah.asp].

Richard Rogers and Mark Fisher, *A New London*, London: Penguin Books, 1992.

Richard Sendi, "Housing Reform and Housing Conflict: The Privatisation and Denationalisation of Public Housing in the Republic of Slovenia in Practice", *International Journal of Urban and Regional Research* 19(3), 1995, pp. 435–446.

Richard Sendi, "Housing Construction in the Transition Period: Slovenia's Non-starter Situation", *Housing Studies* 14(6), 1999, pp. 803–819.

*Spatial Policy in Warsaw*, Warsaw: Promotion Department of City of Warsaw, 2001.

Karel Stejskal, "Town and Country Planning in the Czech Republic", *Latest Developments in the Field of Housing and Planning*, The Hague: IFHP, 2000.

Luděk Sýkora, "City in Transition: The Role of Rent Gaps in Prague's Revitalization", *Tijdschrift voor Economicshe en Sociale Geografice* 84(4), 1993, pp 281–293.

Luděk Sýkora, "Local Urban Restructuring as a Mirror of Globalization Processes: Prague in the 1990s", *Urban Studies* 7(31), 1994, pp. 1149–1166.

Luděk Sýkora, "Prague", in Jim Berry and Stanley McGreal, eds, *European Cities, Planning Systems and Property Markets*, London: E & FN Spon, 1995.

Luděk Sýkora, "Commercial Property Development in Budapest, Prague and Warsaw", in Geörgy Enyedi, ed., *Social Change and Urban Restructuring in Central Europe*, Budapest: Akadémiai Kiadó, 1998.

Luděk Sýkora and Zdenek Cermák, "City Growth and Migration Patterns in the Context of 'Communist' and 'Transitory' Periods in Prague's Urban Development", *Espace, Populations, Sociétés*, 1998.

Hanna Szemzò, "Facing Homelessness in the Countries of Central and Eastern Europe," paper presented at ENHR-MRI Conference, Balatonfüred, 1999, 25–29 August, unpublished.

Mojca Šašek Divjak, "The Settlements Development in Ljubljana Region in the Corridors of the Railway Transportation", *Planum*, 2002, pp. 1–14 [http://www. planum.net].

Luděk Sýkora, "Changes in the Internal Spatial Structure of Post-Communist Prague", *GeoJournal* 49(1), 1999, pp. 79–89.

Francis Tibbalds, *Making People-Friendly Towns: Improving the Public Environment in Towns and Cities*, London: Longman Group UK Ltd, 1992.

Sasha Tsenkova, "Policy Shift and Housing Market Responses in Slovakia and Lithuania", paper presented at ENHR Conference, Gävle, 2000, June 26–30, unpublished.

UNCHS (Habitat), *Global Strategy for Shelter to the Year 2000. GSS in Action*, Nairobi: United Nations, 1992.

UNECE, *Annual Bulletin of Housing and Building Statistics for Europe and North America 1998*, New York, Geneva: United Nations, 1999.

*VISION PLANET: Strategies for Integrated Spatial Development of the Central European Danubian and Adriatic Area, Guidelines and Policy Proposals*, Vienna, 2000.

Nick Wates, *Action Planning*, London: The Prince of Wales's Institute of Architecture, 1996.

# Part 2

## Inter- and intra-urban transformation of captial cities

# 7

# Berlin: From divided to fragmented city

*Hartmut Häussermann and Andreas Kapphan*

## The Uniqueness of Berlin

Berlin's situation is quite unlike that of any other city within the Federal Republic of Germany. Until 1990, the city was divided into two: the West, which belonged to the political system of the Federal Republic of Germany; and the East, which served as the capital of the German Democratic Republic (GDR) or East Germany. In 1990, Berlin became the capital of a reunited Germany. Since then, a tremendous change in the economic and political sphere, as well as in housing and the social structures of the districts, can be observed. Furthermore, the social composition of the neighbourhoods has undergone a transformation as a result of recent migratory movements in and out of the city.

Today, the City of Berlin has 3.36 million inhabitants, living in an area of 889 sq.km, with 63 per cent of them in the West of the city. Berlin is one of 16 *Bundeslander* (federal states) in Germany with 12 districts in the West and 11 in the East. Following the radical political collapse of the GDR in 1989 and the reunification of both cities in 1990, there has been continuous economic, social, and spatial transformation affecting both parts of the city. The eastern half is harder hit, however, in that virtually all conditions for urban development have changed: redistribution of property, new planning laws, new players, new investors (private investors, the federal government, the federal state, the borough administrations, and citizen interest groups), and new planning concepts. The old quarters which were largely neglected or cleared near the Wall during GDR times now lie at the heart of the city's reconstruction and modernization. Furthermore, the city centre in the former East is partly under redevelopment.

The present transformation in East Berlin can be described as "marketization", which is the opposite of its development for 40 years between 1949 and 1989 – "demarketizing" or "decommodification" are the terms which come closest to describing the basic transformation undergone during the transition from capitalism to socialism. East Berlin's development can only be described to a certain extent as that of a "socialist city", since the "Capital of the GDR" was erected on the soil and structures of the old city, and so was made up of both old capitalist and new socialist structures. The "demarketizing" process was guided by centralist planning, which aimed for a representative city form on the one hand, and yet for the prerequisites of a "socialist way of life" on the other. Private ownership and a market economy were then reintroduced, which led to radically different control over the city and the re-evaluation of many areas. The labour market was, of course, also deeply affected by the political change of 1989 – the East is now witnessing extreme job losses (in industry and public administration) and increasing numbers of industrial areas are becoming derelict.

For the time being, changes in West Berlin also mean a re-evaluation of land, which will produce new use patterns in the medium term. Land prices rose sharply immediately after the unification, along with rents upon the agreement of new tenancies. Following the decision to make Berlin the seat of the federal government again, a boom exploded in the West in real-estate investment, which was speculated mainly on the city's new functions. At the same time, structural economic changes took place that soon compensated for the changes in the city economy that West Berlin had experienced in the last 20 years. The West is also suffering from the new financial basis of urban policies, as all the subsidies that were bound to its role as the "Outpost of the Free World" during the Cold War period rapidly disappeared. The loss of subsidies for industry and public administration resulted in the loss of many jobs and led to even higher unemployment rates in the West of the city.

The following discussion of transformation and globalization processes in Berlin outlines, first, the starting point of both halves of the city, and second, an analysis of the city's position in the global and regional system. The third section deals with the economic transformation and changes in the built environment, especially in property distribution, restitution of private property, and the ways in which new players became active in urban development. In the fourth section we focus on spatial structure and transformation, and present research results on aspects of social and ethnic segregation, new mobility structures, and the social transformation of the city's districts. The last section deals with the question of how best to manage the transformation and what the international position of Berlin in the cities network will be in the future.

## Heritages

During 40 years of division, both halves of the city had to fulfil all the functions of a capital city: West Berlin had almost 2 million inhabitants, East Berlin some

1.5 million. The city centre belonged to the East after the division, which for the West meant relocating the central establishments of a city government and creating a new central business district (see Heineberg, 1979).

## East Berlin

The old centre of the capital of the German Reich formed the territory on which buildings for the new socialist capital would be erected. The fundamental design of the new city centre was a demonstration of political power over market values for urban land. Land was no longer a commodity. Thus, new plans for the city were realized, and new streets and buildings constructed, whose dominance was designed to mark the victory of socialism.

The centre resumed its function as a base for state political and economic administration, as well as high-grade commercial establishments. The more centralized an establishment was, the more important and symbolic its location in the city. Unlike the tendency in capitalist cities to displace residential use from the centre and adjacent quarters by expanding tertiary uses, multi-dwelling buildings in the socialist city were indeed built on purpose in the centre and surrounding districts. Of course, the new, centrally located flats were reserved for top officials only.

While construction investment was channelled into major, representative political and economic buildings, and as flats were being built in residential quarters in certain inner city areas (and especially on the periphery of the city), the old quarters were left to decay. Building grand new areas while neglecting old quarters is a characteristic of socialist urban policy. Suburbanization by means of single-family housing – as was and still is typical in Western cities – did not occur in the socialist city, since modern, compact, high-rise estates were built on the periphery. As a result of this type of urban expansion, the previous high density in inner city districts fell from 179 inhabitants per hectare in 1950 to 111 by 1988. On the other hand, population density in the outer boroughs rose from 17 to 20 per hectare, reaching 43 per hectare in the newly constructed estates.

## West Berlin

West Berlin lost all its political functions after the Second World War and could not gain major importance in the Federal Republic of Germany since it was only an associate member. Furthermore, a new city had to be developed in the West after the division, yet West Berlin's structure was deliberately made or kept decentralized. New city functions sprung up around the Zoo station area and Kurfuerstendamm, but the city structure still lacked a distinct centre.

Reconstruction of the city's master plan after the severe damage caused by the Second World War adhered quite closely to the original. There were actually some changes made to street networks and building structures in the redevelopments of the 1960s, but the switch to careful renewal through the redevelopment and modernization of old buildings was not made until the 1980s.

Suburbanization did not occur in West Berlin as it did in other Western cities, since the city was closed in by the Wall from 1961. Furthermore, there were very few private investments and nearly all investments in housing were subsidized by the state. The construction of flats in the West also took the form of compact new housing estates built on open space in the periphery. One could say that housing estates in the dispersed city form – which is so typical of modern urban development – was not the typical form of suburbanization in Berlin. Today, therefore, the extensive city of Berlin is confined by a relatively clear city boundary surrounded by sparsely populated land. Since the reunification, however, suburbanization in the form of single-family housing has begun.

## The Berlin-Brandenburg Region

Berlin is a city-state and thus it is a municipality and one of the 16 Bundeslander of the Federal Republic of Germany. This is important for policy-making because policy strategies can be formulated on the state level much better than in a municipality. Berlin formulates its own programmes for labour market, housing, education, and so on. The 23 districts of the city are only local administrative units without municipal rights.

With its 3.36 million inhabitants, Berlin is the largest city in Germany and exceeds the population of the two next largest cities, Munich and Hamburg, put together. As a state its turnover is small in size compared to other Bundeslander. After unification, efforts were made to merge with the surrounding state of Brandenburg. The state of Brandenburg is not very densely populated and, with its 2.54 million inhabitants (1995), is smaller than Berlin. The merging of the two states was expected to reduce administrative costs and local competition, and thereby help formulate common planning strategies. Especially because of suburbanization of people and industries, Berlin wanted to get back the taxes it had lost from those who left the city (Fig. 7.1).

At the beginning of the 1990s, experts expected immense growth of the Berlin-Brandenburg region. The city was forecast to expand population from 3.4 to 3.8 million, while the surrounding municipalities of Berlin in the Brandenburg state were expected to increase from 0.9 to 1.9 million inhabitants by 2010 (von Einem, 1991: 60). All in all, this would mean a total population in the Berlin agglomeration of 5.7 million inhabitants by 2010. Another prediction expected only 4.9 million inhabitants, though this still represented an increase in population.

Population in West Berlin began to increase again after 1985, long after a steady decline from 1961 when the Wall was built. In East Berlin, by contrast, population was constantly rising after 1961. However, population began to

Fig. 7.1  Berlin and surrounding municipalities in the state of Brandenburg.

decline after 1993 in both parts of the city as a result of suburbanization in the neighbouring areas of Brandenberg (see Table 7.1).

Other migration flows are of minor importance for Berlin. Like most other European cities, Berlin loses inhabitants by natural decrease. There are more deaths than births among urban populations, and stable numbers of inhabitants are only possible through migration (see Table 7.2). In the beginning of the 1990s, immense movements from other areas of Germany to Berlin were expected because of the relocation of government functions there, but this did not actually happen. In fact, 150,000 persons came from outside the Berlin

Table 7.1   Population in the Berlin-Brandenburg region

| Year | Berlin | | | Surrounding municipalities in Brandenburg | Berlin-Brandenburg Region |
|---|---|---|---|---|---|
| | Total | West | East | | |
| 1980 | 3,211,991 | 2,059,462 | 1,152,529 | 798,108* | 4,010,099 |
| 1985 | 3,243,469 | 2,027,883 | 1,215,586 | 805,489 | 4,048,958 |
| 1991 | 3,443,575 | 2,164,131 | 1,279,444 | 779,925 | 4,223,500 |
| 1993 | 3,461,421 | 2,170,411 | 1,291,010 | 780,525 | 4,241,946 |
| 1995 | 3,446,039 | 2,156,943 | 1,289,096 | 806,386 | 4,252,425 |
| 1998 | 3,358,235 | 2,103,190 | 1,255,045 | 887,433 | 4,245,668 |

Notes: *Figure of 1981.
*Source:* Statistisches Landesamt Berlin, Landesamt für Datenverarbeitung und Statistik Brandenburg.

region to Berlin, but only 10,000 of them from other parts of Germany. The figures show that in 1998 especially there was an enormous increase of migrants from other parts of Germany to Berlin, but this is only a statistical artefact. Due to a new tax on residents who have to pay their income tax in another city, most of these "second residents" decided to change their official residence to Berlin.

Migration into Berlin mostly comprises foreigners who came from Eastern European countries during the 1990s, including Russia, Kazakhstan, Poland, and countries of the former Yugoslavia. The migrant population in Berlin is increasing, as a result of migration and higher natural increase. The number of non-Germans – according to citizenship – is stable, because naturalization among non-Germans became more and more accepted between the migrant and the German populations. Their number in 1998 was 440,000 or 13 per cent of the population, being 17 per cent in West Berlin and 5.4 per cent in East Berlin. While the old migrant groups settled in the West before 1990 and have stayed there since, new migrants settle in both halves of the city so that the share of migrants is now also increasing in the East. However, numbers of migrants continue to be relatively small in the East, and ethnic communities like the Turkish in Kreuzberg (in the West) have yet to develop.

## The Economic Transformation

The year 1990 was a year of big expectations for the growth and development of Berlin. Because of the decision that the city would become the new capital of a united Germany, an enormous increase in population and employment was expected. But the reality turned out to be very different, and the 1990s in Berlin saw a decrease in population, labour force, and employment followed by a rise in unemployment and poverty.

Table 7.2 Migration to and from Berlin, 1991–1998

| | 1991 | 1992 | 1993 | 1994 | 1995 | 1996 | 1997 | 1998 | 1991–1998 |
|---|---|---|---|---|---|---|---|---|---|
| Net migration within surrounding municipalities | 158 | −787 | −3,938 | −9,752 | −14,522 | −18,884 | −28,471 | −30,300 | −106,496 |
| Net migration with rest of Germany | 823 | −1,436 | −3,031 | 1,356 | 2,304 | 103 | 1,305 | 9,300 | 10,724 |
| Net migration with foreign countries | 24,447 | 34,277 | 29,162 | 17,248 | 22,224 | 14,265 | −962 | −400 | 140,261 |
| Sum net migration | 25,428 | 32,054 | 22,193 | 8,852 | 10,006 | −4,516 | 28,128 | −21,400 | 44,489 |
| Net migration per 1,000 persons | 7.4 | 9.3 | 6.4 | 2.6 | 2.9 | −1.3 | −8.3 | −6.4 | 13.2 |
| Inhabitants | 3,443,575 | 3,456,891 | 3,461,421 | 3,452,284 | 3,446,039 | 3,428,644 | 3,387,901 | 3,358,235 | −85,340 |

Source: Statistisches Landesamt Berlin.

Table 7.3  Employed persons and the labour force in Berlin

|  | Berlin | | West Berlin | | East Berlin | |
|---|---|---|---|---|---|---|
|  | Employed persons in 000s | As % of labour force | Employed persons in 000s | As % of labour force | Employed persons in 000s | As % of labour force |
| 1991 | 1,690 | 78.1 | 1,028 | 74.8 | 662 | 83.6 |
| 1994 | 1,610 | 76.5 | 994 | 75.3 | 617 | 78.6 |
| 1998 | 1,477 | 74.4 | 875 | 71.8 | 602 | 78.6 |

*Source:* Statistisches Landesamt Berlin: Micro-Census.

The labour force decreased from 1.88 million in 1991 to 1.82 million in 1997. Employment declined from 1.69 million in 1991 to 1.48 million in 1998 (see Table 7.3). This trend already indicates the economic crisis taking place in Berlin after unification. In East Berlin, the decrease in employment was 9 per cent between 1991 and 1998, the collapse occurring especially between 1990 and 1992 and stabilizing in the following years. It would have been even more extreme if there had not been a possibility for East Berliners to commute to work in West Berlin. In 1998, one-third of the employed persons of the East commuted to West Berlin. Correspondingly, the decrease in employment in West Berlin may be described as a process that occurred especially after 1995, with a loss of 15 per cent of jobs in 1995–1998. These trends can be seen in all the individual districts, but job decline can be said to be considerably high in the inner city districts of West Berlin, e.g. in Neukoelln, the number of jobs declined by 22 per cent from 1991 to 1998.

So, one may definitely speak of a general decrease in employment, but a closer look shows divergent patterns of development in different economic sectors, and this offers additional information. In fact, job loss is concentrated in several sectors and branches. Data on employment by economic sector are available for those who are registered as "liable to social security". Their number declined from 1.38 million in 1992 to 1.16 million in 1997 (see Table 7.4). In contrast to the figures mentioned above (Table 7.3), these data do not include a large proportion of part-time jobs, self-employment, and civil service, and thus the number of employed is smaller. Due to suburbanization, the slight decrease in the economically active population cited above accompanies the decrease in employment. The decrease between 1992 and 1997 is particularly noticeable in the manufacturing industries, where more than one-third of the 270,000 jobs have disappeared. In East Berlin, however, about 80 per cent of manufacturing jobs were already eliminated before 1992 (see Fig. 7.2), with steep declines in manufacturing and public administration (with the loss of the GDR capital function).

A similar decline in employment can be observed in nearly all other economic sectors. Only the services with a diverse range of blue- and white-collar jobs

Table 7.4 Employed persons liable to social security according to economic sectors, Berlin (000s)

| Year | Total | Production industry* | Construction industry | Trade | Transport and communication | Financial and insurance companies | Services | Public administration** |
|------|-------|----------------------|------------------------|-------|------------------------------|------------------------------------|----------|--------------------------|
| 1992 | 1.378 | 301 | 113 | 170 | 112 | 43 | 421 | 218 |
| 1994 | 1.294 | 248 | 118 | 153 | 100 | 43 | 434 | 198 |
| 1997 | 1.162 | 205 | 103 | 137 | 79 | 42 | 427 | 169 |

Notes:
*Including agriculture, forestry, energy, and mining.
**Including social insurances and non-profit organizations.
*Source:* Statistisches Landesamt Berlin.

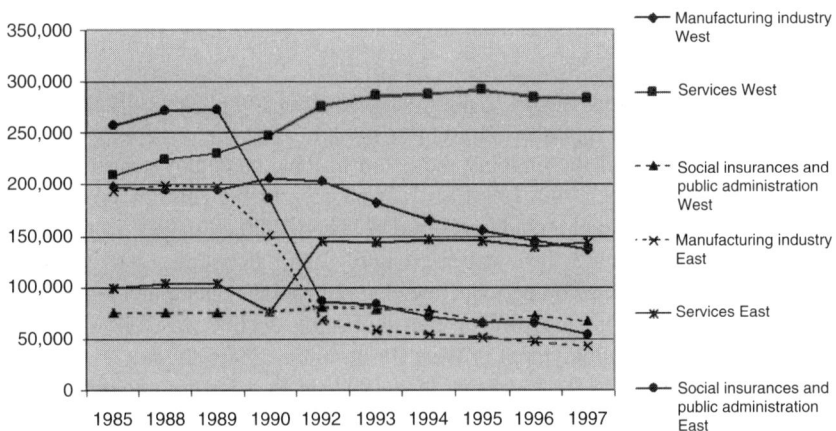

Fig. 7.2  Employment according to economic sectors, East and West Berlin.

have gained employment between 1992 and 1997, both in East and West Berlin. Figs 7.2 and 7.3 illustrate the developments mentioned: extreme loss of jobs in the production industries in both parts of the city, and a growth in the importance of the service industries, where the main expanding branches are consultancy, cleaning, and security services (Kraetke, 1999).

To explain the phenomenon of the sharp decrease in manufacturing in both parts of the city, one has to consider the different political and social preconditions in East and West Berlin. In West Berlin before the unification, manufacturing used to rely heavily on public subsidies. After 1990, however, when the public subsidies were stopped, the sector lost competitiveness. The situation of East Berlin's manufacturing, on the other hand, was determined by a

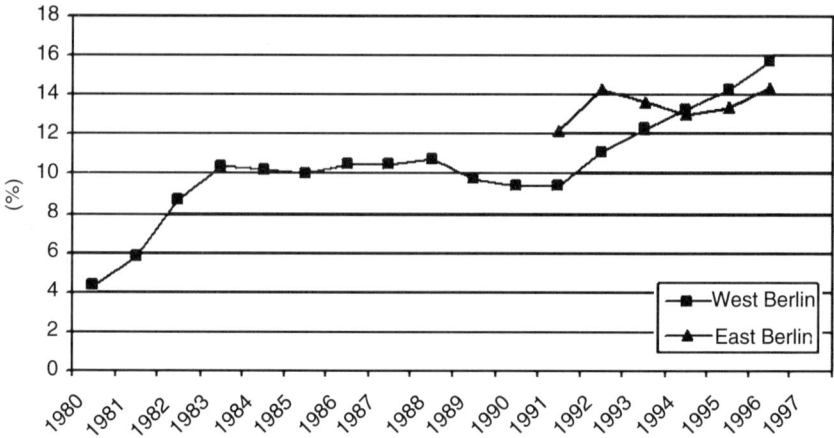

Fig. 7.3  Unemployment rate in East and West Berlin, 1980–1997.

radical structural change caused by the transformation from a centrally managed socialist economy to a capitalist free-market model.

As a consequence of the ongoing reduction in jobs, unemployment increased continuously during the 1990s (see Figs 7.2 and 7.3). In West Berlin, however, a rise in unemployment had already occurred between 1980 and 1983, from 4.3 to 10.4 per cent; the figure then stabilized until 1990. Economic activities and investments in the unification period somewhat reduced the unemployment rate to 9.4 per cent in 1990–1991. However, this short-term decline was followed by a continuous rise in unemployment in West Berlin in the 1990s, the latest available figure being a rate of 17.9 per cent in June 1997. In East Berlin, unemployment rose from 12.2 per cent in 1991 to 14.3 per cent in 1992, hovered between 13 and 14.4 per cent until 1996, and then increased to 16.5 per cent in June 1997. Since 1994, a higher unemployment rate was observable in the West than in the East. Since 1997, no separate figures for East and West Berlin have been available. The 1999 unemployment rate for Berlin as a whole was 17.6 per cent. This was considerably higher than the average rate of Germany and the rates of the West Bundeslander.

As a consequence of the decreasing number of jobs, access to the labour market gets more difficult for the unemployed and new migrant groups from abroad. Thus the number and proportion of long-term unemployed (more than one year) grows constantly: in 1991 it was 27.9 per cent of the unemployed, in 1999 34.1 per cent. Long-term unemployment is more serious in the Western districts, where it grew from 34.6 per cent in 1995 to 38.5 per cent of the unemployed in 1998. In the Eastern districts it was 19.6 per cent in 1995 and increased to 26.2 per cent in 1998. The structure of unemployed according to gender is also different in the two parts of the city. Since 1994, redundancies in the manufacturing industry have been increasing, so the majority of unemployed in Berlin are male (56 per cent in 1998), especially in the inner city districts of West Berlin. However, in the new districts of East Berlin (e.g. Marzahn), more women are unemployed than men. This can be explained by the higher labour-market participation of women in the former GDR, which now results in higher unemployment in East Berlin. The major groups affected by unemployment are unskilled workers, young people, people over 50 years old, and migrants. Those who combine two or three of these characteristics are much more likely to be unemployed, e.g. young unskilled migrants.

## Will Berlin Become a Metropolis Again?

The term "metropolis" must be understood as the heart of a network of cities, the dominant centre of a region. For a city to be a true metropolis, the centres of different functional areas must overlap: it must be not only the political centre but also the economic and cultural centre of the country. Then and only then does it make sense to call a city a metropolis. Prior to the Second World War, Berlin was doubtless such a metropolis, although this did not mean that other German cities such as Hamburg, Leipzig, Frankfurt, and Munich were on the level of provincial cities in the way that was true for every large city in France or England outside Paris or London.

To help answer the question posed, it is necessary to provide a historical overview first, followed by an assessment of developments in the service sector during the last 10 years, to assess where Berlin stands today compared with other service industry centres, and analyse potential fields of growth that may occur in the city. Despite powerful tendencies in the direction of spatial decentralization and suburbanization of economic activities, high-level service functions in the world's large cities are still concentrated in central locations. Ideas about the future function of the city within the German and European city system are thus closely linked to perspectives for the old and new centre of Berlin. In the 1920s and 1930s, the Mitte district was the expression of Berlin's economic vitality, and even today, economic rebuilding is concentrated around symbolic sites such as Friedrichstrasse and Potsdamer Platz. Because of this, the question of where in Berlin the spatial "focus points" for the service sector were, are, and could be, will also be discussed here.[1]

### Historical Overview

An indicator of the great economic importance of Berlin in the pre-war period is the city's share of total employment in Germany. In 1939, more than 10 per cent of all employed persons in Germany worked in Berlin (see Table 7.5). The city even accounted for 9 per cent of all German manufacturing jobs, with large

Table 7.5  Berlin's share of employment in Germany, 1939–1989 (%)

|  | 1939 | 1961 | 1989 |
|---|---|---|---|
| Industry | 8.7 | 4.7 | 3.8 |
| Trade and transport | 10.6 | 5.5 | 5.3 |
| Service enterprises | 15.9 | 8.3 | 5.0 |
| Government and organizations | 16.5 | 7.7 | 7.1 |
| Total | 10.3 | 5.6 | 5.0 |

*Sources:* Workplace censuses, employee surveys, national accounts of the federal states, authors' calculations, and estimates.

electrical and machinery companies such as Siemens, AEG, Osram, and Borsig contributing significantly to the city's economic clout. An 11 per cent share in the fields of trade and transport was largely a result of the big department stores and the headquarters of federal infrastructure companies such as the national railway company (Reichsbahn), postal service (Reichspost), and airline (Lufthansa).

Berlin's role as a metropolis in that period is most clearly visible in the sphere of private service enterprises. The city was the German centre for banks, insurance companies, publishers, and cultural institutions. Looking at the development of the culture industry, which at that time was in its germinal stage, Berlin was in fact a European metropolis. It was the centre of the glittering, glamorous world of film, radio, and television – more than any other city in the world at that time. This high concentration of services is reflected in the employment rate as well: 16 per cent of all persons in Germany employed in the service sector were employed in Berlin. This was nearly as high as the share of government and public organizations, where 16.5 per cent of all jobs were in the capital city.

When examining the spatial distribution of private and public services in the city at that time, it is particularly striking that they were highly concentrated in a relatively small area. The business life of the city was in the immediate vicinity of the government offices, which were located on Wilhelmstrasse – the German Downing Street – in the baroque quarter known as Friedrichstadt, between Friedrichstrasse station and Leipziger Strasse. Because of this proximity of business and government, the area became known as "the city" during this period. There were different quarters within Friedrichstadt: the hotel quarter was north of the street Unter den Linden; the banking quarter was on Franzoesische Strasse and the streets Unter den Linden/Behrenstrasse; the insurance companies were clustered around Mohrenstrasse, south of the banking quarter; the fashion/designer clothing quarter had established itself around the Hausvogteiplatz plaza; and south of Leipziger Strasse, a new quarter was emerging with offshoots reaching into the newspaper quarters and the new film quarter. This "mixed use" in Friedrichstadt was complemented by the University, elegant shops and department stores, bars, cafés, operas, revue theatres, cabarets, and so on. Thus, at any given time of day, different functions dominated within the same space.

It is well known that the Nazis wanted to make Berlin the centre from which they would dominate the world, and that because of this, Berlin soon lost most of what it had possessed before. After the end of the Second World War, the city was divided into four zones among the four allied powers occupying it, and was placed under international law. The banks moved to Frankfurt on Main, most insurance companies relocated to Munich, and both Hamburg and Munich became the media centres of West Germany. The large industrial companies left Berlin as well and greatly contributed to the development of Munich and Stuttgart as modern industrial centres. Not least in importance, the political leadership of West Germany was taken over by the region of Bonn/Cologne. East Berlin, on the other hand, was the capital of the GDR, but suffered severe population losses. In 1961, the year in which the Berlin Wall was built, the city's share of total employment in Germany was only 5.6 per cent, about half of the 1939 level.

The decline in the economic importance of Berlin continued until the phase immediately preceding German reunification. In 1989, Berlin's share of total employment was only around 5 per cent. This decline is particularly conspicuous when looking at the development of West Berlin, which lost almost all of its supra-regional economic importance. The only exceptions were the cultural sector, which received large federal subsidies, and the also heavily subsidized industrial sector, which was still manufacturing products that were long since being made outside large cities elsewhere. The share of unqualified employees in West Berlin was three times as high as in comparable regions. In West Berlin, the main employer was the city administration, which received 50 per cent of its funding from West German taxpayers.

East Berlin, by contrast, had been transformed into the absolutely dominant metropolis of the GDR at the expense of the Saxon cities of Dresden and Leipzig. In 1989, one-third of the employed persons in the GDR who could be identified as working in the service sector were concentrated in East Berlin. However, because the process of tertiarization – that is, the increase in the importance of services compared to the production of goods – turned out to be much higher in West Germany than in the GDR but for the most part left West Berlin behind, the city completely lost its special function in the area of service enterprises. This area's share of total employment in 1989 was, at 5 per cent, close to the average for all sectors, but two-thirds lower than in 1939. Only in the fields of government and public organizations, with an employment share of 7 per cent in both East and West Germany, could one speak of a functional surplus – and this was reached thanks to Berlin's role as an outpost of the West and as capital of the GDR.

The loss of Berlin's economic importance was also conspicuous when looking at the cityscape (see also Heineberg, 1979). The vital downtown area of the pre-war metropolis became, through its division, a border zone. In the East, large parts of Friedrichstadt were abandoned following the 17 June 1953 demonstrations, due to the area's "dangerous" proximity to West Berlin. Shortly thereafter, both the Potsdamer and Leipziger Platz became border zones and the quarter around Leipziger Strasse was torn down. The GDR built a new centre further to the east. Marx-Engels Platz was designed to be the centre of political power, while Alexanderplatz, with a large department store, a high-rise hotel, representative offices of the nationalized industrial complexes, and pedestrian zones, was to be a consumer and communications centre. Between these two prominent points, a large open space was created, and the television tower (Fernsehturm) was placed in its centre. During the GDR period, the historical remains of mediaeval Berlin were almost completely wiped out and Friedrichstadt was largely emptied. In the Western part of the city, on the other hand, the area around the tree-lined avenue Kurfuerstendamm was developed into the centre because it had historically been a central entertainment and shopping quarter. The new downtown grew up around the Gedaechtniskirche (Memorial Church) and the intersection of Joachimstaler Strasse and Kurfuerstendamm, although this area never had the multifunctional network that is typical of city centres. It could not have such a network: aside from small regional branches of banks, insurance companies, and publishing houses, there were no more supra-regional services left in West Berlin.

## Development after Reunification

Immediately after the reunification of Germany and of Berlin, experts all over the world assessed the economic perspectives for development of the city to be extremely positive. Whether in politics, science, or real estate, there were almost euphoric expectations of growth based above all on a foreseen expansion of services in Berlin. Thus, forecasts from the early 1990s predicted growth in employment of more than 200,000 new jobs by the year 2000. These high expectations of growth are manifested particularly in the numerous new building projects that have been undertaken – especially offices, not only downtown, where a "new age of expansion" on Friedrichstrasse was being spoken of, but also on the outskirts and in former industrial areas. Examples of the latter are the AEG (Nixdorf) factory grounds in Wedding, the old Borsig grounds in Tegel, and the redefined use of the industrial grounds in Oberschoeneweide and near the Oberbaum Bridge; once extensive production areas for electronic devices, light bulbs, machines, and other such products, these have now become spaces for services and contain offices, loft apartments, small businesses, and cultural establishments. The grounds of the EAW (Elektroapparatewerke) in Treptower Park are a prototype of this development. For numerous decades, switches, manometers, and instruments were produced in an attractive turn-of-the-century brick building. Today, this is the site of Berlin's largest office building, Allianz Insurance, which was designed to partially integrate the original building. Two further office buildings – the Twin Towers – are located near there on the extensive industrial grounds.

Actual economic development after 1989 looks quite different, however, and initially contradicts the forecasts on all fronts: total employment did not increase, but rather, the number of jobs sank yearly. Economic development in Berlin – like that in Germany as a whole – can be divided into two different phases. The first phase was defined by a severe disparity between development in East and West Germany; the changes in employment associated with this lasted from 1989 to 1992. With the political and economic collapse of the GDR, East Berlin lost its leadership role in politics, the party, and the economy. By 1992, nearly 40 per cent of jobs had been lost. This is much more than in other areas of the former GDR, even though employment fell by almost 30 per cent in some of the new federal states. In the former West Berlin, 1989 brought a phase of economic boom to the city. Because of high demand from the "accession area" GDR, employment figures, especially in trade and services, skyrocketed. Berlin had retrieved its function as the centre in relation to the outlying suburban areas through the fall of the Berlin Wall. In only three years, from 1989 to 1992, employment grew by nearly 15 per cent. In the old federal states this growth rate was, at less than 7 per cent, not even half as high during the so-called "boom years".

Since 1993, employment developments in West and East Berlin have increasingly aligned themselves with one another. In both halves of the city, a single negative development can be observed up to 1997, which at the end of the period was again marked by higher losses in employment. Once again, from 1993 to 1997, nearly 15 per cent of jobs were lost. In West Berlin, the decline amounts to a total of little more than 8 per cent – which corresponds to about half of the gain in jobs between 1989 and 1992. The reduction of employment in East Berlin is still high compared to that in the new federal states, and West Berlin also remains well behind the progress being made in the other old federal states. The years 1996 and 1997 show that West Berlin's economic ties with economic development in the West were severed because of the loss of large segments of industry.

In sum, Berlin's economic weight within Germany has further declined in relation to the situation prevailing prior to reunification (see Table 7.6). Berlin's share of total employment shrank from 5 per cent in 1989 to 4.6 per cent in 1992, and further to 4.3 per cent in 1997. The decline is particularly severe in manufacturing, crafts, and construction. Here, the positive effects of the construction boom in Berlin were more than counterbalanced by the negative effects of the slump in Berlin's industry. Large parts of West Berlin's industry cut back production in the wake of the new federal policy of subsidy reduction.

Table 7.6  Berlin's share of employment in Germany, 1989–1997 (%)

|  | 1989 | 1992 | 1997 |
| --- | --- | --- | --- |
| Industry | 3.8 | 3.2 | 2.8 |
| Trade and transport | 5.3 | 4.8 | 4.0 |
| Service enterprises | 5.0 | 5.6 | 5.5 |
| Government and organizations | 7.1 | 5.9 | 5.7 |
| Total | 5.0 | 4.6 | 4.3 |

*Sources:* National accounts of the federal states, authors' calculations, and estimates.

Others used the opportunity presented by the opening of borders to move production into outlying areas. In East Berlin, only a few businesses or parts of businesses managed to make the leap out of technologically obsolete GDR industry and into the market economy. New industry rarely came to the city – especially because a severe recession had begun in West Germany.

In the area of government and organizations, Berlin's share is also on the decline. This is above all an expression of the "liquidation" of the party and state apparatus of the GDR, which was particularly labour-intensive, but it is also a result of the increasing financial problems of the city-state of Berlin, which today has to fund its own budget largely single-handedly. The western part of the city is no longer the showplace and eastern outpost of the Federal Republic of Germany. Accordingly, less tax funds flow from the national government to the Berlin senate now than before 1990. This, too, has led to reductions in public spending.

The boosted development in the area of supra-regionally orientated services described here has perceptibly improved Berlin's potential for future development. Even the simple increase in the number of supra-regionally orientated service enterprises provided more opportunities for internal networking and training of specialists, giving Berlin added agglomeration power. However, one must also recognize that with the end of the boom resulting from reunification, Berlin is now entering more and more into "normal" competition with other service industry centres. In a national framework, mostly cities in West Germany appear as competitors. These are the cities that had taken over the central functions from Berlin after 1945 and expanded them successfully. In the area of administrative functions, the decision to move parliament and the government prepared the way for Berlin; today, the city is once again the centre for high-level national functions of the government and political parties. Economic organizations, too, are now returning to Berlin. The Association of German Chambers of Industry and Commerce (DIHT) and the Confederation of German Employers' Federations (BDA), for example, have moved into elegant quarters with a close spatial relationship with the government.

There is no question that in the German parliamentary democracy, economic associations play an important role. The real decision-making power, however, rests with businesses, especially in the current age of globalization. Thus, in Berlin's economy, economic associations have only minor significance. With regard to the economic functions that were at least as important as government functions in defining Berlin's position in pre-war times, the perspectives for the future are still largely open – if not to say vague.

In a system of increasing international networking and decentralized organization, Berlin cannot and will not be the pre-eminent centre of supra-regional services that it was before the Second World War. Thus, Berlin will not again become *the* metropolis of Germany. Nevertheless, Berlin is the largest German city and has a higher population density in its inner city districts than any other city in Germany. The surplus value of such a large city lies in its unique quality of encouraging and cultivating diversity and eccentricity – a process that is almost "natural" in such a large group of people, with their various lifestyles and cultures. The great theoretician of cities and cultural philosopher Georg Simmel recognized this at the beginning of this century. The heterogeneity and diversity of a large city is fertile ground for economic and cultural innovation. Berlin must, however, be prepared to allow variety and to make spaces available within the city where the synergy of economic, cultural, and social tensions – in a positive sense – can be lived out and utilized. And where would that be more possible, one must ask, than in the city's centre?

Despite – or perhaps because of – the emptying of the city's centre that was executed by socialist city planners, the opportunity now exists to allow not merely a mono-functional office district to develop, but rather a heterogeneous space containing residential functions, culture, shopping, entertainment, and tertiary services in a lively mixture that does not bear the stamp of state planning. Newly erected building complexes such as those at Potsdamer Platz or around Hackescher Markt give a glimpse of how the downtown of the 2000s could differ from that of the 1960s and 1970s: its texture is defined not simply by office buildings, but by residential areas, entertainment establishments, and shopping areas, along with services with a supra-regional orientation.

The projects that have been carried out or finalized thus far are only a beginning. The decisive factor will be whether other key locations – such as Alexanderplatz or Leipziger Strasse – will create potential for an even greater mixture of uses. Planning along these lines has already taken place. The Berlin Senate's "Downtown Project" (*Planwerk Innenstadt*) in particular will create new possibilities through changes to the public space and elimination of urban wasteland areas. Project Downtown is intended to undo or repair unhealthy modern interventions for the sake of urban vitality, without tearing down buildings. The destruction of street space through the widening of city streets to near freeway dimensions is to be stopped, and instead, streets will be reconstructed. On the property reclaimed by this project, new buildings will be built for both residential and tertiary uses.

In the district of Mitte, a truly "post-modern mix" of functions could develop, based on the advantages of spatial proximity that no other city has to offer. This "creative mixture" could become a focus point for Berlin's future development as a competitive service metropolis within a network of national and international centres.

## The Built Environment

### Housing

Berlin has 1.8 million dwellings; 62.4 per cent of them are in the West, 37.6 per cent in the East. The inner city area consists of old houses – most of them with four or five floors – that were built between 1860 and 1914. Indeed,

28.5 per cent of all dwellings in the city were built before 1918, and another 16 per cent in the inter-war period. Half of the dwellings were built in the period of division – in the East, most of them in a pre-fabricated manner – another 6.5 per cent in the 1990s.

Traditionally, Berlin is a city with a proportionately very large rental sectors, mainly flats; by contrast, owner-occupied flats play a minor role. Very little private housing existed in East Berlin before 1990. In West Berlin, according to the Census in 1987, 11 per cent of the flats were owner-occupied; by 1993, the rate had risen to 12.5 per cent, whereas in East Berlin, it was only 5.5 per cent (BMRBS, 1995). Thus, the Berlin housing market may be described as a renter's market with a strong tendency towards privatization. This trend can be seen in all segments of the housing stock: old (pre-war) houses as well as pre-fabricated houses constructed under the socialist regime, communal housing stock as well as the newly developed private housing areas. It should also be noted that, during the 1990s, the pre-war housing stock in East Berlin was restituted to the former owners, which usually resulted in reselling to private profit-orientated housing companies and developers.

Despite this, the share of public housing stock in Berlin is still very high compared to other German cities, but has declined through privatization. In 1997, 30 per cent of West Berlin housing stock can be said to have been built with public subsidies and because of that is subject to a rent ceiling. In East Berlin, the only type of housing built in the GDR was public and is equal to half the East Berlin housing stock. Another 17 per cent was built between 1919 and 1948 and is therefore also predominantly communal, owned by public housing companies or *Genossenschaften* (private non-profit housing cooperatives). In the 1990s, however, due to the financial problems of the City of Berlin, public companies were forced to privatize 15 per cent of their housing stock by selling it (prior to the *Altschuldenhilfegesetz*).

Of the 1.8 million households in Berlin in 1998, 46 per cent are single and only 10 per cent consist of four or more persons. The number of single households was already high in West Berlin in the 1980s and remains stable at about 49 per cent. In East Berlin, data show an increase in single households in the 1990s, but their share still lies below the average of Berlin as a whole: in 1991 it was 36 per cent, growing to 42 per cent by 1998. Most of the single households are in the inner city districts. By contrast only a small (but rising) number of single households and a much higher proportion of large households characterize the outlying districts, especially Zehlendorf (in the south-west of Berlin), as well as Marzahn, Hellersdorf, and Hohenschoenhausen, where the big housing estates with pre-fabricated housing blocks of the GDR period are located. The spatial distribution of households in Berlin is directly related to the number of rooms in the apartments located in the districts. The inner city areas host dominantly pre-war houses with small number of rooms but large floor space. The supply of dwellings with more than two rooms is small, except in the old West (Charlottenburg and Wilmersdorf). In the outlying districts, the apartments consist of larger numbers of smaller rooms.

Larger households live there, while single households are concentrated in the inner city areas. The highest rate of single households can be found in Tiergarten, Charlottenburg, and Schoeneberg, all of them being inner city districts in West Berlin.

Remarkable differences between East and West can be seen with regard to households with four or more persons. In West Berlin, the rate was 10 per cent in the 1990s, while in East Berlin, after a decline of about 4 per cent since 1991, it was 11 per cent in 1998. This trend resulted from the out-migration of large households, and a high level of divorce and broken families in East Berlin. Thus, the average household size in East Berlin was slightly higher but decreasing. A rise in single-person households and a decreasing in size of households should affect housing demand, but population decline meant that the number of households in Berlin did not rise during the 1990s. As we will see, the structure of the housing market is changing mainly due to privatization and new housing being built.

During the 1990s about 120,000 new dwellings were built in Berlin, and approximately another 90,000 in the suburbs. Most of them came on the market after 1993 when the population peaked in Berlin. Since then the white population has been decreasing, and the supply of dwellings has been rising continuously. As a consequence, prices for middle-class housing were much lower at the end of the 1990s than at the beginning when there was a shortage of dwellings. Vacancy rates have become a serious problem in several neighbourhoods where more than 10 per cent of the dwellings are unused. Increasing supply, however, has offered new opportunities for mobility in Berlin: the mobility rate increased from 10.7 per cent of the population in 1991 to 17.5 per cent in 1997. This means one in six persons moved in the year 1997.

On the other hand, the sector of low-standard housing at cheap rents is declining, too. Urban renewal and modernization is taking place especially in the inner city districts. In East Berlin a high share of the old pre-war houses are low-standard, i.e. without a toilet and bathroom inside the dwelling, and with carbon stoves. Several neighbourhoods are utilizing special regulations for urban renewal, and public subsidies are spent in these areas. In West Berlin, where urban renewal started in the 1960s, modernization of the housing stock is mostly done nowadays by private capital. Most urban renewal actually takes place in the East and goes hand in hand there with the restitution and privatization of old pre-war houses (Fig. 7.4).

*Restitution of Private Property*

Land was nationalized in the GDR. Although property mostly belonged to private owners, it was at least placed under state administration. When both states were united in 1990, it was agreed that former owners should be given

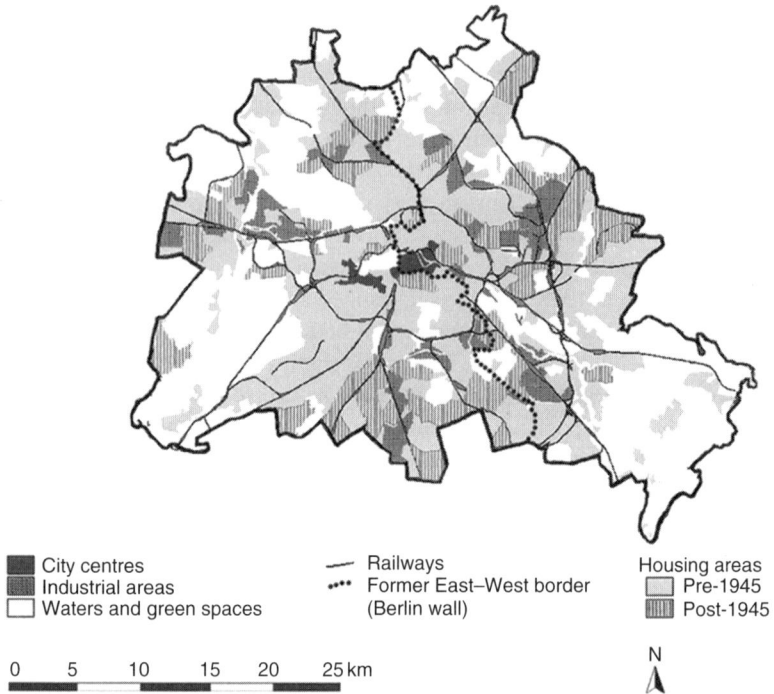

City centres
Industrial areas
Waters and green spaces

— Railways
•••• Former East–West border
(Berlin wall)

Housing areas
☐ Pre-1945
▥ Post-1945

0   5   10   15   20   25 km

N

Fig. 7.4  Spatial structure of Berlin.

back their rights. The intention of rehabilitating the victims of Fascism and Stalinism was part and parcel of the political aim to undo revolutionary socialist changes and to restore the former distribution of property. It was also hoped that the Jewish culture, whose disappearance was caused by mass extermination and emigration, could be brought back to life in Berlin. Prior to Fascism, the large Jewish community in Berlin had been particularly important to cultural life in the city. They were centred, on the one hand, in the bourgeois borough of Wilmersdorf in the West, and in the old inner city districts of the East. It now turns out that up to 90 per cent of private landowners were Jewish. Their heirs are now entitled to claim their land or house back.

Instead of restoring the Jewish culture, however, restitution of private property has led to a massive transfer of property. The now very old survivors of the Holocaust or their heirs usually put the property they have reclaimed straight on to the market either because they have no roots any more in Berlin, or because they want to have nothing more to do with Germany. If no living heirs can be found, the Jewish Claims Conference can place an application. If successful, they have to sell the land or house immediately and give the profits to a fund for victims of the Holocaust. Above all, restitution regulations result in the mobilization of private land, which brings with it two incisive changes for urban development.

First, the social structure of the landowners changes. Before Fascism, individual ownership of land was widespread and formed a material basis for the so-called middle classes. Shopkeepers and landlords were often one and the same, which contributed to the wide variety of land use and allowed non-profit motifs to exert an active influence on urban structure. Marketing this property brings about a new ownership structure as the new owners include investors, international companies, and other such buyers, all of whom are interested in tax savings and capital spending. Large investments cause rents to rise and lead to an extensive exchange of inhabitants because local authorities have extremely limited power to protect low-income tenants.

Second, restitution claims cannot be granted if high-capital investors wanting to buy land in the city centre propose an investment and usage plan which is favoured by the city administration. The *Investitionsvorranggesetz* ("priority of investment law") enables the political authorities to grant the land to these investors, and merely remunerate the former owners. Critics are now talking of a "second expropriation". This process gives the land new dimensions – partly because high-capital investors buy up land that has been put on the market, and partly because new investors can prevent the enforcement of the old ownership rights by means of this priority of investment law. By putting forward a plan that encompasses several properties, and being granted rights of purchase, they can buy up large investment space in the centres of large cities in the eastern regions (Berlin, Leipzig, Dresden). This space can then be used by national or multinational joint-stock companies, who usually tend to build offices (often with retail trade on the ground floor). In this way, a uniform structure of huge dimensions is developing in the new centre of Berlin.

Housing and land were divided into separate categories of ownership in the GDR – state property for public buildings, and then public property, including in particular new flats; economic establishments and enterprises owned by combines; and some flats belonged to workers' cooperatives (AWG). This property was eventually handed over to new owners: the municipalities received the flats; state property was shared between the local and state levels; and enterprise property was marketed by the *Treuhandgesellschaft* (trust company), generally at top prices.

During this process of property transfer and restructuring land ownership, new players entered the field of urban planning. For the first time since the *Gruenderzeit* (the last third of the nineteenth century) in Germany, real-estate capital was a deciding factor in urban development in Berlin. Major investments enabled multinational joint-stock companies to secure the most important sites, thanks to the priority of investment law. Anonymous real-estate funds are important investors in office and flat construction. West German and West European investment companies are in general occupying the central and high-grade areas of Eastern cities. And the inner city areas of East German cities are being sold to Western joint-stock companies. A similar result can be seen when flats have to be privatized by local housing cooperatives in accordance with the *Altschuldenhilfegesetz*.

The new inner city structure thus differs significantly from that of the "old European city": investors and users are no longer the same people, and a neutral and flexible property structure now exists on a large scale. As opposed to earlier, real-estate investments are now pure capital spending, which is manifest in a regular exchange of ownership during planning and construction. Investment is encouraged by high-depreciation gains, meaning that it becomes irrelevant what is built – the main thing is that losses are made.

Sometimes chaotic processes occur in the old quarters, in which non-investment and investment in modernization measures are closely linked. Restitution and reinvestment create a sense of great insecurity for the residents. Stocks are still dilapidated and flats remain empty because cooperative housing only manages old buildings adequately once a restitution claim has been filed. Although investments have been put into lasting modernization and restoration projects, these are still isolated cases. This inequality stems mainly from the varying speeds at which decisions on restitution claims are made. What is more, the lack of public funding for cooperative housing means that investments in privately owned flats are now 10 times as high as in publicly owned flats.

## New Planning in the Old Centre: Government Locations and the "Planwerk Innenstadt"

After reunification in October 1990, the historical centre of Berlin, which had been the capital of the GDR over the past 45 years, became the capital of a united Germany once again, and in 1991 Berlin was designated as the seat of the federal government.

Looking at the locations of the governments of the different political systems Berlin has experienced, some highly symbolic features can be seen: the Chancellery, the biggest new central building being constructed today by the state, is not located in any of the historic government districts; it is supposed to form a symbolic clamp between East and West, and is being built over the river Spree (according to the design competition's jury decision). The new federal government is using two remaining Nazi buildings in the centre: the Reichsbank, where the central committee of the party (ZK der SED) used to reside, and the House of the Ministries (the former Nazi ministry of aviation or Reichsluftfahrtministerium). Obviously these latter buildings have been "decontaminated" by their interim use by the government of the socialist GDR.

An important part of the change in public space in the inner city after the end of socialism was the renaming of streets and the removal of monuments. More than 60 streets and squares, most of them named after socialist politicians, communist philosophers, and anti-fascists, were renamed. A lot of plaques on houses where important socialists once lived or worked disappeared, but neighbours and activists have replaced many of them. One significant monument that was removed is the 25 m-high statue of Lenin, formerly standing in the middle of Lenin Square (today the square of the United Nations).

The reconstruction carried out by state socialism has mainly been left untouched, apart from the Wall. Only the GDR Ministry of Foreign Affairs has been torn down, and grass grows there now. The destruction of the city by modernist urban design and state centralism from 1950 to the 1980s can be cured only gradually and carefully. So, the Planwerk Innenstadt has a special significance for the transformation of public space in the centre of Berlin. This master plan is aimed at repairing the destruction of the GDR period, but without pulling down a single house or building. The destruction of street space can be seen in the Eastern inner city areas of new buildings, and in the traffic constructions of the Western centre. Their harmful effects are to be restricted by reducing their width. The monumentality of the streets in the East is to be reduced – that is, hidden – by reconstruction. Areas reserved for cars are planned to become smaller, while pedestrians and cyclists will gain possibilities to stay in the inner city again and will be encouraged by street pedestrianization and provision of cycle paths.

The Planwerk Innenstadt is, however, also a socio-political project, which could deeply affect public spaces by re-establishing the urban citizen and by privatizing and dividing the land into small plots. This, as well as small investors (if possible only for self-use), should generate a section of the urban public that was lost through the nationalization and expropriation of land during the GDR regime. A counter-revolution is intended, through which the *citizen* shall become the subject of the city again. This becomes very clear in the new images of public space that have been created by the Planwerk Innenstadt. An example of this is the Spittelmarkt, which used to be a typical example of early bourgeois public areas with its varied mix of uses. In the Planwerk Innenstadt, the restoration of this square, which had completely disappeared under GDR urban planning, is expected to be reconstructed in its basic structure.

The Planwerk is an aesthetic project, which goes against the destruction of streets and monumentalism of GDR town planning. Pedestrians are to come back into the urban space, but for this to happen that same space needs to be created again. The Planwerk Innenstadt does not contain any new public building. Thus private actors are to be mobilized, mainly by regaining or newly creating public spaces, also with catering facilities. In so far as a new urban planning project is being mapped onto the structure of the socialist capital city, the Planwerk Innenstadt can be called "winners' planning" – especially there, where empty spaces, which manifest the historically unique intervention of socialism into a capitalist inner city, are supposed to be destroyed and rebuilt.

All new buildings that had been completed by 1998 were projects driven by private investors. They are also classic examples of private urban developments,

Fig. 7.5 Images of Berlin. (a) The Reichstag, German parliament. (b) Contrasts in the city centre: reconstituted versus non-reconstituted old building in Prenzlauer Breg. (c) Palast der Republik and the television tower, symbols of "socialist superiority". (d) Plattenbau, pre-fabricated housing in the city centre from the 1980s. (e) Plattenbau housing estate in Leipziger Strasse. (f) New Sony centre at Potsdamer Platz.

whose importance for urban space is already very high and could become even higher. Some examples of this are the projects at Hackesche Hoefe, Friedrichstrasse, and Potsdamer Platz (Fig. 7.5 [a–f]). Big investors have created spaces that are being filled by a responding public. In terms of economics, they already work very well. This is about economized spaces, which are strictly supervised and guarantee safety for the experience provided. Carefully calculated uses of land and the allocation of floor space to chains of stores show the reduction of urban citizens to the status of clients. The public spaces of the street are put into the hands of the private sector, or are privately controlled, and come in the form of shopping malls and underground walkways that connect places for consumption, with security guards and closed-circuit cameras. They are clean and warm and "consumer friendly". These are clear signs of an increase in the consumer public at the expense of the civil–social public.

# Socio-spatial Changes and Social Cohesion in Berlin Since 1990

*The Historic Patterns of Social Spaces in Berlin*

The inner city area of Berlin is characterized by densely built houses of the late nineteenth and early twentieth century. These dwellings had been built for working-class families, the proletariat who came to Berlin during the period of industrialization. The former suburbs where the bourgeois classes lived are now located inside the city borders. The historic pattern of social segregation shows two poles. The west and south-west was bourgeois, the east and north predominantly proletarian and lower middle class. This structure was dependent on exchange and segregation taking place across the whole city, and had to change, therefore, when both halves of the city reorganized themselves as one. For a while, both East and West contained the whole social spectrum, which is usually to be found in any big city. One of the most interesting questions surrounding restructuring after the reunification is how social segregation in the East will change, and whether the old socio-spatial pre-war pattern will re-emerge after 40 years of division.

The most significant change for the West after 1945 was the arrival of foreigners filtering into the old districts near the centre. Immigrants congregated in the northern and southern peripheral areas of the inner city, which had been established as working-class areas in the nineteenth century. The German population gradually moved to the periphery when these areas were pronounced redevelopment zones, and as the new estates were completed. The working-class districts in the north and the lower-middle-class areas in the south (Kreuzberg), which were also the quarters with the poorest living conditions, acquired the lower classes made up of foreign guest workers and unskilled labourers. The newly constructed estates on the periphery predominantly fostered the social mix that was typical of the social structure of post-war society: lower and upper middle classes with a large share of public employees and skilled workers. But the south-west kept its bourgeois structure throughout the time of the divided city.

The process of segregation worked differently in the East. The exclusive bourgeois residential areas of former times, which were also to be found in the East, were occupied by the nomenclature of the state leadership and the Party (SED). Housing in the new estates was allocated according to a state-governed distribution system and favoured young families. Income played no role in the allocation of the new flats, which explains the unusual social mixture which formed in these areas and which still exists today. Newly constructed estates are segregated primarily by the age of the residents: younger families moved in as the new flats were completed and grew up along with the estates. Those remaining in the old districts had either been at a disadvantage when the flats were allocated, or they wanted to avoid the way of life and the living conditions that the newly constructed estates symbolized. Hence, marginal groups and political opponents or cultural dissidents were typical residents in the old districts. Socio-spatial segregation was much less marked in the East than in the West, partly because the flats and features of the districts varied much less from each other, but also because socialist society in general was less differentiated.

How is the socio-spatial structure developing now, and how will it develop in the future? Socio-spatial differentiation depends on various developments: on income trends and rent prices, on the opportunity to choose where to live, and thus on the availability of additional flats. In the medium term, however, differentiation of income – which is advancing greatly in the East, where there are large numbers of unemployed – is a deciding factor. The effects of lifestyle and the features of residential areas take only second place. Socio-spatial differentiation thus becomes a function of trends in mobility, pressure from new investment, and the ability of residents to choose to live in the various milieus:

(a) The pattern of social segregation in the West did not change during the 1990s, but the social differences between neighbourhoods are deepening. The most common form of inner city mobility between East and West was, and still is, commuting. Some 150,000 citizens – one-third of East Berlin's employed persons – commute daily from East to West. The Wall prevented Easterners commuting across the border before 1990. Another 50,000 persons commute from West to East and another 160,000 come from outside the city, most of them from neighbouring municipalities. Mobility between East and West has emerged and is becoming more normal. Since neither the East nor the West of the city were showing signs of suburbanization following the usual Western pattern for reasons already discussed, a "jam" has built up, which will be cleared by people moving into the surrounding region. Suburbanization is in fact now under way in both the East and the West of the city.

(b) The old districts in the East, which, as already mentioned, were severely neglected by socialist urban policy, and consequently were in terrible condition by 1990, are now undergoing lasting changes: the process of restitution accelerates and at the same time slows down the modernization of old houses. There are, in addition, redevelopment programmes which involve the majority of local cooperative housing. Real-estate owners are speculating on the gentrification process, demand for which is still too low on the one hand, and which is restricted by redevelopment regulations on the other. Gentrification is encouraged by speculative expectations, which latch on to the city's prospective growth and its new significance; but the process stopped when district councils in the East attempted to retain control over living space.

(c) Social transformation is also to be expected in the pre-fabricated housing estates on the periphery. During the GDR period, they were highly attractive and there were long waiting lists for living space, which was allocated in order of urgency. The new flats were characterized by high construction standards and modern comforts (hot water supply, bath and WC, central heating). Since income played no role in the allocation of these flats, the social structure in these areas was very heterogeneous. Transformation here, above all, is a matter of available alternatives and of income trends. Income levels and structure will, undoubtedly, change mainly in accordance with trends in the job market. What is to become of these large housing estates from the GDR era will not be determined in the estates themselves, but rather by the new districts in the surrounding region and by the old city quarters. The highest wage earners will almost certainly move out of the pre-fabricated housing estates if single-family housing becomes available in the new districts in the region. If, at the same time, gentrification and modernization (thus a rise in prices) proceeds in the old quarters, the affordable housing segment will become smaller, the number of households depending on being allocated a flat by the local housing agent will grow, and these households will be forced to turn to the pre-fabricated housing estates. Then any remaining pockets of poverty could develop in the neglected old housing areas, while low-income households could conglomerate in the estates on the periphery. Rights of occupation, which are still possessed by the local housing office, guaranteeing accommodation to low-income groups and homeless households, will determine the structure.

## The Spatial Segregation of Migrants

The recruitment of labour force from southern Europe from the 1950s to overcome labour shortages in the period of the "economic miracle" brought thousands of citizens from other countries to Germany. At first these groups were regarded as "guest workers" (*Gastarbeiter*). They were expected to stay only for a short time and then return to their home countries – this did not turn out to be the case, however. When recruitment was stopped in November 1973, because of economic recession, guest workers began to stay and settle in Berlin, and brought their families too. In contrast, the 1980s were characterized by refugee migration. Migrants came from Lebanon, Iran, Vietnam, and Poland.

The city of West Berlin has about 2 million inhabitants. The total non-German population there was only 22,000 in 1960 but rose to 190,000 – i.e. about 9 per cent of the population – in 1975, after the recruitment period. The so-called "guest workers" arrived particularly from 1968 onwards, mainly from Turkey and Yugoslavia. In this period, German inhabitants moved out from the inner city areas and rented apartments in the big estates that had just been built at the fringes of the city. Migrant workers from Turkey and Yugoslavia concentrated in the urban renewal zones in the inner city districts. They had been regarded as temporary settlers due to the rotation principle that had been established as part of the guest worker recruitment policy.

Areas where migrant households settled in the 1980s mirrored the concentrations of the late 1960s and the early 1970s. The number of migrants nearly doubled between 1975 and 1990, especially the number of Turkish, but also Arabian, Iranian, and Polish citizens. Before 1990, of course, the concentration of migrants only occurred in the West of the city, while the rate of migrants in East Berlin was below 2 per cent in 1990. In 1998, the share of non-Germans in Berlin as a whole was 13 per cent, but was three times higher in West Berlin (17 per cent) than in East Berlin (5.4 per cent).

During the 1990s, new migrant groups came from Eastern Europe, especially Poland, the former Soviet Union, and Yugoslavia. These also settled in East Berlin. There, empty, run-down old housing could be found, and nowadays the urban renewal zones are concentrated in the East. The number of migrants increased in the beginning of the 1990s, and because of out-migration of households from the inner city areas and social housing stock, an enormous mobility has affected segregation patterns since then. Migrant families filled vacant housing, and German households do not want to live in this social housing any more. The social housing estates thus underwent a deep social change in the 1990s.

## Social Segregation

The labour market situation of migrants in Berlin is very bad. Because of declining job opportunities, unemployment is increasing amongst migrants. The guest worker migrants who had found work mainly in the manufacturing industries were often dismissed in the 1990s, and it is not easy for new migrants to get into any kind of job. The economic crisis in Berlin has resulted in bad labour market opportunities for migrants and young people who try to enter the labour market. The same holds true for low-skilled and unskilled labourers. Because of the high segregation of the migrant population in the same areas where German low-skilled workers live, unemployment is very high in the inner city areas of West Berlin.

Figure 7.6 shows the spatial dimension of unemployment. In the inner city districts of Berlin, a much higher percentage of unemployed persons are resident than in the outlying districts. In West Berlin, the northern part of Neukoelln and the districts of Kreuzberg and Wedding have the highest unemployment rates, whereas in south-west Berlin, high-status neighbourhoods show a considerably lower unemployment rate. East Berlin does not exhibit a similar spatial division: unemployment is high both in the inner city districts with old housing stock and

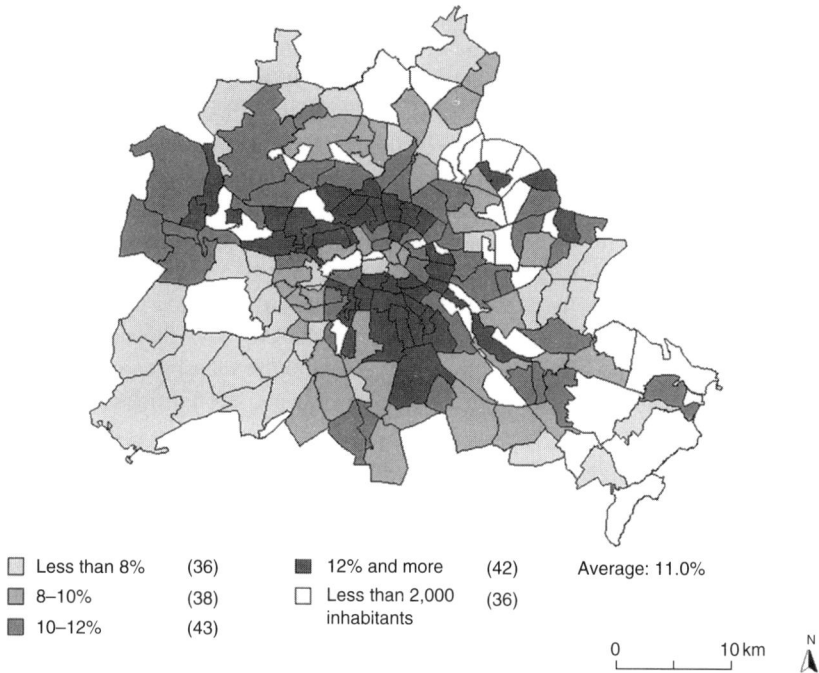

Fig. 7.6 Unemployment in the statistical areas of Berlin, 1998: unemployment as percentage of labour force.

*Source:* Statistisches Landesamt Berlin.

in the outlying districts with big housing estates built in the 1980s (Marzahn, Hohenschoenhausen, and Hellersdorf).

The variances described above hold true for youth unemployment, where differences can be said to be even more distinct.

The inner city districts of Neukoelln and Kreuzberg are as highly affected by youth unemployment as the neighbourhoods with big housing estates in East Berlin, while youth unemployment is lower in the inner city districts of East Berlin and the south-west districts. The trend of increasing unemployment in the inner city districts and in the social housing estates is worsened by selective mobility between neighbourhoods. Those neighbourhoods that are well off will attract high-income groups, while those that have already suffered from unemployment will attract only low-income groups and the unemployed.

## New Mobility Trends in Berlin: Changes in the Social Composition of Districts

Mobility increased enormously in the 1990s. As mentioned above, the increasing supply of housing has offered new opportunities for people to move in Berlin.

The mobility rate rose from 10.7 per cent of the population in 1991 to 17.5 per cent in 1997. Between 1991 and 1998, therefore as a statistical average, everybody had moved to a new dwelling in Berlin. In 1997 and 1998, it was one-third of the population. It is not surprising that within this process, patterns of segregation do change. Those who are willing to find a new dwelling for cheaper rent or in a better neighbourhood can improve their housing situation.

The highest rates of mobility can be found in the inner city districts. Here, more than 20 per cent of the inhabitants move to a new flat every year. About one-third of the moves stay in the same district, but as a consequence of this, population decreases in these areas. In the East, suburbanization plays a central role; families are drawn towards the edge of the city and the neighbouring municipalities. The highest rates of out movement to the suburbs can be found in the inner city districts of East Berlin as well as in the pre-fabricated high-rise estates on the fringe.

Suburbanization follows the logic of augmenting living space that is only possible where land is still cheap and available. While families leave the unattractive dense inner city and the high-rise areas, migrants, the unemployed, and the poor gather there. Besides the marginalized, urban professionals stay in the centres, demanding luxurious flats. These households usually have no children and possess a lot of disposable income. But this process of gentrification only exists in some small pockets of the inner city. Gentrification occurs under the assumption of a growing service sector of well-paid jobs, but actually this sector is not increasing as much as has been supposed. The demand of the service elite is therefore too small to cause widespread gentrification in the inner city districts.

The process of selective mobility can be shown by the moves of employed persons (the best figures that are available according to social status). Of all moves in and out of a neighbourhood, only a part of the persons involved are employed. While there are neighbourhoods where the share of the employed amongst the moving population of economically active age (15–65 years) is quite high, in others it is very low. But it is not the share itself that is important, but whether those who move out have a higher share than those who move in. Figure 7.7 indicates the quotient among the labour force of the moves in and the moves out of a neighbourhood. Where the index is less than 100 the share of unemployed is increasing by moves, if it is more than 100, e.g. 120, those who move in are 20 per cent more often employed than those who move out. As a result, employment increases and the social status of the neighbourhood improves.

Mobility deepens social polarization in Berlin by its selectivity. This can be shown especially for the social housing stock in the West that was built mostly in the post-war period. In the 1970s, housing market discrimination led to a concentration of migrants in the old housing stock in the West. In the 1980s, access to social housing became possible for migrants in the West, but discrimination often stopped such entry. In the 1990s, both social housing in the West and the pre-fabricated housing units in the East were subject to change.

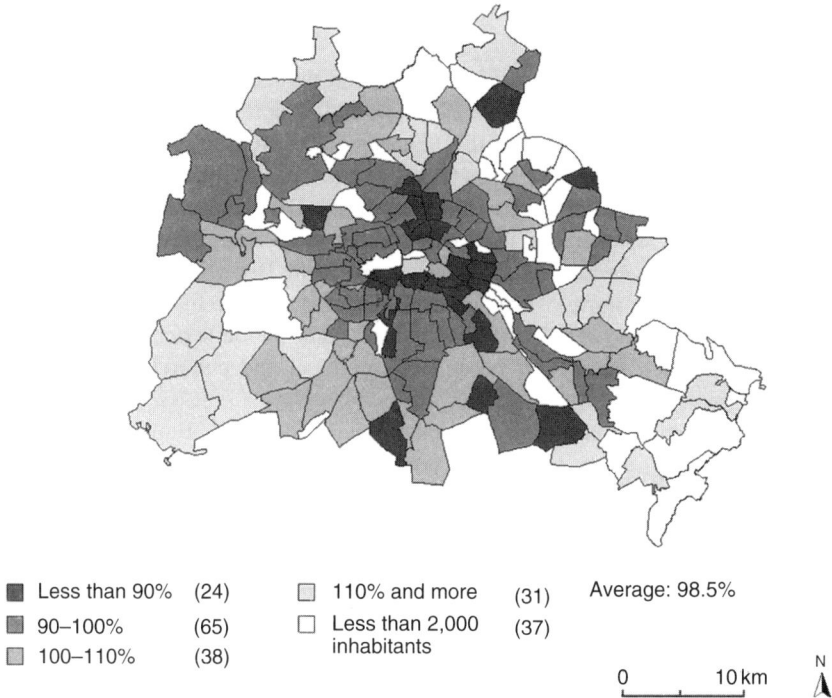

Fig. 7.7 Social selectivity index: those employed amongst the moving labour force, quotient of move-ins/move-outs, 1994–1997.

*Source:* Statistisches Landesamt Berlin.

The proportion of migrants and unemployed increased, and in some neighbourhoods migrant households are the only ones to apply for dwellings. Since vacancy is a serious problem, migrants and the unemployed move in, and such areas are often seen to become disadvantaged.

The situation is worsening, both in the East and in the inner city areas of West Berlin. The concentration of the unskilled, migrants, and the poor leaves little hope for the future. As long as unemployment is increasing and money for social infrastructure is reduced, strategies for "social development" cannot achieve big results. Hope is vanishing, and apathy and discouragement are taking its place, especially amongst the youth. The decay of the inner city of the West is not just limited to substandard and non-modernized housing units, but also affects social housing and urban renewal zones. Wherever poverty increases and the well-off are moving out, the supply of services and the diversity of shops – as well as the general opportunities of an area – decrease. Local shopkeepers have to close down and a decline in purchase power offers few possibilities for new entrepreneurship.

## Concluding Remarks

With the collapse of the communist regimes and the fall of the Wall, Berlin has lost its two earlier positions – West Berlin as a "frontier of the free world", East Berlin as the capital city of the GDR. During the Cold War period, Berlin was separated from the dynamic growth economies of the Western world, and because of its extraordinary geopolitical isolation the economy of West Berlin was nearly fully dependent on payments and subsidies from West Germany. The relocation of the government and parliament from Bonn to Berlin has been accompanied by the move of federal institutions from Berlin to Bonn, so that the balance of exchange was zero. Berlin did not gain public service jobs, it only gained importance, because it became the political and cultural centre of the united Germany.

Since unification, Berlin has regained the potentiality of a European political centre, and also of a place of exchange of ideas, people, money, and commodities between Eastern and Western Europe. The economic change in Berlin has been dramatic, and this change has had powerful effects on the socio-spatial structure of the city. At the same time, unemployment and new employment in modern services are growing. Polarization of income distribution is rising as a consequence of de-industrialization and of growth of service jobs. Income inequality is increasing, and the rising proportion of long-term unemployed might lead to a new urban underclass. Berlin is quickly adopting a post-modern class structure and also post-modern urban policies.

Because the city aspires to the status of a global city, a lot of public investment is aimed at the creation of a new economy, based on new technologies, communication services, and international exchange functions. But this growth does not trickle down to the less educated unemployed manual workers. Because of the deficit of the public budget, the Berlin government (the Senate) is selling public property – after the water and energy supply agencies, now the publicly owned housing companies are for sale. This will lead in general to a reduction of public influence on housing provision, and the two markets – the labour market and the housing markets – are becoming linked more closely because the stock of social housing is declining from year to year (through privatization), and almost no new social housing is being added to this stock any more; the private sector mainly provides new housing.

Growing inequality of incomes, declining state intervention into the housing supply, and the growing mobility of private households, possible through the temporary oversupply of housing – all of this leads to a polarized socio-spatial pattern, as is occurring in other big cities in Europe. But until now there are only a few initiatives or approaches to tackle these new social problems. It will be necessary to develop a globally orientated policy for connecting the local economy with the wider world as well as a strictly locally orientated policy for the protection of the losers of the contemporary change.

# Note

1  This chapter is drawn from an unpublished paper by Martin Gornig and Hartmut Häussermann on "Berlin: Economic and Spatial Change", written in 1999.

## REFERENCES

Berliner Festspiele, Architektenkammer Berlin, *Berlin: offene Stadt. Die Erneuerung seit 1989* [Berlin: The Open City. Urban Renewal since 1989], Berlin: Nicolai, 1999.

Bundesministerium fuer Raumordnung, Bauwesen und Staedtebau (BMRBS), *Haus und Wohnung im Spiegel der Statistik 1995/96* [House and Flat in the Statistics 1995/96], Bonn: BMRBS, 1995.

Eberhard von Einem, "Berlin Szenario 2010 – Flaechen und Standorte" [Berlin Scenario 2010 – Spaces and Locations], in Senatsverwaltung fuer Stadtentwicklung, Umweltschutz und Technologie, *Metropole Berlin: Mehr als Markt!* [Metropolis Berlin: More than Market!], Berlin: Kulturbuchverlag, 1991, pp. 59–89.

Christof Ellger, "Berlin: Legacies of Division and Problems of Unification", *Geographical Journal* 158, 1992, pp. 40–46.

Christof Ellger, "Berlin – Metropolis in Transition: The State of Urban Development in 1994", in Gerhard Braun, ed., *Managing and Marketing of Urban Development and Urban Life,* Berlin: Geographical Institute FU Berlin, 1994, pp. 9–19.

Martin Gornig and Hartmut Häussermann, "Berlin: Economic and Spatial Change", *European Urban and Regional Studies* 9(4), 2002, pp. 331–341.

Hartmut Häussermann, "From the Socialist to the Capitalist City: Experiences from Germany", in Gregory Andrusz, Michael Harloe, and Ivan Szelenyi, eds, *Cities after Socialism. Urban and Regional Change in Post-Socialist Societies*, Oxford: Blackwell, 1996, pp. 214–231.

Hartmut Häussermann, "Social Transformation of Urban Space in Berlin since 1990", in Ove Kaelltorp, Ingemar Elander, Ove Ericsson, and Mats Franzén, eds, *Cities in Transformation – Transformation in Cities. Social and Symbolic Change of Urban Space*, Aldershot: Avebury, 1997, pp. 80–97.

Hartmut Häussermann and Andreas Kapphan, "Berlin: Bilden sich Quartiere sozialer Benachteiligung" [Berlin: Do Neighbourhoods of Social Disadvantage Develop?], in Sebastian Herkommer, ed., *Soziale Ausgrenzung – Gesichter des neuen Kapitalismus* [Social Exclusion – Faces of the New Capitalism], Hamburg: VSA, 1999, pp. 187–208.

Hartmut Häussermann and Andreas Kapphan, *Berlin: von der geteilten zur gespaltenen Stadt. Sozialraeumlicher Wandel seit 1990* [Berlin: From the Divided to the Fragmented City. Socio-spatial Change since 1990], Opladen: Leske + Budrich, 2000.

Heinz Heineberg, "West-Ost-Vergleich grosstaedtischer Zentrenausstattungen am Beispiel Berlins" [An East–West Comparison of the Composition of Metropolitan Centres – The Example of Berlin], *Geographische Rundschau* 31(11), 1979, pp. 434–443.

Andreas Kapphan, "Nichtdeutsche in Berlin-West: Zuwanderung, raeumliche Verteilung und Segregation 1961–1993" [Non-Germans in Berlin West: Immigration, Spatial Allocation, and Segregation 1961–1993], *Berliner Statistik* 12/1995, 1995, pp. 198–208.

Andreas Kapphan, *Das arme Berlin: Sozialrauemliche Polarisierung Armutskonzentration und Ausgrenzung in den 1990er Jahren* [The Poor Berlin: Socio-spatial Polarisation, Poverty Concentration and Exclusion in the 1990s], Opladen: Leske + Budrich, 2002.

Stefan Kraetke, "Berlin's Regional Economy in the 1990s: Structural Adjustment or 'Open-ended' Structural Break?", in *European Urban and Regional Studies* 6(4/99), 1999.

Brian Ladd, *The Ghosts of Berlin. Confronting German History in the Urban Landscape*, Chicago: Chicago University Press, 1997.

Friedrich Leyden, *Gross-Berlin: Geographie der Weltstadt* [Big-Berlin: Geography of a World City], Berlin: Gebr. Mann Verlag, 1995 (reprint from 1933).

Walter Momper, Juergen Kromphardt, Georg Dybe, and Rolf Steinke, eds, *Berlins Zweite Zukunft. Aufbruch ins 21. Jahrhundert* [Berlin's Second Future. Breakup into the 21st Century], Berlin: edition sigma, 1999.

Bettina Reimann, "The Transition from People's Property to Private Property: Consequences of the Restitution Principle for Urban Development and Urban Renewal in East-Berlin's Inner-City Residential Areas", *Applied Geography* 17(4), 1997, pp. 301–314.

Senatsverwaltung fuer Stadtentwicklung und Umweltschutz, "Metropole Berlin: Mehr als Markt!" [Metropolis Berlin: More than Market!], *Proceedings from the Conference November 26–27, 1990*, Berlin: Kulturbuchverlag, 1991.

Senatsverwaltung fuer Stadtentwicklung, Umweltschutz und Technologie, written by Hartmut Häussermann, Andreas Kapphan, Gabriele Mersch, and Christof Speckmann, *Sozialorientierte Stadtentwicklung* [Socially Orientated Urban Development], Berlin: Kulturbuchverlag, 1998.

Senatsverwaltung fuer Stadtentwicklung, Umweltschutz und Technologie, *Planwerk Innenstadt Berlin. Ergebnisse, Prozesse, Sektorale Planungen und Werkstaetten* [Concept City-Centre Berlin. Results, Processes, Sectoral Plannings, and Workshops], Berlin: Kulturbuchverlag, 1999.

Senatsverwaltung fuer Stadtentwicklung, Umweltschutz und Technologie, written by Hartmut Häussermann, Andreas Kapphan, and Rainer Muenz, *Migration. Berlin: Zuwanderung, gesellschaftliche Probleme, politische Ansaetze* [Migration. Berlin: Immigration, Social Problems, Political Approaches], Berlin: Kulturbuchverlag, 1995.

Werner Suess and Ralf Rytlewski, eds, *Berlin. Die Hauptstadt* [Berlin. The Capital], Berlin: Nicolaische Verlagsbuchhandlung Beuermann, 1999.

# 8

# The Warsaw Metropolitan Area on the eve of Poland's integration into the European Union

*Grzegorz Weclawowicz*

## Regional Differentiation and the Position of the Warsaw Metropolitan Area in Poland

The spatial structure of Poland has been shaped in the past by strong ideological preferences of egalitarianism. However, under communism the policy of even distribution of productive forces became only partly effective. After 1970, the concept of a moderate polarization tended to support the development of urban agglomerations. As a result, Warsaw remains one of the most important economic centres, but does not dominate the rest of the country like the capitals of Hungary and the Czech Republic.

Currently, the new regional structure under formation will be shaped by two basic trends: the collapse of old industrial regions and the further underdevelopment of already underdeveloped areas, and the formation of the new prosperous regions with production adapted to the requirements of the new economic conditions, i.e. competitive domestic and international markets. It will also continue to enforce the traditional disparities between rural and urban areas, and between small and larger cities, which have already increased substantially.

In 2002, regional differentiation had not changed radically, but the position of some regions had become stronger than that of others. Particularly the position of Warsaw, as the leader of transformation, had led to the region becoming not only the place with the highest concentration of rich people, but also the largest contributor of GDP on the regional scale in Poland (12.5 per cent in 2001).

Despite substantial domination in the social, economic, and administrative domains, Warsaw has never developed as a typical primary city. Furthermore, in the 1990s, the pre-eminent position of Warsaw was challenged by Krakow on the grounds of cultural, scientific, and spiritual values, then by Gdansk on the grounds of political power, and by Poznań, based on its economic leadership in the transformation. As a great economic centre and the capital city, Warsaw has a substantial influence on the diffusion of the modernization process in the eastern part of the country. Another significant factor contributing to increased regional disparities is the spatial concentration of economic activities.

Warsaw and its metropolitan area are accumulating a large share of Poland's foreign investment. The other winners are Poznań, Gdansk, and Krakow. The prosperity generated by transformation along the western border sharply contrasts with stagnation and constant high unemployment along the eastern border with the former Soviet Union.

On the losing side are the majority of industrial towns, particularly those connected with the heavy industry located in Upper Silesia, as well as with the military industry, scattered all over Poland. The restructuring process has not yet started properly in the largest industrial cities, and is significantly delayed in the remaining medium-sized and small industrial cities.

European integration and globalization processes will have a substantial impact on the future development of the Warsaw Metropolitan Area (Jałowiecki, 2000; Kukliński, 2000; Furman, 2000; Kukliński et al., 2000; Korcelli, 1997; Węcławowicz, 1998a).

On the regional – Central European scale, the Warsaw Metropolitan Area could be perceived as the "eastern end of the trajectory" of economic development (Korcelli, 1999), or as a potential gateway to Eastern Europe for the European Union (Węcławowicz, 2002).

## Inherited Constraints: Historical Overview of City Development

The introduction of communism in 1945 had decisive consequences for the formation of the internal spatial structure of all cities in Poland, as well as for the character of the entire urban network in Central Europe. It involved the transformation of several elements, such as the social structure of urban areas, the physical fabric of cities, their position in the settlement network, and their administrative functions.

Explanations of the urban settlement network's origin and intra-urban disparities are based on the hierarchy of social and economic processes. From the beginning of communism, ideological priorities were of the utmost significance. Decisions concerning the nationalization of the means of production and the choice of overall economic goals in terms of imposed industrialization were made on purely ideological grounds. Their aim was the creation of a socialist society – an urban society, with the domination of the proletariat as the main social class. The objective was obviously to create a social stratum that would support communism. Thus, by fulfilling economic functions, industrialization became the main process through which ideological vision was being implemented. The subordination of the whole economy to the requirements of heavy industrialization resulted in severe disproportions in the national economy. The increasing lag of urbanization in comparison with the pace of industrialization was the most pronounced inequality, as exemplified by the discrepancy between the share of GDP invested in the productive sector and the share allocated for the improvement of living conditions.

Under the command-rationing economy, urban and regional planning was subordinated to economic planning and also became a part of ideologically determined social engineering. Its main concern in urban areas was the implementation of the socialist housing policy with its strong egalitarian tendency. Nonetheless, over time, the aforementioned policy has slowly become neglected in favour of a more selective allocation policy. As a result, socialist housing policy could not prevent the preservation and emergence of intra-urban disparities (Węcławowicz, 1998b).

In the process of rebuilding Warsaw after the devastation of the Second World War, a substantial role was played by the Decree on Communalization of 1945, abolishing private ownership of the land. Nevertheless, since 1989, property rights have become one of the main obstacles of urban development in Warsaw, particularly in its central part.

## The Evolution of Socio-spatial Differentiation under Socialism

The central function of Warsaw, as the capital city, in a natural way generates the steady increase of social categories connected with bureaucracy (Węcławowicz, 1992). Under communism this phenomenon was additionally amplified by the control system of the centrally planned economy, political management, and the enormous development of the surveillance system. The capital city's social structure became the object of social engineering, which aimed at "improving" the ratio of working-class persons on the one hand to bureaucrats and the intelligentsia on the other. The working class was given the advantage with the introduction of socialist industrialization in Warsaw. Another important element of post-war transformation was the disappearance of ethnic differentiation, and the substantial elimination of certain social categories from urban areas.

The roots of contemporary disparities can be easily traced to the post-war reconstruction. It is worth mentioning that many European cities suffered wartime devastation and many have been subsequently redeveloped, but none on such a scale as Warsaw. On the eve of the Second World War, Warsaw was populated by 1,300,000 inhabitants. In 1945, there were only 162,000 people who survived the bombing, the street combat, and the planned extermination carried out by Germans. The physical structure of the city was also destroyed.

The resettlement and reconstruction of the socio-spatial structure of Warsaw after the Second World War has been quite well documented by several factorial analyses (Węcławowicz, 1975, 1981, 1988; Dangschat 1987). After the basic reconstruction of the 1950s and 1960s, the 1970s and 1980s had a basic differentiating influence on the contemporary urban structure of Warsaw.

The 1970s were characterized by rapid expansion of housing construction and a substantial increase in the number of new dwellings. Allocation policies for new housing have favoured not only young families with children, and the waiting lists of housing cooperatives have not really been respected – political criteria and corruption have dramatically influenced the chances of individuals. The criterion of the social value of the labour force, determined arbitrarily by political bodies, was given priority in the central allocation system (Węcławowicz, 1988, 1996). Therefore, egalitarian trends characteristic of the 1960s and the early 1970s were abandoned during the late 1970s. The general tendency of increasing intra-urban disparities has been augmented. However, the general socio-spatial structure of the 1970s has evolved radically only in the areas where new housing was introduced. The preservation of old structures is the result of housing shortages and very low intra-urban mobility. Areas of high status in the 1970s became generally more segregated socially and absorbed more representatives of higher social groups. As a result, socio-spatial disparities increased even further in the 1980s.

Since 1970, Warsaw has been treated as a "socialist city", the type of city developed in Poland under communist rule, as distinct from the Western European capitalist cities (Węcławowicz, 1988, 1996). The most characteristic features of such cities were:

1. Domination of employment in the industrial production sector and the low percentage of middle-class persons (townspeople) meant that the majority of city inhabitants consisted of the working class (proletariat). The egalitarian principle and class homogeneity of socialist ideology resulted in a relatively low level of wealth differentiation. Egalitarian principles, however, were relatively easily modified or omitted.

2. The central allocation of inhabitants in relation to localization of dwelling often forced citizens to live in undesirable social surroundings, shaped by the idea of social mixing, or in areas of professional and social homogeneity. This artificial and forced segregation, or social mixture, augmented by the organization of the social life of urban dwellers around the place of work, diminished the chances of creating local communities.

3. Cities were absolutely dependent on central government for their finances and were "organizationally divided". The centralized authoritarian system had split different decisions concerning the cities, which came from different government departments and, at the smaller scale, from the authorities of

particular cities. The mayor represented the interests of the state against the citizens, rather than the interests of the citizens against authority. Even the elected city councils represented no local interests; their first allegiance was to the central government and its policies. Lastly, municipal offices became units subordinated to the state administration.

4. Uniformity of architecture and urban landscape created a higher proportion of wasteland, and led to the deterioration of the old quarters of cities (except for the cultural heritage parts of the old towns). The objective of the ruling communist regime, which was imposed on planners and builders, was to provide housing for the labour force in the quickest way. Therefore, the construction of large and homogenous estates, frequently inhabited by more than 100,000 people in the biggest cities, became the dominant pattern. The construction of adequate service facilities usually lagged behind, due to constant investment shortages.

5. Ignorance of land value, particularly in central locations, resulted in the emergence of empty areas that were used only extensively, even in the districts with very good technical infrastructure.

6. Ignorance of the impact of industrial and urban development on the environment led to ecological catastrophes in some industrial regions.

7. Attempts were made to permanently redistribute or eliminate non-communist symbols from the urban environment.

8. Attempts were made to control, by administrative means, the inflow of people into the city. The authorities recruited mostly the members of the labour force and those social categories that were acceptable from an ideological point of view.

9. Forced industrialization introduced a high share of migrants from rural areas without any prior urban experience. The phenomenon of ruralization of some cities resulted in a higher cost of adaptation to urban life.

## The Post-1989 Transformation of the Warsaw Metropolitan Area

The transformation of Warsaw into a post-socialist city involves all the most important elements responsible for urban development. In the case of Warsaw, similar to other large Polish cities, the following political and economic processes have a direct impact on the transformation of the urban space:

1. the return of market mechanisms and particularly the importance of land rent;

2. changes in the ownership of land structure, from state ownership or not strictly defined ownership, to local government and private ownership;

3. the shift of control over space from a central to a local level, mostly by the return of self-government and the formation of new local interest groups;

4. the radical increase in the number of actors competing for particular locations in urban space;
5. changes in the dominant rules of spatial allocation of people and economic activities from political to market criteria;
6. transformation of the employment structure from domination of the production sectors (mostly industry) to the service sector; and
7. the formation of a new social structure generated by a shift in the employment structure.

In general, adaptation to market economy conditions generated the currently visible processes of reurbanization. This is part of a bigger trend following the general European pattern (with some delays), and connected to the processes of European integration and globalization. Both optimistic and pessimistic outcomes are possible. In the optimistic scenario, the Polish urban system will adapt quickly to the European one, in which it will find the niche of its specialization and will contribute to the prosperity of the common market. In the pessimistic scenario, the Polish urban system will be subordinated and pushed to the periphery of the economic core of Western Europe, fulfilling only the secondary functions that would not be accepted in the core region.

One of the most important assets for future development is the current land-use pattern, with abundant space for possible investment. The most important types of land use within the city are the residential areas and big territories used by agriculture, forests, meadows, and wastelands open for future investment (Table 8.1). Property development studies have identified several categories of zones and strategic areas in Warsaw:

1. Category I – zones and strips of land with particular natural and scenic value (Vistula valley, Warsaw Scarp);

Table 8.1 Warsaw city: major demographic data

|  | 1980 | 1985 | 1990 | 1995 | 2000 | 2001 |
|---|---|---|---|---|---|---|
| Population as of 31 December in 000s | 1596.1 | 1659 | 1655.7 | 1635 | 1611 | 1609.8 |
| Population per sq.km | 3,289 | 3,419 | 3,412 | 3,308 | 3,258 | 3,257 |
| Females per 1,000 males | 114 | 114 | 114 | 116 | 117 | 117 |
| Live births per 1,000 population | 13.8 | 12.6 | 9 | 7.2 | 7.3 | 7.2 |
| Deaths per 1,000 population | 10.6 | 11.5 | 11.7 | 11.6 | 11 | 10.8 |
| Natural increase per 1,000 population | 3.2 | 1.1 | −2.7 | −4.2 | −3.7 | −3.6 |
| Infants deaths per 1,000 live births | 19.3 | 17.2 | 14.5 | 13.3 | 7 | 8.1 |
| Marriages per 1,000 population | 9.4 | 6.9 | 5.4 | 4.9 | 5 | 4.6 |
| Net migration | 14,437 | 1,678 | 5,014 | 2,360 | 3,243 | 4,439 |

*Sources: Statistical Yearbook*, Mazowieckie Voivodship, Statistical Office of Warsaw (2000, 2001, 2002);
*Statistical Yearbook of Warsaw* (1998, 2000); Statistical Office of Warsaw (2001).

2. Category II – zones of particular historical, cultural, and architectural value;
3. Category III – zones requiring structural transformation and modernization in regard to existing investment (mostly post-industrial and multi-family housing); and
4. Category IV – "unconstrained" zones for future development.

## The Impact of Economic Restructuring on Employment Structure

The important economic challenge, not only for Warsaw, has been set forth by the decline of industrial production in the state sector, which has become the most important factor in the transformation of the labour market.

Transformation of the industrial function in the post-war period is characterized by two stages. The first is socialist-imposed industrialization, which resulted in the creation of an irrational structure of industrial production in Warsaw. Moreover, it also had a whole set of negative consequences for the organization of the urban space and the social and natural environment. The second stage of de-industrialization can be subdivided into two substages; first, after 1976, characterized by deep economic recession and the collapse of the centrally planned economy; and second, after 1989, characterized by still incomplete adaptation to the market economy, and a slow recovery.

The impact of the market economy transformation has resulted in basic changes in the ownership structure of industry by a radical increase in privatization and the downsizing of industrial plants. The shift in the production structure occurred through a substantial growth in consumer goods production and a decline in manufacturing of the "means of production" (Misztal, 1998). In general, the 30 per cent of Warsaw's workforce employed in industry by the end of the communist period has dropped to only about 18 per cent today.

The process of de-industrialization has an ample impact on the transformation of urban structure. The industrial area in Warsaw's Centrum borough accounted for over 37 per cent of the borough's total area. The collapse, downsizing, and restructuring of large factories resulted in the sudden creation of large "new urban territories" equipped with the urban infrastructure, now accessible for alternative functions such as retail, business parks, housing, shopping centres, and communication. Simply, large under-utilized or extensively utilized areas of industrial plant have been released for other uses. As a result, the former industrial areas represent important territorial resources for prospective use.

In spite of the de-industrialization process, the Warsaw Metropolitan Area will remain one of the largest industrial concentrations in Poland. The rapid modernization of industrial production and increasing foreign direct investment in industrial development, including green-field developments, will very soon create a new specialization. In spite of the large internal market and resources of skilled labour, and the concentration of high-tech institutions in Warsaw, the formation of a modern industrial structure characterized by relatively high and competitive technological standards is still very limited. However, competition on the global market makes the scenario of a shift towards a handicraft type of industry also possible.

Nonetheless, employment and economic activity have been substantially diminishing for several years and particularly since 1989, as a result of restructuring and the economic crisis. The economic recession has additionally reduced the number of jobs and presses for changes in occupation. The reduction and increased efficiency of industry in the city improved the ecological situation. Despite these changes, industry remains important for the city and the national economy. It also needs further modernization in order to be competitive in the conditions of a market economy.

The evolution of labour demand was caused by the economic recession and the economic de-activation of the population, but first of all by the ownership transformation. The expansion of the private sector is of primary significance. New employment opportunities have emerged for highly qualified candidates in the banking sector and different financial institutions, as well as in management and consulting. The expansion of the private sector also created the demand for other demanding jobs like vendors, clerks, financial staff, secretaries, and semi-skilled labour. In this sector, employees are better paid and became more efficient compared with the public sector. In general, the share of the service sector (including retail) has increased in 2001 to 70 per cent of the total working population.

As far as employment and production are concerned, the "shadow economy" has an important share in building the prosperity of Warsaw. It is not only a mass of street vendors or the notorious "Russian Market", but also an enormous sector of illicit trade and production with a turnover that is difficult to measure directly.

The expansion of the private sector in Warsaw ensured that the city would have one of the lowest unemployment rates in Poland. The expansion of the private sector concerns mostly manual workers with only primary or vocational education. The increasing numbers of unemployed youth and the long-term (over one year) unemployed could lead to serious problems of poverty, particularly because the "permanently" unemployed lose the right to receive benefits after one year. The threat of unemployment, however, becomes not only a new factor of social consciousness, but also an additional indicator of poverty.

## Social Cohesion: The New Rich and the Poor in the Urban Space

The well-established socio-spatial structure of Warsaw as a whole was to some extent inherited from before the Second World War, but mostly formed under communism. Transition erased the administrative restriction for the settlement, therefore opening Warsaw but leaving it economically closed. For a lot of its citizens the city became too expensive to live in, but due to housing scarcity and unemployment there was no chance to move. For the new and poor migrants,

Warsaw became inaccessible; or, these migrants were marginalized into badly paid jobs and poor housing in emerging slum areas. At the same time, the inflow of wealthy population additionally created new polarization.

One of the basic indicators of transformation is the situation in housing. After the constant decline in housing construction in the first half of the 1990s, a gradual increase could be observed in the second half. In 2001, the index of new dwellings supply reached 10.1 per 1,000 inhabitants, compared with only 2.5 in 1997. Despite the new housing production boom, nearly 30 per cent of Warsaw's inhabitants still live in the pre-fabricated apartment blocks that form large housing estates in all districts.

Nowadays, access to housing is regulated by a rigid market mechanism. New housing construction represents better quality and has to an increasing extent been reorientated to social groups of a higher income. Generally, this increase in standards has resulted in the new housing stock being inaccessible to households of an average income. On the other side, the limited number of rich consumers limits the growth of housing construction. The cheap housing construction that was subsidized by the state has vanished; the existing housing is unaffordable for the majority.

The most dramatic changes occurred in the production of new cooperative housing, which still accounted for 47.3 per cent of total new housing production in Warsaw in 2001, while the private investors and developers' share was 44.6 per cent. The new tenants represent a social category with an income well above the average. Therefore, cooperative housing, egalitarian in principle, became the major source of income segregation among its tenants, or has been transformed into a cooperative of the rich. The new phenomenon in Warsaw is the existence of empty new flats waiting for tenants, while the waiting list of members is still very long.

Another important factor of the socio-spatial disparity disclosure is the housing situation. The state of housing in Warsaw indicates that in spite of all transformations, Warsaw still has a very large housing problem.

The quality of the existing stock, as well as accessibility to the new dwellings, is quite low. Intra-city discrepancies in housing quality are growing, with a lack of rehabilitation of "old" public stock on the one hand, and visible improvement of the quality of estate builds in the 1990s on the other. The specific pressure on Warsaw's housing market comes from a relatively high demand for rental and owner-occupied units. Due to the unstable market, both the costs of new units and the rents on the secondary market are about two times higher in Warsaw than in other large Polish cities (Table 8.2).

In principle, the housing finance system has been adjusted to market conditions, but persistent high inflation makes it unaffordable to the population. The introduction of new legislation on rents and housing allowances has rationalized communal services. On the other hand, this market-orientated reform led to an increase in rents and a partial withdrawal of some subsidies. The social effect was then amplified by the lowering of the average household

Table 8.2  Housing in Warsaw

| Specification | 1995 | 1999 | 2001 |
|---|---|---|---|
| *Dwellings* | 614,734 | 638,640 | 668,772 |
| Per 1,000 population | 376 | 396 | 415 |
| Average useful floor area per dwelling, sq.m | 48.7 | 50.2 | 51.4 |
| Average number of rooms per dwelling | 3.0 | 3.1 | 3.1 |
| *Ownership structure of dwellings, %* | 100 | 100 | 100 |
| Cooperative | 48.4 | 48.5 | 48.5 |
| Municipal | 25.2 | 19.5 | 18.6 |
| Enterprise | 8.4 | 8.3 | 8.0 |
| Private (individual) | 17.9 | 23.0 | 22.3 |
| Other | — | 0.7 | 2.6 |
| *Housing construction completed within the year* | 3,877 | 9,920 | 16,278 |
| Structure of completed dwellings, % | 100.0 | 100.0 | 100.0 |
| Cooperative | 72.0 | 55.9 | 47.3 |
| Municipal | 0.5 | 0.3 | 0.0 |
| Enterprise | 4.6 | 1.0 | 0.2 |
| Private (individual) | 19.0 | 8.8 | 8.0 |
| Other | — | 34.0 | 43.5 |
| Per 1,000 population | 2.3 | 6.1 | 10.1 |
| Per 1,000 new marriages | 484 | 1,222 | 2,199 |
| Average useful floor area of a dwelling, sq.m | 94.2 | 77.1 | 72.3 |
| Average value (according to cost calculation) of 1 sq.m of a dwelling in the 4th quarter | 1,170.0 | 2,862 | |
| Average gross monthly earning ratio/average price of 1 sq.m of a dwelling | 0.78 | 0.91 | |

*Source: The Warsaw Housing Report, Housing Conditions Needs – Dwelling Construction Housing Policy*, 16th issue 1999, Capital City of Warsaw, September 2000.

income, causing the emergence of systematic arrears in rents. In 2001, over 35.9 per cent of cooperative tenants were not paying rent, whereas 7.5 per cent were indebted for longer than three months. In municipal housing the situation is even worse. In 2001, the extreme was the case of the Ursus commune, where as much as 71.5 per cent of the inhabitants of municipal dwellings were in arrears for more than three months. In the commune of Centrum, where municipal stock still represents a high proportion, as much as 31.7 per cent of the inhabitants had financial problems, and as much as 12.3 per cent were in arrears for more than three months (*The Warsaw Housing Report*, 2002). These numbers reflect the poor economic condition of households and could be the first approximation indicator of poverty.

Rent reform in housing caused rent increases in cooperative and municipal dwellings, resulting from the partial withdrawal of direct and indirect subsidies.

The new Law on Renting Residential Properties and on Housing Allowances, introduced at the end of 1994, affected mostly the lower income social categories. Together with the declining income of many families, the problem of rent arrears has emerged.

Social support from local authorities addressing housing costs has been allocated mostly to the elderly and unemployed. It can be expected that the introduction of the housing allowance system, focused mostly on the lower-income families that occupy relatively small dwellings, should smooth the economic disparities. On the other hand, it will force a lot of other families onto less favourable housing estates, possibly resulting in an increase in socio-spatial polarization.

One social effect of rent reform and the privatization of the housing stock, particularly in the central part of Warsaw, is the process of subletting of flats by the elderly. This is the first stage of an intra-urban migration of a lower-income social category from the most prestigious and centrally located areas to the peripheries, frequently to live with their children or in cheaper accommodation. Subletting of centrally located flats by elderly or other lower-income families is treated as an additional source of income, sometimes the only economic asset of survival.

As a result of privatization and the boom in the private sector, a new social class has emerged, influencing the social structure of the city. The increase in the numbers of self-employed persons and the diminution of working-class groups are two opposite social tendencies that are slowly gaining very visible spatial expression. The widening of the impoverished strata in Warsaw has been very evident, and it includes the homeless, the elderly, and pensioners. In addition, a huge number of people employed in the administration or dependent on the state budget are generally badly paid. At the same time, Warsaw is slowly becoming a very expensive place to live for an ever-increasing proportion of its citizens. At the moment, these citizens still survive using a niche in the informal sector of the economy. This phenomenon contributes substantially to increases in social polarization and spatial segregation (Węcławowicz, 1998c, 2001).

In general, the socio-spatial polarization formed in the middle of the 1990s (Fig. 8.1) is not only the result of past socio-spatial stratification, but also a result of a new differentiating process. The quickest formation of a new socio-spatial structure occurred in the central part of the city. The new elite enclaves were created in the redeveloped areas inside or next to the deteriorating neighbourhoods and devastated housing inhabited by the poor and elderly.

The expansion of the new and very expensive housing development and the revitalization of the old housing stock in the central part of the city are indeed very similar to the gentrification processes described in many Western cities. Also in the peripheral suburban areas, expansion of luxury housing designed for the wealthiest social categories radically and quickly diversified many former low-status areas.

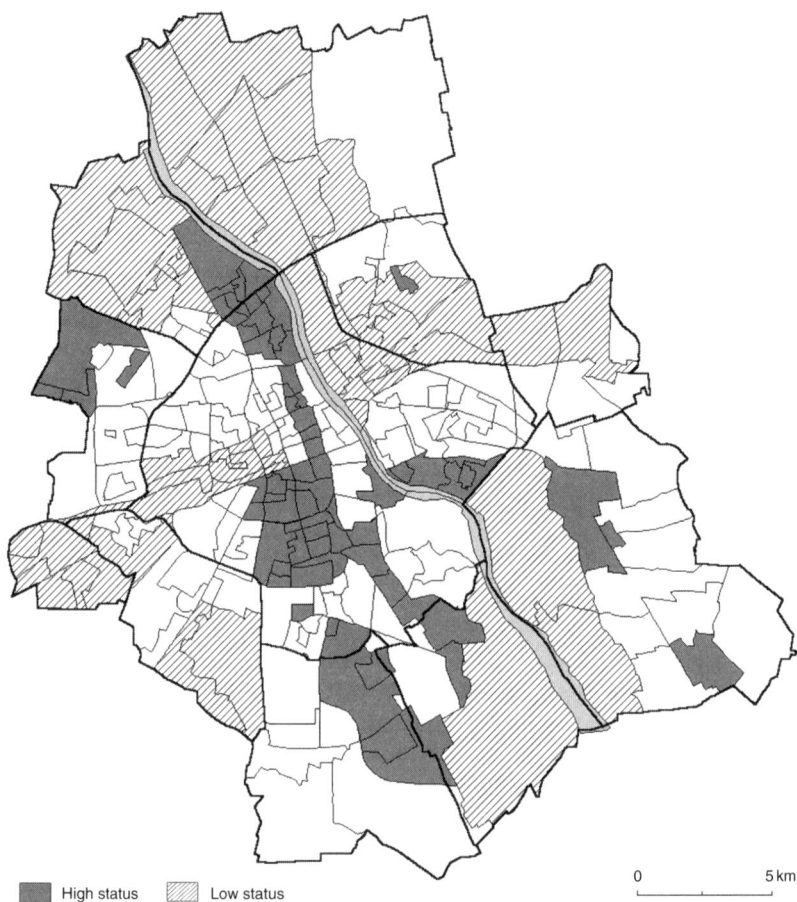

Fig. 8.1 Main social areas in Warsaw.

The increasing scale of social and wealth contrasts in spatial proximity creates a sort of a dual city, where the poor and rich live in the same areas. However both groups use distinct spaces: luxury shops as opposed to street bazaars; public transport in contrast to private cars; different places to work and find services. The spatial separation of different social categories accelerates significantly with time.

Research on poverty and wealth in Warsaw has been based on surveys conducted among social workers (in all 11 communes of Warsaw and 7 districts of the Centrum commune) in December 1996 (Fig. 8.2). This research monitored the current evolution in structure of those phenomena (Fig. 8.3).

The Warsaw communes have a degree of specificity, despite being internally diversified, and we can identify three main types: (i) the peripheral suburban

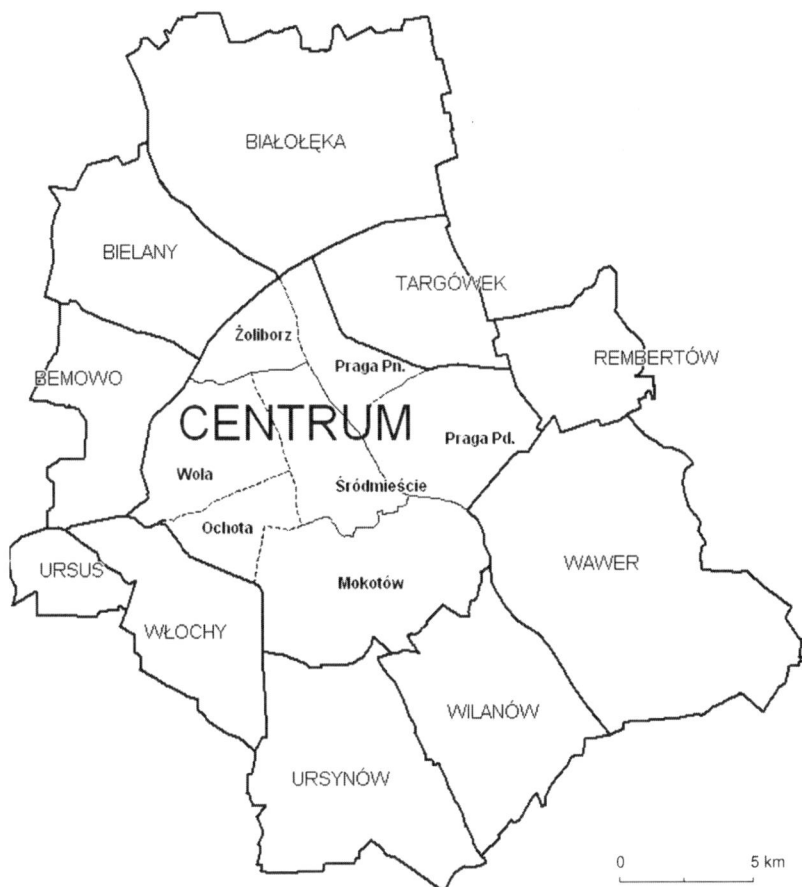

Fig. 8.2  Warsaw administrative and territorial division, 1994–2002.

zone; (ii) the zone dominated by new housing estates; and (iii) the districts of the Central Commune (Gmina Centrum) characterized by a mosaic urban texture. The peripheral communes have very different origins. Some of them are simply rural areas included in the administrative boundary of Warsaw, others are former small suburban towns, and others are a mixture of rural areas with housing estates or suburban settlements. Generally, the discriminatory factors of the socio-spatial structure of the whole peripheral zone were communication with the centre and environmental conditions.

The increase of poverty in the urban space can be treated as a result of radical changes in social relations and the evolution of the government of urban space.

▽ ▨ Enclaves of poverty and poverty areas   ● Enclaves of wealth

0 ——————— 5 km

Fig. 8.3  Poverty and wealth areas in Warsaw, 1997.

We can also identify the two main causes of poverty: systematic error and personal error. The first concerns the majority of the elderly population, mostly pensioners and the retired, with very low income determined by government policies inherited from the communist period. Social workers indicated when interviewed that the minimal social benefits are enough to cover running expenditures like housing, and electricity, but leave nothing for food and other maintenance expenditures. In the case of systematic error, state policy can also be blamed for an increase in poverty among the majority of unemployed and the under-paid employees of the public sector. Personal error concerns the long-term "pathological" groups, and situations caused by individual choice or social inertia.

The emergence of poverty areas close to the booming development of luxurious estates generates political tensions, particularly in a society with still very egalitarian attitudes. On the other hand, it also generates attitudes opposing passivity and other traits inherited from the previous system, creating proactive ideas.

The emergence of large-scale areas of prosperity is still in its initial stage. One of the first indicators of this is the high concentration of new and very expensive luxury housing, partly in the central part of the city, in close proximity to the new commercial and business areas. The processes of creating the new enclaves are much faster for the areas of prosperity and much slower for the poor areas. At the same time, the wealthiest segment of society tends to form new areas outside Warsaw, giving new momentum to the process of suburbanization. The areas favoured usually have similar pre-war traditions, and in the case of Warsaw they are Konstancin (also known as the "Polish Beverly Hills"), Podkowa Leśna, Milanówek, and Łomianki. The suburban zone also experiences the emergence of very segregated and poor areas, formed by poor migrants with no opportunity to settle in Warsaw itself. For the reasons mentioned above, the space of suburban communes has become very differentiated in terms of social status.

## Economic Assets for the Reintegration of the Capital City Region into the European City System

The new international context has created a challenge for the Polish urban system, as it needs to compete for a place in the emerging urban hierarchy of Europe (Dematteis, 1996; Korcelli, 1997). The outcome of this competition will determine the prospects of all urbanized centres for their prosperous development in the beginning of the new century. In spite of the legacy of the past, primarily the socialist period, the cities of Poland – and the Warsaw Metropolitan Area in particular – have many important assets (Zalewski, 1997). These include the relatively good quality of the labour force, favourable geographical and geopolitical locations, urban and industrial structures that are easily adaptable to the new requirements, and lastly, a relatively low level of intra-urban disparities, in fact much lower than that of comparable cities in Western Europe. Nonetheless, the objectives and demands of a market economy raise the question of modernization in Polish cities, and of whether the process of reurbanization and re-industrialization should be introduced.

The significance of the notion of political decentralization, introduced at the beginning of the transition, has been limited recently. The Polish poly-centric urban system, with several large urban centres and agglomerations, is advantageous for the proposed regionalization of the country.

For the entire period of transition that begun in 1989, the Warsaw Metropolitan Area remained the region of the booming economy. Foreign investors became the new actors in Polish regional development (Fig. 8.4), and the highest share of their direct investment has been absorbed by the Warsaw region.

The attractive business environment has been quickly supported by the emergence of modern office space, financial centres, and good access to

(In million US$)

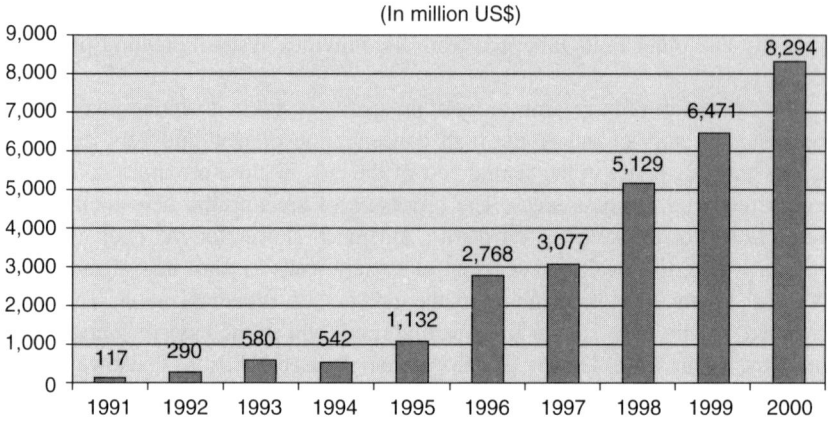

Fig. 8.4  Foreign direct investment in Poland.
*Source: Yearbook of Foreign Trade Statistics*, Central Statistical Office, Warsaw, 2001.

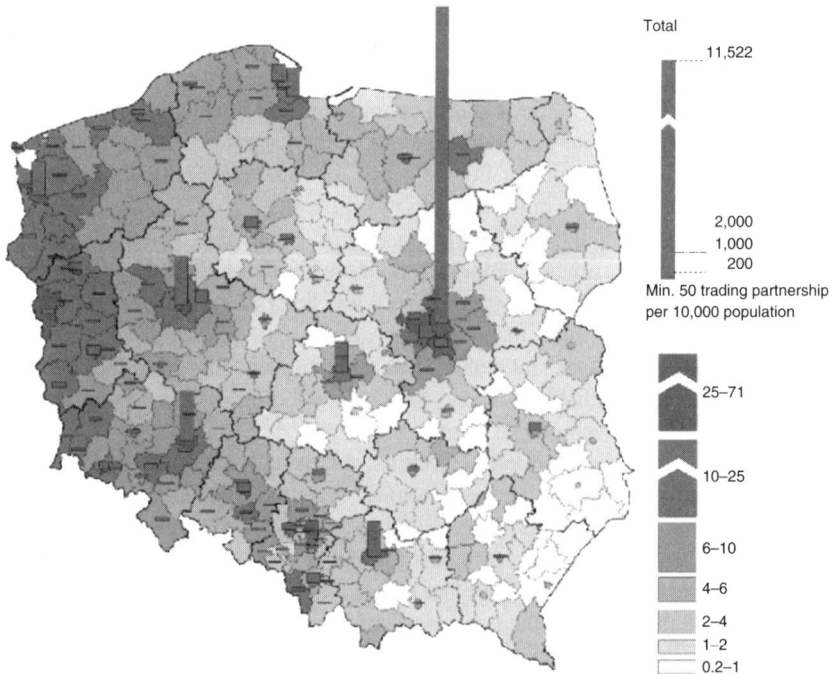

Fig. 8.5  Commercial partnerships with foreign participation.

well-trained professionals. In effect, the international business sector soon recognized Warsaw as an interesting focal location for this part of Europe, as well as an important consumer market. Over 30 per cent of all foreign capital companies in Poland have registered in Warsaw (Fig. 8.5). At the same time, because of the attractive labour market in Warsaw (almost free of unemployment), over 20 per cent of Warsaw's population has a university degree.

Warsaw has also become the financial centre of Central Europe, attracting 27 international banks, 206 of the largest Polish banks, and numerous international and domestic trusts and insurance companies. The National Bank of Poland and the Stock Exchange are also located there. The real-estate market still manages to attract foreign investors, even though Warsaw has a relatively high office space vacancy rate of 17 per cent. Nevertheless, in the second half of 2001 alone, 400 million euros have been invested. According to the official data, the average prime rent for office space in Warsaw is around 28 euros, being higher than in Prague or Budapest.

The retail trade was the first and the quickest economic activity to adapt to the market economy. Currently it is entirely private, and generally flourishing. At the same time, the large consumer market of Warsaw over the last four years attracted another 26 supermarkets with 500,000 sq.m of retail space.

The development of the business environment is best illustrated by the expansion of commercial office space in Warsaw (Fig. 8.6). On the regional level, the high concentration of new investment in Warsaw created the largest market of commercial office space in Central Europe. Despite that fact, the office market seems still to be undergoing the transition. The unduly expensive office rents of the beginning of the transition were the result of the shortage of the proper office space needed by foreign and domestic companies. Since 1989, over 120 office buildings have been constructed, which augmented office space in Warsaw to roughly 1.9–2.1 million sq.m of usable space (Śleszyński, 2002). As a result of this development, the rent level dropped from 60 euros per sq.m in the beginning of the 1990s, to below 30 euros per sq.m in 2002. The average rent for office space outside the centre is even lower, and varies from 15 to 19 euros per sq.m.

The spatial concentration of commercial offices has a direct impact on internal structure through the formation of new commercial headquarters in the urban space (Fig. 8.6). The relatively large dispersion of new office facilities, particularly in locations far from the traditional downtown areas, forced the reorganization of the entire central part of the city. Only in 2002 were as much as 197,000 sq.m of the city's office space built, of which 169,000 sq.m have been located outside the city centre. During 2003, another 50,000 sq.m of office stock will be added.

The former socialist centre of the city remained economically weak, whereas the historical and cultural heritage areas have been restored and prepared to fulfil more tourism-related functions. The new centre of economic activity has shifted westwards, taking over the former industrial areas. On the other hand, the prospects for completion of 125,000 sq.m of office space in the city centre might

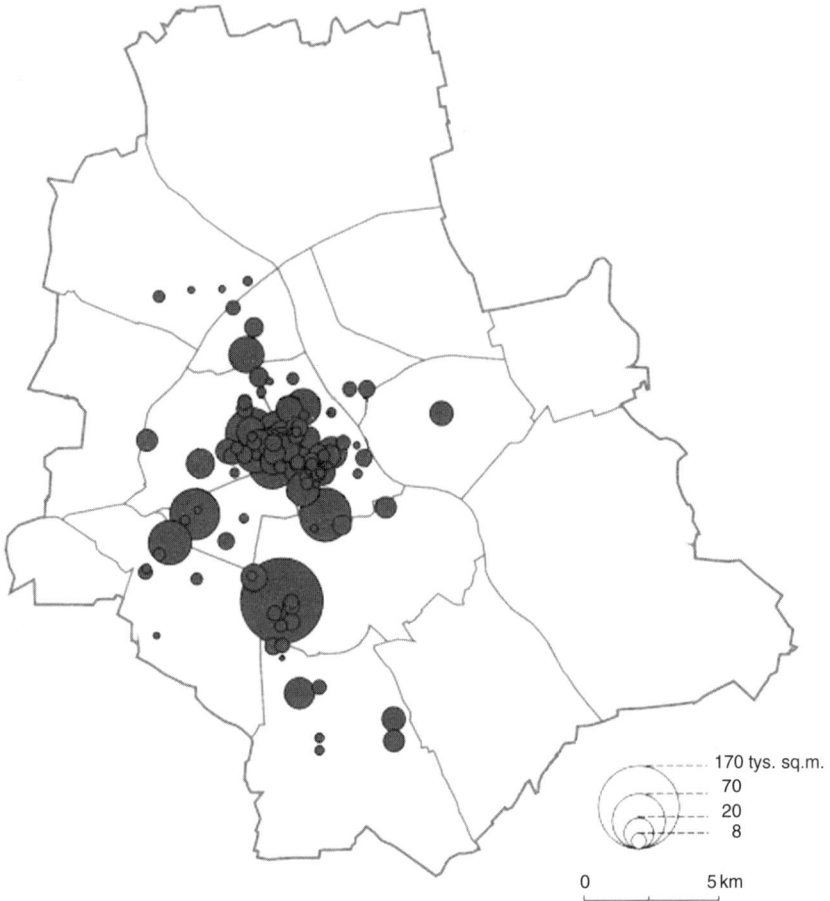

Fig. 8.6  Modern office space constructed in Warsaw, 1989–2001.
*Source:* Sleszynski, 2002.

partly reverse this trend. The only constraint, a legacy of the socialist past, is that in Warsaw after the Second World War most of the privately owned land was communalized for the sake of the planned development and restoration of the city. The extent of this communalization was much greater than in other cities. This problem of land ownership within Warsaw's pre-war administrative boundaries remains unsolved to this day. Restitution claims concern a total of 14,000 hectares, of which 12,200 are located in the central borough alone. In total, over 25 per cent of Warsaw's most strategic zones have a questionable legal status. As a result, various legal solutions are still under discussion, but it is possible that the city council might be forced to pay substantial compensations in the near future (Muzioł-Węcławowicz, 2001).

An important element of the general goals of the "Warsaw Development Strategy until 2010" is the improvement of living standards and the general appeal of the city. The largest asset in terms of environmental conditions is the fact that the Warsaw Metropolitan Area has retained its extensive green areas. The most important are the Kampinos primeval forest, also known as the "green heart" of Warsaw's agglomeration, and the forested areas on the eastern side of the Vistula River, known as the city's "green lung". Warsaw has also preserved corridors of open space, which function as an important climate-shaping element. All together, the river valley, the forested ring surrounding the city, the valuable areas of nature conservation, and other areas covered by the various protections cover about 47 per cent of the Warsaw Metropolitan Area (Degórska, 2002) (Fig. 8.7a – f ). These environmental resources are unique to Warsaw and

Fig. 8.7  Images of Warsaw. (a) Old town, Royal Castel, and Castel Square. (b) Old town, Vistula River banks. (c) The old "capitalist" and new "socialist" constructions of Kosciol Ewangelicki, Zacheta, and the Palac Kultury. (d) Inner city, large housing estate. (e) City centre, commercial street of Nowy Swiat. (f ) The new CBD under formation.

cannot really be compared with the other largest European metropoles. They are also very advantageous in terms of facilitating the sustainable development of the whole metropolitan area.

## Towards a New Function of the Warsaw Metropolitan Area

Transport and communication are recognized as the key factors in modern economies. However, according to the "European Transport Policy for 2010: Time to Decide" (White Paper), the Europe of the 1990s began to suffer from traffic congestion in certain areas and on certain routes. Furthermore, congestion in the centre goes hand in hand with excessive isolation of the outlying regions. This situation will dramatically deteriorate with the eastern enlargement of the European Union. Substantial improvements in modern transport and communications between the European core and the enlarged peripheries are necessary to ensure regional cohesion within the European Union.

The concept of the Warsaw Metropolitan Area as a future gateway to the European Union could be easily combined with the much wider concept of "The Eastern Gateways of the European Union". The proposed extended idea of the new East–West transport network, known as the "Eurocorridor", offers a unique historical chance for the economic and social progress of the Central European metropolitan areas.

The Warsaw Metropolitan Area is situated, similarly to the other Central European metropoles, immediately on the fringe of the enlarged European Union. This highly developed region faces basic constraints in expansion further to the east due to a lack of appropriate transport facilities. Poland in particular lacks a modern network of motorways. On the European scale, there is a difference in gauge between the railway network in post-Soviet countries and the rest of the trans-European network. The Eurocorridor project aims to improve economic conditions and social cohesion, maintain a positive environmental context through more sustainable modes of trade and transport, and enhance prosperity and quality of life in the fringe regions. It offers probably the best way of facilitating economic expansion further to the East, enhancing the basic assets of the entire European Union in global competition. The existence of a good facility for further economic expansion across the new Member States to Eastern Europe (Russia, Belarus, and Ukraine) and beyond should prove profitable for the core of economic development in the European Union. All together, this concept might positively contribute to the new shape of Europe in the future.

Between the different concepts generated by the political and economic sciences, describing current, historical, and potential axes or belts of communication and development, one of the most popular is the idea of an East–West flow of information, innovation, invasions, migration, and other elements. The huge Eastern European Plain stretching from the Ural to the Atlantic is one of the obvious physical factors facilitating intense communication.

The intensification of economic and cultural exchange between the EU Member States and the process of enlargement creates a growing need for a new trans-European transport network. These axes or corridors are of strategic importance for the future. At the moment, the East–West links between the European Union and the candidate countries are rather poorly developed. They are designed to remove bottlenecks of economic exchange and of the regional development of the peripheral regions.

Suggested structural investment in the east of Warsaw, composed of the Warsaw Metropolitan Area beltway connected with the intersections of Via Baltica and Via Intermare, gives the regional policies a geopolitical meaning. The borders are no longer lines to be defended, they are rather corridors of open passage. In the case of Poland, they will be slightly asymmetric. The border with the European Union will cease to exist, whereas the eastern border will remain open, but at the same time, will be more controlled. It is quite likely it will not be as freely accessible as the other borders. This of course will have a strong impact on regional development, as border crossings tend to facilitate local growth.

The formation of the communication and infrastructural facilities concentrated in the east of Warsaw (generally between Minsk Mazowiecki and Siedlce) should be part of the new development axes (Via Baltica and Via Intermare), together with the A2 motorway (the main East–West project under construction, connecting Warsaw and Berlin) proposed a long time ago, leading to the Poland – Belarus border (Fig. 8.8).

The first axis is the Via Baltica. It envisions the construction of a motorway leading from Warsaw to Tallinn in Estonia, and even further (by ferry) to Helsinki, Finland. This proposal is indeed in the best interests of all countries concerned (Poland, Lithuania, Latvia, and Estonia), as well as in the interests of Finland. Also its construction is in the interests of Russia, with a possible extension of the motorway to St Petersburg in and to the Kaliningrad district. In terms of regional development, it will create a belt of prosperity across one of the most underdeveloped regions of north-eastern Poland.

In a similar way, the construction of the Via Intermare (between the Baltic and the Black Sea) connecting Warsaw with Ukraine will function as an alternative connection of the core economic area of the European Union with the south-east of Europe and the Black Sea and Caucasian countries. Its specific route is suggested to lead from Gdansk to Odessa, and further through the Black Sea, Georgia, Armenia, and Azerbaijan, to Central Asia. It was also suggested to use the already existing parts of this route in its construction. The idea was fairly successful and initiated the emergence of additional concepts such as the construction of a gas pipeline from Central Asia. In effect, in 2001, the first rail freight connection was opened from Gdańsk to Odessa.

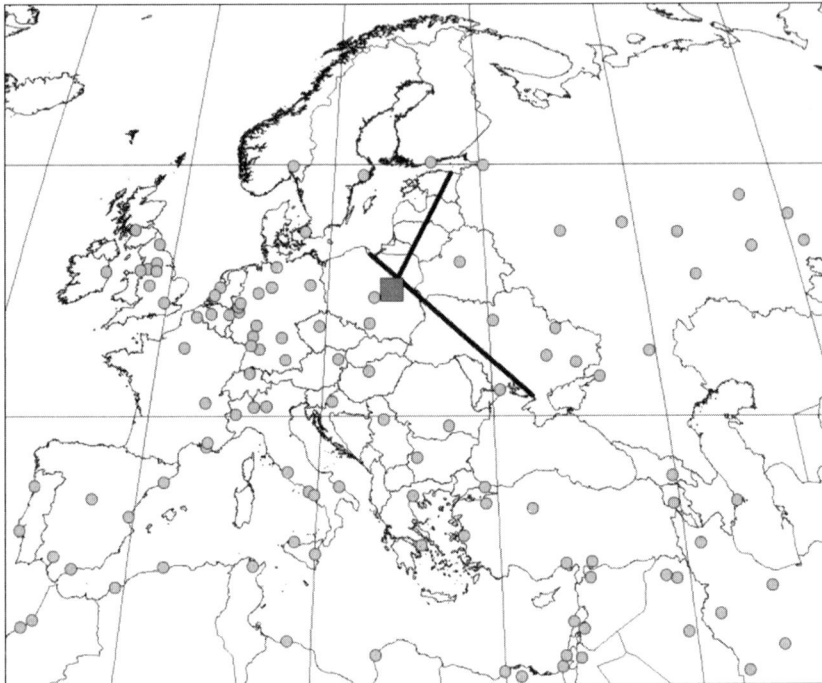

Fig. 8.8  New axes of development: Via Intermare and Via Baltica.

As of today, the Via Intermare is not the focus of EU policy-makers, but still might become a crucial element for future Polish development strategies. At the same time, it provides the Ukraine with the quickest access to the European developed markets. It is also to be expected that the European Union will eventually decide to expand to the Ukrainian market using the same corridor. The proposed route omits the politically unstable Balkans and opens new possibilities for the dynamic Turkish economy. The construction of the Via Intermare should enable the Scandinavian countries to avoid the crowded motorways of Germany and Austria and provide them with better opportunities of cooperation with the Black Sea region. It should also be noted that the proposed connection does not interfere with the planned trans-European A1 motorway from Oslo, through Gdynia to the Balkan countries and Turkey. Lastly, the Via Intermare should provide a better opportunity to cooperate with Romania, as the port of Konstanza would gain an alternative connection with Western Europe or the Scandinavian Peninsula through the proposed Via Baltica. The Via Intermare supplements the European Union's already approved A4 motorway, leading through southern Poland to Ukraine.

The creation and development of infrastructural and transport corridors should prove one of the most important means of utilizing the strategic geopolitical location of Poland. In this manner, Poland might become a bridge between the East and the West, rather than a separating buffer zone.

## Conclusions: The Chances of Warsaw in Capital City Competition in Central and Eastern Europe

The greater integration of the Polish settlement system with that of Western Europe is inevitable. Looking at the relationship between the post-communist and Western European cities, it is apparent that the former perhaps fulfil the suburban function for the Western metropoles within close proximity (e.g. Bratislava as a suburb of Vienna). A similar situation could develop with the Polish cities of Poznań, Szczecin, and Wrocław, in their relation to Berlin. In the context of European integration and the decentralization of the national administration, it is possible that some alternatives to Warsaw in terms of close economic cooperation might develop. For example, Gdańsk could become a partner for Copenhagen, Wrocław could become a partner of Prague, and Kraków could establish closer ties with Vienna and Budapest. Therefore, the challenge for Warsaw, and for the regional policies of Poland in general, is whether to make Warsaw more attractive than the other large Polish cities, or to leave it as a mere "capital" for eastern Poland. The possible economic integration of the Polish regional system, particularly with neighbouring Germany, could also create a counter-reaction to the increasing functional integration of the national system in political and cultural terms.

Warsaw's position in the European urban system will probably be based on the regional development of Poland and the creation of the "core development area" between Warsaw, Łódź, and Poznań, as well as on its location on the West–East axis (Paris–Berlin–Warsaw–Moscow). In the future context of the European Union, Warsaw will serve as a gateway to Eastern Europe.

In spite of the quickness of transition, the social and economic activity of urban dwellers will, for a long time yet, be carried out in a physical structure created for other economic and ideological objectives. Unfortunately, the formation of a post-socialist city is still far from complete.

Warsaw's position and international image have improved in recent years, and Warsaw has become classified as one of the European centres, together with Prague and Budapest. One of the substantial contributing factors for this is the success of the Polish transformation. Warsaw as a centre of economic, financial, and managerial decision-making attracted a large share of foreign investment. Nonetheless, the dynamic development of the city presents a challenge for urban managers, politicians, and urban planners. The "Warsaw Development Strategy until 2010" indicates its basic goal as "Warsaw as a European metropolis with a rapidly growing economy and a steadily increasing standard of living". This goal, however, calls for a substantial increase in the city's competitiveness in relation to other European cities.

## REFERENCES

Jeans Dangschat, "Socio-spatial Disparities in a 'Socialist' City. The Case of Warsaw at the end of the 1970s", *International Journal of Urban and Regional Research* 11, 1987, pp. 37–60.

Bożena Degórska, "Kształtowanie terenów otwartych na obszarze metropolitalnym Warszawy – rozpoznanie problemów" [Shaping of Open Spaces in the Warsaw Metropolitan Area – A Preliminary Study], in Grzegorz Weclawowicz, ed., *Warszawa jako przedmiot bada w geografii społeczno-ekonomicznej*, Warsaw: Prace Geograficzne, 184, Instytut Geografii i PZ PAN, 2002, pp. 37–54.

Giuseppe Dematteis, "Towards a United Metropolitan System in Europe: Core Centrality versus Network Distributed Centrality", in Denise Pumain and Therrese Sant-Julien, eds, *Urban Networks in Europe*, Paris: INED/John Libbey, 1996, pp. 19–28.

Stanisław Furman, "Globalizacja metropolii warszawskiej. Ogólny szkic problemu", in Antoni Kukliński, Jerzy Kołodziejski, Tadeusz Markowski, and Wojciech Dziemianowicz, eds, *Globalizacja polskich metropolii*, Warsaw: Euroreg, 2000, pp. 421–447.

Bogdan Jałowiecki, "Warszawa jako metropolia europejska?" [Warsaw as a European Metropolis?], in Antoni Kukliński, Jerzy Kołodziejski, Tadeusz Markowski, and Wojciech Dziemianowicz, eds, *Globalizacja polskich metropolii*, Warsaw: Euroreg, 2000, pp. 24–80.

Piotr Korcelli, "The Urban System of Poland in an Era of Increasing Inter-Urban Competition", *Geographie Polonica* 69(1), 1997, pp. 45–54.

——, "Warsaw: The Eastern End of the Trajectory", in *The Changing Map of Europe, the Trajectory Berlin–Pozna –Warsaw–A Tribute to Antoni Kukli ski*, Warsaw: Oficyna Wydawnicza Rewasz, 1999, pp. 141–150.

Antoni Kukliński, "Metropolia Warszawy wobec wyzwań procesów globalizacji", in Antoni Kukliński, Jerzy Kołodziejski, Tadeusz Markowski, and Wojciech Dziemianowicz, eds, *Globalizacja polskich metropolii*, Warsaw: Euroreg, 2000, pp. 13–23.

Antoni Kukliński, Jerzy Kołodziejski, Tadeusz Markowski, and Wojciech Dziemianowicz, eds, *Globalizacja polskich metropolii*, Warszawa: Euroreg, 2000.

Stanisław Misztal, "Przekształcenie struktury przemysłu Warszawy" [Transformation in the Industrial Structure of Warsaw], in *Atlas Warszawy* 8, 1998.

Alina Muzioł-Węcławowicz, "Property Development and Land Market in Warsaw – A Challenge for Urban Planning", manuscript, 2000.

Ôleszyński Przemysław, *"Office Space Investments and the Development of Management Space in Warsaw in the Period of Transformation (1989–2001)"*, *Europa XXI, Institute of Geography and Spatial Organization, Warsaw: Polish Geographical Society, 7*, 2002, pp. 87–99.

*The Warsaw Housing Report: 20th issue 2001*, Warsaw: Capital City of Warsaw, 2002.

Grzegorz, Weclawowicz, "Struktura przestrzeni społeczno-gospodarczej Warszawy w latach 1931 i 1970 w świetle analizy czynnikowej" [The Structure of Socio-economic Space in Warsaw in 1931 and 1970 in the Light of Factor Analysis], *Prace Geograficzne* 116, Wrocław: IGiPZ PAN Ossolineum, 1975.

——, "Phóba teorii struktury wewnetrznej miast Polski. Studium z ekologii czynnikowej" [Towards a Theory of Intra-urban Structures in Polish Cities], in Kazimierz Dziewoński and Piotr Korcelli, eds, *Studia nad migracjami I przemianami systemu osadniczego w Plosce*, *Prace Geograficzne*, Wrocław: IGiPZ PAN 140, Ossolineum, 1981, pp. 234–267.

——, *Struktury społeczno-przestrzenne w miastach Polski* [Socio-spatial Structures in Polish Cities], Wrocław: Prace habilitacyjne IGiPZ PAN, Ossolineum, 1988.

——, *"Die Sozialraumliche Structure Warschas. Ausganglage und Postkommunisstische Umgestaltung"*, Wien: Herausgegeben vom Institut Fur Stadt-Und Regionalforschung, Osterreichische Akademie der Wissenschaften, 1992.

——, *Contemporary Poland. Space and Society*, London: UCL Press, 1996.

——, "Varsovie, future metropole europeenne?", *Le courrier des pays de l'Est* 430, 1998a, pp. 52–65.

——, "What to do with the Post-socialist Cities? – Towards a New Policy", in Ryszard Domański, ed., *Emerging Spatial and Regional Structures of an Economy in Transition*, Warsaw: Wydawnictwo Naukowe PWN, 1998b, pp. 163– 182.

——, "Social Polarization in Post-socialist Cities: Budapest, Prague and Warsaw", in György Enyedi, ed., *Social Change and Urban Restructuring in Central Europe*, Budapest: Akademia Kiado, 1998c, pp. 55–66.

——, "Przestrzeń ubóstwa – nowy czy stary wymiar zró nicowania społeczno-przestrzennego w miastach Polski" [Areas of Poverty – New or Old Dimension of Socio-spatial Differentiation in Polish cities], *Przeglad Geograficzny* 73(4), 2001, pp. 451–475.

——, "From Egalitarian Cities in Theory to Non-egalitarian Cities in Practice: The Changing Social and Spatial Patterns in Polish Cities", in Peter Marcuse and Ronald van Kempen, eds, *Of States and Cities: The Partitioning of Urban Space*, Oxford: Oxford University Press, 2002, pp. 183–199.

Andrzej Zalewski, *Economic Transformation in the Warsaw Agglomeration during the 1990s*, Warsaw: Polish Academy of Science, 1997, pp. 19–36.

# 9

# Post-socialist Budapest:
# The invasion of market forces and
# the response of public leadership

*Iván Tosics*

## Introduction

Although Budapest was one of the biggest cities of central Europe throughout the twentieth century, events in history have changed its relative position many times in the local, national, and international contexts. The second largest city of a once much larger country (Austro-Hungarian Monarchy), Budapest acquired a strong dominant role as capital within the much smaller Hungary after 1920, but lost much of its earlier international reputation. The socialist period initially brought severe isolation, which was gradually eased from the 1960s. Following the reforms of the 1980s, the political changes of 1989/1990 opened up a wealth of opportunities for the city to regain its earlier powerful position in the Central European region. As the capital of a small but open, foreign-trade-orientated economy, market-orientated changes in Budapest were quick, and the development of the city soon became dominated by the processes of globalization and EU accession.

From 1989 until the middle of the 1990s, Budapest received far more FDI than other cities in the Central European region (except East Berlin). Consequently, Budapest exemplifies some of the accelerated restructuring processes that are not yet as advanced in many other capital cities of the region. The following analysis of the last 12 years of change in the city also aims at answering the question: to what extent is the liberal, non-interventionist strategy of leadership successful, and what are those factors and reasons that would make a more active public leadership necessary?

The structure of this chapter is as follows: after a very brief historical review, the main factors of transition are discussed, summarizing the political, institutional, administrative, and economic changes that have occurred. In analysing the trends at the end of the 1990s, particular attention is paid to migration processes and their causes and effects on different parts of the city as well as on the metropolitan region. A detailed account is provided of the new concepts discussed at the municipal level about future urban development, and the relationship of the capital city to the regional level.

## The Heritage of the Past: A Historical Overview of City Development

Buda and Pest developed for a long time as separate cities on opposite banks of the Danube. Buda became the diplomatic centre of the country, and in many respects of an even bigger area in the late 1300s. After a "golden age" of one-and-a-half centuries the city lost most of its international importance during the Turkish occupation and also during the reign of the Habsburgs. Real development of the city restarted with the technical–industrial innovations of the nineteenth century. Budapest was established administratively with the unification of Óbuda, Buda, and Pest in 1873. The "Compromise" with Austria in 1867 created favourable circumstances for development, and the half-century from that date until the First World War was the most dynamic period of development in Budapest's history.

In the inter-war period, Budapest became the capital of a country that lost not only the war, but also two-thirds of its former territory. National independence came together with a small-nation status, so Budapest could only very slowly and gradually try to regain its importance on the international scene (Beluszky, 1998: 43).

The 44 years of Soviet dominance and the imposition of the socialist system created at the beginning very unfavourable conditions for Hungary and its capital, which became very isolated from the Western world. From the 1960s onwards, however, Hungarian politics achieved a gradual opening-up of its foreign relations and by the end of the 1980s, Budapest was almost regarded as a "European city" again. Thus, the collapse of socialism and the change of the political and economic system were of relatively less importance for Budapest than for the other capitals of the Central and Eastern European countries. However, it was only after 1989 that Budapest could again become an integral part of the European urban system.[1]

## The Transition: The Main Factors of Change

The fundamental changes in the political, economic, and institutional conditions for city development in Eastern Europe are discussed in Chapters 3 and 4, so topics specific to the development of Budapest will be analysed in this chapter.

## Political and Geo-strategic Change, and Local Government Reforms

### The First Decade of the Democratic Political System: Changes at the National and Local Levels

As one of the most important steps of the political transition, the first free parliamentary elections took place in Hungary in April 1990 and were won by the Conservative – Christian Democratic coalition.[2] The new parliament adopted – as one of its first activities – the Law on Local Governments. This brought very substantial changes at the local level, the previous council system being replaced by independent local governments. As a result, in practice, the previous strong party domination over local politics was dissolved and political power at the local level was passed to locally elected politicians. In October 1990, the first free local elections took place and the liberal parties won in almost all of the bigger cities. In Budapest, 21 out of 22 districts elected a mayor from either the Alliance of Free Democrats or the Federation of Young Democrats. Consequently, the leadership of the Budapest municipal government has also become liberal in opposition to the national government.

After the first four-year term, the second free elections took place in 1994. The leading coalitions changed at both the national and local levels; the parliament became dominated by the Socialist party, which formed a coalition with the Alliance of Free Democrats. The same coalition was formed also at the Budapest level, and there the previous mayor of the municipality was re-elected (this was the first time that the mayors had been elected directly). In 1998, in the third free elections, nothing changed in Budapest (both the mayor and leading coalition were re-elected) but at the national level a right-wing coalition took over power from the socialist–liberal coalition. Thus Budapest – with unchanged local politicians – came for the second time into opposition with the national government (as it had been between 1990 and 1994). Finally, in 2002 the situation of 1994–1998 returned: the still unchanged Budapest coalition (with Mayor Demszky starting his fourth term) now has a national government consisting of the same parties. This is the second period of potentially friendly relations with the central government.

## The Law on Local Governments: New Administrative Structure

### The Two-tier Administrative Structure of Budapest

In 1950, a two-tier administrative structure with elected municipal and district councils was introduced in Budapest, parallel to the creation of a "greater Budapest" (through the annexation of surrounding settlements). The system of municipal and district councils, however, did not function in the socialist period as a real two-tier system, as there were no real roles and rights given to the districts; the important decisions were taken at the municipal and in many cases even the national level.

The 1990 Law on Local Governments reinforced the previous two-tier administrative structure of Budapest. The municipal government and the 22 (later 23) district governments were all considered to be local governments, having their assemblies of elected politicians and their mayors. This highly complicated system had at least two in-built conflicts: the first between the municipality and the districts, the second between the mayor and the assembly (since 1994 mayors were elected directly and it happened frequently that they did not come from the party that was strongest in the local assembly).

The 1990 Law delegated very important functions to the lower district level (all local, neighbourhood public services), while the municipality became the owner of the public utilities and assumed the tasks related to the whole or a large part of the capital (see the detailed description in Bird, Ebel, and Wallich, 1995: 122). The municipality and the districts also became independent in an economic sense, as they acquired their own assets and the right to establish their budgets independently.

The two-tier administrative structure of the municipality and the districts functioned with great difficulties in the first years. The administrative system contained elements of at least three different models simultaneously: it was centralized, as the big infrastructure networks and public works became municipality-owned; it was federal, as the allocation of normative state subsidies between the municipality and the districts was subject to negotiations; and finally, it was also decentralized, as the districts obtained substantial independence (Perger, 1999: 197). It is no wonder that there were ongoing debates between the actors and several modifications to the system were necessary:

*1990–1994*: the period of equal rights in municipal–district relations meant that the two actors could successfully block each other (e.g. the municipality had zoning rights, while the district issued building permissions, so each actor had a strong tool to stop the ideas of the other).

*1994–1998*: a modification of the Law on Local Governments gave the municipal level some more rights, especially in planning for the whole city.

*1998*: new ideas emerged to increase the role of the districts, especially in the allocation of central budget transfers (e.g. the allocation of shared financial means requires the approval of the majority of the districts as well as the municipality).

The decentralized, fragmented character of the administrative system is even more true when taking local elections into account. The "electoral map" of Budapest shows clearly how strong a "demarcation line" the Danube is, since the right-wing parties dominate richer Buda districts, while the majority of the more problematic Pest areas belong to the centre–left wing coalition (since 2002, however, even some of the Buda districts have come under centre/left control.)

## Budapest and its Agglomeration

The structure of the Budapest agglomeration can be interpreted as a series of concentric circles or sequential rings (Schuchmann, 1992: 1):

- the earlier "Little Budapest," i.e. the city within its border until 1950;
- Budapest within its current administrative border (together with the settlements attached in 1950, which could be called "the inner agglomeration zone");
- the suburban area around Budapest with very intensive connections to the city: a zone with 600,000 residents living in 78 suburban settlements defined since the mid-1990s as the "agglomeration zone"; and
- the outer ring, a larger surrounding area, which acts as "a protecting zone" in many respects.

Figure 9.1 shows first three concentric rings or zones, while the last and biggest unit is Budapest and the whole of Pest County (together called the Central Hungarian Region). In addition to the ring-based structure, a radial structure can also be observed, which means that the agglomeration can be divided into sectors and that it also extends the boundaries of the rings out along the main transportation routes (Pestterv – MTA RKK, 1995: 7).

Previously, the "suburban belt" included 44 settlements. There were no empirical criteria in determining the borders of the agglomeration, because this group of settlements was not "institutionalized." The Act on Local Governments of 1990–1991 created a decentralized administration system, concentrating very much on the local government level and not at all on the "middle level" of county or regional functions. Accordingly, no regulation was passed on competencies related to urban development or agglomeration relations around big cities.

Changes concerning the definition and institutionalization of the agglomeration came only in the second half of the 1990s. On the one hand, the definition of the Budapest agglomeration was revised, and a bigger settlement group with 78 settlements was officially declared – for statistical purposes only – as an agglomeration. On the other hand, the Act on Urban Development was approved, establishing county development councils and regional development councils in the country. One of those was the Budapest Agglomeration Development Council, including Budapest and its agglomeration (with 2.6 million inhabitants).

Despite the official acceptance of the existence of a "Budapest agglomeration" or metropolitan region and the establishment of the Budapest Agglomeration Development Council, the system around Budapest remained fragmented and relations between the city and its surroundings remain highly problematic. As the rights of the county self-governments were minimized in 1990, Pest County had practically no power to influence any of the decisions made by the settlements. Thus, the surrounding area can be regarded as a fragmented system: individual settlements are weak as regards any serious negotiations with Budapest, there is no formalized "agglomeration" structure, and not even the county can (or wants) to represent the interests of the

Fig. 9.1   Administrative structure of the Budapest agglomeration.

agglomeration (Perger, 1999: 198). On the other hand, the settlements around Budapest are very strong, as no one can influence in any way their individual development decisions.

To sum up, the new administrative structure of 1990 favoured the local governments as the lowest level of the settlement hierarchy, and gave much less rights to the middle level (almost nothing to the counties, and only restricted rights to the municipal level in Budapest). This made coordination above the district level very difficult, and coordination between Budapest and the neighbouring settlements became totally impossible.

*Municipal Finance Issues*

The Hungarian municipal finance system was already reformed four years before the political changes: in 1986 the "expenditure regulation" system (in which expenditures had to be negotiated with the National Planning Office and the accepted expenditures got automatic financing from the budget) was replaced with a much more democratic "resource regulation" system (in which the resource levels of the local governments were regulated and it was up to the local level how to spend the accepted resources).

Decisions of major importance to the creation of more independent local governments at the beginning of the 1990s included the Property Transfer Act, transferring the ownership of previously state-owned retail and commercial units, vacant land, and public rental housing stock to the local level; and the Law on Local Taxes, which gave local governments the right to impose certain taxes. Despite legal efforts to increase the possibilities for raising local revenues (Bird, Ebel, and Wallich, 1995: 93), in the early 1990s central budget sources dominated the revenue side. It was only in the second half of the decade that locally sourced revenues exceeded central resources, because of a dynamic increase in the business turnover tax (i.e. local tax with the highest importance for the local governments).

Due to the difficulties of the two-tier administrative system, in which both levels were entitled to own some revenues, a special construction of financial resource allocation between the municipality and districts has been introduced in Budapest. This system, aiming to create more equal financial opportunities for the districts to perform the same tasks, is subject each year to lengthy and difficult political debate between the districts and the municipality.

The allocation of central budget resources has taken a definite change in the 1990s: compared to the previous period, smaller settlements have received more support. This had important consequences in the suburban area around Budapest. Local governments in Pest County completed major development projects during the period of 1990–1994. According to an empirical survey (Pestterv – MTA RKK, 1995: 78), half the local governments launched five or more investment projects (gas and mains water establishments, sewage, gymnasiums, road construction, telephones etc.). The majority of development was related to infrastructure and two-thirds of the settlements chose debt financing to complete the projects. At the same time, one-quarter of the local governments could only manage their operations with the help of loans. The survey indicated that the ongoing burdens of these development projects launched during the period of 1990–1994 meant that approximately one-quarter of the settlements did not plan any further development for the following four years. Nevertheless, approximately 50 per cent of the settlements came up with new ideas, too, besides infrastructure projects. Settlement reorganization and local economic development (creating industrial sites, shopping centre construction etc.), crucial for the purpose of attracting entrepreneurs, began to play a very important role among these other objectives.

## Economic Reforms: Patterns of Change

### Economic Development in the City and its Metropolitan Region

Before the changes to the political system, business relations between Budapest and its surrounding area moved primarily in one direction. During the industrialization of the country in the 1960s and 1970s, administrative regulations prohibited the establishment of industrial plants, even sites of larger companies, within a 50-km radius around Budapest. Thus, the settlements of the agglomeration became mostly related to the industry of Budapest through commuting (Pestterv – MTA RKK, 1995: 7) and the proportion of those commuting to Budapest has reached 61 per cent within the actively employed population of the agglomeration.

In 1990, the Budapest economy provided more than 1 million jobs, 82 per cent of which were filled by people living in Budapest and 18 per cent by commuters. Nevertheless, between 1970 and 1990 the number of Budapest jobs decreased by 20 per cent, reducing the proportion of all Hungarian jobs located in the capital from 26 to 23 per cent (Barta, 1998: 204). The decrease in the number of jobs continued also in the 1990s (1994: 876,000 jobs in Budapest; 1996: 779,000 jobs).

Regarding the restructuring of the job market, the crisis in Budapest's traditional industries and the development of the new economic structure are the most important factors in the relationship between Budapest and the agglomeration (Pestterv – MTA RKK, 1995: 10).

The crisis in the traditional Budapest industries can be illustrated with the following data: between 1983 and 1993, the number of industrial jobs in Budapest fell from 347,000 to 128,000. Obviously, this also involved a decrease in opportunities for commuters (between 1990 and 1992, the number of people commuting to Budapest decreased by 13–15 per cent). The crisis had a further direct impact on those settlements where Budapest companies had a site (primarily larger settlements outside the close agglomeration, such as Vác, Cegléd, and Nagykôrös), and on the settlements where additional cooperative activities, contracted by Budapest industry, developed.

Private businesses could be created as early as at the beginning of the 1980s (in the first few years only small enterprises were allowed, but from 1985 onwards the upper limit for the number of employees of a private firm was increased to 300). The number of individual businesses grew faster in the agglomeration; this was an advance sign that a new, cooperation-based type of work distribution was developing, replacing the former one-sided labour attraction.

The new economic structure has developed faster in Budapest and its surrounding area than in other parts of the country. Consequently, the local economy became stronger in settlements surrounding Budapest relatively fast. This provided jobs for many of those who were previously commuting to Budapest. The degree to which the former state-owned and cooperative plants and additional industrial structures were transformed was also an important issue. These structures represented the most important opportunity for the initiation of new private businesses, since very few Hungarian small enterprises had sufficient equity for green-field investments, typical only for enterprises owned by foreigners.

In settlements where the former industries were revitalized in the form of private businesses and even new, green-field jobs were created, the one-sided relationship between Budapest and the agglomeration has ceased. The former direct controlling role of Budapest is becoming more and more indirect and is being replaced by the capital, money, and information market.

Together with privatization, and partly related to it, the influx of foreign investments was the most important driving force for economic change. By October 1999, about US$20.5 billion of FDI came into the country, more than half of it to Budapest. A substantial part of this investment came as machinery, which contributes to the fact that the efficiency of this region is higher.

It is possible to estimate the share of public versus private investments in city development. Total investment in the city can be estimated to be around 600 billion HUF (US$2.4 billion) per year. The budget of Budapest, municipality and districts together, is around 400 billion HUF per year, i.e. US$1.6 billion at the end of the 1990s, of which – in many years' average – 15–20 per cent (US$240–320 billion) is designated for development purposes. If the investment of other public bodies (central government etc.) was of similar magnitude, the share of the private sector in total investment could be estimated as 70–85 per cent. Taking another source of information, according to official statistics (*Statistical Yearbook of 1998*), 13 per cent of total investment came from the central government, 6 per cent from the local governments, and 81 per cent from the private sector.

The data in Table 9.1 indicate that Budapest and its surrounding area benefited significantly from foreign investments. Considering the number of companies with foreign investment and the registered capital amount, Budapest has a 54 per cent respectively 53 per cent share (while Pest County has a 7 per cent respectively 14 per cent share) of the national data. This shows that in the 1990s the highest number of companies with foreign investment operated in Budapest and Pest County and the largest amount of foreign working capital was also invested there. However, the data indicating large concentrations need to be approached with care because they are all based on the records of company head offices. Practice shows that in many cases the sites in the countryside are large because the trans-national companies place their routine manufacturing activities in the countryside even if their head offices are established in Budapest, and therefore all their activities are statistically recorded in the city (Barta, 1992: 1).

After the dynamic rise in the first two to three years in the number of companies with foreign ownership, this number stabilized; the amount of equity capital, however, continued to increase, as a result of the efforts of foreign owners to increase their shares in and the capital of their ventures.

Table 9.1 The impact of FDI in Budapest and its agglomeration: the number and equity capital of the foreign-owned companies

| | Number of companies | | | | Equity capital (in million US$) | | | |
|---|---|---|---|---|---|---|---|---|
| | Budapest | Pest County | Hungary | The share of Budapest in the country (%) | Budapest | Pest country | Hungary | The share of Budapest in the county (%) |
| 1992 | 8,907 | 1,081 | 17,182 | 51.8 | 5,055 | 526 | 8,913 | 56.7 |
| 1993 | 10,953 | 1,312 | 20,999 | 52.2 | 7,882 | 647 | 12,100 | 65.0 |
| 1994 | 12,838 | 1,461 | 23,557 | 54.5 | 9,142 | 712 | 13,574 | 67.3 |
| 1995 | 12,150 | 1,550 | 25,096 | 48.4 | 8,812 | 1,169 | 15,825 | 55.6 |
| 1996 | 12,923 | 1,638 | 26,130 | 49.5 | 8,149 | 1,042 | 14,930 | 54.6 |
| 1997 | 13,349 | 1,691 | 26,529 | 50.3 | 8,588 | 1,275 | 15,432 | 55.6 |
| 1998 | 13,410 | 1,720 | 25,992 | 51.6 | 7,807 | 1,162 | 13,800 | 56.6 |
| 1999 | 13,964 | 1,881 | 26,433 | 52.8 | 7,600 | 1,206 | 13,428 | 56.7 |
| 2000 | 14,322 | 2,007 | 26,645 | 53.7 | 7,208 | 1,570 | 12,783 | 56.4 |
| 2001[*] | 13,584 | 1,864 | 25,365 | 53.6 | 6,608 | 1,716 | 12,380 | 53.4 |

Note: [*]Preliminary data.
*Source: Statistical Yearbook of Hungary.*

In 1991, only around 15 per cent of the companies with foreign capital were owned 100 per cent by foreigners. Recently this share increased to 60 per cent, and in another 33 per cent of the companies foreigners are in a majority ownership position (Barta, 2000).

The tendencies of the 1990s show that besides Budapest, the economy of Pest County has also become very active and there are a lot of new businesses. "Yet these business projects do not promote the modernisation of the economic structure of the county, they rather help to maintain the former economic structure (for example companies do not need many specialists with higher degrees, the largest demand exists for trained young blue-collar workforce)." (Pestterv – MTA RKK, 1995: 63) The significant differences in investment patterns between Budapest and Pest County are shown in Tables 9.2 and 9.3. In Budapest, the newly established foreign-owned companies start their activities mainly in the service sectors: financial services, commercial activities, and the real-estate business (13–15 per cent each). In the case of Pest County, manufacturing is the leading edge of investment (here most of the investments come from Hungarian-owned companies – partly MOL, the biggest oil company in Hungary – while in the case of Budapest, most of the investors are largely foreign-owned). The difference is very substantial: the share of service-related investments is around 60–70 per cent in Budapest, while only around 20–30 per cent in Pest County.

Table 9.2 The share of the different sectors in investment of the partly or fully foreign-owned companies in Budapest (total amount of investment in million US$)

|  | 1992 | 1993 | 1994 | 1995 | 1996 | 1998 | 1999 | 2000 | 2001 |
|---|---|---|---|---|---|---|---|---|---|
| Agriculture, hunting, forestry | — | — | — | — | — | 0.2 | — | — | — |
| Mining and quarrying | — | — | — | — | — | — | — | — | — |
| Manufacturing | 24.5 | 21.0 | 28.7 | 24.8 | 19.0 | 19.3 | 23.9 | 22.7 | 30 |
| Electricity, gas, sewage, and water supply | — | 0.2 | — | 4.8 | 4.7 | 7.2 | 8.2 | 8.8 | 11.9 |
| Construction | 2.1 | 1.6 | 3.0 | 10.0 | 16.8 | 2.4 | 2.1 | 1.5 | 1 |
| Wholesale and retail trade | 14.9 | 6.1 | 10.7 | 6.0 | 10.6 | 9.4 | 12.3 | 13.6 | 15 |
| Hotels and restaurants | 18.7 | 1.6 | 1.5 | 1.6 | 2.0 | 2.1 | 1.7 | 2.8 | 2.6 |
| Transport, storage, and telecommunications | 4.0 | 45.4 | 36.9 | 31.5 | 33.9 | 23.6 | 25 | 29.4 | 27.8 |
| Financial intermediation | 16.9 | 11.8 | 8.9 | 16.2 | 9.5 | 16.0 | 12.3 | 7 | n/a |
| Real estate, renting, and business activities | 17.6 | 11.5 | 9.5 | 4.4 | 2.8 | 19.0 | 14.1 | 13.7 | 11.2 |
| Public administration, defence, and compulsory social security | — | — | — | — | — | — | — | — | — |
| Education | — | — | — | — | — | — | — | — | — |
| Health and social work | — | — | — | — | — | 0.1 | — | — | 0.2 |
| Other community, social, and personal services | 0.8 | 0.3 | — | — | — | 0.3 | 0.4 | 0.5 | 0.3 |
|  | 100 | 100 | 100 | 100 | 100 | 100 | 100 | 100 | 100 |
| Total | 435 | 884 | 1,014 | 1,098 | 1,139 | 1,240 | 1,114 | 1,089 | 860 |

Note: No data are available for 1997.
*Source:* Statistical Yearbook of Budapest.


Thus, we can conclude that institutional and service supply relations between Budapest and the settlements of the agglomeration have loosened compared to the former rigid limitations. At the same time, "the intermediary and higher level health, educational and cultural institutions are still concentrated in Budapest. Therefore Budapest has remained as attractive as before in that aspect" (Pestterv – MTA RKK, 1995: 11).

*Economic Development by Sectors*

**Industry**

This sector has substantially decreased in size. Only those parts of industry that have high efficiency and low territorial demand – e.g. chemistry and some forms of machinery – have developed. Industry has reduced significantly from the beginning of the 1990s, as evidenced by falling employee numbers and amounts of industrial territory. The privatization process could explain the concentration of multinational industrial firms in Budapest. Since a large share of the former

Table 9.3 Share of different sectors in investment of partly or fully foreign-owned companies in Pest County (total amount of investment in million US$)

| | 1992 | 1993 | 1994 | 1995 | 1996 | 1998 | 1999 | 2000 | 2001 |
|---|---|---|---|---|---|---|---|---|---|
| Agriculture, hunting, forestry | — | 0.5 | 0.2 | 0.2 | 0.48 | 0.5 | 0.6 | 0.8 | 0.4 |
| Mining and quarrying | 2.6 | 4.2 | 1.7 | 0.6 | 0.4 | 1 | — | — | — |
| Manufacturing | 66.5 | 32.9 | 63.1 | 49 | 45.6 | 55.8 | 79 | 60 | 68 |
| Electricity, gas, sewage, and water supply | — | — | 0.1 | 30 | 23.5 | 10.4 | 6.5 | 7.2 | 10.8 |
| Construction | 5.5 | 0.4 | 1.2 | 0.6 | 2.7 | 8.5 | — | — | — |
| Wholesale and retail trade | 10 | 6 | 1 | 3.7 | 6 | 11.4 | 5 | 16 | 9.2 |
| Hotels and restaurants | — | — | — | 0.5 | — | — | — | — | — |
| Transport, storage, and telecommunications | 0.2 | 38.9 | 15 | 12.4 | 12.6 | 10.6 | 7.3 | 14.4 | 9.1 |
| Financial intermediation | 5.9 | 1.6 | 0.6 | 0.9 | 0.7 | 0.4 | — | — | — |
| Real estate, renting, and business activities | 9 | 15.2 | 7 | 1.9 | 7.5 | 1 | — | — | 1.6 |
| Public administration, defence, and compulsory social security | — | — | — | — | — | — | — | — | — |
| Education | — | — | — | — | — | — | — | — | — |
| Health and social work | — | — | — | — | — | — | — | — | — |
| Other community, social, and personal services | — | — | — | — | — | — | — | — | — |
| | 100 | 100 | 100 | 100 | 100 | 100 | 100 | 100 | 100 |
| Total | 56 | 92 | 226 | 334 | 224 | 476 | 484 | 468 | 467 |

Note: No data are available for 1997.
*Source: Statistical Yearbook of Pest County.*

socialist industries was concentrated in Budapest, the privatized industries were also located there. But after the privatization process lessened, since 1997–1998, the new green-field investments have been concentrated mainly in the north-western part of Hungary.

## Services
In Hungary, the privatization of banks was carried out relatively quickly, and some foreign-owned new banks also became active. The share of foreign ownership of Hungarian banks exceeded 50 per cent by 1997, and this is an important factor in the establishment of modern banking technologies that were totally absent previously. Other conditions are also improving (stable macro-economic environment, more and more multi- and trans-national companies present, improving communication and transport infrastructure, still low price of manpower, stable legal system). Still, the size of the Hungarian economy and financial market is small, in itself not enough of a foundation for Budapest to

become a regional financial centre, so the expectations of some Hungarian politicians in this regard might be too ambitious. It is not even sure that the dynamism and direction of the development of the Eastern European region will require quick intensification of financial services – and even if this occurs, new technical development in the financial sector will most probably lead to a situation where most of the functions of a regional financial centre will be taken over by the existing Western centres, and the Central European metropoles will only play the role of sub-centres, specialized for some selected services (Bellon, 1998: 66).

## Commerce

The main tendencies in the commercial sector, especially regarding offices and shopping centres, are analysed in Chapters 3 and 6, where substantial examples are given from Budapest. Analysing the development of the retail sector, the Budapest case has been classified as an example of the "uncontrolled invasion of retail chains." It is the retail sector where foreign investments are the quickest and the highest – at least in the first several years of transition (the telecommunications sector, banking, and real-estate sectors follow with a small delay – see Nagy, 1998: 102). Foreign investments were concentrated initially in the biggest urban centres – by 1996, 91 per cent of new foreign investment into the Hungarian retail sector was directed to privatized and green-field projects in Budapest and Pest County. This first, concentrated wave of investments increased temporarily the share of the capital city: Budapest (having a share of 19 per cent of the Hungarian population) reached 62.5 per cent of the Hungarian total in the turnover of commercial units in 1997. Since then the level of this concentration has decreased, and foreign investments have started to be spread out to the second layer of Hungarian settlements, the medium-sized cities.

According to an analysis of changes in the retail sector (Baross, 1999), there has been a huge transformation since the socialist era, when commerce was concentrated in the local centres of new housing estates. In the 1990s, the two extremes of the spectrum of commerce were developing the fastest: little private shops in the local centres and side streets of densely populated living areas, and the new products of foreign investment – the big hypermarkets, mega-shops, shopping centres etc., in specialized "big boxes". Hungarian retail chains were quickly privatized to foreign investors. As a result of this concentrated activity of foreign chains, the share of shopping centres within overall retail activity reached 16 per cent by 2000, a higher share than that of Greece or Germany (see Baross, 1999: V-5).

## Real Estate

As mentioned in Chapter 3, the socialist period can be described as planned city development, in which the state was the biggest – and almost the only – investor. In the transition period the municipalities had the ruling power, but in a much more limited sense, as it was the private sector which decided about most of the investments. The new market mechanisms brought up new phenomena, like quick suburbanization and "over-construction."

In Budapest, the most dynamic parts of the real-estate sector are office and commercial investments. After a short period of internal restructuring (converting flats into offices) at the beginning of the 1990s, the office market became very active and there has been an annual construction of about 50,000–60,000 (in some years even 100,000) sq.m since then. As a result of this dynamic enlargement, the office market is by now close to being full in Budapest (about 18 per cent of the stock was empty in the first half of 1999). In the last 10 years, not only the inner city but also some parts of the "transitional belt" with good public transportation have become target areas for office investments. New phenomena, like office parks – "Graphisoft" in District III – or even technopark-technopolis, higher education, and offices together – like "Infopark" in District IX – are emerging.

Besides the new office buildings there are new shopping centres, which mark the new period of development of Budapest. Between 1990 and 1999, almost 500,000 sq.m of new retail space was built, 76 per cent within the city, the rest in the agglomeration belt.

Much less dynamism can be observed in the sector of industrial real estate. Many of the big premises of the former socialist industry have been shut down, occupying huge areas in the transitional belt of the city; some 4–8 km form the CBD area. It is rare that foreign investors take on the burdens of brown-field restructuring, including the problems of contaminated soil – their usual method is to invest in green-field areas around the city, making use of the discounts and tax-exemptions offered by the agglomeration settlements. Especially dynamic is the development of the south-western agglomeration area of Budapest, where the motorways from the west and from Balaton unite to create the "Western Gate" of the capital.

Since 2000, the new area of dynamism has been housing: due to new regulations and subsidies, private banks have become interested in lending, and competition between banks has even broken out.

### Favourable Economic Conditions

Budapest was very successful in the last decade in attracting foreign investments. The majority of capital investment projects were completed within the town boundaries, especially the investments of the service and office sectors were significant.

According to a recent research Budapest was the third on the list of European cities – after London and Stockholm – when surveying "competitiveness/business climate," i.e. the conditions for economic investments. The main factors of attractiveness of Budapest, besides the stable political and macro-economic environment, were the low price of labour and the improving real-estate conditions.

## Housing Policy and the Built Environment

### Transition with Massive Privatization of Housing

In Hungary since 1952, the year of nationalization, the housing stock of bigger cities was dominated by the public rental sector, although the private (owner-occupied) sector was always substantial in the form of single-family housing and new multi-family cooperatives and condominiums. Up until 1990, there was a centrally regulated housing policy determining the rent level for the whole country, and financial means for new construction and renovations were allocated from the central budget through planning decisions.

In the transition period, all these conditions changed. The public stock was transferred to the local governments, and with this, rights and responsibilities also became a local matter. Between 1990 and 1993, there was practically no central-level housing policy (responsibility for housing was split between six ministries) and there were also uncertainties about the role that the local governments should play in housing policy. The new owners of the public rental stock initially found themselves in a contradictory situation, as legal regulations were unclear about the rights of landlords (e.g. one of the laws would have allowed a rent increase, while another allowed freezing of public rents).

Finally, a Rental Housing Act was approved by parliament in 1993, which – in its final form – introduced the right to buy for tenants in public rental units. The responsibility for housing was given to the Ministry of Finance (since then this responsibility has moved again, to the Ministry of Economy, and lately to the Ministry of the Interior). Following the period of 1994–1995, when a moratorium on rent increases and the right to buy regulations showed a strong central influence, local governments finally became the main actors of housing policy. Since 1996, local governments have practically been free to decide on their local housing policy. Not even central budget transfers determine their decisions, as these transfers are not tied to purposes – normative grants according to objective criteria (e.g. the number of residents between the age of 18 and 35) for housing can freely be used at the local level for any other purposes.

By the time local governments got power over local housing policy, however, the structure of the local housing markets had changed substantially, and the real possibilities for a publicly led local housing policy became very limited. As a result of comprehensive housing privatization, the share of the public rental sector dropped in Budapest from over 60 to below 10 per cent of the housing stock. Most rented dwellings were sold for 15 per cent of their market value, this being the selling price of any public dwelling that had not been extensively modernized during the previous 15 years. Moreover, tenants had only to pay 60 per cent of the discounted sales price if they paid in cash. The other option was to pay by instalment: in this case 10 per cent of the sales price had to be paid in cash, and the remainder in monthly instalments over 35 years at a low fixed interest rate (the interest rate was set at 3 per cent for the whole repayment period, even though inflation was between 20 and 30 per cent from the end of the 1980s).

According to the regulations, privatized apartments could be resold or rented out by the owner immediately following purchase, without any restrictions (except for the obligation to repay the instalments in the case of properties resold within five years). Moreover, there was no restriction on turning the apartments into offices or shops, and these changes did not even have to be reported to the local authority.

The main push for this "give-away privatization" (see the debate on the evaluation of this policy in Alm and Buckley, 1992; Hegedüs et al., 1993) came, on the one hand, from the local governments, and on the other, from the main beneficiaries, the families living in the best public rental flats. As a result, the public rental sector practically disappeared from the housing stock, leaving much less opportunities for local governments to fulfil a social function in housing policy.[3]

*Housing construction and infrastructure*

After the transfer of public rental housing to the local level, all direct state subsidies for the housing sector have been withdrawn. As a consequence, and also due to high inflation, new housing construction decreased to historically low figures in most parts of the country. New construction became much greater in the agglomeration than in Budapest and, in contrast with Budapest, even increased around the middle of the 1990s (see Table 9.4). In an agglomeration of 600,000 people, the number of newly constructed homes was almost identical to the figure in Budapest, where the population was above 1.8 million. Around 2001–2002 the situation changed again – due to favourable government subsidies and steeply growing bank lending, new construction increased, and this increase was more substantial in Budapest than in any other part of the country.

The settlements of the agglomeration had, at the turn of the 1980s and 1990s, rather old-fashioned infrastructure, the standard of which was sometimes even lower than the national average. However, many of the agglomeration settlements managed to catch up within only five years. With state subsidies, using their own resources, and in most cases with contributions from the population, the local governments have completed large infrastructure projects. Between 1991 and 1995, primarily those utility investments were completed which also involved central budgetary subsidies and for which the consent of the population was easiest to get. Typically, such projects included the construction of gas mains, because the population had an interest in contributing financially

Table 9.4 Housing construction per 1,000 residents

|  | 1990 | 1995 | 1998 | 1999 | 2000 | 2001 |
|---|---|---|---|---|---|---|
| Budapest | 3.3 | 1.8 | 1.6 | 1.6 | 1.7 | 2.5 |
| Agglomeration | 5.6 | 6.5 | 5.0 | 4.5 | 5.3 | 5.1 |

*Source: CSO Pest County Statistical Year Book.*

(cheaper heating). Parallel with the large volume of gas projects, but at a slower pace, water mains were extended, and costly sewage network extensions followed. Today, in numerous settlements around Budapest, basic infrastructure services are at the same level as those of Budapest.

*The Condition of the Built and the Natural Environment*

The housing stock of Budapest has serious deficiencies. One-quarter of flats are to be found in buildings that are more than 80 years old and have never been substantially renovated. The majority of the 200,000 flats in these buildings have a low comfort level: either the bathroom or the toilet, or both, are missing. The concentration of these low-quality flats is much higher in Budapest than the national average.

Besides housing, the environment also faces big problems in the capital city. The quality of air, the level of noise, and the intensity of car traffic create much more unpleasant circumstances in Budapest than in other parts of the country. Only the quality of air has improved a little in the last decade, due to the bankruptcy of the most polluting big state enterprises.

In contrast to the growing problems of Budapest, the situation of the surrounding settlements improved substantially in the 1990s. The existence of the full scale of services, together with the more pleasant residential environment, represents a substantial attraction to those planning to change their residence, especially the inhabitants of Budapest.

Under such circumstances, it is no wonder that from the mid-1990s the previously positive migration balance of Budapest turned into a negative. The loss of 10,000–15,000 mainly middle- and upper-class population per year not only means lower PIT tax revenues and growing expenditures (due to increasing traffic and subsidies for services used by commuters) for the local government but also leads to further deterioration of the more densely built parts of the city from where out-migration is the highest.

## Social Cohesion

The social conditions of the inhabitants of Budapest are relatively good compared to that of the rest of the country. Notwithstanding the share of homeless people, which is currently the highest in the country, various social indices are more favourable in the capital: unemployment is half as high in Budapest than in other parts of the country, and the same applies to the share of people living below subsistence level; the share of disabled and permanently ill persons is also below the national average.

Even so, the inhabitants of Budapest list social problems as being among the gravest problems of the city. The main reason for this is not the absolute level of these problems, but rather their uneven spatial distribution across the city. Within the city there are very significant differences among the districts with respect to the social position of the inhabitants; in some districts, social indicators are especially bad:

- the difference in life expectancy between the "best" and the "worst" district of Budapest is six years – this means that the inhabitants of Buda District II are on the level of Belgium, while the inhabitants of Pest District X are on the level of Syria;
- there is a three times difference in the share of families receiving continuous social benefit and a four times difference in the share of families receiving unemployment benefit between the "better" and "worse" districts;
- the share of flats without comfort is 17 per cent in the group of "better" districts, while above 40 per cent in the group of "worse" districts.

Differentiation in the social position of inhabitants, as well as in the social subsidy potential of districts, is growing fast. Moreover, those districts where most people need social benefits are in the worst financial situation. As a consequence, the likelihood of residents of Budapest getting social benefits depends more and more on which district they inhabit.

The social protection system underwent significant changes in the course of the 1990s in Budapest. Some of its elements were developed rapidly (e.g. care for homeless people). At the same time, however, the district-level fragmentation of the social care system creates growing problems. The opportunities of the municipal level are very much constrained, both from above (the national level) and from below (the districts).

## Processes and Tendencies at the End of the 1990s

### Directions and Tendencies in the Migration of Population

The population of Hungary has been decreasing since 1980. Similar processes have taken place in Budapest too. Compared to the rest of the country, the decline in population is much faster in Budapest, amounting to 8 per cent in seven years as opposed to the 2 per cent national decline (see Table 9.5). However, the population of the agglomeration is increasing (9 per cent growth for the same period). Pest County, which covers the entire agglomeration zone (this represents two-thirds of the population of the county), is the only medium-level unit in the country, the population of which has grown for the last few years.

The natural decline in Budapest's population began as early as the beginning of the 1970s and was related to the ageing of the population. Even so, the number of inhabitants of Budapest was constantly growing until the end of the 1970s, due to the strong positive balance of migration. However, since 1993 the consolidated index of changes of permanent and temporary residence between Budapest and the rest of the country has become negative for Budapest (the balance of change of permanent residence has been negative already since 1991).

Both migration into and from the capital city fell until 1994, but the decline was larger in the case of migration to Budapest. In 1995, however, there was a large increase in the number of people out-migrating from Budapest.

The analysis of the balance shows that the positive migration balance was mainly the result of temporary migration, to the extent that in 1991 and 1992 the temporary migration balance was able to offset the negative permanent migration balance and even result in a positive balance in consolidation. The balance of temporary migration was negative for the first time in 1995. Of the two measures of migration it is permanent migration that is more important, because this reflects the impact of long-term decisions. However, the various sub-types of temporary migration could also be important for the assessment of future migration.

The negative migration balance of Budapest applies almost exclusively to Pest County (in 1995 nearly 28,000 people moved out from Budapest into Pest County and only 15,000 replaced them from the county).[4] Since 1993, however, more and more counties have become "net receiving counties" compared to Budapest. The extent of out-migration from Budapest is not yet significant in the case of the other counties, but the tendencies definitely deserve attention.

Out-migration – where to? More detailed data indicate that the close agglomeration has lost its former hegemony considering the scope of migration difference.[5] During the last two years the dynamism of settlements was the highest in the region situated between the close and extended agglomeration, and even the more extensive zone has by now reached the growth rate of the close agglomeration (Table 9.6).

Since the change in the political system, differences have increased between the more and less dynamic parts of the agglomeration. The group of settlements that are able, to a certain extent, to share the dynamism of Budapest through its multi-functional, bilateral, and intensive relations, involves 32–36 settlements. It may be assumed that this close and intensive agglomeration represents also a potential location for trading and service activities. However, the various housing functions (e.g. separate luxury residential parks) are better suited to settlements that offer adequate size and quality land, and they are not necessarily included in this group of the closest and most dynamic settlements.

Out-migration – where from? Until 1992–1993, the inner districts and the best Buda green-belt districts, with rapidly rising property prices, were the main "issuing/sending districts" (higher out- than in-migration) and the outer districts were still "receiving districts" (higher in- than out-migration). During the last few years, however, trends have changed significantly, and by now the migration balance has fallen into the negative in all parts of the city, without exceptions.

Summarizing the migration trends, it may be concluded that, following a decline of a few years, migration of population has increased again in Budapest and the surrounding area. Budapest's population will, due to migration, decline by 15,000–20,000 residents a year (in addition to natural decline) in the next few

Table 9.5 Population in Hungary, Budapest and its agglomeration, and other towns, 1993–2000*

|  | Hungary | | Towns excluding Budapest | | Budapest | | Budapest agglomeration zone (78 settlements) | |
|---|---|---|---|---|---|---|---|---|
|  | (000) | Change % | (000) | Change % | (000) | Change % | (000) | Change % |
| 1993 | 10,310 | | 4,701.4 | | 2,008.5 | | 579.5 | |
| 1994 | 10,277 | −0.3 | 4,697.8 | −0.1 | 1,995.7 | −0.6 | 585.1 | +1.0 |
| 1995** | 10,246 | −0.3 | 4,662.8 | −0.7 | 1,930.0* | −3.3 | 588.8 | +0.6 |
| 1996 | 10,212 | −0.3 | 4,650.8 | −0.25 | 1,906.8 | −1.2 | 598.1 | +1.6 |
| 1997 | 10,174 | −0.3 | 4,636.7 | −0.3 | 1,886.2 | −1.1 | 607.9 | +1.6 |
| 1998 | 10,135 | −0.4 | 4,617.5 | −0.4 | 1,861.4 | −1.3 | 618.3 | +1.7 |
| 1999 | 10,092 | −0.4 | 4,596.9 | −0.4 | 1,838.7 | −1.2 | 628.6 | +1.7 |
| 2000 | 10,043 | −0.5 | 4,576.9 | −0.4 | 1,811.6 | 1.5 | 640.5 | +1.9 |
| Total | | −2.6 | | −2.6 | | −9.8 | | +10.5 |

Notes:
* At the beginning of the year.
** This dramatic decrease in population was mainly due to a change in the statistical system.
Agglomeration zone, 1993–1996: Calculated data.
*Source: Budapest Statistical Yearbooks 1992–2000.*

years. On the other hand, the settlements of the agglomeration show increasing growth, and this is not restricted to the close agglomeration zone any more. Also taking into consideration the fact that the first major actions of parcelling out of land took place in the agglomeration belt only in the middle of the 1990s, and that there are much more aggressive extensions planned for the near future, migration from Budapest may increase even more.

Table 3.2 in the comparative city-development chapter in this volume (Chapter 3) shows that among the Central European capitals, it is Budapest where suburbanization is expected to continue the fastest, despite the fact that Budapest is not a very densely populated city (i.e. there would be plenty of space even within the city to improve the living and housing conditions of the population).

The restructuring of the population of the capital does not solely depend on suburbanization. As mentioned earlier, there is also an "inner suburbanization" going on, in the process of which inner areas lose population to the outer parts of the city. The main cause is the "push factor" of the offices and other business and administrative functions occupying inner city areas, but the "pull factor" of the outer districts – which offer plenty of opportunities for new construction of semi-detached and detached houses – is also important.

Table 9.6 Balance of migration between Budapest and Pest County

| | 1990 | 1992 | 1993 | 1994 | 1995 | 1996 | 1997 | 1998 | 1999 | 2000 | 2001 |
|---|---|---|---|---|---|---|---|---|---|---|---|
| Permanent inhabitants | −2,203 | −5,918 | −8,106 | −10,856 | −10,778 | −11,601 | −11,864 | −13,442 | −15,433 | −16,981 | −14,300 |
| Temporary inhabitants | 682 | 811 | 129 | −1,740 | −1,469 | 1,022 | −1,194 | −278 | −1,076 | −733 | −924 |
| Together | −1,521 | −5,107 | −7,977 | −12,596 | −12,247 | −10,579 | −13,058 | −13,720 | −16,509 | −17,714 | −15,224 |

Source: KSH Budapest Statistical Yearbooks 1990–2001 (no data were available for 1991).

Due to all these reasons, during the 18 years between 1980 and 1998, the population of the whole city decreased. This decline, however, was not the same in all parts of the city:

- 69.9 per cent in the CBD area of Budapest (districts I and V);
- 75.4 per cent in the inner city (VI–IX districts);
- 82.8 per cent in the transitional belt (X, XIII, XIV);
- 91.3 per cent in the high-quality Buda side (II, III, XI, XII, XXII); and
- 105.6 per cent in the outer districts (IV, XV–XXI).

These data (and Fig. 9.2) refer, besides suburbanization, to substantial internal restructuring, leading to a quick decline in the population of the inner areas while the outer parts were growing.

As already mentioned, trends in new housing construction changed around 2001–2002, as growing state subsidization of new housing and more willingness on the part of the banks to give loans for housing resulted in growing new construction, especially in Budapest. It remains to be seen whether this new dynamism is only temporary, or if not, whether suburbanization can be lessened in this way.

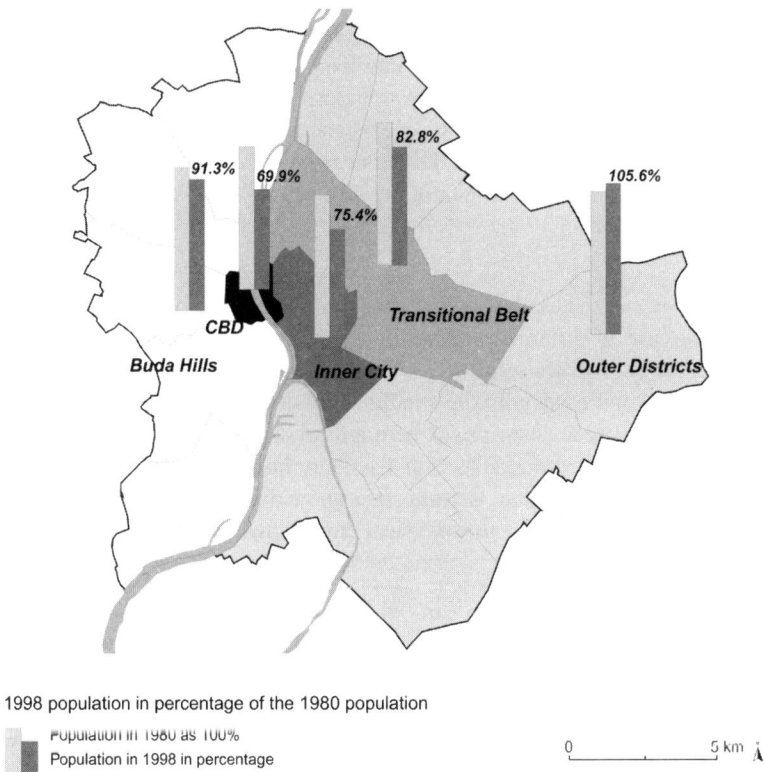

1998 population in percentage of the 1980 population

Population in 1980 as 100%
Population in 1998 in percentage

0          5 km

Fig. 9.2  Population in the city of Budapest, 1980–1998.

## Effects of the Transition on the Various Parts of the Transforming Post-socialist City

The various parts of the socialist city became subject to vastly diverging processes after the change of the political regime. The effects of the economic, social, demographic, and population changes can be categorized by city area as follows:

*Inner city areas.* Privatization had a strongly diversifying effect. In the prosperous parts of the inner districts (within the central business area or in its immediate vicinity) privatization has been almost wholesale and the rehabilitation of houses is under way, as a large majority of the population can afford to invest in renovation. In the less advantageous high-density areas, private apartments also prevail, but as the low-quality rental units are concentrated in this zone, there is hardly any hope that the new condominiums with mixed ownership will create the uniform will of the owners which is required for reconstruction. Thus, the moving-out of the middle class is quite predictable and it will eventually lead to the deterioration of these areas.

*Transitional zone.* Certain elements of the mixed functions (e.g. major factories) of this zone were almost universally going bankrupt and closing down. Only a tiny part of the industrial areas can be transformed, and this transformation is controversial too (condominium-like coexistence of small enterprises in large halls, previous industrial premises). This zone, 4–8 km away from the CBD area, is the biggest adjacent problem area of the city. At the same time, however, this is its biggest and one of its most well-located territorial (re/development land) reserves as well.

*New housing estates.* These have also witnessed large-scale privatization, which led to an increase in differences. The higher-quality blocks (those built in the 1950s from bricks, and those of the 1980s built to a higher standard, in better parts of the city) and especially the smaller four-storey houses have a relatively better position, and real-estate prices here are relatively high. The high-density housing estates built in the 1970s, with 10-storey houses and high maintenance costs, are in the worst situation. Certain signs show that the middle classes began to abandon the area, which in this physical environment can very easily lead to the emergence of slums.

*Elite green-belt areas.* These areas can only further develop in a qualitative sense (along with some increase in density) because of a lack of space supply. Qualitative changes entail the disappearance of problems in areas such as telephone, road, and commercial services. As a rallying place for high-quality private services (e.g. private schools, private clinics) since the change of the regime, these areas retain firmly their dominant role among urban classes of housing, a role that might be challenged only by some luxurious suburban housing parks.

*Outer single-family housing areas.* These are most stable where there are only gradual changes in infrastructure (telephone and perhaps sewage). Private construction activity is continuously going on and leads in some areas to densification.

In the case of *suburban settlements* the newly won municipal independence, the new financial redistribution system that favours the smaller settlements, and the high priority given to infrastructure developments had the consequence that these settlements have managed to overcome their infrastructure backwardness in the course of six to eight years and are able to provide very good infrastructure conditions to the population and certain types of enterprises. There are also some poorer settlements towards which less affluent families move out from the city, mainly from high-cost flats on housing estates.

Polarization – that is, the increase of differences according to type of housing, housing environment, and differences in the incomes of the population – is a universal phenomenon in nearly all the structural elements.

Within the inner districts, the transitional zone, and the new housing estates, certain areas have begun to deteriorate. On the other hand, the CBD area, the surroundings of the new shopping centres, the green-belt areas, and many of the suburban settlements are the places where positive tendencies dominate (Fig. 9.3).

## Plans and Cooperation for the Future

### New Strategy for Development

As a logical consequence of the collapse of the socialist system and the total change in political, administrative, and financial relations at the city level, the system of economic–social planning has also changed. The five-year plans of the socialist period were prepared according to the political intention of the central planning body, in an iteration process between the central and local levels. From the second half of the 1980s, the local governments were given more freedom to establish their plans within the framework established at the central level. After the 1989–1990 changes the independence of the local level, including planning, became one of the cornerstones of the new political and administrative system. Parallel to the disappearance of all forms of central guidelines (top-down planning), all forms of forecasting have also been discredited. As a result, local governments base their activities on yearly prepared, budget-orientated plans.

In the case of the Budapest municipality, around 1993–1994, the first medium-term financial and investment plans were created (first for three to four years ahead, later for seven), in order to forecast the effects of new investments on the city budget. In the second half of the 1990s, when the period of consolidation was finished – the institutional set-up and the financial roles and responsibilities have

Fig. 9.3 Image of Budapest. (a) Inner city, Buda side. (b) Elizabeth Bridge, Pest side across the Danube. (c) Havana housing estate, District 18, built in the 1970s. (d) Urban renewal in District 9, Raday Street. (e) Lurdy ház, new shopping centre, District 9. (f) Suburbanization north-west of Budapest, Cosbánka village.

been clarified in the complex, two-tier Budapest local government system – the leaders of the city went another step forward and initiated the preparation of a long-term Strategic Development Concept for the city.

The Budapest Strategic Development Concept – the preparation of which started in October 1997 – is aimed at a period of 15 years. Its objective is to identify a conceptual framework for city development – there will be no definite conclusions drawn on any specific area or technical problem, but the Concept will outline the main trends in the most important sectors of city development and no sectoral concept should be passed which would be in contradiction to the Strategic Development Concept. The Concept focuses on city development primarily from the point of view of the public sphere, analysing especially the role to be played by the municipality (and occasionally by the districts). The

Budapest Strategic Development Concept suggests, as a starting point, a balance of three main strategic aims: economic efficiency, sustainability/quality of life, and solidarity.

To increase the efficiency of the city would mean to:
- promote the efficiency of the economy;
- develop the macro-regional connections of the city; and
- improve inner traffic conditions (efficient connection of public and individual traffic, ring-road development).

To improve quality of life in the city would mean to:
- help to preserve the compactness of the city;
- speed up urban renewal, in both the inner city residential and transitory industrial areas;
- improve housing conditions, ensuring favourable terms for new construction;
- develop public spaces and green areas; and
- help environmental sustainability (develop infrastructure, protect green areas).

To ensure the solidarity aspect of city development it is necessary to:
- improve the social situation of poor people and poor areas (decrease inequalities between districts, fight against ghettoes).

The basic approach of the new Budapest Strategic Development Concept is quite different from the previous development ideas. It is obviously different from the socialist planning ideas, in so far as it accepts the existence and leading role of the market economy and the big (in some regards decisive) role that private and market actors play in city development. On the other hand, it also differs from the more or less "laissez-faire" ideology of the 1990s, as the new Concept aims for more active, initiating public policy in city development.

The active role of the public sphere can be categorized in three quite different forms:[6]
- regulating the market: to cooperate with market forces, to help and regulate their activities;
- initiating the market: to make basic improvements to and investments in the infrastructure, as a result of which market forces will become interested in further developments; and
- replacing the market: to carry out developments that are not in the interest of market actors but are very important for the city.

In the socialist period, city development and planning was totally dominated by the public sphere; market forces were suppressed even in those areas where their higher efficiency was obvious. In "laissez-faire" type urban development strategies, the role of the public sphere is minimized, constrained purely to the market-replacing function.

The new Budapest Strategic Development Concept aims to remain in between the two extreme alternatives. The Concept suggests applying all three forms of public involvement in a differentiated way, depending upon the criteria of the optimal share of roles for the given tasks. Regarding the concrete statements made by the Concept, the following examples can be given of the different roles the public sphere should play:

- regulating the market by supporting the most innovative sectors of the economy and offering regulatory and financial help for the preparation of new multi-family housing and urban renewal;
- initiating the market by restructuring the distressed transitional belt of the city (to initiate new private investments with the publicly financed development of a new ring road and improvements to the basic infrastructure of the area); and
- replacing the market by giving public support to distressed areas of the city and developing basic conditions for cooperation with the agglomeration belt.

From this overview it can be seen that the Concept suggests proactive city policy even in some sectors which do not belong to the mandatory tasks of the municipality. The suggestion of new roles for the municipality to play is the essence of the new Concept: the municipality should take the initiative not only in market replacement but also in market regulating and market initiating tasks.

The Concept involves strongly defined spatial priorities, the following areas being of primary concern for future public development policy:

- the restructuring of the transitional belt: to develop a new circle-road around the inner city, mainly on the Pest side, with two new bridges at the two ends, in order to bring new life to the whole transitional belt dominated today by derelict industrial land, mostly out of use;
- improvement of the banks of the River Danube as one of the main attractions of Budapest, connected with suggestions for waterfront housing and renovation of the existing physical structure;
- continuation of urban renewal in the inner city areas, in parallel with efforts for traffic reduction, new parking policy, the reduction of density, and improvement of public spaces; and
- upgrading of the outer areas, especially the centres of the outer districts (having been independent settlements in the past), helping also to overcome infrastructural backlogs and preserve still-existing natural values.

The main long-term goal of the Concept is the redevelopment of the transitional zone, which also means exploitation of land for future development in the under-utilized brown-field area. The development of the zone along the River Danube and the continuation of urban rehabilitation in the inner city are the other two main aims, also with short- and medium-term relevance. The intertwining of the different goals is also very important: the restructuring of the transitional zone will ease the load on the inner city by supplementing its functions and improving its quality. At the same time, the improvement of public transport, the new ring road, and the suggested inter-modality centres will also promote the integration of the outskirts into the city. Thus, the development outlined above is beneficial for almost all districts of the capital, as their own population will gain, either directly or indirectly, by having new local centres and inter-modal nodes, and by the restructuring and strengthening of the economic functions of the transitional zone.

The Draft of the Strategic Development Concept was discussed on a political level in the municipality and sent out to the districts, relevant ministries, and some other key actors of city development for official discussion. On the basis of the comments received, a new version of the Concept was prepared and submitted to the Municipal Assembly.

## The Region: Cooperation between Budapest and the Surrounding Area

The Strategic Development Concept focuses primarily on the problems and development of Budapest. It is obvious, however, that Budapest is going to become an EU capital city in the near future. Therefore, EU legislation and the aid system of the structural funds promoting accession will be of primary importance.

By the time Hungary becomes an EU Member State, the NUTS 2 regions will be the main depositories of investments. According to the present law, Budapest and the surrounding Pest County form the Central Hungarian Region. Thus, after EU accession, most probably not Budapest itself but the region will be the subject of EU programming and will be in competition with other European regions. For all these reasons the Budapest Strategic Development Concept needs to consider national, regional, and agglomeration coherence.

Efforts must be made in order to have the main elements of city planning in tune with the regional development concept currently under preparation.

The role and functioning of the NUTS 2 regions is one of the most important questions for the candidate countries. This is especially true for Hungary, where, after several years of uncertainty, the lower subnational level, the 19 counties, became very strong again politically (having elected self-government). As a result, by the end of the 1990s the Hungarian regions could not be defined as completely new units with new borders, but only as a certain grouping of the counties (three counties form one region). The new socialist-liberal government (2002) aims to change the present system into a new arrangement with self-governing regions, which would have a stronger status than their present "planning-statistical" one. This would need strong political will and also the support of the opposition parties, however. To replace the counties with self-governing regions will not be easy: all the presidents of the Regional Development Councils are presidents of the Development Council of one of the counties belonging to the given region, which clearly indicates the strict control of counties over the regions. Counties always emphasise their "1,000 years of existence" and would fight very hard to preserve their self-government status, thus hindering the regions from achieving this status.

It is clear that accession countries need, on the subnational level (between the national and local governments), well-functioning planning capacity. At the same time they also need democratic, elected subnational government. In the optimal case, efficient planning capacity and democratic government are created on the same subnational level, as the creation and fulfilment of plans needs strong legitimacy. To reach this optimal case, however, is not easy. Recently only the Polish regions fulfil this criteria, while in the Czech Republic and Hungary these two functions are on different levels (EU planning on the regional level, self-government on the county level). In these countries the unification of the two functions on the same level could be a longer process, where the final outcome is uncertain.

Capital cities are always in a special situation regarding the regional system. Many of the capitals create regions themselves (Vienna, Berlin, Prague, Bratislava), while there are also examples of regions including the capital and its surrounding area (Warsaw, Budapest). It is uncertain which version will apply to Budapest by the time the regions achieve self-government in Hungary.

The Strategic Development Concept of the city aims at cooperation with the agglomeration and other parts of the region, accepting the fact that city development is a multi-player game. In order to ease the tensions between the city and its surrounding areas, the Concept assigns a central position to the establishment of the institutional system of participation, the strengthening of partnership relations and cooperation, the development of market-conform, investor-friendly regulatory instruments, the development of a predictable system of decision-making, and the adequate communication thereof.

## The Position of Budapest in the Competition of Cities

City competition does not necessarily or exclusively mean the competition of two neighbouring cities. When talking about city competition in relation to Budapest, most people concentrate on the competition between Budapest and Vienna. In certain aspects, however, Budapest is more in competition with Warsaw, Prague, and Bratislava (or in even broader context, with Bucharest and Sofia) than with Vienna – e.g. regarding potential investment by overseas investors (shopping centres, car factories, etc.).

The chances of Budapest in competition with the other mentioned cities are not bad. Budapest is in a good geopolitical situation to become, on the one hand, the gateway for Western influence towards South-east Europe, and on the other hand, the transfer city of South-east European culture and values towards the West. Being closer to the Eastern neighbours of the European Union to be enlarged, Budapest has a good chance of taking over most of the gateway functions of Vienna.

Besides pure competition, it is also worth discussing the relationship between competition and cooperation. In order to increase the attraction of bigger geographical areas, cities should cooperate, whereas within smaller areas the same cities might compete. If we take again the example of Vienna and Budapest, it is in the interests of both cities that Central Europe becomes more attractive, leading to increasing overseas investments, tourism, and so on. It is already now the case that many overseas visitors come for combined visits to Prague, Vienna, and Budapest within a one- to two-week schedule. In this sense these cities should cooperate, to increase the joint capacities of their infrastructure (e.g. cooperation between airports, fast rail link, split of tasks instead of direct rivalry).

## Conclusion

Budapest belongs to the group of Central European cities whose transition from an already more reformed socialist city towards the market was fairly quick. Not only the speed but also the extent of market-orientated changes is of importance, as almost all forms of public control have been withdrawn.

Due to its favourable geopolitical position, the stability of its political system and economic regulation, its improving macro-economic situation, and the above-mentioned "liberal" policy towards the market, Budapest has received by far the most FDI in the region in the first six to eight years of transition. Thus Budapest is among the "first runners" in the "restructuring race", on the example of which the main tendencies of the change from the socialist to a market-orientated model of city development can be well illustrated.

As result of the huge amount of FDI coming into Budapest, market services and their related infrastructure (telecommunications, financial services, different types of commercial real estate – petrol stations, shopping centres, offices) were developed the fastest, and these were the areas on which most foreign investment was spent. As the public sector was recovering relatively slowly, was fragmented and blocked by internal debates, and had only limited investment possibilities, city development soon became dominated by the market – the share of the private sector in total investment can be estimated to reach as high a share as 70–85 per cent! The domination of city development by private investments came very quickly and was very much concentrated in some areas of the city – for these reasons, some analysts talked about the "invasion" of the capital.

The strategy of the political leadership of Budapest in the 1990s can be considered as quite "liberal"; there were very few planning constraints raised and even most of the municipal works were offered for privatization, in order to overcome the difficulties in infrastructure services and get capital for the necessary investments. The only method the municipality did not use to attract foreign investment was tax concessions. The belief of the leaders of Budapest was that the city is very attractive and that many investors and developers would come, even if the level of local tax (the business turnover tax) was fixed at the highest level allowed by the national Law on Local Taxes.

This strategy can be evaluated in general as successful. Although there are cases known of companies moving out of the capital or new investments being placed into the agglomeration belt instead of the capital, all in all the influx of investments into Budapest was not substantially hindered by the relatively high local tax rate. On the other hand, this quickly increasing tax revenue presented good opportunities for the capital to improve the basic infrastructure of the city. While the amount of business turnover tax was in 1996 only around the half of the amount Budapest has got from the central budget, this proportion has changed and since 1999 business turnover tax revenue surpassed the support Budapest is getting from the central level (partly as a result of the increase of this tax but also due to the efforts of the central government to equalize budget allocation, favouring less-developed settlements and areas of the country).

Thus, the liberal, non-regulatory approach of the Budapest municipal leadership has resulted in good economic results so far. There were, however, also problems with this approach. Investors were not constrained at all in their efforts to find the easiest solutions for their investments, and in this way they could avoid more difficult, more costly, but at the same time more sustainable solutions. This caused, for example, growing problems with the brown-field zone (instead of investing into existing rundown industrial premises, investors chose green-field sites within or around the city) and a decrease in green areas. Additionally, the liberal approach has led to a sharp increase in inequalities between the different strata of society, and among the different areas of the city.

The basic consideration of the new Budapest Strategic Development Concept is the suggestion that the public hand should change its strategy, playing a more active role in the future in shaping urban development, including the build-up of a new type of supporting, initiating, and control function of the public sector over market forces. Although Budapest is not at all as rich as the very powerful municipality of Moscow, the decade of liberal handling of private economy has brought some financial means, forming an initial base for the new, extended role of the public sector.

Thus, the future of Budapest depends very much on the capability of the municipality to establish this new type of public leadership (regulating, initiating, and in some regards controlling market processes) in order to support economic growth, help the fulfilment of the sustainability criteria of urban development, and ensure the maximum level of solidarity (handling the problem of growing disparities between the districts, between the richer and poorer sides of the Danube, etc.). This new type of public leadership must also take cooperation on the regional level as an important goal, ensuring the optimal development of Budapest and its surrounding area, as the central region of Hungary.

What are the lessons we can learn from the case of Budapest's development in the last decade? There are at least two. The first is the necessity of replacing all the important parts of the political, decision-making, institutional systems of the socialist city very quickly by new market-orientated establishments. Empirical experience shows that there is a very low chance for success with "third-way" solutions, i.e. any combination of socialist and market principles. However, there is also a second lesson: in the new, market-orientated political and institutional structure it is absolutely necessary very quickly to "build up" again the public sector, i.e. to establish a new, legitimate, strong institutional structure which can – in a market-conform way – successfully represent the public interest in the market-orientated city development process.

## Acknowledgement

Thanks for the contribution of Éva Beleznay and Éva Gerőházi.

## Notes

1  For further discussion of the urban history of Budapest, readers are referred to Enyedi and Szirmai (1992) and Enyedi (1997).
2  Six political parties managed to get into parliament, three of which (Hungarian Democratic Forum, Smallholders Party, Christian Democratic Party) formed the above-mentioned coalition, while the remaining three (Alliance of Free Democrats, Federation of Young Democrats, Socialist Party) were in opposition.
3  For a more detailed analysis of the changes in housing policy see e.g. Hegedüs and Tosics (1992, 1994).
4  KSH Budapest Yearbooks only contain data on inner migration within Budapest. However, the total migration difference may also be calculated from population figures and natural multiplication data; inner migration may then be eliminated and the approximate balance with the country can be formed.
5  See note 4, above.
6  This idea has been developed in conversations with Paul Baross.

## REFERENCES

James Alm and Robert Buckley, *Privatization by Local Government in Reforming Economies: A Net Worth Perspective*, Washington D.C.: The World Bank, 1992.
Pál Baross, "Kiskereskedelem: átalakuló kínálati struktúra?" [Retail Sector: Changing Structure of Supply?], in *Budapest Városfejlesztési Koncepciója, Kézirat* [Budapest Strategic Development Concept], manuscript, 1999.
Györgyi Barta, "Budapest helyzete az országban," [The Situation of Budapest in the Country], in *Fővárosi reform. Területi megalapozó tanulmányok* [Background Papers for the Administrative Reform of Budapest], manuscript, Budapest: Pylon Kft, 1992.
———, "Industrial Restructuring or Deindustrialization?", in György Enyedi, ed., *Social Change and Urban Restructuring in Central Europe*, Budapest: Akadémiai, 1998.
———, "Újra 'boom' a budapesti gazdaságban" [Boom Again in the Budapest Economy], in *Budapest Városfejlesztési Koncepciójáról* [About the Budapest Strategic Development Concept], Budapest: Budapesti Negyed, 2000.
Edit Bellon, "Lesz-e Budapest pénzügyi központ?" [Will Budapest Become a Financial Centre?], in Ferenc Glatz and Györgyi Barta, eds, *Budapest – nemzetközi város* [Budapest – International City], Budapest: Magyar Tudományos Akadémia, 1998.

Pál Beluszky, "Budapest – nemzetközi város. Történeti áttekintés" [Budapest – International City. Historical Overview], in Ferenc Glatz and Györgyi Barta, eds, *Budapest – nemzetközi város* [Budapest – International City], Budapest: Magyar Tudományos Akadémia, 1998.

Robert M. Bird, Robert D. Ebel, and Christine I. Wallich, eds, *Decentralization of the Socialist State. Intergovernmental Finance in Transition Economies*, Washington D.C.: World Bank Regional and Sectoral Studies, 1995.

Project managers Iván Tosics, Metropolitan Research Institute (Kft Városkutatás), and Katalin Pallai, F38 Kft (up till 2000), project team Pál Baross, Budapest Kolpron, Györgyi Barta, MTA Reg. Kut. Központ, Éva Beleznay, Kft Városkutatás, Zoltán E ő, Kft Palatium, Lajos Koszorú, Kft Teampannon, Gábor Locsmándi, BME Urbanisztikai Int., László Molnár, Fő Rt., Katalin Pallai, F38 Kft (up till 2000), Péter Schuchmann, Kft Pestterv, János Schulek, Főmterv Rt, and Iván Tosics, Kft Városkutatás, *Budapest Strategic Development Concept*, printed version, Budapest: Municipality of Budapest, 2002.

György Enyedi, "Budapest: Return to European Competition," in Christopher Jensen, Alan Butler, Jan van Weesep, and Arie Shachar, eds, *European Cities in Competition*, Aldershot: Avebury, 1997.

György Enyedi and Viktória Szirmai, *Budapest. A Central European Capital*, London: Belhaven Press, 1992.

József Hegedüs, Katharine Mark, Raymond Struyk, and Iván Tosics, "Local Options for Transforming the Public Rental Sector," *Cities* 10(3), August 1993, pp. 257–271.

József Hegedüs and Iván Tosics, "Housing Reforms in Hungary," in Bengt Turner, József Hegedüs, and Iván Tosics, eds, *The Reform of Housing in Eastern Europe and the Soviet Union*, London: Routledge, 1992, pp. 151–179.

József Hegedüs and Iván Tosics, "Privatization and Rehabilitation in the Budapest Inner Districts," *Housing Studies* 9(1), 1994, pp. 41–55.

Sándor Gy. Nagy, "A külföldi mulködőtőke a budapesti agglomeráció kereskedelmében" [Foreign Direct Investment in the Retail Sector of the Budapest Agglomeration], in Ferenc Glatz and Györgyi Barta, eds, *Budapest – nemzetközi város* [Budapest – International City], Budapest: Magyar Tudományos Akadémia, 1998.

Éva Perger, "Közigazgatási dilemmák" [Dilemmas of Public Administration], in Györgyi Barta and Pál Beluszky, eds, *Társadalmi-gazdasági átalakulás a budapesti agglomerációban* [Social and Economic Transformation in the Budapest Agglomeration], Budapest: Regionális Kutatási Alapitvány, 1999.

Pestterv – MTA RKK, *Pest megye területfejlesztési koncepcióját megalapozó tanulmányok* [Background Papers for the Regional Development Concept of Pest County], Budapest: manuscript, 1995.

Péter Schuchmann, "A budapesti agglomeráció lehatárolási javaslata" [Proposal for the Territorial Definition of the Budapest Agglomeration], in *A "Fővárosi Reform" javaslat területi megalapozó munkarésze. Kézirat. Fővárosi Reform Területi megalapozó tanulmányok* [Municipal Reform, Territorial Background Studies], Budapest: Pylon Kft, 1992.

# 10

# Prague returns to Europe

*Jiří Musil*

## Prague in the Central European Urban System

If we wish to understand the current transformations of Prague we have to view them in their proper geographical and historical contexts. These changes are part of a more general process seeking to restore democracy and a market economy in the Czech Republic, and to secure a place in the European Union for the Czech state. They also aim at finding an appropriate response to the impact of globalization on this city.

Before 1918, Prague was an integral part of the Habsburg monarchy, and thus of the Austrian urban system that was dominated by Vienna. This can be readily seen from the communications network – illustrated, for example, by the railroad maps of the period. Prague was the capital of Bohemia, then one of the Austrian provinces. It was also a component of an urban system that differed from its West European counterpart, consisting of a number of small- and medium-sized towns. The only large city in the Czech territory – which comprises Bohemia, Moravia, and Silesia – was Prague. Yet, due to the specific features of the Austrian urban system, Prague was at the same time the third largest city of the Habsburg Empire, after Vienna and Budapest (Melinz and Zimmermann, 1996; Weber, 1989).

However, Prague was also part of a wider system of Central European cities, which after 1918 consisted of a network of capitals of the newly established states on the one hand, and of the capital of Germany on the other (i.e. Prague, Vienna, Budapest, Warsaw, and Berlin). At the beginning of the twentieth century, Berlin and Vienna dominated the entire Central European urban system quite markedly. Their inhabitants represented roughly 70 per cent of the total population of the five capital cities. The key role was played by Berlin, whereas the position and status of Prague was weak, that of Warsaw only a little stronger, and that of Budapest rising but not much stronger (see Table 10.1).

Table 10.1  Growth of Central European capital cities (population in 000s)

| City | 1910 | 1920 | 1930 | 1950 | 1970 | 1980 | 1990 |
|---|---|---|---|---|---|---|---|
| Prague | 667.6 | 729.6 | 949.2 | 1,047.4 | 1,140.7 | 1,182.2 | 1,212.0 |
| Vienna | 2,084.0 | 1,910.0 | 1,935.6 | 1,616.0 | 1,580.0 | 1,531.0 | 1,488.0 |
| Budapest | 1,110.4 | 1,232.0 | 1,441.6 | 1,590.3 | 1,940.2 | 2,060.0 | 2,115.0 |
| Warsaw | 764.1 | 972.0 | 1,277.0 | 819.0 | 1,315.6 | 1,596.1 | 1,671.0 |
| Berlin | 3,734.0 | 3,804.0 | 4,243.0 | 3,335.0 | 3,207.0 | 3,211.9 | 3,443.5 |

Note: All figures refer to results of censuses taken approximately in the year as stated in the table.
*Source:* Census data from individual countries.

Table 10.2  Rank of Central European capital cities by population size

| Rank order in | Prague | Vienna | Budapest | Warsaw | Berlin |
|---|---|---|---|---|---|
| 1910 | 5 | 2 | 3 | 4 | 1 |
| 1990 | 5 | 4 | 2 | 3 | 1 |

The status of Vienna, measured by population size, declined considerably during the course of the twentieth century. Berlin, too, was losing population, but not to the same extent as was Vienna. Indeed, Vienna is now smaller than Budapest and Warsaw. By contrast, Prague, Warsaw, and Budapest experienced quite a significant growth at this time. All three approximately doubled their population between 1910 and 1990. The result of these changes – since population size does determine and express the status of a city to a notable extent – is a new order of importance in the Central European capitals. At present, the situation clearly differs from that prevailing at the beginning of the century (see Tables 10.1 and 10.2). Among the consequences of the uneven development of these five cities during the last one hundred years was a considerable reduction in the differences in their relative population size. The new scale of importance of the Central European capital cities at the end of the twentieth century, based on population size, is evident from Table 10.2.

These shifts occurred in spite of relatively modest growth of the total population of these five capitals, from approximately 8.4 million people in 1910 to 9.6 million in 1990. The share of the three fastest-growing cities thus rose from 30.4 per cent in 1910 to 52.1 per cent by 1990. However, it should be emphasized that the picture of the Central European urban system changes when another six cities are added to this list: Munich, Frankfurt on Main, Nuremberg, Leipzig, Dresden, and Wroclaw. We then find that, for example, Munich now has a larger population than Prague and is surpassing Vienna. On the other hand,

Table 10.3 Population and territory of selected Central European cities and urban regions, 1996

| City | City | | | Region | |
|------|------|------|------|--------|------|
|      | Population (000s) | Percentage of national population | Territory (sq.km) | Population (000s) | Territory (sq.km) |
| Prague | 1,215 | 11.8 | 496.4 | 1,740 | 3,920 |
| Berlin | 3,472 | 4.3 | 889.1 | 4,262 | 5,369 |
| Budapest | 1,930 | 18.8 | 525.2 | 2,474 | 2,548 |
| Warsaw | 1,641 | 4.3 | 495.0 | — | — |
| Vienna | 1,640 | 20.4 | 415.0 | 2,106 | 5,079 |
| Munich | 1,370 | 1.9 | 310.0 | 2,397 | 2,336 |
| Dresden | 469 | 0.5 | 153.0 | 1,110 | 4,300 |
| Leipzig | 471 | 0.5 | 226.0 | 1,500 | 3,300 |
| Wroclaw | 642 | 1.7 | 293.0 | 1,076 | 6,287 |
| Krakow | 746 | 2.0 | 326.8 | 1,220 | 3,254 |

*Source:* Czech Statistical Office and UN data.

there has been a relative decline of cities such as Leipzig and Dresden over the same period of time (see Table 10.3).

There can be no doubt that the collapse of communism, the societal transformations of the former communist states, the unification of Germany, and the transfer of the seat of the German federal government from Bonn to Berlin, as well as the slow process of integrating central European cities into the entire European urban system, will initiate a reordering of the rank of various cities in this part of the continent.

In order to better understand Prague's present urban status, the data on the changing relative positions of the Central European capitals have to be augmented by those that relate to Prague's position in the settlement systems of both the Czech territories and the former Czechoslovakia. The most rapidly expanding cities in the period 1910–1991 were, in fact, the two largest Slovak cities, Bratislava and Košice. During these years, these two cities increased their population four- to fivefold (Table 10.4). Yet, Prague was the most rapidly growing Czech city and almost doubled its population between 1910 and 1991. Other larger Czech cities such as Brno, Ostrava, and Plzeň grew more slowly throughout this whole time. In fact, most Czechoslovak cities grew extensively in the inter-war period (during the so-called First Republic) from 1918 to 1938, and most particularly in the years between 1921 and 1930. Yet the overall conclusion is that all indices used in Tables 10.4 and 10.5 show that from 1910 to 1950 the position of Prague was relatively improving in the Czechoslovak urban system. Since then, Prague's place in the urban system of large Czechoslovak cities, as well as in the general system of settlements, has been declining.

Table 10.4 Growth of the six largest cities in Czechoslovakia, 1910–1991 (population in 000s)

| City | 1910 | 1921 | 1930 | 1950 | 1961 | 1970 | 1980 | 1991 |
|---|---|---|---|---|---|---|---|---|
| Prague | 667.6 | 729.6 | 949.2 | 1,057.4 | 1,132.9 | 1,140.7 | 1,182.2 | 1,212.0 |
| Brno | 216.7 | 237.7 | 284.0 | 299.0 | 324.2 | 344.2 | 371.5 | 388.0 |
| Ostrava | 186.6 | 198.5 | 219.5 | 215.8 | 254.3 | 297.2 | 322.1 | 327.6 |
| Plzeň | 111.0 | 121.3 | 133.0 | 126.5 | 139.1 | 152.6 | 170.7 | 173.1 |
| Bratislava | 104.9 | 122.2 | 170.3 | 210.0 | 261.0 | 305.9 | 380.3 | 411.5 |
| Košice | 54.3 | 63.1 | 81.8 | 75.3 | 97.0 | 149.6 | 202.4 | 234.8 |

Note: All data except for 1991 are comparable. They refer to the same territory of individual cities as defined in 1980. The data for 1991 do not include local communities that have split from the core city.
Source: Alois Andrle et al., Vývoj československých měst, 1869–1980 [Development of Czechoslovak Cities, 1869–1980], Prague: TERPLAN (1986) and Census of the Czech Republic (1991).

Table 10.5 Indices of Prague's position in the settlement system of Czechoslovakia, 1910–1991

| Indices | 1910 | 1921 | 1930 | 1950 | 1961 | 1970 | 1980 | 1991 |
|---|---|---|---|---|---|---|---|---|
| Proportion of Prague in the national population | 5.13 | 5.61 | 6.78 | 8.57 | 8.24 | 7.95 | 7.74 | 7.79 |
| Ratio of the first city to the second city | 3.08 | 3.07 | 3.34 | 3.54 | 3.49 | 3.31 | 3.11 | 2.75 |
| Ratio of the population of the first city to the five largest ones | 0.99 | 0.98 | 1.07 | 1.14 | 1.05 | 0.91 | 0.82 | 0.77 |

## Prague and Socialism

The data quoted in the previous section indicate that, compared to other European capitals, Prague remained a relatively small capital city, as well as a capital with a low primacy within the Czechoslovak and even the Czech urban systems. This was partly caused by historical factors, but in the years 1950–1989 these features were strengthened by political decisions rooted in socialist urban ideology. An important part of this ideology was a critical attitude towards large cities, which was put into operation by policies to control their growth and to close the gap between town and the country. By contrast, the role of medium-size cities was evaluated positively by this ideology (see Chapter 3).

One of the most efficient instruments used to control the growth of Prague – mainly in the 1950s and 1960s – was the successful limitation of migration into the capital city through controls over the issue of work permits. Only people who, from the perspective of the planners, were "needed" in Prague were allowed to move and acquire a dwelling there. Other factors that contributed to low growth rates were certain elements of state housing policy, such as the concentration of housing construction in the then expanding industrial regions (like Ostrava; see Table 10.4) or the ideologically motivated policy of reducing the construction of family houses in Prague.

One fact should especially be stressed in this context. Regional and planning policies, as well as the absence of market mechanisms, combined to arrest the process of metropolization in Czechoslovakia for many decades. Prague ceased to function as a growth pole.[1] Indeed, Ryšavý and Link (1976) made clear that "polarization effects", which had been strongest in the period between 1910 and 1930 and medium to strong in the years 1869–1910, almost vanished in the period between 1950 and 1970. Suburbanization processes, too, almost stopped under socialism, particularly in its first 25 years – the population growth rates of Prague's suburban communities were much lower during the socialist period before 1975 than in the last three decades of the nineteenth century.

Prague, like most large cities in the Habsburg monarchy, was a city with a strong industrial base. However, during the inter-war period of 1918–1939, after having become the capital of a new state as well as a regional business centre (Ullrich, 1938), it began to change into a service centre. But even then, typologically, Prague belonged in the category of industrial – service and commerce centres. According to the classification method used by the International Institute of Statistics in The Hague, cities with 20–50 per cent of the population employed in industry, 20–33 per cent in commerce and transport, and 20–33 per cent in service should be included in this category.

This trend was stopped by the Second World War and by the economic strategies applied after the communist takeover in 1948.

A new socialist industrialization wave, with strong emphasis on steel production and engineering, could not fail to have an impact on the city of Prague. The absolute number of persons employed in the industry, as well as the ratio of industrial workers to the entire economically active population, started to rise again. In fact, the number of people employed in Prague's industry more than doubled in the period 1949–1961, and half of this labour force worked in engineering. This process of re-industrialization reached its peak at the beginning of the 1960s. According to the 1961 census data on Prague, the working class in that year represented 61 per cent of the economically active population. The emphasis on industrialization was also politically motivated. The aim was to keep the proportion of industrial working class among the total population of the city as high as possible. All these policies, to be sure, blocked the development of Prague into a service centre of any higher order. So, the city, as well as most other cities, suffered from an underdevelopment of the service sector during the whole socialist period. Many of the changes that have occurred since 1989 can be understood as reactions to such circumstances.

## The End of Ethnic Diversity

One of the most important changes that Prague has been undergoing since the second half of the nineteenth century up to the present time has been the transformation of its ethnic structure. It changed from an ethnically heterogeneous city in which Czechs, Germans, and Jews had cooperated, competed, and vied together for primacy, to one of the most ethnically homogeneous capital cities of Europe. After the Second World War it became an exclusively Czech city for all practical purposes. Commercial, cultural, and social interaction with other countries, which had also been formerly mediated by Prague's Germans and Jews, considerably weakened. Thus, the city entered the post-communist era and faced the current globalization process seriously impoverished. There are fewer mediators available for this interaction. To a certain limited degree, the role of cultural mediators has been taken over by the Czechs who returned from exile after 1989, or who continue to live abroad but have renewed contacts with their native country.

According to most estimates, about 60,000 German-speaking people lived in Prague in the middle of the nineteenth century. This number subsequently declined to 38,600 in 1880, to 32,000 in 1910, and to 28,300 in 1921, but it rose again to 41,000 in 1930. After the post-1945 expulsion of the German population from Czechoslovakia, the total dropped to 1,126 in 1961.

It is very difficult to estimate the number of Jews who lived in Prague at various points in time. According to McCagg (1989), there were 7,700 Jews living there in 1857 and 19,000 in 1880. According to Votrubec (1965), as many as 35,000 Jews were living there in the 1930s and their number notably increased to 47,000 by 1941, mainly as a result of immigration from Germany and Austria. The majority of the Prague Jews later died in the Holocaust or emigrated during the first post-war years. Pěkný (1993) estimates that only about 1,000 persons of Jewish origin now live in the city.

Both minorities mentioned above had lived in Prague for centuries and enriched the city economically as well as culturally, but they disappeared in a few years during and after the Second World War. By 1961, Prague became a virtually mono-ethnic city, with 97.6 per cent Czechs and 1.3 per cent Slovaks who at that time formed the largest ethnic minority. Foreigners – i.e. those who were not Czechoslovaks – accounted for 1.1 per cent of the city's inhabitants (Pěký, 1993).

## Factors of Change after 1989

The changes in the urban system of the Czech Republic after 1989 can only be understood in the contexts of the transformation of the political and social system of the country after the "Velvet Revolution" (1989–1991) and the "Velvet Divorce" which split Czechoslovakia in 1992 into two sovereign states, the Czech and Slovak Republics. The following survey tries to describe as briefly as possible the main changes that have had urban and regional impacts, such as the transformation of a centralist state into a democratic one, the transformation of the centrally planned economy into a market economy, and changes in the labour and housing markets, in transport policies and in regional and local self-government, as well as new patterns in foreign investment.

## The Transformation of the Political System and the Opening of Prague

After the elections in 1992 the Czech Republic changed into a fully fledged democratic party system with a right-of-centre orientation and a strong commitment to a neo-liberal concept of economic transformation. The main general features introduced after 1992 can be summarized as follows:

- emphasis on the diminishing role of state and other public bodies in the economy, social policy, health, and culture, with the aim of reducing public expenditure;
- formation of a relatively strong, centralist-orientated state administration, without influential intermediary regional and association units;
- a neo-liberal conception of economic transformation stressing privatization, deregulation, liberalization of prices, step-by-step reduction of state subsidies in all parts of economy, and internal and external convertibility of the Czech crown;
- emphasis on social consensus, and carefully balancing the interests of the emerging new upper and middle classes;
- ideological neutrality, stressing a formal conception of democracy, and the negative concepts of freedom, e.g. "freedom from" (R. Aron, R. Dahrendorf); and
- the transformation of territorial government and administration (i.e. the dismantling of regional administration, territorial decentralization, and the introduction of territorial self-government at the level of municipalities), leading to a rapid fragmentation of existing territorial administrative structure, so in Prague the 10 existing boroughs were replaced by 46 suburban self-governed communities (*Numeri Pragensis*, 1999: 36; Barlow, Dostál, and Hampl, 1994).

The main political transformations that have already changed the cities and urban systems of Central Europe consist in the geopolitical reorientations caused by the collapse of the communist regimes. Part of this involved dismantling Comecon, the Warsaw Pact, and other similar economic, political, and military organizations. Soon after 1989, most post-communist countries applied for membership of the European Union, and three of them (Czech Republic, Hungary, Poland) became members of NATO in 1999. Foreign trade orientations changed radically as well; before 1989, 45 per cent of Czechoslovak foreign trade was with the former Soviet Union, whereas by 1998 it had dropped to about 6 per cent and had been substituted by trade with Germany.

The most powerful impact on the city of Prague was caused by the opening of its borders, which had been one of the first political acts after the Velvet Revolution of 1989. Prague quickly became the destination for millions of tourists, students, business people, politicians, and scientists – and also, unfortunately, for drug dealers, criminals, and international mafia.

## The Transformation of the Economy

The transformation of the economy was based on price liberalization, the liberalization of foreign trade, the introduction of internal as well as external convertibility of the Czechoslovak currency (crown), and critically on a radical change in ownership towards privatization (Vačernik and Matěju, 1999). Three methods of privatization were applied: privatization of smaller state or cooperative enterprises by auctions; privatization of larger units by two waves of voucher privatization; and privatization by property restitution. The pace of privatization can be described as relatively quick. In legal terms, at the end of 1998 almost 94 per cent of enterprises in the Czech Republic were private business companies and partnerships, 5.28 per cent were cooperatives, and only 0.75 per cent of legal units remained state-owned enterprises. However, the voucher privatization that facilitated this only led to a legal change in the structure of ownership (e.g. the transfer of ownership rights directly performed by the state to the investment funds and banks, which were to a large extent controlled by the state). The actual ownership rights of the individual owners of vouchers or shares were not realized, and management remained ineffective.

In spite of the fact that after 1995 industrial output in the Czech Republic started to grow, the proportion of GDP produced by the industrial sector has been systematically decreasing since 1994 and by contrast, the proportion of GDP produced by services is growing. The Czech economy is definitely going through a process of de-industrialization. At present many old and famous large industrial firms are facing bankruptcy or closing down, and some of them are located in Prague. In 1990, approximately 2 million people were employed in industry and their number declined to 1.6 million in 1998. By contrast, the number of employees in services increased from 2.3 million (43 per cent of employees) to 2.6 million (54 per cent) people. After 1989 the service sector is the only one which has been growing in absolute as well as relative terms, in spite of a general decline in the number of people working in the Czech economy (from 5.4 million in 1989 to 4.8 million in 1998). These changes are reflected in the changing structure of economically active people in Prague (Table 10.6). The unemployment rate in the whole country was relatively low in the first years of the transformation, fluctuating between 2 and 4 per cent, but since 1996 a systematic increase has occurred, reaching 9.2 per cent in 1999.

After an initial slump in the years 1990–1993, household real incomes are rising so that present real income levels per capita have returned to those before the collapse of the communist regime – in Prague, however, they are now much higher. At the beginning of the millennium, GDP per capita in Prague was higher than the average European Union GDP per capita. At the same time, inequalities in income have grown and can be observed between sectors, types of employees, and regions, and especially with increasing distance from Prague.

Table 10.6 Structure of economically active population according to the main sectors in Prague, 1950–1998

| Year | Percentage of population | | |
| --- | --- | --- | --- |
| | Agriculture | Industry and construction | Services, administration, etc. |
| 1950 | 2.8 | 37.8 | 59.4 |
| 1961 | 1.0 | 45.7 | 53.3 |
| 1970 | 1.3 | 36.2 | 62.5 |
| 1980 | 1.3 | 35.4 | 63.3 |
| 1995 | 0.2 | 26.1 | 73.7 |
| 1998 | 0.2 | 23.5 | 76.3 |

*Source:* Czech Statistical Office.

Among other economic changes that impact on urban processes, special attention must be paid especially to labour and housing markets, transport, foreign trade, and foreign investments.

The post-1989 transformation embodied the changes in the labour code and other legal norms that led to a liberalization of the labour market and opened the door for labour mobility and migration. This potential, however, has not as yet been realized because of growing constraints in the housing market. Housing construction declined from 55,000 dwellings handed over for use in 1955 to 12,600 in 1995, and that increased only to 22,300 in 1999. Thus, the housing shortage is growing, mainly in large cities and in the metropolitan region of Prague where the highest demand for labour occurs. This disequilibrium, caused by the fact that the old, socialist housing system was not quickly substituted by a new, well-thought-through system, became a bottleneck, which has slowed the processes of structural economic transformation. The housing situation has become a serious barrier to the mobility of labour.

Most often, economies that go through extensive structural or systemic changes experience increased mobility of labour and hence geographic migration. Data from the Czech Republic show that the opposite has occurred, with a constant decline in migration rates after 1989: in 1989 24.7 persons per 1,000 inhabitants moved, in 1993 23.4, and in 1998 only 19.8. At the same time, the spatial pattern of migration has changed in important ways. Until 1990 the number of migrants "from district to district in the same region" did not substantially differ from the number of migrants "from municipality to municipality in the same district" or even from the number of migrants "from region to region" (i.e. long-distance migration), which was quite high. Since 1989, however, long-distance migration has declined, while short-distance migration has started to rise. Table 10.7 expresses some effects of this on Prague.

Table 10.7 Population changes in Prague, 1991–1998

| Year | Mid-year population (000s) | Population change | | Population of working age (000s) |
|---|---|---|---|---|
| | | By natural increase (%) | By net migration (%) | |
| 1991 | 1,214.9 | −2.85 | 4.41 | 706.0 |
| 1992 | 1,217.0 | −3.39 | 3.81 | 715.7 |
| 1993 | 1,217.9 | −3.57 | 3.28 | 724.7 |
| 1994 | 1,216.6 | −4.55 | 2.11 | 732.8 |
| 1995 | 1,212.7 | −5.72 | 0.97 | 737.0 |
| 1996 | 1,207.3 | −5.65 | 0.77 | 739.7 |
| 1997 | 1,202.6 | −5.12 | 0.62 | 740.7 |
| 1998 | 1,196.9 | −4.68 | −2.51 | 736.7 |

*Source: Numeri Pragensis* (1999: 12).

The state and municipalities monopolized the transport system in the pre-1989 regime. It was a highly subsidized sector of the socialist economy; transport was cheap for the users and thus daily commuting to work was very intensive in the Czech Republic. The public has reacted to the privatization of bus transport, mainly outside the cities, to declining state subsidies to railway and bus transport, and to the resulting rise in fares, by limiting their use of public transport and by starting to use private cars for journeys to work. These changes were facilitated and also stimulated by a rapid increase in the number of private cars from 2.4 million cars in 1990 to 3.7 million in 1998. At present Prague has one of the highest car-ownership rates among European metropoles (Table 10.8).

The transformation of railways is facing difficulties and its future is uncertain. This is partly due to the very high density of railways inherited from the past in the Czech territories, in common with other parts of Europe including Belgium, the Netherlands, Germany, and Britain. The need to reduce the number of small railway lines run by the state is evident. In the future, however, the Czech urban system will experience important beneficial effects from high-speed railways. With the help of the European Union the state is concentrating its resources on building up a system of semi-high-speed railways. At present two such "corridors" are under construction: Berlin–Prague–Brno–Vienna (started functioning in 2003), and Warsaw–Ostrava–Vienna. A third is supposed to connect Prague with Linz, and a fourth will link Prague to Nuremberg, Frankfurt, and Paris.

Even more important for cities in the Czech Republic will be motorways. The existing national system of highways is already linked to the West European highway system by the motorway Prague–Plzeň–Nuremberg. In the near future it will be linked by the Prague–Dresden–Berlin and Katowice–Brno–Vienna motorways as well.

Table 10.8 Trends in the socio-economic structure of the active population in Prague, 1995–1998 (%)

| Sector | 1995 | 1996 | 1997 | 1998 |
|---|---|---|---|---|
| Industry | 17.2 | 16.2 | 16.1 | 16.1 |
| Construction | 8.9 | 8.5 | 8.1 | 7.4 |
| Wholesale and retail trade, repair of automobiles, household goods | 6.3 | 6.1 | 13.2 | 12.0 |
| Hotels and restaurants | 2.8 | 2.6 | 3.6 | 3.8 |
| Transport, communication, storage | 12.2 | 12.9 | 11.2 | 11.5 |
| Financial intermediation | 6.9 | 7.5 | 6.3 | 6.6 |
| Real estate and business activities | 12.1 | 12.4 | 12.6 | 13.3 |
| Public administration | 7.6 | 8.2 | 6.8 | 7.1 |
| Education | 10.6 | 10.7 | 9.0 | 9.3 |
| Health and social work | 7.9 | 7.7 | 6.4 | 6.4 |
| Other community services | 7.5 | 7.1 | 6.4 | 6.2 |

*Source:* Calculated from Table 5.1 in *Numeri Pragensis* (1999).

Air transport developed rapidly in the Czech Republic and the number of passengers using Prague airport per year has doubled since 1989 from about 2.5 million to 5 million. It is estimated that in the next five years this number will rise to 10 million. Changes in the geography of Czech Airlines destinations are also important – in fact, they mirror the changed geopolitical linkages after 1989. Flights to some former destinations in Eastern Europe and the former Soviet Union were cancelled and updated by new routes to Western Europe, especially to German cities such as Frankfurt, Düsseldorf, Berlin, Stuttgart, Hamburg, Hanover, Munich, and Cologne-Bonn.

One of the factors of globalization shaping Prague since 1989 which should not be ignored is the renewal of intellectual contacts with the outside world, contacts from which the city was isolated by the Iron Curtain for more than 40 years.[2] After 1989 one can observe a rapid growth of cooperation and contacts among Prague universities, institutes of the Czech Academy of Sciences, and other research institutes, as well as laboratories and their partners in the West. Similarly, contact of Prague writers, artists, and musicians with colleagues all over the world quickly expanded. And, especially importantly, within 10 years Prague became a city of international congresses, conferences, exhibitions, fairs, and the exchange of ideas. There is no doubt that this growing international role of Prague has been stimulated, among other factors, by its rediscovered attractiveness as a beautiful city. And yet one should not forget that similar ambitions to become an international meeting place are also nurtured by other cities in the region which opened themselves up to the world, or which had played this role already in the past: Berlin, Vienna, Budapest, Krakow, and Warsaw.

## New Polarities and Integration within Europe

All the changes mentioned above in the political, economic, and social systems of the Czech Republic have started to transform the cities and the regional structure of the country. The locus of the most essential changes, however, has been Prague. Two main concepts help to explain the growing organizing functions of large cities in the post-communist countries: the theories of the diffusion and the selectivity of regional and urban development. The large cities always function as gateways, though in a time of radical societal changes their role in this respect is substantially enhanced. This is because large cities, and especially the capital cities, are the origins of the new rules, new legal forms, new institutions, and new patterns of social organization, which are diffused to other parts of the country and assist wider regional international integration (Drbohlav and Sýkora, 1996). Fundamental changes in political, legal, and economic mechanisms "triggered many necessary structural changes and increased selectivity of development also from the regional point of view" (Hampl et al., 1999: 62). In most general terms the reintroduction of a market economy and pluralist democracy engendered unevenness in regional processes and polarization in regional development. Two kinds of polarization reveal themselves as most relevant: polarization between the

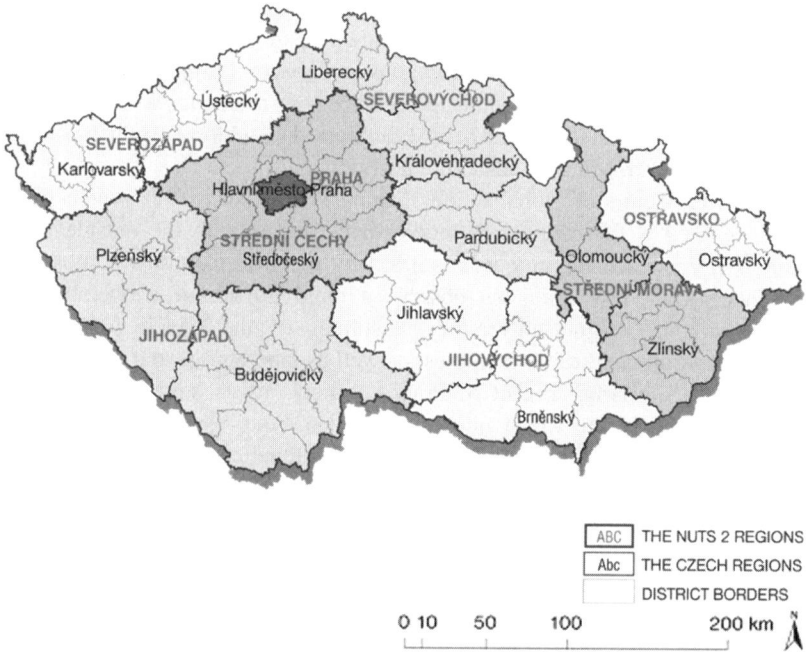

Fig. 10.1  The Czech regions and NUTS 2 region.

*Source:* Prague City Hall, City Development Authority Section, Strategic Planning Department.

Prague metropolitan region and other Czech regions; and polarization between the metropolitan and non-metropolitan Czech regions.

Statistical data comparing the pre- and post-1989 regional developments unequivocally show that after 1989 the Prague metropolitan region's position among other Czech regions was considerably strengthened (Fig. 10.1). One can describe this process as polarization. However, because of the specific Czech situation, namely stagnant population and a housing shortage, the "stronger" position of Prague is not reflected in the growing size of her population – in contrast, for example, to Warsaw in Poland. But data on the processes of concentration of jobs, of jobs in the service sector, and of financial activities, and data on growing earnings, permanently low unemployment rates, and other indicators as summarized in the Tables 10.9–10.12, quite convincingly document the specificity of urban processes after 1989. Prague started to differ much more from the rest of the country than in the pre-1989 period.

Table 10.9  Rank order of Czech districts with highest wages

| 1989 | | | 1998 | | |
|---|---|---|---|---|---|
| Rank order | District, city | Ratio to the Czech Average | Rank order | District, city | Ratio to the Czech average |
| 1 | Karviná | 122.0 | 1 | Prague | 135.6 |
| 2 | Ostrava | 112.3 | 2 | Mlada Boleslav | 117.1 |
| 3 | Most | 109.9 | 3–5 | Prague – West | 107.9 |
| 4 | Frydek-Mistek | 109.8 | 3–5 | Ostrava | 107.9 |
| 5 | Sokolov | 107.0 | 3–5 | Most | 107.9 |
| 6 | Kladno | 106.9 | 6 | Pilsen | 107.1 |
| 7 | Prague | 106.4 | 7 | Prague – East | 107.0 |

*Source:* M. Hiršl, unpublished report.

Table 10.10  Polarization processes in the Czech Republic (Czech Republic = 100)

| Territorial unit | Indicators of polarization | | | |
|---|---|---|---|---|
| | Relativized intensity of jobs | Relativized job development index 1989–1996 | Wages level 1996 | Relativized index of wages development 1989–1996 |
| Metropolitan areas – total | 110.4 | 103.0 | 109.7 | 105.4 |
| Prague | 127.0 | 113.8 | 127.6 | 120.0 |
| Non-metropolitan areas | 90.7 | 96.9 | 90.3 | 94.3 |
| Bohemia | 104.2 | 101.8 | 103.3 | 103.9 |
| Moravia and Silesia | 93.3 | 96.9 | 95.4 | 94.5 |

*Source:* Hampl et al. (1999).

Table 10.11 Regional differentiation of total economic development (Czech Republic = 100)

| Territorial unit | Total economic level 1996 (EA/population) | Index of total economic development 1989–1996 |
|---|---|---|
| Metropolitan areas – total | 120.5 | 108.1 |
| Prague | 161.4 | 136.3 |
| Non-metropolitan areas | 81.6 | 91.0 |
| Bohemia | 107.3 | 105.4 |
| Moravia and Silesia | 88.6 | 91.2 |

*Source:* Hampl et al. (1999).

Table 10.12 Development of concentration of the financial sector in six major Czech metropolitan areas

| Metropolitan area | Share in the CzR of jobs in finance and insurance (%) | | | | Share (%) in population of the CzR, 1996 |
|---|---|---|---|---|---|
| | 1989 | 1992 | 1996 | Difference 1989–1996 | |
| Prague | 28.86 | 31.40 | 36.61 | 7.75 | 13.32 |
| Brno | 5.49 | 5.02 | 5.62 | 0.13 | 5.28 |
| Ostrava | 5.62 | 5.34 | 6.02 | 0.40 | 8.13 |
| Pilsen | 3.31 | 2.96 | 4.29 | 0.98 | 3.01 |
| Hradec Kralove | 3.59 | 3.93 | 4.02 | 0.43 | 3.15 |
| Total (metropolitan[*]) | 59.06 | 60.88 | 69.40 | 110.34 | 47.08 |
| Total (non-metropolitan) | 40.94 | 39.12 | 30.60 | 210.34 | 52.90 |

Note: [*]Includes six other metropolitan areas.
*Source:* Hampl et al. (1999).

Prague has "moved" in its standard of living, lifestyles, and socio-economic structure, nearer to the Western neighbouring cities. Prague started, as shown by the growth of foreign investments, with a change in its economic base, and with tourism, which helped it integrate into the European system of cities.

## Politics and the Built Environment Under Socialism

Recent theories stress the cyclical nature of urban processes. Periods of longer or shorter upsurges are often followed by periods of stagnation or even decline. The smaller the city and the narrower its economic base, the bigger are the risks that such cyclical ups and downs will occur. Growth and stagnation periods in large cities are, however, most often linked to their political functions and to the historical fluctuations in the wealth and power of the country where they are located. During the twentieth century, few European metropoles experienced such frequently alternating periods of growth and expansion with periods of stagnation and decline as did Prague. Another phenomenon is correlated with this cyclical nature of Prague's twentieth-century history: a high degree of societal discontinuity. The citizens of Prague lived, in this period, under nine different political regimes. The systemic differences among these regimes were quite considerable, e.g. from a corporate monarchical regime (before 1914) and liberal democratic republic (1918–1938), to a Nazi protectorate (1939–1945), people's democracy (1945–1948), unitary socialist Czechoslovakia (1948–1968), and a socialist federal state (1969–1989), to a post-communist democracy since 1989.

This societal discontinuity was, however, combined with an unusual physical, demographic, morphological, and architectural stability (Moscheles, 1937). Prague was not damaged by war actions in 1939–1945 – unlike Warsaw, Berlin, Vienna, Budapest, or Dresden. Prague, especially its centre, was also not destroyed by post-1945 reconstruction and expansion as so many German cities were, and hence it retained in physical terms the features of a Gothic, baroque, and nineteenth-century Gründerzeit city. The timeliness of morphological and architectural stability and continuity on the one hand, and of societal discontinuity on the other, created a specific tension that is a particular feature of Prague, and it has influenced inter-urban social and spatial processes in different periods of the twentieth century.

Before discussing the transformation of Prague's socio-spatial structures after 1989 (i.e. after the reintroduction of a democratic and market-economy system), it will be useful to summarize the main features of the city's social geography under socialism. Of crucial importance were the factors that "socialized" the housing system step-by-step. Private ownership of apartment houses was abolished; legal norms enabling the local authorities to regulate the housing system (moves, changes of dwellings, etc.) were introduced. Existing housing space was redistributed by dividing large upper- and middle-class dwellings and houses. Rent control[3] was continued and buttressed by the introduction of the policy of cheap state-subsidized housing, the abolition of a land property market, and the introduction of administratively set prices of land. The nationalization of retail businesses, trades, services, and restaurants, an emphasis on heavily subsidized urban public transport, the introduction of more egalitarian distribution of incomes, and the introduction of unified prices of food and consumer goods – all these policies expressed an intention to minimize the urban inequalities engendered by capitalism. All urban conditions – housing, services, transportation, and even environment – should be similarly equitably arranged and available (Carter, 1979). After the first period of revolutionary fervour, however, these socialist ideas were gradually eroded and abandoned.

Supporting these socio-economic changes were, as Häusermann has stressed, the instruments of central planning which replaced market mechanisms:

The socialist city developed in a completely different framework; ... all investments were state controlled, decision processes were organized in a strictly hierarchical way, and were centrally co-ordinated. The functions of the city, the timing, and the extent of investments were completely a state matter – these were ideal prerequisites for urban planning. The final product (the city) could be designed according to theory and thereupon be realized according to the plan, for the state was in charge of all means necessary to implement it. In former times, not even the sovereign rulers disposed of such great power over urban development. (Hausermann, 1996: 215–216)

Yet, it must also be stressed that the socialist society inherited an existing material, social and spatial structure in Prague that had neither been damaged as severely as Berlin or Budapest, nor had seen destruction comparable to that of Warsaw. In many cities of Central and Eastern Europe, the post-war renewal of their physical structure paralleled in large measure the transformation of an entire social system. But, this was not the case in Prague. The new social structure and content was realized mostly within old, inherited ecological structures that had been moulded or created during the preceding century by a capitalist-type society. New parts that were gradually added to these old structures formed a relatively small "layer" in the overall city fabric.

The obvious continuity and stability of Prague's morphology and built environment was combined with quite extensive changes in the spatial distribution of social strata and social groups. These changes happened mainly in the first 10–15 years of the socialist period. The common denominator was a trend towards the social homogenization of urban space. The social differences between individual parts of Prague under socialism decreased. Empirical studies document that the residential segregation of manual workers in 1950 was considerably lower than in 1930 (Musil, 1968). "The main axis of spatial differentiation in pre-war Prague was class dichotomy: this determined the profile of concentric zones and divided their territory into predominantly bourgeois and predominantly working class districts" (Matějů et al., 1979). In 1970, the socio-spatial structure of the city was also dichotomized, but the dichotomy was of a different type. It can be described as "genetic" in socio-demographic and in physical terms. According to a study based on factor analysis, family and age structure of population and the age structure of housing explained more than the half of the variance in 1970. The socio-economic (class) structure in Prague under socialism became a relatively unimportant factor and its role diminished compared with the pre-war years. By contrast, demographic factors, especially age structure and family status, gained in importance, to a large extent as a result of housing policies that preferred young families with children, and as a result the construction of large new housing estates on the outskirts of Prague (Smith, 1989).

The trend towards desegregation slowed down in the 1960s and 1970s, and new socio-spatial differences started to emerge. Most important was the decay of the inner city. Social processes developed in parallel with the deterioration of the built environment in these inner areas. They experienced depopulation, and most of those who remained – who were "trapped" there – were old people, pensioners, widows, and unskilled workers or employees. In pre-war capitalist Prague, by contrast, affluent households and especially German and Jewish minorities inhabited the central areas of the city. At the same time, these inner parts of Prague served as the business and financial centre. And, in the inter-war capitalist period of growth of the city, these central areas of Prague underwent extensive changes, with many new office buildings, shopping centres, and apartment houses being built. Nothing comparable happened under socialism. Socialist urban policy concentrated its energy on building new housing estates on the periphery, and neglected the central and inner areas. Post-socialist Prague has returned to the pre-war trajectory, and thus today the central zones of Prague are experiencing a new upsurge of activities, construction, and renewal. Again, the structural and functional changes are being accompanied by a transformation of the socio-spatial pattern of the city. But it is not just a return to the pre-socialist social geography of inter-war Prague.

## Impacts of Transformation and Globalization on the Built Environment

Ten years after the breakdown of the communist regimes in Central and Eastern Europe, Prague is again in the middle of a major transformation of its internal spatial structure and morphology, and of many features of its built environment. At present it is too early to see the new features of the emerging urban pattern very clearly. Physical and spatial elements of societies change much more slowly than political, economic, and social factors. And we still lack reliable data for small geographical units that would enable us to compare the present situation with the past. On the other hand, however, we can visually observe the effects of the new mechanisms that started to restructure the city after 1989. And there are also reliable but more general data that document these changes. The observable morphological effects of the transformations that are leading to a system based on pluralistic democracy and market economy can be linked to the synergy of the following specific factors:

- privatization and restitution of property;
- reintroduction of a property market;
- successive deregulation of rents;
- growing income differences;
- sectoral changes in the economy, especially de-industrialization;
- weakening of the welfare state system;

- decentralization of city governments;
- more emphasis on environmental quality; and
- liberalization of immigration policies.[4]

Ten years in the life of a large city is too short a period for substantially changing its morphology. But the societal transformations the Czech Republic underwent in the 1990s were so extensive and intensive that already after these 10 years many changes in the internal socio-spatial patterns of the city are clearly visible (Fig. 10.2). The main changes, discussed in more detail below, are:

- internationalization and globalization of the city;
- growing socio-spatial disparities;
- revitalization and commercialization of the inner parts of the city;
- the formation of tourist Prague; and
- suburbanization and commercialization of peripheral zones.

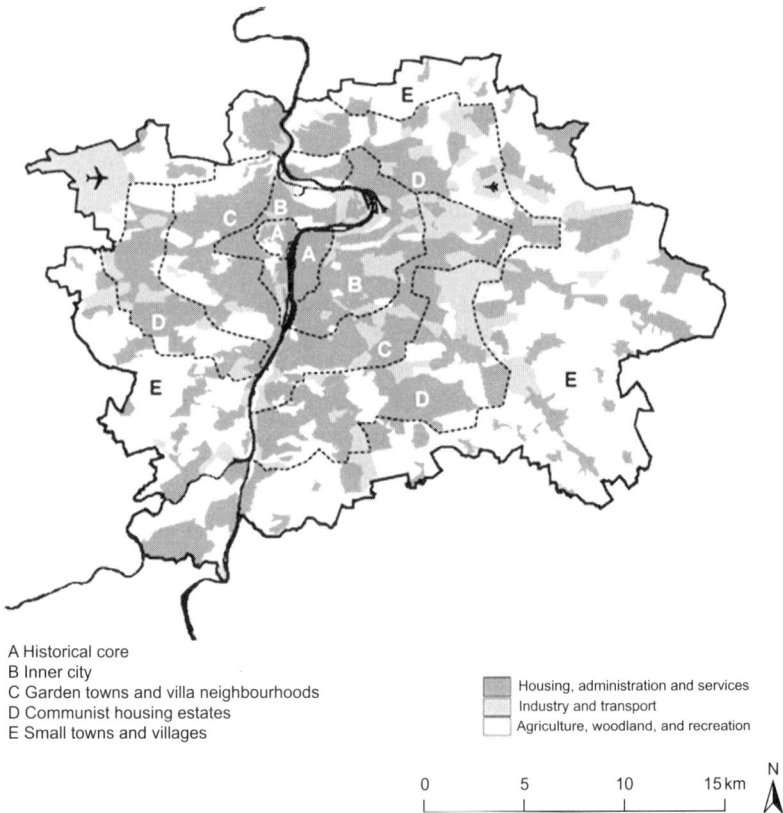

A Historical core
B Inner city
C Garden towns and villa neighbourhoods
D Communist housing estates
E Small towns and villages

Housing, administration and services
Industry and transport
Agriculture, woodland, and recreation

0    5    10    15 km    N

Fig. 10.2  Prague: urban spatial structure and land use.

*Source:* Prague City Hall, City Development Authority, Section Strategic, Planning Department.

## Internationalization and Globalization

As Sýkora (1999) observes, the internationalization and globalization of Prague's economy, lifestyles, and culture were started by the political transformations that began in 1989 and that were speeded up by the transformation of the Czech economy:

The most important of these was internationalization through capital investments by foreign companies, which expanded their operations in the Czech Republic and Prague. In Prague, foreign activities were particularly important in trade and advanced services, such as finance, audit, consultancy, real estate development and marketing, public relations, media, etc. Foreign companies demanded office, retail, and warehousing premises for their operation and foreign developers become very influential actors in the commercial property development process. In many cases, attractive properties gained in restitution by domestic private persons were quickly sold to foreign investors and developers, who supplied office and retail space for lease to foreign firms. The segment of the property market with high specification office and retail space is dominated by foreign owners, investors, developers, consultants, brokers, and users. (Sýkora, 1999)

So, in this segment of Prague's property market, both Italian and German firms are quite active and successful. These developments, as well as those linked to political institutions, culture, teaching, and research, led to an inflow of Western professionals and employees, and their families. According to the estimates worked out by the Magistrate of the City, there are at present approximately 50,000 Western employees working in Prague. To them should be added members of their families and those who live in Prague, but are not employed.

The numbers of Western residents at any one time, however, is significantly larger than this as one must also add as many as 10,000–14,000 American students who lived in Prague at the beginning of the 1990s. In addition, there are manual workers from Eastern Europe, mainly from Ukraine, Russia, Poland, and the former Yugoslavia, together with small shopkeepers, traders, and vendors who have come from China and Vietnam. There are no reliable data on the number of people in this group. The only reliable statistics are those on foreigners registered as permanently employed. Compared with socialist Prague, when the number of Western citizens – including the members of Western embassies – living permanently in Prague did not exceed 2,000 people, the post-1989 years brought immense changes in this respect (Drbohlav and čermák, 1998).

The other factor contributing to the globalization of Prague is tourism. Official statistics show that tourism grew dramatically after 1989, and the city became one of the most frequently visited cities in Europe and the highest-ranked tourist destination among the former socialist cities. Tourism-linked business thus became one of the main economic activities of the city and substantially escalated the internationalization of Prague.

The growing number of Western employees and tourists, along with the growing import of Western consumer goods, American movies, and Western TV programmes, started to change the consumption patterns, fashion, lifestyles, and values of the local population (see Demetz, 1997). Most of these changes in cultural patterns, mainly those symbolizing the links to the West, are already reflected in the architecture semiotics of the city, the streets, and other public spaces. Some commentators therefore speak about the Westernization or Americanization of Czech culture. Even if one does not accept this critical connotation, there is no doubt that Prague's cultural life became more varied and diversified after 1989. Contemporary Prague is full of large and small expatriate communities. Some people even speak about the "Paris of the 1990s" and document this trend by avant-garde publications, coffee houses, pubs, and foreign language journals: five English newspapers and two English journals, alongside French and German periodicals, are published in Prague. On the other hand, the Czech publishers, reacting to the emerging new demand, started to publish many English, German, and French translations of Czech literature, or books of authors belonging to the "Prague circle" of German writers (see Brod, 1966). Paradoxically, Prague's move forward in this respect means, at the same time, a return to its cultural past.

## Growing Socio-spatial Disparities

The dismantling of central planning, the reintroduction of the market economy, the liberalization of foreign trade, and the free movement of labour led within a few years to observable changes in the Czech urban system. The intra-urban structure of Prague reacted to these systemic changes even faster. Initially, the spatial distribution of activities and functions changed. In the last 10 years, however, even the socio-spatial structures of the city – which are relatively rigid – underwent considerable transformation. Despite the fact that census data on population and housing for small geographical units (e.g. for census tracts) are not available, some special surveys hint at the main transformations which are taking place.

Two parallel processes primarily caused changes in the socio-spatial structure of Prague: growing disparities in income and wealth, and increasing differentiation of housing quality in individual localities of the city.[5]

The main results of surveys prove that the city is in the middle of a substantial transformation, which can be described in the following way. Since the start of economic reform after 1989, a process of increasing differentiation of population according to income and wealth has emerged. The reforms brought about divergences in incomes and earnings, and privatization has created a new social group of property owners. Some of these are now quite wealthy people. On the other hand, the emergence of unemployment – which is still relatively low in Prague – the transformation of the social welfare system, and the rising costs of housing and transport contributed to the growing social inequality and even poverty. It should be stressed, however, that income distribution in the

Czech Republic, as compared with Hungary, Poland, and other post-communist countries, retained more of the features of the egalitarian pattern so typical for socialist Czechoslovakia.

Table 10.10 illustrates the increasing social disparities in the Czech Republic after 1989. This is due mainly to the fact that growth in the real value of the wages was more dynamic in Prague than in other Czech districts. Nevertheless, it should be stressed that real income in 1998 was higher than in 1989 in only eight Czech districts. In the remaining 69 districts, real incomes have as yet not regained their 1989 levels.

However, not even in Prague do all citizens benefit from these higher incomes. The retired, unemployed, and those dependent on other social benefits have the same level of earnings as people in the other parts of the country. Thus, income disparities are higher in Prague than in the other regions of the Republic. Sýkora (2000) stressed that the income differences would be even bigger if we included the strong group of affluent Western foreigners brought to the city by internationalization and globalization.

Growing disparities in wealth and earnings alone would not be able to initiate a process of substantial socio-spatial differentiation. Changes on the supply side (i.e. in the housing system) were an essential factor as well. While communist housing policy attempted to reduce differences in access to housing and to homogenize housing supply through the provision of standardized dwellings, the post-communist governments aimed to alleviate public intervention into housing and to create conditions for market-based housing supply. They used three instruments to do this: privatization of part of the housing stock, rent deregulation, and a withdrawal of the state from direct housing provision. The combined effects of the growing income disparities and the new housing policies stimulated the increase of socio-spatial disparities. Rent deregulation has started a new type of internal migration within the city. According to Sýkora, low-income households are seeking smaller flats in localities where rent is not likely to increase at the rate that it will in the city centre.

Privatization (i.e. restitution of property) has been another factor in the growth of socio-spatial disparities. Valuable properties often become the subject of renovation and refurbishment into luxury housing, offices, or hotels. This process has often resulted in the removal of all the original tenants, and has reduced the proportion of the less affluent households living in attractive locations. The replacement of the original population by high-income tenants, quite often foreigners, has contributed substantially to a change in the social profile of the city's neighbourhoods.

The withdrawal of the state from direct housing provision and termination of state support for the construction of new cooperative housing caused a rapid decline in apartment construction. Preference given to subsidizing mortgages has been unable to reverse the slump in state-supported house building. In 1991, some 7,200 dwellings were built in Prague, but in 1997 the number dropped to

1,800. Yet, the first signs of recovery were registered in 1998 when 3,600 new dwellings were completed. Most newly constructed private housing is affordable only for the highest-income group of households, however, because there is a large disparity between the prices of residential real estate and the income of the population. The non-existence of state support for non-profit housing is another factor that contributes to the socially one-sided character of new housing. And yet two factors restrict the processes of socio-spatial differentiation in post-communist Prague: the first is the very low house-building rate, which blocks the movement of households, and the second is rent control, which embraces nearly 60 per cent of all apartments in 1998 in the city. Even so, the rent ceiling has been deregulated step by step and deregulation will continue until the market determines rents in all locations. Sýkora (2000) estimated that the rent ceiling in Prague increased more than 14-fold between 1991 and 1998, resulting in an increase of almost 500 per cent in real terms.

## Revitalization and Commercialization of the Central Parts of the City

Eleven years ago, when the post-communist cities in Central Europe had just started their transformations, I expressed the view that "the introduction of the market economy is already changing the behaviour of urban actors ... the market economy has changed the centres of cities in Czechoslovakia, Hungary, Poland, and eastern Germany. In all these countries the process of revitalization of old historical centres can be observed and, in combination with growing tourism, this process will continue" (Musil, 1993: 902).

Physical revitalization is occurring across all of the central and inner city of Prague, but the most visible changes have happened in the old historical areas (i.e. in the Old Town and in the Lesser Town). However, the spatial distribution of the revitalization processes has been rather uneven, and has mainly been concentrated along streets with shops. These were quite often previously "dead" streets where shops from pre-war times had been changed during the socialist period into stores and where the facades of historical buildings were crumbling. Now they have been transformed into fashionable lanes with art galleries, exclusive boutiques, and good restaurants. Historical slums have been converted into attractive spaces with cafés, shops, and galleries, as well as offices. One of the best examples of such revitalization is the complex known as "Ungelt" near the Old Town Square. Ungelt was a ruin during the decades of socialist rule. Revitalization and rehabilitation were not always motivated only by commercial purposes. Many gardens on the slopes of the Lesser Town were reconstructed with a simple aim: to save these gardens and to open them to the public (Fig. 10.3[a–f]).

The attitudes of the residents, of the professionals, and of city authorities towards the combination of revitalization and massive commercialization are ambivalent. There are those who believe that too much preservation hinders the

Fig. 10.3 Images of Prague. (a) Old City Square, the Town Hall, and the Cathedral. (b) Old city, new hotel on the embankments of the Vltava river. (c) Inner city, Hotel International, new classicism ("Stalinist style"), 1950s. (d) South-west city, housing estates built in the late 1970s. (e) Inner city, the "Dancing House" (new administrative building). (f) Inner city, Golden Cross, new housing estate.

transformation of the historic core into a functional part of the city. In this point of view, tourism, combined with privatization and development, is the main factor reviving the historic core. This is because these economic activities bring renewed vitality to old buildings, which again become viable economic units as they begin earning money in the form of shops and cafés. This, they suggest, has led to a more effective revival of Prague's "historic slums" than have any of the formal mechanisms of planning or legal protection used by the previous socialist regime, which ironically were a factor in the neglect and subsequent decline of these areas. On the other hand, there are those who worry that the historical centre is, due to this radical revitalization, overburdened and threatened. They have already expressed several times their disagreements with change and have managed to stop some extravagant projects (mostly hotel building).

The result of these efforts to find a balance between the preservation of the historical beauty of the old centre and its necessary revitalization by means of commercialization and tourism could be called "the Prague compromise". Among the best accounts of these efforts are the words of Hungarian observer and commentator Ilona Sármány-Parsons:

A local specialty is to place new business or bank centres in refurbished palaces, which usually date from the Baroque era or the turn of the century ... Very often Czech developers choose to revitalize lovely old buildings, but even for some foreign investors, it seems to be considered worthwhile financially to restore the old fabric, since this brings both prestige and business confidence. For example an Italian developer restored the Charles Bridge Centre in 1994. (Sármány-Parsons, 1998, p. 226)

Another example of the change of old historical or nineteenth-century buildings from residential to commercial use is the placement of the Dresdner Bank in a formerly rich apartment house on the banks of the Vltava river. In addition, though, two other procedures of commercialization have been applied: (a) the demolition of existing structures containing residential and commercially less intensive uses and their replacement by new, taller and larger buildings; and (b) land-use intensification through new commercial developments of vacant land. Both these procedures are used predominantly in the nineteenth-century residential districts rather than in the historic core.

Commercialization in Prague has been driven mainly by the development of offices, multipurpose commercial centres, and tourism-orientated facilities such as hotels, restaurants, and souvenir shops. As Sýkora (1998) states: "The development of office space was stimulated by rapidly increasing demand from foreign trade and business firms expanding to East Central Europe and domestic, especially financial sector, companies." Comparative studies carried out by developers Jones Lang Wootton on Prague, Budapest, and Warsaw have shown that annual office supply during the years 1993–1997 was highest in Prague, followed by Budapest and Warsaw respectively. In Prague, office space went from 50,000 sq.m in 1993 to 110,000 in 1997, while in Budapest it rose from 50,000 to only 85,000 sq.m.

Recently, two new phenomena can be observed. The first derives from the fact that possibilities to find space in the centre of Prague are now nearly exhausted, and as a result reconstruction and new construction are moving into the zone of nineteenth-century suburbs. Some parts of this zone changed in the past into "transition zones" with decaying property and infrastructure. After 1989, in some of them (Žižkov), a dynamic redevelopment process started, and the old transition zones are being slowly transformed into parts of the expanding business centre. Most often a similar process as in the historical core of the city has been set in motion: a change from residential to commercial use within the existing building stock. However, new office and commercial buildings are constructed in these older suburbs than in the historical core.

Since 1999, a second new phenomenon can be observed in the nineteenth-century zone of Prague. This is the construction of large, new commercial and leisure/entertainment centres on land used in the past by industry, stores, and other non-residential functions. The best example is the construction of a new multifunctional centre in Prague 5, called the Angel Centre. The redevelopment and development of real estate in Prague's centre, as well as in the zone surrounding the centre, undoubtedly brought new life to many parts of the inner city, and revitalized the physical appearance of buildings and streets. At the same time these developments caused many problems: a considerable reduction of the residential function, rapidly increasing car traffic, and often damage to the historical heritage.

## The Formation of Tourist Prague

Already by 1993, Prague was one of the most frequently visited cities in Europe, first among the former socialist cities and a rising international tourism star.[6] Using the official Czech government definition of a tourist – a person who stays overnight in a registered bed – approximately 10 million visitors per year visit Prague as tourists. For a city of only 1.2 million residents this is a high number, and there is no doubt that tourism is a phenomena that radically changed Prague after 1989 (Hoffman and Musil, 1999) (Table 10.13).

The Prague experience represents a different phenomenon from that of cities that are restructuring to capture tourism or have been built as tourist centres. For Prague, tourism has been an integral part of post-1989 democratization,

Table 10.13 Basic data on tourism in Prague, 1996–1998

| Indicator | 1996 | 1997 | 1998 |
|---|---|---|---|
| Total number of accommodation establishments | 734 | 993 | 983 |
| Collective accommodation establishments – | 381 | 472 | 464 |
| in hotels | 189 | 233 | 226 |
| Individual accommodation | 363 | 521 | 519 |
| Total number of guests (000s) | 2,570.8 | 2,826.4 | 2,781.6 |
| International guests (000s) | 2,168.3 | 2,252.0 | 2,075.2 |
| Total days of stay (000s) | 9,509.9 | 10,842.0 | 11,013.2 |

*Source: Numeri Pragensis* (1999).

marketization, and privatization. In this sense, Prague represents a naturally occurring experiment, which permits us to examine the interplay of history, culture, and political economy, and to see more clearly how tourism articulates with global market forces. More than in other cities, tourism in Prague represents one of the most important factors of globalization. As it has opened up to the world, Prague has become a destination for an international flow of travellers whose motives for visiting the city have ranged from work and culture to play and nostalgia. People may travel exclusively for pleasure or in connection with work; between these two poles there are travellers who combine work, play, and nostalgia. This last group of people has been particularly important for Prague. Groups attracted by Prague include the international corporate and business class – consultants, lawyers, accountants, developers, and entrepreneurs – for whom the city is a venue for business and professional activity. This group has fuelled demand for upgraded accommodation and services, thereby changing not only the "atmosphere" of Prague but also the socio-spatial structure of the city, while simultaneously linking it with the globalizing world. Business and commercial tourism has also been stimulated by Prague's return to its pre-war tradition of hosting fairs and exhibitions. After 1989, the number of such events increased dramatically. In 1995, for example, one of the two major exhibition halls held 50 fairs – approximately one a week – and the other held 40. Also, Prague quickly joined the ranks of the top 20 conference sites worldwide to become an intellectual meeting place and centre, hosting hundreds of lectures, congresses, and professional meetings each year. This is enabled, in part, by Prague's convention infrastructure. The 6,000-seat Convention Palace, the former Palace of Culture, is, ironically, a legacy of the communist regime and was originally planned for the uses of the Communist Party. In a year, approximately 60,000 conference participants spent an average of US\$623 in this one building. Top political meetings, congresses, and professional meetings have helped the incorporation of local politicians, professionals, and business people into the mainstream, and helped to open the Czech Republic to Western models and training. In the autumn of 2000, Prague hosted the annual meeting of the World Bank and International Monetary Fund, and in autumn 2002 a meeting of NATO. Since 1997, Prague has also been the venue of annually organized Forum 2000 conferences, which are attended by Nobel Prize winners, world-renowned politicians, and scientists who discuss various aspects of globalization processes in the contemporary world. President Václav Havel himself is the host of these Forum 2000 conferences, which take place at the Prague Castle and which are sponsored predominantly by a Japanese foundation, the Nippon Foundation, Tokyo. Here we have a promising example of world cooperation and globalization. To a large extent even the attendees of business and professional meetings are motivated to come to Prague because of its beauty as a city. This is one of the main assets of the city.

There exists still another motif, not often mentioned, which brings a specific category of people to Prague. It is rather a mixed group of people who have one common feature: nostalgia. Among them are Prague Jews who survived the Holocaust but emigrated, their children, expelled Prague Germans and many other people who went through the city as emigrants, and students who studied at Prague's university. Some of the oldest of these individuals want to see the city again after more than 50 years. And of course, there are the intellectuals who were never personally linked to the city but whose relation to the city is built upon an understanding of old Prague's literature, music, and art.

The effects of the opening up of Prague and of the inflow of millions of tourists are obvious. Already in 1994 foreign currency revenue from tourism reached approximately US$2 billion, equivalent to 14 per cent of the export earnings of the Czech Republic and 6 per cent of the GDP. By 1996 these revenues had climbed to US$4 billion, and they stabilized in subsequent years in the range of US$3.5–3.7 billion. Yet, over and above the official figures, there is an underground tourist economy estimated at over US$1.5 billion per year. And more than two-thirds of the total Czech tourist income is generated in Prague.

Under conditions of quickly growing demand for tourist services, Prague needed and pursued foreign capital. Tourism in general and accommodation in particular attracted more foreign investment than other branches of the economy, and this has triggered a dramatic cycle of hotel building and reconstruction. By 1995, tourist accommodation in Prague was comparable statistically to that of European cities like Munich and Vienna, with 170 hotels and between 35,000 and 50,000 beds, a major increase over the 10,000 hotel beds available in 1989. At present the number of beds in hotels, boarding houses, and hostels has risen to 65,000. Most of the older hotels had been renovated during the 1990s, and at least 30 were newly built or converted from apartment buildings or dormitories. Major international chains that have competed to build or acquire hotels in Prague include Four Seasons, Möuenpick, Ritz-Carlton, Hilton, Holiday Inn, Best Western, Radisson-SAS, Barcelo, and the Renaissance chain.

To these large investments in hotel accommodation should also be added the investments in the catering industry. Hundreds of new restaurants, bars, bistros, pubs, and cafés have arisen during the last 10 years. They are a very important element of revitalization, especially of old parts of Prague, and they have contributed to the transformation of the economic base of the city. Foreigners own many of them.

There are also costs of this globalization through tourism, however. They are being borne most directly by residents of those parts of Prague where the tourist activities concentrate. One can speak already about "the tourist Prague", a similar area to that of Paris or Vienna, where the services for tourists as well as the attractive spaces for them are concentrated. They are located in the old, historical parts of the city, in the Old Town and the Lesser Town. Reflecting the urban ecology of the former regime, the residents of these parts of Prague were mainly old and relatively poor. The sudden, dramatic change in the character of their districts makes them commute for cheaper food and basic services elsewhere in the city. Although rents are still partly regulated, these long-time residents are nonetheless being forced out as buildings are bought, sold, and renovated for expanding commercial and tourist-related activities. Overall in the tourist Prague, residential use is rapidly declining, and retail and commercial space increasing. Another cost lies in the public amenities that have been forgone. Others more directly related to tourism are rises in crime, crowding, noise, loss of privacy, gambling casinos, and various types of informal economic activities, such as prostitution and street vending.

In this chapter on Prague, we have devoted a relatively extensive section to tourism. In the cities of post-communist countries in Central Europe the role of tourism in the globalization processes is extraordinarily important, and it has some specific features. It is the more complex form combining work, play, and nostalgia that gives post-communist tourism its dynamic character. One factor differentiating tourism in Prague from that in Paris and London is Prague's status as a newly opened economic, political, and cultural frontier. Professional and cultural interactions in particular have helped to integrate Prague quickly into international circuits. The study of Prague allows us to view tourism as a cultural mechanism that accompanies and enables political and economic globalization.

## Suburbanization and Commercialization of Peripheral Zones

The lack of suburbanization was one of the generic features of Prague's urban development under socialism. The planners were afraid of the economic costs of urban de-concentration, and for the politicians, the single-family houses normally built in suburbs represented physical symbols of the bourgeois lifestyle. The result in Prague was that for decades almost no house building was undertaken in the peripheral zone of the city. It was expected that after the demise of the socialist regime suburbanization would become the most dynamic urban process in the Prague region. As Sýkora rightly observes:

Residential suburbanization has not developed as quickly as was expected at the beginning of the 1990s. The expectations were based on public opinion polls, which said that people prefer single-family homes, and in comparison with western cities, where suburbanization developed. However, the development of residential suburbanization has been very slow, limited by the low purchasing power of the population. Suburban housing is affordable only to affluent households. Even the introduction of mortgages, which are supported by a state contribution that covers part of the interest, has not stimulated massive development of suburban family housing. Mortgages for new single family houses are available only to households with three times higher than average incomes. (Sýkora, 2000)

Nevertheless, statistical data indicate that the suburbanization of large Czech cities after 1989 is more intensive than it was under socialism. Around all large Czech cities a "migration wreath" developed during the years 1991–1998, a kind of a continuous circular zone with the highest population growth rates. This growth is a result of several processes: the movement of affluent households to new housing built by developers for sale; individual developments which transform existing communities in the suburban zone as households purchase vacant lots and construct new houses; households that purchase existing property, demolish it, and replace it with new houses, or who reconstruct existing houses and modernize them.

These suburbanization processes do not result only from housing preferences; they reflect one of the feasible housing paths in the environment of contemporary labour and the housing market in the Czech Republic. In large cities, and especially in Prague, the following phenomena are correlated: a high concentration of jobs and a relatively high demand for labour, extensive commuting from districts and communities outside the urban territory, and high migration out of cities, mainly due to the scarcity of affordable housing in the cities. Households react to this situation by trying to find housing or invest in housing outside the cities within a bearable commuting distance to the cities offering them jobs. As already said, the contemporary housing crisis starts to become a bottleneck of the economic development of large cities, and consequently of the whole country. Table 10.14 illustrates these trends.

Commercial suburbanization has more visible impacts on the transformation of the suburban zone than does residential development, and it is also easier to explain. In such a compact city as Prague, there are very few vacant spaces for constructing large supermarkets or regional shopping centres. In this situation, investors concentrate their interest on two categories of locations. First, they begin to concentrate their projects in complexes built along highways and near important transport intersections. Second are locations near underground (metro) stations or near the termini of the underground transport lines. Some analysts stress the fact that the quick development of these large suburban centres in the last two to three years has begun to be felt in the inner parts of Prague – many small and mainly Czech retail shops are being closed because they are not able to compete with the big (foreign-owned) chains. Until recently most retail turnover

Table 10.14  Population growth in zones in Prague, 1995–1998

| | Population | | Difference | Index of change |
| Zone of Prague | 1995 | 1998 | 1995–1998 | (1995 = 100) |
| --- | --- | --- | --- | --- |
| Historical core | 38,698 | 36,372 | −2,326 | 94.0 |
| Business centre | 56,627 | 53,934 | −2,693 | 95.2 |
| Nineteenth- and twentieth-century middle- and lower-middle-class zones | 561,719 | 549,469 | −12,250 | 97.8 |
| Nineteenth-century working-class estates | 151,846 | 148,552 | −3,294 | 97.8 |
| Zone of housing estates (socialist period) | 279,276 | 280,700 | +1,424 | 100.5 |
| Peripheral communities | 121,664 | 124,243 | +2,579 | 102.1 |

*Source:* Calculated from data published in table 2–10 of *Numeri Pragensis* (1999).

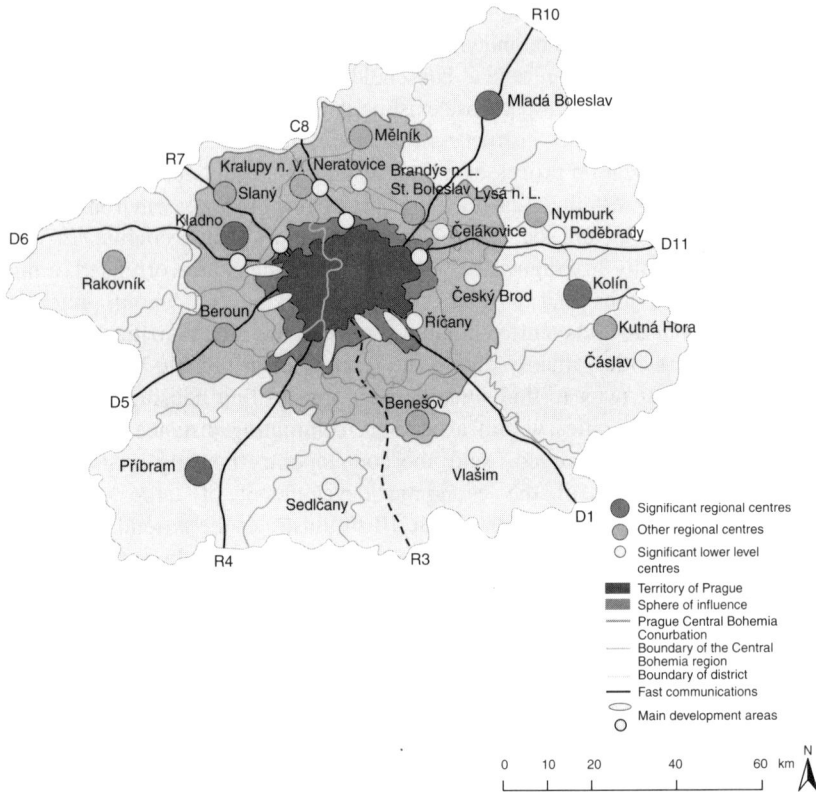

Fig. 10.4 Prague in the Central Bohemia Region.
*Source:* Prague City Hall Development Authority Section, Strategic Planning Department.

was concentrated in the city centre – nearly 50 per cent in 1989 – but now a significant proportion of shopping is moving to the suburban zone (Fig. 10.4).

The next step will most probably be the suburbanization of offices. The first symptoms of such a development can be seen near Prague's international airport. All the examples mentioned above of Prague's suburbanization demonstrate the fact that market mechanisms and economic behaviour patterns function in a new environment in a similar way as in Western countries. The new commercial suburban zone will probably become the most Westernized part of Prague.

## Conclusions

In the twentieth century, Prague's position in the urban hierarchy of Central Europe remained relatively stable despite experiencing cycles of growth and stagnation. Nevertheless, its urban status has been to some extent transformed by changes in its political and economic functions. In the first two decades of the twentieth century, Prague was, first of all, the capital of the Czech Lands. The main change that the city went through was becoming the capital of a new medium-sized state, Czechoslovakia, in 1918. This state was established by uniting formerly separated parts of the Habsburg Empire (i.e. Czech territories and Slovakia). This new role stimulated a rapid development of Prague during the inter-war period, and growth even continued during the Second World War so that there was a moderate but continuous improvement of the position of Prague in the hierarchy of Czechoslovakia, as well as that of European cities, up to the year 1950. Even so, Prague remained a relatively small capital city.

Socialism changed the trend and initiated a process of weakening Prague's position in the urban system of Czechoslovakia, as well as of Europe. The city entered a new trajectory, which involved the decline of its role as a political and macro-regional service centre and the strengthening of its industrial base. The period after 1948 thus saw Prague decay into provincialism and into a state of relative isolation. It was a kind of return to previous developmental phases. There was, however, one important difference: it was not a return to ethnic diversity. On the contrary, ethnic homogeneity – unusual under European conditions – began to prevail.

The political and economic transformations after 1989 returned Prague to the developmental trajectory abandoned after the Second World War. It was a kind of "rectification process". As the capital city of a relatively small country that depends on foreign trade and on a good position in the international markets, Prague began to cultivate a gateway function and to develop the role of receiver and transmitter of innovations in technologies, science, lifestyles, and culture. So since 1989, another function of Prague has been strengthened, namely that of mediator between Western and Eastern Europe. In this sphere, Prague faces strong competition from Budapest, Vienna, Berlin, and Warsaw. All these cities live in a kind of symbiotic competition, which gained in importance after the removal of the Iron Curtain. Prague's new intensive interaction with Western Europe is caused mainly by the expansion of three elements: foreign trade, cultural and scientific contacts, and tourism. In the near future – after the enlargement of European Union – another factor, politics, will gain in importance. All three above-mentioned elements have become more diversified as compared with the pre-1989 situation, and the city has developed into a conference centre and a meeting place for writers, artists, students, and tourists. Prague's attraction as a cultural centre has been enhanced by tradition and architectural heritage, as well as a good tourist infrastructure. Last but not least, Prague's status has been enhanced by its advantageous location in Central Europe. Yet Prague's role as a regional Central European financial centre has not evolved as successfully as that of Budapest.

Globalization and growing integration with Europe has led to a rapid growth of air and road traffic, which has made it necessary to continuously expand Prague International Airport and construct motorways connecting Prague with Western Europe. In 2003, a corridor of high-speed railway, which is under construction at present, will link Prague with Berlin and Vienna.

The process of globalization also engendered a regional polarization within the Czech Republic. Economically, culturally, and socially, Prague is moving away from other regions of the country. This is evident from the growing disparities in GDP, earnings, and infrastructure. Undoubtedly, a long-term concentration of financial, political, and cultural activities in Prague is occurring, and to some extent the capital has begun to be separated from the rest of the country. It can be hypothesized that Prague's growing interaction with cities outside the Czech Republic is correlated with a certain alienation from cities and regions inside the country.

The development of the market economy, growing contacts with the world, and Prague's role of gateway and mediator have also engendered changes in the internal socio-spatial structure of the city. Prague's social geography started to return to the pre-socialist pattern. Diversification has emanated from increasing disparities of income and wealth, the gradual deregulation of rents, property restitutions, and the building of some luxurious neighbourhoods of apartment houses, and by the withdrawal of the state from direct housing provision. Yet, this process is still rather slow because house building is sluggish, and rent control still exists for some parts of the housing stock, restricting extensive migration within the city.

Globalization processes are also changing the spatial patterns of the city through the revitalizing and commercializing of the central and inner parts of the city, through tourism, and through commercialization of the city periphery. The increasing differentiation and pluralization of all spheres of urban life are also reflected in the social geography of the city. A remarkable renewal, revival, and enrichment of many central areas of Prague is occurring. Yet some parts of the city are excluded from this positive urban transformation, and they stagnate or decay. Signs of new forms of urban poverty have become indisputable.

How will the linkages between Prague and the West European urban systems be affected in the future, and what role can Prague's local potential play in strengthening these links? It is likely that a highly urbanized European zone will spread its tentacles east as far as Berlin and Vienna and, maybe, also Prague as a result of growing trade, cultural and scientific contacts, tourism, and political interaction, and also due to the integration of some post-communist countries such as the Czech Republic, Poland, and Hungary into the European Union in 2004. To some extent therefore, the West European urban system will be partly extended by means of a kind of secondary urban zone to the east. Proof of such trends can be seen in the regional and urban processes that arose within Germany after reunification in 1990. It must be explicitly stressed, however, that the impact of the existing West European spatial organization and urban and regional structures on both the Eastern metropolis and on urban systems in general, is much stronger than vice versa. The main impulses come undoubtedly from the West, but their absorption and their effectiveness will depend also on some endogenous factors existing in the East. Internationalization and globalization processes always have external and internal aspects that can be described as local urban potentials.

Local potential is often described as a composite of resources, which function as catalysts for innovation, factors helping to make the control functions of cities more efficient, and factors promoting contacts with the outside world (globalization). The following resources are most often quoted as positive, innovative, and interactive:

1. advantageous geographic location, accessibility;
2. diversified economic activities, sectoral mix;
3. strong internal and external political roles (e.g. capital cities, presence of the headquarters of major industrial or financial groups);
4. efficient urban infrastructure, mainly transport and communication infrastructure;
5. social factors (i.e. human potential, flexibility, readiness to accept change, knowledge of languages, and intellectual openness);
6. good technological, legal, marketing, and other services, and the existence of diversified scientific research;
7. the presence of strong cultural and intellectual traditions, and an abundance of cultural and intellectual activities;
8. architectural qualities, genius loci;
9. good quality of municipal administration and general political stability;
10. good quality of housing, diversified forms of housing; and
11. easy access to educational, cultural, recreational, and leisure facilities.

The knowledge available on urban dynamics shows that factors 4, 5, 7, 10, and 11 are the most important for the innovative functions of cities. Factors 2, 3, 4, 6, and 9 are decisive for enhancing the control function of cities, and factors 1, 3, 5, 6, 7, and 8 for stimulating globalization processes.

Qualitative estimates of the potentials of Budapest, Prague, and Warsaw document the fact that these three capitals to some extent differ in comparison, with Budapest and Prague being rather similar and Warsaw having slightly weaker general developmental potential than the other two capitals. Budapest ranks most probably first among the three capitals in its innovative and control functions, while Prague is the strongest in its globalization potential.

From all the available data on the changes after 1989, it is clear that a new pattern of division of labour between the Central European capital cities, including Vienna and Berlin, is slowly emerging. It is also a pattern that can be described by the terms symbiotic competition or complementarity, cooperation, and competition. All these types of relationship are beginning to emerge and express, to some extent, a return to the pre-1914 situation.

What does this mean in terms of the spatial pattern of the Central European urban system? The most realistic concept in this respect is a theory that assumes that some urban regions within post-communist Central Europe will become linked, as peripheral units, to the "European megalopolis". The Eastern parts of this megalopolis are, in any case, already expanding to the east, as seen in Eastern Bavaria (Nuremberg, Furth, Passau). Some old, industrial, highly urbanized regions before seen in Saxony will be reunited with the core growth zone running through Western Germany as the most Eastern outposts of the main European urban growth zone, and these will profit from their geographical location as well as from some other advantages (such as lower land prices, smaller scales, skilled and relatively cheap labour, and good intellectual infrastructure). This school of thought can be described as one of "peripheral development". Prague, being connected by new motorways and other infrastructure elements with both of the above-mentioned German regions, would undoubtedly profit from its links to these two economically strong regions.

After 1989, Prague entered the international or European competition of cities, as did all the large post-socialist cities in Central Europe. The capital cities of the region have started to perform the functions of receivers and transmitters. At the same time, in order to have success in the competition, they have to cultivate their connections with West European cities. In estimating the general effects of this new and competitive situation one can agree with Conti (1994) that only Prague, Budapest, and Warsaw have good chances to participate in the European urban competition and that these three capitals will become – in the near future – members of the second division of Western European metropoles (such as, for example, Lyon and Turin). We can only add that in a long-term perspective some of these cities probably also have the chance to become members of the first division.

## Notes

1 According to François Perroux ("Note sur la notion de pole de croissance", *Economie Applique* 7, 1955, pp. 307–320), a large city stimulates the growth of towns in its vicinity, and thus he applied the term "growth pole" to large cities.
2 Although in the 1980s the situation began to improve, Czechoslovakia, together with the former USSR and GDR, was undoubtedly the most closed state within the Soviet bloc.
3 See Jiří Musil, "Housing policy and the Socio-Spatial Structure of Cities in a Socialist Country: The Example of Prague", *International Journal of Urban and Regional Research* 11(1), 1987, pp. 27–36.
4 In 2000, they began to again become more strict.

5 Ludek Sýkora, from the Charles University in Prague, has written the best Czech studies on the socio-spatial structure of Prague after 1989 (see Sýkora, 1994, 1996). With the kind permission of the author, I reproduce some of his findings, supplemented by my own analyses.

6 The following section is based on the paper: Lily Hoffman and Jiří Musil, "Culture Meets Commerce: Tourism in Post-Communist Prague", in Dennis R. Judd and Susan S. Fainstein, eds, *The Tourist City*, New Haven: Yale University Press, 1999, pp. 179–197; and on my recent research.

## REFERENCES

Gregory Andrusz, Michael Harloe, and Ivan Szelenyi, eds, *Cities After Socialism*, Oxford: Blackwell, 1996.

Max Barlow, Petr Dostál, and Martin Hampl, eds, *Development and Administration of Prague*, Amsterdam: Universiteit van Amsterdam, 1994.

Antonín Boháč, *Hlavní město Praha – studie o obyvatelstvu* [The Capital City Prague–Study of Population], Prague: State Statistical Office, 1922.

Max Brod, *Der Prager Kreis* [The Prague Circle], Frankfurt on Main: Suhrkamp, 1966.

Frank W. Carter, "Prague and Sofia: An Analysis of their Changing Internal City Structure", in Richard. A. French and F. E. Ian Hamilton, eds, *The Socialist City: Spatial Structure and Urban Policy*, Chichester: John Wiley & Sons, 1979, pp. 429–460.

Sergio Conti, *La citta e la transizione post-socialista in Europa Centro-Orientale* [The City and Post-Socialist Transition in East Central Europe], Turin: DIT Working Papers, No.1, 1994.

Peter Demetz, *Prague in Black and Gold. Scenes from the Life of a European City*, New York: Hill and Wang, 1997.

Dušan Drbohlav and Zdeněk Čermák, "International Migrants in Central European Cities", in György Enyedi, ed., *Social Change and Urban Restructuring in Central Europe*, Budapest: Akadémiai Kiadó, 1998.

Dušan Drbohlav and Ludek Sýkora, "Gateway Cities in the Process of Regional Integration in Central and Eastern Europe: The Case of Prague", paper presented at the WIFO-OECD seminar, Vienna, February 1996.

György Enyedi, ed., *Social Change and Urban Restructuring in Central Europe*, Budapest: Akadémiai Kiadó, 1998a.

György Enyedi, "Transformation in Central European Post-Socialist Cities", in György Enyedi, ed., *Social Change and Urban Restructuring in Central Europe*, Budapest: Akadémiai Kiadó, 1998b.

Heinz Fassmann and Elisabeth Lichtenberger, eds, *Märkte in Bewegung: Metropolen und Regionen in Ostmitteleuropa* [Changing Markets: Metropoles and Regions in East Central Europe], Wien, Köln, Weimar: Böhlau, 1995.

Pierre George, *La position de Prague: Précis de géographie urbaine* [The Position of Prague: Outline of Urban Geography], Paris: Presses Universitaires, 1961.

Martin Hampl et al., *Geography of Societal Transformation in the Czech Republic*, Prague: Charles University, Faculty of Science, 1999.

Hartmut Häussermann, "From the Socialist to the Capitalist City: Experiences from Germany", in Gregory Andrusz, Michael Harloe, and Ivan Szelenyi, eds, *Cities After Socialism*, Oxford: Blackwell, 1996.

Lily Hoffman and Jiří Musil, "Culture Meets Commerce: Tourism in Post-Communist Prague", in Dennis R. Judd and Susan S. Fainstein, eds, *The Tourist City*, New Haven: Yale University Press, 1999, pp. 179–197.

Milan Kučera and Zdeněk Pavlík, "Czech and Slovak Demography", in Jiří Musil, ed., *The End of Czechoslovakia*, Budapest, London, New York: Central European University, 1995, pp. 15–39.

Otto Lehovec, *Prag, eine Stadtgeographie und Heimatkunde* [Prague, Geography and Ethnography of a City], Prague: Volk und Reich, 1944.

Elisabeth Lichtenberger, *Metropolenforschumg* [Research of Metropoles], Vienna: Böhlau, 1993.

Petr Matějů, Jiri Vecerník, and Hynek Jerabek, "Social Structure, Spatial Structure and Problems of Research: The Example of Prague", *International Journal of Urban and Regional Research* 3(2), 1979, pp. 181–202.

William O. McCagg, Jr, *A History of Habsburg Jews 1670–1918*, Bloomington, Indianapolis: Indiana University Press, 1989.

Gerhard Melinz and Susan Zimmermann, *Wien, Prag, Budapest – Urbanisierung, Kommunalpolitik, gesellschaftliche Konflikte (1867–1918)* [Vienna, Prague, Budapest – Urbanization, Communal Politics, Social Conflicts (1867–1918)] Vienna: Promedia, 1996.

Julie Moscheles, "The Demographic, Social and Economic Regions of Greater Prague: A Contribution to Social Geography", *Geographical Review* 27, 1937, pp. 414–429.

Jiří Musil, "The Development of Prague's Ecological Structure", in Ray E. Pahl, ed., *Readings in Urban Sociology*, Oxford: Pergamon, 1968.

——, *Sociologia della citta* [Urban Sociology], Milan: Franco Angeli, 1970.

——, "Housing Policy and the Socio-Spatial Structure of Cities in a Socialist Country: The Example of Prague", *International Journal of Urban and Regional Research* 11(1), 1987, pp. 27–36.

——, "Changing Urban Systems in Post-Communist Societies in Central Europe: Analysis and Prediction", *Urban Studies* 30(6), 1993, pp. 899–906.

Jiří Musil, ed., *The End of Czechoslovakia*, Budapest, London, New York: Central European University Press, 1995.

Christian Norberg-Schulz, *Genius Loci*, London: Academy Editions, 1979, pp. 78–111.

*Numeri Pragensis*, Prague: Czech Statistical Office, 1999.

François Peroux, "Note sur la notion de pôle de croissance" [Note on the Term Growth Pole], *Economie Applique* 7, 1955, pp. 307–320.

Tomáš Pěkný, *Dějiny židů v echách a na Moravě* [The History of Jews in Bohemia and Moravia], Prague: Sefer, 1993.

Violette Rey, ed., *Transition, Fragmentation, Recomposition, La Tchéco-Slovaquie en 1992* [Transition, Fragmentation, Recomposition, Czechoslovakia in 1992], Fontenay–St Cloud: ENS Editions, 1994.

Zdeněk Ryšavý and Jirí Link, "Vliv polohy měst v sídelní síti českých zemí na jejich vývoj" [The Impact of Location of Cities in the Settlement System of the Czech Lands on their Growth], in Jiří Musil, ed., *Otázky urbanizace* [The Questions of Urbanization], Prague: VÚVA, 1976.

Ilona Sármány-Parsons, "Aesthetic Aspects of Change in Urban Space in Prague and Budapest During the Transition", in György Enyedi, ed., *Social Change and Urban Restructuring in Central Europe*, Budapest: Akadémiai Kiadó, 1998.

Carol Skalnik Leff, *The Czech and Slovak Republics. Nation Versus State*, Boulder: Westview Press, 1997.

David M. Smith, *Urban Inequality under Socialism: Case Studies from Eastern Europe and the Soviet Union*, Cambridge: Cambridge University Press, 1989.

——, "The Socialist City", in Gregory Andrusz, Michael Harloe, and Ivan Szelenyi, eds., *Cities After Socialism*, Oxford: Blackwell, 1996.

Walter Sperling, *Tschechoslowakei; Beiträge zur Landeskunde Ostmitteleuropas* [Czechoslovakia; Contributions to Geography of East Central Europe], Stuttgart: Verlag E. Ulmer, 1981.

Luděk Sýkora, "Local Urban Restructuring as a Mirror of Globalization Processes: Prague in the 1990s", *Urban Studies* 31(7), 1994, pp. 1149–1166.

Luděk Sýkora, "Prague", in J. Berry and S. McGreal, eds, *European Cities, Planning Systems and Property Markets*, London: E&FN Spon, 1995.

Luděk Sýkora, "The Czech Republic", in P. Balchin, ed., *Housing Policy in Europe*, London: Routledge, 1996, pp. 272–288.

Luděk Sýkora, "Commercial Property Development in Budapest, Prague and Warsaw", in György Enyedi, ed., *Social Change and Urban Restructuring in Central Europe*, Budapest: Akadémiai Kiadó, 1998.

Luděk Sýkora, "Changes in the Internal Spatial Structure of Post-Communist Prague", *GeoJournal* 49(1), 1999, pp. 79–89.

Ivan Szelenyi, "Cities under Socialism – and After", in Gregory Andrusz, Michael Harloe, and Ivan Szelenyi, eds, *Cities After Socialism*, Oxford: Blackwell, 1996.

Zdenek Ullrich, ed., *Soziologische Studien zur Verstädterung der Prager Umgebung* [Sociological Studies on Suburbanization of Prague] (*Bibliothek der sozialen Problemen*, Vol. 6), Prague: Charles University, 1938.

Jiří Večerník and Petr Matějů, eds, *Ten Years of Rebuilding Capitalism. Czech Society after 1989*, Prague: Academia, 1999.

Ctibor Votrubec, *Praha, Zem pis velkom sta* [Prague, The Geography of a Metropolis], Prague: SPN, 1965.

Adna F. Weber, *The Growth of Cities in the Nineteenth Century*, reprint, Ithaca, N.Y.: Cornell University Press, 1989.

Sharon L. Wolchik, *Czechoslovakia in Transition: Politics, Economics and Society*, London and New York: Pinder Publishers, 1991.

# 11

# Ljubljana: From "beloved" city of the nation to Central European "capital"

*Nataša Pichler-Milanović*

## Introduction: The "Global–local" Nexus

The aim of this chapter is to analyse the most important effects of globalization and "EU-ization" on the transformation of Ljubljana,[1] capital city of the Republic of Slovenia. Those impacts are commonly perceived as a successful transition from socialism to a democratic society and market-based economy, and internationalization – independence from the former Yugoslav Federation together with prospective membership of the European Union. Globalization has also enhanced the position and role of cities as the most important locations of economic activity, decision- and policy-making institutions, and cultural and civic organizations. Cities are interacting through the flow of capital, labour, goods, and information linked through networks and spatial hierarchies. The transformation of the city of Ljubljana in the 1990s was influenced by these external (i.e. "global") pressures for political, economic, and institutional reforms matched with specific local responses in the form of the independence of Slovenia from Yugoslavia, efforts in capital city formation, and specific local policy responses such as privatization, deregulation, and administrative reforms. Geo-strategic location, historical development, demographic and socio-economic development, and the process of policy formulation and implementation are also important local factors. Therefore, this chapter represents an attempt to explain the features of both global (external) pressures and specific local (internal) responses – i.e. the "global–local nexus" – on the transformation of Ljubljana from "socialist to post-socialist" city and from regional centre to capital city, and the position and role of the city in the national and international contexts.

# Heritage of the Past: Historical Overview of City Development

With a population of almost 300,000, Ljubljana is the largest and the most important city in Slovenia, a state of only 2 million inhabitants, squeezed between the southern Alps, the northern Adriatic, and the edge of the Pannonian plain, bordering with Italy, Austria, Hungary, and Croatia. In the European context, Ljubljana is only a medium-sized city and one of the smallest capitals, but represents an important crossroads between Central Europe, the Mediterranean, and South-east Europe. As a consequence of its "optimal city size" and geo-strategic location, Ljubljana, the "beloved city of all Slovenes", in many ways "does not look like an industrial 'post-socialist' city of national importance, but a pleasant, self-contended little town with responsibility only to itself and its citizens . . . a little Prague without the crowd" (Fallon, 1995: 5).

Despite differences embedded in spatial, temporal, and local policy contexts, Ljubljana's urban development also resembles other Central European cities in terms of their shared experiences of (i) historical dominance of the Austro-Hungarian Monarchy until 1918; (ii) post–Second World War socialist ideology; and (iii) the onset of democratic and market economy forces caused by transition reforms and EU requirements for fully fledged membership in the 1990s (Fig. 11.1).

Ljubljana contains the remnants of its historic appearance from Celtic and Roman times to the present. In the century before the birth of Christ, the Romans built military fortification known as Emona, which developed into a thriving town and strategic crossroads on the routes linking Roman Pannonia in the south with colonies in the north. The Slavs settled there in the sixth century and prince Kocelj briefly established an independent state of Slovenes in Lower Pannonia (869–874). Thereafter, Slovenian lands were ruled by Bavarian, Frankish, and Czech masters. Ljubljana first appeared in print in the year 1144 as the German town of Laibach. The most important change occurred in the year 1335, when the city became a hereditary possession of the House of Habsburg. With the short intermezzo of Napoleon's rule in the nineteenth century (1809–1815),[2] the Habsburgs remained the masters of Slovenia until the end of the First World War. They turned Ljubljana into an important trading centre with an episcopate that in the sixteenth century became the centre of the Protestant Reformation in Slovenia.[3] The reconstruction of the city in the seventeenth and the eighteenth centuries after the earthquake of 1511 left many of its baroque (both Italian and German) features. The political, administrative, cultural, and economic development of Ljubljana began in the second part of the nineteenth century as a provincial capital in the Habsburg (known from 1867 as Austro-Hungarian) Monarchy. The railway linking the capital Vienna with its port Trieste on the Adriatic Sea reached Ljubljana in 1849 and stimulated industrialization in the town. By 1880, Ljubljana, despite its small size of 25,000 inhabitants, was already cosmopolitan in ethnic structure. In 1895, another great

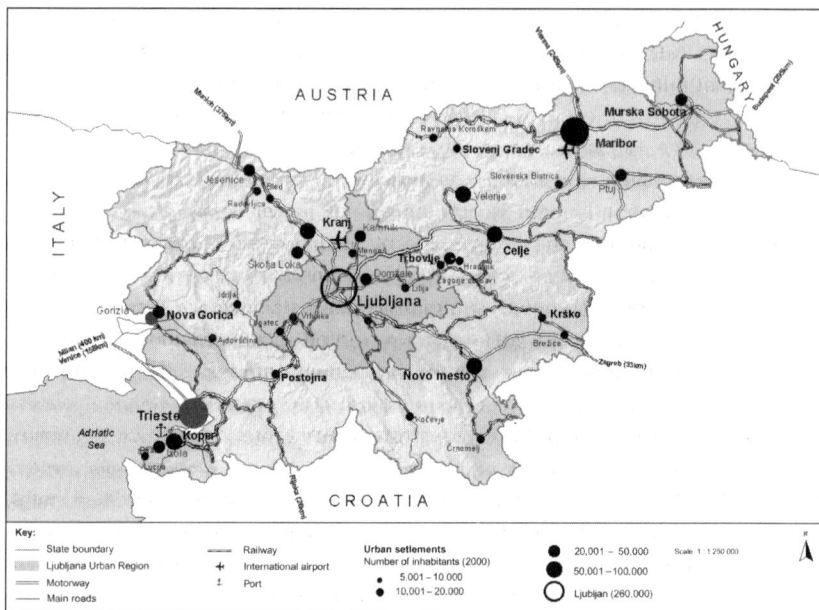

Fig. 11.1  Urban system and transport infrastructure of Slovenia.
*Source:* Surveying and Mapping Authority of the Republic of Slovenia, Ministry of Environment, Spatial Planning and Energy.

earthquake forced Ljubljana to rebuild again, this time in the art nouveau (secessionist) style that became a trademark of Central Europe at the beginning of the twentieth century (Mihelič, 1983; Vodopivec, 1993).

The breakpoint in then administrative and political system occurred in 1882 when Slovenes achieved a majority on the city council with their first (non-German) mayor, Peter Grasseli. Before or by that time several financial institutions were established, such as City Saving Bank (Mestna Hranilnica) in 1820 and the Ljubljana City Bank in 1887, both in the hands of the local capital (Starič -Strajnar, 1995). Most important factories were also built in the second half of the nineteenth century, like the Union Brewery (1868) and tobacco factory (1873). At the same time, Ljubljana was equipped with electricity (1888), a water system (1890), telephones (1897), public transport (tramway in 1901), and a cinema (1896, a year after Paris). Kranjska Building Society (Kranjska stavbna družba), established in 1871 with a majority of German capital, played a key role in housing development for the middle and upper classes (Mihelič, 1983). Despite intensive development on the eve of the First World War, Ljubljana was still a small provincial administrative centre within the Austro-Hungarian Monarchy with only 60,000 inhabitants.

After the collapse of the Austro-Hungarian Monarchy in 1918, the Slovenes joined the neighbouring Croats and the victorious Serbs to form the Kingdom of Serbs, Croats, and Slovenes under the Serbian royal family, renamed the Kingdom of Yugoslavia (1929–1941). The Slovenes entered the new state with a reduced territory, about 500,000 people being left in Austria, Italy, or Hungary.[4] Ljubljana became the third largest city in the new state after Belgrade and Zagreb. As a consequence, Ljubljana's former close connections with towns in Italy (Trieste, Gorizia, Udine) and Austria (Klagenfurt, Graz, Villach) were replaced or substituted by those Yugoslavian cities. The old trade links have only been renewed since the 1960s, and have been further strengthened since the end of the 1980s.

In the Kingdom of Yugoslavia, Ljubljana had only the status of administrative centre of the Province of Drava (Dravska banovina), where Slovenes enjoyed cultural and linguistic autonomy. There were no major changes in Slovenia's political status, as the state administration was located in the Yugoslav capital, Belgrade. But the inter-war period was important for the accelerated cultural development of Ljubljana, transforming it from a provincial centre in the Austro-Hungarian Monarchy into a national (Slovenian) centre. It was also "the golden age" for city development, with the establishment of a series of national foundations – i.e. University, Academy of Science, National Library, museums and other administrative, cultural, health, and sports institutions. Most of these buildings were designed and built by the world-renowned Slovene architect Jože Plečnik,[5] who was responsible for the comprehensive (re)development of the inner city of Ljubljana between the 1920s and the 1950s. This inter-war city development represents today a world-renowned example of fine architecture and urban planning in Central Europe. Ljubljana became the centre of art, culture, and trade, in contrast to its "new rivals" – Belgrade, the political centre, and Zagreb, the industrial centre. As a consequence of these new developments Ljubljana grew rapidly, reaching a population of 90,000 in the year 1940.

In April 1941, at the outbreak of the Second World War, Slovenia was divided between Nazi Germany, Italy, and Hungary. Italians (1941–1943), then Germans (1943–1945) occupied Ljubljana, transforming the city into an "urban concentration camp" encircled with 36 km of barbed wire. In comparison with some other capital cities in Central and Eastern Europe (like Belgrade or Warsaw), Ljubljana was not bombed and survived the war with only limited physical destruction. After the Second World War, Yugoslavia was reconstituted as the Socialist Federal Republic of Yugoslavia, in which Slovenia was one of the six republics with a substantial amount of autonomy. But the leading role and power of the ruling Yugoslav Communist Party (known as the League of Communists) implied a central and supra-national, ideologically based authority. President Tito played an instrumental but authoritarian role in balancing demands for national autonomy with an interest in keeping Yugoslavia as an integrated state. After his death in 1980, tensions between the republics increased, leading to collapse, disintegration, and ethnic conflicts in the 1990s.

Until the end of the 1980s, Ljubljana developed close relations with other cities and regions in the Yugoslav Federation, but not with other Eastern European cities that were under the political and economic influence of the Soviet Union.[6] Industrialization became a priority from 1947 onwards, followed by an intensive process of urbanization influencing the growth of larger towns as dominant locations of economic activity. As a consequence, Slovenia, which was predominantly a rural country in 1948 with 47 per cent of the population involved in agriculture, became by the 1990s rather urbanized, with less than 10 per cent agricultural population. During the 1960s and 1970s, new manufacturing industries were established in Slovenia to meet local consumption needs and to increase exports. Open borders and trade with Western European countries, a limited market economy, and cross-border links with Austria, Italy, and Germany allowed Slovenia to become highly industrialized and the most prosperous of the six republics by the late 1970s (Simmie and Dekleva, 1991; Svetlik, 1992). In 1990, with less than 8 per cent of the total Yugoslav population, Slovenia produced 20 per cent of the GDP and 29 per cent of exports, and productivity was twice that of Yugoslavia as a whole (Pichler-Milanović, 1996) (Table 11.1).

In the 1970s, the most important economic activity in Ljubljana was manufacturing. This created 45 per cent of the city's GDP, especially the metal-processing and electrical industries. Manufacturing employed 31 per cent of the active population, followed by producer services (23 per cent) and the construction industry (12 per cent). Relatively high numbers were employed in cultural and educational activities (10 per cent) as a result of Ljubljana's position as capital of the Republic of Slovenia within the Yugoslav Federation. Jobs in education, health, and administration remained relatively stable during the 1980s with only a slight tendency for growth, whereas employment in industry and construction declined. At the same time, jobs were increasing in financial services from 13,000 in 1980 to 16,000 in 1990, indicating a new role of Ljubljana as a centre of finance in Slovenia (Gantar, 1994).

Table 11.1  The position of the Republic of Slovenia in the former Yugoslavia (1991)

|  | Slovenia | Yugoslavia |
| --- | --- | --- |
| Area (sq.km) | 20,251 | 255,804 |
| Population (mil.) | 1.91 | 23.7 |
| Share of agriculture population (%) | 9.1 | 19.0 |
| Employed/1,000 inhabitants | 437 | 290 |
| Unemployment rate (%) | 3.2 | 14.9 |
| Exports (% of GDP) | 22.2 | 17.9 |
| Cars/1,000 inhabitants | 284 | 140 |

Source: Pichler-Milanović (1996: 30).

# The Effects of Inter-Urban Transformation and City Competitiveness: Back to "Europe"?

Economic transition in Slovenia initially started with reforms in the former Yugoslavia in 1987, characterized by stabilization policies and an initial phase of enterprise privatization. The reforms started under the internal pressures of high inflation, unemployment, foreign debt, and economic differences between the Yugoslav republics. At the same time, the rise of Serbian nationalism and its leader Slobodan Milosevič only aggravated the disintegration of the Yugoslav Federation. One reason for the disintegration of the Yugoslav Federation was also that the Yugoslav federal government was unable to take the necessary steps to complete its political (democratic) and economic reforms at the end of the 1980s and to establish closer connections with the European Community. Slovenia's national interests became threatened by the Yugoslav economic, political, and ethnic crisis, lagging behind political developments in other Eastern European countries. In Slovenia, this was interpreted as an exclusion from the process of Europeanization, and the path towards independence was often characterized in terms of "Slovenia going back to Europe".

## Independence, Sovereignty, and Democratic Reforms

Claims for sovereignty of the Slovenian nation had existed from the nineteenth century. These were mainly in the form of requests for national autonomy, first within the Austro-Hungarian Monarchy and later within both the Kingdom of Yugoslavia and Socialist Federal Republic of Yugoslavia. Democratization in Slovenia began with civic movements and their associations exerting pressure for political reforms at the end of the 1980s.[7] In 1989, the liberal group within the Communist Party of Slovenia won political control in the republic. Slovenia's proposal for restructuring Yugoslavia as a democratic confederation of sovereign republics or asymmetric federation was rejected, marking the beginning of the end of the common state (Svetlik, 1992). In 1990, the Slovenian National Assembly (Parliament) accepted amendments to the Constitution of the (Socialist) Republic of Slovenia enabling political pluralization, introduction of a market economy, and the first multi-party elections. In a referendum in December 1990, the overwhelming majority of Slovenia's population voted in favour of a sovereign and independent state. On 26 June 1991, Slovenia proclaimed independence from the Yugoslav Federation; this precipitated a short but fierce war between Slovenian territorial forces and the Yugoslav Army, ending in a debacle for the federal military forces. In October 1991, Slovenia established control over its border crossings; it then introduced its own currency, and passed the new Constitution in December 1991. Ljubljana became the capital city of an independent state which began building and strengthening its international status while at the same time struggling with economic transition to transform itself from a "socialist industrial city" to a "post-socialist" Central European capital city, the process known as capital city formation.

## Macro-economic Stabilization and Privatization

In the 1990s, military and ethnic conflict in the former Yugoslavia caused severe disruptions to individual republics in the form of casualties and refugees, disruption of trade and capital flows, and loss of infrastructure and supply linkages. The disintegration of the Yugoslav Federation led to a sharp decline in Slovenia's trade with other republics, from an equivalent of 83 per cent of GDP (1990) to only 30 per cent (1992). Slovenia no longer enjoyed its traditional sources of raw materials or markets for its products in Yugoslavia. Concerning markets for industrial goods, the links were even stronger, as about one-third of all sales were realized in other Yugoslav republics (OECD, 1997).

But in comparison with other Yugoslav republics Slovenia embarked on its transition process from the best starting position, as the most economically developed and with relatively minor war damage during the move to independence. Many of the distinctive features of Slovenia's economic success in the 1990s were due to its development prior to the transition reforms. The first concerns were the openness of the economy and the freedom of circulation of people and goods across the borders, especially with Western European countries. In the 1980s, around 70 per cent of Slovenia's foreign trade was with the European Community (about 50 per cent of its total exports were to Germany and Italy) and EFTA countries, while only 16 per cent was with former CMEA countries. Second, Yugoslavia was characterized by a system of self-management, social ownership, and so-called "market socialism". The system of decentralized control, where markets were allowed to play a significant role in the allocation of resources, was in stark contrast to the more centralized systems that prevailed in other Eastern European countries, except Hungary. But the inefficiency of market socialism, combined with economic recession in the 1980s and the collapse of the Yugoslav Federation, left a legacy of difficulties at both the macro-economic and structural levels.

The process of transition from socialist to market economy has led to important structural changes characterized by a shift from social to private ownership, from industrial to service economy, from large to small companies, and from a supply- to a demand-orientated economy, and by a reorientation of trade from Yugoslav to EU markets. Independence from the Yugoslav Federation required changes from the development of a regional (i.e. federal republic) to a national economy, and an integration of Slovenia into international organizations and associations. It also meant setting up new public administration and institutions, the establishment of a monetary system and the introduction of a national currency (tolar), and prospective accession to the European Union.[8]

The economic situation started to improve at the end of 1992 when international banks such as the World Bank and IMF, and foreign markets,

Table 11.2  Selected macro-economic indicators of Slovenia

|  | 1992 | 1994 | 1996 | 1998 | 2000 |
|---|---|---|---|---|---|
| GDP per capita (US$) | 6,275 | 7,233 | 9,481 | 9,878 | 10,109 |
| GDP at PPP (US$) | 8,847 | 9,917 | 11,608 | 13,755 | 15,600 |
| Inflation rate (%) | 201.3 | 19.8 | 9.7 | 8.5 | 8.4 |
| Share of GDP (%): | | | | | |
| Exports | 63.1 | 58.9 | 55.8 | 56.7 | 59.0 |
| Gross fixed capital formation | 18.6 | 19.7 | 22.5 | 24.6 | 26.7 |
| Agriculture | 4.9 | 4.9 | 4.8 | 4.6 | 3.3 |
| Industry | 35.0 | 34.4 | 33.2 | 32.1 | 32.0 |
| Services | 60.1 | 60.8 | 62.0 | 63.4 | 64.6 |
| Foreign exchange reserves | 9.5 | 19.2 | 21.9 | 25.6 | 34.3 |
| Registered unemployed (%) | 11.5 | 14.5 | 14.4 | 13.9 | 12.2 |
| ILO Unemployment rate (%) | 8.3 | 9.1 | 7.3 | 7.1 | 6.4 |
| Average exchange rate SIT/US$ | 81.3 | 128.8 | 135.4 | 166.1 | 222.7 |

*Source:* Institute of Macroeconomic Analysis and Development (IMAD) (various years).

slowly opened for Slovenia. As Table 11.2 shows, after 1993 the positive effects of macro-economic stabilization, restructuring, and micro-economic reforms gradually came into force, with the growth of GDP, productivity, exports, and foreign exchange reserves. The level of inflation in Slovenia was reduced from 267 per cent in 1991 to less than 10 per cent in 1996. Thus, Slovenia regained the development level of 1990 in 1994. Since 1994, economic and institutional reforms in Slovenia have been under the influence of EU recommendations for achieving Maastricht (1992) convergence criteria, harmonization of legislation, standards, norms, and policies, as requirements for Slovenia's fully fledged membership of the European Union in 2004. In the late 1990s, Slovenia was considered the most successful Central and Eastern European transition country by international organizations such as the World Bank, IMF, OECD, and EBRD.

The privatization of social enterprises, formally entitled the "Enterprise Ownership Transformation Act", was implemented in Slovenia in May 1993, after privatization of public rented housing (1991–1994). The legislation allows all socially owned (eligible) enterprises to select their own privatization strategy from several models provided by the law,[9] and subject to approval by the Agency for Privatization of the Republic of Slovenia (Cvikl, Kraft, and Vodopivec, 1993). The privatization law provided a combination of free transfers of capital and commercial privatization methods, supported by a number of programmes aimed at reforming enterprises, reducing their losses, and developing an institutional and legal framework for the market economy. At the same time, all citizens of Slovenia were given certificates that could be used to obtain/buy shares. Almost all of the 1,380 companies eligible for privatization submitted their programmes.

These companies employed about 50 per cent of the labour force, achieved 40 per cent of sales, and represented 45 per cent in total capital of the economy. At the end of 1996, about 65 per cent of these companies were privatized.

The new ownership structure indicates the dominance of internal owners (e.g. employees and management), accounting for 24 per cent of equity, followed by investment funds (19 per cent), state investors (14 per cent), and small investors (12 per cent). The remaining 31 per cent of equity was kept in the ownership of miscellaneous owners such as the state, cooperatives, and local communities (OECD, 1997).

Privatization of enterprises in Slovenia has been criticized by international organizations as being slow and without possibilities for foreign participation. This may be partly due to the unique ownership structure of the former "self-managed socially owned enterprises" and the strong feeling that employees were the de facto owners of (their) companies. At the same time, by adopting this cautious approach, Slovenia has avoided some of the privatization mistakes that have occurred in other Central and Eastern European countries.

The ownership transformation of the two largest banks – Nova Ljubljanska banka and Nova Kreditna banka Maribor (which together hold a 40 per cent share in assets and capital in Slovenia) – with foreign participation started in 2002. The privatization of public utilities and services left under direct government control, like energy, water supply, public transportation, ports and airports, and telecommunications, is still in the first phase of implementation.

## Economic Integration: The "Emergence" of the Ljubljana Urban Region

In the early 1990s, the city of Ljubljana and its urban region experienced one of the deepest economic recessions in its history as a consequence of the disintegration of, and war in, the former Yugoslavia. At the same time, the introduction of a market economy, structural adjustments, and government budget constraints with strict monetary policy (to reduce inflation), constrained investments in large social enterprises. Overall economic restructuring was evident in the decline of output, employment, and productivity in the first part of the 1990s. Between 1989 and 1993, the number of jobs in Ljubljana had declined by nearly 20 per cent, while the share of manufacturing in total employment fell from 41 per cent (1989) to 34 per cent (1994) and unemployment suddenly rose from 3 per cent to more than 10 per cent. Most companies lost their export markets and subsidiaries located in other republics of the former Yugoslavia. As a result, some companies became insolvent or were on the verge of bankruptcy (Gantar, 1994).

### Employment Structure and Companies' Performance

The Central Slovenian Region or Ljubljana Urban Region (Ljubljana City Municipality and other 23 municipalities), together with the Coastal Region between the Italian and Croatian borders, is the most prosperous region in

Table 11.3 Population and employment structure in Ljubljana (2000)

| Administrative units | Population (2002) | Number of jobs* | Employment sectors (%) | | | | Active working population** | Employed in city of Ljubljana*** |
|---|---|---|---|---|---|---|---|---|
| | | | I | II | III | IV | | |
| Slovenia | 1,948,250 | 768,172 | 5.6 | 31.2 | 40.1 | 23.1 | 768,172 | 170,234 |
| Ljubljana Urban Region | 485,843 | 218,361 | 2.1 | 29.3 | 40.4 | 28.2 | 211,018 | 144,717 |
| City Municipality of Ljubljana | 264,269 | 174,466 | 0.4 | 24.4 | 44.8 | 30.4 | 115,708 | 105,569 |

Notes:
* Persons in paid employment.
** Resident population.
*** Ljubljana urban settlement ("city proper").
Employment sectors (NACE classification): *Primary* (I) (agriculture, forestry, fishing); *Secondary* (II) (manufacturing, mining, construction); *Tertiary* (III) (utilities supply, construction, trade, hotels and restaurants, transport and telecommunications; financial, real-estate, and business services); *Quaternary* (IV) (public administration, defence, social security; education, health, social work; sport, recreation; other public and private services).
*Source:* Statistical Office of the Republic of Slovenia (SORS): Register of Active Working Population; Pavlin and Sluga (2000).

Slovenia.[10] Total employment in the Ljubljana Urban Region declined throughout the 1990s, with growth recorded only in public administration and financial services.

As shown in Table 11.3, most people in the Ljubljana Urban Region are employed now in producer services (40 per cent) such as trade, catering, transport, infrastructure, and financial, real-estate, and business services. A further 30 per cent are employed in consumer services such as public administration, education and research, and health services, while less than 30 per cent are employed in industrial activities. More than 40 per cent of all jobs in consumer services in Slovenia can be found in the Ljubljana Urban Region, in comparison with less than 25 per cent of the total Slovenian population. With respect to employment, key features are the concentration of services in the inner city of Ljubljana (i.e. the Ljubljana urban settlement or "city proper"), while secondary activities, especially manufacturing, still dominate in municipalities outside the city agglomeration.

More than 60 per cent of all Slovenian banks and insurance companies are also located in the city of Ljubljana, showing the transformation of the former socialist city to a national capital of finances, trade, and business services. The importance of public administration in Ljubljana is a direct result of capital city formation after Slovenia's independence in 1991 (Pichler-Milanović, 2001b).

Despite its decline, manufacturing in the Ljubljana Urban Region is more effective than the national average, with higher economic growth and productivity but lower export orientation (i.e. only 37 per cent of goods go abroad). The most

important value-added sectors are chemicals (and pharmaceuticals), paper
and pulp (together with printing and publishing), and the food and electrical
industries. The chemical industry is the most export-orientated (70 per cent of its
production), while the food and printing and publishing industries are orientated
towards the domestic market (Pichler-Milanović, 2001b).

Table 11.4 shows that the most important companies in Slovenia according
to sales, exports, number of employees, capital, and net profit are actually based
in Ljubljana and the nearby cities (regional centres) of Kranj (25 km north of
Ljubljana) and Novo mesto (60 km south of Ljubljana) (see Fig. 11.1). Some of
these companies, such as ELES (distribution of electricity) and Telecom
(telecommunications), are public utility companies still in state ownership. The
most important manufacturing companies according to net profit in Ljubljana are
Lek (pharmaceuticals), Pivovarna Union (beverages), Kolinska (food), and Julon
(chemicals). Other important service companies are Telecom and Mobitel
(telecommunications), Adria Airways (air transport), and Petrol (wholesale/retail).

Table 11.4  Top 10 companies in Slovenia (1995–2000)*

| Company | City | Sector | Number of employees | Sales (mil. US$) | Profit (mil. US$) | Export (mil. US$) |
|---|---|---|---|---|---|---|
| Petrol | Ljubljana | Wholesale/ retail (gas) | 2003 | 1,163.8 | 8.6 | 44.1 |
| Revoz | Novo mesto | Manufacturing of transport equipment | 2327 | 907.3 | 85.7 | 824.2 |
| Eles** | Ljubljana | Production/ distribution of electricity | 496 | 531.0 | 12.2 | NAV |
| Gorenje | Velenje | Manufacturing of electrical equipment | 5365 | 484.2 | 14.5 | 406.2 |
| Mercator | Ljubljana | Wholesale/ retail | 3308 | 463.3 | 18.8 | NAV |
| Telekom** | Ljubljana | Telecommu- nications | 2938 | 379.7 | 23.2 | — |
| Prevent | Slovenj Gradec | Manufacturing of transport equipment | 252 | 340.5 | 5.4 | 316.6 |
| Krka | Novo mesto | Pharmaceuticals | 2775 | 295.6 | 32.1 | 256.9 |
| Lek | Ljubljana | Pharmaceuticals | 2489 | 273.0 | 25.3 | 151.4 |
| Merkur | Kranj | Wholesale/retail | 1433 | 274.2 | 6.9 | 25.3 |

Notes:
* Data for the year 2000/01; location of companies (cities) shows the economic importance of
central Slovenia: Ljubljana–Kranj–Novo mesto.
** Companies in state ownership (not yet privatized).
*Source:* http://gvin.com (own calculations).

In January 2001, Lek joined SKB (bank) and BTC (shopping and recreation centre) at the London Stock Exchange.

*Trade Patterns*

As already mentioned, Slovenia suffered a particular collapse in trade due to the break-up of Yugoslavia, military conflict, and associated sanctions in the Balkans in the 1990s. Therefore, the prime objective of trade policy was to raise the share of exports in GDP and develop alternative markets. The Co-operation Agreement of 1983 between the former Yugoslavia and the European Community helped Slovenia to increase its share of foreign trade to the EU market after its independence.[11] The expansion of foreign trade and economic cooperation with Western Europe (see Table 11.5) has made the question of membership of international organizations, especially the European Union, of vital importance for Slovenia. Since 1992, about 70 per cent of the total Slovenian trade in goods and services, as well as virtually all foreign direct investment, has been realized with EU countries, most notably Germany, Italy, Austria, and France. This means that Slovenia's trade is predominantly cross-border and with nearby regions, such as the Friulia-Venezia-Giulia and Veneto

Table 11.5  Foreign trade of Slovenia (million US$)

| Foreign trade of Slovenia with: | 1992 | | | 2000 | | |
|---|---|---|---|---|---|---|
| | Exports | Imports | Trade balance | Exports | Imports | Trade balance |
| Total | 6,681 | 6,141 | 540 | 9,252 | 9,492 | −240 |
| EU(total)* | 3,668 | 3,078 | 590 | 5,758 | 6,532 | −774 |
| Germany | 1,805 | 1,394 | 411 | 2,428 | 2,206 | 222 |
| Italy | 880 | 839 | 41 | 1,158 | 1,611 | −453 |
| France | 616 | 493 | 123 | 628 | 798 | −170 |
| UK | 141 | 74 | 67 | 259 | 190 | −69 |
| Austria | 341 | 500 | −159 | 693 | 919 | −226 |
| EFTA* | 461 | 689 | −228 | 120 | 237 | −117 |
| US | 195 | 167 | 28 | 244 | 291 | −47 |
| Former Yugoslavia | 1,508 | 1,218 | 290 | 1,564 | 671 | 893 |
| Croatia | 952 | 852 | 100 | 799 | 576 | 223 |
| Former Soviet Union | 226 | 251 | −26 | 410 | 275 | 135 |
| Russia | 130 | 132 | −2 | 281 | 241 | 40 |
| CEFTA** | 257 | 324 | −67 | 751 | 707 | 44 |
| Rest of the world | 366 | 414 | −48 | 405 | 779 | −374 |

Notes:
* EU 15 (2000): with Austria, Sweden, and Finland; EFTA (1992): without Austria, Sweden, and Finland.
** CEFTA: Hungary, Poland, Czech Republic, Slovakia, Bulgaria, and Romania.
*Source:* SORS (various years).

Provinces (Italy), Carinthnia and Styria (Austria), and Bavaria (Germany). Trade with France is sector-related – Revoz (car production) in Novo mesto is a subsidiary of Renault. Trade with neighbouring Croatia represents 60 per cent of trade with the former Yugoslav market and less than 10 per cent of Slovenia's total exports. High export concentration is recorded in four manufacturing sectors: transport and electrical equipment, chemicals, and clothing. Despite some expectations, CEFTA[12] is not an important trade partner of Slovenia (8 per cent of total exports) but represents a major substitute for the former Yugoslav market in selective goods (i.e. food, raw materials, etc.) (Svetličič, 1996).

Analyses of trade specialization (see Gross and Vandille, 1995; Aiginger and Wolfmayr-Scnitzer, 1996) show that Slovenia possesses the comparative advantages of a skilled and productive labour force combined with a relatively high degree of product differentiation in quality rather than low prices.

During the second half of the 1990s, the trade patterns of the Ljubljana Urban Region contributed 15 per cent of Slovenian annual exports and absorbed 34 per cent of total annual imports due to the location of companies' headquarters in the city, and imports of consumer goods to satisfy local demand. In 2000, the most important export-orientated companies from Ljubljana were Lek and Adria Airways. If we also take into consideration the two neighbouring cities of Novo mesto with Revoz and Krka (pharmaceuticals), and Kranj with Iskraemeco (electrical appliances) and Sava Goodyear (car tires), it is evident that central Slovenia, with the capital city of Ljubljana, is the most important location of economic activity in the country (*Gospodarski Vestnik*, 1999).

*Foreign Direct Investment*

Foreign trade is not the only instrument of functional integration with global and especially EU markets – FDI also plays this role. The first joint venture in Slovenia was based on foreign investment legislation introduced in 1967 in the former Yugoslavia. In addition, several Slovenian firms had already started to internationalize their operations in the 1960s, establishing representative offices and setting up firms abroad. Since independence, FDI has not been significant in Slovenia in comparison with Hungary, Poland, and the Czech Republic. The main reasons lie in the unstable political situation in the Balkans in the 1990s, followed by Slovenia's restrictive property legislation, a rather slow privatization process which did not favour foreign buyouts, higher property prices and labour costs, and inadequate (deferred) spatial planning legislation.

Capital investments began to flow into Slovenia in 1993; EU countries (mainly Austria, Germany, France, and Italy) account for about 75 per cent of their total. Between 1993 and 2000 the stock of inward investments rose threefold from US\$954 million to US\$3 billion (i.e. 12 per cent of GDP). This, however, represents a modest 5.5 per cent of all FDI in Central and Eastern Europe. At the end of the 1990s, Austria became the most important foreign investor in Slovenia with 40 per cent of total FDI, mainly in banking, trade, business services, and the

Table 11.6 FDI in Slovenia's largest towns

| Largest city municipalities/towns[*] | 1996 mil. US$ | 1997 mil. US$ | 1998 mil. US$ | Total mil. US$ | Number of companies with FDI[**] | Most important sectors/activities (NACE) with FDI |
|---|---|---|---|---|---|---|
| Ljubljana | 875.4 | 1010.6 | 1306.7 | 1236.2 | 586 | – Financial services<br>– Trade[***]<br>– Real estate, business services |
| Kranj | 36.3 | 51.8 | 167.3 | 161.0 | 26 | Manufacturing of:<br>– rubber and plastics<br>– textile and leather |
| Novo mesto | 146.6 | 162.5 | 216.0 | 153.0 | 17 | – Manufacturing of vehicles |
| Koper | 155.4 | 178.2 | 226.2 | 237.5 | 148 | – Real estate, business services<br>– Trade |
| Maribor | 84.8 | 111.9 | 138.1 | 123.0 | 95 | – Manufacturing of chemicals, plastics<br>– Trade |
| Celje | 25.2 | 22.5 | 32.0 | 31.9 | 32 | – Wood processing<br>– Trade |

The "1999" label spans the "Number of companies with FDI" and "Most important sectors/activities (NACE) with FDI" columns.

# Table 11.6 (continued)

| Largest city municipalities/towns* | 1996 mil. US$ | 1997 mil. US$ | 1998 mil. US$ | 1999 | | |
|---|---|---|---|---|---|---|
| | | | | Total mil. US$ | Number of companies with FDI** | Most important sectors/activities (NACE) with FDI |
| *Total (1–6)* Slovenia (total) | 1323.7 2062.8 | 1537.5 2207.7 | 2086.3 2765.5 | 1942.6 2683.6 | 904 1524 | Sectors/activities with most FDI in Slovenia: <br>– Manufacturing (46%) <br>– Financial service (18%) <br>– Trade (17%) <br>– Real estate, business services (13%) |
| Share of largest towns (1–6) in total FDI in Slovenia | 64.2 | 69.7 | 71.8 | 72.4 | 59.3 | |
| Share of Ljubljana in total FDI in Slovenia | 42.4 | 45.8 | 47.3 | 46.0 | 38.5 | Financial services (98%) <br>Trade (58%) <br>Real estate, business services (54%) |

Notes:
* Central Slovenia: Ljubljana-Kranj-Novo mesto; western Slovenia: Koper; eastern Slovenia: Celje-Maribor.
** Number of companies with more than 10 per cent of FDI in portfolio.
*** Trade: wholesale, retail, car repair.
*Source:* Internal data: Bank of Slovenia: Agency of Payment of the Republic of Slovenia; IMAD; own calculations.

paper industry. Most European FDI comes from SMEs with long-standing business relations. US-based multinationals play only a minor role in Slovenia. According to UNCTAD's *World Investment Report* (UNCTAD, 1999), five companies from Slovenia were among the 25 largest companies with FDI in Central and Eastern Europe: Gorenje (electrical appliances) from town of Velenje was ranked third, and Adria Airways from Ljubljana was in the eighth position.

As shown in Table 11.6, FDI in Slovenia could be found primarily in manufacturing, financial services, trade, real estate, and business services. More than 70 per cent of all FDI in Slovenia is concentrated in the six largest towns located at the main transport routes: Ljubljana, Kranj, Novo mesto (central Slovenia), Koper (port town at the Adriatic coast), Maribor, and Celje (eastern Slovenia). Furthermore, almost half of total FDI in Slovenia is concentrated in the city of Ljubljana, which is also the most important recipient of FDI in financial services (98 per cent of total), and of more than half of FDI in trade, real estate, and business services.

In the long run, more FDI is seen as a key factor in Slovenia's further integration into global and, more specifically, EU markets. At the same time FDI could also stimulate internationalization of Slovenian companies, and their own outward investment (Rojec, 1995). In 2001, Slovenia's direct outward investments were estimated at US$800 million, directed mainly towards the traditionally known former Yugoslav market, i.e. Croatia, Bosnia-Herzegovina, Macedonia, and Serbia.

The other important market for Slovenia's outward investment consists of the CEFTA countries (25 per cent), most notably Poland, and traditional trading partners in the European Union (10 per cent) such as Germany. These investments are directed primarily towards the manufacturing industry, e.g. food, electrical appliances, pharmaceuticals (57 per cent), retail and wholesale (30 per cent), and financial services (15 per cent). The value of outward investment in the late 1990s was relatively high in comparison with other Central and Eastern European countries (i.e. US$23 per inhabitant in Slovenia against US$5.7 per inhabitant in Central and Eastern Europe), but low in comparison with the EU average (US$1,032 per inhabitant) (*Delo*, 26 April 2000).

According to World Bank experts, the main obstacles to FDI in Slovenia are rather inflexible (urban) land-use planning legislation, an out-of-date property register, and high land prices.[13] As in the case of privatization, emphasis was put on the protection of national interests rather than an active role for FDI.

*Tourism and Cultural Links*

The globalization and internationalization of Ljubljana can also be analysed through numbers of foreign visitors and the role of tourism in the city economy. During the 1990s, numbers of foreign tourists stagnated as a consequence of the conflict in the Balkans. In 1999, sales revenue from tourism in Slovenia was US$1 billion (3 per cent of GDP), with a total of 1.8 million registered visitors spending an average of 3.5 days in the country. Ljubljana mainly attracts business and conference tourism (80 per cent of total sales revenue) (Pichler-Milanović, 2001b). At present, most foreign visitors come from neighbouring countries: Austria, Italy, Germany, and Croatia. One of the reasons for this is that Ljubljana has not been "discovered" by "global" tourists as yet, quite unlike Prague or Budapest in the 1990s. As a result of the international promotion of Ljubljana (and Slovenia) in recent years, and close proximity to and accessibility from well-known tourist destinations in Italy, Austria, the Adriatic, and Central Europe, the city began to attract many other European, American, and Japanese visitors.

The other visible form of Ljubljana's internationalization and capital city formation in the 1990s can be seen in the presence of new embassies and consulates, and representatives of international organizations and foreign companies.

Ljubljana is also a cultural and research centre, playing host to many important cultural events and organizations, such as the International Biennale of Graphics, International Summer Festival and International Jazz Festival, the UNESCO Centre for Chemical Studies, the Jožef Stefan Institute and International Cooperation and Development Centre, and the World Trade Centre. This "knowledge-based" infrastructure and unique natural and cultural heritage at the crossroads of Alpine, Mediterranean, and Balkan cultures supports the specialization of Ljubljana in congress tourism, which is a competitive advantage in the global and European city networks.

## The Effects of Transformation on Social Cohesion

In the context of economic transition it is also important to review in brief the effects of transformation on social cohesion, such as growing unemployment, social and spatial polarization, homelessness, and effects on the status of ethnic minorities. Until the Second World War, Slovenia was a country of emigration with significant diasporas in Europe, the US, Argentina, and Australia. As the most industrially developed republic of the Yugoslav Federation, high demand for labour force in construction and manufacturing from the 1960s onwards drew in immigrants from other Yugoslav republics. Despite this high inflow, Slovenia remained ethnically the most homogenous of all Yugoslav republics with only 12 per cent of the population being non-Slovenes. A rather liberal law on citizenship granted immigrants from the former Yugoslavia with permanent residence and employment in Slovenia the right to apply for Slovene citizenship. As a result, 95 per cent of the total population has Slovenian citizenship. Italians who traditionally live in western (coastal) regions and Hungarians in north-east Slovenia have the status of autochthonous minorities enjoying all the privileges of citizenship and special minority rights. In the capital city of Ljubljana less than 3 per cent of the population are foreigners, but when other ex-Yugoslav nationalities (Croats, Serbs, Muslims, Albanians, etc.) are included the number increases to 18 per cent of the city population.

During the 1990s, refugees fled to Slovenia first, from Croatia (1992), then from Bosnia-Herzegovina (from 1993) and from Kosovo (1999). The official figures ranged between 40,000 and 70,000 people (1994), but most have returned to their homes or emigrated to other countries, leaving behind only around 4,000 people with acquired refugee status. Since 1998, there has also been an increase in asylum seekers from Asia and Africa. Slovenia became a rather prosperous and attractive country with external borders with various EU Member States, which in most cases are the final destination for these refugees.

The other important problem is that a direct consequence of transition reforms and economic restructuring is the level of unemployment that affects all social groups. Before 1990, Slovenia suffered from considerable hidden unemployment, partly because of political pressures to hire during the socialist period. The official (registered) unemployment rate was less than 3 per cent in the 1980s, but it rose to 9 per cent in 1991 and 15 per cent in 1994 (OECD, 1997).[14] Unemployment remains high and has a strong regional dimension. In contrast, unemployment in Ljubljana has declined from 22,000 in 1993 to 15,000 on average from 1996, or only 7 per cent of the labour force, or half the national average.

As a consequence of unemployment, job insecurity, income differentiation, and high costs of living, the numbers of households living below the poverty line has increased, but remained stable from 1994. Health care, social security, and the pension system have also been under revision since 1996, but with a high political importance that preserves the increase of social and spatial differentiation. Personal safety in Ljubljana and other cities in Slovenia is still at high levels despite an increase in criminal charges due to the social effects of economic transition in the 1990s. Most of the crime is performed against property and none of the areas in the city are considered as dangerous or "no-go" zones (Hanžek et al., 1999; Kreitmayer, 2001).

## A "Story of Success"?

Regional differences in Slovenia existed even before the 1990s. However, these differences have grown even more during the transition period, confirming the fact that market forces increase rather than decrease regional disparities. The Ljubljana Urban Region, with 13 per cent of national land and 25 per cent of total population, represents the most important location of economic activity, generating 35 per cent of the country's GDP. In 2000 its GDP per capita was 30 per cent higher than the national average. This urban region accounts for 27 per cent of exports and 37 per cent of country's imports respectively, 40 per cent of total value added, and almost half of all foreign investments in Slovenia. Productivity (e.g. value added per employee) is more than 25 per cent higher than in Slovenia, while the average salary is 20 per cent above the national average, mirroring the concentration of employment in higher-value-added activities (i.e. banking, insurance, public administration, pharmaceuticals) and showing a rather successful transformation from the "socialist industrial city" to the "post-socialist service and knowledge-based city" (Pichler-Milanović, 2001b).

The Eurostat's "Europe of Regions" survey at the end of the 1990s has shown that the Ljubljana Urban Region would have ranked 144th among the 281 (EU) regions at the NUTS 2 level, including some "first-wave" accession candidates to the European Union: the Czech Republic, Estonia, Hungary, Poland, Slovenia, and Cyprus. Among Central and Eastern European city regions the level of development was slightly higher only in the Prague region (index 103) and was well ahead of Budapest (index 80) and Warsaw (index 73) (Strmšnik, 1998). Ljubljana is one of the most competitive capital cities in Central and Eastern Europe, without entering the process of more intensive internationalization (city exports, FDI, foreign tourists, international events, etc.) as in Prague, Budapest, or Berlin (Pichler-Milanović, 2001).

## Global "Connectivity": Memberships, Cooperations, Links, and Networks

The process of the internationalization of Slovenia and its (re)integration into the world economy has been reinforced since independence (1991), not only through economic development, trade (re)orientation, FDI, privatization, tourism, and cultural links, but also through memberships, links, and cooperations within global (e.g. World Bank, IMF, UN, OECD, WTO, NATO) and European organizations and institutions (e.g. EU, European Council, WEU, EBRD), and regional and cross-border associations (e.g. CEFTA, Alps-Adriatic Working Community, SECI, Pact of Stability for South-east Europe), including different sectoral links and networks with professional associations and individuals. The other impact of internationalization, or rather implicit globalization of the economy and society, is the development in transport infrastructure and telecommunications, numbers of air passengers, trans-national inter-city flights, and recently the importance of the information society (i.e. number of Internet connections, importance of the e-society in commerce, banking, governance, etc).

### Internationalization of Links and Networks

Some of the above-mentioned connections of Slovenia resulted from links established before the demise of the former Yugoslavia, but also from new foreign policy goals set after independence in 1991. These goals are:
– strengthening the international position of Slovenia;
– good relations with neighbouring countries;
– full membership of the European Union, NATO, and WEU;
– closer cooperation with CEFTA countries; and
– normalization of relations with all new countries that have emerged from the former Yugoslav Federation.

The most important foreign policy goal since 1990 has been fully fledged membership of the European Union. Orientation towards the European Union is not only the result of political, economic, or security interests, but also of the cultural heritage of Slovenia as a European country.[15] After signing the Accession Treaty in Athens (April 2003), Slovenia became a member of the European Union in May 2004. Slovenia has been traditionally active in regional and cross-border organizations and associations such as the Alps-Adriatic Working Community and Central European Initiative. From January 1996, Slovenia became a member of CEFTA, the Free Trade Association of Central European countries. Slovenia also participates in the South-east European Cooperation Initiative (SECI) launched in 1996 by the US with the assistance of UNECE to strengthen economic cooperation with the Balkans and Black Sea regions, and in the South-east European Reconstruction Initiative (Pact of Stability) launched in 1999 for the Balkan countries in order to achieve democratic, political, and economic reforms.

Slovenia, in comparison with the Czech Republic, Hungary, Poland, or Slovakia, is still not a member of the OECD and NATO, despite the fact that the former Yugoslavia was the only Central and Eastern European country with a special status within the OECD (from 1973 to 1991). In 1994, Slovenia signed NATO's *Partnership for Peace* and in 1996 the WEU Council welcomed Slovenia as an associate partner. Despite expectations, Slovenia was not accepted in the first round of NATO enlargement (1998). As part of the former Yugoslav Federation, Slovenia never belonged to the "Warsaw Pact", and it was not involved in military and ethnic conflicts in the Balkans during the 1990s. Above all, Slovenia's NATO membership was the only one not opposed by Russia and supported by the EU member states.[16] NATO's invitation for Slovenia's membership came at last at the Prague Summit (2002), and was also confirmed at the country's referendum in March 2003.

In Ljubljana, the process of internationalization is still under the shadow of capital city formation where most formal international links exist at the state, but not as much at the local (city) level. In the former Yugoslavia, Ljubljana was a regional (republic) centre and all formal international contacts were established through the federal capital, Belgrade. Another reason for the somehow delayed internationalization of Ljubljana was the local government reform at the end of 1994, precipitating the establishment of the City Municipality of Ljubljana with a new administrative structure and different role of the city government. Before Slovenia's independence, Ljubljana had close connections with cities in the former Yugoslavia, mainly the capitals of the constituent republics (Zagreb, Belgrade, Sarajevo, Skopje). During the 1980s, Ljubljana was also involved in twinning and cooperation partnerships with foreign cities such as Bratislava (Slovakia), Chengdue (China), Parma and Pesaro (Italy), Thilisi (Georgia), Chemnitz (East Germany), and Leverkusen and Wiesbaden (West Germany). The most intensive relations were with the West German cities, Leverkusen and Wiesbaden, as a result of close economic (trade) connections between Slovenian industrial enterprises and their foreign partners. There are also traditional connections with the strong Slovene community in Cleveland (US). Connections with the nearby or cross-border cities (in the radius of 150 km) of Trieste, Gorizia and Udine (Italy), Klagenfurt, Graz, and Villah (Austria), and Zagreb (Croatia) have been changing over time under the influence of history, politics, international borders, and trade relations. Some of these cities have a large Slovene minority, and they are also considered traditional competitors of Ljubljana.

Most of these past international connections of the city of Ljubljana were rather protocolar (i.e. diplomatic), economic, less cultural, or strategic. It is interesting that among 25 bilateral partnerships (twinnings) between Ljubljana and other European cities between 1985 and 1995, about 18 links were established with cities in the EU Member States, most of them as cross-border links with cities in Italy, Germany, and Austria (Hočevar, 2000). These city links and networks confirm the importance of the "cross-border regionalization" already visible in the 1990s in foreign trade, FDI, and tourist patterns. But the new international status of Ljubljana as the capital city of an independent state has reinforced the establishment of contacts and partnerships with capital cities and important regional centres in Europe: Berlin and Munich (Germany), Vienna (Austria), Budapest (Hungary), Prague (Czech Republic), Bologna, Milan, and Turin (Italy), Zagreb (Croatia), and Sarajevo (Bosnia and Herzegovina). Recently, the emphasis has been on establishing firmer connections with capital cities of the EU Member States in support of Slovenia's accession to the European Union. Ljubljana is also participating as a member or observer in the United Towns Organization (the only "global" city connection) and World Health Organization (Healthy Cities Programme). The other multilateral connections are more of European importance – Eurocities, European Council Standing Conference of Local and Regional Authorities, European Cultural Cities, Ecos-Ouverture, and regional (or cross-border) networks such as the Working Community of Alpine Towns, Cities' Forum (Central European), and the Association of Four Cities (Klagenfurt-Graz-Ljubljana-Trieste) (Hočevar, 2000; Pichler-Milanović, 2001a).

## Accessibility: Transport Infrastructure and Telecommunications

As already mentioned, Ljubljana is located at the intersection of important transport routes from Northern and Western Europe to the Mediterranean, Balkans, and the Middle East. A national motorway network, known as the "Slovenian Motorway Cross", is currently under completion. It is one of the major investment projects in Slovenia funded also by the European Union and EBRD as part of the E5 corridor (Barcelona–Kiev) and one of the nine priority corridors through Central and Eastern Europe. This transport network is orientated in two major directions: (i) west–east (E5) – Vienna–Graz–Maribor–Ljubljana towards Gorizia/Trieste–Venice–Genoa – and (ii) north–south (E10) – Munich–Salzburg–Ljubljana to Zagreb–Belgrade–Athens/Istanbul. At the EU level, attention is being devoted to new corridor E10: Salzburg–Ljubljana–Zagreb–Belgrade–Thessaloniki, once known as the "Balkan Route", which is expected to regain its importance after stabilization of conditions in the former Yugoslavia. Ljubljana is also the railway junction between Austria, Italy, the Adriatic Sea, and the Balkans. At the moment it is only of local (or regional) importance for flows of passengers and mainly for freight from the ports of Koper or Trieste to other Central European destinations. Connections between Ljubljana and other cities in the cross-border region such as Trieste, Klagenfurt, Graz, or Zagreb are not well developed by public transport due to the long journey time in comparison to accessibility by car. Until recently, there was no direct rail connection between Ljubljana and Hungary passing through northern Croatia. The construction of the direct rail link between Slovenia and Hungary (25 km) was the most important railway project at the end of the 1990s, and this will be the fastest link between the ports of Koper (Slovenia) and Trieste (Italy) in the northern Adriatic, and the Central and Eastern European countries (see Fig. 11.1).

The specific connectivity of Ljubljana with international destinations in Europe is shown by the patterns of air routes. The international airport (Brnik) located 20 km north of Ljubljana has contributed to development of modern passenger and freight air transport. In the year 2000, more than 900,000 passengers passed through the airport, an increase of 30 per cent in comparison with 1996. From this airport Ljubljana is connected with more than 30 cities abroad. The most frequent daily flights connect Ljubljana with:

- cross-border EU "hubs" such as Munich, Frankfurt, Zurich, and Vienna;
- EU capitals and "world cities" such as London, Paris, and Brussels;
- other large cities which are important destinations for Slovenian exports, like Moscow and Istanbul;
- cities in the nearby region (former Yugoslavia): Sarajevo (Bosnia and Herzegovina), Skopje and Ohrid (Macedonia), Split (Croatia), Podgorica and Tivat (Montenegro), Priština (Kosovo); and Tirana (Albania).

There are also weekly flights to other EU capitals such as Stockholm, Copenhagen, Amsterdam, Dublin, and Athens, and important tourist destinations such as Barcelona, Catania, Malta, Dubrovnik, and Tel Aviv. Ljubljana's airport is a major hub (together with Vienna and Zurich) for Balkan destinations. These air connections confirm close links with cities primarily with EU countries such as Frankfurt, Munich, Vienna, and Zurich. London is also an import destination for tourists, business, and trans-continental connections. Since 1996, Brussels has gained importance because of its status as the "capital of the EU", and the process of Slovenia's accession to the European Union. What is missing is the absence of direct air connections with Central and Eastern European capital cities such as Budapest, Berlin, Sofia, and Warsaw. The first direct flight with Prague was opened in the year 2001. There are no direct connections with Italian cities due to the close proximity of Ljubljana (120 km) to Trieste's airport. Adria Airways is the national air carrier that was established while Slovenia was part of the former Yugoslavia. Foreign air companies like Swissair/Crossair, Lufthansa, Austrian

Airline, and Sabena, and cross-border (regional) airlines such as the Montenegro and Macedonian airlines, also have direct flights to Ljubljana.[17]

The other sign of "connectivity", or a direct effect of technological improvements and globalization, is the importance of telecommunications and the information society. At the end of the 1990s, there were more than 90 telephone connections per 100 households and more than 1.4 million mobile phone connections (70 links per 100 inhabitants) in Slovenia. The number of ISDN lines is also growing rapidly. In 2000, there were more than 300,000 (active) Internet users in companies, educational institutions, and households. E-commerce is a relatively new activity among 10 per cent of active Internet users, with the average purchase costing US$200. E-banking (i.e. bank transactions, payment of bills and invoices) is becoming more common, especially with the largest banks.[18] In comparison with other Central and Eastern European countries, Slovenia has highly developed its information profile. As a consequence of its importance, the Slovenian government established the new Ministry of Information Society in January 2001.

## The Effects on Intra-Urban Transformation: City Fragmentation and Reorientation

The effects of globalization and internationalization are also visible on the inter-urban transformation of the post-socialist city, in the administrative, morphological, demographic, and functional changes that have taken place in the intra-urban form of Ljubljana.

One of the specific features of Slovenia is its dispersed settlement structure. This consists of close to 6,000 settlements, of which less than 200 have the status of urban settlements (3 per cent of the total), but contain half the population of Slovenia.[19] After the Second World War the urbanization rate rose from 27 per cent (1953) to 33 per cent (1961), 49 per cent (1981), 51 per cent (1991) – and down to 49 per cent (2002)! The reverse trend is due to intensive suburbanization in the 1990s, and statistical fallacy due to the official classification of "urban and rural settlements" based on deferred criteria from the 1950s (see Table 11.7). But this rather low level of urbanization must be compared with the number of active population in agriculture. In 1971, Slovenia had 20 per cent agricultural population, which decreased to about 10 per cent in 1991, and further down to 5 per cent in 2001. The difference means that, overall, Slovenia is a highly urbanized country, but with one of the highest proportions of deagrarized population in Europe.[20] The population in rural settlements are employed in secondary and tertiary activities in the nearby urban centres, commuting daily from private, predominantly self-built family detached houses constructed on their own land.[21] The close accessibility of urban settlements (employment, services, education centres), ownership of private land (inheritance

Table 11.7 Population of largest towns in Slovenia*

| Census years | 1900 | 1931 | 1948 | 1953 | 1961 | 1971 | 1981 | 1991 | 2002** |
|---|---|---|---|---|---|---|---|---|---|
| Total urban population (%) in Slovenia | 17.5 | 22.7 | 26.9 | 29.1 | 33.2 | 38.7 | 48.9 | 50.5 | 49.0 |
| Ljubljana | 45,017 | 79,391 | 98,914 | 113,666 | 135,806 | 173,853 | 224,817 | 267,008 | 257,338 |
| Maribor | 31,337 | 46,251 | 62,677 | 70,815 | 82,560 | 96,895 | 106,113 | 103,961 | 92,284 |
| Celje | 9,471 | 13,576 | 16,083 | 18,549 | 22,424 | 31,305 | 33,033 | 40,710 | 37,547 |
| Kranj | 5,220 | 8,308 | 15,981 | 17,827 | 21,477 | 27,211 | 33,520 | 36,456 | 35,237 |
| Koper | 8,230 | 8,035 | 7,381 | 6,666 | 10,512 | 17,116 | 23,581 | 24,704 | 23,285 |
| Novo mesto | 2,750 | 4,173 | 4,218 | 5,134 | 6,885 | 9,668 | 19,741 | 22,333 | 22,368 |

Notes:
* Population in officially defined urban settlements.
** Census 2002; rate of urbanization (49 per cent) is based on own calculations using the same number (and area) of urban settlements as in Census 1991.

Source: Natek and Natek (1998); SORS (www.sigov.si/popis2002).

or purchase), availability of detached family houses (self-built or inherited), and overall quality of life in rural areas were the most important "pull" factors, first for "urbanization of the countryside" in the 1960s and 1970s, and then from the 1980s for the process of suburbanization.

It is not surprising, therefore, that despite being the largest city in Slovenia, Ljubljana contains only about 15 per cent of the total Slovenian population. This relatively low primacy rate of the capital city is directly related to the specific settlement network of Slovenia and to urbanization (or regional) policy from the 1970s; this is known as the concept of poly-centric development.

This concept was based on the principle of "equal distribution" of industry and services (central place theory), not favouring the growth of Ljubljana but concentrating on regional centres and, in the 1980s, other municipal centres (towns). Emphasis was put on transport infrastructure, services, and employment growth in secondary and tertiary activities to eliminate differences between regions, and to curb housing demand in larger urban areas. The other "push" factor was the introduction of the self-management system by the Federal Constitution (1974) which had emphasized decentralization and the role of local communes (authorities) in individual republics of the Yugoslav Federation. These characteristics and tendencies are illustrated in Table 11.7. However, this also shows that Ljubljana continued to grow substantially throughout the socialist period until the mid-1980s.

## Administrative Reforms: The City Municipality of Ljubljana

In December 1994, the new Local Government Reform Act changed the local administrative division of Slovenia from 62 communes to 147 (and further to 192 municipalities in 1998) local authorities, of which only 11 were granted the official status of urban municipalities. At the same time the state (re)created 58 local administrative units (*upravne enote*) equivalent to the previous communes (with the exception of the Ljubljana five communes; see below). Ljubljana City Municipality, with more than 250,000 inhabitants in 1995, became the largest local authority in Slovenia. The first democratic local elections in December 1994 brought directly elected mayors and local councils. But the process of decentralization (or democratization) with the establishment of new local authorities has not been completed as yet (Table 11.8).

As a consequence, the process of regionalization (i.e. establishment of regions or provinces as intermediate administrative entities between the state and local authorities) has been postponed until the year 2004.

From the 1950s until the end of 1994, the city (agglomeration) of Ljubljana was administratively divided into five communes – Center, Bežigrad, Šiška, Moste-Polje, and Vič-Rudnik – which expressed the diversity of the city's geographic location and morphological form. The division of the city was made in the context of decentralization (i.e. self-management) reforms to achieve

Table 11.8 Administrative division of the "city" of Ljubljana

| Characteristics of administrative city of Ljubljana | | Ljubljana agglomeration* | | | | | City Municipality of Ljubljana |
|---|---|---|---|---|---|---|---|
| | Total | Center | Bežigrad | Šiška | Moste polje | Vič-Rudnik | |
| Area (sq.km) | 902 | 5 | 46 | 156 | 152 | 544 | 272 |
| Population (1991) | 321,607 | 28,351 | 58,150 | 82,845 | 72,081 | 80,180 | 272,637 |
| Density (Pop./sq.km) | 357 | 5670 | 1264 | 531 | 474 | 147 | 1002 |
| Settlements | 292 | 1 | 8 | 54 | 38 | 189 | 38 |

Notes: * Ljubljana agglomeration (1955–1994) (former communes: Center, Bežigrad, Šiška, Moste-Polje, and Vič-Rudnik); Ljubljana City Municipality (1994 onwards).

*Source: Statistical Yearbook of Ljubljana* (various years).

"even" redistribution of resources (services, housing, industrial investments, etc.), despite disadvantages for urban planning and management. In 1991, the territory of the Ljubljana agglomeration (five communes) comprised 902 sq.km and 321,607 inhabitants (356 inhabitants per sq.km). The "city proper" (i.e. officially defined urban settlement) occupies only 147 sq.km, while its built-up area only 65 sq.km, of which 50 sq.km is for residential use. Local government reforms in late 1994 transformed the capital city administratively and spatially. The official city territory was reduced from 902 to 272 sq.km. The administrative division of the agglomeration into five communes was abolished with the establishment of the Ljubljana City Municipality and nine surrounding small municipalities – Brezovica, Dobrova-Horjul-Polhov Gradec, Dol pri Ljubljani, Ig, Medvode, Škofljica, Velike Lašče, and Vodice – with their own mayors and local councils.

## Population Change: Suburbanization and Residential Mobility

After the Second World War the fastest population growth occurred in the territory of the Ljubljana urban settlement ("city proper"). The number of inhabitants more than doubled as a result of industrialization, and immigrations from other parts of the Slovenia city area outside the city core experienced the most rapid population growth in the 1970s (about 40 per cent) as new housing estates were constructed on green-field sites in the inner city periphery. Population growth in settlements outside the inner city (built-up) area (i.e. Ljubljana urban settlement) was less than 10 per cent in the 1960s, but rose to 25 per cent in the 1970s. This was due to private land ownership (self-built housing).

Population in the city core (former Center commune) declined in the 1960s due to ageing of the population, lack of new housing, and conversion of existing residential stock to commercial uses. The settlements that attracted most of these new developments are located alongside the main transportation lines in the north and west of the Ljubljana agglomeration (Bežigrad, Šiška). In the 1980s, population growth occurred also in smaller settlements in the southern (Vič-Rudnik) and eastern (Moste-Polje) parts of the city agglomeration. In the late 1980s, the Ljubljana agglomeration experienced a diminished rate of population growth as a result of the process of suburbanization and development of smaller towns in the functional urban region such as Vrhnika, Škofja Loka, Domžale, Kamnik, and Grosuplje (see Table 11.9) (Fig. 11.2). From 1987 onwards, population decline in the Ljubljana agglomeration became absolute for the first time, indicating a shift from a (sub)urbanization to a desurbanization phase – a trend which was further reinforced in the 1990s.[22]

In comparison with the decline in population, the rise of daily commuters and traffic congestion is one of the most negative effects of intra-urban transformation in the 1990s (Fig. 11.3). Good transport connections, a dispersed settlement network, and deferred supply and high cost of housing in the inner city area have all impacted on the increase in car ownership – from 320 cars per

Table 11.9 Characteristics of the "city" of Ljubljana and Urban Region

| Administrative and functional classification of the city of Ljubljana | Area (sq.km) | Population | | Density (Pop. per sq.km) | Annual population change (%) | | | |
|---|---|---|---|---|---|---|---|---|
| | | (1991) | (2002) | | 1961–1971 | 1971–1981 | 1981–1991 | 1991–2002 |
| Ljubljana Urban Settlement | 147 | 267,008 | 257,338 | 1,750 | 2.86 | 2.09 | 0.25 | -0.34 |
| Ljubljana City Municipality | 272 | 272,637 | 264,269 | 972 | 2.84 | 1.90 | 0.41 | -0.28 |
| Ljubljana agglomeration | 902 | 321,607 | 321,235 | 356 | 2.44 | 1.86 | 0.54 | -0.01 |
| Ljubljana Urban Region | 2,555 | 463,802 | 485,843 | 190 | 2.10 | 1.84 | 0.67 | 0.43 |
| Metropolian Region | 4,990 | 617,892 | 646,868 | 130 | 1.63 | 1.58 | 0.66 | 0.42 |

Notes:

Inner city: Ljubljana Urban Settlement ("city-proper").

Administrative city (1994 onwards): Ljubljana City Municipality.

Administrative city (1955–1994): Ljubljana agglomeration (five communes).

Ljubljana Urban Region (statistical region) (>2000).

Metropolitan region (FUR): Ljubljana Urban Region and municipalities within administrative districts (*upravne enote*) of Kranj (6) and Škofja Loka (4) in Gorenjska Region, and Kočevje (4) and Ribnica (2) in South-East Region.

*Source: Statistical Yearbook of Ljubljana* (various years); SORS (various years), Census 2002 (www.sigov.si/popis2002).

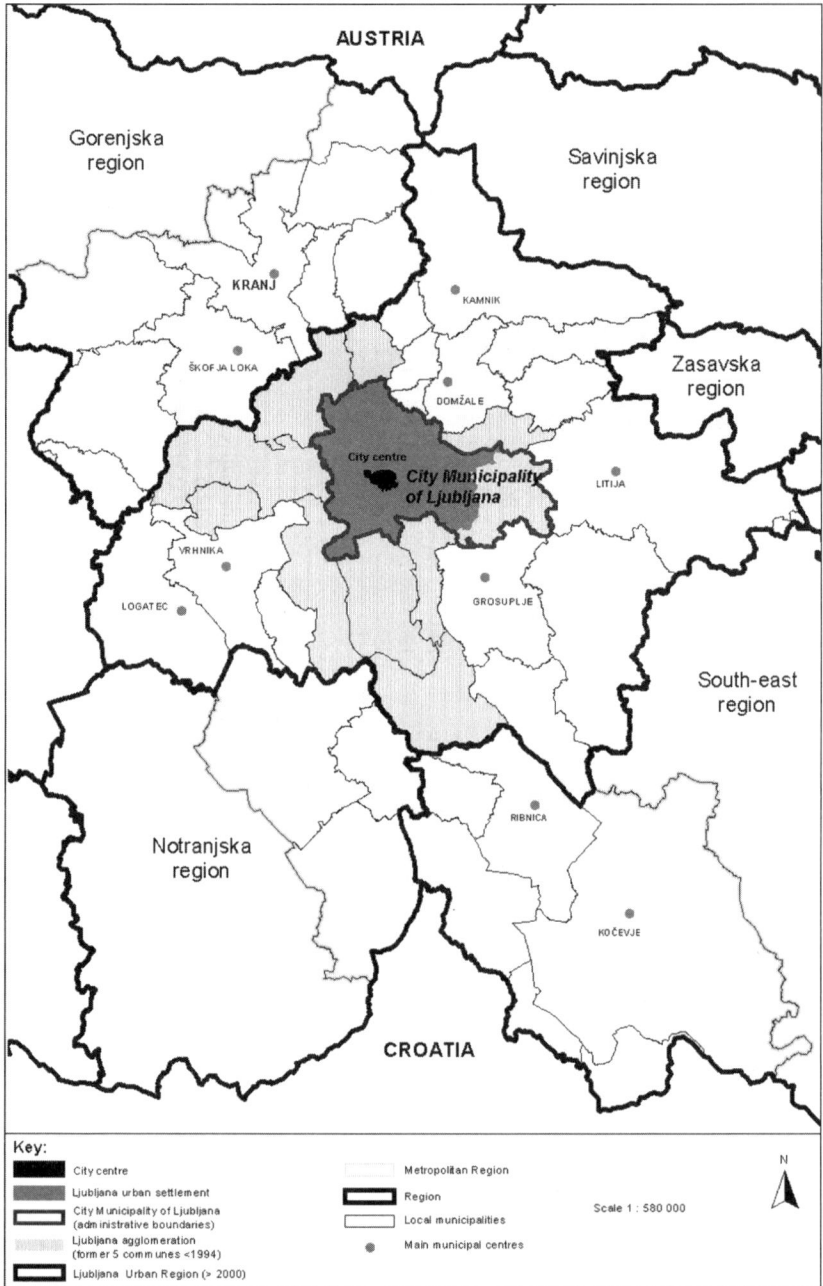

Fig. 11.2 The "city" of Ljubljana and Urban Region.

*Sources:* Surveying and Mapping Authority of the Republic of Slovenia; Urban Planning Institute of the Republic of Slovenia.

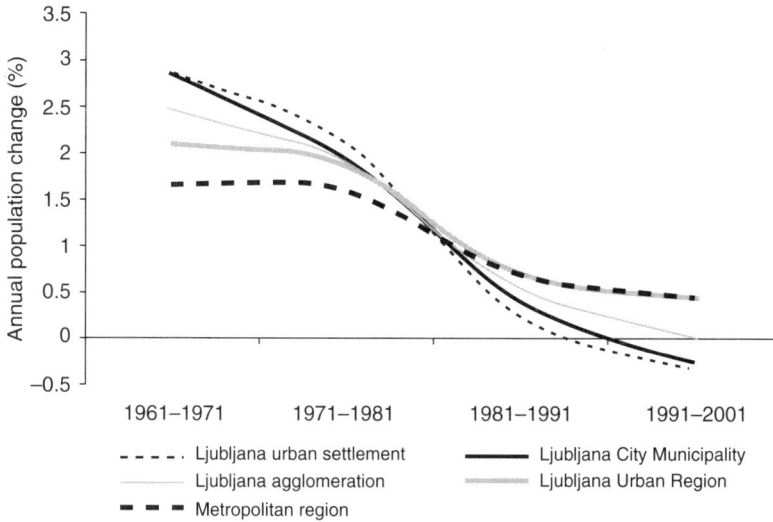

Fig. 11.3 Population change in the "city" of Ljubljana and Urban Region.

1,000 inhabitants in 1989 to 480 cars per 1,000 inhabitants in 2000. The high number of private vehicles also reflects an inflexible public transport network. Buses are the only means of public transport in Ljubljana (agglomeration), while the suburban railway system is still not well integrated. As a consequence the rate of daily commuters (for employment, education, shopping purposes, etc.) is estimated at between 90,000 and 120,000, of which more than 65 per cent use private cars (Dekleva, 2000).

*Land Use and the Built Environment: Market versus Planning*

The morphological form of the city of Ljubljana and its agglomeration is in the shape of a "star", where urban development historically followed main transport and infrastructure corridors towards smaller towns in the urban region, such as Kranj, Grosuplje, Domžale, Litija, and Vrhnika (see Figs 11.1 and 11.2). The most intensive land-use development occurred after the Second World War, more specifically the growth of residential and industrial areas first in the inner city of Ljubljana and then in other (urban)settlements in the agglomeration, and in the urban region.[23] Thus, publicly organized construction of multi-dwelling housing and industrial estates occurred mainly where land was available after nationalization or compulsory purchase according to the master plans made in the name of the "public interest", as defined and implemented by the former political elites. Land remained in private ownership in suburban and rural settlements where transactions were not completely regulated. Self-built construction of private single-family houses (for personal use) was intensified from the 1960s using the "informal" or "semi-formal" (private) land market as a result of housing shortages in urban areas (Dekleva, 1991).

The urban development of the inner city of Ljubljana was mainly influenced by the Master Plan (1966). The built-up area was enlarged more than three times from 1952 to 1995. More than 50 per cent of the current built-up area was created between 1952 and 1975, in comparison with only 15 per cent between 1975 and 1995. In 1995, land used for residential purposes occupied 55 per cent of the area, followed by land for industrial use at 15 per cent, while tertiary and quaternary activities made up about 10 per cent of land use. The following changes in land use and the morphological structure of Ljubljana are most notable (Dimitrovska-Andrews, 1998):

- physical urban growth on the inner-city periphery ("green-field" development) from 1960 to 1985;
- increased density of development in existing built-up areas, especially before 1965 and after 1985;
- urban growth of the inner city areas through "in-fill" development and transformation (demolition and reconstruction) of existing land use ("brown-field" development) – i.e. new housing estates and shopping centres replacing military barracks, industrial premises, and warehouses – after 1985 and, most extensively, after 1991; and
- urban growth by "satellite" extension of new suburbs in the existing city neighbourhoods and settlements (villages) at the city periphery or in the surrounding municipalities of Vrhnika, Domžale, and Grosuplje, from 1985, and most extensively after 1991.

*Housing and Property Markets*

Reintroduction of land and housing markets in post-socialist cities is the main element of urban transition in the 1990s (Pichler-Milanović, 1994, 2001a). The effects of political, economic, and institutional reforms are profoundly visible on the transformation of the built environment in Ljubljana. The most important "push factors" are housing privatization reforms (restitution, sale of public rented housing, new housing provision system, etc.), constrained provision of affordable housing, selective reurbanization (and gentrification), and property market developments such as expansion of office and commercial activities (upgrading of hotels and transport infrastructure, new shopping centres and hypermarkets at the inner city periphery, growth of retail shops, cafés and restaurants, etc.). These changes are mostly visible through upgrading and renewal of existing buildings, and new "in-fill" developments on unused or "recycled" land ("brown-field" areas). The other significant effect of internationalization and the capital city formation of Ljubljana is demand for adequate property for new foreign embassies and consulates. Most of them are located in the city centre, with an impact on the formation of the new embassies quarter and renovation of (restituted) historic buildings in the old town (Stara Ljubljana) and villas in prestigious residential areas (Rožna dolina, Mirje, Vrtača, Poljane, etc.) near the city centre.

Housing stock in the city of Ljubljana is characterized by either multi-dwelling buildings in middle and high-rise housing estates (up to 400 inhabitants per ha), built mostly after the Second World War, or private single-family houses on the inner city periphery with a low density (20–40 inhabitants per ha). A much higher proportion of the housing stock in the city centre was built before the Second World War. Most of these multi-dwelling houses were confiscated or nationalized in the 1940s and 1950s. Deferred maintenance and low quality were significant characteristics of these buildings by the late 1980s. Most housing estates were constructed between 1960 and 1985, with the use of pre-fabricated or "in situ" construction methods, for 5,000–15,000 new inhabitants, usually in buildings ranging from 4 to 12 storeys high. The average size of dwellings in these buildings is 55 sq.m, compared to the national average of 68 sq.m, which includes single-family houses. Terraced and atrium houses ("bungalows") were rather rare forms in the built environment before the 1990s. After the 1960s, construction of private detached family houses intensified in the inner city periphery and in settlements (villages) in the agglomeration. In the 1980s, and most notably the 1990s, new housing construction increased more in municipalities outside the Ljubljana agglomeration such as Škofja Loka, Kranj, Domžale, Kamnik, Vrhnika, Logatec, and Grosuplje (see Figs 11.1, 11.2, and 11.4).

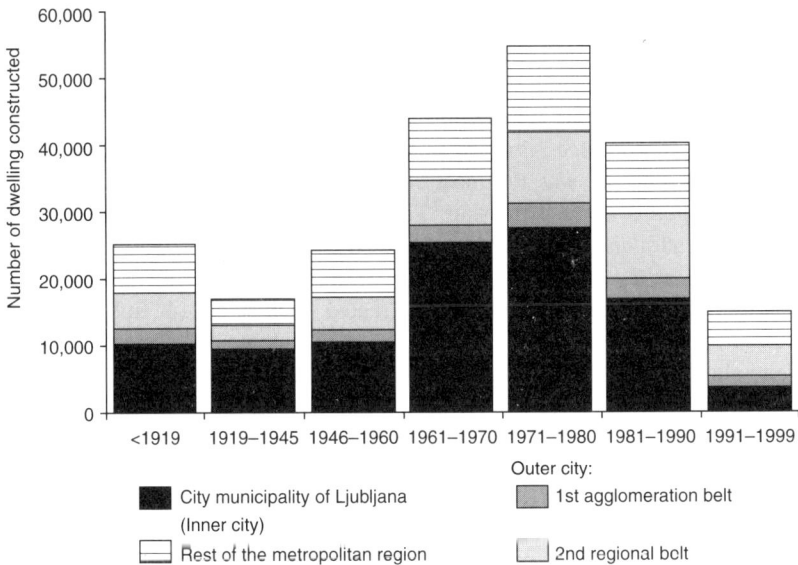

Fig. 11.4 Housing stock increase in the "city" of Ljubljana and Urban Region; housing by age of construction in the "city" of Ljubljana and Urban Region.

The share of public rented housing was higher in large and especially capital cities of Central and Eastern Europe, which reflected the importance of the "socialist" cities as industrial and employment centres (see French and Hamilton, 1979). Before housing privatization (1991–1994), 38 per cent of the housing stock in Ljubljana (agglomeration) was tenured as public rented housing, of which 90 per cent was in multi-dwelling buildings. And yet the proportion of public rented housing in 1991 in Ljubljana was lower than in Prague (59 per cent), Budapest (54 per cent), Bratislava (51 per cent), or Warsaw (45 per cent) (Pichler-Milanović, 2001).

Privatization of public rented housing in the 1990s has been one of the most important political and economic decisions in support of private property rights and a market economy in Central and Eastern Europe. The long-term objective of housing (privatization) reforms is a more efficient housing provision in production, distribution, and maintenance, than during the socialist period. But the general tendency in the 1990s was the reduction of government budget expenditure and a shift of responsibilities for social policy to the local level, and of housing maintenance costs to private owners (Hegedüs, Mayo, and Tosics, 1996). In this respect, housing privatization (including restitution) has significant effects on changes in ownership patterns, prices, value and use of property, commercialization, selective new construction, urban renewal/rehabilitation activities, and increased residential mobility. The change in – or rather, neglect of – urban planning regulation in the 1990s had a direct impact on land-use development and the architectural design of new buildings.

In Slovenia, it was precisely in the housing sector where public ownership – the symbol of collectivism and the self-management system – was first abolished and privatized. In October 1991, the Housing (Privatization) Act not only granted the "Right to Buy" to sitting tenants in public rented housing, but also completely changed the institutional structure of housing provision. The low-cost sale of public rented housing was the most effective housing policy instrument in the 1990s in support of home ownership.[24] The full discount price of up to 60 per cent of the book (administrative) value represented only 10–15 per cent of the housing market price at the time of sale in late 1991. The demand for sale was high, resulting in 67 per cent of the total public rented stock being sold in Slovenia, and around 75 per cent in the capital, Ljubljana. As a result the rate of home ownership rose to almost 90 per cent, and this is now one of the highest levels in Europe (see Starič-Strajnar, 1995; Mandič, 1996; Mandič and Stanovnik, 1996; Pichler-Milanović, 2001a,b). The Restitution Act passed in November 1991 included the return of property (e.g. agriculture and building land, housing, forests, companies, shops) confiscated or nationalized by the Yugoslav socialist government to the original owners or their heirs. The most profound effects of restitution in Slovenia can be observed in the inner city of Ljubljana. But it is estimated that about 3 per cent of the total public rented stock in Ljubljana (before privatization) was restituted by the end of the 1990s (see Pichler-Milanović, 2001a).

The formulation and implementation of the new housing policy has continued with the amendments to the Housing Act (1994–2000), legal acts and regulations, and finally the approval of the National Housing Programme (2000). The major negative effects of housing privatization have been the decline in new housing construction and the rise of house prices; both caused problems in housing availability and affordability, a feature in common with other Central and Eastern European cities (see Hegedüs, Mayo, and Tosics, 1996; Struyk, 1996; Pichler-Milanović, 2001a). As a consequence of housing privatization and financial reforms, organized (not individual) housing construction in Ljubljana in the 1990s declined to approximately 450 dwellings annually, compared with an average of 2,750 dwellings between 1970 and 1985. About 50 per cent of these new dwellings built by (private or public) developers are predominantly for sale to "better-off" owner-occupiers. The only significant new development throughout the 1990s was the construction of owner-occupied detached family houses at the city periphery and in surrounding (rural) settlements, or high-quality (but expensive) terraced, semi-detached, and low-rise multi-dwelling houses in private ownership (e.g. "condominiums") in attractive inner city locations.

Some of the best examples are: Bežigrajski dvor, a mixed-use development completed in 1996 at the site of the former military barracks; Nove Poljane, mixed-use development with different tenure types (owner-occupied, private rented, non-profit, and social rented housing) built at the end of the 1990s, at the former military site; and Koseški bajer and Nova Grba, recently completed estates built on former industrial premises near attractive inner city green areas (see Fig. 11.5). Therefore, profitability of location became the most important factor of urban development in Ljubljana in the 1990s.

In Slovenia, as in other Central and Eastern European countries, housing rehabilitation has increased through renovation of restituted houses or upgrading of old and neglected historic buildings. This has influenced only a small part of the housing stock, and in a selective spatial pattern. Urban renewal of the central city area is rather a step-by-step continuation of the local authority programmes from the 1980s known as *"Ljubljana – My City"*.

Due to recent problems with restitution and property rights, a lack of new planning regulations, and insufficient investment funds, renovation of many buildings was postponed. Those renovated were mainly facades of historic buildings of national importance such as the Slovenian Philharmonia, Academy of Music, Academy of Sciences and Arts, etc., government offices (i.e. new ministries), and buildings used for other public administration purposes. The most important task now for the state, local authorities, and individual owners is the comprehensive revitalization of the inner city area and the refurbishment of (privatized) housing estates; this is needed to improve not only the city's image and competitiveness, but also the identity and sustainability of the built environment in Ljubljana (Cerar, 2002; Dekleva, 2002).

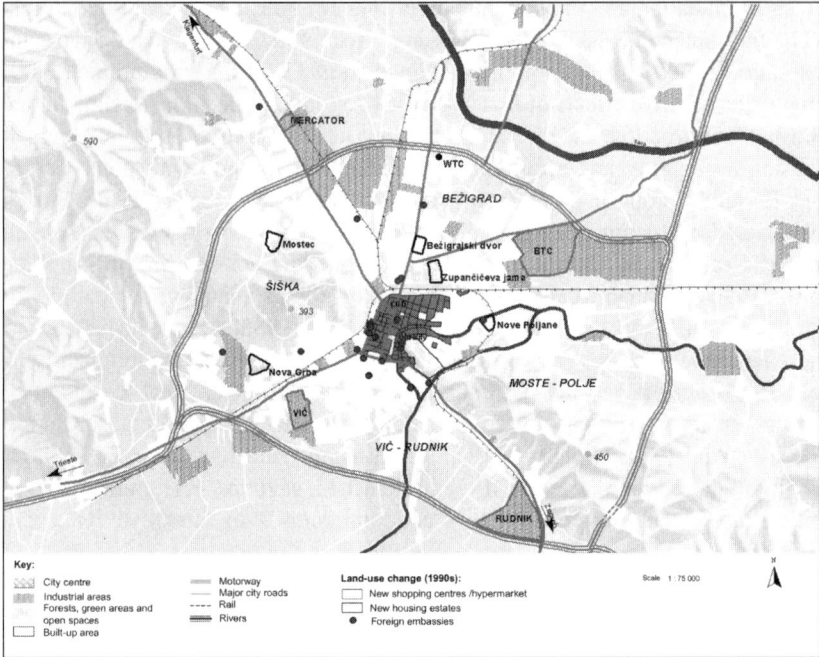

Fig. 11.5 New land-use patterns in the inner city of Ljubljana.

*Source:* Surveying and Mapping Authority of the Republic of Slovenia, Ministry of Environment, Spatial Planning and Energy.

As a consequence of deferred supply, house prices have risen faster than either the official rate of inflation or the foreign exchange rates of the tolar during the 1990s. House prices in Ljubljana are the highest in Slovenia and are matched only in towns on the Adriatic coast like Koper, Piran, and Portorož, or in some other attractive tourist resorts. House prices rose from US$1,000/sq.m (1991–1992) to almost US$2,000/sq.m (2000) for new dwellings, and from US$700 to US$1,800/sq.m on average for older housing, stock depending on location. Prices near Ljubljana are US$700–1,400/sq.m, while in other larger cities (regional centres) the average price is US$500–1,300/sq.m; yet in some industrial towns in decline and with low housing demand (e.g. Trbovlje, Velenje, Jesenice) prices are even below US$500/sq.m (Pichler-Milanović, 2001b).

Slovenian house prices are the highest in Central and Eastern Europe, most notably in Ljubljana, ranging from US$800/sq.m for new non-profit construction to more than US$2,500/sq.m for new terraced or (semi-)detached houses, or higher-quality multi-dwelling houses in attractive city locations. Since 1993, location has become the most important variable of house price formation as it reflects demand, accessibility, dwelling size, age and type of building, quality of

Table 11.10  Real estate prices (US$/sq.m) in Ljubljana and other larger towns (2000)

| City | Commercial property | | | Residential property* | | |
| | Offices | Restaurants | Retailing | Houses | Small dwellings | Large dwellings |
|---|---|---|---|---|---|---|
| Ljubljana (inner city) | 1,195 | 2,640 | 1,730 | 1,600 | 1,585 | 1,170 |
| Ljubljana (periphery) | 1,030 | 2,000 | 1,280 | 1,555 | 1,335 | 1,110 |
| Maribor | 920 | 1,970 | 1,445 | 1,555 | 695 | 585 |
| Koper | 1,250 | 1,500 | 1,750 | 890 | 1,360 | 860 |
| Celje | 670 | 780 | 945 | 500 | 720 | 665 |
| Kranj | 945 | 620 | 750 | 555 | 835 | 665 |
| Novo mesto | 1,030 | 1,305 | 1,195 | 530 | 780 | 610 |

Note: *Houses: terraced/atrium and (semi-)detached houses (average price); Small dwellings: studios and one-room dwellings; Large dwellings: dwellings with three and more rooms.
Source: SLO-NEP (Slovenian Real Estate Association); own calculations.

neighbourhood, and the socio-economic characteristics of its inhabitants. As a consequence, price differentiation of the housing stock between local districts is increasing now in Ljubljana. Table 11.10 shows, however, that differences are also now clearly apparent in the commercial property market.

In Ljubljana the spatial impact of trade patterns and FDI could be seen in the increased number of new commercial premises and change in urban land use that is a direct result of transition, capital city formation and local demand for goods and services. Four large new shopping centres/hypermarkets were built in the inner city periphery near the intersections of the ring road (motorway) with major urban transport routes. The BTC shopping and recreation centre in the north-east part of the inner city of Ljubljana occupies 50,000 sq.m, with more than 300 shops that attract 30,000 visitors per day. BTC was initially developed in the early 1990s through the transformation of the former warehouses into retail shops. Interspar (Austrian supermarket chain) first opened its premises there in 1993. In late 1990, BTC further expanded with transformation of further industrial premises and new "in-fill" developments such as supermarkets, furniture stores, designer clothes outlets, multiplex cinema, fitness centre, fringe theatre, restaurants, kindergardens, etc. Rudnik, the second largest commercial area, has been under construction since 1999 at unused industrial land in the southern part of the inner city of Ljubljana. Leclerce (French supermarket chain) first opened there in 2000 at 8,000 sq.m premises, followed by Rutar (Austrian furniture stores), Merkur (Slovenian DIY store), and other outlets with shops, restaurants, services, etc. Interspar opened its second hypermarket in 1997 in the eastern part of the inner city at former industrial premises (Vič), followed by the

Fig. 11.6 Images of Ljubljana. (a) Old city at the banks of Ljubljanica river. (b) City centre, Noboticnik ("The Skyscraper"), built in the 1930s. (c) Inner City, the Smelt and World Trade Centre (WTC) office blocks built in the 1980s. (d) Trnovo, housing estate (mixed tenure) built at the end of the 1970s near the city centre. (e) Mercator, new shopping centre (hypermarket) opened at the end of the 1990s at the edge of the inner city. (f) Inner city, Bežigrajski dvor, new housing estate (private ownership) built in the 1990s on former military premises.

Mercator (well-known Slovenian foodstuff distributor and retailer) hypermarket in 2000 at unused industrial premises in the north-western part (Šiška) of the inner city periphery of Ljubljana (see Fig. 11.6[a–f]).

## Urban Planning Reforms: Towards Sustainability?

During the socialist period, urban planning regulation in Slovenia operated through: nationalization of urban land and housing; administrative control of property transactions; land expropriation and compulsory purchase for construction of housing and industrial estates, roads, and communal infrastructure;

limits on land and housing in private ownership; preservation of agricultural land and restriction on its change to other land uses; and control over land in public ownership. Urban planners tried to control the post-Second World War development of Ljubljana primarily through the Master Plan (1966) and long-term planning document called *Ljubljana 2000*. The latter was initially approved in 1986 but partly revised in 1995 after reforms in line with market ideology and property rights (restitution, privatization, abolishment of compulsory purchase, etc.). The revised master plan proposed densification and "recycling" of the existing urban built-up area and renewal or rehabilitation of the built environment from the 1950s and 1960s. The greatest deviation from the original plan occurred in the form of "illegal and semi-legal" construction of individual (family) houses without planning or building permission on land not designed for that use. In Ljubljana, however, the scope and scale of this type of development was less significant than in other large cities of the former Yugoslavia such as Zagreb or Belgrade. The other related phenomenon that has occurred due to this unplanned dispersed housing development is the large scale of suburbanization that occurred in the late 1980s and the 1990s, with insufficient provision of communal infrastructure (water supply, sewage system) and services and increased individual motorization, daily commuting, and transport congestion.

Urban planning has been neglected in the 1990s because of the priorities of macro-economic reforms and the connotation of such planning with the former socialist regime. Market forces, not planning, prevailed until the end of the 1990s, when the need for planning regulation to control and direct the spatial development of Slovenia and its local communities and settlements was recognized. The Ministry of Environment, Spatial Planning and Energy has been preparing the new planning legislation with the Strategy of Spatial Development of Slovenia in cooperation with researchers, professional planners, and other national and local authorities. Local authorities are also obliged to formulate and adopt their own long-term development strategy, mid-term plans, and detailed site plans. The plans adopted in the 1980s were mainly in use in the 1990s, with only minor changes to accommodate some ad hoc projects that were not in accordance with the original plans (new commercial areas). At the same time, local authorities still do not have a wide enough spectrum of needed land policy and fiscal instruments such as local property taxes, compulsory purchase rights, and land banks, to be able to implement these policies into practices (Kreitmayer, 2001).

The new comprehensive development strategy and new spatial development concept for the city of Ljubljana was adopted in June 2002 under the paradigm of sustainable development as part of the new Spatial Development Plan of the City Municipality of Ljubljana. It specifies programmes and projects that are needed for the improvement of city competitiveness, quality of life, and sustainability (see Cerar, 2002; Dekleva, 2002).[25] In 2002, the Regional Development Agency of the Ljubljana Urban Region was also established, with its first task being to prepare regional development strategy as a joint project between the City Municipality of Ljubljana, its surrounding municipalities, and other stakeholders in the urban region (larger employers, public and private institutions, non-government and civic organizations, etc.).

The main objectives of these national, regional, and local strategies are to facilitate future development of Ljubljana as "competitive and sustainable Central European capital city in an enlarged Europe". The most important new programmes and development projects will be targeted towards improvement of transport infrastructure (master renovation of the main rail and bus station, public transport, parking garages, etc.), new "in-fill" low-density multi-dwelling houses, improved waste management, and new recreational areas. For implementation of these strategies, programmes, and specific projects, a set of effective policy instruments still need to be defined together with financial resources and specific partnerships between different stakeholders. This will guarantee their successful implementation and enhance city attractiveness, while at the same time preserving city identity, sustainability, and quality of life for local citizens.

## "Between Venice and Vienna": Globalization, Cross-Border Integration, or "Eu-ization"?

Ljubljana, the "beloved city of the nation" and historical cultural capital of Slovenia, was exposed in the 1990s to the international challenges of globalization and intense inter- and intra-urban transformation. The most important aspects of these processes are: capital city formation – strengthening of the city's administrative, financial, and business functions; and internationalization – strengthening of cross-border links with cities and regions in Italy, Austria, Croatia, and Germany; the emergence and growth of new political, economic, and cultural links with EU Member States and Central and Eastern European countries; and (re)establishing contacts with other cities and regions of the former Yugoslavia.

Ljubljana is a typical Central European city regarding its cultural and architectural heritage. Despite some socialist city heritage in its land-use patterns (e.g. zoning) and modern building forms (e.g. housing estates), Ljubljana is rather an example of a "socialized" (and not socialist) city in comparison with other Central and Eastern European capitals. Because of its small size and recently acquired status as a capital city, it is somehow difficult to compare Ljubljana directly to the larger and well-known Central European capitals like Berlin, Prague, Budapest, and Warsaw. But Ljubljana also has substantial comparative advantages relative to those cities on the basis of its strategic geographical location, strengths of the national and city economy, quality of life, and institutional capacity for reforms.

The independence of Slovenia and break-up of the former Yugoslavia in 1991 was an important "trigger" for the capital city formation and internationalization of Ljubljana. In the early 1990s, Slovenia had the image of the country "between Brussels and Bosnia", i.e. between "Europe" and ethnic and military conflict(s) in the Balkans. Slovenian diplomacy and economic success during the transition have managed to create a perception that Slovenia is quite different from the rest of Yugoslavia – that is, ethnically homogenous, culturally and historically part of Central Europe but with proximity to EU markets. Prospective fully fledged membership of the European Union will further reinforce the position of Ljubljana in the European network of capital cities and the Central European urban network, and will strengthen its role vis-à-vis other nearby cities in the region, especially Zagreb (capital of Croatia), Trieste (Italy), and Graz (Austria).

Since 1995, Slovenia has appeared to be the most successful transition country in implementing political and economic reforms and managing its own domestic and foreign affairs. Historically, Slovenia was the most developed republic of the former Yugoslav Federation, and a market- and export-orientated country even before 1990 due to its geographical location, former self-managed system of exposing companies to international competition, and business relationships with European partners. Slovenia has the most outward-orientated economy, with a relatively narrow technological gap. GDP per capita is compatible with Greece and Portugal and two or three times higher than other Central and Eastern European countries (see comparative tables in Chapters 3–5). Slovenia possesses the advantage of a skilled and productive labour force with a relatively high degree of product differentiation, which enables companies operating in niches to be competitive in rather sophisticated segments of the economy. Harmonization of legislation is currently the most important goal of the pre-accession strategy for EU membership and improved export competitiveness. In this sense the process of transition is perceived as a necessary step towards accession to the European Union, and hence reintegration into the global market.

All these processes of political, economic, and institutional reform in Slovenia have shaped the transformation of inter- and intra-urban patterns in Ljubljana. The most important comparative advantage for Ljubljana is its strategic location at the crossroads of Central, South-East, and Western Europe, preferential macro-economic situation, social cohesion, and environmental quality. The process of globalization is manifested primarily through Europeanization and Slovenia's membership of the European Union in 2004. Strengthening political, cultural, and transport links to support well-established economic relations with cross-border cities and regions in Austria, Italy, Germany, new countries on the territory of the former Yugoslavia, and other Central and Eastern European countries, are of critical importance for the future role of Ljubljana in European urban networks.

Ljubljana is a middle-sized capital city of a rather small country. Despite its central functions, concentration of local, regional, national, and recently, international institutions, dynamic economic activities, transport accessibility, quality of its built environment, close proximity to attractive natural environment, and relatively high quality of life, Ljubljana is still a rather "provincial" city in a European context. The most important impediments to its development are a lack of more propulsive FDI and the benefits of urban tourism (as in Prague), and a lack of principal multinational organizations and companies. Ljubljana is the most expensive Central and Eastern European city – this is a direct result of higher incomes and the macro-economic situation. Prices are driven by local market demand, and not as much by foreign organizations as in Prague or Budapest. But new investments are needed for creating jobs, revitalizing inner city areas and housing estates on the city periphery, recycling industrial land, and upgrading services. New trends such as city competition with other Central and Eastern European capitals and nearby cross-border cities like Trieste, Udine, Venice, Klagenfurt, Graz, Rijeka, and Zagreb, for investment, tourists, and overall "prestige", represent a new challenge for the city government, which is occupied with strategic thinking for the future of the city. The successful implementation of this strategy depends upon the ability of local leaders to encourage the active involvement of professions and local communities. Political leadership and commitment are critical for progress, which is often lacking. Cooperation and partnership between different public and private institutions and other stakeholders is essential for the implementation of national, city, and regional strategies in the twenty-first century.

Ljubljana may never become the "capital" of Central Europe – as might be the result of "global city formation" and competition with Vienna, Berlin, Prague, Budapest, and Warsaw. Yet, as a result of cultural heritage, stable political and economic conditions, social cohesion, quality of life, local identity, and geo-strategic location in Europe, Ljubljana has the opportunity to become an attractive meeting place and tourist destination between two "global" cities in the region – Venice and Vienna. At the same time, the city can preserve the quality of life for local citizens to avoid the problems of homelessness, urban decline, social and spatial polarization, crime and vandalism, and over-congestion known to many other European cities.

## Acknowledgements

The author wants to thank Mr Jože Dekleva, from the Ministry of Environment, Spatial Planning and Energy, Dr Janez Šušteršič, from the Institute of Macroeconomic Analyses and Development, and the City Municipality of Ljubljana for their support and assistance while conducting this research. Thanks also to Professor Sir Peter Hall from the University of London, and the late Professor F.W. Carter and Dr F.E. Ian Hamilton, for their valuable comments on earlier drafts of this chapter.

# Notes

1 The name of Ljubljana, the capital city of Slovenia, was first mentioned in the year 1144 as the German town of Laibach, and two years later as Luwigana (Slovene/Roman variant). The exact origin of this name is not known and it has been disputed ever since. According to Anton Tomaž Linhart (1756–1795), Slovenian poet, writer, historian, linguist, and educator, the name of the city – "Ljubljana" – comes from the word of Slovene (and Slavic) origin "ljubljena" (or "beloved" in English), notifying the cultural importance of the "city of all Slovenes" at the time when German was the official language in the Habsburg province of Carinthia (Carniola or Kranjska).

2 Napoleon established the Illyrian Provinces (1809–1913) with Ljubljana as the capital in an attempt to cut the Habsburgs' access to the Adriatic Sea. In 1821, members of the Holly Alliance of Austria, Prussia, Russia, and Naples met at the Congress of Laibach (Ljubljana) to discuss measures to suppress the democratic revolutionary and national movements in Europe.

3 The sixteenth-century Reformation in Slovenia was closely associated with the nobility and the emerging middle class, and generally ignored by the rural population. Reformation brought a new impetus to Slovene culture and a high awareness of its own language. The first book in Slovene, *Catechismus*, was translated and published by Protestant minister Primož Trubar (1551), followed by Jurij Dalmatin's translation of the Bible (1584). The Counter-Reformation by the Catholic Church, fiercely supported by the Habsburgs, resulted in only 1 per cent of the current population of Slovenia being Protestant. In respect of this important period for the cultural enlightenment of the Slovene nation, 31 October, Reformation Day, is now a national holiday.

4 In the west the coastland was lost to Italy as a reward for shifting its alliance during the First World War, while in the north in Carinthnia population voted in a plebiscite to remain in Austria.

5 Jože Plečnik, the most famous Slovene architect, was born in 1872 in Ljubljana. He was a student of Otto Wagner in the Viennese School of Architecture, and was also responsible for the renovation of the Prague Castle. After his return to Ljubljana (1921) until his death (1957) he almost single-handedly transformed the inner city of Ljubljana, adding Byzantine, Islamic, ancient Egyptian, and folkloric motifs to the city's classical, Greek, and Roman architecture and baroque and art nouveau features. Plečnik's eclecticism in his lifetime led to him being "rediscovered" in the 1980s as a prophet of post-modernism.

6 Yugoslavia was a specific case among socialist countries. The party leadership broke political ties with the Soviet Union in 1948, and the country was not a member of the Comecon bloc, developing only bilateral agreements with other Eastern European countries. Yugoslavia was trading with Western Europe, Eastern Europe, and the Middle East. In international politics it was a leading member of a non-aligned movement while developing a specific "self-management" model of socialism.

7 What made Slovenia also different within Yugoslavia was the very specific process of democratization in the 1980s. The new civic movements (environmental, cultural, feminist, alternative, etc.) were the embryo of the emerging civil society, encouraging the development of various associations with more specific political demands. Political pluralism emerged as a result of pressures and cooperation between the civil society and the rather open-minded reformist Communist Party elite in Slovenia and, under external pressure from centralist and conservative forces in the former Yugoslavia, most notably the nationalist forces in Serbia under the leadership of Slobodan Milošević.

8 The most important goals of transition and Slovenia's integration into the European Union are: (i) development of international relations characterized by trade liberalization and intensification of trade with EU countries; (ii) macro-economic stabilization to satisfy conditions for joining the EMU; (iii) structural reforms to complete the economic transformation and development of a well-functioning market economy; and (iv) stimulation of the competitiveness of Slovenian enterprises to perform successfully within the single market (*SEDS*, 1995).

 9 The regulation allows sale of enterprises, employee buyout, or transfer of shares requiring 10 per cent of the book (administrative) value of social capital to be distributed as shares to the Slovenian Pension and Disability Fund, Compensation Fund (10 per cent), and authorized investment funds (20 per cent), with 20 per cent going to employees and 40 per cent to the population.

10 Since the 1970s, Slovenia has been divided into 12 regions for planning and statistical purposes. Until the end of 2002, there were no officially defined administrative regions (provinces) at the intermediate level between the state and local authorities.

11 It was amended (1993) with a special Co-operation Agreement between Slovenia and the EU based on the preferential trade agreement, except for the free movement of labour.

12 The Central European Free Trade Agreement (CEFTA) replaced the initial 'Visegrad' group of Czechoslovakia, Hungary, and Poland. Slovenia became a member of CEFTA in 1996, followed by Romania (1997), Bulgaria (1998), Estonia (1999), and Croatia (2002). The main purpose of CEFTA is abolishment of custom barriers between its members and joint preparation for accession to the European Union.

13 The World Bank: Foreign Investment Advisory Service (FIAS) Report (1999) on FDI in Slovenia.

14 According to international (ILO) standards, the unemployment rate in Slovenia is only 7 per cent.

15 Relations between Slovenia and the European Union were governed by the Trade and Co-operation Agreement (1993). In 1995, the signing of the Europe (Association) Agreement was postponed by Italy's pressure on Slovenia to change restitution law and foreign property legislation. In July 1997, the Slovenian Parliament approved the proposal for new property legislation with modification of the Constitution (Article 68). The Europe Agreement was then ratified by the European Parliament and respective parliaments of the EU Member States.

16 On his visit to Ljubljana (June 1999), former US President Bill Clinton emphasized Slovenia's unique role as a peaceful and most prosperous transition country, with stable democracy and institutions, as a model for the other countries in the Balkans. Mr Bruce Jackson, US chairperson for NATO enlargement, on his visit to Slovenia (April 2000) stated that Slovenia was not accepted in the first wave of NATO enlargement due to the country's not well-recognized international image and geographical proximity to conflict zones in the Balkans.

17 In 2000, British Airways cancelled its flights from London to Ljubljana and Trieste (Italy) respectively due to low profitability and competition from national carriers Adria Airways and AlItalia. In December 2002, after 11 years, direct air connections have been established between Ljubljana and Belgrade, the former Yugoslav capital.

18 From 1996, annual research on the use of the Internet in Slovenia includes monitoring of the official statistical data on users (households, companies, and educational institutions), Internet providers, e-commerce, and e-banking activities. International comparisons are available in the OECD's *European Information Technology Outlook 2000*.

19 According to the Census 1991, in settlements with less than 500 inhabitants (92 per cent of all settlements) lived 34 per cent, while in 15 urban settlements with more than 10,000 inhabitants lived 32 per cent of all inhabitants of Slovenia.

20 The term "deagrarized population" has been widely used in the former Yugoslavia to describe population living in officially classified rural settlements, but working in secondary and tertiary activities in towns. The new classification of "urban areas" has been implemented for the last Census (April 2002) in order to encompass this phenomenon more precisely. The "real" urbanization rate is expected to be around 75 per cent.

21 In Slovenia more than 80 per cent of land was in private ownership even during the socialist period.

22 According to Drewett et al. (1992) and Pichler-Milanović (1994), analyses of European urbanization trends (1950–1990) based on official national statistics, the process of "desurbanization" (i.e. absolute decline of population in the city agglomeration) first occurred in Ljubljana (agglomeration) at the end of the 1980s, and only later appeared in other Central and Eastern European capital cities.

23 Two other periods are also important for the inner city development of Ljubljana in the twentieth century. After the Great earthquake (1895), Camillo Sitte and Max Fabiani (an architect of Slovene origin), both students of Otto Wagner from the Viennese School of Architecture, were invited to Ljubljana to incorporate modern urban planning ideas with the traditional values of city development. The result was the first comprehensive urban development plan that envisaged city growth, land-use structure, transport corridors, and morphological forms. The other important urban development period was between the First and Second World Wars, known today as "Plečnik's Ljubljana". The post-war (1945–1990) urban planning and development of Ljubljana was marked with the work of modern architects, urbanists, and planners from the "Plečnik" School of Architecture (University of Ljubljana) – Ivan Vurnik, Edvard Ravnikar, Šarjan Tepina, Marko Šlajmer, Vladimir Braco Mušič, etc. (see Tepina, 1996).

24 Location was not considered a factor in determining a dwelling's book (administrative) value, which represented only about 50 per cent of the housing market price in 1991.

25 The most important strategic development goals, as formulated in these two documents of the City Municipality of Ljubljana, are focused on improvement of the international competitiveness of Ljubljana, entrepreneurial and business culture, inter-modal public transport, residential environment, social inclusion of deprived groups, development of the information society, and reduced pressure on the natural environment.

# REFERENCES

Karl Aiginger and Yvonne Wolfmayr-Schnitzer, *The Qualitative Competitiveness of Transition Economies*, Vienna: WIFO, 1996.

Marjan Cerar, ed., *Prostorski plan mestne občine Ljubljana: Prostorska zasnova* [Spatial Development Plan of the City Municipality of Ljubljana: The Concept of Spatial Development], Ljubljana: City Municipality of Ljubljana, 2002.

Milan Cvikl, Emil Kraft, and Milan Vodopivec, "The Cost and Benefits of Slovenian Independence", *Policy Research Working Paper*, Washington, D.C.: The World Bank, 1993.

Jože Dekleva, ed., *Dejavniki razvoja poselitve Ljubljane* [Land Use Patterns and Settlement Development in Ljubljana], Ljubljana: Urban Planning Institute of the Republic of Slovenia, 1991.

Jože Dekleva, "Ljubljana – Strategy for Sustainable Development of Ljubljana Metropolitan Region", in *Intelligent Mobility: Towards Sustainable Urban Development*, Vienna: City of Vienna Planning Bureau, 2000, pp. 55–57.

Jože Dekleva, ed., *Strategija trajnostnega razvoja mesta Ljubljana* [Sustainable Development Strategy of the City of Ljubljana], Ljubljana: City Municipality of Ljubljana, 2002.

"Prodor slovenskih kapitalistov" [The Penetration of Slovenian Capitalists], *Delo*, 26 April 2000, p. 6.

Kaliopa Dimitrovska Andrews, ed., *Zasnova urbanizacije* [Urbanisation Trends in Slovenia], Ljubljana: Urban Planning Institute of the Republic of Slovenia, 1998.

European Bank for Reconstruction and Development (EBRD), *Transition Reports*, London: EBRD, 1996–2000.

Roy Drewett, Samantha Mason, and Nataša Pichler-Milanović, "Population Dynamics of European Cities 1970–1990", in Roy Drewett, Uwe Schubert, and Richard Knight, *The Future of European Cities: the Role of Science and Technology*,

Brussels: URBINNO/FAST Monitor Programme, DG XII, Commission of the European Communities, 1992.

Steve Fallon, *Slovenia*, Hawthorn: Lonely Planet, 1995.

Anthony R. French and F. E. Ian Hamilton, eds, *The Socialist City: Spatial Structure and Urban Policy*, Chichester: John Wiley & Sons, 1979.

Daniel Gros and Guy Vandille, "Slovenian and European Trade Structures", *IB Revija, Journal of the Institute of Macro-economic Analysis and Development* 8–9, 1995, pp. 13–23.

Pavel Gantar, "Decentralisation of Administrative and Political Authority to Promote Regional Economic Development: The Case of Ljubljana", in David A. Rondinelli, ed., *Privatisation and Economic Reform in Central Europe: The Changing Business Climate*, Westport, Connecticut, London: Quorum Books, 1994, pp. 107–121.

"The 100 top companies in Slovenia," *Gospodarski Vestnik* 29, 1999.

Matjaž Hanžek, eds, *Human Development Report for Slovenia*, Ljubljana: Institute of Macro-economic Analysis and Development (IMAD) and United Nations Development Programme (UNDP), 1999.

József Hegedüs, Steven Mayo, and Iván Tosics, "Transition of the Housing Sector in the East Central European Countries", *Review of Urban and Regional Development Studies* 8(2), 1996, pp. 101–136.

Marjan Hočevar, *Novi urbani trendi: prizorišča v mestih – omrežja med mesti* [New Urban Trends: Locales within Cities – Networks between Cities], *Znanstvena knjižnica Fakultete za družbene vede* 43, Ljubljana: Faculty of Social Sciences, 2000.

Institute of Macro-Economic Analysis and Development (IMAD), *Economic Mirror*, Ljubljana: IMAD, 1992–2001.

Janja Kreitmayer, ed., *"Istanbul +5": The Slovenian National Report on the Implementation of the Habitat Agenda*, Ljubljana: National Office for Spatial Planning, Ministry of Environment and Spatial Planning, 2001.

Srna Mandič, "Slovenia", in David Clapham, Jószef Hegedüs, Keith Kintrea, Iván Tosics, and Helen Kay, eds, *Housing Privatisation in Eastern Europe*, Westport, Connecticut, London: Greenwood Press, 1996, pp. 151–169.

Srna Mandič and Tine Stanovnik, "Slovenia: Fast Privatisation of the Stock, Slow Reform of Housing Policy", in Raymond Struyk, ed., *Economic Restructuring of the Former Soviet Bloc: The Case Study of Housing*, Washington, D.C.: The Urban Institute Press, 1996, pp. 139–170.

Breda Mihelič, *Urbanistični razvoj Ljubljane* [Urban Development of Ljubljana], Ljubljana: Partizanska knjiga, 1983.

Karel Natek and Marija Natek, *Slovenija: geografska, zgodovinska, pravna, politična, ekonomska in kulturna podoba Slovenije* [Slovenia: Geographic, Historical, Legal, Political, Economic and Cultural Image of Slovenia], Ljubljana: Mladinska knjiga, 1998.

Organisation for Economic Co-operation and Development (OECD), *Economic Survey of Slovenia*, Paris: OECD, 1997.

——, *Economic Outlook*, Paris: OECD, 1998.

Branko Pavlin and Gregor Sluga, "Ljubljana kot zaposlitveno središče" [Ljubljana as Employment Centre], in Matej Gabrovec and Milan Adamič Oražen, eds, *Ljubljana, geografija mesta* [Ljubljana: Urban Geography], Ljubljana, Ljubljansko geografsko društvo, ZRC-SAZU, 2000, pp. 259–267.

Nataša Pichler-Milanović, "The Role of Housing Policy in the Transformation Process of Central-East European Cities", *Urban Studies* 31(7), 1994, pp. 1097–1115.

——, "Slovenia in the New Geopolitical Context", in Francis W. Carter and H.T. Norris, eds, *The Changing Shape of the Balkans*, London: UCL Press Ltd., 1996, pp. 25–51.

——, "Urban Housing Markets in Central and Eastern Europe: Convergence, Divergence or Policy Collapse", *European Journal of Housing Policy* 1(2), 2001a, pp. 145–187.

Nataša Pichler-Milanović, ed., *Primerjalne prednosti mesta Ljubljane v procesu EU integracij* [Comparative Advantages of the City of Ljubljana in the Process of EU Integration], Ljubljana: Urban Planning Institute of the Republic of Slovenia, 2001b.

Matija Rojec, *Neposredne tuje investicije v slovenskem gospodarstvu in njihov razvojni potencial* [Development Potentials of FDIs in the Slovenian Economy], *Delovni zvezek* 6, Ljubljana: Institute of Macroeconomic Analysis and Development, 1996.

James Simmie and Jože Dekleva, eds, *Yugoslavia in Turmoil: After Self-management*, London, New York: Pinter Publishers, 1991.

*Slovenia: Strategy for Economic Development. Approaching Europe – Growth, Competitiveness and Integration (SEDS)*, Ljubljana: Institute of Macroeconomic Analysis and Development, 1995.

Barbara Starič-Strajnar, "New Forms of Housing Provision – Problems and Policies", *Urbani izziv* 28–29, 1995, pp. 68–72.

Statistical Office of the Republic of Slovenia (SORS), *Statistical Yearbook*, Ljubljana: SORS, various years.

Mestna občina Ljubljana, *Statistični letopis Ljubljane* [Statistical Yearbook of Ljubljana], Ljubljana: MOL, various years.

Igor Strmšnik, *Slovenija v Evropi regij: regionalne strukture razširjene evropske zveze* [Slovenia in Europe: Regional Structures of Enlarged EU], *Delovni zvezek* 6/97, Ljubljana: Institute of Macroeconomic Analysis and Development, 1998.

Raymond Struyk, ed., *Economic Restructuring of the Former Soviet Bloc: The Case of Housing*, Washington D.C.: The Urban Institute Press, 1996.

Ivan Svetlik, ed., *Social Policy in Slovenia*, Ashgate: Avebury, 1992.

Marjan Svetličič, "A Small Country Going Into Europe: Economic Pragmatism and Nationhood", in Danica Fink-Hafner and Teddy Cox, eds, *Into Europe: Perspectives from Britain and Slovenia*, Ljubljana: Faculty of Social Sciences, 1996, pp. 189–224.

Marjan Tepina, *Prostor in čas urbanizma in Ljubljane urbane: ob stoletnici urbanizma 1895–1995* [The Space and Time of Urbanism and Ljubljana 'Urbana': 100 Years of Urban Development 1895–1995], Ljubljana: ČZP Enotnost, 1996.

United Nations Conference on Trade and Development (UNCTAD), *World Investment Report 1999*, Geneva: United Nations, 1999.

Peter Vodopivec, "Slovenes in the Habsburg Empire or Monarchy", *Nationalities Papers* 21(1), Association for the Study of the Nationalities of the USSR and Eastern Europe, 1993.

# 12

# Mixed success: Economic stability and urban inequality in Sofia

*Elena Vesselinov and John R. Logan*

## Introduction

This chapter focuses on the changes that have been taking place in Bulgaria's capital city of Sofia since 1989, the year symbolizing the shift from socialist planned economy to market-based economy and from one-party political system to parliamentary democracy. In particular, we are concerned with the process of urban transformation in the era of economic globalization. For us, economic globalization mostly relates to the macro-economic policies orientated towards economic growth in the process of Bulgaria's accession to the European Union.

Scholars and observers argue that macro-economic stability has been reached in Bulgaria in the last three years, largely attributed to the introduction of a Currency Board (CB) in July 1997. The most serious economic crisis to date has been successfully overcome, but the long-term consequences of dramatic changes in the housing system since 1989 are acute indicators of a future urban crisis. The central argument of this chapter is that, although a severe economic crisis in Bulgaria has been overcome, urban disparities in the capital of Bulgaria are increasing and silently building up to a possibly serious urban crisis.

To study the signs of a mounting urban crisis is especially important given the fact that Sofia is in the process of becoming the regional centre of the Balkan Peninsula. Bulgaria has proven its ability to retain peace and stability throughout the worst calamities of the Yugoslav conflict and to make economic progress despite the sanctions imposed by the United Nations. Therefore Sofia, as the capital and the most dynamic city in the country, has every chance of becoming the leading urban centre of the Balkans, and thus an important hub in the network of the largest European cities and one of the major communication and transportation centres of the new and integrated Europe.

The process of market transition and the effects of European integration in Bulgaria define the same dimensions of change in the country. For Bulgaria, as for the other East European countries, the process of integration into the world economy happens mostly through integration into the economic and political structures of the European Union. Accession to multinational and regional organizations set the macro-economic agenda for the country, aimed at restoring the leading role of market signals in resource allocation (Ljubomir Hristov, in Centre for the Study of Democracy, 1998). In this respect joining the IMF and World Bank in September 1990, entering into an association agreement with the European Union in February 1995, joining the World Trade Organization in December 1996, and beginning the official negotiations for accession to the European Union in February 2000, in general have put similar pressures on the Bulgarian government to implement measures of market-orientated reforms. The Copenhagen Council of June 1993, which set the criteria for the countries of Central and Eastern Europe to join the European Union, explicated unequivocally that prospective members have to demonstrate "the existence of a functional market economy, as well as the capacity to cope with competitive pressure and market forces within the Union" (Ljubomir Hristov, 1998: 54).

In 1998, it was decided which countries would be able to join the European Monetary Union (EMU) (Priemus, 2000) and on 1 January 1999 the fixed exchange rate was set within which the various European currencies were linked. The Maastricht Treaty specified the criteria that a country must satisfy to be able to join the EMU – the convergence criteria. These criteria concern the inflation rate, the bank rate, the government deficit; the government gross debt, and the exchange rate. Reflecting the most important aspects for future EU integration, the criteria thus become part of the major macro-economic indicators that are monitored for each negotiating country. There is no doubt that becoming an integral part of Europe is a sound political and economic goal for Bulgaria. Nevertheless, in the process of market transition and accession to the European Union there are a few other indicators that should be monitored. In terms of urban space those indicators relate mostly to distribution of housing, residential location, and land property, for these factors determine to what extent the larger economic forces affect people's daily lives. It is also important to monitor changes in the housing system because it is there that urban policy-makers can exert power and good political will at the time of market transition.

The analytical duality between macro-economic and urban indicators will play out in the structure of this chapter. First, we will examine the larger macro-economic context in Bulgaria as well as the specific social and economic changes in Sofia after 1989. Since there is a noticeable gap in scholarly literature that explores the current urban developments in the Bulgarian capital, it is necessary to outline the broader socio-economic context. In the second section of the chapter we discuss the more important changes in the housing system since 1989 and focus on those changes that we find to be the most problematic in the future urban scene. The third section discusses the urgency of facing those challenges in the context of Sofia's evolving position as a leading and lively centre of stability in the Balkans.

## Socio-economic Context

### Macro-economic Stability in Bulgaria

The Maastricht Treaty set down the criteria (Priemus, 2000) that a country must satisfy to be able to join the EMU: inflation may not be higher than the average inflation in the three Member States with the lowest inflation, plus 2 per cent; long-term interest may not be higher than the average of the interest rate in the three Member States with the lowest inflation, plus 2 per cent; the government deficit may not be greater than 3 per cent of GDP; the government gross debt must be less than 60 per cent of GDP; and the exchange rate of the country concerned must have remained for two years within the EMS band. There can be no question of devaluation on a country's own initiative. The risk of Bulgaria devaluating its currency at the moment is near zero because since July 1997 the Bulgarian National Bank (BNB) functions as a CB, with a fixed exchange rate.

Table 12.1 registers the major macro-economic indicators for Bulgaria between 1991 and 2001. Most of them reveal the acute economic crisis of 1996–1997: negative economic growth, negative rate of capital investment, skyrocketing inflation, a bank rate that reached 140.9 in 1996, and a government budget deficit of 15 per cent of GDP in 1996. After the introduction of the CB, the Bulgarian economy is already showing signs of stability, and the macro-economic situation in Bulgaria seems to have dramatically improved.[1] A comprehensive reform programme was introduced, with strong measures for fiscal consolidation and a number of targets for structural reform. By 1998, CPI inflation had declined to negligible levels, budgetary balance was achieved, domestic interest rates had declined remarkably, and output had shown some signs of recovery (OECD, 1999). Positive changes can be readily observed from the basic macro-economic indicators after 1998.

Two major processes very much determine the above changes in the country's macro-economic climate: the process of privatization, and the functioning of the CB. Both are also indicative of economic globalization. Privatization is regarded as a key feature of globalization concerning transition economies and the way it relates to the foreign direct investments (FDI) (Sassen, 1999). The CB on the other hand signifies the changes that are taking place in the sphere of monetary

Table 12.1  Basic macro-economic indicators for Bulgaria

| Indicators | 1991 | 1992 | 1993 | 1994 | 1995 | 1996 | 1997 | 1998 | 1999 | 2000 | 2001 |
|---|---|---|---|---|---|---|---|---|---|---|---|
| GDP growth, % | -8.4 | -7.3[3] | -1.5 | 1.8 | 2.9 | -10.1 | -6.9 | 3.5 | 2.4[6] | 5.8 | 4.5 |
| Fixed capital investment growth, % | -19.9 | -7.3 | -17.5 | 1.1 | 16.1 | -21.2 | -23.9 | 16.3 | 25.3[5] | 8.2 | 11.5 |
| Inflation (CPI Year, %) | — | 91.3 | 72.8 | 96 | 62.1 | 121.6 | 1,058.4 | 18.1 | 2.6 | 10.3 | 7.3 |
| Unemployment rate[1] (%) | — | 15.6[3] | — | — | 14.7 | 13.7 | 15.0 | 16.0 | 17.0[6] | — | 7.3 |
| Rate of registered unemployment[2] (%) | — | — | 16.4 | 12.8 | 11.0 | 12.5 | 13.7 | 12.2 | 14.0[6] | 16.3 | 19.4 |
| Annual interest rate of the BNB | 49.5 | 45.0[3] | 48.2 | 63.3 | 49.1 | 140.9 | 35.8 | 5.4 | 4.7[4] | 3.9 | 4.5 |
| Gross foreign reserves (million US$) | — | — | — | — | 1,236 | 751 | 2,482 | 3,051 | 3,222[6] | 3,460 | 3,229 |

Notes:
[1] Percent of labour force, ILO definition.
[2] National Office of Employment at Ministry of Labour and Social Affairs (2000), Sofia: Bulgaria.
[3] Bulgaria's Capital Markets in the Context of EU Accession: A Status Report, Centre for The Study of Democracy.
[4] Bulgarian National Bank Annual Report for 1998 (1999).
[5] National Statistical Institute, Preliminary Results (2000).
[6] Business Survey Series, Bulgaria 1999 Economic Series, Agency for Economic Analysis and Forecasting.
Source: OECD Economic Surveys: Bulgaria (1999); National Statistical Institute (2002); Bulgarian National Bank Annual Report (2002).

policy, which is a central issue in the context of the IMF agenda in promoting international financial integration based on fewer and fewer obstacles for free capital flows (Vesselinov, 2000a). In this section, therefore, we will focus our attention on these two larger processes – privatization and the functioning of the CB – for they link the macro-economic state of affairs in Bulgaria with the larger extra-national economic forces to which the country is subjected.

Privatization in Bulgaria has been pursued along three separate lines (OECD, 1997): (a) restitution of land and urban property to former owners and their heirs; (b) cash sales of state assets; and (c) mass (voucher) privatization. It is important to note that the first privatization initiative in Bulgaria was associated with restitution of urban property. It was also one of the first legislative acts of the first radical anti-communist government in Bulgaria, elected in October 1991, and can be viewed as an attempt to satisfy the urban supporters of the Union of Democratic Forces (UDF). Restitution was either in kind, or through securities for property that had been substantially upgraded or extended (Bobeva and Bozhkov, in Zloch-Christy, 1998). As of September 1996, close to 90 per cent of all submitted claims had been resolved, involving the restitution of more than 22,000 sites with an estimated value of approximately US$200 million to previous owners or their heirs (OECD, 1997). Roughly half of these sites are shops. The transfer of assets has provided the infrastructure for the explosive growth of private trade and services. Inefficient state trading and service companies, not being in a position to pay market-based rents, seem to have left restituted commercial buildings largely to new private entrepreneurs.

The Law on Transformation and Privatization of State and Municipal Enterprises was passed in April 1992. This law provides for a wide range of privatization methods: auctions, tenders, direct negotiations, debt/equity swaps, public offering of shares, management and employee buyouts, sales of separate parts of enterprises, and (after 1994) mass privatization. Bobeva and Bozhkov (in Zloch-Christy, 1998) argue that the privatization process in Bulgaria is decentralized, and various state agencies are entitled to initiate privatization deals: the ministries, the Privatization Agency, the Council of Ministers, and municipalities (for municipal-owned enterprises). The Privatization Agency seems to play a controversial role in this process, and it also had changed personnel several times, corresponding to changes in government. It handles the privatization of large enterprises (with over 50 per cent of state assets) and by law does not need a formal approval by the Council of Ministers. However, the Council of Ministers had rejected or postponed transactions already approved by the Agency (OECD, 1997).

Different agents of privatization did not have very strong interests in getting things done. For line ministers, for example, privatization threatens to limit directly their influence over firms in their industry. Moreover, a number of senior ministerial officials serve on the boards of directors of state-owned enterprises, typically receiving pay or perquisites that far exceed their ordinary wages as civil servants. In addition to delaying the privatization of enterprises under their jurisdiction, ministries have also lobbied the government on occasion to obstruct potential deals of the Privatization Agency. Thus, an overall common process for transition economies and a key feature of economic globalization becomes conditioned, at times forestalled, by private interests. This argument can be supported also by the fact that each of the seven governments since 1989, supporting general market reforms, had its own agenda in terms of privatization; this, as argued by Wyzan (in Bell, 1998), is one of the reasons for privatization delay as part of structural economic reform in the country. Economic restructuring cannot be isolated as an independent determinant of social processes (Logan and Molotch, 1987; Logan and Swanstrom, 1992), simply because in itself it is shaped by the local interests and political power of certain groups. The immediate implication of this argument for urban studies is that places are not just passive recipients of the inevitable economic restructuring; specific local policies and struggles produce the economic changes.

As argued above, the delay in privatization is one of the major reasons for the delay in structural economic reform and consequently a reason behind the economic crisis of 1996–1997. The malfunctioning state-owned enterprises accumulated large non-performing loans in commercial banks, which were established after 1990. The government continued to subsidize these enterprises, whereby large government deficits were produced; this, together with the bad loans, led to the collapse of the banking system in 1996–1997. A third feature of the economic crisis was political instability, reflected in the fact that from 1989 to 1997 there were seven governments with their own administration that came in and out of office. This perpetual political change made adopting a consistent legal and administrative regulatory framework almost impossible.

Policy changes in the last years addressed some of the earlier controversies of privatization. The Privatization Agency now has responsibility for privatizing the largest companies in two groups, Group A and Group B,[2] while the line ministries can take charge of the smaller firms' restructuring. The multiplicity of possible privatization approaches foreseen by the Privatization Law and the "Strategy for Accelerating Privatization", including debt/equity swaps using either Brady (external) or ZUNK (domestic) bonds, delegates responsibilities to various state bodies, causing problems of coordination. Therefore the "Strategy" has upgraded the status of the Privatization Agency as a coordinator of the whole privatization process. As a result of policy accent on privatization, the figures from 1997 were significant: the Privatization Agency and the line ministries contracted for payments, corporate liabilities assumed by buyers, and investment commitments for a total of US$1.5 billion, an amount roughly equal to the cumulative sum of such contracts from 1993 to 1996 (OECD, 1999). Cash payments contracted in 1997 reached US$608 million as compared to US$442 million in 1996. A large part of the acceleration in cash privatization came from sales to foreign investors. The sale of MDK Pirdop copper mine to Belgium's Union Miniere alone brought payments and contracted investments totalling US$300 million. Bulgarska Roza Svetopolis, which produces the famous rose oil, was sold to an Irish company, while a consortium led by the Banque Nationale de Paris acquired a 33 per cent stake in the Albena Black Sea tourist complex, the first resort to be privatized (OECD, 1999).

The completion of the programme for the privatization or liquidation of loss-making state-owned enterprises is considered to have contributed to the recent economic recovery. The year 1999 was marked by the highest number of deals concluded since the launch of the privatization process in Bulgaria in 1992. It also witnessed the largest number of sales of large-scale state-owned enterprises and of heavily indebted state-owned enterprises included in the Liquidation Programme of firms in grave financial straits. The highest rate of cash privatized assets was also reported in 1999. As of the end of 1999, over two-thirds of all state-owned assets allocated for privatization had been transferred to private hands. As a result, 1999 turned out to be the most successful privatization year in Bulgaria (Agency for Economic Analysis and Forecasting, 1999). The privatization of several large state-owned companies – Balkan Airlines, Kremikovtzi, Neftohim, Petrol – was the most important reform step. The high speed of privatization and the liquidation of loss-making companies in the last two years initiated a high-intensity process of restructuring and labour productivity improvement (Agency for Economic Analysis and Forecasting, 1999).

The positive role of privatization in 1999 notwithstanding, the major stabilizing influence behind the positive economic changes is attributed to the introduction of the CB. A caretaker government was appointed in the spring of 1997 and negotiated with IMF the terms for the CB. This radical step came in response to hyperinflation in early 1997, drastic depletion of foreign currency reserves (to a critical level of US$440 million without monetary gold), closure of 14 commercial banks (comprising 25 per cent of the consolidated bank balance sheet), and fully disrupted functions of the national currency (Nenovsky and Hristov, 1999). A central feature of this programme was the replacement of active monetary policy with a CB to defend a fixed exchange rate of 1,000 lev to the DM. Bulgarian currency was pegged to the euro on 1 January 1999 for the indefinite future. Confidence in the CB is maintained by promising never to change the exchange rate and allowing the public to openly exchange as much local currency for reserve currency as they wish. Thus, even prior to membership of the European Union, Bulgaria will have achieved an irreversible fixing of its exchange rate – a condition that should be met by all full members of the European Union and European Monetary Union.

With the introduction of the CB, the BNB becomes independent of the Bulgarian government's control and at the same time it ceases to have independent regulatory functions in setting the national monetary policy. Those functions are relegated to external financial, European, and international authorities (Avramov, 1999). The CB institution at the same time directly affects national government and banks, as they should translate hard budget constraints to state-owned enterprises and (through banks) to the private sector. The central bank itself faces new constraints because it is deprived of the inflation tax, which is a major source of income in a classical central bank model. The economy cannot adjust to external shocks through the exchange rate; thus their impact on economic agents is direct. The burden of adjustment falls on the real sector and financial variables such as interest rates, incomes, output volumes, productivity growth, and employment, which are among the main shock absorbers.

The new BNB policy is in compliance with the Protocol on the Statute of the ESCB that central banks should conduct their monetary policy using, in effect, market instruments, thus implying that administrative instruments ought to be excluded. No recourse is made to administrative instruments to intervene in financial markets (Roussenova and Yordanova, in Centre for the Study of Democracy, 1998). One peculiarity of the CB is that unlike the "classic case" it has some limited ability to act as a lender of last resort. The BNB extends credits in levs to solvent banks only when there is a credit risk, which affects the stability of the banking system. The restriction on the BNB's function as lender of last resort makes the banks more cautious when they apply for and give credits, which in turn reduces the probability of a new wave of non-performing loans (or bad credits). At the same time, reluctance to lend among banks may cause delays in the processes of privatization and economic restructuring. It seems that a possible "catch 22" is forming in the context of the CB and emphasis on privatization: in order to undergo a successful round of economic restructuring most enterprises need external funding. Given the low development of credit and equity markets in Bulgaria and the constraints imposed by the CB, external finance other than foreign investment for restructuring remains quite scarce. Therefore, a centre in the national economy process of economic restructuring seems dependent on foreign resources, putting additional pressure at the same time on the state budget, because the budget is to assume the operating losses and liabilities.

Another controversy relates to the role of the CB in ensuring the primacy of market mechanisms over administrative regulation. On the one hand, there is growing unemployment and low levels of output in Bulgaria, dramatically increasing income inequality (OECD, 1999). On the other hand, it is argued that since its establishment, the CB has been a success (Avramov, 1999; Miller, 1999): from hyperinflation in February 1997, inflation fell to a record low in 1998–1 per cent, and 1.8 per cent in 1999 (see Table 12.1). The dramatic fall in basic interest rates made it possible for the government to reduce the large government deficit (OECD, 1999). The introduction of the CB necessitated strong supporting measures for fiscal consolidation. A consolidated budget deficit of over 15 per cent of GDP in 1996 was reduced to 3 per cent in 1997, and entirely eliminated in 1998, representing one of the most significant accomplishments of the economic programme. Of course, the reduction in budget deficit was related to severe subsidy cuts in a variety of social programmes, housing being the first area to experience these cuts. As a direct consequence of economic globalization, at the urging of IMF no further subsidies for housing have been included in the state budget from as early as 1992 (Hoffman and Koleva, 1993). The dramatic change in the level of subsidies for housing puts immediate constraints on urban policy.

Urban policy-making faces limitations within the specific, rather narrow scope of policy-making under the conditions of the CB. Establishing a fixed exchange rate, the CB relies on automatic mechanisms to restore macro-economic equilibrium. In theory, just like the gold standard, the money supply will automatically adjust when balance of payments disequilibria arise (Miller, 1999). A CB restores confidence by relying on these automatic mechanisms and severely limiting the discretion of policy-makers. However, the credibility of a CB depends on both economic and political factors. Avramov (1999) argues that the success of a CB depends on broad political consensus at its adoption as it represents a specific public contract and a basically new monetary constitution. To sustain confidence the CB must have sufficient foreign currency reserves to honour the pledge to exchange local currency for reserve currency. Politically, the government must be prepared to maintain the fixed exchange rate when adverse circumstances arise. This argument is particularly important in the context of the food riots in Latin America accompanying the austerity measures of the IMF (Walton and Saddon, 1996) and the protests in Seattle during the WTO meeting in 1999 (*New York Times*, November 1999). Another example of civil unrest in Bulgaria is the teachers' strike national alert in 2000, because under the municipal budgetary constraints the teachers' salaries are usually not paid on time (*Standart*, 2000).

As it has been proven during political demonstrations and meetings since 1989, the most politically active population in Bulgaria lives in big cities and in Sofia in particular. Therefore, in order to have a sustained economic recovery, the constraints put on urban policy by demands for stable national macro-economic performance have to be regularly re-examined, taking into account the effects of larger economic changes upon urbanites' daily lives. The next section of this chapter takes the reader from the changes in macro-economic environment to the level of changes in Sofia's urban context, and then goes into further detail to examine the specific housing conditions within which *Sofiantsi* (residents of Sofia) experience urban change.

## Sofia's Administrative and Socio-demographic Profile

Sofia shares common and distinctive features within the lager network of East European cities. Most post-socialist city typologies are still based on national political and socio-economic conditions, rather than on the urban form per se (see Chapter 4). German cities are usually regarded as a class on their own, because of the specific context of East–West unification. Czech, Polish, Hungarian, Slovenian, and Slovakian cities are considered to be a second group, with a larger share of FDI in the countries as a whole, larger capital investment in offices and the urban commercial market, more rapidly increasing and differentiating population incomes (see Chapter 3), and a faster pace of housing privatization. Bulgaria, Romania, Lithuania, and Latvia form a third group of countries, where there is a considerably lower level of FDI (see Chapter 5), and institutional and legislative environments are less developed, which resonates in the establishing of new controls over land and property markets. Among all post-socialist countries, however, Bulgaria comes second in Eastern Europe, after the Czech Republic, in its level of urbanization: about two-thirds of the Bulgarian population live in urban areas and are therefore profoundly affected by the transformation of the cities. As of 1997, 1.2 million people, or 14 per cent of the Bulgarian population, lived in the Sofia Municipality. The primacy of the capital in population, economic development, and future prospects sets it as a leading example for cities in the country. Therefore it is particularly important to discuss the changes taking place there. The position of Sofia within the national urban system is shown in Fig. 12.1, together with the country's major roads and administrative divisions.

*Government and Administration*

In October 1991, the Great General Assembly adopted the Law of Local Government Autonomy and Administration (LLGAA), based on the principles of the new Constitution. In 1996, the law was expanded on the basis of the

Fig. 12.1  Cities and traffic system in Bulgaria.
*Source:* National Statistical Institute, 2001.

experience of the first democratically elected local and central government officials. The principles of the European Charter of Local Government Autonomy, ratified by the Bulgarian Parliament in 1995, were also taken into account. Paragraph 136, notation 1 of the Constitution and paragraph 5 of the LLGAA stipulate that "the municipality is the basic territorial unit, within which the local governing takes place". The municipal territory includes the smaller districts and towns. Local government autonomy means that municipality residents, through their elected officials, have the right to decide on questions related to municipal property, local businesses, taxes and tariffs, education, health care, social services, and cultural institutions (UNDP, 1997).

The Sofia City Council has 61 members. These are elected through proportional party representation, whereas the Mayor is elected through general elections. The mandate of the mayor and the council is four years. The mayor is the most powerful executive officer, whereas the 24 district mayors have a much more limited scope of decision-making. In the last local elections, held in October 1999, Mayor Stefan Sofiyanski was re-elected for a second term, representing the Union of Democratic Forces. In the boundaries of the Sofia Municipality are included 24 districts with 4 cities and 34 villages. The cities are: Sofia, with a population of 1,114,168; Bankja, with 8,342 inhabitants; Novi Iskar, with 13,570 inhabitants; and Buhovo, inhabited by 3,286 individuals.[3]

The preliminary work on the new Master Plan for Sofia, the first comprehensive urban planning strategy in the last 20 years, recognizes the need to change the administrative divisions of the city. The Plan suggests dividing the Sofia Municipality into 10 new districts, 6 of which will encompass the territory of Sofia compact city and the other four of which will incorporate the suburban territories. The central advantage of the new administrative division is a decrease of bureaucracy and therefore improved services for Sofiantsi. Another advantage is found in the administrative consolidation of the city centre and the organization of districts along the five most important road arteries in Sofia. The new administrative structure is still under construction, however, as is the whole plan, and will be enforced only after the bill is passed by the Parliament.

The city municipal budget is formed on the basis of: percentage of profits of the municipally owned enterprises, 6.5 per cent of the profits of all businesses on its territory, inheritance tax, tax buildings, 50 per cent of the state-administered individual income taxes, property taxes, taxes of real-estate transactions, and other factors not unlike those of any contemporary city. The important part is that unlike in the communist era, where state subsidies constituted the major part of the city budget, now 87 per cent (1996) of the city budget comes from local taxes. The government subsidies for 1998 slightly increased and constituted about 22 per cent of the revenues in the municipal budget, whereas in 1999 the level of subsidies was again lower – 12 per cent of municipal revenues.

According to Ministry of Finance officials, about 80 per cent of municipalities in Bulgaria experience a shortage of funds. The National Association of Municipalities says in a report that priority expenditures constitute close to

92 per cent of all municipal revenues, which means that some necessary but not of the highest priority budgeted expenditures like construction and building maintenance are not covered. According to the report, there is a growing disparity between what municipalities are mandated to spend according to normative regulations and what revenues they are able to generate. Municipalities are supposed to be financially independent, but they can actively exercise power over no more than 10–15 per cent of their own budgets. By the end of 1999, for example, municipalities were short of 166.4 million levs, and did not cover even priority expenditures such as salaries (including teachers' salaries), medical supplies, and social security, or other expenditures like construction and building maintenance (Alexandrova, 2000b).

*Social Characteristics, Economic Structure, Employment, and Unemployment*

Reflecting the overall positive changes in the country, the economic environment in the Bulgarian capital during 1998 and 1999 can be characterized as very dynamic, where the defining feature was the increasing role of private businesses and its impact on the city. In comparison with the previous two years, public sector firms have declined in number from 977 in 1996, to 696 in 1997, to 632 in 1998, whereas private sector firms have increased: from 26,540 in 1996, to 29,578 in 1997, to 32,143 in 1998 (National Centre for Regional Development and Housing Policy, 1999c). The increase in the number of private firms reflects the changing economic structure, as well as providing evidence of the firms' capacity to register with the National Statistical Institute. Registration speaks about the common standards applied in reporting business information and about conducting business activities in compliance with official regulations. This is a very important indicator for the stability and legitimacy of the business environment at the state and local levels.

During 1998, the structure of Sofia's economy shows that almost 50 per cent of all registered firms in Sofia work in the area of trade and repairing activities.[4] The second largest concentration of firms is in the real-estate sector, constituting 17 per cent of all firms. The third place from the top is taken by the non-governmental agencies (9.58 per cent), and the fourth is manufacturing (8.76 per cent of all firms). In the industrial sector of Sofia's economy, only the mining and quarrying industries increase their relative weight in the industrial output, when comparing output in 1994 and 1997 (National Centre for Regional Development and Housing Policy, 1999c). All other industrial branches show signs of absolute decline. In this way Sofia resembles many other cities of the post-industrial age, where employment in industrial plants and enterprises has decreased as opposed to employment in the service sectors.

A feature that affects and will continue to affect the quality of life in the capital is that the industrial zones are spatially close to residential and/or recreation zones. This will be a definite area of future careful consideration for urban planners. Those industrial zones that will decline further in the future have

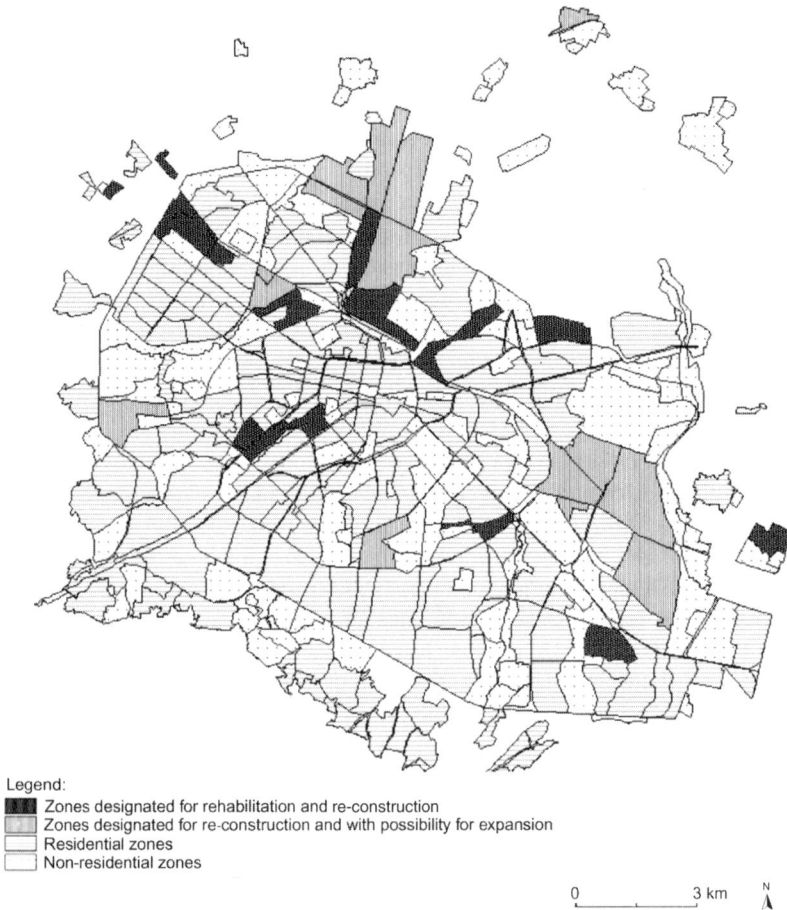

Fig. 12.2  Industrial zones for reconstruction and development in Sofia compact city.
*Source:* National Centre for Regional Development and Housing Policy, 1999c.

the potential to be a factor in the city's spatial differentiation. As we can see in Fig. 12.2, the industrial zones[5] that need rehabilitation and reconstruction are well incorporated and spread out within the compact city boundaries. Having a mixture of industrial and residential zoning enables people to live close by their jobs, but at the same time, the decline of the industrial plants may contribute to the decline of the residential areas where the plants are located.

Even though the output of most industrial branches shows signs of absolute decline, the manufacturing industry still constitutes to be the second largest sector of employment in Sofia's economy. The structure of employment in Sofia for the period after 1989 reveals that the dominant proportion of people are employed in the service sector. The percentage employed in the primary sector (forestry and agriculture) was 3 per cent, in the secondary sector (industry) 19 per cent, and in the tertiary (service) sector 78 per cent in 1998 (Obshtina, 1999).

In contrast to other major European cities, budgetary constraints prevent a rapid increase in the number of people employed in government-sponsored service sectors. Nevertheless, there is a tendency to find more people employed in the expanding banking and insurance sector. The new sector of advanced services, such as management consulting, legal and accounting services, and architecture and design, also creates new opportunities for qualified workers. Another area of opportunity, characteristic of the transition from state to private ownership, is that of private consulting in medicine, education, and construction. As a rule, professional people who work as consultants in these various areas of expertise are employed mostly in the city public sector (UNDP, 1997).

The economic sectors of trade, health care, education, construction, and transportation, together with employment in the government sector, business services, manufacturing, and finance, constituted 69.25 per cent of the labour force in 1996 and 70.07 per cent in 1997.[6] Employment in the public sector is very dynamic and rapidly changing, whereas employment in trade, business services, finance, and transport is taking the major share. There is also a slight increase in employment in the private manufacturing sector from 2.46 per cent in 1996 to 4.27 per cent in 1997. Overall, as in other post-socialist countries, employment in the public sector has decreased rapidly over the last decade, reaching a par with employment in the private sector (Fig. 12.3).

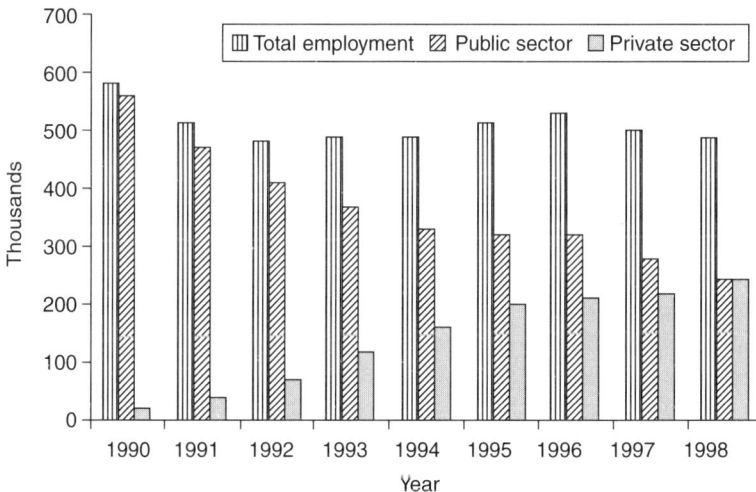

Fig. 12.3 Employment by sector in the Sofia Municipality.
*Source: Sofia: Report on the Regional Economy in 1998*, Sofia Municipality, 1999.

At the opposite side of the employment spectrum, in ways similar to "global" cities (Sassen, 1991) and other post-socialist cities (Busse, 2000), is the market of low-qualified labour, very often employed in the informal economy. Data from a survey in 1996 reveals the extent to which Sofia residents are involved in activities of the informal economy. There are several forms of activity that "informal economy" encompasses as a term. On the one hand, many people work in official businesses and enterprises without official labour or civil contracts, which in turn means no social security. On the other hand, there are businesses functioning with no state or local registration, which means no protection of any sort, but also no liability for paying taxes. A third small sub-sector of the informal economy is populated by people with qualifications such as auto repair technicians, plumbers, tailors, and electricians, who offer private but un-institutionalized and unregistered services (UNDP, 1997).[7]

Employment in the informal economy sectors has the positive feature of being an employment opportunity for people with no other choices. It is good as a temporary working condition. If it turns into a long-term prospect, it contributes to the polarization of the labour force, where there is a "higher" tier of professional, well-paid positions and a "lower" level of dead-end jobs with no benefits or career prospects (Sassen, 1999). Therefore, a policy goal for urban planners, especially in a manageable city like Sofia (with a population of 1,199,708), should be to regularize as many sectors of the informal economy as possible, working with employers, in order to prevent the escalation of off-the-books employment.

From artificially created conditions of full employment, the market transition led to the restructuring of the organization of work. The process of privatization and a cost/benefit approach forced many businesses to lay off labour force. The unemployment levels shot up to 21.4 per cent for Bulgaria and 15 per cent for Sofia in September 1993. From 1993 to 1995 there is a steady decline of unemployment in Sofia, after which there is still a decline in 1998 and 1999, but the general levels are pretty stable across the months and come to an annual rate of 5 per cent in 1998 and 4.1 per cent in 1999.

Unemployment is still a major problem in Bulgaria, associated mainly with the privatization and closure of state-owned enterprises. Compared to other cities in the country, Sofia and the Sofia Municipality have the lowest levels of unemployment, certainly considerably lower than the national rate of unemployment of 16 per cent in 1998 and 18 per cent in 1999. Together with the disproportionate concentration of FDI in Sofia, and the highest number of jobs being available there,[8] together with the concentration of the most educated and professional people, we can easily see support for the argument about bifurcation or polarization of places within regions in the current era (Sassen, 1991; Frey, 1993). The population and demographic structure described in the following paragraphs also attest to a high probability of uneven development, where Sofia and possibly other large cities like Varna and Plovdiv will continue to draw population and capital from the smaller places, which in turn may lead to further depopulation and underdevelopment of smaller urban and non-urban areas.

There is a tendency of decrease in the Bulgarian urban population, and three processes account for this: low natural increase, emigration, and migration to Sofia. Sofia is the only city that is still gaining population rather than losing it. As of the end of 1998, the population of Sofia Municipality was 1,199,708, 52.4 per cent of which are women. In 1991, the natural increase rate was of negative value ($-1.2$ per 1,000 people) for the first time, and this fact has become a steady trend, reaching a negative peak of $-5.6$ per 1,000 in 1997 and slightly declining to $-3$ in 2000 but still remaining negative.

The density of Sofia's population is the largest in the country. The fertility rate (as measured by the birth rate in Table 12.2) has been constantly decreasing since 1980, but the infant mortality rate is decreasing also. Sofia is the only city in Bulgaria to retain its population in the last democratic decade. The forecast for 2030 is that despite the natural decrease, Sofia's population will stabilize at around 1.2–1.3 million people because Sofia will retain the attractiveness of a capital city.

Comparisons between 1990 and 1998 show considerable changes in the age structure of the Bulgarian capital. The number of people below economically active age (15 years of age) declined by 53,000 and as a proportion of Sofia's population decreased from 19.9 to 15.5 per cent. The number of people of economically active age increased by 41,000 people and from 58.4 to 62 per cent of the population. There is also an absolute increase $-9,000$ – of people above the economically active age group, which now constitute 22.5 per cent of the total population as opposed to 21.7 per cent in 1990. The ageing of the population in Sofia may create a situation where less young people will replace

Table 12.2 Basic demographic indicators for the Sofia Municipality

| Indicators | 1980 | 1985 | 1994 | 1995 | 1996 | 1997 | 1998[*] | 1999[*] | 2000[*] |
|---|---|---|---|---|---|---|---|---|---|
| Population density (per sq.km) | 826.5 | 916.8 | 909.2 | 909.9 | 907.1 | 908.3 | 892.2 | 901.1 | 909.1 |
| Sex ratio (women to 1,000 men) | 1,110 | 1,066 | 1,085 | 1,090 | 1,092 | 1,097 | 1,102 | 1,104 | 1,102 |
| Birth rate (per 1,000 inhabitants) | 13.8 | 12.1 | 8.6 | 7.9 | 7.9 | 7.2 | 7.8 | 8.0 | 9.1 |
| Death rate (per 1,000 inhabitants) | 8.7 | 9.3 | 11.5 | 11.9 | 12.1 | 12.8 | 12.5 | 12.0 | 12.1 |
| Natural increase (per 1,000 inhabitants) | 5.1 | 2.8 | −2.9 | −4.0 | −4.2 | −5.6 | −4.7 | −4.0 | −3.0 |
| Infant mortality rate (per 1,000 live births) | 18.9 | 13.4 | 12.1 | 12.9 | 12.4 | 11.7 | 11.1 | 10.8 | 7.9 |
| New marriages per year (per 1,000 inhabitants) | 9.6 | 7.8 | 5.2 | 5.5 | 5.2 | 5.0 | 5.6 | 5.7 | 5.3 |

Note: * National Statistical Institute (2002).
*Source:* National Centre for Regional Development and Housing Policy (1999c).

their older counterparts on the labour market. At the end of 1996, every third person in Sofia was of retirement age or older (UNDP, 1997: 107). Another fact that attests to population ageing is the increase in the mean age of Sofia's population – it changed from 37.3 years in 1990 to 39.1 years in 1998 (Obshtina, 1999).

As outlined above, the city's profile points to some of the positive changes taking place in the capital and at the same time speaks about the problematic areas in this conurbation. The industrial plans are closing down due to either liquidation of loss-making enterprises or downsizing in the process of privatization and optimization of production and labour costs. Unemployment in Sofia, however, is still the lowest because of its lively economic environment, where most government jobs are located, as well as the new sectors such as banking and finance, insurance, and real estate. The spur of private economic activities endows the city with a dynamic face; at the same time it creates conditions of informal economy, where workers have no social security, no health insurance, and no retirement plans. Sofia is the only city in the country to gain population; at the same time, the population of Sofia is ageing, and this will put additional pressure on the city government to expand its social programmes. Meanwhile, the city government can no longer rely on state government subsidies: as of 1999 government subsidies made up only 12 per cent of municipal revenues.

The next section's inquiry into the specific housing conditions in Sofia extends further the logic leading us from the larger national macro-economic context through the socio-economic context in the capital to the daily lives of Sofiantsi.

## Housing Conditions

How did the radical macro-economic and political changes reflect upon the housing sector? There seems to be a general consensus among housing scholars that the reforms in the housing sector of most East European countries are still not a high national priority and were delayed by the overhaul of macro-economic policy and industrial privatization (Andrusz, Harloe, and Szelényi, 1996; Clapham et al., 1996; Hegedüs et al., 1996). Most changes, in both policies and outcomes, have occurred as a result of new macro-economic and fiscal realities or social and economic pressures (Struyk, 1996). Clapham (1995) reinforces Kemeny's (1995) stand that political choices and commitment to a market economy have led to a move towards a dualistic housing model in East Europe, which emphasizes private ownership and market allocation. In the dualistic model dominant in the Anglo-Saxon world and most Western European countries, private and public rented housing are distinct and the public sector is prevented from effectively competing with the owner-occupied sector. The result is a residual public sector, which serves the needs of the poorest households. By contrast the unitary system has integrated the public and private sectors and housing policies, and tenure-neutral public rental systems house a large and diverse segment of the population (as in Sweden, the Netherlands, and Germany). It seems to us, however, that at least in Bulgaria the dualistic model was not chosen because it represents a clear break from the past, as Clapham (1995) argues. Neither has it been chosen for the symbolic value of a move towards a market-orientated economy. The emphasis put on housing commodification since 1989 is driven by the overall market transition in the conditions of fiscal crises and subsidy cuts. The impact of market reforms on the housing system is especially profound given the previous heavy state subsidies. As a direct consequence of economic globalization, at the urging of the IMF, no further direct subsidies for housing are being included in the state budget (Hoffman and Koleva, 1993). The cut in subsidies affected dramatically the number of housing units built, which is shown in Table 12.3.

The impact is so dramatic in part because of prior investment in big housing estates, a common feature for all former socialist countries. The process of building housing estates on a mass scale started in the mid-1960s in many large Eastern European cities (French and Hamilton, 1979; Koleva and Dandolova, in Turner, Hegedüs, and Tosics, 1992). For more than 20 years the relative share of state housing construction (municipal dwellings, dwellings for compensation of owners after reconstruction, dwellings for sale, state organizations' dwellings)

Table 12.3  Basic housing indicators

| Housing indicators | Bulgaria | | Sofia | |
|---|---|---|---|---|
| | 1990 | 1997 | 1990 | 1997 |
| Number of housing units | 3,387,000 | 3,434,000 | 487,000 | 480,000 |
| Number of housing units built by state-owned enterprises | 13,267 | 1,974 | 4,586 | 1,228 |
| Number of housing units built by private builders | 12,777 | 5,478 | 1,965 | 98 |
| Total number of units built | 26,044 | 7,452 | 6,551 | 1,326 |
| Public rental sector (%) | 6.6 | 7.1 | 11.6 | 12.8 |
| Private rental sector (%) | 1.5 | 3.2 | 1.8 | 4.0 |
| Privately owned (%) | 91.7 | 89.4 | 86.4 | 83.2 |
| Number of households | 2,964,600 | 2,979,600 | 461,700 | 472,400 |
| Housing utility expenditure to average annual household income,rental sector (%) | 6.4 | 11.6 | 7.2 | 12.3 |
| Housing utility expenditure to average annual household income, privately owned sector (%) | 7.2 | 14.5 | 8.0 | 15.9 |
| Average market price of housing unit to average annual income of household (%) | 474 | 700 | 987 | 1,416 |

Source: National Centre for Regional Development and Housing Policy (1999c).

exceeded 75 per cent. In certain periods more than 68,000 dwellings were built annually, which illustrates exactly the great social and economic commitment of the state (UN/ECE, Committee on Human Settlements, 1993). Also, the state-owned enterprises which built them were heavily subsidized by the government on many levels: fuel subsidies for material production and transportation, direct funding of materials production companies to cover operating losses, the provision of land and units at prices below the state's cost, and artificially low interest rates on construction and mortgage loans (Strong, Reiner, and Szyrmer, 1996; Clapham et al., 1996). The cuts affected all those subsidized areas.

As evident in Table 12.3, the number of housing units built by state-owned enterprises sharply declined between 1990 and 1997, both for Bulgaria and for its capital, Sofia. The number of housing units built by private builders has also decreased substantially from 12,777 to 5,478 for Bulgaria and from 1,965 to 98 for Sofia. Two other very specific features of Bulgaria's housing system are shown in the numbers in Table 12.3. First, the number of units in the country built by state-owned enterprises (13,267) was almost the same as the number of units built by private builders (12,777) in 1990. Since 1990 is very close to the beginning of market reforms, this illustrates the fact that the private production of housing was a significant part of the country's socialist housing provision. The proportion of private construction varied throughout the socialist period, but private housing cooperatives and individually built houses were always part of the housing production.

The second specific feature of Bulgaria, until the massive housing privatization in other East European countries in recent years, is the high rate of private homeownership. Sofia shares many common features with other East European cities, yet is a specific case of the highest homeownership rates in the former socialist bloc. In East Berlin, for example, only a small amount of private housing existed before 1990; the rate as of 1995 is reported to still be 5.5 per cent (Haeusserman and Kapphan, 1999). In West Berlin the rate of owner-occupied housing is not very much higher – 12.5 per cent in 1993. Thus, the unified Berlin housing market may be described as a renter's market with a strong tendency towards privatization. In Budapest the state rental sector constituted 52 per cent of housing units in 1990 (Bodnar, 1996). In Czechoslovakia, owner-occupied housing was at 49 per cent in 1992 (Peter Michalovich, in Clapham et al., 1996), but still public rental and cooperative housing had substantial shares, 21 and 18 per cent respectively. Poland's ownership was also split in a similar way in 1988 – private housing constituted 43.5 per cent, municipal housing 19.4 per cent, and cooperative housing 24.3 per cent (Strong, Reiner, and Szyrmer, 1996). These examples illustrate why privatization of housing plays a central role in the urban transitions of East Europe. Even though there is a process of housing privatization and restitution of pre-1944 real-estate property in Sofia, this process is not as important for the urban landscape as it is in most former socialist cities.[9]

Previous research has pointed to evidence of increasing urban polarization in Sofia after 1989, when communist rule was peacefully abolished and the first democratic parliament was voted in (Vesselinov, 1998, 2000a). This increase in urban polarization is based on several factors: increases in income inequality, increases in housing costs (prohibitively high for most people), fiscal and home financing constraints, and a sharp decline in housing construction. Another acute problem in conditions of market transition is the increasing price of electricity, heating, and other housing costs such as building maintenance. As shown in Table 12.3, the proportion of annual average household income in Sofia (and Bulgaria) to cover housing costs doubled between 1990 and 1997 for private owners, and almost doubled for renters. The prices of electricity and heating increased numerous times in this period and after that as well. In 2000 the planned division of the state electric company (NEK) was postponed, because the adequate legal and price regulatory controls had not been passed by the national legislature (Alexandrova, 2000a). In the programme for the division, however, it is mandated that prices for electricity will continue to increase, so that they cover the private investors' costs and profits. Until 1 July 2001 the electricity prices for commercial and private users have to merge at US$0.04 per kWh. The state subsidies still allocated to the industry will be for capital investment and restructuring and not to subsidize user costs. On the other hand, however, the government succeeded in negotiating with the IMF a price increase for private users of only 4 per cent as opposed to 7.54 per cent starting 1 August 2000 (Alexandrova, 2000b). In return for the deal, the government takes responsibility for ensuring complete price liberalization of electricity by 1 January 2002 and guaranteeing transparency in the restructuring processes of NEK.

Another piece of success in the last negotiations with the IMF is the freezing of the heat price paid by private users in the winter season, which was supposed to be subject to increase. The problem with heating remains acute in Sofia, however, because the housing units with central heating are 77.2 per cent of all units in the city, as opposed to 18.1 per cent in the country. A project developed by the World Bank has postulated that for financial betterment of the heat-producing industry about 244 million lev (US$150 million) will be needed. The suggestion is to borrow these funds from private investors (the World Bank and European Bank for Reconstruction and Development) under government guarantees (Alexandrova, 2000c). The credit, however, means increasing the country's indebtedness to international financial institutions, whereas the foreign debt, at the same time, is limited under the conditions of the IMF. The more important problem is that if the profits after the restructuring of the industry are not high enough, the payments on the credit will have to come from the government budget. Either way, consumers will have to cover the costs, which will continue to increase.[10] The consumers themselves in the last few years have reacted to the price increases by discontinuing the heating in their apartments or simply by not paying their bills. By the end of 1999, the amount of unpaid bills for the seven largest heating plants is above 101 million lev or about US$46 million (Alexandrova, 2000c). One way to address this problem is the introduction of special tariffs for heat, where one component of the price is fixed and the other varies according to consumption (Alexandrova, 2000b).

The problem of maintenance of housing units comes to the fore as well, with major issues surrounding the maintenance of housing estates. A substantive number of housing units in Sofia (46.4 per cent) are part of the big housing estates and constitute the basis for thinking about "humanization" of the urban environment (Master Plan of Sofia, 2000). Given the change to municipal fiscal solvency, the municipalities can no longer allocate subsidies for the maintenance of housing estates (National Centre for Regional Development and Housing Policy, 1999a). Housing estates continue to deteriorate because the large majority of owners are unable to afford the maintenance by themselves. The parts that are common, like staircases, electricity in staircases, and elevators, have to be maintained with mutual agreement and equal financial participation of the homeowners. Any renovation that has to take place in common areas, such as painting of walls, has to be agreed upon and paid for by all families. The local associations of homeowners, however, do not have a legal status that could give them the power to enforce the common property rules and regulations. And in times of financial hardship, maintaining common spaces is the first family expenditure to be reconsidered. A sociological survey based on a national sample for Bulgaria, conducted in June 1999, shows that 34.4 per cent of people in the country and 49.6 per cent of Sofiantsi are not satisfied with the way common areas are maintained (National Centre for Regional Development and Housing Policy, 1999b). The respondents said that this was because homeowners did not have enough means to spare for maintenance (22 per cent of all respondents), and because homeowners did not give their share to maintain the shared spaces (15.4 per cent of all respondents).

The difficulties in maintenance and rehabilitation of housing are reflected in the spatial distribution of housing as well. The most problematic areas in the city in terms of quality of housing are shown in Fig. 12.4.[11] Some neighbourhoods in the central part of the city and to the north of this area, shown as the zones with the most damaged housing on the map, are of a high level of depreciation and dilapidation. The buildings there need a complex programme of rehabilitation, including infrastructure renovation. The "black zones", as they are called, are three neighbourhoods where there is a high concentration of Gypsy/Roma population. The housing in these parts is in the worst condition for the city, with slums and shanty housing, and very poor infrastructure. Also, these neighbourhoods lack social services and have high self-occupancy and crime rates, compared to the other parts of the city. Even though they are relatively few in number, measures have to be taken to preclude these areas from further deterioration.

The most striking spatial pattern is the one related to differentiation of neighbourhoods in the capital and based on housing prices. There have been

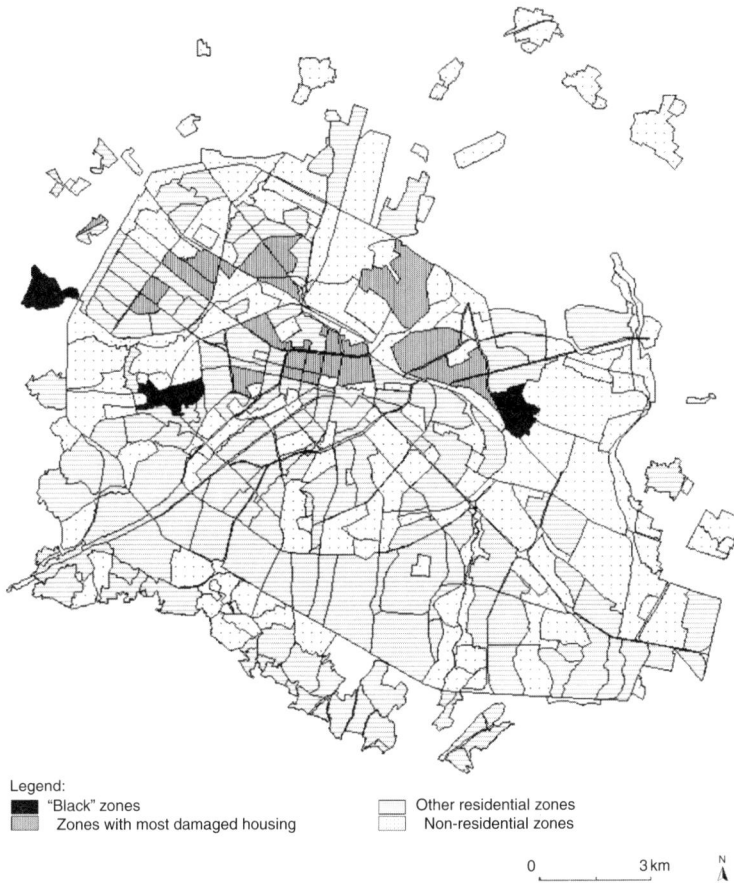

Fig. 12.4  Problem neighbourhoods in Sofia compact city.

*Source:* National Centre for Regional Development and Housing Policy, 1999c.

distinctions between different parts of the city before, especially between centre city and the more prestigious neighbourhoods on the one hand, and the housing estates on the other during the socialist period. The distinctions in quality of housing and the surrounding environment have happened largely because of the way the city developed. The central parts were built by the 1960s and consist mostly of buildings of up to eight storeys, with large open spaces for parks and recreation. The technology developed in the former Soviet Union during late 1960s to early 1970s allowed for building of big housing estates, constructed by pre-fabricated building blocks. The housing estates were built throughout the areas surrounding the city centre.

These distinctions notwithstanding, the current housing prices by neighbourhood not only express a pattern of differentiation, but also of clustering.

Fig. 12.5  Housing markets in Sofia compact city.

*Source:* National Centre for Regional Development and Housing Policy, 1999c.


Fig. 12.5 shows the asking price per square meter for housing units in each residential zone, which is the closest approximation of a neighbourhood in Sofia.[12] As is clearly seen in the map, the first two categories outline the central areas of the city, reflecting mostly the older city parts. The city core is where a lot of commercial property is located. There is a growing demand for office space for national and international businesses with the formation of a central business district in the centre of the city, which in turn increases the price of housing in that area as well. The images of Sofia in Fig. 12.6 (a–f) demonstrate the mixture of ancient Sofia with the government buildings of the socialist era, the existence of open spaces and trees even in the very heart of the city, and the

Fig. 12.6 Images of Sofia. (a) St George Rotunda, fourth century, in the midst of the Presidency and Government Offices. (b) Slavejkov Square, book market in front of typical city centre housing. (c) The former Communist Party Headquarters, now Parliament Offices. (d) City Centre, commercial street Vitsha. (e) Inner city, mixed-use housing neighbourhood complex Lagera. (f) Post-Socialist suburban gated mansion on Dragalevsi street.

mixture of new fashion shops like Max Mara and old building style on the busiest commercial street of Sofia, Vitosha Street.

Several characteristics make the neighbourhoods in the price range of US$303 to US£396 per square metre attractive to Sofiantsi. There are three parks in this area – the Borisov Garden, the Loven Park, and the Southern Park – and these neighbourhoods are part of the era previous to the pre-fabricated estates, with relatively low-rise brick and stone housing, more spacious apartments, and easy access to the centre and thus to entertainment and cultural institutions, universities and schools, and medical facilities.

The third price category, from US$224 to US$291 per square metre, is mostly a mixed area of relatively higher-status housing estates and some family housing. And the last category, from US$154 to US$218 per square metre, represents the wide belt of housing estates. With the exception of places like Vrazhdebna, Poduene, Gorubljane, and Bankja, where people live in single-family houses, most of the neighbourhoods in this belt are high-rise, pre-fabricated, big housing estates. Transportation to the centre is rather difficult and slow, the choices for shopping and entertainment are limited, and access to hospitals is also limited. Thus, the price differentiation between sections of Sofia reflects a complex set of circumstances relating to quality of housing, access to the city centre, and the location of green zones in the city. Differentiations between urban neighbourhoods and segmented urban housing markets have long been observed in scholarly literature (e.g. Logan and Bian, 1993; Zhou and Logan, 1996; Marcuse and van Kempen, 2000). The danger in Sofia is of having the housing estate area further decline and become socially and functionally separated from the older parts of the city. Since more than 50 per cent of Sofia's residents live in housing estates, the further deterioration of those areas will adversely affect most urbanites' daily lives.

Coming from the larger scope of macro-economic reforms through the changes at city level, in this section of the chapter we discuss the more striking urban transformations related to the housing sector. The transformations in housing are important because housing is part of every person's everyday life and because the life chances of people in the current era are becoming more and more entangled with the qualities of their immediate urban living space – where the residents live in the city determines their access to a particular lifestyle, to time spent travelling to and from jobs, to air quality, etc. In Sofia, as much as in many other post-socialist cites, increased differentiation is taking place between neighbourhoods (Pichler-Milanović, 1998; see also Chapters 3 and 8), between people who can afford to live in better neighbourhoods and those stuck in deteriorating housing estates and "black" areas, and between those who will continue to own valuable property and those who will either cease to be homeowners or whose property will depreciate.

These changes have to be considered when we talk about the role of economic globalization, because the agents of globalization are not only the larger financial institutions and the trans-national companies. The processes of privatization and FDI are not the only aspects involved in globalization. The most important agents of globalization are people, and it is the daily lives of people that are most affected by globalization. As urban sociologists, we argue that *people* weld together national economic prosperity and sustainable economic growth. The disparity in urban conditions affects directly and adversely most Sofia residents' lives and thus is contradictory to the happy merging of rising national and urban development.

If urban disparities are taken seriously and prevented with sound urban policy, the relative macro-economic stability achieved in Bulgaria in recent years can be coupled with the strategic geopolitical position of the Bulgarian capital, leading to the firm establishment of Sofia as a powerful node in the new European urban network. In the next section we will outline the evolving position of the city in the changing European urban landscape.

## Sofia: Regional Centre in the Balkans and Hub of the New Europe

The new Master Plan for Sofia (Master Plan of Sofia, 2000) addresses both the problematic aspects of city development and the strong chances of Sofia as a transportation, communication, and information centre of an integrated Europe. The major goals set in the Master Plan for urban policy-makers are to find solutions regarding "humanizing" of the big housing estates environment, to deal with the intensely built parts of the central city, to address the problem of "black" neighbourhoods, and to zone new territories for housing within the city limits. The prognosis, based on expert evaluation and assessment, is that Sofia will not need to expand beyond its current territory at least until 2020. The threat of sprawl is thus deterred for the future, but at the same time sociological surveys have determined, as we saw with the prices of housing detailed above, that depressed areas are forming in the city, and that new richer areas are under formation as well. There is no specific policy delineation, however, of how and when this process will be addressed.

On the other hand, a clear understanding comes through of the new place for the city in the process of European integration. Future policy, it is argued, will revolve around and incorporate the new realities of (a) the emerging role of Sofia as a regional centre in the Balkans, (b) the increased transportation and communication importance of the city in Europe, and (c) the city as the most dynamic economic region in the country. In recognition of the need for a larger policy framework within which to address urban disparities, consideration of the new role of Sofia in the larger European context is unequivocally based in the national economic and political strategy.

As we have argued, the two central goals of Bulgarian economic and political strategy connected with prospective membership of the European Union are (1) meeting the Maastricht criteria for membership of the economic and monetary union, and (2) establishing Bulgaria as an infrastructure centre in South-east Europe (Triffonova and Kashoukeeva-Nousheva, 1999). The priority fields within the second goal are road transportation, railway and airport management, development and modernization of the transport network in sections of mutual interest, and the adoption of a consistent transport policy compatible with EU policies.

The purpose of EU transport policy in general is to secure possibilities for the movement of people and goods within the united internal market and to and from third countries, the optimization of the technical and organizational aspects of transport between various regions and across borders, and guarantees for the ecological dimensions of the field. Particular attention is paid to the development of combined transport, or multi-modal transportation links, whereby the goal is to have competition between various operator services and not so much between various types of transportation. In essence the policy states that pan-European transport corridors should be multi-modal, although on the basis of concrete socio-economic and environmental analysis one type of transport may be given priority.

The most important development in the 1990s was the Trans-European Transport Network of the European Union, adopted in 1996 by the European Parliament and the Council of Europe. The Trans-European Transport Network will contribute to the main goals of the European Union, creating a working internal market and strengthening the economic and social cohesion of the regions. With respect to countries external to the European Union, a process is taking place for integration with the Trans-European Networks through the Transport Corridor System. This was initially orientated towards the physical connection of the transport systems of Western and Eastern Europe, following the decision taken on the island of Crete, Greece, in 1994, to construct nine coordinated corridors. At a later stage, at the Third Pan-European Transport Conference in Helsinki in 1997, the network was supplemented and orientated as a route to the zones of trans-continental cooperation. Of particular interest is the Eastern section, because of the greater commodity flows expected in the future from Central Asia to Europe. The concept of "transport corridors" represents a new area of cooperation, which serves not only to stimulate economic development and employment, but also to assist in the integration process.

Five of the proposed 10 corridors pass through Bulgaria: No. 4 (Berlin–Dresden–Prague–Vienna–Budapest–Belgrade–Sofia–Thessaloniki–Istanbul), No. 7 (goes along the River Danube), No. 8 (Durres–Tirana–Skopje–Sofia–Plovdiv–Burgas–Varna), No. 9 (Helsinki–Kiev–Kishinev–Bucharest–Dimitrovgrad–Alexandroupolis), and No. 10 (Salzburg–Ljubljana–Belgrade–Nis–Sofia–Istanbul). The development of the European transport corridors is led by the Transport Working Group of the G-24; the international financial institutions (European Bank for Reconstruction and Development, European Investment Bank, World Bank) fund and observe the process of construction. The memorandums of understanding between the countries of a certain corridor emphasize the will of all the participants to coordinate the development of these routes and to direct necessary resources. Despite the profit-making interests of all financial institutions that sponsor the project, the development of these transport networks does in fact stimulate cooperation between the countries, which in the Balkan region is of particular importance.

In the above context, having Sofia as a connecting point in three of the five corridors that pass through Bulgaria illustrates the already increasing importance of the city in the European urban network. Sofia is becoming an important factor in connecting the regions of Western and Central Europe with Ukraine and Russia on the one side, and Middle and Near East Asia on the other. One of the EU's priorities is to establish a reliable system of transportation and information exchange, through which goods and services can move fluidly back and forth between Europe and Asia. Sofia thus has a strategic place and a new role to play in the context of intensification of the links between the two continents. The city's strategic role is based on three factors: first, the city's geographic position as a crossroads between Northern Europe and the southern parts of the Balkan Peninsula, between Central Europe and Turkey, and between Western/Central Europe and Asia through the Black Sea routes. The second factor is that Sofia has become a centre where international relief organizations are stationed helping the revival of the regions struck by the war in the former Yugoslavia. And third, the Balkan region is rapidly changing and regional interactions are increasing. Bulgaria has played a central role in bringing the cooperation of the Balkan countries to a new level, and Sofia has hosted many regional political and economic initiatives and meetings in the last 10 years.

Of particular importance for Sofia is the European transport corridor Adriatic Sea–Black Sea, corridor No. 8. It will connect southern Russia and the Caucuses region, as well as the Middle East, with Italy and southern Europe. It will include rail, road, and sea routes in the multi-modal fashion described above. The development of Eurocorridor No. 10 was added during the pan-European conference in Helsinki and in the section Budapest–Belgrade–Sofia–Istanbul is the shortest and most convenient road linking Western Europe and the Middle East. The integration of Bulgaria into the river transport routes in corridor No. 7 (Rain–Main–Danube) presents an excellent opportunity to develop further the links between river and road routes that already exist in Bulgaria. Thus the Bulgarian transport system will connect the Danube River route with the Aegean and Adriatic Sea routes, which will strengthen further Sofia's "middle-man" position in the route Vidin–Sofia–Thessaloniki. Sofia is not only emerging as a central dispatcher city in the Balkans, the links it facilitates between three continents – Europe, Asia, and Africa – will bring more revenue for the city and add to its leading economic position in the country.

The strategic role of Sofia in the Balkan region and in the new, integrated Europe is defined also by two other more important factors: the number of

Table 12.4  Percentage of students enrolled in Sofia's educational institutions

| Year/educational institutions | General schools | Special schools | Vocational schools | Art schools | College | Universities | Number of students |
|---|---|---|---|---|---|---|---|
| 1991/1992 | 55.9 | 0.4 | 5.4 | 7.4 | 3.1 | 27.8 | 263,281 |
| 1992/1993 | 55.6 | 0.5 | 5.4 | 6.7 | 2.8 | 29.0 | 256,538 |
| 1993/1994 | 53.9 | 0.4 | 5.2 | 6.2 | 2.7 | 31.5 | 257,699 |
| 1994/1995 | 52.5 | 0.4 | 4.5 | 6.4 | 2.4 | 33.7 | 262,855 |
| 1995/1996 | 51.2 | 0.4 | 3.7 | 6.7 | 2.4 | 35.5 | 267,030 |
| 1996/1997 | 50.4 | 0.4 | 3.0 | 6.8 | 2.6 | 36.7 | 262,434 |
| 1997/1998 | 50.2 | 0.4 | 2.5 | 6.8 | 3.2 | 37.0 | 264,055 |
| 1998/1999* | 48.0 | 0.5 | 2.0 | 6.3 | 3.4 | 39.0 | 269,560 |
| 1999/2000* | 48.7 | 0.5 | 1.9 | 6.6 | 3.0 | 38.4 | 261,468 |
| 2000/2001* | 48.8 | 0.5 | 2.2 | 6.9 | 2.6 | 38.1 | 258,018 |

Note: *National Statistical Institute, Sofia (2002).
Source: National Centre for Regional Development and Housing Policy (1999c).

educated and professional people living in the capital, who can perform the functions of the new information economy, and the increased level of FDI in the last few years. The largest proportion of professional schools, colleges, and universities of higher education is concentrated in Sofia: 13 per cent of all professional schools in the country (a total of 337) are in Sofia. The runner-up is Plovdiv, with 6 per cent. 19 per cent of all colleges (a total of 47) that confer associate degrees are in Sofia; the next in line is Varna, with 8.5 per cent. And lastly, 51 per cent of all higher education institutions (a total of 41) are in Sofia; next is Plovdiv with 12 per cent (as of 1994; National Centre for Regional Development and Housing Policy, 1999).

The number of students in educational institutions by type of education also reveals the high concentration of schools and universities in Sofia, as well as the increasing proportion of people each year who are in the process of obtaining their Bachelor's or higher degrees (Table 12.4).

Even in the most difficult crisis years, 1996 and 1997, the proportion of students enrolled in universities continued to rise, following a trend starting in 1991. In the current information age, having an educated workforce is far more important than having a cheap workforce, as was the case with FDI in Latin America and other third world countries. The high percentage of economically active population with higher and professional education (66 per cent) in Sofia is a serious advantage in attracting the high-technology, communication, and information industries. Another advantage of the Bulgarian education system is that the higher education institutions in Sofia have a long tradition of educating students from all Balkan countries, from many African countries, and from the countries of the Middle East. The educational system has changed a lot in the last decade, but education remains an important social value and will undoubtedly play a significant role in establishing the city's position on the European market.

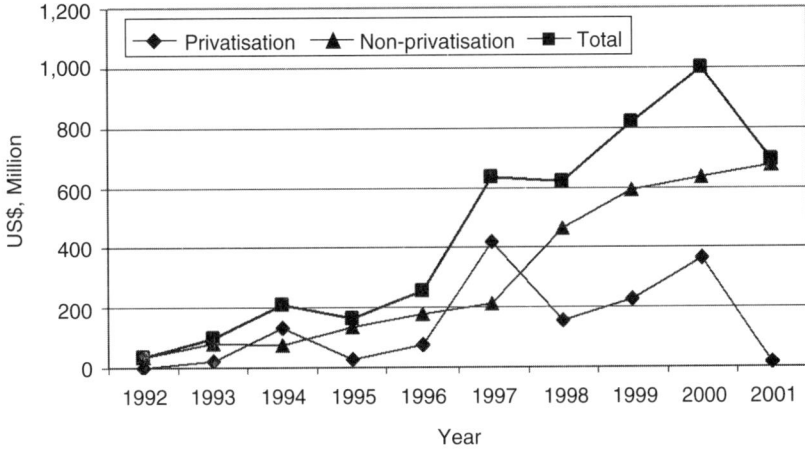

Fig. 12.7  FDI inflows in Bulgaria.
*Source:* Agency for Foreign Investment, 2002.

Investments in transportation and information technologies (see Triffonova and Kashoukeeva-Nousheva, 1999) add to the higher level of FDI in Bulgaria and Sofia since 1995 (Fig. 12.7). While the war in Kosovo has strengthened Bulgaria's position in its negotiations to obtain additional funds from the international financial institutions, it has made it more difficult to attract private capital flows. In 1997, FDI was US$636.2 million, which was the highest amount since 1989 and more than double the amount for 1996. In 1998 the level of FDI slowed down, due mainly to the crisis in the emerging markets (Miller, 1999) as well as problems in privatization, and reached US$436 million total (Agency for Foreign Investment, 1999). The confidence of investors returned in 1999 and 2000, whereby FDI peaked to slightly over US$1 billion in 2000. Germany, Belgium, the US, and the Netherlands take the four leading positions in total FDI for the period from 1992 to 30 September 1998, investing respectively 17.56, 16.48, 9.19, and 6.21 per cent of all FDI in Bulgaria.

An interesting comparison constitutes the structure of FDI by economic sector in Bulgaria and Sofia. The bulk of all FDI in Bulgaria for the period from 1992 to 30 September 1997 was in industry, 49.7 per cent. The sector drawing the second largest proportion of FDI is trade – 16.6 per cent – while the third largest amount goes to finance, credit, and insurance – 11.13 per cent. The structure of investment in Sofia reflects the investors' desire to have a secure and fast return on their investments. For the period from 1992 to 1998 the bulk of investments in the capital city is in the trade sector – 37.3 per cent of all investments. The second place is taken by the finance, credit, and insurance, sector with 21 per cent, and third comes the industry sector with 12.9 per cent (Obshtina, 1999a).

The leading role of these three sectors – trade; finance, credit, and insurance; and industry – both at the national and local levels, signifies the modern stage of Bulgarian macro-economic environment.

For the whole period from 1992 to 1999 the capital city of Bulgaria has attracted 44.6 per cent of all FDI in Bulgaria. The urban region second in scale and importance, the coastal city of Varna, attracted four times less than the investments made in Sofia. The third largest total foreign investments are made in Plovdiv – about 12 times less than in the Sofia region. Therefore, the strength of Sofia in attracting FDI undoubtedly points to the leading role of the capital in the urban hierarchy of Bulgaria.

Another act of international recognition for the new role of Sofia is the ranking of cities, based on the level of functions cities are expected to perform in the twenty-first century. The cities are ranked mainly according to their performance of national and regional functions, and the extent to which they are establishing a reputation as centres of European or international significance (*Perspectives and Strategies of Spatial Development Policy in the Central European, Danubian, and Adriatic Area*, 1998). According to this perspective, Sofia, together with Prague, Budapest, Warsaw, and Bucharest, is expected to rise in its role from a city of national importance to a city of European importance.

## Conclusion

In the context of economic globalization and transition to a market economy, the city of Sofia is ready to take on new responsibilities for the twenty-first century based on the leading role it already plays in the Balkans and based on the processes of policy harmonization of the new and integrated Europe. In order for the city to live up to the new realities and successfully enhance its leadership as a centre of prosperity and stability in the Balkans, the policy-makers in Sofia must address promptly the increasing urban disparities. The changes in the city, and particularly the changes in housing and neighbourhood conditions, affect directly and adversely most residents' daily lives. Increases in urban inequality jeopardize the cohesiveness and continuity of the urban space, at a time when cohesiveness and continuity are most needed. Only an integrated city can fulfil the new demands of an integrated Europe.

Integration and cooperation are also concepts central to the overall process of globalization. Globalization means integration; it means connectivity not only of capital flows, goods, and services, but more so of people. Globalization means the increased consciousness of the world as a whole (Harding, 1996). Increased social divisions, spatial differentiations, and urban disparities are in fact inherently contradictory to the whole globalization project.

The institutional agents of globalization in Europe set a policy agenda intended to bring cohesion and even development to all parts of Europe. The same agents, then, should be alarmed at the signs of rising disparities in the post-socialist capital cities. These disparities are particularly disturbing because cities usually represent the leading economic regions in the national economic space. Sofia is one of those regions, the most economically developed and dynamic region in Bulgaria at a time of macro-economic stability in the country. Sofia, as much as all other post-socialist cities, has a serious stake in European prosperity and is in a position to make a significant contribution to it. The question to think about is how to ensure that there are no born losers on this speedy urban highway to Europe.

## Acknowledgements

We are indebted to many people in Bulgaria who generously provided data and advice during the period of conducting this research. In particular, we would like to thank Dr Ognyan Minchev, Director of the Institute for Regional and International Studies in Sofia, and his staff for their continuous support. We are very grateful to Peter Dikov, Alexander Mihajlov, Dimiter Dimitrov, Stojcho Motev, and Sergey Tsvetarski.

## Notes

1 Many macro-economic analysts attest to this fact; see Bulgarian National Bank Annual Report for 1998; Report of the Agency for Economic Analysis and Forecasting (1999); Miller (1999).
2 State-run enterprises were placed in two groups depending on their size and importance. Group A included 30 key enterprises in infrastructure (mines and heating companies, the national railway, and Sofia municipal transport companies). Group B consisted of 41 enterprises, which in the final stage of the rehabilitation process had to be either privatized or liquidated (Agency for Economic Analysis and Forecasting, 1999).
3 Based on data from the National Statistical Institute as of 31 December 1997.
4 The data describing the economic characteristics of Sofia's economy are based on generalized statistical data from the annual income statements of 32,775 firms from the public and private sectors.
5 Based on data from Master Plan of Sofia, 2000.
6 Economically active population consists of all people older than 15 and has the same meaning as the country's labour force, which encompasses employed and unemployed people.
7 This is believed to be one reason for the larger rate of unemployment in Bulgaria as a whole; see OECD Economic Surveys: Bulgaria (1999).
8 According to an estimate, 9.3 per cent of all available jobs in 1999 were located in Sofia (data from the National Statistical Institute).
9 The restituted state-owned housing units in 1994 were 4.95 per cent for Bulgaria and 9.41 per cent in Sofia; the privatized units in 1993 were respectively 9.5 per cent and 12 per cent.
10 Heat prices for private users were as follows: 1997 – 16.94 lev per mWh; 1998 – 29.04; 1999 – 31.77; and 2000 – 36.97 (*Capital*, 8–14 July 2000).
11 Based on data from the National Centre for Regional Development and Housing Policy (1999).
12 Based on expert estimates, National Centre for Regional Development and Housing Policy (1997).

REFERENCES

Agency for Economic Analysis and Forecasting, *Annual Report*, Sofia: Bulgaria, 1999.

Galina Alexandrova, "MWF: Otlagame Razdeljaneto na NEK" [IMF: Postponing the Division of NEK], *Capital*, 6 February 2000a [http://www.capital.bg/].

——, "Pravitelstvoto Ne Otstapi Za Cenite Na Toka i Parnoto" [The Government Did Not Give in About the Costs for Electricity and Heating], *Capital*, 27 July 2000b [http://www.capital.bg/].

——, "Dojde li Vreme Razdelno Za Toplofikaciite" [Is it Time for Dividing NEK yet?], *Capital*, 11–17 March 2000c [http://www.capital.bg/].

Gregory Andrusz, Michael Harloe, and Iván Szelényi, *Cities after Socialism: Urban and Regional Change in Post-Socialist Societies*, Oxford: Blackwell Publishers, 1996.

Rumen Avramov, *The Role of a Currency Board in Financial Crises: The Case of Bulgaria* (Discussion Papers), Sofia: Bulgarian National Bank, 1999 [http://www.bnb.org/].

John D. Bell, *Bulgaria in Transition: Politics, Economics, Society, and Culture after Communism*, Boulder, Colorado: Westview Press, 1998.

Judith Bodnar, "He That Hath to Him Shall Be Given: Housing Privatisation in Budapest after Socialism", *International Journal of Urban and Regional Research* 20, 1996.

Centre for the Study of Democracy, *Bulgaria and the European Union: Towards an Institutional Infrastructure*, Sofia, 1998.

——, *Bulgaria's Capital Markets in the Context of EU Accession: A Status Report*, Sofia, 1999.

Sarah Busse, "Social Capital and the Informal Economy in Novosibirsk, Russia: Some Preliminary Observations", paper presented at the American Sociological Association Meeting, Washington D.C., 2000.

David Clapham, "Privatisation and the East European Housing Model", *Urban Studies* 32(4), 1995, pp. 679–694.

David Clapham, József Hegedüs, Keith Kintrea, and Iván Tosics, eds, *Housing Privatisation in Eastern Europe*, Westport: Greenwood Press, 1996.

Robert A. French and F. E. Ian Hamilton, eds, *The Socialist City: Spatial Structure and Urban Policy*, Chichester: John Wiley & Sons, 1979.

William Frey, "The New Urban Revival in the United States", *Urban Studies* 30, 1993, pp. 741–747.

H. Harussermann and A. Kappham, "Berlin", draft for the city chapter of UNU/IAS Book Project, *Project Globalization and Urban Transformations in Central and Eastern Europe*, 1999.

Alan Harding, "Is there a New Community Power and Why Should We Need One?", *International Journal of Urban and Regional Development* 20, 1996, pp. 637–655.

József Hegedüs, Stephen E. Mayo, and Iván Tosics, "Transition of the Housing Sector in the East Central European Countries", *Review of Urban and Regional Development Studies* 8, 1996, pp. 101–136.

Michael L. Hoffman and Maria T. Koleva, "Housing Policy Reform in Bulgaria", *Cities*, August 1993, pp. 208–223.

Jim Kemeny, *From Public Housing to the Social Market: Rental Policy Strategies in Comparative Perspective*, London, New York: Routledge, 1995.

John R. Logan and Yanji Bian, "Inequalities in Access to Community Resources in a Chinese City", *Social Forces* 72(2), 1993, pp. 555–576.

John R. Logan and Harvey L. Molotch, *Urban Fortunes: The Political Economy of Place*, Berkley: University of California Press, 1987.

John R. Logan and Todd Swanstrom, eds, *Beyond the City Limits*, Philadelphia: Temple University Press, 1992.

Peter Marcuse and Ronald van Kempen, eds, *Globalizing Cities: A New Spatial Order*, Oxford: Blackwell Publishers, 2000.

Jeffrey Miller, *The Currency Board in Bulgaria: The First Two Years* (Discussion Papers), Sofia: Bulgarian National Bank, 1999 [http://www.bnb.org].

National Centre for Regional Development and Housing Policy – Preliminary Research Phase, Master Plan of Sofia, Working Group, leading author Stoicho Motev, *Predvaritelni Prouchvania na OGP – Sofia, Razdel Obitavane i Zhilishten Fond, Etap Analiz i Diagnoza*, Sofia, 1999a.

National Centre for Regional Development and Housing Policy, *Otnoshenie kam poddrazhkata na obshtite chasti v zhilishtnite sgradi* [Attitude Towards Maintenance of Common Property in the Housing Estates], Sofia, 1999b.

——, *Plan Za Regionalno Razvitie na Oblast Sofia*, [Plan for Regional Development of Sofia], Sofia, July 1999c.

*New York Times*, "A Turbulent Trade Meeting", Editorial Desk, 28 November 1999.

Nikolay Nenovski and Kalin Hristov, *Monetary Policy Under the Currency Board: The Case of Bulgaria* (Discussion Papers), Sofia: Bulgarian National Bank, 1999 [http://www.bnb.org/].

Master Plan of Sofia: Draft, Project Director P. Terziev, Sofia, 2000.

*OECD Economic Surveys: Bulgaria*, Centre for Co-operation with the Economies in Transition, Organization for Economic Co-operation and Development, 1997.

Stolichna Obshtina, Otdel Pazarni Prouchvania I Analizi, *Sofia: Obzor za Sastojanieto na Regionalnata Ikonomika prez 1998 godina* [Sofia: Report on the Regional Economy in 1998], Sofia: Sofia Municipality, 1999.

*Perspectives and Strategies of Spatial Development Policy in the Central European, Danubian and Adriatic Area*, Bonn: European Commission, 1998.

Nataša Pichler-Milanović, "Globalisation, Regionalization and The Transformation of Central and Eastern European Cities Toward the 21st Century", paper presented at the conference "City, State and Region in Global Order: Toward the 21st Century", Hiroshima, Japan, 1998.

Hugo Priemus, "European Housing Policy: A Ten Points Program", keynote address at the European Network for Housing Research conference "Housing in the 21st Century: Fragmentation and Reorientation", Gavle, Sweden, 26–30 June 2000.

Saskia Sassen, *The Global City. New York, London, Tokyo*, Princeton: Princeton University Press, 1991.

——, *Globalisation and its Discontents*, New York: The New Press, 1999.

Standart-Comentary, "Uchitelite v Cjalata Strana Gotvjat Stachka," *Standart*, 4 September 2000 [http//www.standardnews.com/].

Ann Louise Strong, Thomas A. Reiner, and Janusz Szyrmer, *Transitions in Land and Housing: Bulgaria, The Czech Republic, and Poland*, New York: St Martin's Press, 1996.

Raymond Struyk, ed., *Economic Restructuring in the Former Soviet Bloc: Evidence from the Housing Sector*, Washington D.C.: The Urban Institute, 1996.

Elena Triffonova and Vanya Kashoukeeva-Nousheva, eds, *Regional Infrastructure Projects in South-Eastern Europe*, Sofia: Institute for Regional and International Studies, 1999.

Bengt Turner, Jozsef Hegedüs, and Iván Tosics, *The Reform in Housing in Eastern Europe and the Soviet Union*, London, New York: Routledge, 1992.

United Nations Development Program (UNDP), *Doklad za Razvitieto na Choveka: Grad Sofia*, [Report on Human Development: Sofia], Sofia, 1997.

UN/ECE, Committee on Human Settlements, Habitat Housing Workshop, *Evaluation of the Present Condition of the Bulgarian Housing Sector. Financial and Economic Aspects of Housing Reform in the Transition Countries of Europe*, Sofia, 1993.

Elena Vesselinov, "Housing Policy in Bulgaria: The Case of Sofia", paper presented at the conference "City, State and Region in Global Order: Toward the 21st Century", Hiroshima, Japan, 18–20 December 1998.

——, "The Continuing 'Wind of Change' in the Balkans: Globalisation and Housing Transformations in the City of Sofia", paper presented at the American Sociological Association Meeting in Washington D.C. (winner of the Outstanding Student Paper Award for 2000 of the Community and Urban Sociology Section of the American Sociological Association), 2000a.

——, "Housing Inequality in Sofia, Bulgaria", paper presented at the European Network for Housing Research conference "Housing in the 21st Century: Fragmentation and Reorientation", Gavle, Sweden, 26–30 June 2000b.

John Walton and David Saddon, *Free Markets and Food Riots: The Politics of Global Adjustment*, Oxford: Blackwell Publishers, 1996.

Min Zhou and John R. Logan, "Market Transition and the Commodification of Housing in Urban China", *International Journal of Urban and Regional Research* 20, 1996, pp. 400–421.

Iliana Zloch-Christy, ed., *Privatisation and Foreign Investments in Eastern Europe*, Westport, Conn.: Praeger Publishers, 1995.

——, ed., *Eastern Europe and the World Economy: Challenges of Transition and Globalization*, Cheltenham, UK: Edward Elgar, 1998.

# 13

# Baltic orientations: Globalization, regionalization, or "EU-ization"?

*Martin Åberg*

## Introduction: A Brave New World?

"The times they are a-changing"[1], so we have been told on a daily basis for the last 10 years or so. And undoubtedly, it is the case that deregulation, the IT revolution, and the internationalization of economies, or in one word "globalization", is producing – at an ever-increasing speed, it would seem – profound economic and social changes in a number of ways. This is particularly true of the world's major cities, the very nodes linking flows of capital, information, and commodities together and into the "New Economy" (Sassen, 1991). Yet, whether or not we remain partly suspicious about the eventual "net" results of globalization, or valiantly hail it as a new era for the increased prosperity of mankind, one thing is beyond doubt: paths towards globalization, and the new network patterns between cities which they produce, have so far varied quite considerably from region to region and from country to country. Such variation has been due to the historically specific economic, cultural, and political conditions – what Friedmann once summarized as the "endogenous conditions" – of cities (Friedmann, 1986: 69 71).

Turning our attention to the post-socialist Baltic state capitals, three sets of such circumstances can be highlighted as being particularly important for structuring globalization trends and, in the long run, their effects on the growth and performance of the local economies. First has been the scope and pace of transition to market economy institutions in Estonia, Latvia, and Lithuania since the early 1990s. Small as these economies might be, there are nevertheless variations between them in this respect, including the extent to which they have attracted foreign capital in recent years. Second, the position of each capital city within the structure and hierarchy of the European urban system is an important feature to consider. Both flows of capital and the patterns by which Tallinn, Riga, and Vilnius are gradually integrating with new inter-urban transportation and communication networks reveal certain spatial properties. These, in turn, reflect what to some extent remain the inherited positions of these capitals relative to other European cities. And third, the impacts of a range of political factors associated first and foremost with the eastward enlargement of the European Union need to be stressed. Post-1989 forms of international cooperation between the Baltic capitals and other cities endow globalization in its post-Soviet Baltic context with a different and distinctly "regional" character compared to what is emerging in world cities in Asia or in Latin America.

## Globalization in the Baltic Context

To begin with, the building of market economy institutions is obviously of immense importance to the competitiveness of the Baltic State capitals. The scope and pace of this process, though, differs between countries. Thus the local economies of the respective capitals have also responded differently to globalization trends regarding changes in the local labour market and the assignment of new roles and functions. Estonia was the quickest Baltic State to adopt and, more importantly, to implement a radical programme for market reforms, including selling off enterprises to foreign investors. Thus, Estonia also attracted larger amounts of FDI compared to Latvia and in particular Lithuania during the initial phase of transition following independence in 1991. Similar differences also occur regarding other endogenous conditions, such as new emerging forms of local self-government (i.e. the institutional framework for the implementation of proactive policies in response to globalization and increased market competition). A specific aspect of institutional reform pertains to the problem of bureaucracy and corruption. Although corruption is presumably at a lower level in the Baltic States compared, for example, to Russia, the unofficial sector of the economy still amounts to a considerable share of GDP in all three cases.[2]

Economic globalization in the Baltic region, however, has specific spatial properties for a variety of reasons other than the purely institutional. These may be clustered together in two major categories, one being geographical and related to certain historical and cultural particularities, the other one being overtly political. Still, in our "global era", classic geographical criteria such as accessibility (in its various dimensions) continue to play a part in determining who decides to invest where on the globe, and why corporate key functions tend to end up located in a particular place rather than somewhere else. However, as well as "hard" variables such as transportation costs and travel times, "softer" and less tangible but nevertheless important factors such as "cross-cultural distance" also define accessibility. Knowledge and familiarity on the part of prospective investors regarding not only possibilities but also difficulties tied up with potential target areas is always important in overseas business. For such reasons, companies in neighbouring countries have proved to be among the major investors in the Baltic States.

For example, the linguistic kinship between the Finnish and Estonian languages plays an important role in this context. Another aspect is that, like the Scandinavian countries and northern Germany, both Estonian and Latvian society are Protestant, while Lithuanian society – like Polish society, with which it had close historical ties – is firmly embedded in Catholic culture. Yet, apart from geographical proximity and certain cultural similarities, there is also a more general tradition of commercial and other contacts across the Baltic Sea that encompasses connections of a far more recent nature than those captured by the simplistic and long over-exploited symbol of the Hanseatic League. Commercial vessels from Russian and Baltic ports were a common enough sight in Scandinavian and north European harbours at the turn of the last century. As the Estonian and Latvian provinces together with the neighbouring St Petersburg region became industrialized during the late nineteenth century, further commercial importance was added most notably to Reval (Tallinn) and Riga (Misiunas and Taagepera, 1983; Kirby, 1995). Or, as Eduard Vilde, an Estonian writer, put it somewhat exuberantly at the end of the nineteenth century: "Tallinn is becoming a metropolis, Tallinn is rising to be one of Russia's most important factory cities, Tallinn will become a second Manchester! Hurrah!" (quoted in Pullat, 1998: 115). Of course, the imperial Russian markets were important to foreign investors, too. The Riga–Dünaburg (Daugavpils) railroad, completed in 1861, was financed and constructed by British companies (Kirby, 1995: 168) and the first major foreign undertaking of the Swedish telephone manufacturer L.M. Ericsson was to establish a new production plant in St Petersburg in 1887. Although the Russian Revolution of 1917 and, later on, the Soviet annexation of the Baltic States in 1940 curtailed the majority of such ventures, Baltic exile communities in Scandinavia, the US, and Canada maintained a nucleus of contacts with the eastern Baltic which continued to play a part in post-1991 developments.[3] Indeed, the extent to which economic dependencies and contacts similar to those mentioned are currently patterned in the Baltic Sea area does to some extent rely on the inherited position of its cities in relation to the European urban system. Most European cities are relatively small and have, historically speaking, served as regional or cross-border regional centres rather than as all-European – let alone global – metropoles, a trait recognized not least by Christaller (1950, 1966 [1933]) when probing his famous central place theory. Today many cities continue to be embedded within such relatively stable and regionally based economies. In turn, this reflects the persistence of functional urban hierarchies established mainly during the industrialization of the eighteenth and nineteenth centuries. Although the pattern is gradually changing as a result of, among other things, new networks of transportation and communication, the old hierarchies in many cases prove to be relatively stable (Törnqvist, 1996; Kunzmann, 1998). Yet, from our perspective the lingering effects of the political division of the Baltic Sea area before 1989 must also be taken into account. The Soviet period resulted not only in undermining the established positions of Tallinn, Riga, and Vilnius within the Baltic and wider European contexts, but also gave them a specific and, indeed, important role in the Soviet urban system for four decades. This must be taken on board if we are to appreciate correctly the drive "back towards Europe" among contemporary Baltic policy analysts and key decision-makers.

Circumstances of this kind of globalization structure in the Baltic Sea area, albeit for different reasons than is the case with institutions, regional hierarchies, and inequalities, are in a sense analogous to institutions by their qualities of representing spatial "path dependencies" (North, 1990). As the American Sun Belt cities phenomena and, indeed, the models of "uneven urban development" launched in the 1970s to explain it illustrate (Watkins and Perry, 1977), drastic changes are often required to break up old dependencies such as those represented by the state socialist legacy in the Baltic States. Thus, not only do endogenous conditions, including the pace of market transition, become important, established functional urban hierarchies also play a role. In this respect, too, the Baltic state capital cities differ from each other, in terms of their pre-Soviet heritage as well as their Soviet legacies. They represent different types of post-socialist cities and acquire differentiated roles and positions in the new regional urban network that started to form after 1991.

Geopolitics and state-building processes are another set of circumstances that add further impetus to the regionalizing effect of globalization among the Baltic capitals. Whereas globalization brings challenges to modern nation states, in certain respects resulting in the erosion of national borders, the Baltic States illustrate the reverse trend. That is, the birth pangs associated with creating new nation state structures have occurred simultaneously with trends towards increased international and global dependency. To begin with, this is of importance from an economic perspective: market reforms and institutional change in transitional societies is certainly contingent on the national context and on state intervention, as much as it is on the policies and pressures brought to bear by international actors such as the IMF, World Bank, and EBRD. And as the building of nation states and the implementation of market reforms are connected phenomena, this also means that the latter concern becomes indirectly tied to security policy and security issues in the region. This, in turn, is reflected in the activities on a number of partly intersecting and overlapping levels, from Nordic–Baltic regional cooperation specifically to the broader EU and NATO levels. Thus, the joining of the Baltic States with an enlarged European Union as well as the issue of NATO membership becomes significant (Jopp and Lippert, 1998; Knudsen, 1998). But as these authors emphasize, one should also note the differences and – often – the lack of coordination between Baltic policies and approaches to the roles of the European Union and NATO.

As is the case more generally in Central and Eastern Europe, this process is shaped by real as well as by imagined historical "legacies" among the Baltic peoples themselves (Åberg, 1997). Indeed, the opening note of Latvian Prime Minister Maris Gailis at a 1995 Riga conference on NATO and EU enlargement and the Baltic States serves as a pertinent illustration to these perceptions.

The only constant factor in Latvian foreign policy is geography. . . . Two different worlds have always come into contact in Latvia: Northern democracy and Eastern authoritarianism, Western constitutionalism and Eastern despotism, the market economy and socialist thriftlessness, Protestant rationalism and Byzantine mysticism, the inheritance of German culture and Slavonic tradition. [sic] (NATO and EU Enlargement: The Case of the Baltic States, 1996: 11)

Thus, recent experiences pertaining to the inter-war period and the Soviet era are decisive. In particular, in Estonia and Latvia discussions concerning the possibility of a "Baltic League" comprising the three Baltic States, Finland, and Scandinavia played an important part in the internal political debate in the early 1920s (Lehti, 1998) – and, indeed, to key decision-makers in contemporary Estonia the words of Ants Piip probably still ring true. Piip, Estonian foreign minister in the 1920s, concluded in 1934 that "the law of history is the following: if the nations inhabiting the shores of the Baltic Sea are not able to create between themselves a stronger organization, they are doomed inevitably to submit to a stronger European power of the respective period" (quoted in Lehti, 1998: 11).

The main difference today compared with the inter-war period, though, is that the Baltic Sea area actually now has working structures which might eventually facilitate the realization of such visions. Another crucial difference is the enhanced importance of cities in the renewed attempts at cross-border integration. This is illustrated, for example, by the role played by cities and city networking in the VASAB 2010 (Vision and Strategies Around the Baltic Sea) policy document on spatial planning in the Baltic Sea area (for a brief overview, see Fischer, 1998). Indeed, cross-border cooperation between cities, in such matters as city twinning, has come to constitute an increasingly important aspect not only of economic transition but also as part of emerging patterns for collective security in the region (Joenniemi and Sweedler, 1995; Johansson and Stålvant, 1998). Taken together it is likely – in the long run – that these processes will strengthen the poly-centric tendencies of the European urban system, much in line with the policy of the European Union to create "a Europe of regions" (Pichler-Milanović, 1998).

The following sections correspond to the three-dimensional characteristic outlined above. Consequently, three indicators will be used to outline globalization and cross-border regionalization processes from the perspective of the Baltic capitals. The next section includes an analysis of institutional change and FDI flows in Estonia, Latvia, and Lithuania, and – as far as current empirical data allow – focuses on the local level. This is followed by an assessment of the air transportation network in the Baltic Sea area – measured in terms of the extent and patterning of airline connections – and the relative accessibility or "centrality" of the Baltic State capitals within this network. Finally, some of the political implications of urban regionalization in the Baltic States are discussed with particular emphasis on the twinning patterns involving Tallinn, Riga, and Vilnius.

## Institutions and Economy

The Baltic Republics ranked among the most highly developed and urbanized regions within the Soviet Union, although there were differences between the three countries.[4] In the early 1980s, 70.1 per cent (Estonia), 69 per cent (Latvia), and 62 per cent (Lithuania) of the population were living in cities and towns (Misiunas and Taagepera 1983: 290–291). In contrast to Estonia and Latvia, Lithuania had experienced a more belated industrialization that by and large did not occur until the Khrushchev period (1956–1964). In addition, there were other significant differences. In Estonia and Latvia the urban system was largely mono-centric, a trait that remained characteristic to these countries both during and after the Soviet period. Apart from Tallinn and Riga, with 427,000 and 820,000 people respectively in 1996, only Tartu in Estonia and Daugavpils and Liepaja in Latvia exceed 100,000 in population. In Lithuania, on the other hand, the urban system has been and still is more clearly poly-nuclear. Whereas Vilnius has about 584,000 inhabitants (1995), the cultural centre of Kaunas and port city of Klaipeda are also key cities in Lithuania and, along with Siauliai and Panevezys, form a group of five cities exceeding 100,000 people.

Once laid down these patterns remained fairly stable until the late twentieth century. Despite policy efforts to the contrary, regional differentiation and inequalities were always great within the Soviet Union. Added to this was an endemic imbalance between industrial growth and spatial planning (Musil, 1980; Morton, 1984; Dellenbrant, 1986; Medvedkov, 1990: 58–79). In other words, economic and regional planning in the Soviet Union contributed in many respects to the inherited differences between the Baltic Soviet republics by enhancing (albeit varying) levels of specialization among cities and regions. In particular, Tallinn and Riga strengthened their positions as major manufacturing centres, although the focus gradually shifted towards heavy industry. By contrast, post-war industrialization in Lithuania resulted in the transfer of new functions to Vilnius as the local economy gradually modernized, but the contrast between the capital city region and the rest of the country did not become as sharp as in Estonia and Latvia. Yet, further specialization and concentration of key functions occurred, for example, as a result of transport policies adopted on an all-union basis: beside Tallinn and Riga, other port cities – in particular Ventspils and Klaipeda, Latvia – became central nodes in the Soviet transportation network (Brodin, 1997) (Fig. 13.2).

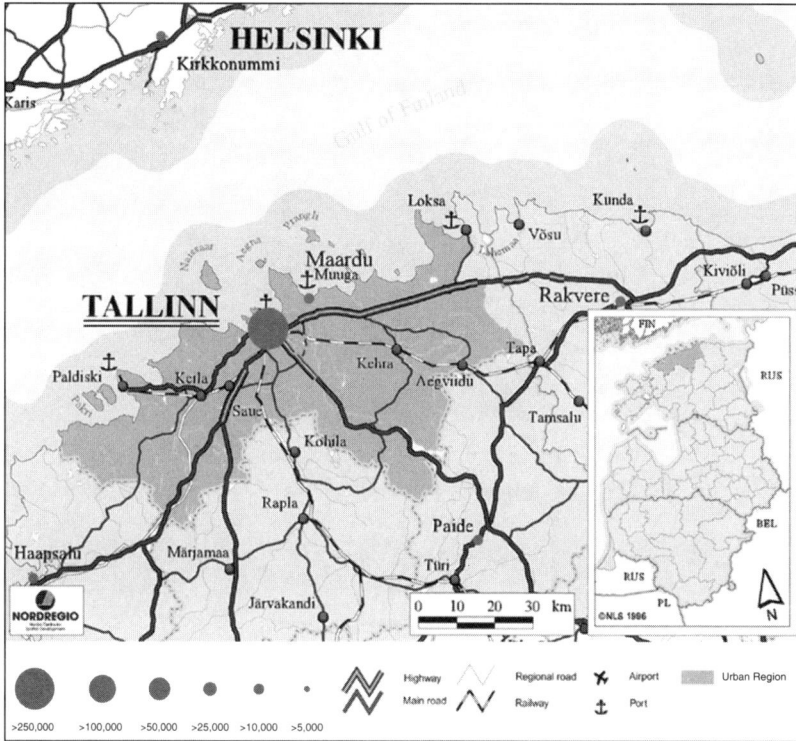

Fig. 13.1  The City of Tallinn and Urban Region.
*Source:* Nordregio at www.nodregio.se.

Changes occurring after 1989 must be judged against this background. Estonia may in general be considered a more successful case of transformation than either Latvia or Lithuania, although economy and society in all three countries went through great ordeals in the 1990s. Production declined rapidly, triggering unemployment and increased social stratification. GDP dropped significantly in all three countries – data on the share of GDP by city level is generally not available – and projections for 1999 showed that real GDP would still amount to only 79 per cent of the 1989 level in Estonia.

Latvia and Lithuania fared even worse, the same projections being set at only 60 and 65 per cent respectively by the EBRD (*Transition Report*, 1999: 6, Table 1.1).[5] While this certainly put the Baltic States as a whole ahead of countries such as Moldova, Ukraine, and Russia, the situation in Latvia and Lithuania is in some respects still in stark contrast to the relative success stories of Estonia, the Czech Republic, and Slovenia.

As for the social effects, unemployment in all three countries soared by the mid-1990s. When peaking in 1996, though, it had struck hardest in Latvia at a

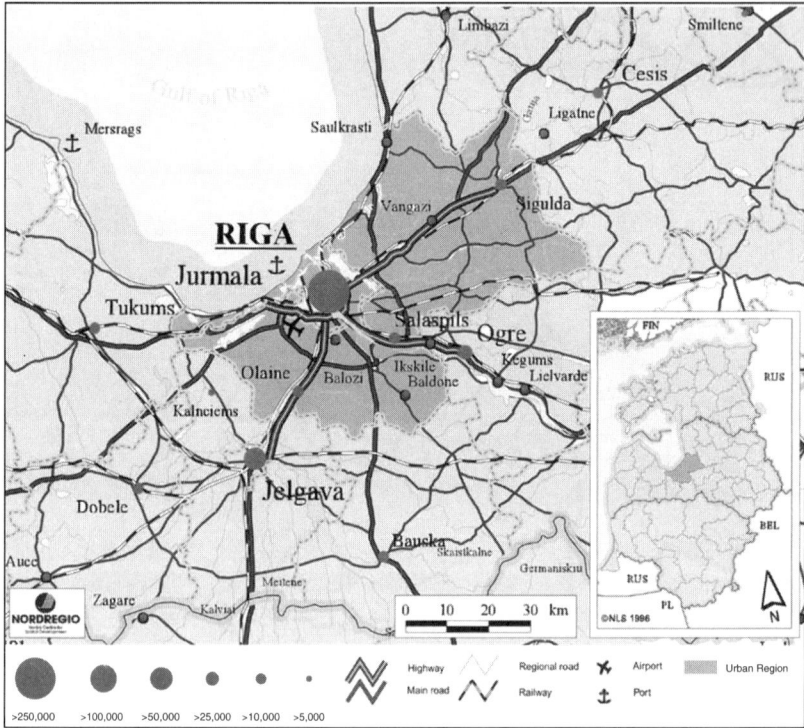

Fig. 13.2  The city of Riga and Urban Region.
*Source:* Nordregio at www.nodregio.se.

record 19.4 per cent. At the same time, data for Lithuania indicated 7 per cent unemployment, whereas the Estonian economy took up a middle position with a calculated 10 per cent unemployment. This ranking held for the following year as well, although at lower levels and with the most significant improvement of the situation occurring in Latvia (*Transition Report*, 1999: 56, 62, 63). As for the capital cities, estimates for 1997 put unemployment at generally lower levels although in an almost reversed pattern compared to national levels, i.e. 1.8 per cent in Tallinn, 3 per cent in Riga, and 4.6 per cent in Vilnius (*Economic Profile of Tallinn*, 1998) (Fig. 13.3).

All three capital cities had their fair share of difficulties as a result of decline and restructuring. A most obvious sign of this has been the decline in population, when the national and local levels are compared. Summarizing the 1991–1998 period, the trend still pointed towards decline in Estonia by the end of the period, in the country as a whole as well as in Tallinn. Indeed, projections made by the city council have varied between a further decline of the population down to 400,000 people and a slight increase and stabilization at 440,000 people by

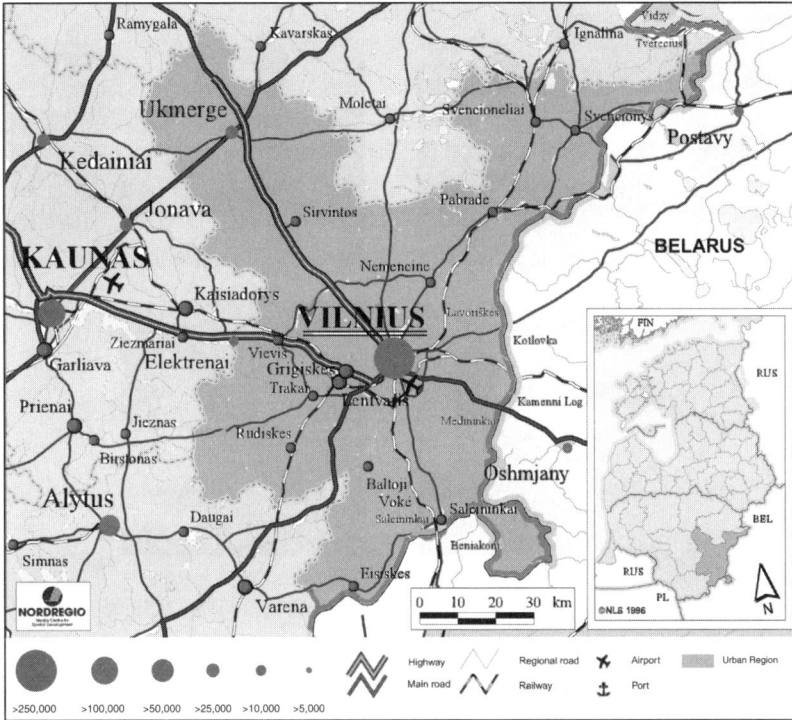

Fig. 13.3 The city of Vilnius and Urban Region.
*Source:* Nordregio at www.nodregio.se.

2010; note however that the latter scenario implies only a very modest increase compared to the 1996 level (*City of Tallinn Development Plan*, 1997: 5). In Latvia, the drop in population was initially more dramatic but then tended to stabilize at around 2.5 million by the mid-1990s. The urban population, however, has continued a slow decline. No data for small towns and communities are available, but between 1993 and 1998 the share of urban population in Latvian cities with more than 40,000 inhabitants fell from 73.4 per cent to 72.6 per cent. During the same period the share of Riga's population fell from 48.2 per cent to 47.2 per cent (*Latvia Human Development report 2000–2001*, 2001: 153). In Lithuania, finally, population decline was comparatively modest during the first decade of transition, both on the national level and in Vilnius (Fig. 13.4).

Population growth trends taken together seem to indicate that transitional changes were initially more dramatic in both Tallinn and Riga than in Vilnius. Still, the data leave room for interpretation. Although the precise effects of the transition phase so far are extremely difficult to evaluate, at least two sets of circumstances should be taken into account.

Fig. 13.4 Images of Baltic cities. (a) View to old Riga. (b) Old city gate, Tallinn. (c) Old city of Vilnius. (d) New office block, Riga. (e) New shops and offices, Riga. (f) New row of houses, Riga.

First, there is the problem of initial differences between the three economies as outlined above. That is, Vilnius had in a sense "less to lose" from the breakdown of the Soviet industrial system due to its belated industrialization. The concentration of manufacturing in the big-city regions after 1945 was a more pronounced trend in Riga and Tallinn. Whereas the prominence of manufacturing in those capital city regions gave Estonia and Latvia a "competitive edge" in relation to Lithuania during the Soviet period, in a sense that very same edge also left these countries more vulnerable to transitional changes after 1991. Indeed, still in 1997 Tallinn's and Riga's shares of national industrial production were, with some reservation for the accuracy of the data, estimated to be as much as 54 and 52 per cent respectively, but the share was only 14 per cent in the case of Vilnius (*Vilnius Market Profile*, 1997). The same conditions are also reflected

Table 13.1 GDP per capita in Estonia, Latvia, and Lithuania, 1990s (US$)

| Country | 1992 | 1995 | 1998 | 1999 | 2000* |
|---|---|---|---|---|---|
| Estonia | 663 | 2,405 | 3,607 | 3,563 | 3,409 |
| Latvia | 578 | 1,779 | 2,494 | 2,799 | 3,019 |
| Lithuania | 514 | 1,623 | 2,904 | 2,874 | 3,045 |

Note: *Figures for 2000 are estimates.
*Source: Transition Report* (1999: 56, 62, 63; 2001: 75, 77).

somewhat by the differences in GDP per capita between the countries. Although the initial drop in GDP was biggest in Lithuania, it also occurred from a generally lower level than Lithuania's northern neighbours. On the other hand, the fact that estimated GDP per capita in Lithuania had exceeded that of Latvia by 1998 also indicates that some of these initial differences between the countries may have begun to flatten out (Table 13.1).

Second, with regard to the problem of differences at the city level, it is far from self-evident that population decline in Tallinn and Riga has been solely related to economic restructuring. In both cities part of the decline has simply been due to emigration among the large groups of former Soviet citizens living there, mostly Russians. This, in turn, reflects the political pressure brought to bear on these minorities in particular during the first years of independence.[6] Lithuania as well harbours minorities, both Polish and Russian, but the latter did not come to constitute a political trauma to the same extent as they did in Estonia and Latvia.

Differences, then, persist between the three Baltic countries and capitals but are, in certain respects, probably not as dramatic as they seem at first glance – for instance, with respect to average living conditions. As Rose (1995, 1997) has pointed out, using macro-economic indicators such as GDP as a basis for conclusions on the social effects of transition might lead to fallacies, when the Baltic economies are compared with each other. Indeed, Rose's own analysis seems to validate this critique. Using micro-economic surveys, Rose suggests that current differences in wealth between the three countries are actually smaller than expected. "For example, ownership of consumer durables is at virtually the same level in all three Baltic states, and the capacity of individuals to get by is actually higher in Latvia than it is [in] Estonia, notwithstanding the lower reported GDP per capita" (Rose, 1997: 126). However, substantial regional differences within each country should also be added to this picture. For example, in the Estonian countryside – and particularly in the southernmost part of the country – wage levels are considerably lower than in the Tallinn city region (*Estonian Human Development Report 1998*). On the other hand, the fact that living expenses vary between regions must of course also be incorporated into any such calculations.

The issue of national independence, rather than economic considerations, was the decisive factor among the Baltic peoples when seceding from the Soviet

Union. As von Beyme has stressed, however, this was far from always being the case, as economic factors related to the regional inequalities indicated above also played an important role as a leading motive among the republics and regions in striving for increased autonomy or independence (von Beyme, 1996: 270). Yet, even though the Baltic Republics in general were previously among the subsidizers of the poorer regions of the Soviet Union due to their relative wealth, this feature naturally lost significance after 1990–1991. Notwithstanding the attempts at economic restructuring during perestroika, independence basically implied a shift from the possibility of such reforms to the immediate necessity for change. For the first time, the Baltic economies, based as they were on inefficient and outdated production technologies, now took a serious blow from international competition.

Complicating the situation was the fact that independence meant simultaneously severing many of the old trade links with the former Soviet Union, most notably with the Russian Federation, leading to a loss of market as well as to shortages of raw material and energy. Added to this was the political factor. Relations with Moscow had quite naturally turned sour and, as mentioned, in the case of Estonia and Latvia the issue of the large Russian minorities in these two countries repeatedly complicated relations during the first years of independent statehood. Taken together, these were strong enough motives inducing the Baltic States to re-orientate and integrate with the international economy as rapidly as possible. In Estonia and Latvia in particular – since the better part of their national economies was localized in the Tallinn and Riga city regions – the task of restructuring the local economies became one of paramount national importance. The role of the capitals in the Estonian and Latvian transition process, then, was obvious from the very outset. In Lithuania, however, the role of Vilnius is more ambiguous. As has been pointed out, no detailed GDP figures by which the relative importance of the capital cities can be measured have been available for this chapter. But considering trade, for example, and using Tallinn as an illustration, some estimates claim that the city accounted for over 50 per cent of all Estonian exports in 1997 (*Economic Profile of Tallinn*, 1998). For Lithuania we have more detailed information, however. Local GDP in the Vilnius region increased much more rapidly in 1996–1998 (54 per cent increase) than it did in other cities such as Kaunas (39 per cent), Klaipeda (26.6 per cent), and Panevezys (25.6 per cent) (*Lithuanian Human Development Report 2000*, 2000: 101). Although the urban system in Lithuania is more balanced – meaning less dominance for the capital city in terms of population and economy – than that of Estonia or Latvia, Vilnius seems to have taken the lead.

Reconstruction, of course, became the prime task of the new national governments, and in particular the issue of privatization. These efforts were supported by international assistance aimed at stimulating the Baltic economies – for example, within the framework of the Baltic Investment Programme launched in 1992 and jointly implemented by the Nordic Investment Bank, the

Nordic Project Fund, and the EBRD (*Baltic Investment Programme – Evaluation Report*, 1995). In important aspects, however, local governments have come to play a role, too. Changes of this kind, though, do not only involve "pressures" on local government to "reconstruct relations between the public and private sectors on the local level" (Clarke, 1993: 1–2). Indeed, as part of the entire transition to a market economy and local self-government, they imply the very invention, or at least reinvention, of these concepts and the necessary institutional underpinnings during the first years of post-Soviet urban governance. Similar strategies directed at marketing the city, at attracting more FDI to the local economy, at coordinating and assisting new entrepreneurial undertakings, and at improving infrastructure in terms of telecommunications have thus been adopted in all three Baltic capitals, often as part of international cooperation schemes.

The kind of national privatization policies adopted in each country as well as the pace at which these were implemented constituted the single most important aspect of institutional reform after independence. In Estonia changes were quick and drastic, in certain respects inspired by the attempted perestroika economic reforms in the late 1980s. Political discussions during this early phase, however, focused mainly on the issue of employee ownership. After 1992, more and more preference was given to outsiders and, at the same time, privatization was opened up to foreign capital (Mygind, 1997: 134–143). By now Estonian privatization is virtually completed, as far as industrial, commercial, and service companies are concerned. What remained by the turn of the millennium was basically the selling-out of "large-scale infrastructure companies" (*Transition Report*, 1999: 36).

Privatization in Latvia proceeded at a slower pace up to 1994. Contributing to this was the politically volatile situation in the country, largely due to the nationality problem (for an overview of the political system and of political cleavages in Latvia, see Bottolfs, 2000). The following banking crisis in 1995 added further to these difficulties. In Lithuania, finally, legislation on privatization was passed in early 1991 and the following year a programme for selling state-owned enterprises to foreign investors was introduced. However, the new policies were implemented on a broad scale only as late as 1995 (Mygind, 1997: 134–143). Thus, the fact that there are some variations between the countries with respect to FDI is not surprising; by comparison, large volumes of FDI were injected into the Estonian economy as early as 1993–1994, while Latvia and in particular Lithuania lagged somewhat behind. As the process gained impetus in Latvia in 1994 and in Lithuania in 1996, accumulated FDI actually began to exceed that of Estonia (Table 13.2), although measured per capita the level is still higher in Estonia. The economic turmoil in Russia in 1998 complicated the picture, however. Annual FDI certainly peaked in both Estonia and Lithuania in 1998, but at the same time the Russian crisis led the EBRD to substantially lower the growth projections for all three states (*Business Central Europe*, May 1999).

Obtaining reliable full-coverage FDI data pertaining to the local level is more difficult. Occasionally, too, the data refer to accumulated FDI over longer

Table 13.2  FDI in Estonia, Latvia, and Lithuania, 1992–2001 (million US$)

| Country | 1992 | 1993 | 1994 | 1995 | 1996 | 1997 | 1998 | 1999 | 2000* | 2001* |
|---------|------|------|------|------|------|------|------|------|-------|-------|
| Estonia | — | 157 | 212 | 199 | 111 | 130 | 574 | 222 | 241 | 300 |
| Latvia | 43 | 50 | 279 | 245 | 379 | 515 | 303 | 331 | 399 | 350 |
| Lithuania | 25 | 30 | 31 | 72 | 152 | 328 | 921 | 478 | 355 | 300 |

Note: *Figures for 2000 are estimates and figures for 2001 are projections.
*Source: Transition Report* (1999: 56, 62, 63; 2001: 61, 75, 77).

Table 13.3  Share of FDI in Baltic capital cities, 1996–1998

| % share of FDI | 1996 | 1997 | 1998 |
|----------------|------|------|------|
| Tallinn | n/a | 73.0 | n/a |
| Riga | 65.8 | 62.9 | 50.5 |
| Vilnius* | 41.4 | 51.6 | 59.3 |

Note: *Figures for Vilnius are courtesy of Ms Egle Samsonaviene, Economic Development Division, Vilnius City Municipality.
*Sources: Economic Profile of Tallinn* (1998); *Investment in Latvia* (1999: Table 1.5).

periods and, furthermore, is compiled in a manner that makes it impossible to break up the volumes for each respective year. However, these contingencies duly considered, it is still clearly the case that the major share of investments have so far been funnelled to the capital city regions. From the two cases where data across several years are available – Riga and Vilnius[7] – it is however also obvious that the pattern again varies between the Baltic countries. Whereas the share of FDI directed to Riga declined between 1996 and 1998 – from 65.8 per cent to 50.5 per cent – Vilnius reveals an opposite pattern (Table 13.3). This difference is the more paradoxical considering the differences between the Latvian and Lithuanian urban systems. Latvia is completely dominated by Riga as a commercial and financial centre, whereas the urban system in Lithuania is more balanced, including as it does a smaller capital city balanced by other large and medium-sized cities such as Kaunas, Klaipeda, and Panevezys. Yet, in the case of Latvia, the share of total FDI per annum fell not only in Riga but also in cities such as Daugavpils and Liepaja between 1996 and 1998. By contrast, smaller towns and communities such as Valmiera in northern Latvia or Bauskas in southern Latvia did increase their (albeit modest) share of FDI (*Investment in Latvia*, 1999: Table 1.5). In Lithuania, on the other hand, the increasing importance of Vilnius as a receiver of FDI between 1996 and 1998 (Table 13.3) went hand in hand with a decline in the share of FDI in, for example, Kaunas and Klaipeda.[8] The development in Vilnius with respect to FDI, then, is similar to the city's increased share of GDP in the second half of the 1990s.

If we compare the origins of investments, interesting differences can be noted – however, precisely as an effect of globalization, the practice of putting labels of nationality on economic actors is not entirely without pitfalls if we start to consider variables such as ownership. In this respect, however, we also face the problem of a lack of data but for one exception (Vilnius). Considering the importance not only of Tallinn and Riga but to some extent also Vilnius in their respective national economies, though, it would be tempting to hypothesize that the pattern for the national level is reflected in the local pattern as well. Indeed, as the case of Vilnius illustrates, this assumption is probably correct to some extent (see Tables 13.4 and 13.5).

On the whole, the FDI pattern on the national level echoes what has previously been indicated about the geographical orientations of the Baltic countries. Some differences should be noted, however, and a quick country-by-country tour is illuminating. In Estonia, Finnish, Norwegian, and Swedish enterprises, in that order, have so far been the most prominent investors. Together they are responsible for a 61 per cent share of all FDI until 1998. Most dominant in all respects are Finnish companies, with 30 per cent. Although the pattern is more dispersed in the case of Latvia, similar roles are played there by Danish (15.5 per cent), American (10.7 per cent), and, importantly, Russian

Table 13.4 FDI structure in the Baltic Republics by country of origin (% share of accumulated FDI in 1998)

| Country of origin | Estonia* | Latvia | Lithuania** |
|---|---|---|---|
| Denmark | 6.0 | 15.5 | 6.6 |
| Estonia | — | 3.4 | 4.3 |
| Finland | 30.0 | 4.4 | 9.6 |
| Germany | — | 8.4 | 3.4 |
| Ireland | — | 5.4 | 2.8 |
| Luxembourg | — | — | 3.0 |
| Netherlands | 6.0 | 2.6 | 0.2 |
| Norway | 21.0 | 3.8 | 2.1 |
| Russian Federation | — | 8.7 | 0.4 |
| Sweden | 10.0 | 6.9 | 13.2 |
| Switzerland | 6.0 | 2.3 | 0.4 |
| UK | — | 7.5 | 6.8 |
| US | — | 10.7 | 9.9 |
| Other | 21.0 | 20.4 | 37.3 |
| Total | 100.0 | 100.0 | 100.0 |

Notes:
*1997.
**1 January 1999.
*Source: Economic Profile of Tallinn* (1998); *Investment in Latvia* (1999: Table 1.3); figures for Lithuania are courtesy of Ms Egle Samsonaviene, Economic Development Division, Vilnius City Municipality.

Table 13.5  FDI structure in Vilnius by country of origin (% share of accumulated FDI in 1998)

| Country of origin | % |
| --- | --- |
| Denmark | 4.9 |
| Estonia | 5.4 |
| Finland | 16.2 |
| Germany | 5.8 |
| Ireland | 2.7 |
| Luxembourg | 5.1 |
| Norway | 3.5 |
| Sweden | 22.3 |
| UK | 7.1 |
| US | 16.6 |
| Other | 10.0 |
| Total | 100.0 |

Note: Only the top ten countries have been included.
*Source:* Figures for Vilnius by courtesy of Ms Egle Samsonaviene, Economic Development Division, Vilnius City Municipality.


interests (8.7 per cent). In Lithuania, Swedish, American, and Finnish investors top the list (Table 13.4). Hidden in the data (under "other"), though, are also investments made by Polish businesses in Lithuania, a feature that probably reflects the renewal of the old ties between the two countries. Examples in recent years include the purchase by Polsat of a 51 per cent share in the Baltijos TV (BTV) company (*Warsaw Business Journal*, 26 April–2 May 1999).

All in all the regional sourcing character of FDI flows into the Baltic States is quite predictable. Including the countries already mentioned – Poland and the US excluded – the lion's share of investments derive from actors either in Scandinavia, or in other northern European countries such as Germany, the Netherlands, and the UK. It is also representative of the relatively successful restructuring of the Estonian economy that Estonian investors themselves have started to operate in the other two Baltic countries. Shifting the perspective to our one local case, finally, we may note that in Vilnius the same countries as on the national level top the list, although in a different order (Table 13.5): Swedish, American, and Finnish companies rank as the three most important investors.

Foreign investments also tend to focus on certain sectors of the local economies. To be sure, many of them have been made through take-overs of old manufacturing industries, which assists higher productivity and important spillover effects from foreign companies to domestic ones. One such case is the Latvian food and beverage industry (Rucevska and Cuntonova, 1998: 37–39). Other investments, though, are more clearly part of the restructuring of the local economies towards increased importance of the trade and service sectors, including transportation and telecommunications. Thus, whereas in Tallinn 37 per cent of all FDI between 1992 and 1996 were made in manufacturing, 25 per cent were made in the wholesale and retail trades. Another 18 per cent, finally, went into transportation and telecommunications, the investments by Swedish Telia AB and Finnish Telecom in the Eesti Telefon and EMT AS mobile telephone companies in 1996 being two major undertakings (*Economic Profile of Tallinn*, 1998). A similar pattern is discernible in Riga as well as in Vilnius, although investments in trade seem to play, relatively speaking, a more prominent role than is the case in Tallinn (*Investment in Latvia*, 1999: Table 1.5; *Vilnius Market Profile*, 1997).

All in all, FDI trends in the Baltic States reflect variations on one theme. On the one hand, a cheap and well-educated labour force has served to attract many foreign investors. On the other, the input of new capital in what traditionally were underdeveloped sectors during the Soviet period has contributed to and gone hand in hand with a break-up of old economic dependencies. Whereas in the late 1980s "85–95 per cent of Baltic trade [took place] with other Soviet republics" (see Arkadie and Karlsson, 1992: 172), this picture has since been altered dramatically. Western countries, including the neighbouring Scandinavian countries, have become the most important trading partners, although the Russian Federation continues to play a role. One can therefore speak of a break with established path dependencies in at least two respects. One, of course, is purely institutional. The other is geographical, and pertains to the international reorientation of the Baltic economies. Importantly, the latter process has unfolded parallel with and, indeed, profited from readjustment of the transportation networks in the Baltic Sea area and a gradual improvement in the position, or relative "centrality", of the Baltic capitals in these networks.

## The Baltic Sea Area Air Transportation Network

It is tempting here to contemplate for a moment the European urban hierarchies as outlined by Walter Christaller half a century ago (Christaller 1950, 1966 [1933]). Drawing on pre–Second World War data and applying the notion of major functional urban centres being "fixed" at certain distances in relation to each other, Christaller proposed that Baltic Sea area cities fell by and large within either one of two clusters. One cluster centred on Scandinavia, the other one on the Baltic Republics and Poland, with groups of German and Russian cities intersecting at the south-west and north-east fringes of this structure. In the Scandinavian cluster, Copenhagen and Stockholm played the role of metropoles, while most notably Warsaw and, in the case of the Baltic countries, Riga took up similar positions in the southern and eastern Baltic (Christaller, 1950). Basically this pattern indicated by Christaller would later become even more pronounced, at least as far as the Baltic state capitals were concerned, although for completely different reasons, i.e. the political East–West division of the Baltic Sea area. To some extent this division is still reflected in the patterning of transportation links, particularly the air transportation networks.

Networks and functional hierarchies, theoretically speaking, epitomize two different concepts of "distance". The importance of geographical distance as reflected by the position of cities in an urban hierarchy can occasionally be seen as being offset by proximity between the very same cities or nodes in networks of transportation and communication (Törnqvist, 1996). Thus the relative accessibility or "centrality" of cities that are otherwise at an equal geographic distance from each other may vary, depending on their position in such networks. For example, Helsinki and Tallinn are both equidistant from Stockholm, but when accessibility is measured by air transport accessibility, contemporary Helsinki is considerably more "central" in relation to Stockholm than is Tallinn (see Table 13.6 and Fig. 13.5).

During the post-1945 period, Scandinavian cities integrated with the expanding west European flight network, blurring the distinction between this group of cities and the urban hierarchies on the main continent. For the Baltic States, though, the Iron Curtain served to deepen the East–West division depicted by Christaller. Low flight density combined with a dependency on Moscow and St Petersburg as central nodes in the Soviet air transportation network left the Baltic capitals fairly isolated from the rest of Europe (Erlandsson, 1991). As the Baltic States entered the long and winding road towards market reforms in the late 1980s, their capitals ranked right at the bottom of the European scale in terms of air transportation accessibility. Tallinn, Riga, and Vilnius were all less accessible than other Soviet cities such as Tbilisi and Baku, and they ranked on

Table 13.6 Inbound and outbound accessibility or "centrality" of top ten Baltic Sea area cities, June 1999 (measured by number of daily non-stop flights)

| City | State | Outbound accessibility | Inbound accessibility |
|---|---|---|---|
| Copenhagen | Denmark | 70 | 75 |
| Stockholm | Sweden | 41 | 40 |
| Helsinki | Finland | 37 | 26 |
| Malmö | Sweden | 14 | 13 |
| Riga | Latvia | 11 | 12 |
| Göteborg | Sweden | 10 | 8 |
| Hamburg | Germany | 7 | 9 |
| Tallinn | Estonia | 7 | 7 |
| Jönköping | Sweden | 4 | 4 |
| Oulu | Finland | 2 | 5 |

Note: Nodes/cities below cut-off value (e.g. cities connected by less than one direct connection operating seven days a week) are excluded from the graph.
Source: Data collected from the respective timetables of SAS, Lufthansa, British Airways, Finnair, Braathens, LOT, Estonian Air, AirBaltic, and Lithuanian Airlines (June 1999).

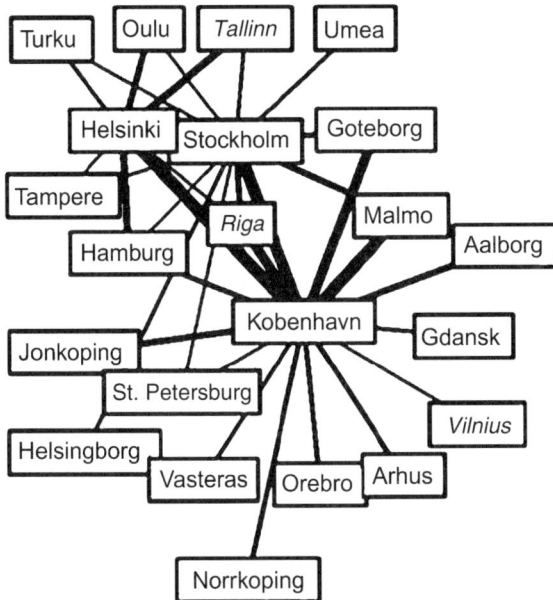

Fig. 13.5  The Baltic Sea area flight network, 1999.

Notes: Nodes/cities connected by less than direct connection operating seven days a week are excluded from the graph.

*Sources:* See Table 13.6.

roughly the same level as cities such as Reykjavik or Leipzig. Indeed, in terms of inbound accessibility, in 1988 all three cities had degraded into even lower positions compared with the mid-1970s. Other Baltic Sea area capitals (e.g. Copenhagen and Stockholm) ranked on roughly the same level as Zürich, Hamburg, or Rome (Erlandsson, 1991: 11; see also Chapter 4).

Although such traits have persisted into the transition period, significant changes have nevertheless taken place during the past decade. The Baltic State capitals have improved both inbound and outbound accessibility in a manner that reflects the impact of globalizing tendencies. To illustrate this, the extent of airline connections between a number of Baltic Sea area cities is used in Table 13.6 as a measure of their relative accessibility or "centrality" within a larger regional network. Variables such as travel time (which Erlandsson applied), though, have not been included in the calculations; flight frequency alone is used as a measure of accessibility.[9] Thus the results are not directly comparable to those of previous research, most notably that of Erlandsson (1991) and Nilsson (1997).

While Erlandsson studied a selection of 97 European city regions, our survey (see Table 13.6) is limited to 44 Baltic cities with 100,000 or more people in their administrative areas (1996–1997) in Denmark, Sweden, and Finland.[10] The survey also includes St Petersburg, Estonia, Latvia, Lithuania, the Kaliningrad (Russian Federation) enclave, and the seven northernmost voivodships of Poland (based on the administrative structure before the 1998 regional reform).

Hamburg, Schleswig-Holstein, and Mecklenburg-Vorpommern in Germany are also included.[11] All direct flights between these cities as of June 1999 have been included to measure inbound and outbound accessibility, although the cut-off value regarding the frequency of connections has been set at a higher level than that used in the Erlandsson (1991) study. Only those direct connections that operated on a daily basis on all seven days of the week are included.[12]

Table 13.6, which ranks the top ten cities by accessibility and centrality, suggests a distinctive pattern. First and foremost, the Scandinavian capitals rank high in both inbound and outbound accessibility, which means that they are nodes with a high degree of centrality in the air transportation network. Most importantly the data reveal the strong position of a core of three cities in the transportation network, i.e. Copenhagen, Stockholm, and Helsinki, in that order. This reflects the positions of traditionally dominant urban centres in the Baltic Sea area context as once proposed by Christaller, as well as to some extent airline company policies – most notably, the fact that SAS deliberately concentrates air traffic at Copenhagen and Stockholm (see also Nilsson 1997: 64). For example, despite the close geographic proximity of Helsinki and Tallinn (lying merely 100 km from each other across the Bay of Finland), there were, at the time of the present survey, no direct SAS flights between these two cities. Instead, SAS flights on the Helsinki–Tallinn route were directed via Stockholm airport. Finally, we should note that there are – most notably in the case of Helsinki – significant differences between inbound and outbound accessibility (Table 13.6). This also holds true for several non-capital cities in the sample, such as Helsingborg (Sweden) and Oulu (Finland). This means, as in the case of Helsinki, that there are better communications from the latter cities to other urban regions than the other way around.

The structure in Table 13.6 is depicted graphically in Fig. 13.5; this has been created by "annealing", meaning that certain features of the graph have been optimized.[13]

Table 13.6 and Fig. 13.5 also reveal interesting contrasts to the late 1980s regarding the position of the Baltic State capitals. The breaking down of the old East–West division is obvious in the case of Tallinn and Riga, despite the high cut-off value imposed when gathering the data on flight connections. These two cities have taken up new positions and are gradually improving them, at least considered in a Baltic context. Riga is the most central of the three capital cities concerned and it ranks on roughly the same level as traditionally well-connected regional centres in Sweden such as Malmö[14] and Göteborg. Tallinn, on the other hand, has – once again in a strictly Baltic Sea area context – a position similar to Hamburg and is more centrally positioned in the network than most Scandinavian regional centres. Straightforward comparisons with Erlandsson's

(1991) analysis are impossible, but some parallels may be drawn. In 1988, all three Baltic State capitals scored the lowest indices even if only other Baltic cities in his sample are considered (Erlandsson, 1991: 11). Judging by the situation in mid-1999, however, Tallinn and Riga now both take up middle positions. So, put in perspective, there are interesting similarities between the new role of these capitals as markets for foreign investors, and their improved position in relation to other Baltic cities in the air transportation network.

Cities such as Vilnius or Gdańsk, on the other hand, are positioned at the fringes of the network, but the survey of course does not take into consideration their connections with cities on the main continent, which is an important feature regarding at least Polish cities. To some extent, therefore, the low centrality of Vilnius and of cities like Gdańsk is probably somewhat misleading. For example, in contrast to Tallinn and Riga, Vilnius is as much a "Central European city" as it is a "Baltic city". By way of illustration, this is also indicated by the contrasting pattern of inter-urban cooperation linkages in terms of city twinning between Vilnius and other European cities and the cities of Tallinn and Riga.

## Inter-urban Cooperation in the Baltic Sea Area

A network pattern similar to that described above consists of different forms of cooperation between Baltic Sea cities and municipalities. Among the numerous forms of cooperation which have more or less successfully gained impetus on various levels since 1989, two are particularly important: (1) international aid programmes directed at the transformation of Baltic State municipalities; and (2) city-to-city cooperation. Among the former type of initiatives we should, for example, note the Canada Baltic Municipality Assistance Programme (CBMAP), specifically targeted at the three Baltic State capitals. This initiative is aimed at formulating proactive policies and implementing new strategies for city governance to cope with the marketization of the post-Soviet economies. Other examples include most notably the Union of Baltic Cities (UBC), founded in Gdańsk (1991). Considering city-to-city cooperation specifically, however, the phenomenon of city twinning becomes important. Such endeavours in the Baltic Sea area have to some extent even spilled over into the field of international security. Drawing on European post–Second World War experiences of city-to-city cooperation, twinning at an early stage of transition became a natural post-1991 measure for bridging decades of political hostility and suspicion originating from the former political division of the Baltic Sea area.

As a rule, localities do, of course, only have more limited powers and means to act trans-nationally, restricted as they are by national institutions and foreign policy considerations. Occasionally, local initiatives of this sort may even be at loggerheads with national policies, as was the case with German–Polish city twinning in the 1970s (Wagner, 1998), for example. On the other hand, city-to-city cooperation through twinning undoubtedly serves as an important means by which to strengthen cross-border cohesion and may ultimately stimulate local as well as regional economic development. In a wider sense, even "security" may play a role on the local level, implying exchanges and cooperation as a means for trying to remedy transitional "diseases" such as increased crime rates and solve social problems following the transition process in the post-socialist cities.

Cooperation and assistance initiatives such as CBMAP notwithstanding, in all the above respects new interaction patterns and dependencies still remain more regional than global by nature, e.g. the pattern is roughly similar to those of economic exchange and modified air transportation networks. Boosting city twinning, at least from the perspective of the Baltic peoples themselves, is, not surprisingly, the strongly developed feeling of belonging to a more or less distinct "Western" cultural sphere, although with the unfortunate geographical drawback of being uncomfortably close to Russia. Looked at from the opposite perspective this view, of course, is countered by equally strong "Western" incentives for bringing not only the Baltic States but also Russia closer to the European Union, and this is something that is clearly reflected by the twinning pattern that evolved during the 1990s. Again, therefore, we have to acknowledge that globalization and cross-border regionalization in the Baltic Sea context have overt cultural and political implications alongside the purely economic ones.

To provide a context for the general features of city twinning involving Baltic Sea area countries, it is instructive to note that the four Nordic states (Denmark, Finland, Norway, and Sweden) and Germany had a total number of 7,378 twinning agreements around the world by the mid-1990s. Of this total roughly half of all twinnings (51 per cent) involved other Nordic or Baltic countries. Twinnings initiated by the five above countries with the three Baltic States exclusively accounted for 4.8 per cent of the total number of recorded agreements. However, if twinnings involving Russia and Poland and those initiated by the Nordic countries with German municipalities are included, this proportion rises to 14.7 per cent (Johansson and Stålvant, 1998: 153, Table 2).[15]

Twinnings specifically involving Tallinn, Riga, and Vilnius based on more recent data need to be considered also, although the regional bias in the overall pattern is again clear. Table 13.7 includes the number of twinning agreements involving the Baltic capitals and other European municipalities by country as recorded by the Council of European Municipalities and Regions (CEMR) up to 1999. Yet, the data should be interpreted with caution (not all of the agreements included had actually been confirmed by both parties involved at the time of the survey).[16] No distinction is made between proposers and acceptors. Even so we can note that a total of 36 agreements involve the three Baltic State capitals, the majority of which (24) are with partners in other Baltic Sea countries, most notably Sweden, Germany, and Denmark (Table 13.7).

As expected there are differences between the Baltic States in this sphere too, although the numerical data does not allow any more far-reaching conclusions. Still, among the 15 twinning agreements involving Tallinn, six of these connect

Table 13.7 Baltic twinnings: number of twinning agreements between Baltic capital cities and other European Municipalities by country, 1999

| Country | Tallinn | Riga | Vilnius |
|---|---|---|---|
| Austria | — | — | 1 |
| Belgium | 1 | — | — |
| Denmark | 1 | 1 | 2 |
| Finland | 1 | 1 | 1 |
| France | 1 | 1 | 1 |
| Germany | 2 | 2 | 2 |
| Greece | — | — | 2 |
| Italy | 1 | — | 1 |
| Poland | — | — | 3 |
| Spain | 1 | 1 | — |
| Sweden | 6 | 2 | — |
| UK | 1 | — | — |
| Total | 15 | 8 | 13 |

Note: The data include links that in some cases had not been confirmed by both parties at the time of the survey.
*Source:* Data are courtesy of Ms Sibylle Weber, Council of European Municipalities and Regions, Paris.

the city to various Swedish municipalities, such as Stockholm, Göteborg, and Malmö, while one includes cooperation with Kotka on the southern coast of Finland. One third of the links connect Tallinn to European cities outside the actual Baltic Sea area, including Ghent (Belgium) and Dartford (England) (Table 13.7). In the case of Riga the pattern is more dispersed but still with a bias for the regional level. Links in this case include agreements with Stockholm, Norrköping (Sweden), Pori (Finland), Aalborg (Denmark), Bremen, and Rostock (Germany) in the Baltics, but also Calais (France) and Alicante (Spain). The same is true of Vilnius, albeit with a stronger orientation towards Poland (Kraków, Lódź, Suwalki). The pattern of Vilnius, though, does also frequently include cities elsewhere in Europe, such as Salzburg (Austria) and Strasbourg (France), including the Mediterranean, Patras and Piraeus (Greece), and Pavia (Italy) (Table 13.7). Taken together with the Polish connections the pattern suggests a significant impact of the traditionally more "Continental" or "Central European" ambience and orientation of Vilnius as compared with the relatively more Baltic orientation of both Tallinn and Riga.

"Twinning" patterns may be interpreted as one of several possible indicators of how cities choose to respond to accelerating changes on the international and global scale. Underpinning such choices and responses are, of course, the more elaborate strategies and limitations of local self-government and urban governance that pertain to each of the Baltic State capitals – factors that lie beyond the scope of this chapter. Nevertheless, the manner in which the Baltic capitals have entered the arena of international cooperation during the last decade does represent an important piece of empirical evidence regarding how local decision-makers and policy analysts perceive the role and position of "their" cities in the European context as new opportunities and challenges appear. For historical reasons and due to economic and political considerations these roles and the ambitions associated with them are – at least as a first step – limited partially to the cross-border regional level. The long-term ramifications of this strategy by the Baltic capitals are a far cry from becoming "global" in any sense of the word. Rather, what is taking place on the verge of the new millennium is their integration, or perhaps reintegration, with a fairly durable European urban structure.

## Conclusions

The previous sections have outlined the extent and patterning of a few key dimensions of "globalization" with a focus on the three Baltic State capitals, and more precisely, in terms of FDI and economic development, air transportation connections, and city networking. Do the trends suggest any signs of the Baltic capitals becoming "global", or does increased internationalization above all mean "EU-ization" and "cross-border regionalization"? It is fair, considering the data available, to arrive at the latter conclusion, which is particularly strongly supported by the FDI pattern. Regardless of what the outcomes may eventually be, the integration of the Baltic capitals within an established but gradually changing Baltic Sea network of linkages and dependencies is likely to represent one of the main trends for the twenty-first century.

And yet there are and will be differences in the paths followed by the various cities in the future. Regarding globalization – defined very generally as "the spatial organization of the new international division of labour" (Friedmann, 1986: 69), or as "a process extending the determinative frameworks of social change to the world as a whole" (Mlinar, 1992: 19) – these changes have affected Tallinn, Riga, and Vilnius differently. For one thing, in the longer perspective, existing urban hierarchies in Europe have played and continue to play a part. This feature should be considered not only as a potential but also as a contingency. As reflected by the changing air transportation network in the Baltic Sea region, it is thus only very recently that the old and established geographical divisions pre-dating the Second World War and reinforced during the "Cold War" period have begun to break up. This break in the cases of Tallinn and Riga is especially clearly visible.

From this perspective, above all, the inter-war situation in the region and the Soviet experience provide a historical antecedent for Baltic policy analysts and decision-makers to intervene with the basically economy-driven processes of globalization and cross-border regionalization. Such considerations play an important part also at the local level and are reflected in the manner by which the Baltic cities connect to new partners on the international arena. As in the case of air transportation linkages a significant difference seems to run between Tallinn and Riga in the capacity of typical "Baltic Sea cities" on the one hand, and Vilnius with its more Continental or Central European traditions, on the other.

All three cities experienced economic difficulties as a result of the transition, albeit with some differences. Although the variation between the three Baltic States should not be exaggerated, the conventional interpretation of Estonia as the most successful country still holds, with Latvia in an intermediate but ambiguous position between Estonia and Lithuania. Indeed, the Latvian road to a market economy has been laden with problems – regarding the current situation, most notably that of corruption. Compared to Lithuania, however, data on population dynamics and in particular FDI also seem to suggest that smaller towns and communities in Latvia actually may have been, relatively speaking, more dynamic compared to the capital city region, at least during the second half of the 1990s.

Considering the introductory typology of post-socialist cities posited in this volume (see Chapter 1), then, Tallinn clearly figures among a group of type 2 "fast-track" cities. The pattern for Tallinn has been characterized by "great drama" and the breakdown of old structures during the initial transition, but also relatively speedy recovery subsequently. On the other hand, Riga, our second typically "Baltic State capital", and Vilnius tend so far to remain type 3 cities with stalled or incomplete transition. But data also suggest important differences between Riga and Vilnius, differences that may in the long run indicate a more dynamic role than was perhaps expected for Vilnius in its national urban system.

## Notes

Originally this chapter was written in 1999. By courtesy of the editors it has been possible however to update some of the data in face of recent developments in the Baltic Sea area. I am also in gratitude to the late Dr F.E. Ian Hamilton, LSE, for valuable comments on earlier versions of the manuscript.

1  A phrase from the Bob Dylan song of the same name (1964).

2  Estimates for 1995 ranged between 35.3 per cent (Latvia) to 11.8 per cent (Estonia). (*Transition Report*, 1997: 37–39, 74). Compared to Estonia and Lithuania, Latvia is also ranked as more corrupt by Transparency International (Lambsdorff 2001: 234–235).

3  It should be stressed however that these communities to a considerable extent pre-dated the 1940s. Misiunas and Taagepera refer to estimates claiming that one out of three Lithuanians were living in North America by 1914 (Misiunas and Taagepera 1983: 7).

4  There are several comprehensive overviews of the social, economic, political, and institutional development in the Baltic States after independence, as well as of the Soviet period in the region, in Lieven (1993), van Arkadie and Karlsson (1992), Smith (1994), Blom (ed.) (1996), and Knutsen and Aarebrot (2000).

5  See also *Human Development Report*, 1999: 14, Table 2.1, which reports a similar pattern. The figures in the two reports do not compare, however, due to the use of different base years etc.

6  Interestingly, recent studies suggest no major economic differences along lines of nationality and citizenship in the Baltic States (Rose 1997: 125).

7  Figures pertain to the administrative city level.

8  Personal communication with Ms Egle Samsonaviene, Economic Development Division, Vilnius City Municipality, June 1999. According to her figures, the share of FDI in Kaunas fell from 15 per cent as reported by 1 January 1997 to 10 per cent as reported by 1 January 1999. The corresponding decline in share was 4.5 per cent for Klaipeda and 8.4 per cent for "other cities and districts".

9  Inbound and outbound accessibility thus defined for all purposes equals the graph theoretical concept of in- and out-degree used to measure centrality in sociological network analysis (Freeman, 1979).

10  In the case of Finland 1997 figures on population.

11  Definitions of the "Baltic Sea region" are abundant. The definition used here roughly equals the one proposed by Kivikari (Kivikari, 1996: 33–35).

12  For this purpose the timetables of the major operators in the area (SAS, Finnair, Lufthansa) were used, as well as Braathens, British Airways, LOT, and the three major Baltic State companies of Estonian Air, Air Baltic (Latvia), and Lithuanian Airlines. In comparison to the data in the ABC World Airways guide some data on flight connections may be lost but not to the extent that the overall structure of the regional air transportation network is distorted.

13  For calculating accessibility/centrality and for drawing the graph in Fig. 13.5, the following software was used: S.P. Borgatti, M.G. Everett, and L.C. Freeman (1992), UCINET IV.1; and D. Krackhardt, J. Blythe, and C. McGrath (1995), Krackplot 3.0. This procedure should not be confused with multi-dimensional scaling (MDS) solutions. The latter measures geodesic path distances between nodes based on the extent of direct as well as indirect links between them. This is an approach that – given the data and methodology used – is less suitable in our case, as it would give a distorted picture of the actual "distance" between different cities. While the centrality measure used here is based on frequency of relations between pairs of nodes, an MDS solution would treat these connections not as separate ones but as links in longer chains of indirect relations. By contrast, annealing simply means structuring the data so as to prevent, in the case of a large number of nodes, their overlapping with each other (which does otherwise often happen in randomly created graphs). Other features include avoiding excessively long lines (edges) in the graph. Importantly however, the software also allows for sub-groups of nodes of a roughly similar degree of centrality to be grouped together. Consequently, in Fig. 13.5 the pattern indicated in Table 13.6 is "enhanced" since the most accessible central cities – as measured by direct air transportation connections – are grouped together in the graph, while less well-connected cities are positioned at the periphery of the graph.

14  It is important to stress that the picture presented will have changed somewhat with the opening of the bridge between Copenhagen and Malmö across the Öresund strait.

15  Data for Germany are uncertain, according to the authors. In addition it should be noted that the overall figure for "Nordic/Baltic" countries includes also Iceland, the Faeroe Islands and Greenland, and the Czech Republic. Taken together, though, the latter countries account for only a minor proportion of all twinnings.

16  Data were obtained from the CEMR by courtesy of Ms Sibylle Weber with this word of caution – it should also be noted that the Baltic States were not originally included in the CEMR's publications on twinning. See *Directory of European Twinnings*, 1995.

## REFERENCES

Martin Åberg, "History, Nationalism and the Rethinking of Cities in the Baltic Sea Area, Implications for Regionalisation and Cross-Border Cooperation", in Martin Åberg and Martin Peterson, eds, *Baltic Cities: Perspectives on Urban and Regional Change in the Baltic Sea Area*, Lund: Nordic Academic Press, 1997, pp. 113–127.

Brian van Arkadie and Mats Karlsson, eds, *Economic Survey of the Baltic States: The Reform Process in Estonia, Latvia and Lithuania*, London: Pinter, 1992.

*Baltic Investment Programme – Evaluation Report*, København: Tema Nord, 1995.

Klaus von Beyme, "A New Movement in an Ideological Vacuum: Nationalism in Eastern Europe", in Gregory Andrusz, Michael Harloe, and Ivan Szelenyi, eds, *Cities after*

*Socialism: Urban and Regional Change and Conflict in Post-socialist Societies*, Oxford: Basil Blackwell, 1996, pp. 268–285.

Raimo Blom, ed., *Regulation and Institutionalization in the Baltic States*, Tampere: Department of Sociology and Social Psychology, University of Tampere, 1996.

Heidi Bottolfs, "Latvia", in Terje Knutsen and Frank Aarebrot, eds, *Politics and Citizenship on the Eastern Baltic Seaboard: The Structuring of Democratic Politics from North-West Russia to Poland*, Kristiansand: Høyskoleforlaget, 2000, pp. 75–104.

Alf Brodin, "Competing Port Cities – Going for Market Shares under a Dark Geopolitical Cloud", in Martin Åberg and Martin Peterson, eds, *Baltic Cities: Perspectives on Urban and Regional Change in the Baltic Sea Area*, Lund: Nordic Academic Press, 1997, pp, 74–96.

*Business Central Europe*, May 1999.

Walter Christaller, *Central Places in Southern Germany*, Englewood Cliffs: Prentice-Hall, 1966 [1933].

——, *Das Grundgerüst der räumlichen Ordnung in Europa*, Frankfurt a. M.: Frankfurter Geographische Hefte, 1950.

*City of Tallinn Development Plan for the Years 1998–2000*, Tallinn: Tallinn City Council, 1997.

Susan E. Clarke, "The New Localism: Local Politics in a Global Era", in Edward G. Goetz and Susan E. Clarke, eds, *The New Localism: Comparative Urban Politics in a Global Era*, Newbury Park: Sage, 1993, pp. 1–21.

*Comparative City Statistics: Major Cities of Scandinavia, Tallinn and St Petersburg 1996*, Helsinki: City of Helsinki, Information Management Centre, 1997.

*Das Grundgerüst der räumlichen Ordnung in Europa*, Frankfurt on Main: Frankfurter Geographische Hefte, 1950.

Jan Å. Dellenbrant, *The Soviet Regional Dilemma: Planning, People, and Natural Resources*, New York: M.E. Sharpe, 1986.

*Directory of European Twinnings* 1, Paris: CEMR, 1995.

*Economic Profile of Tallinn*, Tallinn: Tallinn City Council, 1998.

Ulf Erlandsson, *Kontakt-och resemöjligheter i Europa 1976 och 1988*, Lund: Department of Social and Economic Geography, Lund University, 1991.

*Estonian Human Development Report 1998*, Tallinn: UNDP, 1998.

Helle Fischer, "Urban Networking as Part of a Spatial Vision in the Baltic Sea Region", in Ros-Mari Edström and Gun Frank, eds, *Baltic Cities, Global Aspects on Urban Settlements in the Baltic Sea Region*, Stockholm: Byggforskningsrådet, 1998: 97–99.

Linton C. Freeman, "Centrality in Social Networks: Conceptual Clarification", *Social Networks* 1, 1979, pp. 215–239.

John Friedmann, "The World City Hypothesis", *Development and Change* 17 (1), 1986, pp. 69–83.

*Human Development Report For Central and Eastern Europe and the CIS 1999*, New York: UNDP, 1999.

*Investment in Latvia* 4/1998, Riga: Central Statistical Bureau of Latvia, 1999.

Joenniemi Pertti and Alan Sweedler, *The Role of Cities in International Relations: New Features in the Baltic Sea Region*, PFK-texte 36, Kiel: Christian-Albrecht Universität, 1995.

Torbjörn Johansson and Carl-Einar Stålvant, "Twin City Relationships: A Code for Neighbourhood Co-operation in the Baltic Sea Area?", in Christian Wellmann, ed.,

*From Town to Town: Local Authorities as Transnational Actors*, Hamburg: Lit Verlag, 1998, pp. 141–169.

Mathias Jopp and Barbara Lippert, "Towards a Solution of the Baltic Issue: the EU's Role", in Mathias Jopp and Sven Arnswald, eds, *The European Union and the Baltic States: Visions, Interests and Strategies for the Baltic Sea Region*, Helsinki/Bonn: Institute of International Affairs/Institute for European Politics, 1998, pp. 9–18.

David Kirby, *The Baltic World 1772–1993: Europe's Northern Perifery in an Age of Change*, London: Longman, 1995.

Urpo Kivikari, *The Legacy of Hansa, The Baltic Economic Region*, Helsinki: Otava, 1996.

Olav F. Knudsen, *Cooperative Security in the Baltic Sea region*, Paris: Chaillot Papers, 1998.

Terje Knutsen and Frank Aarebrot, eds, *Politics and Citizenship on the Eastern Baltic Seaboard: The Structuring of Democratic Politics from North-West Russia to Poland*, Kristiansand: Høyskoleforlaget, 2000.

Klaus R. Kunzmann, "World City Regions in Europe: Structural Change and Future Challenges", in Fu-chen Lo and Yue-man Yeung, eds, *Globalization and the World of Large Cities*, Tokyo: UNDP, 1998, pp. 37–75.

Johann Lambsdorff, "Transparency International 2001 Corruption Perceptions Index", in Robin Hodess, Jessie Banfield, and Toby Wolfe, eds, *Global Corruption Report*, Berlin: Transparency International, 2001, pp. 232–236.

*Latvia Human Development Report 2000–2001*, Riga: UNDP, 2001.

Marko Lehti, *A Baltic League as a Construct of the New Europe: Envisioning a Baltic Region and Small State Sovereignty in the Aftermath of the First World War*, Frankfurt: Peter Lang, 1998.

Anatol Lieven, *The Baltic Revolution: Estonia, Latvia and Lithuania and the Path to Independence*, New Haven: Yale University Press, 1993.

*Lithuanian Human Development Report 2000*, Vilnius: UNDP, 2000.

Olga Medvedkov, *Soviet Urbanization*, London: Routledge, 1990.

Romuald J. Misiunas and Rein Taagepera, *The Baltic States, Years of Dependence 1940–1980*, London: C. Hurst and Company, 1983.

Zdravko Mlinar, "Individuation and Globalization: The Transformation of Territorial Social Organisation", in Zdravko Mlinar, ed., *Globalization and Territorial Identities*, Aldershot: Avebury, 1992, pp. 1–34.

Henry W. Morton, "The Contemporary Soviet City", in Henry W. Morton and Robert C. Stuart, eds, *The Contemporary Soviet City*, London: Macmillan, 1984, pp. 3–24.

Jiří Musil, *Urbanization in Socialist Countries*, New York: M.E. Sharpe, 1980.

Niels Mygind, "Privatisation and Employee Ownership: The Development in the Baltic Countries", in Neil Wood, Robert Kilis, and Jan-Erik Vahlne, eds, *Transition in the Baltic States: Micro-Level Studies*, London: Macmillan, 1997, pp. 131–147.

*NATO and EU Enlargement: The Case of the Baltic States* (conference proceedings), Riga: Konrad Adenauer Foundation/Latvian Institute of International Affairs, 1996.

Jan Henrik Nilsson, "Economic Development and Communication Networks in the Baltic Sea Area", in Martin Åberg, and Martin Peterson, eds, *Baltic Cities: Perspectives on Urban and Regional Change in the Baltic Sea Area*, Lund: Nordic Academic Press, 1997, pp. 43–73.

Douglass C. North, *Institutions, Institutional Change and Economic Performance*, Cambridge: Cambridge University Press, 1990.

Nataša Pichler-Milanović, "Globalisation, Regionalisation and the Transformation of Central and Eastern European Cities Towards the 21st Century: An Outline", paper presented at the conference "City, State and Region in a Global Order: Toward the 21st Century", Hiroshima, 18–20 December 1998, unpublished.

Raimo Pullat, *All Roads Lead to Tallinn: History of Old Tallinn*, Tallinn: Estopol, 1998.

*Rocznik statystyczny 1997* [Statistical Yearbook for Poland 1997], Warszawa: GUS, 1997.

Richard Rose, *Micro-economic Conditions of Baltic Nationalities*, Glasgow: Studies in Public Policy, No. 254, University of Strathclyde, 1995.

Richard Rose, "Micro-economic Differences Between or Within Baltic Nationalities", in Neil Wood, Robert Kilis, and Jan-Erik Vahlne, eds, *Transition in the Baltic States: Micro-level Studies*, London: Macmillan, 1997, pp. 109–128.

Evija Rucevska and Anda Cuntonova, *Foreign Direct Investment's Impact on Productivity in Comparison to Domestic Investment: Food and Beverage Industry in Latvia*, Riga: SSE Riga, 1998, p. 7.

Saskia Sassen, *The Global City: New York, London, Tokyo*, Princeton: Princeton University Press, 1991.

Graham Smith, ed., *The Baltic States, The National Self-Determination of Estonia, Latvia and Lithuiania*, London: Macmillan, 1994.

*Statistisches Jahrbuch 1998 für die Bundesrepublik Deutschland* [Statistical Yearbook for Germany], Wiesbaden: Statistischer Bundesamt, 1998.

*Statistisk årbog 1997* [Statistical Yearbook for Denmark 1997], København: Danmarks statistik, 1997.

*Statistisk årsbok '98 för Sverige* [Statistical Yearbook for Sweden '98], Stockholm: Statistiska centralbyrån, 1998.

*Suomen tilastollinen vuosileirja 1998* [Statistical Yearbook for Finland 1997], Helsinki: Tilastokeskus, 1998.

Gunnar Törnqvist, *Sverige i nätverkens Europa, Gränsöverskridandets former och villkor* [Sweden in a Europe of Networks: Frames and Conditions of Cross-Border Transformation], Malmö: Liber-Hermods, 1996.

*Transition Report 1997, Enterprise Performance and Growth*, London: EBRD, 1997.

*Transition Report Update April 1999*, London: EBRD, 1999.

*Transition Report Update April 2001*, London: EBRD, 2001.

*Vilnius Economic Profile '98*, Vilnius: Vilnius City Municipality, 1998.

*Vilnius Market Profile, Foreign Investment and Export Markets*, Vilnius: Vilnius City Municipality, 1997.

Beate Wagner, "Twinnings: A Transnational Contribution to More International Security?", in Christian Wellmann, ed., *From Town to Town: Local Authorities as Transnational Actors*, Hamburg: Lit Verlag, 1998, pp, 37–44.

*Warsaw Business Journal*, 26 April–2 May 1999.

Alfred J. Watkins and David C. Perry, "Regional Change and the Impact of Uneven Urban Development", in David C. Perry and Alfred J. Watkins, eds, *The Rise of the Sunbelt Cities*, Beverly Hills: Sage, 1977, pp. 19–53.

Neil Wood, Robert Kilis, and Jan-Erik Vahlne, eds, *Transition in the Baltic States: Micro-level Studies*, London: Macmillan, 1997, pp. 109–128.

# 14

# Moscow in transition

*Olga Medvedkov and Yuri Medvedkov*

## Introduction

### Moscow in the Urban Hierarchy of Europe

Moscow, in terms of population numbers, has a prominent place in the European urban hierarchy. The city is the second biggest in Europe (exceeded only by Paris), with 8.5 million residents within its municipal borders (*Moskva*, 2002). The daytime population in Moscow, including commuters, is between 11.5 and 12 million (Shvetsova, 2002). For comparing Greater Moscow with other urban agglomerations in Europe we refer to the latest UN survey (United Nations, 2002). This survey shows 8.4 million residents in Greater Moscow and 9.6 million in Greater Paris, the mega-city of the highest rank. The other European mega-cities closest in size are Greater London (7.6 million) and St Petersburg, (4.6 million). Other European urban agglomerations are much smaller, with Greater Berlin, at 3.3 million, being geographically closest. In the Middle Eastern realm the nearest to the Moscow mega-city is Greater Istanbul, at 8.9 million.

### Excellence in Human Capital

In 1997, persons with university-level diplomas represented 43.4 per cent of all working Muscovites (MSE, 1998: 48). In absolute numbers this means an impressive pool of 2,224,000 specialists, i.e. persons who added at least five years of education after high school. For assessing the most frequent specialities we examined records relating to 540,900 persons who were students in the

1989–1990 academic year (Mosgorstat, 1990: 104). The former students are now at the prime age of their life. Most commonly they are engineers in manufacturing (43 per cent), economists and lawyers (19 per cent), school teachers, (12 per cent), engineers in transport and communications, (10 per cent), and physicians, dentists, and pharmacists (4 per cent).

In the years of the transitional economy, good education helps Muscovites to move up in status. Holders of university diplomas account for 55.5 per cent of all employers and self-employed persons in the city (MSE, 1998: 48).

*The Role of Human Capital in Moscow's Globalization*

Human capital is the ultimate resource of Moscow for two reasons. First, Moscow has to deploy its human capital as the trump card for mitigating the severe disadvantages of its geographical location. The circumstances of Moscow's location call for a detailed discussion, found later in this chapter. Second, the overriding factor, the globalization of the world economy, is fuelled by the key role of human capital. Superior efficiency develops because of "the increasing interconnectedness of people and places through converging processes of economic, political and cultural change, through commerce, communications and travel" (Rowntree et al., 2000: 1). According to Clark and Gail (1998: 6): "Human capital, the analytic and information skills critical to the capacity to innovate, becomes a key element of profitability and wealth creation." Due to its human capital, Moscow might obtain desirable globalization rewards such as profitability and wealth creation. However, this is not happening.

*The Paradox of Moscow: Low Competitiveness*

Globalization rewards are measured in several ways. One approach is represented by GNP per capita. For Moscow the GNP becomes the GRP, gross regional product. According to official sources (Goskomstat, 1998 [Vol. 2]: 22) the 1996 GRP per capita in Moscow was two times the average for the Russian Federation. The same source, by its later numbers, which the World Bank accepted for comparisons (Broadman and Recantini, 2001: Table 6), shows that in 1998 Moscow's GRP per capita was 2.3 times the average for the Russian Federation. The estimate for the latter in 2001 was US$8,300 per capita, computed by the purchasing parity power method (CIA, 2002). Consequently, the GRP in Moscow comes at best to US$19,090. This level is exceedingly low for a mega-city in Europe. The per capita performance of Moscow turns out to be similar for the populations of Israel (US$20,000 in 2002), New Zealand (US$19,500), Spain (US$18,900), South Korea (US$18,000), and Greece (US$17,900). The GRP per capita in Moscow is somewhat better than in Slovenia (US$16,000) and the Czech Republic (US$14,600) – the wealthiest countries of Central Europe by GNP per capita (CIA, 2002).

In addition to the GNP approach one can assess Moscow's main activity, which is in organizing efficiency in the overall economy of Russia. There is an index that measures the economy efficiency of countries in terms of international competitiveness. The Harvard Business School regularly computes this index. According to the Competitiveness Index, 2001 (World Economic Forum, 2002), Russia's rank is 58. Russia's competitiveness is not much better than that of the Dominican Republic and Ukraine, which follow at ranks 59 and 60. Among 76 nations included in the comparisons, Russia's Competitiveness Index in 2001 was in the bottom quartile. As a comparison, the ranks of Slovenia (32) and of the Czech Republic (35) were above the median.

These two approaches find an illogical absence of returns on the formidable human capital of Moscow. This is a paradox and it begs explanation. The research thrust in this chapter is to look for this explanation. The search goes in several directions, examining patterns in Moscow's past development, and patterns in transitional changes.

## Patterns of History

The transitions of the 1990s in Moscow were bold and more radical than elsewhere in Russia; this can be understood by taking into account patterns in national history and mentality. Long before the 1990s, Moscow had obtained an aura of glorified exceptions. Leadership in transition came because of similar leadership shown in the past.

The Russian Empire and the Soviet Union made different interpretations of history. Yet, some factors were common. First, rulers in both societies wanted to concentrate power in one privileged city. Second, Moscow maintained its sacred place in the Russian national mentality, rather than St Petersburg, a *parvenu* city built only in the eighteenth century. The history of Russia has created the cumulative causation mechanism (Myrdal, 1957) that gave Moscow a propensity for leadership. Nearly mystical beliefs developed about Moscow's destiny of leading Russia in all urgent moments of history, and these beliefs empower Moscow's elite. Thus, in the 1990s the elite was capable of speeding Russia into radical reforms, when logical minds expected gradualism (Blacklin, 1999).

### The Fighter for Statehood

Moscow is not one of the oldest cities. The earliest reference to "*Moskov*" in a monastic chronicle was in 1747. Several administrative centres in Russia were founded much earlier: Rostov and Smolensk (862), Novgorod (859), and Pskov (903). Moscow outranked older towns in the battles of liberation from the Tatar-Mongolian yoke. These battles occurred over 350 years. Moscow excelled in the fabrication of arms, being at the crossroads of two trade routes, one between the Volga and the Western Dvina (Daugava), and the other between Novgorod and Ryazan (Arsenyev and Petrushevskiy, 1898).

Ivan III, the Grand Prince of Moscow, 1462–1505, accepted the "Third Rome" destiny for Moscow after the fall of Constantinople in 1453. This was the act of proclaiming Moscow the successor to Constantinople and the custodian of orthodoxy. The following quotation on the "Third Rome" is of interest because it is a recent statement of the Mayor of Moscow:

From time immemorial Moscow collected holy things of national and Christian importance together with gathering nations and lands, which had been hostile before . . . Comprehending itself as the "Third Rome", it tried to embody outwardly the ideals of the first Rome and of the "Second Rome", which Constantinople was. The best masters of the East and the West were attracted to the work. In the image of Sacred Moscow Russia accumulated talents and experience of different nations in itself, their strivings for the better, spiritual life, formed a united, unrepeatable look of a Eurasian state, full of dignity and power. (Luzkov, 1996: 3)

The "gathering of nations and lands" proceeded very successfully after Ivan III. Russian troops marched from Moscow to the Pacific Ocean, reaching the Pacific in 1647.

### The Commercial Centre of Russia

Modern times came to Moscow with a setback. In 1712, Tsar Peter I moved the court and the government to St Petersburg. For 206 years the political rank of Moscow became lower. Peter I made a radical geopolitical turn by expanding westward. Moscow was not in the best location for reaping the benefits of this westward expansion. The forward capital and seaport, St Petersburg, better accomplished this.

Nevertheless, in the eighteenth and nineteenth centuries the city was rebuilt as a European city. The fire of 1812 prompted the new construction. Cultural life was active, boosted by the Moscow University (since 1755) and the Bolshoi Theatre (built in 1825). The city became the main hub of Russia's railroads, with 11 lines radiating from it by 1901. In 1897, the population was already above 1 million. Twenty years later, by 1917, the city had over 1.8 million residents. Moscow became the main commercial centre of the Russian Empire.

### The Soviet Capital City

In 1918, the Soviet government moved from St Petersburg to Moscow. The state capital function was again that of the "Third Rome". However, the new government was in no way motivated by the old Russian spiritual significance of Moscow. The Soviets initially ruled in the name of "the world proletariat". Only on the eve of the Second World War did the Soviets accept, reluctantly, the importance of Russian patriotism.

At the beginning of the Soviet period, the social geography of Moscow changed quickly and radically. Before 1918, only 5 per cent of the workers lived in the city's central part, within the Sadovoe Kol'tso or the "Garden Ring". In 1920, that share increased to more than 40 per cent (Khmurov, 1998: 31).

The 1920s were the decade of diversity in Moscow. One could see assertive Red Army commanders in long trench coats, the leather jacketed revolutionaries of domestic and foreign extraction, the colourfully dressed poets and artists surrounded by admirers, the Orthodox priests who dared to challenge Marxism, and the Chinese street vendors. The old elite was invisible. Many were killed in the Civil War, or evicted from the city. The more fortunate emigrated.

In the 1930s, the rag-tag crowd was no more on the streets of Moscow. The Shukhov Tower, 148 metres tall, dominated the Moscow skyline. It was the antenna of Radio Comintern. However, foreign revolutionaries were uncomfortable. The secret police conducted purges of their ranks. Between 1934 and 1937 people disappeared in the fight of Joseph Stalin with the "Trotskyists" and the other old guard of the revolution. Gradually, all non-conforming elements were targeted.

Industrial workers were not numerous in Moscow before the Soviet period. In 1913, they numbered 159,300, or less than 10 per cent of the population (Khmurov, 1998: 45). Factories were nationalized in 1917. The Civil War produced chaos in the economy. By the end of 1925, the number of industrial workers in Moscow was barely 5 per cent more than it was 12 years earlier.

The five-year plans – started in 1928 – boosted growth in Moscow. Between 1926 and 1933, the population of Moscow increased by 68 per cent. The social structure changed, as shown in Table 14.1. The strongest growth was in jobs for workers. Jobs in offices enjoyed the second biggest increase. Private traders and landlords were virtually totally eliminated. The state socialist economy of Moscow was already in place by 1933. The expansion of Moscow's territory went rapidly, being prompted by the construction of new factories. State directorates in charge of the factories could reserve as much land as they wanted, in the absence of charges for land. The Master Plan of Moscow approved by the Supreme Soviet in 1935 allowed a smaller rate of population increase than had already occurred.

Table 14.1 Social changes in the Moscow population at the beginning of the five-year plans, 1926–1933

| Social group | Dec. 1926 (000s) | Dec. 1926 (% of all jobs) | July 1933 (000s) | July 1933 (% of all jobs) | % change 1926–1933 (% of 1926) |
|---|---|---|---|---|---|
| Workers | 293.2 | 33 | 823.4 | 44 | 181 |
| Office staff | 263.3 | 30 | 649.9 | 35 | 147 |
| Service staff | 91.4 | 11 | 214.6 | 11 | 135 |
| Handicraftsmen | 91.1 | 10 | 76.2 | 4 | −16 |
| Domestics | 42.5 | 5 | 52.6 | 3 | 25 |
| Private traders and landlords | 35.0 | 4 | 1.3 | — | 2100 |
| Others | 65.4 | 7 | 59.0 | 3 | 210 |
| All jobs, total number | 881.9 | 100 | 1877.0 | 100 | 113 |

*Source:* Data compiled from *Moskva v tsifrakh, 1934* [Moscow in Numbers, 1934], Moscow: Stroitelstvo Moskvy, p. 16.

The permitted limit of the target year, 1960, was 5 million. In reality, when 1960 came, Moscow's population numbered 6 million.

Moscow feverishly added not only factories but also the monumental buildings along the main streets. The necessity for making main streets straight and wider occurred because of traffic problems in the growing city. However, the remodelling of Moscow's territory also had an explicit ideological dimension. The symbols of the tsarist past had to be weeded out to remove competition for the new symbols of the Soviets. Many treasures of architecture and accumulated monuments of Russian culture were destroyed.

After the Second World War the most significant changes in Moscow were those associated with the rapid accumulation of a well-educated workforce. Mass housing construction started at the end of the 1950s, and it was an act of recognition by the Soviet leaders that the city of specialists required a new social contract. The cost of replacing an engineer, a teacher, or a physician was considerable. Moreover, the arms race left no time for training replacements for existing specialists if those specialists were treated as expendables (as they were, under Stalin). The Soviet leaders gave priority to Moscow's needs because the city contained the population engaged in defence-related research and in the organizational efforts of the arms race. There was also an element of fear, when the 1956 revolution in Hungary was cruelly crushed. The Soviet leaders could see that they were losing trust among Muscovites. The dissidents became a new phenomenon in the city (Alekseeva, 1985).

In the 1980s, jobs in R&D and the sciences were almost as numerous as those in manufacturing. The tertiary sector started to determine the character of Moscow. Several larger industrial enterprises in Moscow assumed the character of research laboratories, because they were busy with the high-technology implementations of the tools of war. Examples are the Dementyev aviation complex, with 16,000 staff, and the Khrunichev complex of space rocketry, with 11,500 staff.

## The Transformation of Governance in Moscow: 1990–2000

### An Overview

After the demise of the Soviet Union, Moscow, together with St Petersburg, received the special status of membership of the Russian Federation. This act gave significant power to Moscow's municipal authority.

Historically, Russia did not have strong municipal traditions. In the Soviet period, the national government institutions dominated Moscow. Just as the regions of Russia did not have powerful leaders, Moscow was deprived of its own strong leadership until the post-Soviet period. All this changed with the rise of the current Mayor of Moscow, Yuriy Luzhkov, who came to power in the early 1990s.

Table 14.2  Distribution of jobs by sectors of economy in the city of Moscow near the end of the Soviet period and later (000s)

| Sectors | 1970 | 1980 | 1985 | 1989 | 1992 | 1997 | 2001 |
|---|---|---|---|---|---|---|---|
| Manufacturing | 1,341 | 1,349 | 1,324 | 1,187 | 1,041 | 773 | 733 |
| Construction | 458 | 566 | 555 | 556 | 631 | 734 | 853 |
| Science, R&D | 774 | 1,022 | 1,035 | 978 | 798 | 542 | 424 |
| Transportation and communications | 418 | 500 | 499 | 424 | 361 | 393 | 441 |
| Information and computing services | 9 | 19 | 21 | 35 | 25 | 65 | |
| Commerce and catering | 406 | 480 | 495 | 480 | 492 | 773 | 1041* |
| Realtors and market services | — | — | — | — | 57 | 284 | |
| Finance and insurance | 20 | 28 | 28 | 27 | 36 | 150 | 149 |
| Public health, sport, and welfare | 193 | 262 | 271 | 299 | 286 | 302 | 325 |
| Education and cultural institutions | 301 | 379 | 418 | 447 | 489 | 491 | 490 |
| Housing maintenance and repair shops | 224 | 253 | 266 | 246 | 187 | 216 | 270 |
| Administration, state, and local | 187 | 246 | 251 | 136 | 173 | 188 | 209 |
| Other | 94 | 105 | 108 | 117 | 165 | 188 | 573 |
| Total employment | 4,425 | 5,209 | 5,271 | 4,932 | 4,741 | 5,099 | 5,508 |

Notes: *Combined employment in three sectors: information and computing services, commerce and catering, and realtors and market services.
Sources: Data compiled and computed from (1) Mosgorstat, Moskva v tsifrakh [Moscow in Numbers, 1989], Moscow: Finansy i statistika, 1989, pp. 24–25; (2) Mosgorstat, Moskva v tsifrakh [Moscow in Numbers, 1990], Moscow: Finansy i statistika, 1990, pp. 24–25; (3) MSE, Mosgorstat, Moskovskiy statisticheskiy ezhegodnik 1998 [Moscow statistical Yearbook 1998], Moscow: Mosgorkomstat, 1998, pp. 43–45; (4) Moskva 2002, Moskovskiy spravochnik [Moscow 2002: Moscow Reference Book], official server of the Government of Moscow, 2002 (www.mos.ru/spr/spr2002/ spr020627009.htm).

## New Power Structure

The Moscow governing body is made up of two major branches: the executive, represented by the city mayor and his subordinates, and the legislative, represented by the Moscow Duma and district assembly members. This new structure was introduced in the summer of 1992 and comprises 10 prefectures (okrugs) and 125 municipal districts (see Fig. 14.1), succeeding 33 former boroughs.

The former 33 boroughs had a very peculiar configuration; 13 of them converged on the downtown area. Since all politically powerful establishments of the Soviet government were in the downtown area, the administrators of each of the 13 boroughs wanted a piece of this lucrative pie. The prefectures left no continuity to the former 33 boroughs. The boundaries of the 10 prefectures follow the historically developed structure of the city. For example, the Central Prefecture boundaries are confined to the borders of the Kamer-Kollezhsky rampart, encircling old Moscow. The prefectures differ in population size, with the Southern Prefecture being twice as big as the North-western (see Table 14.3).

The number of post-Soviet municipal districts was changing over time, initially totalling 143 territorial units, then trimming down to 135 in 1992, 128 in

Fig. 14.1  Moscow administrative territorial division, 1998.

1995, and 125 in 1998. The changing number of municipal districts is explained mostly by local politics. If the head of a specific municipal district was lacking the required managerial skills, this district was merged with its neighbour. If somebody capable and close to the mayor's office needed a high-level position, one district would be split in two to accommodate the newcomer. The names of municipal districts coincide in many cases with their indigenous names, such as Lefortovo, Palikha, and Yakimanka.

A prefect appointed by the mayor heads each prefecture. All 10 prefects have ministerial rank and are members of the Moscow government. They are in charge of their respective regions as top officials. However, they do not have their own budget and depend entirely on the mayor, who can run the city single-handedly by executive directives. As Timothy Colton (1995: 686) puts it: "In the same way as the Yeltsin constitution for Russia is hyper-presidential, these (Moscow) local structures are hyper-mayoral."

Table 14.3 Ten prefectures of Moscow, main numbers

| Prefecture | Territory | | Population 1992 | | Population 1998 | | Change %, 1992–1998 |
|---|---|---|---|---|---|---|---|
| | Sq.km | % of total | 1,000 | % of total | 1,000 | % of total | |
| Moscow, total | 1079.4 | 100 | 8,864.00 | 100 | 8,629.00 | 100 | −2.7 |
| Central | 66.2 | 6.1 | 669.9 | 7.9 | 588.2 | 6.9 | −12.2 |
| North | 112.6 | 10.4 | 967.4 | 10.9 | 884 | 10.4 | −8.6 |
| North-west | 93.4 | 8.7 | 609.2 | 6.8 | 635.1 | 7.4 | −4.3 |
| North-east | 101.9 | 9.4 | 1,114.7 | 12.6 | 1,069.1 | 12.5 | −4.1 |
| South | 131.5 | 12.2 | 1,350.4 | 15.1 | 1,270.6 | 14.9 | −5.9 |
| South-west | 111.7 | 10.3 | 957.7 | 10.8 | 950.3 | 11.1 | −0.8 |
| South-east | 117.3 | 10.3 | 844.7 | 9.6 | 865.3 | 10.1 | −2.4 |
| West | 153 | 14.2 | 975.1 | 11 | 943 | 11.1 | −3.3 |
| East | 154.6 | 14.3 | 1,205.3 | 13.4 | 1,125.8 | 13.2 | −6.6 |
| Zelenograd | 37.2 | 3.4 | 170.5 | 1.9 | 205.8 | 2.4 | 20.7 |

*Source:* Data compiled and computed from Mosgorstat, *Administrativnye okruga Moscovy, 1998* [Administrative Districts of Moscow in 1989], Moscow: Mosgorstat, 1998.

The power structure in 125 municipal districts is made up of sub-prefects, later renamed "chiefs of the municipal assembly". The candidates for these positions are selected by the mayor and are approved by an elected municipal assembly. These municipal assemblies were introduced in December 1997. They are playing a dual role, giving advice to the chiefs of the municipal assembly on the one hand, and channelling local initiatives to the mayor's office on the other. If any grassroots initiatives are possible in this governmental structure dominated by the mayor's appointees, one should look for them at a lower level: the neighbourhood groups.

Very often there is a fuzzy division of responsibilities between the all-city and the lower-level authorities (Bater, 1998: 2). Schools, for example, are under the jurisdiction of the all-city Department of Education but they are also accountable to their municipal district and the prefecture. Residents can be confused about where they should complain if the need arises. The structure of Moscow's authorities has an element of insulating the top officials from the citizens. It is not a unique feature of Moscow; the problem is apparent everywhere in Russia, from the federal level upwards.

The Moscow Duma has 35 deputies who are elected in the districts. The Duma functions since 1993 as the legislative branch of the Moscow government. Very often Muscovites refer to it as a "pocket duma", a reference not only to its size but also to its subordination to a strong mayor, Luzhkov. The Moscow Duma has a complex structure of various committees and subcommittees. The committees deal with matters such as economic policy, the development of self-governance, budgets, housing, and ecology.

## Civic Activity

There are grass roots activities in Moscow that are slowly leading to the emergence of the civic society. The Expert and Consultative Public Council (EKOS) plays a special role in this process. This public organization has the status of a consultative body at the Chief Architectural Agency of the city and includes historians, architects, journalists, sociologists, lawyers, and other experts. Their major task is the protection of cultural and historic monuments (Vinogradov, 1997).

The most notable case of a civic activity led by EKOS was the issue of laying down the Third Transportation Ring through Lefortovo. The highway had to cut through an area with historic buildings. The group of activists succeeded in saving the Shcherbakov's Palatial Chambers and the Old Belief Church.

# Moscow Reinvents Capitalism

If there is any place where the good fruits of the past decade of reforms can be seen, it's in Moscow . . .

(Sergei Kireenko, ex-Prime Minister of Russia, writing in *Noviye Izvestiya*, 1999)

## From Leadership in Reforms to the Greatest Profits in Russia

At the end of the 1990s, Moscow had the most advanced economy among the 89 regions of the Russian Federation. The city contained 5.9 per cent of Russia's population, and it produced a larger share of the national GNP, 11.8 per cent in 1997 (Goskomstat, 1998 [Vol. 2]: 18). This means twice the productivity than the national average.

Russia's press and field observations tell that post-Soviet Moscow offers a haven for the New Russians – the people who make money. Even schoolchildren in Russia are informed of the benefits that Moscow has accumulated after the fall of the Soviet Union. The schoolchildren have a new discipline, *Moskvovedenie*, which in translation means "Learning Moscow". Textbooks are published for explaining developments in the city – guidance in life for the growing generation (Alekseev, 1996; Khmurov, 1998).

## The Mechanisms of Change

During the 1990s, Moscow changed radically and far beyond the incremental adjustments known in social urban ecology (Berry and Kasarda, 1977; Medvedkov, 1978, 1980, 1998). In December 1999, elements of radicalism had to occur in Moscow because the city retired the central institutions of the dissolved Soviet Union. Political power shifted to the governing bodies of Russia, a new nation state.

Reformers consolidated around Boris Yeltsin, the first President of Russia, knew that the old institutions of the Soviet Union were the command economy masters. They also knew that the command economy was causing severe adverse effects. Failed galvanization attempts undertaken in the perestroika years had proven that the command economy was beyond repair. It was political suicidal to tolerate the Soviet Union's central institutions and to continue with attempts at galvanizing the command economy. The reformers found the solution in terminating, as fast as possible, the two-headed monster: the Soviet Union's central institutions and the command economy. The latter had to be replaced by the market economy.

Obviously, the reformers in Moscow understood the situation very well. In moving the market economy to all corners of Russia, the process has to start at the most strategically important place, the capital city. This may explain why Moscow has captured key positions in private banking, real estate, market information processing, and foreign investments so fast. Moscow acts as the commanding pinnacle in Russia's lucrative foreign trade and in domestic commerce. The new wealth, material and spiritual, is impressive in the new Moscow.

Developments in Moscow are not altogether unique. Other nations with transitional economies have capital cities that, as noted by Vardomskiy (Vardomskiy and Mironova, 1999: 56), "gain from the ability of making the fastest adaptations to the market economy". However, people in Russia pay attention mostly to changes in their vast nation. From that point of view, the post-Soviet success of Moscow looks unprecedented. When compared to the perestroika experiments, the current productivity and wealth of Moscow are indeed miraculous. Moscow is widely accepted in Russia as the best evidence of the market economy's superiority over the old Soviet monster. The opinion stated in the above epigraph (Kireenko, 1999) supports this view.

## Housing Privatization: The First Phase of Economic Transformation

Moscow reformers started the privatization of housing several months before the demise of the Soviet Union. This privatization was aimed at creating a propertied middle class and at widening support for the reforms. In September 1991, the decree "Conversion of the State and Municipal Housing Fund of Moscow into the Property of the Citizens" was signed by Gavriil Popov, who at that time was the Mayor of Moscow (Meria, 1991: 9–12). The decree gave nearly any permanent resident of the city the right to obtain ownership for his or her housing unit. The owners of privatized housing units could freely use them or buy and sell them for the market price. The ownership came gratis, with minimum paperwork and a nominal registration fee. One had to pay money only for claiming ownership on exceptionally large dwellings, such as those occupied by higher rank Soviet bureaucrats and by the Communist Party "apparatchiks".

In 1991, nearly 80 per cent of the housing stock in Moscow was announced as eligible for privatization. In 1992, eligibility widened to 90 per cent, because

Boris Yeltsin promulgated a nationwide housing privatization decree. This time, privatization was extended to share apartments (*kommunalki*) in municipal or state housing projects – provided that all the tenants agreed. For condominiums, some 10 per cent of the current housing stock in Moscow, the two decrees permitted owners to trade their property freely and at the market price.

Not all Muscovites rushed into obtaining ownership of housing units. In 1998, the total of privatized dwellings reached 1.36 million, close to 50 per cent of the housing stock in the city. Recently, every year has added 80,000–100,000 dwellings to the privatization. Yet, some households remain undecided about claiming ownership. As Colton (1995: 704) observes: "Many Muscovites have been nervous about future confiscation, possible denial of municipal maintenance and utilities, and onerous property taxation."

## Changes in Business

The privatization of enterprises started in 1992. Prompted by the "shock therapy" of the economy, the privatization hit its highest peak in the same year. When 1992 came to an end the city had 9,486 privatized businesses (*Moskva v tsifrakh*, 1992–1995: 36–38). In 1992, a difficult case was resolved concerning the biggest factory in Moscow, the ZIL automobile works. A joint-stock company, AMO-ZIL, replaced the initial state-owned conglomerate. The AMO-ZIL employees received half of all shares, 25 per cent donated free and 25 per cent auctioned at a discount. The rest was sold to the public (35 per cent), offered to foreign investors (10 per cent), and reserved for the city and the sub-prefectures of Moscow where the AMO-ZIL works were located (5 per cent). An auction with payments in privatization vouchers was used in making private another giant, the Bolshevik Confectionery Factory (Colton, 1995: 710). Joint-stock ventures became popular. By January 1994, the Moscow workforce of 5.1 million had a 50/50 split of jobs between the private sector and state or municipal enterprises.

The second peak was more modest: it came in 1995, when 1,686 enterprises became private. Auction sales and buying initially rented business by instalments became the two leading forms of privatization, and they still predominate today. However, the list of businesses offered for sale by the state or by the city is coming to an end. In January 1998, the city had 560,000 enterprises, and 78.3 per cent of them were private (Goskomstat, 1998 [Vol. 2]: 298).

Retail outlets, restaurants, and repair facilities were the first to go into private ownership. In the Soviet period, the state or municipal agencies owned and ran this sector. Even in 1990, in the late years of Gorbachev's perestroika, the state and municipal outlets concentrated 96.4 per cent of retail sales in Moscow. In 1997, the picture was radically different. Private enterprises made up 96.8 per cent of the city's retail volume. Private or joint-stock businesses made 80.6 per cent of all construction (Goskomstat, 1988 [Vol. 2]: 506, 591). The private sector produced 90.8 per cent of manufacturing output in Moscow, operating with

81.6 per cent of manufacturing labour (Goskomstat, 1998 [Vol. 2]: 336). Labour productivity is apparently better in the private sector than in the remaining non-private enterprises.

The military–industrial sector is, traditionally, very large in Moscow. Until recently it was entirely state-owned. The precise number of current jobs in the military–industrial complex remains secret. These jobs are in manufacturing, and in science and R&D. In 1997 manufacturing kept 15.1 per cent of the jobs in Moscow, whereas science and R&D kept 10.6 per cent. The upper limit for the military–industrial complex cannot be higher then 25.7 per cent of all jobs in the city. The official statistical yearbook shows that civilian goods made up 58.8 per cent of the total output of Moscow's military–industrial complex in 1997. The corresponding indicator for all of Russia is higher: 62.4 per cent (Goskomstat, 1998 [Vol. 2]: 338). One may conclude that some Moscow military enterprises do not rush into the conversion to civilian goods production.

## Changed Employment Structure

Table 14.4 shows the direction and magnitude of changes in two periods – Soviet perestroika and the post-Soviet years. In the terminal period of the Soviet system, 1989 to December 1991, the economy of Moscow suffered greatly. Every year the city lost on average 63,700 jobs. Most jobs were on the state payroll. The Soviet Union central government decided dictatorially how many state jobs to cut and where to cut them. The heaviest losses came in the sciences and the R&D laboratories. Manufacturing faced the second biggest decline in jobs.

Table 14.4 shows that cuts ordered by the Soviet Union government in 1989–1992 hit 6 out of the 13 sectors of employment in Moscow. The liberalized press of Moscow angrily complained about the hectic decisions to abolish many jobs in the state payroll. These were jobs in Moscow's transport and communications, in public health and social benefits, in the maintenance of housing, and in the information and computing services.

The post-Soviet shifts in the economy of Moscow started with "shock therapy". In retrospect, "shock therapy" was a prelude to the successful revival of the city because the doors were opened for the market economy.

Table 14.4 shows the growth in employment for the years 1992 to 1997. New jobs arrived at an average rate of 71,600 per year. All this time, the market economy dominated in the increases in employment. Only two sectors of employment show a continued decline. They are manufacturing and science, both not yet entirely free from the old legacies.

The most sizeable growth occurred in commerce, catering, real estate, marketing, and market services. Expansion also came to construction, information and computing services, transport and communications, housing maintenance, and public health, sport, and welfare. Jobs in producer services are known to be important for improving the competitive advantages of cities. Table 14.4 shows

Table 14.4 Employment by activity sectors: percentage of total jobs and change in jobs (000s)

| Activity sectors | Soviet period | | Post-Soviet period | | | Average change in jobs per year | |
|---|---|---|---|---|---|---|---|
| | 1970 | 1989 | 1992 | 1997 | 2001 | 1989–1992 | 1992–1997 |
| Manufacturing | 30.3 | 24.1 | 22.0 | 15.2 | 13.3 | −48,700 | −53,600 |
| Construction | 10.4 | 11.3 | 13.3 | 14.4 | 15.5 | 25,000 | 20,600 |
| Science and R&D | 17.5 | 19.8 | 16.8 | 10.6 | 7.7 | −60,000 | −51,200 |
| Transport and communication | 9.4 | 8.6 | 7.6 | 7.7 | 8.0 | −21,000 | 6,400 |
| Information and computing | 0.2 | 0.7 | 0.5 | 1.3 | | −3,330 | 8,000 |
| Commerce and catering | 9.2 | 9.7 | 10.4 | 15.2 | 18.9 | 4,000 | 56,200 |
| Realtors and market services | — | — | 1.2 | 5.6 | — | | 45,400 |
| Finances and insurance | 0.5 | 0.5 | 0.8 | 2.9 | 2.7 | 3,000 | 22,800 |
| Public health, sport, and welfare | 4.4 | 6.1 | 6.0 | 5.9 | 5.9 | −4.330 | 3,200 |
| Education and culture | 6.8 | 9.1 | 10.3 | 9.6 | 8.9 | 14,000 | 400 |
| Housing maintenance and repair | 5.1 | 5.0 | 3.9 | 4.2 | 4.9 | −19.700 | 5,800 |
| Administration, state, and local | 4.2 | 2.8 | 3.6 | 3.7 | 3.8 | 12,330 | 3,000 |
| Other | 2.1 | 2.4 | 3.5 | 3.7 | 10.4 | 16,000 | 4,600 |
| Total percentages | 100.0 | 100.0 | 100.0 | 100.0 | 100.0 | — | — |
| Total number of jobs (000s) | 4,425.0 | 4,932.0 | 4,741.0 | 5,099.0 | 5,508.0 | 63.7 | 71.6 |

*Sources:* Data compiled and computed from (1) Mosgorkomstat, *Moskovskiy Statisticheskiy ezwgognik* [Moscow statistical yearbook 1998], Moscow: Mosgorkomstat, 1998, pp. 44–45; (2) Mosgorstat, *Moskva v tsifrakh 1989* [Moscow in number, 1989], Moscow: Finansy i statistika, 1990 p. 24; (3) Mosgorstat, *Moskva v tsifrakh 1990* [Moscow in numbers, 1990], Moscow: Finansy i statistika, 1991, pp. 30–31; (4) *Pravitelstvo Moskvy. Moskovskiy Spravochnik 2002. Statistika* [Moscow Government. Moscow Directory 2002. Statistics], official server of the Government of Moscow, 2002 (www.mos.ru/spr/spr2002/spr020627009.htm).

growing producer services in four rows, from "Transport and communication" to "Finance and insurance". Each year from 1992–1997, the city received, on average, nearly 81,400 new jobs in growing producer services. In the same period over 56,000 new jobs came on average each year in commerce and catering.

Jobs in administration have increased in post-Soviet Moscow, from 174,000 in 1992 to 188,000 in 1997 (MSF, 1998: 44). One might expect a decline after the demise of the Soviet Union, but things went another way. First, the presidential republic, established by the 1993 Constitution of Russia, wanted to build its network of executive agencies. Second, the parliament (Federal Duma) followed the process by hiring staff for numerous committees. Third, Moscow for the first time in its history has a real and powerful self-government. Consequently, the mayor and the municipal parliament of Moscow find that they also need numerous officials. One may wonder, will Moscow climb up to its old 1985 maximum in the number of administrative jobs: 250,800, right before perestroika (Mosgorstat, 1990: 31)?

## Challenged Sectors

Between 1992 and 1997 the manufacturing sector in Moscow lost 268,000 jobs, a decline of 25 per cent. Since 1992, many outputs in Moscow's manufacturing have declined. By 1997, the output of cars declined from 101,900 to 20,600. The output of TV sets declined from 813,800 to 51,300 (Goskomstat, 1998: 398, 401). Output went down in the factories of refrigerators (4.3 times), washing machines (153 times), watches (15 times), footwear (4.2 times), and textiles (6.2 times). The declines have occurred because the consumer now has access to imported goods, and the imports offer better quality. The new middle class enjoys the opportunity of spending on high-quality or novelty goods. The majority of consumers have to economize. They look for the cheapest products, made either in China or in the locally mushrooming sweat shops.

Changes in the sector of producer goods are even more dramatic. This sector suffers both from foreign competition and from a general slump in domestic orders on new equipment. In 1992–1997 the number of metal-cutting machine tools made in Moscow went from 6,500 units to 500. The output of re-programmable automated lines for machine building declined from 1,600 units to 300. Moscow cut down by 60 times the fabrication of industrial electric motors (MSE, 1998: 258). The sales of rolled steel in Moscow went down from 1.1 million metric tons in 1993 to 0.6 million in 1997 (Goskomstat, 1998: 620).

Success stories in Moscow's manufacturing sector do exist. In 1992–1997, output of personal computers increased from 32,000 to 124,000. Moscow chemical factories started to produce modern synthetic materials in volumes that went up three to five times, depending on the brand (MSE, 1998: 258, 261, 264). Upward trends are observable in the production of non-alcoholic refreshments (2.9 times up), canned food (7.8 times), and salami and sausages (1.5 times). As a rule, bigger increases have been experienced by factories with foreign capital participation.

Jobs in the sciences, R&D, and education are not growing in Moscow as they used to in the Cold War years. Many talented individuals have moved to the producer services, to banking, and to marketing. However, in 1995–1998 the number of research centres was fairly stable: between 20,968 and 21,619. The numbers remain impressively high. The same is true of the staff of experts in research: 313,900 and 290,400 for the same years. They can offer very impressive brainpower; there are 54,600 scientists with doctor's degrees (MSE, 1998: 121).

According to Table 14.4, education is a sector with slower than average employment growth. Trends in this sector are complicated. Downsizing factors operate alongside new and exciting challenges. On the one hand, universities cannot count on capturing students from the former Union Republics and dependencies. On the other, universities and colleges are getting more numerous: 77 in 1989, 81 in 1992, and 85 in 1997. Diversity in education has increased; private colleges do much of the pioneering work. They offer training that is in high demand in the job market.

A new skyscraper in the south-west of Moscow has an impressive size and purpose: the Centre for Marketing Research. Run by Abel Aganbegyan, a prominent economist, this centre is ranked higher than Moscow State University in the popularity of its new training programmes. The MBA degree is a notable example.

Moscow contains between 16 and 17 per cent of the students admitted every September to Russia's universities and colleges. From 1994 to 1997 the number of students steadily increased, up to 142,000 (Mosgorkomstat, 1998; Goskomstat, 1998 [Vol. 2]: 201). Nearly 36 per cent of the students take correspondence courses, combining studies with work (Mosgorstat, 1990: 96).

Correspondence courses are more affordable, because the part-time student can earn money and cover their tuition costs. Tuition commonly amounts up to US$400 per quarter in the better schools (Vendina, personal communication, November 1999).

## The Emerging Middle Class

The new middle class of post-Soviet origin struggles with the instability of its status. Perhaps this instability explains why the official statistics fail to identify the phenomenon in a proper way. Moscow statistical yearbooks do not report the size of the middle class. The published tabulation of incomes shows quite a meaningless upper stratum that includes 57.3 per cent of Muscovites (MSE, 1998: 81). The arithmetic average for a stratum that includes the top earnings of multi-millionaires means very little. Besides, reported incomes are of questionable accuracy. Tax evasion is universal in Russia. The discrepancy between the sum of population incomes and population spending in Moscow is astronomically large (MSE, 1998: 72).

For estimating the size of the middle-income stratum, we prefer to rely on indirect but well-maintained statistical records. These are records regarding privatized dwellings, private cars, and private businesses. The circle of households aspiring to the middle class includes more households than those with privatized dwellings. In 1997, the number of those in the latter group was 1,361,000 (MSE, 1998: 190). Discussions with Muscovites show that not all middle class families live in privatized dwellings. Specifically, of about 80,000 federal and municipal officials, few do this. Rather, they live in the dwellings provided as career perks. This 80,000 must be added to the previous figure of 1,361,000 when estimating the number of middle class individuals in Moscow.

Car ownership is another indicator of middle class lifestyles. In January 1998, the number of cars in Moscow households was 1,689,900 or 2.7 more than in January 1992 (MSE, 1998: 295). The numbers in the above text show that well over a million Moscow households belong to the middle class. This number is further confirmed by adding together the groups in population with entrepreneurial functions. The most numerous are self-employed persons, at 575,000 (MSE, 1998: 42). In 1997, Moscow had 174,500 small private businesses with an average staff of 64 per 10 enterprises (MSE, 1998: 190). The number of medium-sized and large businesses is 20,600, considering only manufacturing (MSE, 1898: 234). By assuming two co-owners, on average, in a small business and four executives in a medium-sized or large manufacturing enterprise, we find that owners and executives in small, medium-sized, and large businesses total 431,400 persons. Finally, one has to count 70,900 physicians who now enjoy access to private practice, and 191,200 certified experts in research centres, who today run contract projects (MSE, 1998: 121, 133, 182, 272). The total from adding these numbers comes to 1,268,500. According to this estimate, the middle class breadwinners make 25 per cent of the economically active population, and 15 per cent of all residents in Moscow.

## Unemployment: The Biggest of Social Pathologies

Fast transformations in Moscow have produced casualties. The post-Soviet press honestly and promptly describes these sad events. Negative sides in a transitional economy more readily trigger political debates than accomplishments. Certain casualties look sensational. For example, a terrorist act or a mutiny will surely be reported in internationally distributed TV programmes. Unemployment in Moscow does not cause a sensation. However, that is the very area that is causing the most numerous casualties. And the cause of unemployment can be squarely identified: the blame lies with the new conditions of jobs in the transitional economy.

Officially reported unemployment in post-Soviet Moscow is very moderate. Unemployed persons numbered 280,500 in 1992 and 194,900 in 1997. The unemployment peak, 335,300, came in 1994 (Goskomstat, 1998 [Vol. 2]: 81). All numbers here are for unemployment in the definition of the International Labour Organization. The numbers include persons who may seek jobs but do not register as unemployed. In 1992, the unemployed made up 4.9 per cent of the labour force, and in 1997 the number declined to 3.7 per cent. Moscow's municipal programme for providing unemployment benefits faces smaller numbers. In 1997, applicants for benefits numbered 37,525, and all but 957 received the requested support.

The job market in Moscow usually offers more vacancies than the number of unemployed. In this respect, Moscow is unique in Russia. In 1997, every advertised job vacancy attracted, on average, six jobseekers in Russia.

In Moscow, this ratio was nearly 9 times smaller: 7 jobseekers for every 10 job offers (Goskomstat, 1998 [Vol. 2]: 93). Indeed, unemployment in Moscow is triggered not by the absence of jobs but, rather, by rapid structural changes.

One may ask: has the city a strategy for generating future jobs steadily? The answer is affirmative. The boom in commerce and banking surely strengthens the position of Moscow for adding more jobs. Specifically, commerce and banking do this because of a multiplier effect. The Mayor of Moscow has repeatedly initiated seed investments in new office complexes. The construction phase brings jobs immediately, and more jobs arrive later, when the complex starts functioning. The most ambitious booster programme, a blueprint for the jobs of the next two decades, was approved by the Mayor in December 1998: the new Master Plan of Moscow.

## The Built Environment

The central streets of Moscow are saturated with new foreign stores, ethnic restaurants, casinos, banks, and foreign luxury cars. At night the city shines under a myriad of lights and advertisements, which makes one forget the image of a grey, socialist city as if it were the distant past. Moscow is undergoing a major remaking, with the reconstruction and gentrification of the historic centre, the reconstruction of demolished cathedrals and the building of new churches, the construction of new transportation networks, and the booming construction of high-rise apartment complexes and family houses. These changes are not only about the bricks and mortar; they are also about the people. Moscow is becoming a comfortable city in which to live, to visit, and to have fun. The theatre life in Moscow is magnificent. The central streets of Moscow at night are full of Muscovites and tourists enjoying the city life. The newly built public spaces give people the opportunity to socialize.

The new Master Plan of Moscow, approved by the city government in December 1998, declared its major task to make Moscow a comfortable city in which to live. This was the first time in the history of Moscow's urban planning that the human being was placed ahead of production.

Starting from 1995, more than 600,000 sq.m of housing, public, and business buildings have been reconstructed and built within the Garden Ring. Up to then, no major repair had been done to the old buildings since 1910, just a facelift for some. Unique buildings were neglected during decades of mass housing construction of dull, monotonous architecture. The renovation of Moscow's historic centre is one of the main tasks of the new Master Plan (Fig. 14.2).

Seemingly all downtown is under excavation. The "big projects" include Kitay-Gorod, an ancient cultural, trading and business centre of Moscow since the fifteenth century. The architects undertook the challenge of reconstructing the wall and restoring the famous Guest Court (Gostiny Dvor). The restoration

Fig. 14.2 Images of Moscow. (a) City centre, the Cathedral Square. (b) Mosossovet, the City Hall in the downtown area. (c) Inner city, the first power station of the Soviet period on the Moscow river bank. (d) South-west of Moscow, Soviet mass housing projects implemented in the 1970s. (e) Inner city gentrification. (f) New villas in Moscow's suburbia.

of the Tretiakov Art Gallery and the Bolshoi Theatre on Teatralnaya Square, and the rebuilding of the Red Porch of the Grand Kremlin Palace on Cathedral Square, top the list of projects, which are still continuing. One of the most famous projects is the restoration of the Christ the Saviour Cathedral. The restoration of the Church of Mother of God of Kazan and the Resurrection Gates on Red Square was conducted within the shortest possible time. The Centre is changing not only its appearance but also its functions, giving space to more diverse CBD land users.

Paris may have inspired a number of grand projects initiated by Yuri Luzhkov. The construction of a new business centre at Krasnopresnenskaya Embankment, the "City", has a strong parallel with La Defense in Paris, which is considered to be one of the boldest ventures of French urban planners. Both centres, La Defense and the City, are designed to attract business activity from the congested CBD to more peripheral locations, to take some pressure off the old core. The City will spread over 100 ha along the Moscow River, with numerous office buildings, major Russian and foreign HQs, exhibitions, and hotels. The rapid transit system will connect the City with the major airports of Sheremetyevo and Domodedovo (the latter is now under reconstruction).

A Second World War memorial ensemble has been built in the western part of Moscow, along Kutuzovsky Prospect on Poclonnay Hill (Poklonnaya Gora). This complex consists of the Second World War Memorial, Saint George Cathedral, a mosque, and a synagogue. During Victory Day on 9 May, thousands of Muscovites visit the Memorial to pay respect to those who served and to share their sorrow. It is interesting that a large portion of this crowd are teenagers looking with amazement and great respect at old men and women whose chests are decorated with medals. The place generates a feeling of continuity with the past.

A unique public place has been generated around a newly built commercial centre, Okhotny Ryad. It is an underground shopping mall with luxury goods, restaurants, and cafés at the Manege Square, next to Red Square. This project caused contradictory feelings among Muscovites, just like the creation of the "Pyramids" at the Louvre entrance. The outcome of this project is amazing in a way few expected. A great public space has been born around Okhotny Ryad. There are numerous cafés. It is a meeting place where people interact, watch a concert staged in front of them, or just enjoy viewing the turbulent urban life. The whole stretch of Tverskaya Street from the Manezh Square up to Pushkin Square is the main commercial artery patronized by Muscovites and visitors day and night. The Old Arbat Street, located in the western sector of the Central Prefecture, has been turned into a pedestrian mall with shops, restaurants, artists, and musicians. Russian chain restaurants such as Shury-Myry (Hanky-Panky) and Yolky-Palky are becoming extremely popular.

The centre is becoming a cleaner place to live. A substantial number of industrial land users are getting rid of their most polluting factories. Overall, 25 per cent of the land in Moscow is occupied by industries in comparison with 5 per cent in American cities.

The city is in desperate need of a new transportation system. The number of automobiles during the last decade has increased by roughly 1 million, from 629,000 in 1991 to 1,690,000 by the end of 1998, but the roads inside Moscow are practically the same. This situation creates terrible bottlenecks and congestion, particularly inside the Garden Ring, making it impossible to drive. If one has to cross the city, the subway (metro) is a much better choice. One of the first projects of the 1990s was the reconstruction of the beltway (MKAD) stretching for 109 km around the city. Four lanes in each direction replace two old lanes built in the 1960s, and new glassy overpasses for pedestrians give the beltway a finished look.

The major transportation project reshaping Moscow now is the construction of the Third Ring freeway stretching for 35 km and cutting the city in half. This new freeway will follow an old circular inner railroad (CIR), built in 1908. Positioning the freeway along the CIR has minimized the need to demolish the existing buildings. At the same time, the freeway links such major regions inside the city as Luzhniki, the Kiev Rail Station, "the City", and the All-Russian Exhibition Centre. Parts of the old rail system are being converted into a surface metro badly needed by Muscovites.

By 1999, the residential floor space of Moscow reached 179 million sq.m, averaging 20.2 sq.m per person. In Berlin, this number stands at 39 sq.m, in Paris 28, and in Vienna 36 (Baevskiy, 1999: 25). The rate of housing construction is maintained at the high level of 3 million sq.m per year due to a commercial approach that keeps a balance between the sold and freely distributed municipal dwellings.

Free apartments are allocated to families who have been on the waiting list for many years and cannot afford to buy a new dwelling on the market. Among these are families living in communal flats, particularly in the central part of Moscow. By 1998, more than 182,000 families were still on the waiting list, compared to 216,000 in 1992 (MSE, 1998: 98). The Central Prefecture gained 17 per cent of all new housing in Moscow in 1998, more than any other prefecture, having only.6.9 per cent of city's population. The second largest project, 16 per cent of new houses, came to the Northern Prefecture (its population share is 10.4 per cent). Many communal flats in central Moscow have been remodelled and sold or leased to firms. The residents from communal flats have received apartments, usually on the periphery of Moscow, free of charge.

The new Master Plan of Moscow emphasizes the importance of intensive land-use development inside the current municipal boundaries. Nevertheless, substantial single-housing construction occurs on the periphery of Moscow, particularly beyond the beltway. The single home is a new concept of housing for Muscovites. Travelling outside Moscow, one can be astounded by the striking contrast between the old village landscape with its wooden huts, and the newly built red brick mansions, often with armed guards on duty. Those are the new signs of Russian suburbanization.

## Geo-Demographics and Social Stratification

In the Soviet period it was a privilege to live in Moscow. All power and decision-making activities were concentrated in the capital of the highly centralized state.

The city had the best to offer in education, jobs, culture, science, sports, and services. Not everybody could move to Moscow – to be a part of this privileged place one had to obtain a resident's permit (called a *propiska*). This was ordered by the decree dated 27 December 1932.

After the demise of the Soviet Union much emphasis was placed on the decentralization of power. One might expect that the core–periphery gap would narrow during the first post-Soviet decade. But this did not happen, because Moscow made a gigantic step towards reforms, leaving the rest of the country far behind.

This accelerated change did not come free of charge to Muscovites. It resulted in a sharper social polarization, deepening the core–periphery dilemma inside the city; it also sped up the demographic transition into a negative population growth and an older population structure (Medvedkov and Medvedkov, 1999).

Starting from 1992/93, Moscow lost population due to a negative natural increase (see Table 14.5). Between 1992 and 1996 Moscow lost on average 100,000 residents per year. Looking at the column "Natural increase" in Table 14.5, one can see that in 1993 and 1994 the birth rates were outstripped by the death rates by almost by 10 points. These are the hardest years of the reforms. The later years, and in particular 1999 and 2000, saw an increase in prosperity for some groups of Muscovites and were characterized by a slightly milder negative natural increase (–6.8 and –6.7 respectively). In January 2000, the total population

Table 14.5  The dynamics of natural population increase in Moscow, 1988–1998

| Year | Population millions | Birth rate per 1,000 | Death rate per 1,000 | Natural increase (%) |
|------|------|------|------|------|
| 1988 | 8.9 | 13.1 | 12.0 | 1.1 |
| 1989 | 9.0 | 11.8 | 12.4 | −0.6 |
| 1990 | 9.0 | 10.5 | 12.8 | −2.3 |
| 1991 | 9.0 | 9.2 | 12.9 | −3.7 |
| 1992 | 9.0 | 7.7 | 13.7 | −6.0 |
| 1993 | 8.9 | 7.1 | 16.5 | −9.4 |
| 1994 | 8.8 | 7.6 | 17.6 | −10.0 |
| 1995 | 8.7 | 8.0 | 16.9 | −8.9 |
| 1996 | 8.6 | 7.9 | 15.0 | −7.1 |
| 1997 | 8.6 | 7.8 | 14.4 | −6.6 |
| 1998 | 8.6 | 7.8 | 14.6 | −6.6 |
| 1999 | 8.5 | 7.8 | 14.8 | −6.8 |
| 2000 | 8.5 | 8.5 | 15.2 | −6.7 |

*Sources:* Data compiled from (1) Goskomstat, *Demographic Yearbook of Russia (2000)*, official publication, Moscow: Goskomstat, 2000; (2) *Pravitelstvo Moskvy. Moskovskiy Spravochnik. Statistika* [Moscow Government. Moscow Directory. Statistics], official server of the Government of Moscow, 2002 (www.mos.ru/spr/spr2002/spr020627009.htm); (3) Mosgorkomstat, *Moskovskiy statisticheskiy ezhegodnik 1998* [Moscow Statistical Yearbook 1998], Moscow: Mosgorkomstat, 1998; (4) S.O. Schmidt, ed., *Moskva*, Moscow: Encyclopedia, 1997.

of Moscow reached 8,631,000, practically equalling the figure a year before, which was 8,630,000.

This negative trend cannot be offset by the growing positive migration to the city of 13,000 new dwellers in 1994, 26,000 in 1995, 36,000 in 1996, and 51,000 in 1997. There are numerous illegal immigrants and transients residing in the city who are not included in official data for obvious reasons, but do add to the 8.6 million Muscovites an estimated number of 350,000–400,000. On a daily basis the city is embracing around 500,000 commuters who add another 200,000 cars to the already unbearable traffic (Glushkova, 1999). The busy streets of the capital do not give an impression of a shrinking population. The de facto population of Moscow is well over 9 million, exceeding the official figure of 8.6 million. It is estimated that daytime population in the city is exceeding 10 million.

The declining population of Moscow and Russia in general is influenced by a trend in the demographic transition, with its origin in the 1970s and particularly the 1980s (see Fig. 14.3). This trend is a common feature for European world cities. In the case of Moscow, two curves, birth rates and death rates, are crossing each other, changing direction in 1989.

The overall picture of natural population increase in 125 municipal districts in Moscow should have the reverse title of natural population decrease, since only two newly acquired villages in the west (Mitino and Novoperedelkino) have positive population growth numbers (see Fig. 14.4).

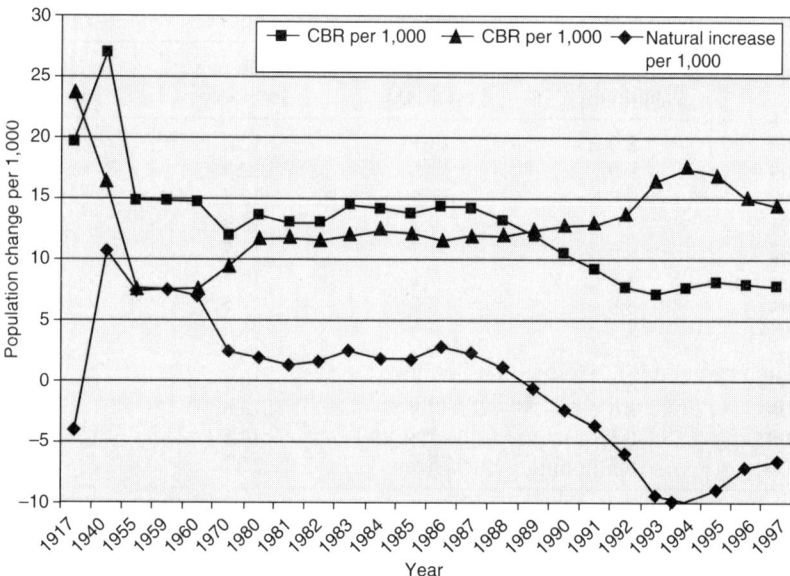

Fig. 14.3  Moscow birth rates, death rates, and the natural increase.
*Source:* See Table 14.5.

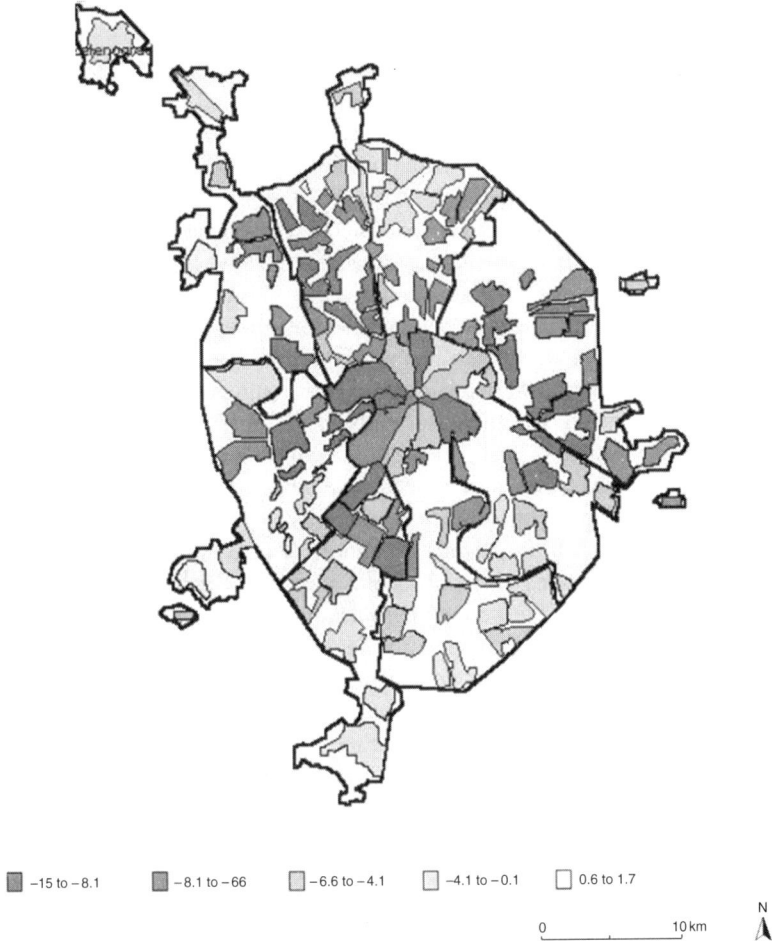

| | −15 to −8.1 | | −8.1 to −66 | | −6.6 to −4.1 | | −4.1 to −0.1 | | 0.6 to 1.7 |

N

0 _____ 10 km   ⋀

Fig. 14.4 Natural population increase per 1,000 people, 1997.

High birth rates are to be found on the periphery, particularly on the outskirts of the North, North-east, East, South-east, and South Prefectures. With the exception of Zelenograd, the north-western suburb of Moscow, the East Side of the city is experiencing higher birth rates. The East Side is much more industrial than the West and is inhabited primarily by workers. This East–West split is repeated in the pattern of many variables, as shall be seen later.

The division into a less privileged industrial East and a more privileged elitist West has occurred over the decades of the Soviet regime. The Soviet nomenclature occupied residential areas adjacent to the Kremlin and along Kutuzovsky Prospect in the Western sector of the centre and extended their turf through the Western Prefecture. The intellectual elite settled in the South-west Prefecture near Moscow State University and numerous Institutes of the Academy of Sciences along Leninsky and Vernadsky Prospects. Military people lived in a concentrated pattern in the North-western and Northern Prefectures. Working class residential quarters were located in the East and South-east Prefectures. At the same time, a casual observer could notice mixed residential neighbourhoods just as well.

During Soviet times the city residents were lacking intra-urban mobility for a very simple reason – an absence of choice and of a real-estate market. The Soviet nomenclature and senior bureaucrats got the best municipal housing in the best city sector because they belonged to the power structure. Currently, the New Russians can purchase the same or better elite housing because they have money. Both categories, old bureaucrats and new entrepreneurs, often end up as neighbours. In the centre the most prestigious areas are the Arbat blocks adjacent to Tverskaya Street, Sretenka, Clean Ponds (Chistye Prudy), and Yakimanka. There are also expensive apartments on Leninsky, Vernadsky, and Kutuzovsky prospects. The western direction is expanding outwards, creating new elite residential blocks along Michurinsky and Mosfilmovskya streets. Some northern directions are considered attractive, such as Mira Prospect, Sokolniki, and the north-west direction following Tverskoy Prospect.

The eastern sector cannot compete on the real-estate market due to the quality of its housing. The middle class perception suggests that only the less fortunate live on the East Side, next to numerous smokestack factories and dumping grounds. The East Side also has dormitories full of illegal residents: foreign refugees, Chinese entrepreneurs, and traders from Central Asia and the Caucasus. The number of unemployed in the Eastern Prefecture is 10 times higher than in the Centre or in the West Side of Moscow. Moscow, during the new market reforms, did acquire the features of world cities: glamorous and sorrowful, all at once.

## Links to Other Cities

### Remoteness

Moscow's location in the network of all capital cities in Europe is distinctly remote. Fig. 14.5 illustrates the point. The area of the most likely mutual interaction among European mega-cities forms a polygon on the map. The shortest polygon side, the London–Paris corridor, is strikingly different from the corridor that links Moscow and Istanbul (1,753 km). Nearly right on the line as the crow flies between London and Moscow sits Berlin. The distance between Moscow and Berlin (1,619 km) is roughly twice that between Berlin and London. Of course, St Petersburg is the mega-city that is closest to Moscow

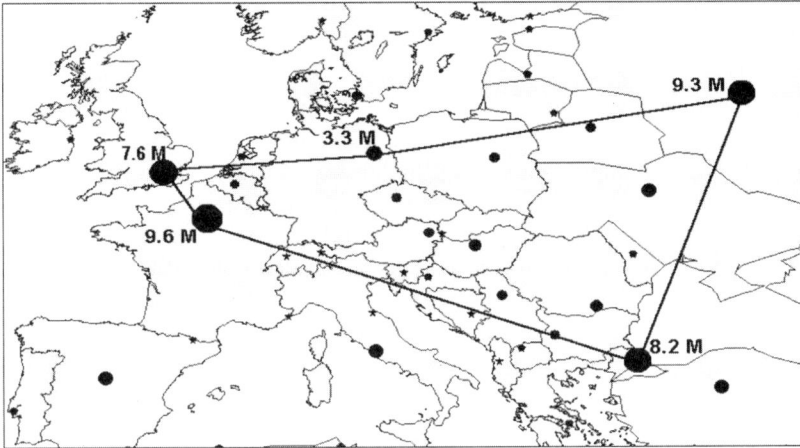

Fig. 14.5  Moscow's location in the network of capital cities in Europe.

(651 km), but it does not offer Moscow the benefits of direct interaction with leading European nations. On the contrary, the proximity of St Petersburg brings an element of competition because foreign investors and other business partners may value its seaport facilities, a feature missing in Moscow. Existing statistical data do not show, however, that St Petersburg successfully attracts foreign direct investments (FDI). For example, in 1998 Moscow captured 23 per cent of all new FDI in Russia, whereas St Petersburg received only 2.6 per cent (Broadman and Recantini, 2001: Table 5).

Inside the polygon one may count 17 European capitals. The capitals make a cluster near the London–Paris corridor and another one in the core of the former Austro-Hungarian Empire. Nothing of this sort is available near Moscow. The polygon corner of Moscow looks strikingly empty on the map. Moreover, the city is remotely located with respect to the sea-lanes of international trade. The nearest seacoast, the Baltic Sea shore, is 651 km away from Moscow. Given these disadvantages, what in geography may suggest alternative partners in playing Moscow's trump card, human resources? The easiest interaction occurs with the human capital in Moscow province.

## Human Resources in Moscow Province

The human capital of Moscow province is formidable in number: 6.6 million persons. The province surrounds the city on all sides, which is good for combining the labour pool of the province with that of Moscow. The province is the most developed part of Russia, both in the Soviet past (Hamilton, 1976) and recently (Ioffe and Nefedova, 1998).

*Limited Commuting*

Geographers in Russia in their recent works rarely merge the city of Moscow and Moscow province into one metropolitan region of 15.2 million residents. When they do, the purpose is not to delimit the city-region. Rather, Moscow and the province make a complex in the national economy (Alekseev et al., 1996: 158) for business outsourcing and subcontracting (Glushkova, 1999: 20). The combined territory of the city and the province, 48,000 sq.km, is similar in size to Switzerland. Less than 9 per cent of residents in Moscow province commute to work in the city of Moscow. The percentage is modest, considering that supply is shorter than demand in the labour market of Moscow (Vardomskiy and Mironova, 1999: 100). One has to remember the general inadequacy of passenger transportation facilities in Russia. The point is that the "friction of distance" is prohibitively high for permitting commuting from the entire province territory. Outsourcing and subcontracting may alleviate the situation because they involve freight movement to substitute for commuting. Unfortunately, freight transportation costs grow in Moscow province at a much faster rate than in the city of Moscow and on average in Russia. This trend has repeated nearly every year since 1994 (Goskomstat, 1998: 778), and it certainly creates obstacles for outsourcing and subcontracting. The abnormally high share, 47–48 per cent, of transportation enterprises in Moscow province worked with financial losses during 1996 and 1997 (Goskomstat, 1998: 709).

*Geopolitics at the Municipal Border*

The city of Moscow has an area of 1,079.4 sq.km. The prospect of Moscow obtaining more land from the surrounding province is very questionable. The federal government cannot change the size of Moscow's territory, as practiced during the Soviet period. The post-Soviet constitution of December 1993 has redefined relations between Moscow and the surrounding Moscow province. There is no subordination between the two. They are equal and self-governed members of the Russian Federation.

Constitutionally, Moscow and Moscow province are exactly similar to states in the US. The number of "senators" they send to the Federal Council is the same (two). Moscow, with its 8.5 million population, can elect more legislators to the Federal Duma. However, Moscow province, with its 6.5 million citizens, makes the second biggest electorate pool in Russia.

*Special Character of Towns in Moscow Province*

The average population density of Moscow is nearly 7,970 per sq.km, much larger than that of Chicago (4,700), according to the 1990 Census of Population. We quote density in Chicago because it is a sister city of Moscow. Implied crowding brings an element of disadvantage for the city. The province surrounding Moscow can more easily provide sites for land-consuming projects such as airports, additional beltways, and complexes of family houses.

Moscow province is rich in R&D staff. Numerous towns are treasure chests of brainpower, and useful managerial skills are also common. Examples are Chernogolovka, Dubna, Friazino, Korolev, and Zhukovskiy. Every one of them has a renowned research centre. While the towns cannot offer Moscow's benefits of size, they attract investors by offering more attractive terms in land renting, longer tax holidays, and low construction costs. Decommissioned military camps saturate the territory of Moscow province. They are for sale. Whereas the property may be federal, it is local support that makes or breaks post-sale developments.

## The Most Developed Province of Russia

Moscow province is the most economically developed part of Russia. The province favourably compares to similar-sized nations in Europe. The urbanization of Moscow province is 80 per cent. By the number of incorporated towns (over 70) the province is unique in Russia. It has 13 cities with a population of over 100,000 in each. The 40 or so largest towns show much similarity in size, in departure from the Rank-Size Rule of urban hierarchy. This peculiar organization of urban hierarchy results from the close interaction of those 40 towns with Moscow, the mega-city.

The population density of Moscow province is 140 persons per sq.km. This is more than that of Denmark (121 persons), which is approximately the same size. For making the comparison on equal terms one has to consider the population in Denmark outside the agglomeration of Copenhagen. In that case the "provincial density" of Denmark steps down to 91 persons per sq.km. The population density of Moscow province is also more then that of the Czech Republic, where "provincial density" comes to 115 persons per sq.km outside the Prague agglomeration and 131 persons in all territory in the republic.

The province is very similar to the city of Moscow in terms of post-Soviet shifts in the structure of economy (see Table 14.6). On the one hand, manufacturing, construction, sciences, R&D, and education have decreased their importance in the job market. On the other hand, transport, communications, retailing, wholesale trade, and catering have increased their share in total employment. Such shifts in employment structure correspond to the general pattern of changes that occur under the influence of globalization.

## Domestic and Foreign Links

In the post-Soviet years, Moscow's commercial banks dominate the economy of Russia. Obviously, the banks have links extended to all corners of Russia. By 1999, the city contained 900 private banks, including 53 per cent of the

Table 14.6 Similarities between Moscow province and the city of Moscow: changes in the structure of employment, 1990–1997

| Sector of economy | Moscow province | | The city of Moscow | |
|---|---|---|---|---|
| | 1990 | 1997 | 1990 | 1997 |
| Manufacturing | 36.7* | 23.5 | 22.6 | 15.2 |
| Construction | 9.5 | 5.8 | 7.8 | 14.4 |
| Transport and communications | 5.9 | 7.4 | 11.8 | 7.7 |
| Education, science, and R&D | 17.8 | 16.6 | 27.4 | 20.3 |
| Retail, wholesale, and catering | 6.7 | 14.6 | 9.4 | 15.2 |

Note: * Numbers show percentage of total employment.
*Source:* Data compiled from Goskomstat (1998 [Vol. 2]: 75).

200 largest banks in the nation. The share of Moscow in all banking accounts of Russia is 65 per cent. The importance of Moscow is even bigger in the total sum of banking credits (67 per cent) and in foreign currency credits (81 per cent) (Vardomskiy and Mironova, 1999: 57). Its leading involvement in credit operations permits it to reap profits from businesses located even in the very distant places of Russia. At the same time, credit operations carry an elevated risk, due to the trial-and-error practice that the transitional economy cannot avoid. Moscow's banks suffered from the financial panic of August 1998. Six banks lost their ratings in the roster of the 100 largest banks of the nation. However, the majority of banks survived the panic. Moscow still has 66 of the 100 largest private banks in Russia (Vardomskiy and Mironova 1999: 67).

Moscow handles the flow of goods in Russia through its commodity exchanges (17 in January 1998). In addition, 2,545 certified brokers trade in goods and 400 trade in securities (MSE, 1998: 214). In 1997, more than 24,500 realtors operated in Moscow. Currently, the Guild of Realtors of Moscow lists property prices in US dollars, a security shield from galloping inflation. So far, land plots in Russia may only be leased, whereas buildings and floor space may be owned. The Government of Moscow permits long-term leases of 49 years or more.

From 1991 to 1997 the share of Moscow in Russia's retail market went up from 11.6 to 27 per cent. The city handles 32 per cent of Russia's exports. Judging by the sum of import duties, one-third of which are collected in Moscow, the city handles at least that much in imported goods (Vardomskiy and Mironova, 1999: 61).

*Foreign Direct Investment*

The city of Moscow is Russia's leader in accumulated FDI, at US$7.76 billion in 1995–1999. Moscow contains 44.2 per cent of all FDI in Russia (see Table 14.7).

Table 14.7 Cumulative inflow of FDI, 1995–1999: distribution by constituent units of Russian Federation

| Constituent units, ranked by FDI | Total FDI (billion US$) | % of total FDI | Rank by FDI |
|---|---|---|---|
| The city of Moscow | 7.76 | 44.2 | 1 |
| Moscow province | 1.72 | 9.8 | 2 |
| Sakhalin province | 1.30 | 7.4 | 3 |
| St Petersburg | 0.94 | 5.3 | 4 |
| Krasnodar kray | 0.70 | 4.0 | 5 |
| Samara province | 0.40 | 2.3 | 6 |
| Novosibirsk province | 0.37 | 2.1 | 7 |
| Tymen province | 0.33 | 1.9 | 8 |
| Sverdlovsk province | 0.28 | 1.6 | 9 |
| Magadan province | 0.20 | 1.2 | 10 |
| Other 79 units | 3.62 | 20.5 | n/a |
| Total | 17.62 | 100.0 | n/a |

*Source:* Data compiled from Harry G. Broadman and Francesca Recantini (2001).

The second place belongs to Moscow province, 9.8 per cent of the total. Obviously, investors appreciate the opportunities of Moscow and of the surrounding province. The oil-rich provinces of Russia, Tymen, and Sakhalin, even when taken together, do not match the FDI accumulated in Moscow province alone, not to mention the city of Moscow. However, the FDI total amounts look ridiculously low, considering the size of Russia.

Trends in FDI are monitored in Russia by the Foreign Investment Promotions Centre (FIPC), which operates in Moscow under the federal Ministry of Economics. The Government of Moscow keeps its own watch on the FDI area, judging by the FDI tabulations published in the very detailed statistical yearbooks of Moscow. For many years, Moscow has steadily increased its share in all FDI within Russia.

In 1994, the city took 18 per cent of all FDI located in Russia. In 1995, the percentage increased to 45; in 1996 it was 60; and in 1997 it was 80. The sum of new FDI received in 1997 was US$3.05 billion, nearly 20 times more than in 1994 (Goskomstat, 1998 [Vol. 2]: 750). The financial crises of August 1998 made a dent in the FDI. In 1998–1999 the share of Moscow in the flow of FDI dropped, reflecting the consequences of the financial crash in 1998 (FIPC, 1999). That decrease was contrary to steps undertaken by the Moscow city government, which wanted to demonstrate that during the crises Moscow offered more security for foreign investors than any other place in Russia. In the fall and winter months of 1998, when Russia's federal treasury stopped paying interest on its foreign loans, there was nothing of this sort in Moscow. The Government of Moscow kept repaying nearly all its foreign debts (Vardomskiy and Mironova, 1999: 66).

*The Growing Globalization Component*

Moscow profits from its old function as a major hub of railroads in Russia and is expanding its new role as a major international airway hub. The geopolitical designs of Moscow politicians reach, at times, very distant corners of the former Soviet Empire. However, the Commonwealth of the Independent States does not bring the best trade partners for Moscow. The main economic and financial links of Moscow are pragmatically different. The shipment of goods from Moscow to former Union Republics went down in post-Soviet years. Shipments to Ukraine reached 2.6 per cent in 1994, compared to those to the domestic market of Russia. In 1997, the Ukrainian share was down to a barely noticeable 0.18 per cent. As of January 1998, investors from the US and Germany led in the number of joint ventures established in Moscow. Investors from the UK, Ukraine, and China made the second tier of leaders (MSE, 1998: 307). Total announced investments in Moscow businesses with foreign partners show the international links of Moscow in another light. The leading links, by volume of investments, belong to Cyprus and Liechtenstein. Moscow, according to this evidence, values links to sources of money with origins that are hard to trace.

Europe contains the most active international links of Moscow served by air transportation. Fig. 14.6 shows the map of 29 popular international destinations accessible through direct flights from the International Airport of Moscow (Sheremetievo). The map is based on the Sheremetievo Airport timetable of flights (www.sheremetyevo.ru/rsp.htm). Every one of the 29 mapped destinations had at least 14 departing flights per week in August 2000. European cities comprise 24 of the 29 destinations mapped. Germany stands out as the only case of multiple destinations, five altogether, in Moscow's air links. European nations east of Berlin harbour 12 popular destinations for air travellers from Moscow. Flights with the highest frequency go to Frankfurt (Germany): 80 departures from Sheremetievo per week. The second and the third most popular places are Prague and London (67 and 62 departing flights). Next in the order of departing flights are Berlin, Stockholm, and Tel Aviv, with 56, 44, and 40 flights per week respectively. Kiev (34), the most populous metropolis among all "borderland" post-Soviet nations, is in seventh place. The weekly number of flights from Moscow to Kiev is nearly the same as from Moscow to Paris (32) and to Hamburg (32). Leading non-European destinations include New York and Tokyo.

We find three components in the geography of destinations shown by Fig. 14.5. The first component consists of links leading to the "alpha" world cities, the commanding centres of the globalization process (Beaverstock, Smith, and Taylor, 1999). London, Paris, Frankfurt, New York, and Tokyo belong to the category of alpha world cities, and they attract 215 flights per week departing from Moscow. Arguably, the globalization component has to include all destinations in nations with alpha world cities: four more cities in Germany and

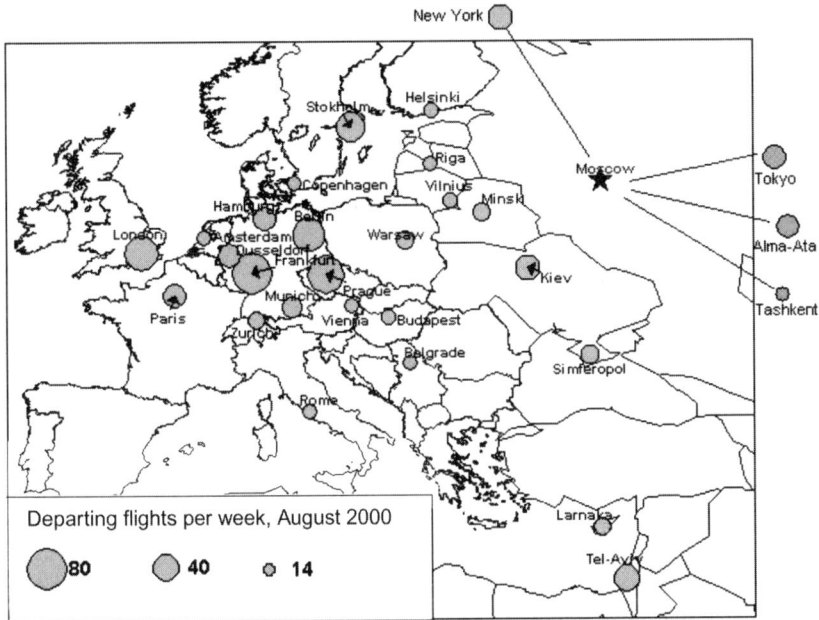

Fig. 14.6  International "hinterworld" of Moscow.

one in Italy. With this approach the number of flights generated by the globalization component steps up to 372. The second component follows legacy links of the former Soviet Union: flights from Moscow to the Baltic States and to the CIS partners. Here Moscow has a weekly total of 141 departing flights. The third component includes legacy links between Moscow and the former "Warsaw Pact" partners. In this case Moscow has a weekly total of 102 departing flights. The globalization component by number of flights is much stronger than the sum of the legacy components (compare 372 to 243). The total number of destinations related to the two legacies is 10, and they receive on average 24.4 weekly flights per destination. The similar average for the first component is 37.2, which is another reason for recognizing the dominating power of the globalization process in Moscow's air transportation geography.

Additional and independent evidence exists regarding the concentration in Moscow of numerous producer services that have been established by transnational corporations in the course of the globalization process. According to the Globalization and World Cities Study Group and Network (GaWC), Moscow is one of the 10 "beta" world cities. This "beta" rank is as strong as that of Seoul in South Korea, but less so than that of the closer situated Brussels, Zurich, and Madrid. At the same time, Moscow's rank in the globalization process is much ahead of that obtained by Prague, Warsaw, and Budapest (Beaverstock, Smith, and Taylor, 1999).

Our own observations support this view. Moscow strengthened its trans-national producer services by the year 2000, compared to the period covered in the GaWC report. In August 2000, the Business Telephone Guide (http://mbtg.net/guide) listed 18 foreign banks that operate in Moscow, including three trans-national giants: Dresdner Bank, Citibank, and Credit Suisse. Accountancy services are provided by four well-recognized leaders in the field: Arthur Andersen, Ernst & Young International, KPMG International, and *Price Waterhouse LLP*. The first three of these corporations have a staff of Moscow associates numbering 500, 320, and 40 respectively. Nine trans-national firms provide advanced legal services. They are Allen & Overly, Baker & McKenzie, Clifford Chance Peunder LTD, and others. Those nine firms with operations in Moscow make the majority of the 16 similar firms that lead the field of international legal services (here and later in the text, the leaders in the field are those defined by the GaWC).

The producer services of key importance for the globalization process also include the field of advertising and Internet consulting. Moscow has attracted two internationally recognized leaders in this field: BBDO and Dentsu Young & Rubicam. A databank of top agencies that provide advertising (www.ou.edu/class/imc3333/russia.htm) shows also such firms as D'Arcy Masius Benton & Bowles, Bates Saatchi & Saatchi, McCann-Ericson, and Olgivy & Mather. All of these companies earn multi-million incomes in Moscow.

To summarize, Moscow has an impressive array of institutions established for purposes of moving ahead the globalization process. To the east of Germany in Europe they are the institutions with the biggest size, expenses, and diversity. On the European scale, however, all this has not lead, so far, to Moscow's prominence in wealth creation.

## Conclusion

Our conclusion focuses on the paradox of low globalization rewards in Moscow. What can explain the low levels in FDI and in GNP generation? There are several explanatory factors, and they mutually strengthen each other.

### Point One

The usual counter-force of globalization is at work. We mean the complex mix of opinions about the paramount and overriding importance of protecting Russian cultural identity from the internalization of global lifestyles. The energetic rush of new ventures and the adoption of the most efficiently working ideas could surely look like a menace for traditionalists. The famous writer Alexander Solzenitsyn exemplifies a negative attitude to the steamroller of globalization.

Globalization enters Moscow in a roaring way, but without a public relations programme. Not every Muscovite interprets the renovated and rebuilt cathedrals as evidence that cultural diversity and globalization profit from each other. Open-air bazaars, over 30 operating day and night, are the main display of globalization that Muscovites know. Unfortunately, these places are ugly and overcrowded. The visual image of the bazaars can therefore strengthen the counter-force against globalization.

## Point Two

The agenda of creating symbols of Russia's unity in Moscow must be considered. The project of returning Moscow to its former holy image of Orthodoxy runs at full speed. Muscovites from other religious denominations rush to the new opportunity of having the symbols of their culture in the city where they live. The statement of Yuri Luzkov regarding the "Third Rome" destiny is quoted earlier in this chapter, and it reflects a strong desire to bring to the foreground historic heritage rather than efficiency in globalization. The Mayor and the Parliament of Moscow are aware that the cultural heritage goal is rich in political rewards. This is a way to enhance the cohesiveness of people and to get political support from the electorate. Both are coming faster than success on the part of the city in upgrading its international competitiveness.

## Point Three

Moscow suffers from the morass of Russian politics. Very few of the 89 regions of the Federation have made the same efforts as Moscow in building the institutional base of democracy and the market economy. St Petersburg and Moscow province did make progress. The third case, examined and documented by Ruble (1995), is the province of Yaroslavl. However, the majority of the other provinces are in a morass of indecision and delays. Moscow cannot be shielded from the difficulties of the surrounding areas. The financial crisis of August 1998 was an example. At that time, setbacks in Moscow's globalization designs were severe.

## Point Four

The gap in innovations between Moscow and the rest of the nation is dangerously wide. The imagination of people from the periphery tends to over-inflate the disparities. People in the peripheral regions of Russia are getting angry. They see that some Muscovites live better and better, whereas they do not. The usual cleavages between the core and the periphery are more noticeable in Russia because of the periphery's vast size.

## Point Five

Many industrial capacities have become outmoded. This is a problem for both Moscow and the peripheral regions. With the end of the Cold War many areas with reduced military outputs are declining. The Urals, East Siberia, and Udmurtia provide examples. New investments are urgent but distant peripheries may not trust Moscow as an investment broker. They do not benefit from the "trickle down" effect that Moscow brings to its immediate surrounding.

## Point Six

Moscow suffers from disadvantages in its geographic location, and mitigating solutions are not yet in view. The location of Moscow is peripheral in relation to the other mega-cities of Europe. The intervening opportunity model, well known to urban and economic geographers, permits one to understand that Moscow is not the first in line for receiving investments. The flow of money originates in wealthier world cities, and they have closer targets for investment than Moscow. No alpha world cities are closer to Moscow than those of Western Europe. However, Central Europe offers numerous targets for Western European investors with better closeness in all aspects.

## Point Seven

Moscow is not yet marketing its human capital aggressively. Domestic efforts in this direction are inadequate. During the Soviet period, R&D and the sciences had little experience in marketing their products outside national borders. Currently, foreign promoters are the most realistic force for bringing Moscow's human capital into the globalization process.

## REFERENCES

Alexander I. Alekseev, ed., *Moskvovedenie* [Learning Moscow], Moscow: Ekopros, 1996.
Ludmila Alekseeva, *Soviet Dissent*, Middleton: Wesleyan University Press, 1985.
Konstantin K. Arsenyev and Fedor F. Petrushevskiy, *Rossia* [Russia], Moscow: Brokhouse & Efron, 1898.
Oleg Baevskiy, "Strategia gradostroitelnogo razvitiya Moskvy v 21 veke" [Strategy in Moscow Urban Development in the 21st Century], *Architektura*, 14(4), 1999, p. 26.
James H. Bater, Vladimir N. Amelin, and Andrei A. Degtyarev, "Market Reform and the Central City: Moscow Revisited", *Post-Soviet Geography and Economics* 39(1), 1998, p. 2.
Jon V. Beaverstock, Richard G. Smith, and Peter J. Taylor, "A Roster of World Cities", *Cities* 16(6), 1999, pp. 445–458.

Scott Blacklin, "The Regions and Russian Political Evolution. President's Reports", *AmCham News* 6, Moscow: American Chamber of Commerce in Russia, 1999.

Brian J.L. Berry and John D. Kasarda, *Contemporary Urban Ecology*, New York: Macmillan, 1977.

Harry G. Broadman and Francesca Recantini, *Where has all the Foreign Investment Gone in Russia?*, Working Paper 2640, World Bank, July 2001.

CIA, *The World Factbook 2002*, Washington D.C.: CIA, 2002.

Susan E. Clark and Gary L. Gail, *The Work of Cities*, Minneapolis: University of Minnesota Press, 1998.

Timothy J. Colton, *Moscow: Governing the Socialist Metropolis*, Cambridge & London: The Belknap Press, Harvard University Press, 1995.

Foreign Investment Promotions Centre (FIPC), *On Foreign Investments Into the Russian Federation*, 1999 [www.fipc.ru/fipc/reviews/statjan99.html].

Vera G. Glushkova, *Sotsialnyi portret Moskvy na poroge XXI veka* [Moscow Social Portrait at the Threshold of the 21st Century], Moscow: Mysl, 1999.

Goskomstat, *Regiony Rossii* [Russia's Regions], Vols 1 and 2, Moscow: Goskomstat, 1998.

———, *Demographic Yearbook of Russia 2000*, official publication, 2000.

F.E. Ian Hamilton, *The Moscow City Region*, London: Oxford University Press, 1976.

David Hooson, ed., *Geography and National Identity*, Oxford: Blackwell, 1994.

Gregory Ioffe and Tatyana Nefedova, "Environs of Russian Cities: A Case Study of Moscow", *Europe-Asia Studies* 8, 1998, pp. 1325–1356.

Alexandr M. Khmurov, *Moskvovedenie, Spravochnik i posobie* [Learning Moscow: A reference book], Moscow: Bookline, 1998.

Sergei Kireenko, "Moskve nuzhna alternativa," [Moscow Needs an Alternative], in *Noviye Izvestiya*, 11 June 1999, p. 2.

Yuri Luzkov, "A Word about Moscow", in *Moscow – 850th Anniversary* 1, Moscow: Moscow Textbooks, 1996.

Olga Medvedkov, "Soviet Cities and their Industrial–Social Performance", *Urban Geography* 9(5), 1988, pp. 487–518.

———, *Soviet Urbanization*, London: Routledge, 1990.

Yuri Medvedkov, *Chelovek i gorodskaya sreda* [Human Actors in Urban Environment], Moscow: Nauka, 1978.

———, "Functioning of Space Modified by its Evolution: The Case Study of Moscow", *Studia Geographica* (Brno) 73, 1980, pp. 65–80.

———, "La geographie dans l'etude et la gestion du melieu" [Geography in the Study of Urban Environment], *Villes en parallele* 26–27, 1998, pp. 119–142.

Yuri Medvedkov and Olga Medvedkov, "Turning Points and Trends in Russia's Urbanization", in G. Demko, ed., *Population Under Duress: The Geo-Demography of Post-Soviet Russia*, Bolder: Westview Press, 1999, pp. 201–230.

Meria Moskvy, *Vestnik Merii Moskvy* [Moscow Mayor's Office Herald], No. 3, October, 1991, pp. 9–12.

Moscow Mayor's Office, *City, Reforms, Life: Moscow in Numbers, 1992–1995*, Moscow: Intergraph, 1995.

Mosgorstat, *Moskva v tsifrakh* [Moscow in Numbers], Moscow: Mosgorstat, 1990.

Mosgorkomstat, *Osnovnye pokazateli sotsialno-ekonomicheskogo razvitiya administrativnykh okrugov g. Moskvy za Yanvar-Dekabr 1998 goda* [Basic Indicators of Social and Economic Development in Moscow Administrative Districts], Moscow: Mosgorkomstat, 1999, pp. 12, 48.

*Moskva 2002: Moskovskiy Spravochnik* [Moscow 2002: Moscow Reference Book], official server of the Government of Moscow, 2002 [www.mos.ru/spr/spr2002/ spr020627009.htm].

MSE, *Moscovskiy statisticheskiy ezhegodnik 1998* [Moscow Statistical Yearbook 1998], Moscow: Mosgorkomstat, 1998.

Gunnar Myrdal, *Rich Lands and Poor: The Road to World Prosperity*, New York: Harper, 1957.

Michael Porter, *The Global Competitiveness Report 1999*, Oxford: Oxford University Press, 1999.

Lester Rowntree, Martin Lewis, Mary Price, and William Wyckoff, *Diversity Amid Globalization: World Regions, Environment, Development*, Upper Saddke River: Prentice Hall, 2000.

Blair A. Ruble, *Money Sings*, Cambridge: Cambridge University Press, 1995.

Sigurd O. Schmidt, ed., *Moskva*, Moscow: Encyclopedia, 1997.

Ludmila I. Shvetsova, "Glabnaya zadacha – zabota o cheloveke," [Population in the Centre of Attention], in *Moscow Reference Book*, Moscow: Government of Moscow, 2000; official server of the Government of Moscow Government, 2001 [www.mos.ru/ spr/spr2002/spr020627006.htm].

Leonid B. Vardomskiy and Valentina A. Mironova, eds, *Moscow on the Background of Russia and the World*, Moscow: IMEP RAN, 1999.

Olga I. Vendina, "Transformation Process in Moscow and Intra-Urban Stratification of Population", *GeoJournal* 42(4), 1997, pp. 349–363.

Vladimir A. Vinogradov, ed., *Moscow – 850th Anniversary* 2, Moscow: Moscow Textbooks, 1997.

United Nations, Population Division, *World Urbanization Prospects, the 2001 Revision, ESA/P/WP.173*, New York: UN Press, 2002.

World Economic Forum, *The Global Competitiveness Report, 2001–2002*, Oxford: Oxford University Press, 2002 [www.weforum.org].

# 15

# Conclusions

*Nataša Pichler-Milanović and Kaliopa Dimitrovska Andrews*

This concluding chapter summarizes some of the main findings of this volume, concentrating on the impact of globalization and EU-ization on the inter- and intra-urban transformation of post-socialist cities in Central and Eastern Europe, as well as current urban development practices and policy networks.

The rapid integration of economies worldwide through globalization has been most notable since the 1980s because of the convergence of trends reflecting structural adjustment and internationalization of production, technological innovation, and knowledge-based activities (Lo and Yeung, 1998). The structural adjustments affecting production, use of resources, financial transactions, and wealth creation have also stimulated the process of "world or global city formation" and the transformation of the economic, social, and physical structure of cities and their competitiveness within various urban networks.[1] Simultaneously, the process of globalization, defined as increasing cross-border functional integration of economic and other activities, is enhancing interdependency among major cities located around the world, as increasingly important nodes for the flows of trade, capital, people, and information (see Friedman, 1986, 1995, 2001; Knox and Taylor, 1995; Sassen, 1991, 1994; etc.).

Since the end of the 1980s, Central and Eastern European countries have undergone a political, economic, and institutional transition from various forms of socialist structures towards democratic and market economy systems. Globalization as a term and concept has not only been used in this volume in an economic context; it also encompasses political, socio-cultural, environmental, communication, and policy dimensions, and it can be interpreted as a twofold process. First, in the form of transition or structural adjustment as a shift from socialist to democratic societies and market-based economies, and internationalization or functional (re)integration into global processes after the demise of the Cold War. Second, the prospective accession of these countries to fully fledged membership of the European Union represents a completely new phase of institutional development. The systematic process of EU enlargement and integration – Europeanization, or rather "EU-ization" of values, standards, norms, and policies – can thus be interpreted as a specific "mode" of globalization in Central and Eastern Europe in a particular macro-regional context, aimed at achieving global competitiveness in the twenty-first century.

In this respect, the underlying pressures of the world economy, particularly in terms of city competition for attracting capital investment and improving one's position within the international urban hierarchy and trans-national and cross-border urban networks, are just as applicable in Central and Eastern Europe as elsewhere in the world (Musil, 1993; Enyedi, 1998; Marcuse and van Kempen, 2000; Keivani, Parsa, and McGreal, 2001). Therefore, the "world city formation" and position of Central and Eastern European capital and other large cities within the wider global and European urban hierarchy are yet to be determined.

In general, "world city formation" can be thought of as the process in which global active capital becomes concentrated in cities (Friedman and Wolff, 1982). World city formation is the process by which the global economy impinges upon cities and transforms their social, economic, and physical dimensions, focusing on the role of "command and control" activities in large urban areas (Friedman, 1986; Sassen, 1991, 1994) – these activities include location of headquarters for trans-national corporations and international institutions; business services; transport access, population size, research, and education facilities; and convention and exhibition functions. This traditional focus, however, limits the number and type of cities included as "world" (or "global") cities – for example, to those that have become major centres of manufacturing and service-related activities (Lo and Yeung, 1998).

But "world city formation" is a continuing and varied process, or multi-faceted process. The emergence of specialized or regional "functional" city systems is defining new roles for particular cities or groups of cities in the global urban hierarchy. Those cities integrated into the "functional city systems" (i.e. "cross-border regional urban networks") are also undergoing the process of world city formation. Their inclusion in the system, or urban networks, has had direct effects on urban form, structure, and development.[2] According to Brenner (1999), "world city formation", as part of "reterritorialization", implies that, in order to be effective in global and regional networks, cities have undergone physical restructuring of their intra-urban patterns. Many urban policies are formulated as a response to global economic pressure, with the objective being to attract capital investments and increase competitiveness in relation to other cities.

Therefore, whether Central and Eastern European capital cities are labelled as "world cities" in a traditional framework of world city analysis is somehow irrelevant. In order to analyse "differentiated" impacts of globalization on the transformation of post-socialist (capital) cities in Central and Eastern Europe in this volume, these cities are examined in their geographical and historical settings, in the context of political, economic, and institutional reforms in the 1990s, and in the context of accession to the European Union. Capital cities are also examined through the interplay between global ("external") and local ("internal") forces on their inter- and intra-urban transformation in the last decade.

## From Capital Cities to "Global" Cities

The globalization of the world economy is also leading to selective development and different locational advantages of particular cities in Central and Eastern Europe. The most important spatial effect of globalization processes is the enforcement or reinforcement of the large metropolitan areas, and capital cities in particular, as a priori key nodes of human activity. These cities play a critical role in the diffusion of economic growth and social and cultural innovations within their national urban systems. The effects of globalization are also visible through the "world (or global) city (re)formation" of the largest and most dynamic metropoles such as Berlin and Moscow, and the Central European capitals of Prague, Budapest, and Warsaw.

Since reunification in 1989, Berlin has regained its potentiality as a European political and cultural centre. The creation of an innovative economy based on new technologies, communication services, and (inter)national functions is aimed at supporting the city's aspiration for the status of a "global" city (Krätke, 2001; see also Chapter 7). The position of Budapest, Prague, and Warsaw has risen from the rank of cities of national importance to cities of European importance. Prague has probably the strongest "globalization potential" (e.g. in tourism) after Berlin.

Looking at their main international activities as described in Chapters 8–10, Prague has become a strong cultural centre in Central and Eastern Europe, while Budapest and Warsaw have become important Central and Eastern European centres in finance and industry respectively. Capital cities in South–east Europe such as Sofia and Bucharest are struggling to improve their status from cities of national to European importance, but they are lagging behind the Central European capitals due to macro-economic constraints and their peripheral location in Europe (see Chapter 12).

Other small capital cities in Central Europe such as Ljubljana and Bratislava, or the Baltic capitals – Tallinn, Riga, and Vilnius – (re)gained their international role through the capital city formation of the new independent states, strengthening their national and international status through cross-border and trans-national cooperation and accession partnerships with EU Member States (as shown in Chapters 11 and 13). For example, Ljubljana has substantial comparative advantages vis-à-vis other Central and Eastern European capital cities on the basis of strengths in its national and city economy, quality of life, and institutional capacity for reforms. Ljubljana is one of the most competitive cities in Central and Eastern Europe, but still has to enter into the processes of more intensive internationalization, overriding its small size and rather low level of recognition within the network of European capitals. In this way it will improve its role in the cross-border "functional city system(s)" as part of the "world city" formation process.

The other new capital cities of the former Yugoslavia – Zagreb, Sarajevo, and Skopje – have improved their status as regional centres to that of cities of national importance. Other capital cities in South-east Europe such as Belgrade and Tirana retain the rank of a city of national importance, as they are lagging behind due to political, economic, and institutional constraints in their respective countries. The new capital cities in East Europe, such as Minsk, Kiev, and Kishniev, are currently isolated from global processes, and "long-term" excluded from the process of EU enlargement and integration. In spite of Moscow's peripheral location in relation to other European cities of similar size – e.g. London, Paris, Istanbul – it has retained the rank of a city of international (if not "global") importance, building on the competitive advantages of its human capital and geo-strategic location between Europe and Asia (see Chapter 14).

At the moment none of the Central and Eastern European capitals can be considered as "world cities" in the traditional sense of analysis – not even Moscow, due to its size and former influence over the former socialist cities in Eastern Europe. The only city that may rise to the role of "world city" in the near future, and join the other two "global" cities in Europe – London and Paris, and to same extent Vienna in a Central European context – is probably Berlin. All the other Central and Eastern European capital cities are still internationalizing their financial, business, or cultural functions, while at the same time searching for a particular "niche" to specialize in trans-national (European) and cross-border (regional) "functional urban systems" or specialized city networks.

## From National Settlement Hierarchy to Cross-Border Urban Networks

The other mode of "world city formation" in a more European context is the establishment of "urban networks" through cross-border and trans-national cooperation, links, and partnerships between different cities in EU Member States and cities in Central and Eastern European countries.

The three Baltic capitals that were formerly part of the Soviet Union geographically and economically belong more to the Northern European (Scandinavian) urban networks. Central European cities in Hungary, the Czech Republic, Slovakia, Slovenia, Poland, and to some extent Croatia have strengthened their linkages most notably with cities in Germany and Austria. Since the demise of the Iron Curtain in 1989 and in the context of cross-border regionalization and EU-ization, closer economic and cultural cooperation and partnerships are now possible between neighbouring cross-border cities of different role and size in their national urban systems, such as Gdansk and Copenhagen, Wroclaw and Prague, Warsaw and Berlin, and Vienna, Bratislava, and Budapest. These different forms of partnerships occur through city twinning, and also through improved infrastructure, trade, joint ventures, education and training, and other projects supported by bilateral or EU funds.

In South-east Europe (i.e. other former Yugoslav republics, Bulgaria, Romania, and Albania), cities are still not well integrated in cross-border and trans-national (institutionalized) urban networks, as a consequence of ethnic conflict, political instability, and economic constraints during the 1990s. They are under growing influence from Italy, Greece, and Turkey in terms of trade and capital flows, but struggling to build or reinforce closer connections between each other or with other Central European and EU cities. One specific case is Sarajevo, which was in the "global eye" for several years in the 1990s during the military conflict in Bosnia and Herzegovina, and its newly established (formal) links with the Muslim world.

Considering their geo-strategic location and economic, transport, or cultural influence in Central and Eastern Europe, cities such as Berlin, Vienna, or Munich could each become a "hub" for Central European cities, Stockholm or Helsinki for Baltic cities, and Rome, Athens, or Thessaloniki for South-east European cities. These different types of cross-border links and networks are also consistent with the subregionalization of Central and Eastern Europe as introduced in Chapter 1, based on historic, cultural, socio-economic, and geographical characteristics, and the role and status of particular cities in their respective national or increasingly trans-national urban systems. At the same time, Central and Eastern European cities are developing complementary links to enhance specialization in different urban networks that offer the opportunity to compete more effectively on the world stage. The formation of urban networks based on integrated transport infrastructure, cooperation, links, and partnerships between firms, governments, knowledge-based institutions, and citizens, are encouraging the emergence of a new European urban hierarchy, and contributing significantly to the creation of an increasingly global society, while at the same time preserving the specificities and identities of particular cities across the national borders.

## From Socialist to "Post-Socialist" Cities

Urban development is a highly interdependent and dynamic process that is strongly influenced by history and inherited structures (e.g. spatial distribution of economic activities, land use and property market, administrative and institutional structure) and the interrelation between them. A historic review of the impact of the socio-political events of the twentieth century on the evolution of the Central and Eastern European cities as shown in Chapters 1–6 of this volume shows some similarities in their intra-urban structures through four distinctive periods: before the First World War (the Austro-Hungarian Empire), between the two World Wars (the newly independent countries), after the Second World War (the socialist period), and after 1990 (the transitional period).

After the Second World War the primary objective of communist governments was to eliminate market allocation of goods and services in favour of more comprehensive, socially effective criteria in distribution of resources (French and Hamilton, 1979). Nationalization of property (land, housing, economic assets, etc.) and redistribution of resources under the auspices of the state had been a common procedure in former socialist countries. Urban policies were shaped by significant political-institutional factors such as direct state control over financial resources and control over city size, domination of manufacturing, significant state ownership of urban land and housing stock, and subsequently direct control over land use and housing markets (see Chapters 2 and 3).

The leaders of Central and Eastern Europe sought to diminish the regional inequalities and urban-rural dichotomy (as a heritage of the past) between and within the socialist countries through the processes of industrialization and urbanization. Regional and urban planning was part of the overall national development strategies, with central authorities as the key decision-maker and collective ownership and control of urban land, housing, and infrastructure. Inherited differences between and within Central and Eastern European countries persisted throughout the socialist period despite the (official) egalitarian ideology and policies of "balanced" regional development and "managed" urbanization. Generally the resulting patterns reflected the attempt to stimulate growth in small and medium-sized cities. It could be said that economically more developed countries in Central Europe such as (former) East Germany, Czechoslovakia, Poland, and Hungary had undergone a significant regional development vis-à-vis South-east European countries. The only country where regional "equalization" was less successful was the former Yugoslav Federation, with persistent differences between more developed republics in the north (Slovenia and Croatia) and other less developed republics in the south of Yugoslavia.

The historical context and political legacies of city development in Central and Eastern Europe, discussed in Chapters 2 and 3, show that the urbanization processes in socialist countries differed from those in capitalist countries. Therefore, development of the inherited urban system in the former socialist countries represented only a modification of a "universal" model of urbanization (see also Kennedy and Smith, 1988; Enyedi, 1992, etc.), which could be rectified in a relatively short period. By contrast, the differences between socialist and capitalist urban development were the most significant at the intra-urban level. The socialist model of housing development and urban planning, the centralized, planned economic system, and the non-existence of (urban) land markets are the most important features that have shaped a distinctive structure of socialist cities, significantly different from capitalist cities in Western Europe. Socialism has left its most lasting imprint on the city's periphery, where large housing estates were built, and also in the inner city areas, dominated by deteriorating historic buildings. The suburbanization process did not play an important role before 1985 in shaping the growth patterns of socialist cities as in the capitalist countries. As a result, socialist cities are more "compact" than capitalist ones.

By the 1990s, the population of Central and Eastern Europe had reached 124 million, with 56 per cent in urban areas. The region had experienced the most rapid post–Second World War growth of any region in Europe in total and urban population, but with large differences between the countries. More than half of the urban population in Central and Eastern Europe live in cities with less than 100,000 inhabitants, while cities with 100,000 or more inhabitants contained a quarter of the region's population.[3] In Estonia and Latvia, as in Bulgaria and Hungary, the high concentration of population is particularly visible in and around the national capitals. The capital cities of Poland (Warsaw), Romania (Bucharest), the Czech Republic (Prague), Lithuania (Vilnius), Slovakia (Bratislava), Slovenia (Ljubljana), and Albania (Tirana) contain far lower proportions of their national population (UNCHS, 1996; UNECE, 1997).

In the 1990s, political, economic, and geo-strategic reforms have led to important structural changes in Central and Eastern Europe, characterized by reorientation of trade to EU markets, price liberalization, economic and therefore industrial restructuring, a shift from an industrial to a service economy, transformation of enterprises, privatization, foreign direct investment, a shift from a supply- to a demand-orientated economy, and the membership of international organizations and associations. The transformation process was the most dramatic in countries with the most radical transition reforms, such as Poland, the Czech Republic, and Hungary. The involvement of "global" (financial) organizations such as the World Bank, IMF, and WTO was equally important at that time, as were the EU accession requirements from 1993 onwards. Intra-city transformation of the post-socialist cities has been influenced particularly by local government reforms, restitution, privatization, and capital investments.

The development of socialist cities was in many aspects unique, which also means that cities in Central and Eastern Europe have had great similarities to each other at the beginning of the transition period in the early 1990s. The differences, such as the speed of transition processes, the domination of private ownership, and the role of foreign capital, are evident among the post-socialist cities. Their impact on the transformation of Central and Eastern European cities has been similar during the first phase of transition (1990–1995), showing some common aspects of city transformation on economic competitiveness, social cohesion, environmental quality, built structures, and the role of urban governance in post-socialist cities (Andrusz, Harloe, and Szelenyi, 1996; Enyedi, 1998: Keivani, Parsa, and Mc Greal, 2001). The effects of different forms of integration into the global and European networks have had negative consequences on the emergence of "winners and losers" – between cities, economic sectors, and social groups – and direct implications for the urban management and planning of post-socialist cities.

## Economic Competitiveness: "Winners and Losers"

Since 1989, the restructuring of the international economy and the weakening of national boundaries has been challenging post-socialist cities. City competitiveness is very much dependent on the strength of the national economies, and consequently political stability in Central and Eastern Europe. Transition reforms and EU accession requirements have also had an important impact on the competitiveness of large and capital cities as centres of political, administrative, commercial, financial, technological, scientific, and cultural activity. Changes in property ownership, public administration and finance, transport and energy costs, and employment and housing opportunities have raised questions about the competitiveness and sustainability of Central and Eastern European cities, and their roles in social, economic, and political affairs within and beyond Europe.

The industrial past of the former socialist cities was infamous for its legacies of poor environmental quality, and environmental quality is a major determinant in both attracting and retaining economic activity and high-quality labour force in the city. City competitiveness emphasizes the effects of transformation on supply and demand constraints for economic development and labour markets. The evidence of patterns, processes, and changes in the international integration of post-socialist cities is shown in Chapters 4–5 through trade flows and FDI, which became a key force in shaping the evolution of "globalization" trends through the decisions and activities of (multi)national firms. Improvements in city accessibility and transport infrastructure are reflected in the number of large-scale projects undertaken in Central and Eastern Europe (upgrading of airport facilities, motorways, ports, intra-city transport, etc.). The majority of transport systems currently operating both in and between post-socialist cities are antiquated, overloaded, and unable to meet the demands of the modern city, and are one of the major causes of environmental deterioration. Air traffic patterns, analysed in Chapter 5, provide important insights into the "connectivity" and internationalization of Central and Eastern European cities in the European and global contexts. Real-estate markets represent a strong link between "external" and "internal" forces of globalization, as examples of the "global–local nexus", linking inter-city transformation processes with changing patterns of intra-urban land use and built structures. These are analysed from different perspectives in Chapters 3–6 of this volume (see also Ghanbari-Parsa and Moatazed-Keivani, 1999; Keivani, Parsa, and Mc Greal, 2001; Sýkora, 1998).

After a decade of post-socialist city transformation, there is today considerable rivalry and competition between Central and Eastern European cities for access to resources, associations, and networks. This could diminish the overall competitive strength and cohesiveness of an enlarged Europe.

## Social Cohesion: Diversification and Fragmentation

The emerging processes of globalization and city competitiveness advantage some areas and disadvantage others, creating uneven economic and social development both between and within cities. Emerging economic reforms such as demand for global and European integration are also diminishing social cohesion and increasing differences between ethnic and socio-economic groups in post-socialist Central and Eastern European cities.

In the 1980s, analyses of the internal structure and socio-spatial differentiation of socialist cities were based on the effects of provision and distribution of housing among different social groups in particular city localities. According to Musil (1993) the analysis of the housing system, housing policy, and urban planning in former socialist countries was more adequate than the analysis of land markets, as key factors explaining the pattern and dynamics of residential segregation in capitalist cities. Hence, residential differentiation in socialist cities did not generally show the extremes of social-class segregation, as a consequence of the egalitarian principles of those cities. Since 1990, socio-spatial differentiation in Central and Eastern European post-socialist cities has been reinforced by industrial restructuring, decentralization of economic activities, stagnation or bankruptcy of enterprises, privatization, rising unemployment levels, growing income differences, etc. According to evidence from the individual city case studies (see Chapters 7–14), the process of selective socio-spatial polarization in post-socialist capital cities has been especially apparent in particular city locations with specific housing, demographic, and social structures, and functional land-use patterns. This transformation process is linked with the growing dependence of post-socialist cities on international resources as well as their local economic and social potentials.

## The Built Environment: Revitalization and Preservation

As a consequence of several decades of strong political, institutional, and economic regulations during the socialist period, the Central and Eastern European cities underwent significant changes in their spatial organization that were most evident in the intra-urban structure of particular socialist cities. Mediaeval historic core and inner city areas built at the end of the nineteenth century, with the exception of modest high-rise office developments, were dominated by a deteriorating building stock nationalized in the 1950s and badly maintained until the 1990s. High-density housing estates were constructed at the city periphery, while high-quality low-rise housing estates for the political end economic elites were located in the green belt. Self-built detached family houses were constructed in suburban settlements (villages) lacking sufficient infrastructure, and largely inhabited by lower socio-economic groups.

The socialist legacies of housing development, architectural design, and urban planning strategies are reflected in the transformation of land-use patterns and morphological structure of post-socialist cities. Political and economic reforms in the 1990s have had important effects on city transformation in Central and Eastern Europe, especially housing privatization and restitution, ownership diversification, urban revitalization, and suburbanization. In the urban context, the reintroduction of land and housing markets in post-socialist cities has been the main effect of transition reforms (Pichler-Milanović, 1994, 2001). A sophisticated system of property prices has developed, reflecting the location, quality, size, accessibility, and level of services in particular city areas. Property prices in capital cities are often 30–50 per cent higher than in other cities. Price increases are most significant in attractive inner city locations and some residential areas at the city outskirts, showing the sharp difference between the city centre and peripheral areas as already described in the city case studies in this volume (see also Struyk, 1996; Hegedüs, Mayo, and Tosics, 1996; Pichler-Milanović, 2001).

City transformation in Central and Eastern Europe is most notably associated with de-industrialization, commercialization, and gentrification of the historic core, reurbanization and revitalization of some inner city areas, and residential and commercial suburbanization in the outer city ("urban sprawl"). The process of housing rehabilitation and revitalization of old historic cores can be observed in combination with growing tourism (e.g. in Prague) and demand for space in central locations for expanding retail and office activities. Reconstruction of historically important buildings and sites is another activity, aimed at preserving cultural heritage and respect for tradition, and raising awareness of environmental quality. The development of offices, multipurpose commercial centres, and leisure facilities through the refurbishment of existing buildings, or new in-fill development and gentrification promoted by the private or public sector, are the predominant interventions in inner city areas. Residential suburbanization has occurred in some socialist cities (e.g. Ljubljana and Budapest) since the 1970s, predominately in the form of "satellite" dormitory neighbourhoods or in the existing suburban villages. Since the late 1980s, these processes have become more profound, and in the 1990s they were followed by industrial and commercial suburbanization mainly along motorways and access roads. The most significant problems of urban sprawl in post-socialist cities are visible in the transformation of existing traditional villages into suburbs, with the resultant loss of identity and cultural heritage, pollution of underground water resources due to insufficient technical infrastructure, inadequate waste management, and increasing private car traffic.

These changes in the land-use pattern, including also growth of the need for transport infrastructure and the growth or decline of particular city locations in the 1990s, were similar to those identified in Western European cities (Kivell, 1993), as a result of the restructuring of economic activities and social changes rather than of demographic growth. Unfortunately, there are also negative consequences associated with post-socialist city transformation, such as a marked decline in residential premises in the city centre, conflicts between the interests of commercial development and the protection of cultural heritage, traffic congestion, and parking problems; all of these issues are leading to the differentiation of the functional uses and socio-spatial patterns of Central and Eastern European cities.

## Urban Planning: From Blueprint to Strategic Policies

The neo-liberal thinking of the early 1990s was characterized by the low political priority given by central governments to physical planning, regional development, and housing policy (Sýkora 1994; Dimitrovska Andrews and Ploštajner, 2000; Pichler-Milanović, 2001). The absence of comprehensive national spatial development strategies and coherent regional policies, together with local and regional government reforms and disputes regarding the basis of new planning legislation (as shown in Chapter 6), has been significantly evident in many former socialist countries (e.g. the Czech Republic, Hungary, Slovenia). Consequently, land-use planning at the municipal level has been characterized by the prevalence of ad hoc political decisions rather than long-term strategic visions, weak development control, and a "laissez-faire" approach to city development.

Since the second half of the 1990s, physical planning in Central and Eastern Europe at the urban level has begun to be supplemented by the emerging strategic planning and renewed attempts to implement economic tools for the stimulation and facilitation of local development. The review of planning documents in Chapter 6 shows that in the last decade urban policies have revolved around the search for comparative advantages and the establishment of a proactive role within the European urban networks. This includes the establishment of transportation networks, recognition of the shift from antiquated industry to service-based economy, and the problems of efficient guidance and regulation of private initiatives in the dynamic process of city restructuring. In addition, city governments in Central and Eastern Europe did not have at their disposal the full spectrum of necessary land policy instruments (i.e. differential taxes, pre-emptive rights, expropriation, compulsory purchase, etc.) for use in the areas of spatial planning and urban regulation. Therefore, their power to influence city development in the 1990s was impaired.

However, recent developments in the urban planning and management of Central and Eastern European cities show positive changes towards comprehensive strategic approaches aimed at the enhancement of the image of those cities as a whole, and of the identity of their characteristic areas. Strategic plans and/or development strategy concepts have been introduced in Prague, Riga, Warsaw, Budapest, and Ljubljana for achieving better effectiveness of the planning process and subsequently better quality of the cities' physical development (Markowski, 2000; Dimitrovska Andrews, 2002). Transparency of the urban planning and management process, public involvement in the decision-making process, integration of physical planning and real-estate regulation, and urban renewal projects have also been introduced in the process of reshaping post-socialist cities.

Since the end of the 1980s most Central and Eastern European post-socialist cities have been competing for international investments and development, which became a matter of national prestige. This requires commitment from the city planning authorities to pursue market-orientated strategies for economic growth, but at the same time to preserve social cohesion and cultural heritage, and improve quality of life. These new developments are also a way of promoting city competitiveness and international image, and are in line with the new planning paradigm of sustainable development. Instead of controlling and distributing growth, the new policies should aim to promote cities by reducing the cost or risk of doing business in the area and by improving the social and economic environment.

## Urban Governance: Decentralization and Cooperation

Successful urban development requires strategic vision and proactive city government in order to (re-)establish city identity, stimulate civic pride, improve international image, and hence, encourage an integrated and multifunctional city. Leadership is a crucial variable in how cities respond to economic and social change. Reorganization of city government structure and the provision or better management of high-quality urban services is a requirement for improving city competitiveness and sustainability in Central and Eastern Europe. Availability of funds is one of the most important requirements for efficient and equitable urban development. City governments in post-socialist cities have neither sufficient authority nor adequate financial capacity to undertake the broad range of activities required to complete transition reforms and achieve EU accession requirements, and they rely on central government budget or FDI. Local authorities in some post-socialist cities are traditionally very strongly orientated towards solving internal problems and are not sufficiently aware of the importance of cities as nodes of international interaction. At the same time the aim of city competitiveness inevitably forces (national) governments in Central and Eastern Europe to direct investments into already dominant capital cities, which indirectly improves their position in trans-national urban networks. The instruments that city governments have at their disposal to improve their international status (e.g. fiscal policy, financial subsidies, public–private partnerships, information and advice services, business infrastructure and facilities, accessibility, property market, tourist attractions, cultural events, and environmental quality) are still not fully developed. The formation of public–private partnerships with foreign investors for individual projects, property market development, cooperation with non-profit organizations, and citizens' participation in the planning process, should be some of the key issues to be tackled in the future.

# From "Urban Nodes" to New "Zones of Metropolitan Cooperation"

The continuing restructuring of the international economy and the weakening of national boundaries gives advantages to some areas and disadvantages to others, creating uneven economic and social development. These processes have fundamentally changed the organization and modes of interaction between Central and Eastern European cities, effecting increased although differential rates of integration within the international system of cities. All of these factors are encouraging the emergence of a new European urban system and specific types and forms of urban networks.

Two issues are important for urban policy-making in Central and Eastern Europe. The first one is the influence of international organizations and agencies on policy formulation. Second, at the implementation level, the forms and functions of the metropolitan and local government(s) and their relation to the (supra-)national bodies (i.e. the European Union and United Nations) are equally important. The administrative structure of city regions, institutions responsible for city management and planning, and relations with local and international financial organizations, especially the World Bank and IMF, are also important factors. The role of international organizations, and multilateral and bilateral agencies, is also important for the process of the intra- and inter-urban transformation of post-socialist cities. This interplay between global forces and local demands – i.e. the "global–local nexus" – could have further implications for the transformation of cities in Central and Eastern Europe.

At the beginning of the 1990s, the World Bank and IMF were the most influential in the process of the formulation of transition reforms in Central and Eastern Europe. Their policy recommendations based on market principles were targeted towards efficiency objectives and a need for budget constraints. In the second part of the 1990s, with selective OECD and NATO enlargements towards Central and Eastern Europe (e.g. the Czech Republic, Slovakia, Hungary, and Poland) and "association agreements" with the European Union, the policy-making process focused more on departmental (re)adjustments, harmonization of legislation, cooperation, and institutional development. The international agencies mentioned above focused their activities on the national level, and not particularly on urban development per se. Their role has been complemented with bilateral and multilateral agreements, links, and networks between local and regional authorities. At the second summit of the United Nations Centre for Human Settlements (UNCHS – Habitat) in Istanbul (1996), urban problems and the policy-making process were "globalized", which resulted in the publication of the *Habitat Agenda*. The current actions of local governments in Central and Eastern Europe to incorporate these recommendations into their development plans differ in terms of benefits for cities, regions, and particular social groups. At the same time, more proactive cross-border and trans-national links and partnerships between different actors from cities and regions of the EU Member

States and Central and Eastern Europe have been stimulated and supported with the availability of EU funds, applied research activities, and development projects, as part of the process of EU enlargement and integration.

The opening of the borders to Central and Eastern Europe, the creation of a European single market (1992), and the accession of the new Member States of Austria, Sweden, and Finland (1995) has intensified the questions about the viability and role of different territorial units (i.e. regions and cities) in social, economic, and political affairs in Europe as a whole. Since the European Council Summit in Copenhagen (1993) the commitment to enlargement towards Central and Eastern Europe has required further economic reforms, harmonization of legislation, and strengthening of institutional development. This was confirmed at the Essen Summit (1994) with the formulation of the pre-accession strategy that was published in 1997 as *Agenda 2000*, also known as the EU Enlargement Strategy. In 1998, formal accession negotiations began with the establishment of Accession Partnerships and Twinning Agreements with the "first-wave entrants" (or negotiating candidates) at that time – Estonia, the Czech Republic, Hungary, Poland, and Slovenia (known as the Luxembourg group), followed by the "second-wave" negotiating candidates in 2000 – Bulgaria, Latvia, Lithuania, and Romania (the Helsinki group). The European Council in Nice (December 2000) reaffirmed as a political priority the success of EU enlargement. Accession negotiations with the Czech Republic, Estonia, Hungary, Latvia, Lithuania, Poland, Slovakia, Slovenia, Cyprus, and Malta were successfully concluded in Athens on 16 April 2003 with the Treaty and Act of Accession.

As part of the process of "territorial integration" the European Union has been increasingly supporting the establishment of different links and networks between cities and regions to cooperate and participate in joint projects under DG XVI (latterly the REGIO directorate). The results of these projects have had an important impact on the formulation of EU "urban and regional agendas", such as *Europe 2000* (1991) and *Europe 2000+* (1994), followed by the *European Spatial Development Perspective* (ESDP) (1999) and the *Second Report on Economic and Social Cohesion* (2001), calling for a "better balance and poly-centric development of a European territory". The ESDP represents the result of a decade-long attempt to prepare a European spatial-planning agenda as a field of policy. The need for policy formulation and coordination at the implementation level has been recognized at the European level, particularly for environmental, transport, agriculture, social, and regional policies. The main aims of this integrated spatial development agenda are: (i) development of a poly-centric and balanced urban system and the strengthening of the partnership between urban and rural areas; (ii) promotion of integrated transport and communication strategies that support the poly-centric development of the European territory; and (iii) development and conservation of natural and the cultural heritage through "wise" management (EC, 1999: 20). Strengthening a poly-centric and more balanced system of metropolitan areas and urban networks is one of the main objectives in shaping the development of a "coherent" European urban system (EC, 1999: 21). The ESDP can also be interpreted as an attempt to address the dual process of "internal" European diversification and "external" pressure of competition from the US and Japan.

## *"Eurocorridors": Transport Links and Access to Knowledge*

The development of "Eurocorridors" represents one of the most important conceptual tool for integrating policies relating to the development of "multi-modal co-operation between cities, the improvement of infrastructure, telecommunication and transport in more peripheral areas, the reduction of congestion and inter-continental accessibility", etc. (ESDP, 1997: 61). Such corridors contribute considerably to the territorial integration of Europe.[4] A number of these transport corridors have already included some of the post-socialist cities in Central and Eastern Europe (e.g. Paris–Strasbourg–Stuttgart–Munich–Vienna–*Budapest*, or Brussels–Cologne–Hannover–*Berlin–Poznan–Warsaw*), but essential missing links still have to be developed. Corridors within the Trans-European Networks with the most important development potential for the Central and Eastern European cities are as follows:

- No. I: Helsinki–*Tallinn–Riga–Warsaw*;
- No. II: Berlin–Warsaw–Minsk–Moscow–Niznji Novgorod;
- No. IV: *Berlin–Prague–Vienna/Bratislava–Budapest–Bucharest–Sofia–*Thessalonici–Istanbul;
- No. V: Venice–Trieste/*Koper–Ljubljana–Maribor–Budapest–Kiev* (with extensions to *Bratislava, Zagreb* and *Sarajevo*);
- No. VII: waterway route on the Danube from Germany to the Black Sea (connecting the capital cities of *Vienna–Bratislava–Budapest–Belgrade*);
- No. VIII: *Durres–Tirana–Skopje–Sofia–Varna*;
- No IX: Helsinki–*St Petersburg–Moscow–Kiev–Kishniev–Bucharest–Dimitrovgrad*–Thessaloniki (with extensions to *Minsk–Vilnius–Kaliningrad*);
- No. X: Salzburg–*Ljubljana–Zagreb–Belgrade–Skopje*–Thessaloniki (with extension to *Budapest, Sofia–Istanbul*).

Cooperation between cities in the EU Member States has been further reinforced by different EU programmes relating to Central and Eastern Europe (e.g. INTERREG, PHARE, TACIS, Ecos/Overture, Framework Programmes) and other forms of bilateral and multilateral cross-border and trans-national cooperation. Cooperation on spatial planning in Europe has given rise to a new planning instrument: the trans-national spatial vision. The two trans-national cooperation documents known as *VASAB 2010+* (for 11 countries in the Baltic Sea Region) and *VISION PLANET* (for 12 countries in the CADSES region: Central European, Adriatic, Danubian, and South-east European Space) offer strategic guidance adapted to spatial needs for the distribution of EU funds for pre-accession assistance to Central and Eastern European countries (PHARE,

ISPA, SAPARD programmes).[5] This is important since it means that the Central and Eastern (accession) countries "would have jointly worked out strategic planning policies at their disposal for a spatially differentiated application of the EU funds within the period 2000–2006" (EC, 1999: 51). For example, the integration of the Baltic capitals within the established but gradually changing Baltic Sea network of linkages and dependencies is likely to represent the main trends of EU-ization and cross-border regionalization, showing significant differences between Tallinn and Riga in the capacity of typical "Baltic Sea cities" on the one hand, and Vilnius, with its more Continental or Central European tradition, on the other (see also Chapter 13). The same is expected for Ljubljana and Bratislava and their (re)integration within the Central European urban network and more active cooperation within the CADSES area.

With regard to spatial development projects, the EU initiatives INTERREG II and subsequently INTERREG III are the most important programmes, dealing with trans-national cooperation, and in connection with the PHARE programme (cross-border cooperation) are an important instrument for the application of the ESDP in Central and Eastern Europe.[6]

The INTERREG programmes focus primarily on regional integration, with the aim of strengthening the development of peripheral areas beyond the European core (Fig. 15.1). Among the other EU funds of particular importance that aim to encourage coherent development of Europe through inter-continental cooperation, are the TACIS programme (for newly independent states of the former Soviet Union and Mongolia) and the MEDA programme (for countries bordering the Southern Mediterranean). These countries will benefit to varying degrees from evolving associations or partnerships with the European Union, but they are not candidates for EU membership in the foreseeable future.

## Europe's Urban Regions: New "Global Integration Zones"?

The ESDP highlights the special role of cities, which could be undertaken by Eurocorridors, global integration zones, gateway cities, urban clusters, and individual urban poles, in support of a better territorial balance within the enlarged European Union. The enlarged European Union will include a number of urban regions, small and medium-sized cities, and a diversity of rural hinterlands, mountain regions, and islands. The new European urban system will include a number of metropolitan areas holding the capital functions and the dominant position in the national urban systems. After the last EU enlargement in 2004, about 70 major cities with more than 500,000 inhabitants will dominate the European urban system. About 20 per cent of the enlarged EU population (i.e. 27 Member States) will live in these cities.

The ESDP designates the "Pentagon", shaped by London, Paris, Munich, Milan, and Hamburg, as the dominant core region of Europe and, at present, the only European "zone of global importance". Taking into consideration the

Fig. 15.1 Trans-national cooperation areas and the INTERREG CADSES and Baltic Sea Region Programmes.

*Source:* CEC, 1994; EC, 1999.

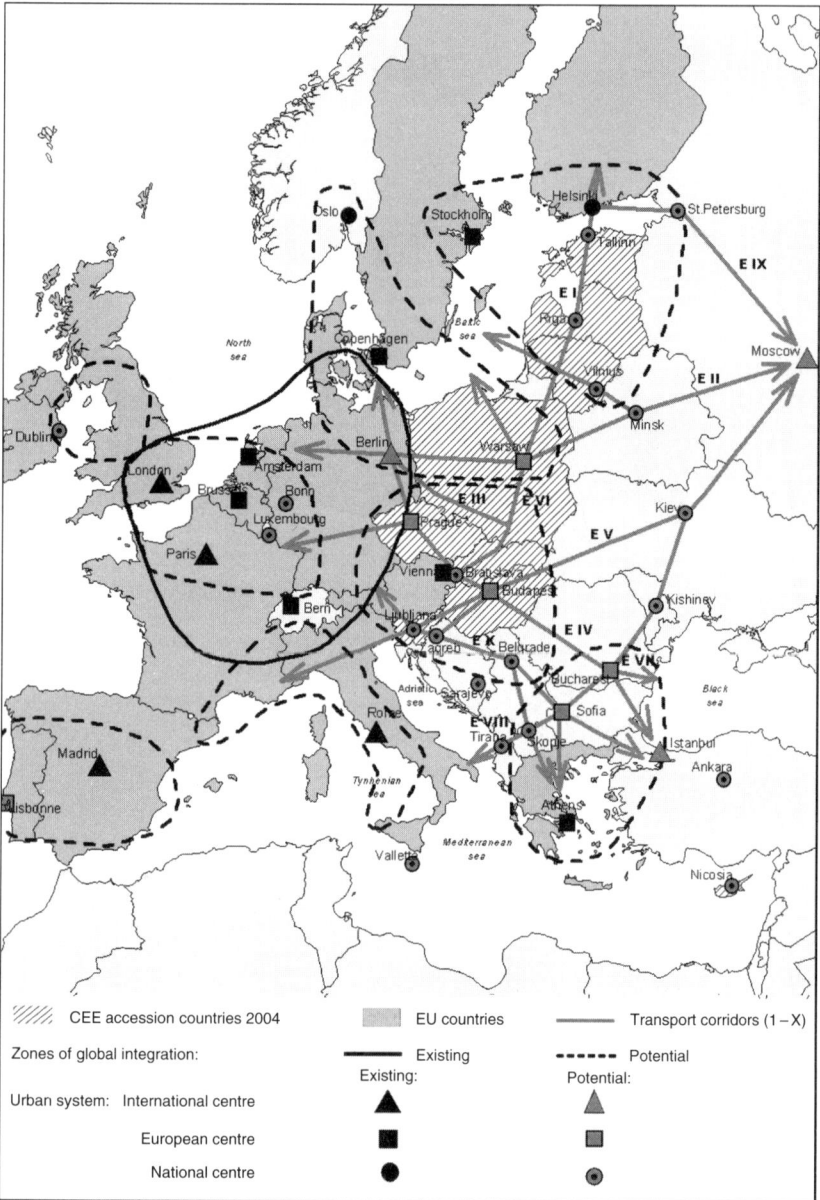

Fig. 15.2 New European urban system or global "integrated zones" of metropolitan cooperation?

*Source:* Based on Read (2000); Mehlbye (2000); Faludi (2002); and EC (1999).

balanced development and poly-centrism of an enlarged European Union, the "Pentagon" core will be coupled by new "zones" of cross-border metropolitan cooperation, which might aspire to the status of "global economic integration zones", as dynamic and global "clusters" of internationally well accessible metropolitan regions, geographically well distributed within the European territory (Fig. 15.2).

New cooperation structures and committed partnerships involving neighbouring (cross-border) metropolitan areas, cities, towns, and rural hinterlands should be stimulated by "top-down" (trans-national) political stimuli, knowledge-based activities, and financial support from the European Union, coupled with the "bottom-up" initiatives process between cities and regions finding partners and establishing institutional links and networks (see Mehlbye, 2000; Faludi, 2002).

There is a growing need these days to clarify territorial characteristics of the globalization process at the European scale, relevant for the evolvement of "global integration zones". Analysis of the socio-economic and territorial specificities and profiles of metropolitan areas of Europe has been undertaken since 2000 in order to improve understanding of the similarities and to make visible the potentials for synergies of cooperation, as declared in ESDP. The current research at the European level concerning "global integration zones" is also the result of a trans-national research network and the establishment of the European Spatial Planning Observatory Network (ESPON).[7]

## Globalization, Europeanization, or Cross-border Regionalization?

Central European countries – the Czech Republic, Slovakia, Hungary, Poland, Slovenia, and the Baltic States (Estonia, Latvia, and Lithuania) – became for political, economic, and strategic reasons fully fledged members of the European Union in May 2004. Bulgaria and Romania will follow them shortly in 2007. The "non-accession" countries of South-east Europe – Albania, Bosnia and Herzegovina, Croatia, FYRoM, and Serbia and Montenegro (recently labelled as the "Western Balkans") – and the East European countries of Belarus, Moldova, and Ukraine are currently excluded from the process of EU enlargement, with the possibility to "join the club" in the decade to come, if EU enlargement requirements are satisfied.

The process of EU enlargement and integration will enhance the position of Europe on the world stage. Accession of Central and Eastern European countries as members of the European Union is dependent on restricted continuation of global forces, or rather globalization through "links and networks" between various partners from European cities and regions. Therefore, from 1994 the forces of Europeanization or EU-ization with cross-border regionalization, or different forms of cooperation between Central and Eastern Europe and EU Member States, are stronger than the forces of globalization or integration of Central and Eastern European cities into the world networks. From this perspective, inter- and intra-urban transformation of "post-socialist" cities in Central and Eastern Europe is perceived not as a unique phenomenon per se, but rather an outcome of global processes within a specific spatial and temporal context.

As indicated in various chapters in this volume, the "end" result of the city transformation process in Central and Eastern Europe is as yet uncertain and might vary in the different "subregions" of Europe (i.e. Central Europe, Southeast Europe, East Europe). As a consequence of both "external" and "internal" forces during the last decade, Central and Eastern European post-socialist cities are somehow becoming more alike, struggling to dismantle the negative effects of socialist development and enhance their international status. The cumulative effect of the transformation process on inter- and intra-urban development is essentially a process of revitalization and "renaissance" of Central and Eastern European cities, emphasizing their cultural heritage, local identity, and a development path towards sustainability.

The future of post-socialist cities depends now not only on their (pre-)socialist legacies, or their success in the adoption of more market-orientated principles, establishment of efficient public regulation/control, and effectiveness of city governance during the transition period, but also on their (re)integration into different European and global networks. The network of capital cities nowadays represents the most dynamic process of territorial integration on the European scale. At the same time, "specialized" and "thematic" cooperations could also diversify forms of urban networking and promote a less hierarchical spatial organization of cities, leading to a more poly-centric structure of Europe. Therefore these cities represent "engines" of territorial integration in Europe. Metropolitan "clustering" of specific cross-border city networks in establishing "global integration zones" is a new territorial concept, as part of the European integration process. It is regarded as one of the most important components in the efforts to ensure sustainable development and a better territorial balance within Europe. Linking towns, cities, metropolitan areas, and their hinterlands with each other via infrastructure and strategic cooperation, and forming poly-centric urban regions, could lead to the formation of dynamic global integration zones. The overall aim is to "trickle down" the benefits of effective social and economic performance across the urban system, while at the same time strengthening Europe's global competitive position as a whole. In that respect, the competitive potentials and the global status of the Central and Eastern European cities will have to be improved if this "vision" of territorial integration is to be realized. What these cities achieve and how they develop will be profoundly shaped by interactions of both global and local contexts and wider developments in economy, politics, and society.

# Notes

1 The integration of the world economy, the emergence of "world" or "global" cities, and the formation of a new urban hierarchy on a global scale have all, since the 1980s, prompted the development of a research paradigm called "world (or global) city analysis". Friedman's seminal paper with G. Wolff (1982) was the first attempt to seek direct connections between urbanization and global economic change in the contemporary world.
2 For a review of the impact of globalization on the transformation of cities in the Asia-Pacific region, see Lo and Marcotullio (2000, 2001).
3 For comparison, in EU Member States (15) half of the urban population live in cities of 100,000 or more inhabitants.
4 The Trans-European Networks initially proposed for Western Europe in 1992 and officially agreed in 1996 were extended as a result of decisions reached at the pan-European Conference of Transport Ministers in Crete (1994) and Helsinki (1997) to include 10 "multi-modal corridors" connecting the infrastructure of Central and Eastern European accession countries.
5 PHARE: Cross-border cooperation programme with accession states from Central and Eastern Europe; ISPA: Instruments for Structural Policy for Pre-accession; SAPARD: Spatial Action Programme for Pre-accession Aid for Agriculture and Rural Development.
6 The INTERREG IIIB programmes have been launched all over the European continent: the Western Mediterranean, Alpine Space, Atlantic Area, South-west Europe, North-west Europe, North Sea Area, CADSES, Northern Periphery, and Archi-Med cooperation areas.
7 ESPON was established in 2001 as a cooperative venture between EU Member States, the European Commission, and accession countries in the elaboration and application of the ESDP through the INTERREG III programme.

## REFERENCES

Gregory Andrusz, Michael Harloe, and Ivan Szelenyi, eds, *Cities After Socialism: Urban and Regional Change and Conflict in Post-Socialist Societies*, Oxford: Blackwell Publishers, 1996.
Neil Brenner, "Globalisation as Reterritorialisation: The Re-scaling of Urban Governance in the European Union", *Urban Studies* 36(3), 1999, pp. 431–451.
Commission of the European Communities (CEC), *Europe 2000: Outlook for the Development of the Community's Territory*, Luxembourg: Office for Official Publications of the European Communities, 1991.
——, *Europe 2000+: Cooperation for European Territorial Development*, Luxembourg: Office for Official Publications of the European Communities, 1994.
——, *European Spatial Development Perspectives: Towards Balanced and Sustainable Development of the Territory of the EU*, Luxembourg: Office for Official Publications of the European Communities, 1999.
——, *Unity, Solidarity, Diversity for Europe, its People and its Territory: Second Report on Economic and Social Cohesion*, Luxembourg: Office for Official Publications of the European Communities, 2001.
Kaliopa Dimitrovska Andrews, "Planning in Flux: Changes in the Spatial Structure of Central and Eastern European Cities – The Case of Ljubljana", *Informationen zur Raumentwicklung* 11/12, 2002, pp. 693–701.

Kaliopa Dimitrovska Andrews and Zlatka Ploštajner, "Local Effects of Transformation Processes in Slovenia", *Informationen zur Raumentwicklung* 7/8, 2000, pp. 435–449.

György Enyedi, "Urbanization in East Central Europe: Social Processes and Societal Responses in the State Socialist Systems", *Urban Studies* 29(6), 1992, pp. 869–880.

Györgyi Enyedi, ed., *Social Change and Urban Restructuring in Central Europe*, Budapest: Akadémiai Kiadó, 1998.

European Commission (EC), *Agenda 2000: For a Stronger and Wider Union*, Brussels: European Commission, 1997a.

——, *European Spatial Development Perspective* (ESDP), first official draft, informal meeting of ministers responsible for spatial planning of the Member States of the European Union, Noordwijk, 9 and 10 June 1997b.

——, *European Spatial Development Perspective* (ESDP), *Towards Balanced and Sustainable Development of the Territory of the European Union*, Brussels: European Commission, 1999.

Andreas Faludi, ed., *European Spatial Planning*, Cambridge, MA: Lincoln Institute of Land Policy, 2002.

R. Anthony French and F.E. Ian Hamilton, eds, *The Socialist City: Spatial Structure and Urban Policy*, New York: John Wiley, 1979.

John Friedman, "The World City Hypothesis", *Development and Change* 17, 1986, pp. 69–83.

John Friedman, "Where We Stand: A Decade of World City Research", in Paul L. Knox and Peter J. Taylor, eds, *World Cities in a World System*, Cambridge: Cambridge University Press, 1995, pp. 21–47.

John Friedman, "World City Revisited: A Comment", *Urban Studies* 38(13), 2001, pp. 2535–2536.

John Friedman and Goetz Wolff, "World City Formulation: An Agenda for Research and Action", *International Journal of Urban and Regional Research* 6, 1982, pp. 309–344.

Ali Ghanbari-Parsa and Ramin Moatazed-Keivani, "Development of Real Estate Markets in Central Europe", *Environment and Planning A*, 31, 1999, pp. 1383–1399.

József Hegedüs, Stephen E. Mayo, and Iván Tosics, "Transition of the Housing Sector in the East Central European Countries", *Review of Urban and Regional Development Studies* 8, 1996, pp. 101–136.

Ramin Keivani, Ali Parsa, and Stanley Mc Greal, "Globalisation, Institutional Structures and Real Estate Markets in Central European Cities", *Urban Studies* 38(13), 2001, pp. 2457–2476.

Michael Kennedy and David A. Smith, "East-Central European Urbanization: A Political Economy of the World-System Perspective", *International Journal of Urban and Regional Research* 13(4), 1989, pp. 597–624.

Philip Kivell, *Land and the City: Patterns and Processes of Urban Change*, London: Routledge, 1993.

Paul L. Knox and Peter J. Taylor, eds, *World Cities in a World System*, Cambridge: Cambridge University Press, 1995.

Stefan Krätke, "Berlin: Towards a Global City?", *Urban Studies* 38(10), 2001, pp. 1777–1799.

Fu-chen Lo and Yue-Man Yeung, eds, *Globalization and the Worlds of Large Cities*, Tokyo: UNUP, 1998.

Fu-chen Lo and Peter J. Marcotullio, "Globalisation and Urban Transformation in the Asia Pacific Region: A Review", *Urban Studies* 37(1), 2000, pp. 77–111.

Fu-chen Lo and Peter J. Marcotullio, eds, *Globalisation and Urban Sustainability in Asia Pacific Region*, Tokyo: UNUP, 2001.

Peter Marcuse and Ronald van Kempen, ed., *Globalizing Cities: A New Spatial Order*, Oxford: Blackwell Publishers, 2000.

Tadeusz Markowski, "Recent Developments in Housing and Planning in Poland", in *Latest Developments in the Field of Housing and Planning*, The Hague: IFHP, 2000.

Peter Mehlbuy, "Global Integration Zones – Neighbouring Metropolitan Regions in Metropolitan Clusters", *Informationen zur Raumentwicklung* 11/12, 2000.

Jiří Musil, "Changing Urban Systems in Post-Communist Societies in Central Europe: Analysis and Predictions", *Urban Studies* 30(6), 1993, pp. 899–906.

Nataša Pichler-Milanović, "The Role of Housing Policy in the Transformation Process of Central-East European Cities", *Urban Studies* 31(7), 1994, pp. 1097–1115.

——, "Urban Housing Markets in Central and Eastern Europe: Convergence, Divergence or Policy Collapse", *European Journal of Housing Policy* 1(2), 2001, pp. 145–187.

Roger Read, "Chances and Potentials of Networks in Supporting Future-oriented Development in Metropolitan Regions", *Informationen zur Raumentwicklung* 11/12, 2000, pp. 737–743.

Saskia Sassen, *The Global City: New York, London, Tokyo*, Princeton, NJ: Princeton University Press, 1991.

——, *Cities in a World Economy*, Thousand Oaks, CA: Pine Forge Press, 1994.

Raymond Struyk, ed., *Economic Restructuring of the former Soviet Bloc: The Case of Housing*, Washington, D.C.: The Urban Institute Press, 1996.

Luděk Sýkora, "Local Urban Restructuring As a Mirror of Globalization Processes: Prague in the 1990s", *Urban Studies* 7(31), 1994, pp. 1149–1166.

——, "Commercial Property Development in Budapest, Prague and Warsaw", in Györgyi Enyedi, ed., *Social Change and Urban Restructuring in Central Europe*, Budapest: Akadémiai Kiadó, 1998, pp. 109–136.

United Nations Economic Commission for Europe (UNECE), *Human Settlement Trends in Central and Eastern Europe*, New York and Geneva: UNECE, 1997.

United Nations Centre for Human Settlements (UNCHS – Habitat), *An Urbanising World: Global Report on Human Settlements*, Oxford: Oxford University Press, 1996.

*VASAB 2010, Vision and Strategies around the Baltic Sea 2010, Towards a Framework for Spatial Development in the Baltic Sea Region*, 1996.

*VISION PLANET: Strategies for Integrated Spatial Development of the Central European Danubian and Adriatic Area, Guidelines and Policy Proposals*, Vienna: [s.n.], 2000.

# Contributors

Dr Martin Åberg
Department for Studies of Work
Economics and Health
University of Trollhättan/Uddevalla
P.O. Box 1236
S-46228 Vänersborg
**Sweden**

Professor Frank Carter (d. May 2001)
Previously at
School of Slavonic and East European
Studies
University College London
Malet Street
London WC1E 7HU
**England (U.K.)**

Dr Kaliopa Dimitrovska Andrews
Director, Urban Planning Institute of
the Republic of Slovenia
Trnovski pristan 2
1127 Ljubljana
**Slovenia**

Professor Hartmut Häussermann
Institute of Social Sciences
Humbolt University
Unter den Linden 6
10099 Berlin
**Germany**

Dr F.E. Ian Hamilton (d. March 2002)
Previously at
Department of Geography and
Environment
London School of Economics
Houghton Street
London WC2A 2AE
**England (U.K.)**

Professor John R. Logan
Department of Sociology
University at Albany
State University of New York
1400 Washington Ave.
Albany, NY 12222
**USA**

Dr Andreas Kapphan
Institute of Social Sciences
Humbolt University
Unter den Linden 6
10099 Berlin
**Germany**

Professor Olga Medvedkov
Chair, Geography Department
Wittenberg University
P.O. Box 720
Springfield, OH 45501
**USA**

Professor Yuri Medvedkov
Geography Department
The Ohio State University
Columbus, OH 43210
**USA**

Nataša Pichler-Milanović
Urban Planning Institute of the
Republic of Slovenia
Trnovski pristan 2
1127 Ljubljana
**Slovenia**

Professor Jiří Musil
Central European University
Ujezd 15
130 00 Prague 3
**Czech Republic**

Dr Iván Tosics
Metropolitan Research Institute
Lonyai utca 34
H1033 Budapest
**Hungary**

Elena Vesselinov
Department of Sociology, Sloan
College
University of South Carolina
Columbia, SC 19208
**USA**

Professor Grzegorz Weclawowicz
Polish Academy of Sciences
Stanislaw Leszczycki Institute of
Geography and Spatial Organization
ul. Twarda 51/55
00–818 Warsaw
**Poland**

# Tributes

Dr F.E. Ian Hamilton (1937–2002)

Frederick Edwin Ian Hamilton (always known as Ian), born in London on 23 May 1937, passed away to the great sadness of friends and colleagues in Guy's Hospital London on 5 March 2002.

Ian graduated at the London School of Economics and Political Science (LSE) with a first class B.Sc. (Econ.) degree in 1958 and continued to study there for his Ph.D. He spent the year 1959/1960 in Croatia based in the Faculty of Economics at Zagreb. This greatly stimulated what became his lifelong interest in economic and regional development in Eastern Europe. He joined the academic staff of LSE in 1961, gained his Ph.D. in 1963, and his first book, *Yugoslavia: Patterns of Economic Activity*, was published in 1968. In 1966, he had the opportunity to become Hayter lecturer (later senior lecturer) jointly at LSE and the School of Slavonic and East European Studies (SSEES). This brought a heavy burden of work but also the opportunity to specialize. He was to become Head of his Department at SSEES. He was a dedicated teacher and research worker and established excellent contacts with colleagues in Eastern European countries. He was fluent in Polish and other East European languages. He also had many opportunities to travel internationally and enjoyed several appointments as a visiting scholar or Professor in the United States, including a Fulbright Scholarship (1968–1970), North-western University, and as a Distinguished Visiting Professor at the University of North Carolina (1992/3), among others. His travels also took him to Hong Kong and China (1985).

He published his findings regularly. These included *Poland's Western and Northern Territories* (1974) and *The Moscow City Region* (1976), and (with R.A. French) he edited *The Socialist City: Spatial Structure and Urban Policy* (1979). He had become an active member (Chairman 1972–1984) of the International Geographical Union's Commission on Industrial Systems and the stimulus thus given to international studies led to further edited work (with G.J.R. Linge) on *Spatial Analysis, Industry and the Industrial Environment* (1979, 1981, 1983). In 1990 (with George Enyedi), he prepared a special issue of *Geoforum* on "East Central Europe in Economic and Social Transition". He also wrote many other chapters in books, articles in journals, and reports dealing with urban development under socialism, industrialization, and regional development in developed and developing economies, and the economic geography of individual Central and Eastern European countries and the former Soviet Union. He undertook consultancy work (much of it with E. Dokopoulou) for bodies such as the European Community, and for other organizations interested in the economies of Central and Eastern Europe. Much new work was in preparation for publication at the time of his death. He was generous with his time in the interests of geographical studies: as an example, he served for many years as Honorary Treasurer of the Geographical Association. Ian was proud to have been elected an Honorary Member of the Croatian Geographical Society.

He will be greatly missed not only for his worldwide contacts and published work but also by those who had the privilege to work directly with him and by his students for the dedication of his teaching.

## Professor Francis W. Carter (1938–2001)

Professor Francis (Frank) William Carter was born in Wednesfield, Staffordshire in July 1938 and died in May 2001 in London, after a long illness. After graduating at Sheffield University and taking a Diploma in Education at Cambridge he spent two years at the London School of Economics (LSE) (1963–1965) and one year lecturing at King's College London (1965–1966) before taking a Hayter lectureship jointly at University College London (UCL) and the School of Slavonic and East European Studies. His work was marked by a brilliant series of dissertations, first with an MA at LSE (1967) and then doctorates at the universities of Prague (1974), London (1979), Cracow (1990), and finally Zagreb (2000). Frank was also a Head of the Social Studies Department at SSEES (1990–1994). He became Reader at SSEES in 1997, and his Professorship in the Geography of Eastern Europe at UCL was announced in 2001, shortly before his death.

Fluent in almost every East European language, Frank was a truly exceptional geographer with close links within a wide network of scholars from Central and Eastern Europe. His academic life was devoted to the study of the economic and historical geography of the region (excluding Russia). In the 1990s, Frank's attention was caught by current problems of regional differences, ethnicity, environmental pollution, the impact of foreign direct investments, and policy-related themes. While most other specialists in this area concentrated on one country, Frank flourished in virtually all of them, although he gravitated towards Bulgaria, the former Czechoslovakia, Poland, and the former Yugoslavia (especially Croatia and Slovenia). He produced two well-known monographs – *Dubrovnik. A Classic City State* (1972) and *Trade and Urban Development in Poland: An Economic Geography of Cracow from its Origins to 1795* (1994) – a pioneering edited work on the *Historic Geography of the Balkans* (1977), and 10 other edited volumes. Amongst them was (jointly with David Turnock) *Environmental Problems in Eastern Europe* (1993, updated edition 1996). He also prepared the section on Eastern Europe for the United Nations Centre for Human Settlements (UNCHS – Habitat), "Global Report on Human Settlements" (1996). Frank also wrote 40 book chapters and 80 academic articles, and his papers appeared in a diverse range of journals, including many published in Eastern Europe. In 1997, Frank received the Edward Heath Award of the Royal Geographical Society. He held the Diploma of the Geographical Institute of the Romanian Academy of Science and was an Honorary Member of the Croatian Geographical Society. In 1999, he was elected President of the British–Bulgarian Society. He was much in demand for lectures, advice and broadcasts on East European issues in North America as well as in Europe.

With Frank's death, geography and European studies have lost a distinguished scholar, a devoted teacher, and a generous friend. His fascination for learning, enthusiasm for life, and enduring sense of humour made him friends wherever he went, and the quality of his research and writing drew students to him. It was an honour and a privilege to have known him personally; indeed, the memory of Frank will live long in the minds and hearts of all who knew him.

# Photographers

**Baltic cities**
Vita Hribar
Janis Krastins
Matej Nikšič

**Berlin**
Stefanie Stolper
Lena Schulz zur Wiesch

**Budapest**
Iván Tosics

**Ljubljana**
Boštjan Cotič
Creativ d.o.o.
Nataša Pichler-Milanovič

Barbara Zajc
Bogo Zupančič

**Moscow**
Olga Medvedkov

**Prague**
Dagmar Novakova
CTK Prague

**Sofia**
Elena Vesselinov

**Warsaw**
Marek Wieckowski

# Index

Foreign Investment Promotions (FIPs),
    centre, 457
nation-wide housing privatisation
    decree, 439
target of FDI, 62
Russian Federation
    cities in, 12
    cumulative inflow and FDI, distribution by
        constituent units of, 457
    empires, 81
    suburbanisation, 448
Ruthenia, 6
Ryšavý, Zdeněk, 38, 285

Saddon, David, 372
Samsung, 145
Sándor, Gy. Nagy, 260
SAPARD programme, 480
Saraceno, Elena, 55, 62
Sarajevo, 468
    upgraded functional status, 17
Sármány-Parsons, Ilona, 304
SAS, 418, 424
Šašek Divjak, Mojca, 173
Sassen, Saskia, 366, 378, 399, 465–466
"satellite" dormitory neighbourhoods, 474
Saxony, 25
Scandinavian and Finnish FDI in Baltic states, 128
Schuchmann, Péter, 251
Second World War, 80, 100
    differential impacts on cities in region, 83
    primary objective of communist
        governments, 470
second-order cities, major 86
Semenov, 158
Sendi, Richard, 169
Serbia, 6, 10
    nationalism, 323
services within Central and Eastern Europe, 109
settlements in suburban region, growth of 51
Shackleton, Margaret, R., 85
Sharp, Christopher, A., 135
Shvetsova, Ludmila, I., 428
Siemens, 141, 145, 200
Šik, Ota, 90
Silesia, 25
Simmie, James, 322
Simonickova, Ivana, 134
Sinn, Hans-Werner, 118
Sitte, C., 156, 360
    objective of urban design, 156
Skoda in Czechoslovakia, 88

Skopje, 468
    upgraded functional status, 17
Slavonia (northern Croatia), 82
Sleszynski, 239–240
Slootweg, Sef, 66
Slovakia/Slovak Republic, 6, 9, 86, 123, 471
    cities, 72
    Meciar government, 141
    Standard & Poor's award of investment grade
        rating, 141
    trade with Czech Republic, 100
Slovenes, in Kingdom of Yugoslavia, 320
Slovenia, 6, 8, 12, 23, 123
    administrative reforms, 342–344
    Agency for Privatisation of Republic of
        Slovenia, 325
    Alps-Adriatic Working Community and, 336
    Building Act (2002), 175
    Central European Initiative, 337
    citizenship, 334
    concept of poly-centric development, 342
    E-banking, 340
    economic integration, 326
    economic, monetary, enterprise
        reforms, 53
    economic transition in, 322
    Enterprise Ownership Transformation
        Act, 325
    enterprise privatisation, 137
    EU Accession Treaty, 336
    and EU, Co-operation Agreement
        between, 359
    European Union membership, 325, 359
    FDI, 330–333
    FDI with EU countries, 329
    FDI in largest towns, 311–312
    foreign trade with European Community,
        324, 329
    Free Trade Association of Central European
        countries, (CEFTA), 333, 337
    GDP per capita, 357
    global "connectivity", 336
    highest proportion of deagrarised population
        in Europe, 340
    house prices, 362
    Housing Act, amendments of, 350
    housing sector, 350
    immigrants from other Yugoslav
        republics, 334
    in Second World War, 321
    independence, sovereignty, and democratic
        reforms, 323